Rave Reviews for *Sinatra! The Song Is You*

"The finest study yet."   —*Wall Street Journal*

"Musicians will appreciate the author's informed appraisals. . . . Many of the small details included will fascinate Sinatra fans."   —*Choice*

"Friedwald's book is the most important and complete documentary of popular American music. . . . It shows that Sinatra alone is the president of all the popular American singers."   **—Tony Bennett**

"A man with unexcelled knowledge of American popular song, Friedwald looks intensively at the career of The Voice, Ol' Blue Eyes, the Chairman of the Board. . . . Along with the serious analysis there's a plentitude of great trivia. . . . This excellent volume is indispensable as a companion to Sinatra's recordings. In our era of biotrash, *Sinatra!* hits a welcome high note."   —*Cleveland Plain Dealer*

"Perceptive, colorful, and prodigiously researched."   —*Publishers Weekly*

"A stimulating guide to Sinatra the artist."   —*Los Angeles Times*

"Sure to delight true Sinatra fans."   —*Library Journal*

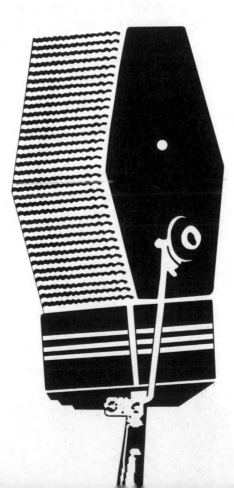

Sinatra!

THE SONG IS YOU

A SINGER'S ART

WILL FRIEDWALD

SCRIBNER

NEW YORK   LONDON   TORONTO   SYDNEY   TOKYO   SINGAPORE

SCRIBNER
1230 Avenue of the Americas
New York, NY 10020

DESIGNED BY ERICH HOBBING

Manufactured in the United States of America

7   9   10   8   6

Library of Congress Cataloging-in-Publication Data

Friedwald, Will, 1961–
Sinatra! the song is you : a singer's art / Will Friedwald.
p.   cm.
Includes bibliographical references and index.
1. Sinatra, Frank, 1915–   . 2. Singers—United States—Biography.   I. Title.
ML420.S565F78   1995
782.42164'092—dc20
[B]
95-11317
CIP
MN

ISBN 0-684-19368-X

In memory of Libby Zion ("Never again")

And to Skeets Herfurt, Alvin Stoller, Deane Kincaide, Johnny Mince,
Yank Lawson, Sammy Cahn, and Jule Styne

And once more for my Babey

CONTENTS

ACKNOWLEDGMENTS

So many people have contributed so much to this book that I'm tempted to ape virtually every other author you've ever read and say I don't know where to begin in terms of thanking people.

Actually, I know exactly where to begin: with the musicians. "I've never heard of a book like that," Al Viola said after we had finished talking, "a book on Frank where they talked to guys like me. The people that were really there with him, sweating it out. That's the one book on Frank that hasn't been written. And I think that's the soul of his music."

First, to the following sidemen and women, who have worked with Sinatra from his big band days up through the '90s: Trigger Alpert, Artie Baker, Julius Baker, Milt Bernhart, Joe Bushkin, Pete Candoli, Page Cavanaugh, John Cave, ("the other") Ray Charles, Mahlon Clark, Buddy Collette, Sid Cooper, Jerry Dodgion, Harry Edison, Alec Fila, Frank Flynn, Stan Freeman, Dave Frisina, Chris Griffin, Bob Haggart, Dave Harris, the late Skeets Herfurt, Jerry Jerome, Deane Kincaide, Harry Klee, Lou Levy, the late Johnny Mince and Betty Williams, Dick Nash, Ted Nash, Loulie Jean Norman, Bobby Pring, Pete Pumiglio, Emil Richards, George Roberts, Don Ruffel, Paul Shure, Eleanor Slatkin, Paul Smith, the late Alvin Stoller, Warren Webb, and Zeke Zarchy.

I'm particularly grateful to the following members of Sinatra's touring rhythm sections, truly the backbone of his music, for sharing their time and memories with me: Johnny Blowers, Vince Falcone, Sol Gubin, Tony Mottola, Al Viola, and, in particular, Bill Miller. (I also made use of a 1979 interview with the late Irv Cottler.)

"A good arranger is terribly vital," Sinatra has said, and I have also found that to be the case. Thanks to the late Billy Byers, Charles Callelo, Robert Farnon, Frank Foster, Neil Hefti, Quincy Jones, Johnny Mandel, Claus Ogerman, Lillian (Mrs. Sy) Oliver, Marty Paich, George Siravo, and especially to Billy May. I was also fortunate enough to obtain a series of interviews with the late Nelson Riddle and the late Gordon Jenkins, and with their sons, Christopher Riddle and Gordon Jenkins, Jr.

9

Thanks also to the singers who shared their reflections and experiences with a man whom they all consider one of the dominant influences on their own work: Eileen Barton, Tony Bennett, Rosemary Clooney, Steve Lawrence and Eydie Gorme, Al Hibbler, Jo Stafford, Louise Tobin, Bea Wain, and Joe Williams.

"And he wasn't singing la-la-la up there," as Sammy Cahn has pointed out. Muchos gracias to the late Mr. Cahn, as well as to his fellow songwriters Alan Bergman, Cy Coleman, Betty Comden, Matt Dennis, Joel Herron, Bart Howard, Jack Lawrence, Lew Spence, and Jack Wolf.

". . . To continue," as Sinatra sings in "Cherry Pies Ought to Be You," my gratitude also to producers George Avakian, Jimmy Bowen, Alan Livingston, Mitch Miller, Phil Ramone, and George Simon, and to engineers Lee Hirschberg and Frank Laico. And also to the following musical giants who've all interacted with Sinatra in one way or another: Les Brown, Milt Gabler, Bill Finegan, Skitch Henderson, Red Norvo, Tito Puente, Pete Rugolo, George Shearing, and the late Paul Weston.

I was also tremendously well served by the army of Frankenmavens out there who provided reams of data and miles and miles of tape. They are: Richard Apt, Ken Carley, Eric Comstock, Bob Conrad, Bill Denton, the late Gary Doctor (of the International Sinatra Society), Ken Hutchins, Kenny Lucas, Sid Mark, Tony Natelli, Ed O'Brien, Rebecca Pranger, Ron Sarbo, Arthur Schell, Jonathan Schwartz, Bobby Sherrick, Jude Spatola, David Weiner, Mitch Zlokower, and especially to the Chairman of Sinatra Scholars, that swinging CPA, Mr. Ric Ross. Very special thanks to the incredibly meticulous Michael Kraus, the monarch and majordomo of musical minutiae, for helping me prepare this paperback edition. Other professionals who have contributed ideas include Stanley Crouch, Nancy Franklin, Herb Friedwald, Gary Giddins, Mary Cleere Haran, Bob Jones, Jim Maher, Dan Morgenstern, and Peter Watrous.

And to Melissa Berger and Ted Panken, for wearing out several computers in pounding out roughly six million pages of transcripts from over two hundred interviews.

Not to mention my editor at Scribner, Bill Goldstein (and his invaluable assistant, Ted Lee), and to my agents, Claire Smith and Phyllis Westberg. (Not to forget Doug Simmons, Joe Levy, and Ann Powers of *The Village Voice* and Fletcher Roberts of the *New York Times*.)

Then too, I can't imagine having undertaken this deal without the help and rolodex of Frank Military, Sinatra's former right-hand man (and today the President of Warner-Chappell's East Coast operations). I also never could have made it without the cooperation of Susan Reynolds and Dorothy Uhlemann, Mr. Sinatra's public relations manager and his personal assistant, respectively, for lo these many millennia. Thanks additionally to Sonny Golden, Mr. Sinatra's business manager, and to Mrs. Nancy Sinatra Lambert for inviting me to participate in *Frank Sinatra: The Capitol Years*.

Most of all to my indefatigable partner in research, Charles L. Granata. Apart from having amassed the most amazing collection of Sinatra material I've ever seen, Chuck has an insatiable desire to know all there is to know about our culture's greatest popular artist. As often as not, his enthusiasm was the spark plug that kept this project going full steam ahead for five years.

And, to use a term of which he would heartily disapprove, "mega-thanks" to Robert Gottlieb. "The smartest man in New York" (as Mary Cleere calls him) extended to me the greatest gift I could possibly have asked for—a week of his time, in order to prevent me, as Bob says, from telling people "more about penguins than they need to know."

And lastly, another special thanks to Babey for not getting too sick of yet another take of "Night and Day."

As Chris Griffin has pointed out, "Frank always gave musicians the credit that they were due, saying, 'I wouldn't be here if it weren't for these guys . . . '" I'm also saying that now.

Sinatra!

THE SONG IS YOU

CHAPTER ONE

"NIGHT AND DAY":
THE SINATRA STYLE

An artist must create a personal cosmos, a verdant world in continuity with tradition, further fulfilling man's awareness, his degree of consciousness, and bringing new subtilization, vision, and beauty to the elements of experience. It is in this way that Idea, powered by conviction and necessity, will create its own style and the singular, momentous structure capable of realizing its intent.

—LEON KIRCHNER
(American composer, born 1919)

"Why is it," one late-night comic recently asked, "that when either Frank Sinatra or the President is in New York, all the hookers suddenly get better looking?" The hubbub regarding a visit from the chief executive can be easily understood. But how can we account for the disruptive power of this swinging septuagenarian, especially in the city that's seen it all? Sinatra is undeniably a dinosaur. But like those two-hundred-million-year-old brontosauri that are let loose in twentieth-century Manhattan in all those 1950s B-movies, he still has the power to trample the city beneath his feet.

The era that spawned Sinatra "is no more," as P. G. Wodehouse wrote of his youth. "It is gone with the wind, it is one with Ninevah and Tyre." If mankind has been around for only a few minutes in the calendar of the cosmos, then the Sinatra epoch flourished and then was finished in a brief, shining microsecond. The concept of something like quality in what we call American popular culture doesn't even amount to a momentary aberration. The idea that music could have substance as well

15

as mass-marketability came into being at the end of World War I. It reached a climax during World War II and slowly fizzled out during the Vietnam War in the 1960s.

The dinosaur metaphor falls apart at this point, because Sinatra can't be compared to a lumbering behemoth who flattened the earth for eons, but rather to some magnificent beast whose entire existence occurred in the twinkling of an eye. Sinatra further represents a unique case where the greatest example of a breed happens to be the one to weather the decades as if in his own personal time capsule—one with hot and cold running babes, a private stock of Jack Daniel's, and no photographers.

The mom-and-pop store that was the music industry in Sinatra's heyday has long since been demolished to make room for the superhighway of lowest-common-denominator culture. Still, Sinatra has dominated the last ten years—the age of digital music software—perhaps even more completely than he has any previous period. (To start with, a search through a database of CDs in print in 1994 yields 283 Sinatra entries.) This trend was apparent long before the recent platinum-selling release of *Duets*, Sinatra's economic zenith, technological masterpiece, and artistic nadir. In the de-ozoned, greenhouse-warmed winter of 1990–91, while the grandchildren of Sinatra's first audience, the World War II generation, prepared for yet another conflict, Sinatra product continued to move in quantities which the music industry traditionally describes in terms of precious metals.

In the early 1990s, Sinatra was not only active but still an irresistible force in pop music: multidisc "historical" packages, normally resistant to big sales, were selling because they were his. Reluctant as Sinatra was to record, it was inevitable that freshly minted Sinatra product would do even better. What was remarkable about the sales of such retrospectives as *The Voice* on Columbia, *The Capitol Years*, and *The Reprise Collection* (as opposed to the exclusively monetary success of *Duets*) was that artistry was once again making enough money to compete with products manufactured solely for economic gain.

Equally remarkable, the success of Sinatra product in the digital decade owes nothing to nostalgia—especially in the early days of the disc format when few survivors of Buddy Holly's generation, let alone Sinatra's, even owned a compact disc player. Now, as he has throughout his career, Sinatra continues to flout convention. The '80s and '90s may be remembered as a period of meaningless technology; we care far more about the recording and marketing of music than we do about its content. When the recordable CD is perfected, thirteen-year-olds will theoretically be able to overwrite the disc containing last year's punk rock with next year's gangster rap (like Roman women who bring the same jars back to the market each week for a refill of honey or jam).

With the release of *Duets* in late 1993, the newspapers were awash in Sinatra "sensitivity pieces." Most of them were by veteran fifty- and sixty-something celebrity journalists, and they almost always followed the same pattern: a reminiscence of their younger days (not necessarily reckless youth but early married life and child-rearing years) interwoven with etched-in-stone memories of Sinatra songs. First, they make plain how much Sinatra has meant to them all their lives, through thirty, forty, or fifty years of listening; then, if they can, they detail the one or two times they had the opportunity to meet the man in the flesh, which they tend to equate with saying howdy to Moses on the mountain. Next, the writer talks about *Duets,* occasionally decrying it as a blasphemously shallow effort from the man who invented depth, but foremostly celebrating the album for its only virtue: a new Sinatra product that is a rip-roaring hit.

So much of our lives has been lived to the soundtrack of Sinatra music, it's hard to tell where our actual experiences end and those we've felt vicariously through Sinatra lyrics begin. Once we reach our thirties, we've long since lost the ability to distinguish whether something really happened to us or we just felt it through the way Sinatra sings, for instance, "It Was a Very Good Year." The Sinatra-inspired "memories" amount to a collective stock-footage library of shared experiences. Most of us can feel the small-town episode of "Very Good Year" amazingly vividly even if we've never been in a village more rural than Greenwich.

The late Gordon Jenkins once explained: "Frank does one word in 'Send in the Clowns,' which is my favorite of the songs we did together, and it's the damndest thing I've ever heard. He just sings the word *farce,* and your whole life comes up in front of you. He puts so much in that phrase that it just takes a hold of you." Where other singers, at best, work with lyrics and melodies, Sinatra deals in mental images and pure feelings that he seems to summon up almost without the intervention of composers, arrangers, and musicians, as vital as their contributions are. In fact, Sinatra is so sure of his relationship with his audience that he gladly acknowledges orchestrators and songwriters in his spoken introductions to each number. How could it take away from what he does to mention the men who put the notes and words on paper when it's he who gives them all meaning?

Sinatra is often larger than life, projecting heightened emotions through intensified vocal gestures. At other times Sinatra is whisperingly intimate, underplaying every note and every emotion to extract the most believability out of a text. At still other times Sinatra is dead-on, having reached a point where we can no longer discern between the part of him that is engaged in what is ultimately a theatrical performance and the real-life man himself. In many numbers—such as "Without a Song," recorded in 1961—Sinatra is all three at different points.

There are times when Sinatra acts as if the lyric doesn't mean anything to him at all, as with a new novelty number (such as "The Hucklebuck") or an archaic throwaway revived as a "rhythm song" (such as "My Blue Heaven") that he just wants to have fun with and not have to take seriously. When Sinatra titled one 1956 album *Songs for Swingin' Lovers!* it wasn't just a marketing hook but an accurate manifestation of his musical-dramatic ambitions; Sinatra showed the world how a singer could be at once romantic and rhythmically playful. His milestone performance of "I've Got You Under My Skin" (on *Swingin' Lovers*) has Sinatra being super-sensitive to the intimate nuances of Cole Porter's lyric at one moment and then, eight bars later, being swaggeringly indifferent to it. When Sinatra adds an ad-lib line, most famously "it repeats—*how it yells*—in my ear," he's simultaneously kidding the text and underscoring it. (These generally are genuinely spontaneous interjections that he varies from performance to performance.)

"Frank's appeal is so great and so wide, I think, because it boils down to one thing: You believe that he's singing [directly] to you," explained Frank Military, Sinatra's former right-hand man (for roughly ten years, beginning in 1951). "If you go to any of the concerts, you'll see truck drivers and prizefighters and all kinds of people, and they just go crazy over him. You'll see people that were there from the beginning, his [original] audience, all those older folks who were there at the [New York] Paramount in 1941 and 1942. You can talk to them, as well as to the new audience that he gets, the young kids today, and every one of them swears that Sinatra sang to them personally."

Sinatra's most appealing talent may be his capacity for emotional expressiveness. As time went on, Sinatra played an increasingly more finely tuned instrument, not only with a broader range at the bottom and top—sadder sads and happier happies—but with more degrees between the peaks. He can develop fifteen different kinds of post–"I've Got You Under My Skin" climax-building euphoria on *A Swingin' Affair*, get you to feel pensive and squirmy twelve different ways on *Where Are You* (both recorded in 1956), splash cold water in your face from twelve surprising angles on *Come Swing with Me,* or simply "kvell" fifteen different finger-snapping ways on the masterpiece *Songs for Swingin' Lovers!* Even more effective are the ways he increases the emotional, no less than the musical, pitch within a single track: "You Make Me Feel So Young" modulates from mere cheerfulness to exalted rapture so overpoweringly it could make a statue want to fall in love.

Sinatra's vocal range extends all the way up to the stratospheric falsetto note that he used to climax the Axel Stordahl arrangement of "The Song Is You"—a very high F (two F's above middle C). In the Capitol and early Reprise eras, his top note would more likely be the high F he hits on "The Tender Trap," going down to the ultradeep, Jolsonian low G that concludes his show-stopping '60s treatment of "Ol' Man River." (He also hits basement-level low notes on the 1959 "Cottage for Sale" and the 1969 "Wave.") That amounts to a span of nearly two octaves, yet as longtime accompanist Bill Miller cautions, he reserves those extremes purely for occasional dramatic emphasis. His "practical range," as Miller puts it, was rarely quite so high or so low.

While Sinatra has a wonderful voice, he is not a vocal virtuoso. There are popular singers whose techniques are superior to Sinatra's, among them Ella Fitzgerald, Nat King Cole, Vic Damone, and Billy Eckstine. Sinatra's spiritual father, Bing Crosby, had a greater gift for resonant melody, and Sinatra seems to have presented himself as a practitioner of pure power singing only in the mid-1940s, when he was promoted as, appropriately, "The Voice." In his personal and professional upheavals of the early '50s, he lost a lot of that wind power and, truth to tell, has gone on very gradually losing more and more of it ever since.

But what he has substituted for pure technique in the very good years since his youth has proved far more meaningful. His ability to tell a story has consistently gotten sharper even as the voice grew deeper and the textures surrounding it richer. Generally, rhythm and dynamics are discussed as if they were two distinct qualities, but with Sinatra they're inseparable. They amount to the primary tools through which he affords varying degrees of weight to key phrases. That weight of emphasis can be applied in terms of both duration—the length of time that he holds the note (rhythm)—or in the volume level at which he chooses to hit it (dynamics). Before Sinatra, loud generally tended to mean long, but The Voice opened up a whole new world of rhythmic-dynamic thinking in which soft notes could be indefinitely extended for greater emotional effect.

Sinatra makes any word sound more like what it is, as the late lyricist

Sammy Cahn observed. "When he sings 'lovely,' he makes it sound '*lo-ovely*' as in 'weather-wise it's such a *lo-ovely* day'" [in Cahn's "Come Fly with Me"], Cahn demonstrated to me, carressing and extending the long soft vowel sound at the center. "Likewise, when he sings 'Lonely' [in "Only the Lonely"] he makes it into such a lonely word."

We could sum up Sinatra's capacity for rhythm with the word "swing," but in saying that we should stay aware that the term means a lot of things. Count Basie's kind of swing is different from Louis Armstrong's, and Sinatra is no less the creator of his own, unique rhythmic idiom. Particularly in conjunction with his longtime colleague and arranger Nelson Riddle, Sinatra masterminded a rhythmic feeling that the team mutually characterized as the "tempo of the heartbeat."

The basic Sinatra-Riddle beat amounts to a bridge between the four-four time signature, played by most swing-era bands, and the two-four beat that an earlier Sinatra collaborator, Sy Oliver, perfected for Jimmie Lunceford and then brought with him to Tommy Dorsey. "Frank likes the Buddy Rich style," said pianist Lou Levy, "the Tommy Dorsey band style, which he was raised on, you could say. The band had so much talent, I'm sure it affected him and stayed with him. I think that's where his taste was formulated. He's a swing-era guy: Tommy Dorsey, Benny Goodman, Count Basie, Duke Ellington."

Even if that *Swingin' Lover*–beat is the one we most identify with Sinatra, he has mastered other time signatures as well, especially the straight-down-the-middle four-four he utilized in albums with Count Basie, Johnny Mandel, and Neal Hefti. Never particularly comfortable with waltzes, Sinatra once made an entire album of ballads, *All Alone* (1962), in three-four time to take emotional advantage of his tentativeness at that signature. He once said of his own sense of swing, "I think that that's kind of inbred. I think you have or you haven't got it. I'm probably one of the fortunate people to whom it was given. I never thought about it much." Typically, Sinatra then gave credit for his success in this area to his accompanists. "If I do a jump arrangement with a band, either on records or on a stage, I find that if the band doesn't settle down into a proper tempo, then you cannot swing. I don't care how good you are, it just doesn't move."

"Once while I was driving I heard an old record by Frank and Nelson, and I had to get out of the car and call the radio station," trumpeter Zeke Zarchy once said. "It was 'The Way You Look Tonight' [from *Academy Award Winners*, 1964], the greatest thing I ever heard! I defy any instrumentalist to swing like he does with his voice on that record."

On another occasion, Billy May, the great big-band writer who frequently worked with Sinatra from the mid-1940s to the mid-1980s, was asked if he considered Sinatra a jazz singer. He answered that it depended. "If your definition of a jazz singer is someone who can approach [a song] like an instrumentalist and get [the written melody] across but still have a feeling of improvisation, a freshness to it, and do it a little bit differently every time, then I would agree that Frank is."

Which isn't to say that Sinatra is strictly a jazz guy all the time, the way Betty Carter is. "I'm not so sure that being a jazz musician is that all-inclusive," trombonist Milt Bernhart, who should know, elaborated. "A jazz musician usually is somebody who refuses to do anything else, like Miles Davis and John Coltrane. But I wouldn't say that Duke Ellington was purely a jazz musician. I mean, when you've got an orchestra and they're all up there playing together and it's so beautiful, I wouldn't nec-essarily call that jazz. I would call that music. I'll bet if you were to ask Sinatra, 'Do you consider yourself a jazz singer?', he would probably respond, 'Hey, I'm a singer.' And even when he sings a song exactly the way it's written, that's good enough for me."

Apart from jazz, big bands, and singers like Ella Fitzgerald, Sinatra's other great musical love is classical music. "He's really interested in good music," May pointed out. "He and his wife and my wife and I have gone to the symphony a couple of times together. He astounds me with how really knowledgeable he is about classical music. We went one night, and he was telling me about how he liked Reinhold Glière. Now, Glière was a contemporary of Rimsky-Korsakov and a fairly obscure Russian composer. For Sinatra to have even heard of him shows he knows a lot." Eleanor Slatkin, who with her late husband Felix (Riddle's preferred concertmaster and the conductor of the Hollywood Bowl Symphony Orchestra) saw quite a lot of Sinatra socially in the Capitol era, remarked, "Every time we went to his house, he always had classical music on. I don't remember hearing anything but classical and opera. And, of course, he's *very* knowledgeable and [knew] many of the artists personally."

While Sinatra may occasionally employ backdrops that reflect his appreciation of European classical music, in his own singing he owes far more to Crosby than to Caruso. Even on the dozen or so songs based on classical themes that Sinatra recorded (mainly in the '40s), he constantly altered the material in a way a lieder or opera singer wouldn't. Even when singing the melodic intervals exactly as notated, Sinatra can't help doing creative and interesting things with the rhythm. He never stops playing with the tempo, whether the piece is serious, romantic, or swinging. In fact, it's easier to list the songs where he does sit squarely on the beat—as on parts of "Whistle a Happy Tune" and his original coda to "Anything Goes" on *Songs for Swingin' Lovers!*—than to cover the endless occasions when he lags behind it or rushes ahead of it for musical and dramatic effect. (Sinatra doesn't fully read music or "sight sing," but it's said that when he sees, for instance, a C next to a D-sharp, he has a vague idea of what that should sound like.)

Sinatra doesn't get as deeply into the groove, so to speak, as Mel Tormé or Nat King Cole, and he isn't a rhythmic chameleon any more than he is a multigeneric musical everyman like Bing Crosby. Nonetheless, he has worked in a wide range of formats; in the '60s, in particular, he kept his art fresh and vital in his third decade at the top by collaborating with orchestra stylists as individual as Basie, Antonio Carlos Jobim, and Duke Ellington, while using a different orchestrator on almost every new album. "I tried to vary the arrangers," he once said, "so that there's a different quality to the songs." But Sinatra's primary focus has been on doing a smaller number of things extremely well. When one experiences Sinatra in concert, essentially one hears two kinds of songs: fast and swinging uptempo numbers and slow, emotionally intense ballads.

A great many classic Sinatra numbers may fall between those two poles ("Witchcraft," "Young at Heart," "Summer Wind"), but these extremes represent Sinatra's two primary musical colors. We can talk about his technical capacities in terms of both pitch and rhythm, and say how this singer might have better intonation or that one swings more, but no one can employ these gifts and put it all together as meaningfully as Sinatra. Earlier, both Jolson and Crosby had developed the idea that a pop performer could be at once a master musician and a great dramatist, but Sinatra brought both ideas to their fruition. His style is, in every sense, the synthesis of fifty years of influences going back and forth between jazz-inspired and mass-media-motivated popular music.

With Sinatra, all vocal considerations—and even all musical considerations—come second to his fundamental mission, which is to tell a story in the most expressive way possible. His formidable musical and dramatic skills immediately blur together. Sinatra has often spoken of his "long breath" technique, which he characteristically identified as the single most essential element of his artistry. "It's important to know the proper manner in which to breathe at given points in a song," he once told friend and interviewer Arlene Francis, "because otherwise what you're saying becomes choppy. For instance, there's a phrase in the song 'Fools Rush In' that says, 'Fools rush in where wise men never go / But wise men never fall in love / So how are they to know?' Now that should be one phrase because it tells the story right there. But you'll hear somebody say, 'Fools rush in' and breathe [right in the middle], 'Where wise men never go'—breath—'But wise men never fall in love . . . ' But if you do it [in one breath], that's the point, you told the whole story."

While Sinatra often discussed his breathing technique in interviews (back when he used to give them), he rarely if ever mentioned any other tools in his kit. The fact of his singing multiple lines on a single breath (actually, in his 1960 version of "Fools Rush In," he divides the four lines into two breaths) may be the least remarkable thing that he does within that eight-bar phrase. It isn't just breathing but a multilayered process involving dynamics, shading, accenting, twisting of pitch and vocal color, all within a single long-breath phrase.

He holds the first "fools" and stretches the "ooo" sound in the middle, then catches up by fittingly rushing through the word "rush." Then he makes it sound as if he's going down a tone on the word "in" even though both "rush" and "in" are actually sung on the same note. The next two lines contain an imitative textual-musical device in which the words "wise men never" are heard in each, and Sinatra phrases each occurrence of the three words so differently that they might as well be completely different. The first time, he puts a slight syncopation on the word "never" by accentuating the first syllable ("NE-ver"). The second time, he emphasizes "WISE men" and then he pauses for roughly half a beat between those two words and the next ("never") so that, rather than stressing the parallel construction of a master lyricist, in this case Johnny Mercer, he makes the lyric seem more immediate, as if it were occurring to him as he's singing it.

Even before this section of the song there's another peerless exhibition of technique, when he connects the end of one word, at the finish of a line, to the start of the next, a device he uses here in the bridge of "Fools Rush In" and more spectacularly in his blockbuster concert piece "Ol' Man River." "Frank used to do one thing that really freaked me out on my ass," vibraphonest Emile Richards recalled. "He would hold his hands behind his back as if he were handcuffed, pull his shoulders forward, or his chest forward and his shoulders back, to get more air. He would go, 'Tote that barge / Lift that bale / Get a little drunk and you land in jailllll . . .' and without a pause for a breath would go right into 'I get weary.' He would go that long without a breath, and then still sing 'I get weary.' And by the time he got there, let me tell you, he was friggin' weary! I tried doing that along with him a couple of times, and it was almost impossible. But he did it with that one breath, and it was so effective, it gave me chills or made me cry every time."

Sinatra's ballads can be intimate, like "Fools Rush In," or larger than life, like "Ol' Man River." Whether he wants it to sound like the working out of an extemporaneous mental process, as in the former, or a proclamation from God, as in the latter, every note, every syllable, every inflection is exactly in place. Contrastingly, on Sinatra's swingers, the singer is just as unflappably informal as he is precise on the love songs. He takes a devilish delight in toying with the tune (not that he doesn't alter melodies on slow numbers, too, though not with the same gleeful audacity), substituting his pet phrases for key words in the lyric, dancing around with it, boxing with it. Sinatra can maintain the inherent intimacy of a piece like "I've Got the World on a String" even at a superfast speed and in spite of his apparent refusal to treat the text as a temple that must be treated as sacred.

The result is total credibility. No popular recording artist has ever been as totally believable so much of the time as Sinatra. "Frank was very attentive to lyrics," explained Alan Livingston, who signed Sinatra to Capitol Records in 1953. "If he was looking at songs, the lyric would be his very first consideration. Frank wanted to know what that song said and whether it appealed to him or not. He said, 'I'll leave the music to somebody else. I pick the lyrics.'" The results come through especially clearly in an overtly autobiographical text like "My Way." Sung by any other interpreter, including the teenage idol Paul Anka (who translated it from the original French), that 1969 hit would sound like an obnoxious joke. In fact, it's a deliberate gag in the messy mitts of Sid Vicious and an unintentional one in the trembling tremolos of Elvis Presley, both of whom recorded it.

"My Way," Livingston said, "is [absolutely] Frank. He's telling you a story there. And it has to be something that he believes in, like 'In the Wee Small Hours of the Morning.' I know Frank [suffered through] many wee small hours of the morning in his unhappy days. Frank has lived through every conceivable emotion. He's had unhappy divorces, and lost women he didn't want to lose, and experienced his career going down the tubes. He went through everything that could happen to a young man who had been *the* teenage idol from the forties. I think that actually gives him his credibility as well as his ability to interpret a lyric and to phrase it. Because he feels it, he understands it."

In contrast, Mitch Miller, who at Columbia produced some of the greatest and worst records of Sinatra's career, warns against over-emphasizing life experiences and undervaluing the technique of a great popular singer. "The ability to bring all your talent together at a certain moment depends solely on craftsmanship," claimed Miller. "Emotion never makes you a hit. I always tell this to singers: Emotion is not something *you* feel. It's something you make the listener feel. And you have to be very cool and know what you're doing. You get a little tear in your voice, you put it there if the lyric calls for it—and little things like that. That's where a good producer comes in. Because now you're going to a nightclub, or you're going to do it on radio or television. What are you going to do? You had a fight with your wife. The kid threw up at you. Comes eight o'clock, you have to go on. You have to put it together! So it's craftsmanship." Miller emphasized that, even in the lowest point of Sinatra's life when his career and his voice were both fading fast, Sinatra always had "craftsmanship."

Irv Cottler, who played drums for Sinatra for nearly thirty-five years, once reported that the singer's passionate involvement with his material immediately communicated itself to both the musicians accompanying him and to the audience. "He gets you up emotionally, because that's what you need to be a player. You have to have a lot of emotion, and he's got that, he projects that. If you don't have that kind of feeling, then forget it, you can't play." As orchestrator Robert Farnon corroborates, "Frank is the inspiration. You know when you're writing for him or in anything you do for him, you have to do your very, very best."

One anecdote will illustrate how Sinatra inspires an orchestra: For one week in the mid to late 1940s, Sinatra served as guest star and host of a nightly radio musical series. The musicians in the show's house band, some of whom had worked with Sinatra before, quickly discovered the difference between Sinatra and the program's regular star crooner, who was out sick that week with a cold. "We're at a rehearsal," recalled lead alto Artie Baker, "and we're playing soft, the way we usually played for the regular star. Frank had his hat over his eyes and was looking very unhappy. He finally stood up and said, 'I would sure like to hear the band. I want to hear the music. Can you guys play a little louder? When I sing, I want to sing *with* the band. And I want the band to swing! So let's take it from there, guys.' That was beautiful. Frank really got the band to swing, and boy, we were swinging like crazy by the time [the regular singer] came back." When he returned, he immediately complained that the band was playing too loud and too intense for him. 'Well, I'm back now,' he announced at the next rehearsal, meaning, 'Knock it off!'"

Bing Crosby once told jazz journalist George Simon, "I like making records even more than making movies. That's because you're constantly creating. And the good thing about it is that when you're finished recording, you've got something that's really your own." The Crooner's greatest disciple shared that opinion. "One thing that impressed me so much in talking with Sinatra from time to time during the [*Great Songs from Great Britain*] sessions," Robert Farnon reminisced, [was that] "he said his favorite method of working was in the recording studio, as opposed to a concert hall or doing films or whatever." No vocalist before Sinatra had so completely fathomed the possibilities of recording and was able to so totally transform the medium.

The first pop singer to bring a consciously artistic attitude to recording, Sinatra developed a sound expressly tailored to the acoustic requirements of microphones and disc-cutting machines—to an even more refined degree than Crosby. He also became the first pop singer to perceive possibilities for record making that went beyond individual songs. Even though Crosby's career as a band vocalist and then a solo star preceded Sinatra's by a decade, The Voice beat Crosby to the punch in the development of what has come to be known as the "concept album."[1]

That first album was *The Voice*, released by Columbia in 1945. Twenty-two years later Sinatra collaborated on the album *Francis Albert Sinatra & Antonio Carlos Jobim* with the Brazilian songwriter Jobim and the German orchestrator Claus Ogerman. Like most of Sinatra's arrangers, Ogerman worked on the charts right up to the last minute. A few hours before the first date, he arrived early at the Western Sound Studios in Los Angeles with the intention of using the time to finish the final arrangement. However, Ogerman recalls, "To my amazement, Frank was already there. He was rehearsing the tunes with [accompanist] Bill Miller, which shows the reason why he's so professional and why he needs only one or two takes—because he works on all the stuff beforehand. I found it remarkable."

Preparation for a Sinatra session, particularly on one of the classic concept albums, always began much earlier. Sinatra starts not so much with an idea but a mood. (Only later in his career, in the sixties, would Sinatra use an extramusical connecting point, on masterpieces like *Academy Award Winners*.) He would then select a set of songs around a particular feeling, as expressed in both tempo (ballads or swingers and all gradations between) and instrumentation (all brass, a string orchestra, a chamber group).

---

1. The statement requires a little qualification: Decca Records had collected some of Crosby's singles into eight-song albums on many occasions, but as far as several astute Crosby scholars can determine, the Bingster never actually sat down and planned a true concept album until after Sinatra had done it. Likewise, jazz chanteuse Lee Wiley had recorded several songbook collections of a single composer's work, but she can hardly be considered a mass-market pop star.

Most important, Sinatra sequenced the songs so that the lyrics created a flow from track to track, affording an impression of narrative, as in musical comedy or opera. "The thing about Sinatra," Frank Military explains, "was that he never went into a record session just to do a record session. He sat down and carefully planned his albums, and lyrically they had to make sense. They had to tell a story. He'd spend days and weeks just preparing this album. Each song would be handpicked, it had a reason for being in the album."

Sinatra selected and sequenced these songs occasionally with the expert assistance of his in-house songwriters, Jimmy Van Heusen and Sammy Cahn. Both were fellow music mavens, and Van Heusen was also Sinatra's close pal for several decades. The composer also served as rehearsal pianist on many occasions when Sinatra was learning new material, primarily because he was on hand more frequently than Bill Miller. In addition to helping him organize albums out of other people's songs, Cahn and Van Heusen made many of Sinatra's concept albums even more conceptual by writing new songs based on the LP's projected title. In the case of *Come Dance with Me* (1958), the twosome took things a step further by providing Sinatra with a closing number, "The Last Dance."

But the majority of the songs are older standard songs, which the Sinatra concept albums made a point of featuring. Beginning in the mid-1940s, Sinatra concentrated (as much as he could get away with) on classic songs that had usually originated in Broadway shows. This at a time, it should be stressed, when *Your Hit Parade* (a radio series that Sinatra starred in for two different stretches) was dominated by ephemeral novelties.

While Sinatra makes a point of featuring great theater songs, he has an affection for practically any half-decent opus from the '20s and '30s, the years he was growing up and first listening to popular music. He is especially fond of Walter Donaldson (including three of the jazz-age composer's "oldies" on the *Strangers in the Night* album, a set ironically subtitled "Sinatra Sings for Moderns") and nearly anything that Bing Crosby sang. (Jimmy Van Heusen was earlier, in fact, half of the team of Burke and Van Heusen, Crosby's own "staff" composer and lyricist for more than a decade.)

Even as Sinatra selected the songs, he had already chosen his orchestrator for any given project. For more than half of his albums it was a given that the arranger would be Nelson Riddle (just as Sinatra almost invariably relied on Axel Stordahl in the 78 era). While Riddle could handle either ballad or swing sets, Sinatra doled out his other assignments according to each writer's key strengths: Billy May for "up" records, Gordon Jenkins for downers. In the post-Capitol years, Sinatra expanded his options to include such specialists as Johnny Mandel (more modern, jazz-styled uptempos), Neal Hefti (more fundamentally earthy swing, with and without Count Basie), and Robert Farnon (almost cerebrally tranquil love songs).

George Siravo, perhaps the most underrated of Sinatra's collaborators, feels that the term "arranger" falls short of doing justice to what he—and Stordahl, Riddle, May, and the rest—actually do. "We're really more like a musical designer, like Christian Dior. The only thing we don't create is the actual cloth itself. But 'arranging,' like they say, requires the same abilities as a composer—you have to create something that will enhance the original melody. It isn't just taking a bunch of chairs and placing them around a table. These guys—like a Nelson Riddle or a Ralph Burns—are true creators."

"On occasions when we were working [in nightclubs or Las Vegas]," guitarist Al Viola, who frequently played for Sinatra during more than thirty years, explained, "we might be warming up in the back room or having a drink. He would look at a tune or he would look at a bunch of songs and say, 'You know, this fits Gordon Jenkins.' Or he would say, 'This would be a great song to do with Nelson.' The *Come Fly with Me* album was typically Billy May, and Frank knew it. Most big-time singers today and even [back then] usually leave those kinds of decisions to their piano players or their musical directors. But Frank used to say, 'I want Nelson to do this album.' Frank was the man who took total charge; he didn't leave it up to the A&R man or anybody. He really thought about his songs. He knew where he was going to go. That's what made him great."

As Sinatra elaborated in the mid-1980s (using the editorial "we" in a genuinely humble fashion), "In ballads, obviously, in the beginning we went with Axel, and then we went to Nelson and then to Gordon Jenkins. And then, [from] the rhythm things, I moved from Billy May to Johnny Mandel to Neil Hefti and people like that. And then came Don Costa into my life."

At this point, Sinatra explains, "We [Bill Miller and Sinatra] would sit down with the orchestrator, and I would give him my thoughts on what the background should be from eight measures to eight measures or four measures to four measures." Sinatra then modestly added, "Then I would say, 'How wrong am I?' And he would say, 'Well, you're about 60 percent all right, but let me explain to you how I think it should be done.' Usually we wind up doing it the way the orchestrator feels it should be done because he understands more than we do about it."

Riddle later gave Sinatra total credit for the tempo and general outline of each number. "Frank would have been thinking about songs for days," the arranger recalled, "and I used to sit there and take notes. And he, in a sideways joke which I think had some validity, said that I was the best secretary he ever had because I'd take notes and three months later we might do the album. And you could never depend on him forgetting what he had said three months previously. I took the notes on what we discussed, and that's what he got."

In the beginning of the Sinatra-Riddle relationship, "as often as not, Nelson hated it," Bill Miller recalled, probably because no other singer had ever made such demands. "But that got to be a habit. He began to expect it." Sinatra would also make changes on arrangements right up until the session. Riddle had originally planned for "Ol' MacDonald" (1960) to commence with an orchestral introduction, but on hearing the chart, Sinatra decided to open more simply with just the rhythm section. Riddle wasn't thrilled with anybody making any kind of change on his work ("Nelson didn't like that at all," said Miller) but ultimately had to concede that Sinatra's way was better.

"Frank has the finest musical taste that I've ever run into, and I've been around for 163 years," Gordon Jenkins told deejay Paul Compton. "I wouldn't question this man's ideas of what's good and bad in music because I've never seen him wrong. Every suggestion that he's ever made to me has been an improvement. He has an unfailing feel for tempos in a song. You might be inclined to think that a ballad is slow, but it's never just slow."

Sinatra didn't always work as closely with his arrangers as he did with Riddle. May and Jenkins, who were known commercial commodities when Sinatra began working with them, were more often left to their own devices. Riddle, however, was barely known even in the music business and at that time had no automatically identifiable style the way May and Jenkins had. In a sense, Riddle was a blank page upon which Sinatra could write, and he inspired the trademark Riddle sound with its colorful emphasis on flutes and bass trombones to blossom.

The ideas that Sinatra did pass along to his other collaborators, however, were generally ingenious, such as the outline for the introduction to "Lonely Town" on *Where Are You?* (1957). He would continually make changes even after initial takes were recorded; in fact, he would implement changes even after the session, in postproduction editing and mixing. If he decided he didn't like an arrangement, he would commission a new one.

Nelson Riddle, only half kidding (in his usual highly caustic fashion), once named *Only the Lonely* his favorite album because he had an entire week, much more time than usual, to work on the arrangements. Arranger Johnny Mandel feels that a month is a respectable interval for the proper writing of an entire album, yet Billy May, in particular, was capable of doing a whole chart in not much longer than it took to play the tune on the piano.

While the arranger was scribbling away, the "contractor," as he was called, would be assembling the orchestra. Riddle hated to record unless Felix Slatkin was available to play first violin, along with his wife, Eleanor, on lead cello; why this was so comes through beautifully in Slatkin's solo on "Close to You." Contrastingly, Gordon Jenkins preferred a classical concertmaster—in particular, Dave Frisina, who served as first violin with the Los Angeles Philharmonic. When Jimmy Bowen produced a series of contemporary pop singles with Sinatra in the mid-1960s, he made a point of using Nashville-style fiddlers, who again brought a completely different, more hillbilly kind of string sound to the proceedings. Likewise, May and Riddle preferred drummers Alvin Stoller and Irv Cottler, as did Sinatra himself, whereas Jenkins' percussionist of choice was Nick Fatool.

Working with musicians-for-hire, Sinatra and his associates were able to maintain the major musical virtue of the swing era—namely, bands that played together night after night for months or years on end made for tighter and more precise ensembles. Sinatra drew from a relatively small pool of musicians and kept these veteran players working together so frequently that they might as well have been a regular "road" band. Johnny Blowers, Sinatra's most frequent drummer in the years 1942 to 1952, recalled that the singer's accompanying musicians were usually referred to as the "Sinatra Band." Since an album typically required three sessions, Sinatra and his contractors made it a particular point to ensure that the same musicians would be available for all three.

These sessions would be scheduled for three hours, with one ten-minute break, as per the union. For this, Capitol Records would expect four sides and the musicians would expect $50 (which would be, according to Bernhart, approximately $150 in '90s dough). "And don't forget, we were based in Los Angeles," Alan Livingston delineates, "where all these great musicians worked in the film studios. They would be at the film studio all day at Paramount or Fox or MGM, and they would come and play at night for us. Most of our sessions were at night."

"There were so many sessions in those days," French hornist John Cave said, "and we'd be playing for the studios all day and then at night working for Sinatra," who, for his part, was also often making movies all day. "We'd all be pooped out, and Sinatra would sometimes sense this. So he'd break out a jug of Scotch or something and start passing it around to the guys. Of course, we all played better after that."

Nearly all the brass, reed, and rhythm players on Sinatra's dates were veterans from varying stages of the swing era. Many, such as guitarist George Van Eps (born 1913) and drummers Nick Fatool (born 1915) and Johnny Blowers (born 1912), were already at the top of their field at the time of the initial explosion of the swing band boom in 1935. (Both Fatool and Van Eps were associated with Benny Goodman's 1930s groups.) By the Capitol era, many musicians in such latter-day swing / proto-"progressive" bands as Woody Herman, Stan Kenton, and Claude Thornhill graduated into Sinatra's studio orchestras. In the '60s, many outright jazz modernists, such as Marty Paich, Bud Shank, and Don Fagerquist, were getting the calls to do Sinatra sessions.

"The thing about Frank," Blowers explained, "was that he knew about everybody, and he handpicked his men. He knew more about you than you ever knew about him. When I first met him, he knew all the things I had done since I had been in New York. Frank is phenomenal that way." Dave Frisina added, "He just made it his business to know everyone."

Sinatra picked up musicians, arrangers, and songs in the same way: he'd hear something he liked and decide if he could use that sound. An admirer of the great Red Norvo–Mildred Bailey band of the late '30s, he used the band's distinctive sound in his 1954 *Swing Easy* and put many of the group's key men on his payroll, including his longtime tenor soloist Herbie Haymer, even longer tenured pianist Bill Miller, and drummer Irv Cottler, and then eventually Red Norvo himself.

A pioneering advocate of racial equality, Sinatra was color-blind in his pursuit of the players he wanted, long before mixed sessions became socially acceptable or even before the musician's union was integrated. Indeed, the most famous of all Sinatra musicians was and is master trumpet obligatist Harry "Sweets" Edison, who had spent several decades on the road with Count Basie. Sinatra also landed Ellingtonians Willie Smith and Juan Tizol (valve trombone, most notably on Sinatra's 1956 "Night and Day"), Plas Johnson (on "That Old Feeling"), and the King Cole Trio's bassist Joe Comfort (who supplies the thunderous "In a Mellotone"–inspired bass breaks on the 1956 "Too Marvelous for Words").

"I think Sinatra never gets enough credit for what he did as far as fighting segregation," said background singer Lillian Clarke, wife of the late arranger Sy Oliver. "He was really in the forefront." Like most of Sinatra's musical associates, Mrs. Oliver feels that "he just got publicity for all the bad news but none of the good deeds."

Sinatra's musicians, in particular the former swing-bandsmen, were truly "his people." When Sinatra felt particularly close to a musician who happened to share his Italian ancestry (among them Al Viola and Emil Richards, who had been born Emilio Radocchia), he had a common nickname for them, "Dago," which he often truncated to "Dag." In Sinatra's parlance it meant "paisano" or "homeboy," and Viola and Richards regarded the epithet as a badge of honor.

"An electrical something or other seems to shoot into the room when he walks in," producer Sonny Burke wrote in 1965. "The musicians, the fans who might be there, and anyone around senses it. However, the tenseness is dispelled with a joke, a warm greeting, or a humorous comment, and everyone has the feeling that something's about to happen."

As much as he enjoyed playing with Sinatra, in sessions trombonist Bernhart was on pins and needles because so many people—apart from the orchestra and engineering team—were always present to witness whatever went down. "There was always a large crowd," Bernhart remembered. "They should have charged admission. There were a hundred, two hundred people sitting in this audience because the recording studio at Capitol on Melrose had been a radio studio, with a very big auditorium. And the place was packed. You weren't just playing a record date; you were playing a performance. They took a great chance on the people applauding because they could get caught up in this thing and ruin a take. I don't know who kept them from applauding, but believe me, they were all sitting on the edge."

On the mid-1960s dates put together by Jimmy Bowen, the producer ensured that no really big celebrities were present, explaining, "I didn't want Frank competing with anybody. I wanted him to have to turn on a crowd because that's when those guys [Sinatra, Dean Martin, Sammy Davis, Jr.] did their best work—in front of people live—and it worked every time.

"I was doing one of the songs with Sinatra, when this real great-looking woman got out of her chair—right while tape was rolling—and walked across the floor in her high heels! You could hear it—click click click click! She opened the door and went out—she had to pee! Well, we lost it, you know. Everybody cracked up, so we had to wait until she came back in and sat down, before we could do the take again. Everybody was laughing too hard."

Typically, the band would play through the chart once, and rarely more than once, to get a feel for it and look for wrongly copied notes. Sinatra, at this point usually in the control room with the engineer, would be checking the recording balances as well as looking for ways to improve the arrangement—as on the 1949 "It All Depends on You," when he edited sixteen bars out of an instrumental chorus. After hearing the arrangement played once, Sinatra would then attempt a vocal, sometimes with the recording apparatus turned on, sometimes not.

"I remember just running the orchestra down," arranger-conductor Marty Paich said of his one session with Sinatra, "and he sang along with it and said, 'Okay, let's do it,' and then he just gave sort of like one or two cracks at it, and that was the end of it." Paich is the only arranger who didn't share Sinatra's preference for working this way. Known for his intricate, modern jazz–oriented orchestrations, Paich wished "that I could have had more time with him. When we went into the studio, it all went by so quickly." However, most musicians (particularly those based in the swing era) preferred doing it Sinatra's way. Trombonist Bobby Pring recalled that many bandleaders or pop singers would insist on running through a number over and over "until it sounded really labored. Frank liked to keep a feeling of freshness, which I agreed with."

Sinatra occasionally went for more takes when it was obviously necessary, most famously on "I've Got You Under My Skin."[2] He found that he could be a perfectionist without sacrificing spontaneity. Bowen remembered, "You'd be going along and he'd say, 'Hold it, hold it just a second. I think there's something "rubbing" there in bar nineteen or twenty.' And sure enough there'd be something wrong, a mistake in copying or something."

"He's very hip about what goes on with a band," observes Billy May. "He knows what to look for. He can look around in the band, and he can pretty much tell if it's a happy band or if there's some bullshit going on."

"Everything was Frank," Eleanor Slatkin explained. "Anything you did with Frank was Frank's idea. To be a producer for him had to be a joke because there was no producing [done by anybody else] to speak of. Anybody who produced with Frank, all he did was announce the takes and say, 'Frank, I think you should hear it.' That's *all*. The input was all Sinatra's. He really ran the session."

"What record producer in the world wouldn't give his right arm to work with Sinatra?" asked Alan Freeman, who received that credit on the 1962 *Great Songs from Great Britain*. Yet, "I can't really say I 'produced' him because Sinatra really produces himself." Freeman also

---

2. While the discographies list twenty-two takes on "Skin," this count must also encompass a high percentage of "false starts" in which a take didn't make it past the first thirty seconds or so.

related [to interviewer Stan Britt] that the act of his which most impressed Sinatra was researching the brand of whiskey that Ol' Blue Eyes preferred and making sure that three bottles of same were within arm's reach between takes.

Tenor saxophonist Ted Nash compares three legends with whom he recorded extensively: Sinatra, Doris Day, and Barbra Streisand. Nash describes Miss Day, with whom he goes back the farthest (they both apprenticed in Les Brown's band) as having the talent to "be a great singer, if only she had been given the right material. But when she started getting big, [Columbia Records] started giving her these crappy songs, which made her a big star, but it took away from her singing ability, because everyone thought of her as a trite 'Que Sera, Sera'-type of singer from then on. She just played it lightly, took it as it came. But she never really had the ambition to be that great. She just sort of floated along with whatever came up.[3]

Jumping 180 degrees in the opposite direction, Nash explains that Ms. Streisand "comes in and takes over the whole scene. From then on, no one has anything to say. She dictates the whole policy of the date." Violinist Dave Frisina agrees. "Streisand is tempermental. She's got her own ideas about music and she's not happy unless it's done exactly the way she wants. I only did a couple of sessions with her because I found her so difficult to work with, but then, so does everybody else."

Sinatra falls right in the middle of the two extremes, being neither too passive nor too aggressive. "Frank was half-and-half," Nash feels. "If he had something going, and it wasn't quite right, all of a sudden he'd stomp down and start laying out the situation. But otherwise, if it was going right, he wouldn't have much to say on some of those dates. He had confidence in his people [whom he had chosen to work with] and let them do their thing, and he did his thing, which was what made him such a success."

Yet while Sinatra had no reservations about changing things that didn't suit him, his first move upon hearing the chart actually played was to figure out exactly what he could do to accommodate it. "He would hear what the arranger had put down, listening while he was thinking and wandering around the studio." Producer Dave Cavanaugh told Paul Compton in 1973. "Dean [Martin] used to kid him and say, 'You're wandering around because you don't know the song.' He knew it all right,

---

3. Pianist Lou Levy offers a similar account of recording with the great Ella Fitzgerald: "Ella would just walk in and do whatever they handed her, under orders from Norman Granz."

but he wanted to figure out where he would sing, and where he would breathe. He had the great flexibility to adjust to what the chart was, and to duck out of the way of the accompanying orchestra (when it) had something to say."

He also knew when the musicians were playing well. "Frank will never come right out and tell you that you swung your ass off," Irv Cottler made clear, meaning that swinging and playing to the best of their abilities was the very least that was expected of musicians. When Milt Bernhart played what might be the world's most exciting and best-known trombone solo (on "I've Got You Under My Skin"), Sinatra invited the brassman to come into the booth and listen to the playback with him. It was the greatest compliment the Chairman could have paid to one of his fellow board members. When Mahlon Clark played a stunning clarinet interlude on "I Couldn't Sleep a Wink Last Night," he asked the singer, "Frank, was the clarinet okay?" Sinatra replied, "You're asking me? You guys are asking *me?* Of course it was all right!"

"Nothing would embarrass him so much as a compliment," said Bernhart. "Once, I was playing with Frank at the Sands, and it was the first time he had done 'One for My Baby' by himself with just piano. Right before, he had said to Bill, 'Just stay with me,' and the two of them came up with this arrangement," a reduction of the one Riddle had written for *Only the Lonely.* "So he did his little acting bit, trembling as if he'd had a few drinks. It was a masterpiece. Afterward, everybody held their breath, and there was a count of about five before they applauded, and then the house came apart.[4] After the show I was still shaking a little bit, it was that moving. So I went up the stairs to his dressing room. Frank was sitting by himself and looking into the mirror, which he rarely did. He was sitting alone, and I just stuck my head in and said, 'That was unbelievable. I'll never forget that, Frank.' And his response was, 'Aah!' He didn't want to hear it." Bernhart got a sample of Sinatra's idea of high praise when the singer was describing a date on which French hornist Vince DeRosa played beyond even his usual impeccably high standards. "I wish you guys could have heard Vince last night," Sinatra said to a small group of brassmen. "[He sounded so good that] I could have hit him in the mouth!"

"And believe me," Bernhart explained, "he reserved [such accolades] for only special circumstances. That's Sinatra. He sings with the grace of a poet, but when he's talking to you, it's New Jersey. It's remarkable."

4. Unbeknownst to Bernhart, Sinatra and Miller had already recorded their duet version of "One for My Baby," which wouldn't be released until 1990. The Sinatra-Miller duo version had its origins in a treatment Sinatra performed with André Previn in the 1955 film *Young at Heart.*

Bernhart's favorite nonprofessional experience with Sinatra occurred at a more formal affair that the singer threw in his legendary Coldwater Canyon compound in 1957. The joint was crawling with luminaries: movie stars, producers, and assorted Los Angelian lunch-doers. Still, the biggest celeb of all, the blue-eyed one himself, spent the entire evening ignoring the Hollywood crowd in order to split a pizza with a handful of studio musicians and their wives, whom he'd also invited.

"Let's face it. That's his great pleasure in life, the music," said Lou Levy. "All the other pleasures are second to that in the long run. Music, that's his great love." The one person who has shared this great love with Sinatra more than any other partner is not an arranger or producer or songwriter but Bill Miller, Sinatra's accompanist and occasional conductor for over forty years. "Bill is the best," said Al Viola, expressing the opinion of every musician to ever play with the two men. "If you listen to the few records they did without any orchestra, like 'Where or When'[5] where it's just the two of them alone, you can hear the strong structure of his harmonies backing Sinatra. It's perfect!"

Yet as adroit as Miller is at minor-mood "saloon piano," let's not forget what a swinging soloist he is on such classics as "The Lady Is a Tramp," "Ol' MacDonald," and "The Lonesome Road," all of which open with Sinatra and rhythm trio only, with the orchestra gradually joining in.

Miller was born in Brooklyn in January 1915, making him almost a year older than the Old Man himself. He landed his first job with a "name" band around 1933, namely Larry Funk and His Band of a Thousand Melodies. In 1935 and 1936, sometimes being listed as Billy Miller, the pianist played for the ahead-of-his-time arranger-bandleader Joe Haymes in a group that included three of Sinatra's future favorite trumpeters: Chris Griffin, Zeke Zarchy, and Lee Castle. From Haymes, Miller moved on to an even more progressive group directed by Red Norvo. In fact, Norvo's music seemed so beautiful and uncommercial that Miller doubted he could ever put a working dance band together.

"When Red first offered me the job, I thought he was kidding," said Miller. "I had earlier worked with Red in a couple of pickup bands, and then he comes out of nowhere and sends me a wire offering $75 a week. That was a lot of money then, and I figured, 'How could Red possibly afford to pay $75 a man?' Then, a couple of weeks later, some of the Haymes guys and I were listening to the radio, and we heard this great band. We couldn't figure out who they were, and the announcer didn't

---

5. Sinatra has also performed "One for My Baby" and "Angel Eyes" as duets with Miller, the latter on a 1965 *Tonight Show*.

come back for a few numbers. When they finally announced that it was Red Norvo, I called him right after the show. I lied and said that his wire had just reached me—which wasn't that unusual since we were on the road—and asked if the job was still available."

Beginning in early 1937, Miller served as pianist in the classic edition of the Red Norvo–Mildred Bailey "Mr. & Mrs. Swing Orchestra," which also featured Sinatra's first favorite saxophonist, Herbie Haymer (as well as that giant of American orchestration, Eddie Sauter). Then, through an equally fortuitous circumstance, Miller did it all over again when he captained the rhythm section of another of the swing era's legendary bands, Charlie Barnet and His Orchestra. By 1939, Mr. & Mrs. Swing's marriage as well as their band was on the rocks, while Barnet's star, in the aftermath of his biggest hit, "Cherokee," was on the rise. "Charlie was kind of a nutty guy off the bandstand," Miller observed, "like all those marriages—he was married eleven times to nine different women—but he was great to work for." As one of Barnet's key men from 1939 to 1942, Miller shared the leader's love for Basie and Ellington, and was called upon to pay homage to their styles in two 1939 instrumentals, "The Duke's Idea" and "The Count's Idea," both written by future Sinatra arranger Skippy Martin. Most of the band's charts, though, were written by trumpeter Billy May. Miller himself contributed several charts to the library, only one of which, the classic "Southern Fried," Barnet's take on a riff by Kansas City's Harlan Leonard, has been identified among the band's recordings.

"In [the summer of] 1940, when we were working the World's Fair, I was driving back into the city with a showgirl that I was dating," Miller recalled. "We turned on the radio, and they were playing 'All or Nothing at All,' the record that Frank made with Harry James. And she said, 'Hey, listen, doesn't that sound good? That's Dick Haymes.' I said, 'No, it's not Dick Haymes. Dick Haymes doesn't sing that good.' I didn't know who it was." Haymes was singing with James then, but "All or Nothing at All," although not released until 1940, had been cut a year earlier when Sinatra was still James's male singer. "And then they announced that it was Frank," Miller said. "That was the first time I was aware of his talent. I thought he was great."

Miller spent World War II with several army bands, although he didn't work in any of the "celebrity service" units like Glenn Miller's AAF or Artie Shaw's Navy bands. Although Barnet had temporarily replaced Miller with early modernists like Dodo Marmarosa and Al Haig, the pianist reclaimed his chair in the spring of 1946, but only briefly. The band business, if not quite on its last legs, certainly didn't have many limbs on which it could stand. Barnet's plans for a band that would stay on the West Coast didn't pan out, and Miller left in the fall of 1947. In the late '40s he subbed with a number of groups, including Tommy Dorsey and Benny Goodman, and then began playing more frequently for Martha Raye, with whom he had worked when she was an anonymous canary on a 1946 Barnet recording session. By 1951, Miller was working in Vegas.

Frank Sinatra played Nevada for the first time in 1951, working the Riverside in Reno in August and Moe Dalitz's Desert Inn in Vegas in September. He had recently parted company with accompanist Graham Forbes, who (the pianist later told maven Bob Sherrick) elected not to travel to the West Coast. Sinatra couldn't have been easy to work for in 1951, when his personal and professional lives had hit correspondingly low notes. He was doing little on records or in pictures, and his major venture of the time, his CBS TV show, was also on the rocks. "You should keep it in mind that Frank was having a rough time," said Al Viola. "His piano players were quitting on him because he didn't have the bucks." According to several sources, it was Jimmy Van Heusen who first "discovered" Miller playing piano in the lounge at the Desert Inn when Sinatra was working in the main venue, The Painted Desert Room. As Viola heard the story, Van Heusen reported to Sinatra, "Frank, I just heard a great piano player. He plays great chords and everything, and he's right here."

Sinatra, naturally enough, knew Miller from his work with Barnet and Norvo. Miller later told friend Mahlon Clark that when he spotted Sinatra, "I immediately started playing solos on songs he liked, and playing the notes that I knew he would like—the pretty notes. And then Frank came up to me and said, 'How would like to work with me, kid?'" Miller began playing for Sinatra at the Desert Inn and soon began accompanying him on the CBS show as well. Miller first recorded with Sinatra on all four of the singer's sessions in 1952, his final year with Columbia.

Miller had gone to work for Sinatra when the career of The Voice was at a low ebb. He was thus in the right place when the tide came back in and swept the Chairman of the Board to new heights. Miller remained *the* Sinatra pianist through the great years of live appearances all over the globe and the classic Capitol and Reprise albums. According to Al Viola, "Frank loved Bill because he was a real character." As Irv Cottler, who played drums next to Miller for so many years, put it, "Bill always looked as if he was falling asleep, but he sure knew what he was doing."

Sinatra initially nicknamed his accompanist "Moonface" Miller and eventually began directing even more attention to the pianist's

bleached-white, prison pallor. For example, here's how Sinatra introduced Miller at the Royal Festival Hall concert of June 1, 1962: "... and
of course my old chum, my right arm, you might say, my accompanist
who is the leader of this infamous group. We affectionately call him Suntan Charlie, and his complexion will explain why we call him that. We
suspect he lives under a rock and comes out at ten o'clock every evening,
but he's a marvelous pianist and a fine accompanist, Mr. Bill Miller."

By 1988, things hadn't change much: "Our pianist is a man who
loathes the sun. You'll see when he gets up. I call him 'Suntan Charlie'
[because] he has never had a suntan as long as I've known him. Mr. Bill
Miller from Burbank, California." As Miller stood and the audience
applauded, Sinatra continued, "See what I mean, folks?" Yet by 1994,
Sinatra in concert was introducing Miller with words that were considerably warmer than anything he was saying about his conductor and son,
Frank Sinatra, Jr., describing Miller, accurately, as "a fine musician, a
wonderful man, and he's my partner at the piano."

Miller was not without his resources, however, if Sinatra took his kidding too far. "Bill always took a lot of flak from Frank, but he had a way of
getting back at him," said Emile Richards. "If Frank said, 'Bill, give me a
tone,' then Bill would just hit one note. One little-bitty 'boop,' and that
would be it. He'd give him just the dinkiest little tone. It's as if Bill were
saying, 'Come on, bitch, find it! You've had it over me all this time, now I
got you!'" In fact, such a moment occurred during one of the sessions (on
an out-take reel) for a Sinatra-Basie album. Miller deputized for Basie on
several tracks of *Sinatra-Basie* and *It Might as Well Be Swing*. At one point
Sinatra asked Miller to help him with a note, and the pianist fed him the
most minuscule—and appropriately Basie-esque—little "plink" you
could possibly imagine. Without missing a beat, Sinatra dropped into his
"Amos 'n' Andy" voice and declaimed, "Man, you economical!"°

In 1969, Miller's house was destroyed in a Los Angeles mudslide. His
daughter managed to get out safely, but Miller's wife was killed, and the
pianist himself wound up in the hospital for several months. "After the
accident," said Viola, "Frank picked up all the medical bills, and he
bought Bill a new set of clothes and a new apartment." Sinatra was making the *My Way* single and album at the time and brought in Lou Levy.
This was the only Sinatra LP up to that time on which Miller didn't play.

In 1967, Miller had become Sinatra's regular road conductor, and he
alternated between the piano and the podium for the next decade. In
that same year, Sinatra and Miller recorded another of their saloon song

°One of the rare Sinatra concerts without Miller illustrates how valuable he was
to the Chairman: when accompanied by old friend Skitch Henderson (who never
claimed to be a jazzman) at a 1963 benefit concert at the United Nations, Sinatra
found it nearly impossible to settle into a swinging groove.

spectaculars, the exquisite "Drinking Again," in which manager Claus Ogerman, Riddle-like, drapes a light sheen of strings behind what is basically all voice and piano. In February 1976, Sinatra and Miller recorded "Empty Tables," which, with "One for My Baby," completed a three-song cycle of Johnny Mercer saloon songs reconceived as duets for the two men.

Both "Empty Tables" and its companion piece, "Send in the Clowns," had previously been taped by Sinatra with full arrangements by Gordon Jenkins, who considered "Clowns" the best chart he had ever written for Sinatra. The singer himself apparently did not share that opinion; although he included "Clowns" on the *Ol' Blue Eyes Is Back* album, the Jenkins treatment of "Tables" has so far come out only on an American 45 and an Italian LP. He redid them both with just Miller for accompaniment, and the difference between the full orchestra and piano-only renditions is as staggering as you'd expect. As good as Jenkins was, there's always an overt formality to his work, whereas the interpretations with Miller (Sinatra introducing "Clowns" with a spoken monologue) resonate as pure drama and emotion.

The only rupture occurred about ten years after the accident. "We just had a falling-out," says Miller, as casually as he says everything else. "What happened was we had been like bucking heads for a little while, six months or a year. I think I was there too long, and so I took him for granted, and he took me for granted." Miller missed Sinatra's last two classic albums, *Trilogy* (1979) and *She Shot Me Down* (1981): however, the two were reconciled by 1985. For two years, Miller conducted while Lou Levy, Bernie Leighton, and others sat at the piano. When Frank Sinatra, Jr., took over the baton in 1988, Miller went back to playing—which he preferred anyhow. Sinatra kept "One for My Baby" out of his book during the few years when Miller wasn't playing for him. Upon the pianist's return, Sinatra not only reinstated the tune in his repertoire, he and Miller recorded it for the third time together[6] in the summer of 1993. It's ironic that their most celebrated latter-day effort together should appear on an album called *Duets*, and even more so that, given all the guest stars brought in on Sinatra's classic songs, the only worthwhile duet is not with a singer at all. The puerile instrumental of "All the Way," torn apart by Kenny G. (who, unlike Miller, gets his name on the back tray card of the CD), unfortunately serves as an introduction to "One More for My Baby." Sinatra and Miller not only overpower the G-man, they transcend his intrusion.

6. Sinatra had originally recorded the Arlen-Mercer tune in 1947; sorely missing the presence of Miller, this Columbia version is by far the weakest of the four versions that he recorded commercially.

Sinatra's vocal here is one of the most painfully moving of his career. His ability to tell a story with a saloon song hasn't diminished. And Miller's accompaniment, as so many of his fellow musicians have said, can only be described as "perfect." Miller plays two roles at once: first, he's providing Sinatra with musical support, harmonies, and rhythm. As engineer Lee Hirschberg put it, "Bill's always has a great sense of what Frank [is] going to do. He always knew exactly where he was going to be, and he was always in the right place."

Second, Miller is a fellow actor "playing," if you will, the role of a piano player in the saloon which Sinatra's character has wandered into and where he's now telling his story. The great pain that Sinatra communicates comes through so strongly partly because it's delivered against such a spare background. What does the guy who is playing the piano in the back care about the drunk who is unburdening himself to the barely interested bartender in the foreground? Miller somehow manages to support Sinatra while all the time sounding as though he's ignoring him. If your heart doesn't stop by the time Sinatra gets to the last line, "that long, long road," then, in the immortal words of Louis Jordan, "Jack, you're dead!" Sinatra lengthens the road by repeating the penultimate phrase over and over—"it's long, it's so long." Every time you think it's going to end, it goes on again until you're dying for Sinatra to resolve the dramatic tension and put himself out of his misery. It's one of the most moving things you'll ever hear because if there are two guys in the world who know how long that road is, it's Frank Sinatra and Bill Miller.

One of Milt Bernhart's all-time favorite records was Sinatra's original Bluebird 78 of "The Night We Called It a Day," cut in 1942. Bernhart's future wife bought it when they were dating, and it became "their song." Bernhart told this to Sinatra at that 1957 party, and, the trombonist recalled, "I expected him to brighten up a little." But instead "his face darkened." Sinatra took out a test pressing of the yet-unreleased album *Where Are You?* that included a remake of "Night We Called It a Day" and played it for Bernhart.

For Sinatra, as Duke Ellington once said of his own work, "the new baby is always the favorite." It's quite beyond Sinatra to fathom why anybody would be sentimentally attached or even interested in his old recordings. He personally has no use for his records after he has finished making them. When Washington deejay Ed Walker asked Sinatra in 1983 to name his favorite albums, he answered, "The ones that stick in my mind are the ones where I think the orchestrator's work and my work came together closely, for instance, *Only the Lonely, Wee Small*

Hours, and one of the jazz things with Billy May." At this point Sinatra paused while he tried in vain to remember more album titles. Sinatra junkies, musicians, singers, and civilians of every stripe have memorized these albums from the first downbeat to the final coda, yet the man who made them hasn't thought about them enough in the years since he finished them to even remember their titles.

"To me, that's the mark of a creative soul," Bernhart said. "It could be a composer, a Rembrandt, or a sculptor. As soon as they're finished with it, they're really through with it. They're finished. They're on to another thing. They'll say, 'Those things are gone, and I am now looking at the next thing to do.'" It has never bothered Sinatra to record some songs two and three times; it has never occurred to him that one reason not to do a song is that he has done it before. Had he not been practically the only one picking his songs, he might have come up with a more varied repertoire, as opposed to so many versions of "The Song Is You." But that seems a small price to pay for the body of work that he has given us.

Which isn't to say that Sinatra ever repeats himself—even by recording multiple versions of the same song. "Frank's the only singer who would take a tune he had already done and completely rework it," Frank Military pointed out. "If he had sung it as a ballad, ten years later he might take it out again and make it a swinger. Or if it had been a fast number, he might redo it into a love song."

One of the qualities of the American popular song is its malleability. The great theater songs by Cole Porter, the Gershwins, Harold Arlen, and so forth, lend themselves to diverse interpretations. They can be played fast, slow, or medium, reconfigured as waltzes, two-steps, or marches, done as bossa novas, mambos, doo-wop, or operetta. However, as Military suggests, when most pop singers are satisfied with one approach to a particular tune, they tend to stick with it. For instance, more than thirty years ago Tony Bennett discovered that there actually was a way to do "One for My Baby" so that it wouldn't make his listeners think of Sinatra's devastating ballad rendition—by belting it as a rock-em, sock-em romper. It worked for him in the mid-1950s, and it still works for him in the mid-1990s. Likewise, Sinatra, with a song that's associated with him and no one else—such as "Strangers in the Night," "Witchcraft," and "New York, New York"—is similarly reluctant to fine-tune the mixture; audiences may not want to hear a new treatment of "My Way."

But Sinatra has taken plenty of songs, particularly classic show tunes, and tinkered with them endlessly. For instance, he's sung "Day In, Day Out" and "The Song Is You" more ways than you or even he can shake a cocktail at. The record-holder, however, would have to be "Night and

Day," which he has treated in nearly all tempos and moods and in every era of his seven decades of performing. By examining the different ways Sinatra has treated the Cole Porter classic, we can find out a great deal about the singer's working methods and how his artistry has evolved from the 1930s to the 1980s.

Porter wrote "Night and Day" in 1932 as a vehicle for Fred Astaire in the Broadway musical *Gay Divorce*. When that show became the basis for Astaire's first starring film, *The Gay Divorcée* (RKO, 1934), "Night and Day" became the sole song from the original score to be retained in the picture. It's not too much of an exaggeration to say that "Night and Day" represents the centerpiece of both Astaire's and Porter's movie careers. The image of Astaire and Ginger Rogers entangling with both passion and sophisticated formality in time to this amazing tune cemented the team as a solid box-office attraction. The song itself appeared in at least four other films (including a wartime short with Dinah Shore warbling special anti-Axis lyrics), not the last of which (if inarguably the least) was *Night and Day*, Warner Bros.' ludicrous Porter biopic in 1946.

Two factors affected the musical shape that the tune eventually took. First, like Duke Ellington, Porter wrote music for specific voices, and in devising a song for Astaire, Porter knew not to come up with anything that would require a multioctave range. Astaire was a great singer (and, like Sinatra, a supremely musical one) but not a great voice, and in writing for him, Porter relied heavily on short, repeated pitches with an infectious rhythmic quality rather than a lot of long-held notes.

Second, in a statement apparently doubted by many scholars, Porter, a noted world traveler, claimed to have been inspired by an Islamic religious chant he had heard in the Middle East. In a conversation with Richard Rodgers, Porter also claimed that he was deliberately trying to come up with tunes that had a "Jewish" feel to them. To Rodgers, "Night and Day" did sound "unmistakeably Mediterranean."

It's easy to see why "Night and Day" would be a standard of lasting value, particularly to jazz-oriented performers: its repeated notes (rather like a Gershwin piece) and bouncy rhythms could swing even though the song is normally done as a ballad. Likewise, its intriguing harmonic pattern, which not only continually shifts from minor to major but cleverly uses major chords as part of minor harmonic contexts, also holds great appeal for improvisers. The song is at once complicated and simple. Ten of the sixteen bars of the verse are sung on one and the same note (emphasizing the "beat, beat, beat" and the "tick, tick, tock" Astaire-style), yet the melody moves primarily in chromatic half-steps, a most unorthodox approach in 1932. Structurally, the piece has an AABA feel, with a clearly defined bridge, yet it actually breaks down into something more like ABABCB, because it doesn't exactly return to the original melody after the bridge but rather to a variation on the second half of the initial opening section, for a total of 48 bars.

Sinatra's personal association with "Night and Day" goes back years before he first recorded it in 1942 and even before the singer himself was "discovered" in 1939 by Harry James. "The song had been written about a couple of years before I decided I'd like to become a vocalist," Sinatra has recollected.[7] "And it was written by Cole Porter. I really believe he was the greatest ever, ever! It's one of the first songs I sang when I was a young, rising singer. I didn't get very far in those days, it took a little while, but as years went by I was using 'Night and Day' a lot wherever I worked."

Around 1937 or 1938, Sinatra was singing with a "club-date" style septet at the Rustic Cabin, a roadhouse near Englewood Cliffs, New Jersey. "On Sunday evenings during the summer months," Sinatra elaborated, "people would come back from the countryside and come through and stop and have a little nip before they went over the [George Washington] bridge to go back into New York." On one such evening "there were about seven people in the audience, and we had a six-piece 'orchestra.' The trumpet player, named Johnny Bucini, said to me, 'Do you know who's sitting out there?' I said, 'Yeah, I know that face. It's Cole Porter!' I couldn't believe it, but he was sitting out in the audience with four or five people. And I said to the orchestra leader, 'I'd like to do one of Cole Porter's songs. Let's do "Night and Day" for him, and I'll talk about it.'

"So I went out and said, 'Ladies and Gentlemen, I'd like to sing this song and dedicate it to the greatly talented man who composed it and who may be one of the best contributors to American music at this particular time in our lives.' I said that Mr. Porter was in the room and I introduced him, and he got up and took a bow. Then the orchestra played the introduction, and I did the first four bars and then proceeded to forget *all* the goddamn words, swear to God. I couldn't think. I just kept saying, 'Night and day, night and day,' for fifteen bars!"

The punchline to the story arrived roughly twenty years later when MGM cast Sinatra as one of the leads in *High Society*, a musical version

7. Sinatra has told the story several times in public (while tape was rolling), and this account is pieced together from several sources, including Sinatra's Yale interview-seminar with Sidney Zion, taped in May 1986, and a 1986 concert, privately issued on the two-LP set *Saloon Singer*. (In that particular concert, Sinatra demonstrated how he sang "Night and Day" on the original night in question, with the aid of the orchestra and the 1956 Nelson Riddle chart.)

of *The Philadelphia Story,* for which the studio commissioned a score from Cole Porter. One evening the composer invited the three principles, Bing Crosby, Grace Kelly, and Sinatra, over to his house to hear the newly written numbers. "He called me inside and said, 'Gee, it's been a long time since we met. I don't know if you remember an evening with me at some nightclub where you worked.' And I said, 'Oh, yeah, I remember very well.' He said, 'So do I. That's about the *worst* performance I ever heard.' But we kidded about it."

Considering his even-then longtime fondness for the song, it's not surprising that Sinatra would choose to include it on his debut session as a solo vocalist in 1942. (What is surprising is that Victor Records allowed him to choose his own material and a ten-year-old tune to boot.) This first of six commercially released Sinatra recordings of "Night and Day," like the second and third, consists of a chorus and half, the half of the refrain that he returns to after a brief instrumental break known as the "outchorus."

Like other songs, "Night and Day" has been published in many keys, including C Major and D-flat; the 1942 version is sung in E-flat. This great orchestration by Axel Stordahl also introduces the great arranger's equally classic countermelody, which pivots on a five-note phrase that the arranger repeats at various intervals and rhythmic durations, generally on the strings. During the years Sinatra used "Night and Day" as his radio theme song, Stordahl's original contrapuntal line became as familiar to listeners as Porter's central melody.

Many of the trademarks of Sinatra's mature Columbia period are already here: the long phrasing—often eight or even sixteen bars to a breath—the tenuous, breathlessly romantic sound, and the deeply felt and communicated recital of the lyrics. He achieves this partly with the aid of slight alterations, at once jazzy and incredibly personal, making the decade-old song sound spontaneous. The outchorus includes subtle grace notes and word-painting, such as "way *down* inside of me" and "this torment won't *ever* be through," both of which Sinatra would keep in the arrangement for years to come. This 1942 disc also includes an extra twist that occurs only here: when the singer gets to "traffic's boom / *or* in the silence" in the first chorus.

The orchestration concludes with another significant melodic alteration. Porter originally set the final three words ("night and day") on the same note—the tonic note, in fact. Sinatra takes the melody down; he sings this climactic "night and day" on three different notes in a descending pattern. Where, in this key, they should be E-flat, E-flat, and E-flat, he makes them D-flat, B, and B-flat. Sinatra would continue to treat the last notes of "Night and Day" in this fashion until the 1956 Riddle arrangement.

The Voice is clearly being pulled in two directions throughout the Bluebird session, his initial impulse being to move beyond the swing band sound. At fifteen pieces, the orchestra is considerably smaller than those Sinatra would use later on a ballad session, yet its combination of strings, woodwinds, and understated rhythm (no drums) is very different from anything any singer was using for accompaniment during this period. At the same time, this especially lilting first rendition of "Night and Day" is clearly part and parcel of the dance band era—the proof lies in the Crosby-like syncopation Sinatra employs on the hard "d" sound at the start of the very final "day." More important, Victor issued this "Night and Day" and the three other tunes from this January 13 session as part of their "Vocadance" series (on the Bluebird subsidiary), which spotlighted star singers from the big bands in vocal recordings designed for dancing. The budding star is therefore obliged to stick to a fairly rigid dance tempo.

Those restrictions gradually diminish with further readings of the classic Stordahl chart, of which more than a dozen additional Sinatra performances have been documented between 1942 and 1950. The second known rendition dates from eight months later, in September 1942. Only two weeks after leaving Tommy Dorsey (their parting performance was another reprise from the Bluebird session, "The Song Is You"), Sinatra prerecorded and then filmed this one song for Columbia Pictures' *Reveille with Beverly*—a B-musical spotlighting several different recording stars. The film's many numbers, done for the most part by popular big bands, had no connection to the picture's plot, which featured Ann Miller as a tap-dancing disc jockey who spins pop hits, each accompanied by the 1942 equivalent of a "music video."

Sinatra appears in the picture for only this number, which, considering how absurdly it's staged, may be something of a blessing: the ultra-thin crooner, clad in what amounts to half a tuxedo (or, as he once said, three sleeves), sings Porter's classic melody in Stordahl's exquisite orchestration for all it's worth while surrounded by a sorority of actresses in formal gowns all pretending to play pianos. This visual inanity unfortunately compromises the sanctity of the sound track; the chart is cluttered up with too many pianos, and, unfortunately, all the *pianos* are much too *forte*.

The arrangement really begins to change in seven performances documented over 1943 (Sinatra's first year of major-league celebrity) and 1944. The lilting dance feeling of the 1942 Bluebird gradually slows away, and Sinatra's interpretation of the orchestration starts to sound more and more like a concert piece. The backdrop gradually assumes the characteristics of a tone poem. It's still the same orchestration on paper, with the familiar countermelody and the "way *down* inside" and "torment won't *ever* be," but it feels completely different. With each successive rendition, the "roaring traffic's boom" gets boomier and "the silence of my lonely room" gets quieter, as the performance as a whole becomes ever more dramatic.

Sinatra "consummated" his relationship with "Night and Day" when he chose it as his opening theme on radio (the closing song was "Put Your Dreams Away"). Each week of *Old Gold Presents Songs by Sinatra* commenced with Sinatra singing the first two lines of the lyric, usually starting the first note by himself, a capella. Earlier versions also exist which utilize "N & D" as both an opening theme and a stand-alone number. Sinatra continued to use "Night and Day" as the opener for both seasons (1945–46 and 1946–47) and returned to it occasionally on later programs.

By 1947 the transformation from "vocadance" disc to concerto was complete—not least because "Night and Day" had by this time highlighted two Sinatra appearances at the Hollywood Bowl; even the radio theme readings are taken much slower than the 1942 version. In 1947, Sinatra rerecorded three of the four tunes from his original Bluebird date for Columbia, including "Night and Day," none of which Columbia released at the time, perhaps for contractual reasons. "The Song Is You" came out in 1958, and the other two, "The Night We Called It a Day" and "Night and Day," lay unissued and even undocumented in Columbia's vaults until 1993.

The 1947 "Night and Day," released at last on Sony's twelve-CD set *Frank Sinatra: The Columbia Years, 1943–1952, The Complete Columbia Recordings,* uses more than twice as many musicians as the 1942 reading. Again essentially the same arrangement, it now takes thirty-six seconds longer (from 3:03 in 1942 to 3:39 in 1947) to get through the same chorus and a half. Thirty-six seconds is a decade in the pop single business, and that extra half-minute may also help explain why Columbia kept it in the can. (Sinatra recorded a second "Night and Day" for Columbia that same day, October 22, 1947, this time with a truncated arrangement. That shorter one still remains unissued.)

Sinatra's style is even more mature by this time; now when he gets to the "boom," the beat is all but entirely suspended, and "the silence" is extended long enough so that we can hear more than the familiar harp but also a celesta in the mix. Where Sinatra was impeccably in tune in

1942, he now sounds more like his older self in that he bobs slightly under the pitch in spots, though one can't be sure if he might be doing this deliberately. He quivers on "spend my life" and bends the notes on the repetition of "under the hide of me" to express his feelings of longing and yearning that much more longingly and yearningly.

Oddly, Sinatra seems not to have sung a complete run-through of "Night and Day" during the entire run of the 1945–47 *Songs by Sinatra*. When he returned to star on *Your Hit Parade* in 1947–49, the advertising agency seems to have insisted on using the Lucky Strike theme ("My Lucky Day") and nothing else. In 1949, Sinatra switched from the *Hit Parade* to *Light Up Time*, a program closer to his own taste, also sponsored by Lucky Strike. Now the Sinatra theme, "Night and Day," could be heard very, very briefly after a line or two of the "Luckies" intro. Since *Light Up Time* rarely used a string section on its nightly fifteen-minute spot, the Stordahl chart had to be rethought once again. For the premier broadcast, the familiar violin countermelody is gone and a trumpet obligato follows Sinatra. (Sinatra apparently did perform a full treatment of "Night and Day" at least once on *Light-Up Time*, but I have not been able to hear it.)

Though "Night and Day" was never a career-making song for Sinatra the way "I Left My Heart in San Francisco" was for Tony Bennett, this is only the first installment of the multigenerational connection between song and singer. Sinatra next tackled "Night and Day" at several junctures in his transition from his young sound (that is, Stordahl) to his mature sound (that is, Riddle). The first is an extremely disappointing rendition from a generally unfortunate concert given in Blackpool, England, in July 1953.

In 1954, Sinatra exhibited an entirely new "Night and Day." This treatment is unique in many aspects, particularly in terms of its breakneck speed, representing the fastest that he would ever attempt the Porter piece (or practically anything else). Then there's also its Latin jazz format, via a small group with bongos and flute, probably the only time Sinatra ever worked in such a context.[8] This 1954 arrangement is also unique in the most literal sense in that Sinatra is known to have performed it once and only once, on his final radio series, *To Be Perfectly Frank* (various sources claim the cut is from June and October 1954).

Like the Stordahl treatment, this version has Sinatra ending on three descending notes; he here includes the verse after the first chorus,

---

8. He did do a session with Xavier Cugat in 1945, which afficionados would probably label as neither true Latin nor jazz; in the mid-1980s he began work on an album that would have been with timbales titan Tito Puente, but it never reached fruition.

before going into the outchorus. This marks the first time we've heard Sinatra sing the said verse, which is included on only one of the five issued studio recordings (the 1961). (Steve Lawrence later recorded an uptempo treatment of "Night and Day" in which he, with a slightly less Latin feel, phrases the verse over bongos in almost exactly the same fashion.) Sinatra's other uptempo readings pointedly omit these sixteen introductory bars.

With this particular performance, Sinatra indicates to us, in hindsight, that he knew that uptempo numbers were going to be a big part of his future. As it happened, this particular outline for a swinging number was not for him: the pace was too fast for Sinatra or anyone else to deploy the emotional expression necessary to get the most out of a Cole Porter love song. Ella Fitzgerald would do only a scat or a nonsense number ("A-Tisket a-Tasket") at this clip, and Jimmy Rushing might do a really fast blues at this metronome reading, but the only way to make the melody move this fast is to totally trash the words. (He also has to fudge some of the notes.) There are times when Sinatra was willing to do that—the Basie albums, for instance—but on most occasions his brand of jazz or rhythm singing was entirely different from anyone else's.

The great Nelson Riddle treatment of "Night and Day," introduced in 1956, illustrates precisely that point. Earlier that year Sinatra had brought his newly minted rhythmic and romantic style to a boil with the appropriately titled *Songs for Swingin' Lovers!* He then revived "Night and Day" for *A Swingin' Affair,* the album that today would have been called *Swingin' Lovers II.* Here's why the "heartbeat" tempo worked so well: it offers all the oomph of a swinger-dinger without Sinatra's having to sacrifice any of Porter's poetry to a horse-race time signature.

Which brings us to the central paradox of Sinatra's two best-known records of "Night and Day": The Stordahl/Bluebird is best summed up as a ballad and the Riddle/Capitol as strictly a swingin' affair. Actually, the first is a concert piece sped up to something close to dance tempo, while the second is a swinger slowed down to a heartbeat. The Capitol is certainly much more of a jazz performance; Sinatra swings a lot more in his phrasing, but ultimately the 1956 track is only marginally faster than the 1942.

The Riddle "Night and Day" exists in two key performances, on the *Swingin' Affair* album and as a run-through from Sinatra's weekly television series (November 29, 1957). Both readings commence with a fanfare—a brief orchestral intro, Sinatra singing "Night and day . . ." and then the orchestra reentering with a "POW!" before Sinatra gets to the next line ("you are the one!"). However, the TV version hits you even harder than the record because, while the commercial recording contains a very brief

pause after the initial "Night and day," the TV one amplifies it into a true
fermata (of a duration to be determined by the conductor), and by waiting
just half a beat longer, the opening becomes far more suspenseful.

The TV version makes one other crucial change from the Capitol. In
the *Swingin' Affair* cut, Sinatra and Riddle drolly refer to the song's
allegedly Middle Eastern inspiration by including a solo by valve-trom-
bonist Juan Tizol. A major voice in Duke Ellington's orchestra, Tizol had
established himself as a specialist in exotica as both a soloist and a composer of such Eastern- and Latin-oriented items as "Bakiff," "Pyramid,"
and the pivotal "Caravan." Tizol's statement in the midsection of "Night
and Day" logically refers to the trombonist's own career. However, the
principals are also alluding to the precedent-setting Sinatra-Riddle-
Porter-*Swingin'* piece "I've Got You Under My Skin" on *Swingin' Lovers*,
which employed a rough-and-ready trombone solo in much the same
fashion in the instrumental midsection. Riddle also reemploys the same
kind of bouncing brass, swinging strings, and overall orchestral coloration that he had pulled off so spectacularly in "Skin." This "Night and
Day," then, could have been called *I've Got You Under My Skin II.*

The nonvocal passage is crucial to the Riddle orchestration because
between first full chorus and outchorus, instead of doing the verse (as in
the 1954), Sinatra changes keys, starting half a step higher in E-natural.
Sinatra concludes with the tonic note as written and goes for a big ending, stretching that last note for dramatic impact. Overall, the TV version
packs a bigger wallop than the Capitol (even if the audio quality on the
commercial version is compensatingly far superior), although it lacks the
Tizol instrumental center—which presents us with a quandary: this
exotic interlude in the middle is quite an entertaining half-time show in
itself, but the chart and Sinatra swing harder without it. (A further live
version of the Riddle chart exists from a concert in the early 1980s, in
which the orchestra plays yet a third variation on the midsection.)

The next variation on the Riddle arrangement uses the interchorus
portion for an even more eventful transition—from small group to full
orchestra. In 1959, Sinatra played a pair of concerts (on March 31 and
April 1) in Australia with Red Norvo's Quintet—or rather, Norvo's group
plus Bill Miller. They open "Night and Day" with an instrumental chorus by Norvo and rhythm trio only in which the vibraharpist adroitly
improvises over the chords yet doesn't so much as drop a hint as to the
melody. Therefore, when Sinatra unexpectedly appears singing "Night
and Day," it exponentially amplifies the drama of his entrance. On both
nights Sinatra went through two full and fast choruses (as opposed to one
and a half) to further build up the momentum.

Sinatra's Australian vocal is even jazzier and packs more punch than the TV reading. Even before he enters on the March 31 performance— the more dynamic of the two—Sinatra can be heard commenting favorably on Norvo's solo ("Marvelous!"). He's like a fan who can't contain his enthusiasm, and that excitement immediately comes through in his vocal. He's enjoying himself so much that he has to force himself to stifle his contagious cackling. He shares an infectious ecstasy with both the musicians and the audience. This contagious euphoria comes through in the singer's especially playful treatment of rhythm. In his most pronounced use of jazz-style "breaks," Sinatra shoots notes back and forth with Norvo—breaking his rule about interrupting a sentence or thought so that the mallet man can zing a few hot licks his way during the fills. (Along with another live item, "I've Got a Crush on You" on *Sinatra at the Sands with Count Basie,* this constitutes Sinatra's greatest instance of interplay with an instrumental obligatist. At the Sands, when tenor saxophonist Lockjaw Davis plays an especially romantic riff behind "Crush"'s reference to "a cunning cottage," the singer responds, "You wanna meet Monday and we'll pick out the furniture?")

In Australia, Sinatra continually accentuates unexpected notes and speeds up and slows down in unpredictable places, particularly in the second chorus when he stretches "why" (as in "why is it so?") and "hide" (as in "under the hide of me") for multiple measures. He spontaneously invents whole new melodies for the phrases "only you beneath the moon" and "in the silence of . . ." Each time he comes to the three words "night and day," he phrases them differently. At times he chomps down hard on "night" and then pauses before the "and day"; elsewhere he accentuates the "and" for absolutely no reason other than that it swings, and he refuses to repeat the pattern he had employed only a few measures before. He throws in classic Frankisms, such as "'neath that moon" and "baby" (rather than "darling"), and he uses the "roaring traffic's boom" as a clever excuse for drummer John Markham to "drop" an unforeseen bebop "bomb." He has to clear his throat in the middle of the second B, mistakenly transposes "night and day" ("day and night") in the outchorus, and drops the "my" in "spend my life." But these minor missteps only endear him to us all the more.

In 1961 and 1962, Sinatra concocted yet another two entirely dissimilar ballad readings of "Night and Day." The 1961 reading amounts to one of twelve lovely charts on *Sinatra and Strings,* Sinatra's first and greatest collaboration with rising writer Don Costa. The Costa treatment doesn't quite qualify as one of Sinatra's many masterpiece readings of "Night and Day," but it's excellent just the same. For the first time

Sinatra includes the verse on a ballad treatment of the tune (this on the same album where he sang the verse—and nothing else—to "Stardust"). Costa's setting of this introduction slowly mounts in dynamics and tension, using the strings of the album's title to voice lots of austere, slow-to-resolve chords. Costa concludes the verse with a device suggesting what Sinatra might have done with Gordon Jenkins: by now far beyond the range of any tempo, each of the three occurrences of "you!" is followed by a very dramatic and dour string flourish.

Costa never had a trademark sound like Riddle, Jenkins, or May, but the soft and flowing use of the guitar (Costa's own instrument as a player) behind the singer signifies a break from anything his predecessors might have written. In this one-chorus orchestration, Sinatra's phrasing on "torment" recalls the Stordahl version, but that's about it, and the new way he finds to sing the notes behind "inside of me" (stretching the "side" syllable) is particularly impressive. The only questionable component of the Costa chart is the surprising heaviness of the ending, which sledgehammers its point home with movie-title-music bombast. The idea may have been, however, to return to the austerity of the verse. Whatever the case, this marks a worthy addition to the ever-increasing pantheon of Sinatra "Night and Day"s.

For his 1962 world tour (done on behalf of children's charities), Sinatra visited six continents with six musicians. He included "Night and Day" from the beginning, initially via a sextet transcription of the Riddle (chorus-and-a-half) arrangement. Two renditions performed in Tokyo on April 20 and 21 are unremarkable; the tune doesn't stand out that much from the rest of the concert. In London, at the Royal Festival Hall concert (June 1, 1962), "Night and Day" is performed stunningly as a duet with guitarist Al Viola. "Instead of doing it with the band," Sinatra said to Viola just before the concert, "we might as well do it with just the guitar. It'll be fresh that way."

Sinatra had begun doing "Night and Day" as a duo (with verse and one chorus only) at least as early as May 25 (at the Ice Palace in Milan). He taped the two best-known performances of the duet a few days later, at the Royal Festival Hall and at the Lido Theatre in Paris on Tuesday, June 5. While the Paris show was to become, incomprehensibly, the first historic (and previously unreleased) Sinatra concert officially released by a major label (in 1994), the London show is superior. Both occurred at the very end of a long and exhausting tour, and by June 5 Sinatra's voice was completely shot. Somehow, those few days (which included two more concerts in England) broke his voice. Sinatra was laboring hard at the Paris concert.

Fortunately, this didn't affect "Night and Day" all that much—although the London rendition still has the edge—because Sinatra played it fairly close to the vest. He was very careful with his intonation throughout, and didn't start anything he knew he couldn't finish. In fact, he stayed very close to the melody, which he stated simply and with great, though not overdone, feeling. Even here, he's not afraid to climb out on the occasional limb, as in the very boomy way he emphasizes the activities of the roaring traffic. Throughout this *mano a mano* rendition, Viola more than holds his own, with graceful and uncomplicated chordal support.

In this effectively minimalist reading, every time Sinatra holds a note a hair longer than we expect, it has a tremendous impact. It's also a tour de force of Sinatra dynamics, as in the way he sings the first line of the verse ("beat, beat, beat") very quietly and the second ("tick, tick, tock") just a few cubic centimeters of pressure more forcefully. As with the best of Billie Holiday, each little pause (as between "stands" and "against" in the verse) and every minute inflection carries with it significant meaning. And, as Viola suggested, if the idea was to help his longtime fans in Europe to recall his original recording, he underscores that idea by reviving the "way *down* inside of me" alteration of twenty years earlier.

We may wish, however, that he had concluded his reimaging of "Night and Day" right then and there, because his final recording of the song is downright embarrassing. In the '90s, Sinatra sold records by lending his vocal tracks to be mutilated by kiddie pop stars in *Duets I* and *II*; in the '60s and '70s, when he tried to reach the youth market, he stooped to their level by dabbling in ephemeral forms that were well beneath his taste and talent. His mercifully brief dalliance in "disco," as it used to be called, represents by far the most execrable example of this trend.

Perhaps in deciding to remake two standards long associated with him rather than a new potential hit or a cover of someone else's chart-topper, Sinatra may have been looking to do damage control even before the damage was done. On February 16, 1977, he and Joe Beck recorded vocal tracks on "Night and Day" and "All or Nothing at All" on top of disco orchestral backings that the producer-arranger had laid down the day before. While "All or Nothing at All" was wisely withheld (released only in 1995 on *The Complete Reprise Recordings* suitcase),"Night and Day" made it out as a single. (Sinatra also performed this version live, even as late as March 1979, at a concert in Valley Forge.)

"Night and Day," unlike "Mack the Knife" or "Come Rain or Come Shine," was not one of the songs you could pretty much count on hearing at nearly every '80s and '90s appearance. In 1982, Sinatra and pianist Vinnie Falcone revived and revised the *Perfectly Frank* small-group version, dropping the Latin elements and retaining the jazzy tempo and the verse in the middle. Sinatra also included the Riddle arrangement in a few concerts. In one October 1986 show (issued privately on the *Saloon Singer* double LP), Sinatra makes his peace with "Night and Day" and brings his relationship with the song full circle. He starts by recapping the story of how he screwed up the tune in the presence of its composer nearly four decades earlier and then uses the first eight bars or so to reenact the screw-up, to the audience's delight. He then gets it more than right for the remaining forty measures. It's a bang-up version; you cannot resist its passion and swing. This rendition of the Riddle version includes yet another middle instrumental section. Make no mistake, Sinatra's interpretations of standard tunes are living, breathing organic entities. He can't help relentlessly fiddling with the arrangements, much the same way he continually comes up with new ways to phrase the individual lines in the best jazz tradition. As long as he's breathing, he'll keep on singing, and as long as he's singing, the music of Frank Sinatra will never stop developing and evolving.

The men who conceived the fashion and form of American popular music, primarily Louis Armstrong, Bing Crosby, and Benny Goodman, who were all born between 1901 and 1910, conceived the American aesthetic in terms of new vocabularies for instrumental, vocal, and orchestral expression. Although many key members of the second generation (generally born between 1910 and 1920), especially Billie Holiday and Ella Fitzgerald, had achieved prominence before Sinatra began attracting attention in 1939, he immediately established himself as the acknowledged leader of the movement to win recognition for this music as an art form. Sinatra and his collaborators mapped out the territory and demonstrated the difference between the one-shot songs that made up Tin Pan Alley's daily bread—served, consumed, and forgotten—and the rich three-layer cakes created by such master chefs as Cole Porter and Harold Arlen.

More than any other artist, Sinatra had both the equipment and the wherewithal to carry out that mission. In the most obvious ways, he stayed in tune with his time or times by being deliberately out of step with it: when America's idea of maleness was John Wayne, he came on as the sensitive and vulnerable type—his sole display of strength was his ability to hold a note in "Ol' Man River" and to cling to his liberal politics despite mounting pressure from the increasingly powerful ultra-right wing. Ten years later, when TV sitcoms trumpeted the ideal of the neutered nuclear family, Sinatra represented the ultimate swinging bachelor, charged with sexual energy and determined to subvert the WASP-y moral code of the Eisenhower era and escape the Tender Trap. (Indeed, Sinatra's 1955 record of "Love and Marriage" has been pressed into service as the opening theme for *Married . . . with Children*, a program that celebrates the dysfunctional family in a funhouse mirror image of the *Donna Reed Show*.)

Sinatra has been completely out of touch with American culture as it evolved from Mitch Miller's era onward. As he consistently achieved higher and higher quality in his recordings, he defied a dichotomy even then encroaching on the American lively arts. Our standard of living rose, and our standard of culture generally plummeted. This was nowhere truer than in pop music, not only in the debasements of the blues that were being packaged for kiddie consumption, but also in the older styles of American pop that were being beaten to death by overpowerful, hit-happy producers. Only Sinatra seemed actually to be getting better with each subsequent release and was truly seeking to reach the highest level of popular music. He rarely underestimated the intelligence of his audiences or talked down to them, and he triumphed commercially over those who did.

One couldn't ask for a body of work that more completely fulfills the potential of twentieth-century popular music than that created by Frank Sinatra, or for more variety within the clearly defined stylistic parameters that Sinatra has established. It upsets all known critical theory when a successful and highly stylized artist doesn't descend into self parody once he passes beyond a certain point. Even considering the very few performers of Sinatra's era who kept their art vital from that time to this (Eckstine and Fitzgerald) and the even fewer artists of the next generation who have achieved extraordinary longevity (Tormé and Bennett), no artist has been able to keep his career snowballing so overwhelmingly. Sinatra's celebrity has long since overshadowed much of his musical accomplishment in the popular mind, but the work stands on its own. The ways he gets under your skin are legion—they repeat, how they yell, in your ear.

EXHIBIT "A"—GRAPH OF SINATRA PERFORMANCES OF "NIGHT AND DAY"

1. The original Axel Stordahl ballad arrangement:
   a. Commercial recording for Bluebird, January 19, 1942 [CD: RCA 2269-2]
   b. Soundtrack recording for film *Reveille with Beverly* (Columbia Pictures) September 17, 1942 [LP: Hollywood Soundstage HS 5014]
   c. Special broadcast presented by the March of Dimes, *America Salutes the President's Birthday*, January 29, 1943*
   d. Concert, The Hollywood Bowl, August 14, 1943
   e. Armed Forces Radio Service broadcast transcription, *Command Performance* #80, September 5, 1943 [CD: Meteor CDMTBS 001]
   f. Commercial broadcast, *Songs by Sinatra*, December 19, 1943 (sustaining—unsponsored) [CD: Jazz Hour JH 1020]
   g. *March of Dimes* fund-raiser transcription, circa December 1943 (made for broadcast in January, 1944) [CD: VJC 1051]
   h. AFRS program, Front Line Theatre, March 6, 1944*
   i. Commercial broadcast, *Vimms Vitamins Presents Frank Sinatra*, undated, circa spring 1944
   j. Commercial broadcast, *Vimms Vitamins Presents Frank Sinatra*, October 4, 1944
   k. Commercial broadcast, *A Date with Judy*, February 20, 1945*
   l. From September 1945 to June 1947, Sinatra used the first two lines from the Stordahl arrangement of "Night and Day" as the opening theme for both seasons of his show *Old Gold Presents Songs by Sinatra*. Sinatra had used "Night and Day" as his program opening music (along with "This Love of Mine") for earlier broadcast appearances, but this is his most celebrated series and use of the Porter song as a theme. (Sinatra further used a different treatment of "Night and Day" as his theme music for an appearance on the Treasury Dept. *Music for Millions* show of September 5, 1945.)
   m. Concert, The Hollywood Bowl, September 29, 1945*
   n. Commercial recording for Columbia, October 22, 1947, "long version." First released in 1993. [CD: CXK 48673 CK 52872]
   o. Commercial recording for Columbia, October 22, 1947, "short version." Still unissued.
   p. Sinatra began using "Night and Day" as his opener again on *Lucky Strike Light Up Time* in 1949–50, using a variant on the Stordahl arrangement, dropping the strings and adding a trumpet obligato.
   q. Sinatra also performed a "full" version of "Night and Day" on *Light Up Time*, in April 1950 (exact date unknown).*
   r. Concert, The Opera House in Blackpool, England, July 26, 1953*

2. a. The *To Be Perfectly Frank* "one shot," radio version, circa June or October 1954 (uptempo with verse).

   b. Concert (audience tape), Buffalo, New York, May 8, 1982, de-Latinized version of small group treatment (with verse in middle).

3. The Nelson Riddle uptempo arrangement:

   a. All-Orchestral version (with at least three different instrumental middle sections):

      i. Commercial recording for Capitol, featuring Juan Tizol, valve trombone, November 26, 1956, for album *A Swingin' Affair* [CD: Capitol CDP 7 94518]

      ii. TV performance, probably broadcast November 29, 1957 [CD: Bravura CD-105]

      iii. TV broadcast, *The Dean Martin Show*, November 1, 1960*

      iv. Concert, Golden Nugget, October 1986 [private double LP: *Saloon Singer*, un-numbered]

   b. Combined small group (quintet) and big-band version, with Red Norvo:

      i. Concert, West Melbourne, Australia, March 31, 1959 [CD: Bravura CD2-104]

      ii. Concert, West Melbourne, Australia, April 1, 1959 [CD: Bravura CD-102]

   c. All small group (sextet) version, 1962 World Tour:

      i. Concert, Hibiya Park, Tokyo, April 20, 1962

      ii. Concert, Mikado Theatre, Tokyo, April 21, 1962

4. The Don Costa *Sinatra and Strings* ballad arrangement, with verse, commercially recorded November 22, 1961 [CD: Reprise 9 27020]

5. As a duet with guitarist Al Viola, ballad with verse, also 1962 World Tour:

   a. Concert, Ice Palace, Milan, May 26, 1962 [part of 3-CD set, Drive CD-534]

   b. Concert, Royal Festival Hall, London, June 1, 1962 [CD: JRR-166-2]

   c. Concert, Lido Theatre, Paris, June 5, 1962 [CD: Reprise 45487-2]

6. Joe Beck "disco" arrangement, commercially recorded February 16, 1977 [issued on 45 single Reprise RPS 1386, Italian Reprise LP W54101]

*Asterisked entries were not available to be auditioned for the purposes of this study, although some may exist in the hands of private collectors.

In addition, Sinatra renditions of "Night and Day" were released on several 16-inch Armed Forces Radio Services BML (Basic Music Library) transcriptions. It's presumed that these duplicate one or more of the performances listed above—but you never know.

THE SKINNY YEARS

CHAPTER TWO

"FOR OLD TIMES' SAKE":
HOBOKEN AND HARRY, 1915–1939

Police Detective: What is that dingus?
Spade: The stuff that dreams are made of.

—DASHIELL HAMMETT,
The Maltese Falcon

As Stanley Crouch once observed, the pre–modern jazz world welcomed innovation with open arms; in the '20s and '30s, Louis Armstrong,
Coleman Hawkins, Art Tatum, and other style setters were seen as making the music more rewarding for players and audiences alike. So it was,
too, in jazz's sister kingdom, mainstream popular music. Once Sinatra
had honed his technique (and this occurred fairly early), it's astonishing
how quick his rise was. Even before anyone had heard of him, at least
four important bandleaders tried to plant him on their bandstands. Once
he had achieved a modicum of exposure with a major band, the public
went for him in a big way.

Francis Albert Sinatra first opened his peepers on the planet on
December 12, 1915, in Hoboken, New Jersey. Though considerably
sheltered and protected as the son of comparatively affluent, powerful parents, Sinatra nevertheless grew up exposed to his share of vio-
lence and hardship in that ethnically dense, blue-collar town. There
were, however, compensating kindnesses as well: Sinatra once told
Manie Sachs (the Jewish godfather of his son, Frank, Jr.) that he was
raised as much by a "kindly old Jewish woman" named Mrs. Golden
as he was by his own mother (who wasn't home much). Sinatra con-

tinued to visit his "Yiddishe Momme" until her death in the early
'50s.[1]

All Sinatra chroniclers, whether seeking to vilify him or deify him, praise
him or bury him, agree that the turning point of his young life was catching a Bing Crosby performance and deciding that he could "do that." They
don't agree on whether it was a live theater gig or a movie in Jersey City
or Manhattan, and whom he was with, but we know that sometime in 1931
or 1932, Sinatra had made up his mind that he was going to be the next
Bing Crosby.

Sinatra graduated from David E. Rue Junior High School in 1931 but
made it through only forty-seven days of high school, and even fewer
than that at his first potential career, working on a delivery truck for the
Jersey Observer newspaper. Early in 1932 the Sinatras moved to their
first house, at 841 Garden Street, where he met his "Garden Street girlfriend," Marian Bush Schrieber. Between 1932 and 1939 he did some
manual labor (at various shipyards), but he also sang whenever and
wherever he could. As Schrieber told the late researcher Herb Kurtin, in
order to find an orchestra to sing with, the young would-be crooner often
had to put it together himself.

"[Frank] didn't have a job at the time, but he loved hanging around
musicians, so I suggested that he get an orchestra together for our
Wednesday night dances," Schrieber said. "In exchange for hiring the
musicians, he'd get to sing a few numbers with the band. I'd take the
money at the door, and when we got enough, we all went to the Village
Inn in New York so that Frank could sing with the orchestra there. We'd
go in to ask the manager beforehand to let Frankie sing. We said that was
the only way we would come in (being under age), and so he usually said
yes. Frank did such a good job for our school dances on Wednesday that
he wanted to take the orchestra to Our Lady of Grace for their Friday
night dances, but the Irish Catholics wouldn't let him in . . . because of
the scandals involving his mother, Natalie (Dolly).[2] They would have
nothing to do with him."

But other musicians would, especially when Sinatra began assembling an arsenal of ephemera essential for club dates, namely a library of

1. This may explain why he speaks better Yiddish than Italian. In 1955, Sinatra captured every Yiddish nuance of "Sue Me" (*nu?*), the most Jewish song in *Guys and Dolls*.
In a 1965 concert, not long after filming *Cast a Giant Shadow* (a war drama about the
founding of Israel), Sinatra "*kvells*" with the audience about how the goyish Duke tried
to "drink a matzoh." At his great Seattle concert from 1957 Sinatra refers to his
musicians collectively as "*klezmer.*"

2. As the Sinatra family officially owned up to in the *Sinatra* TV miniseries, Dolly
Sinatra was arrested several times for performing abortions, one as late as 1950.

stock dance band orchestrations (with vocal parts, naturally), an early portable sound system, and that most indispensable item in the band-leader's bag of tricks, an automobile. On the more typically lesser-bud-get dates, Sinatra worked with just the guitarist Matty Golizio (who would later play on some of his Columbia sessions), his most frequent accompanist for several years beginning in 1934.

In those days, radio stations, even though they constituted the coun-try's number one profit medium, frequently had nonprime airtime that they couldn't sell, which they often gave to young performers willing to work for nothing or next to it. "I didn't have the experience," Sinatra recalled in 1955, "to warrant radio stations paying me." During the evening hours the competition was considerably stiffer even for the non-paying spots; for instance, Glenn Miller and his orchestra might do a sustaining broadcast for the minimum scale from 11:30 to midnight but that same week would do three big-paying fifteen-minute shows for Chesterfield cigarettes.

Long before anyone had ever heard of him, Sinatra sang often on local radio, especially on station WAAT in Jersey City. Herb Kurtin uncov-ered a clip from a 1935 radio guide of a listing from Tuesday, April 16, 1935, of Sinatra appearing on WAAT from 5:15 to 5:30. Kurtin also believed Sinatra went on the air on that station under the nom de plume of "The Romancer." Tony Mottola, three years younger than Sinatra, recalled working with the singer both at WAAT, where Sinatra had his own show (possibly as early as 1932) with a five-piece group, and on club dates.

Occasionally, amateurs and newcomers were able to penetrate the commercially controlled prime-time hours, thanks primarily to Major Bowes. The red-nosed Major launched his *Original Amateur Hour* on local New York radio in 1934 and went national with it a year later. Not long after, Sinatra hooked up with a group of Hoboken harmonizers who sang locally and became part of the Major Bowes radio-based amateur circuit. In addition to his widely heard program, the Bowes empire (later taken over by Ted Mack) consisted of vaudeville appearances, which took the group as far away from home as Vancouver, and several one-reel movie shorts filmed in the Bronx (Hollywood on the Hudson).

According to some accounts, Dolly Sinatra pressured the unit (then a trio) to let "Frankie" join, but he soon became their lead singer and star, and female hearts were already starting to flutter during his solo spots. In all of its appearances with Bowes, the group kept changing its name, most humorously to "The Secaucus Cockamamies" (as Sinatra claimed thirty years later on his *Sands* album) so no one would question their amateur status. It's hard to imagine, however, that that would have been a problem once someone had heard them sing.

Bowes had many performances preserved, including three items by the Hoboken Four: two widely (though unofficially) issued airchecks, a complete "Shine" and "Curse of an Aching Heart," as well as a film of the group doing "Shine," which is not known to have survived. "Shine," broadcast September 8, 1935, reveals a spirited if ragged remake of the then-famous Bing Crosby–Mills Brothers 1932 arrangement of this ancient and even then politically incorrect piece. After ninety embarrassing seconds of banter with the condescending Major (in which Sinatra is introduced as "this fella here" who "never worked at all"), Sinatra can clearly be heard aping Crosby in the solo spots. Overall, the performance bears out Sinatra's statement from 1955 that he "believed, because of [Crosby's] leisurely manner of working, that if he could do it, I could do it. The funny switch is that I've never been able to do it. It's just a trick that he has, a wonderfully relaxed feeling about performing." Overall, the value of the two Bowes airchecks is more historical than musical as the earliest surviving documents of this soon-to-be-famous voice.

Sinatra returned home to New Jersey after growing disillusioned with the good Major, who was as famous for consuming whiskey that, as Sinatra later quipped, "would take the paint off a boat," as he was for his slogan, which referred to "the dizzy spin of the wheel of fortune." For a time Sinatra went back to singing at WAAT, where he played badminton in the record stacks with future producer Gus Statiras. "It didn't take a genius to see that this guy was going to be somebody," Statiras remembered in 1993. "All the girls around Newark were already crazy about him."

In one of his incarnations as a club date (read: bar mitzvah) bandleader and contractor, Sinatra even appeared on Fred Allen's *Town Hall Tonight* show. Unfortunately, Sinatra did not sing on this May 1937 broadcast, although he does banter with Allen and "conduct" an instrumental quartet identified as "The Four Sharps" in a medley of "Exactly Like You" and "Powerhouse" (a composition by future *Hit Parade* compadre Raymond Scott).

In going to work in New Jersey roadhouses, advancing his career at first meant gradually lowering his income, from $50 a week with Bowes to $40 a week at the Union Club (where he worked before and after his stint with the Hoboken Four) to $35 a week at the Rustic Cabin, to whatever he could get at weddings and dances. "Professionally, and I use the word loosely," Sinatra has recalled, "I was working in a roadhouse in Englewood Cliffs, New Jersey, which is about two miles north of the George Washington Bridge, and it was called the Rustic Cabin. I was there for about a year and a half or two. Oh, I was the headwaiter and the chief bottle washer and sweep-up man and everything. It was a great experience, I must say."

According to Harry Zinquist, drummer with the Rustic Cabin band (led by Henry Jacobs, aka Bill Henri), if Sinatra had ever done anything at the Cabin besides sing, he certainly had stopped long before Harry James made his epochal appearance at the Cabin in late spring 1939. The Rustic Cabin, the most famous of Sinatra's Jersey stints, had figured in his life long before he worked there as a single: an early incarnation of the Hoboken Four (then known as "The Three Flashes") had played there several years earlier. The Cabin had one major advantage over the better paying Union Club—the owner had a direct line to radio station WNEW, which broadcast all over the tristate area, whereas the owner of the Union Club refused to spring for such a wire.

By the end of 1938, Sinatra was also doing between three and five quarter-hour shows a week from WNEW's New York studio, including one spot with organist Jimmy Rich that ran "about fifteen minutes apart," in Sinatra's words, from a similar show by fellow future star Dinah Shore. At the same time, he was doing a spot at eight in the morning on WOR in Newark. Both stations paid him little more than carfare, but the Jersey station afforded a compensating virtue. In his 1980 interview with Arlene Francis, Sinatra explained: "I got a job during that period at the WOR Bamberger station in Newark, and I did one show a week with the orchestra there, because they had strings and I wanted to work with strings. I got thirty cents a week for carfare from Hoboken to Newark and back, and that was it, nothing. There was no union, none of that stuff. But out of a half-hour program I had three songs that I did with a string section which to me was a very important thing."

At least one musician who would be important in Sinatra's subsequent career first encountered Sinatra in 1938 or 1939. "The first time I ever met Frank was when I was playing at the Commodore Hotel with Tommy Dorsey," remembered Arthur "Skeets" Herfurt, who would play lead alto on nearly all of Sinatra's Capitol dates a generation or two later. George "Bullets" Durgom, then an "alligator" or band fanatic who later worked in both Miller's and Sinatra's offices, "was a fan of the Dorsey band, and he'd spend most of his nights at the Commodore listening to us. One night he got me a date with a girl in New Jersey, and we went out to Frank Dailey's Meadowbrook on Route 9W. There was a little local band playing there, and guess who was singing? Frankie boy! That's when I first heard him. . . . He sounded just like Frankie. He sounded great."

Proof of how great Sinatra sounded in this period can be found in

"Our Love," a demo disc that the singer is said to have cut on the eve of his wedding to Nancy Barbato on February 4, 1939. The circumstances surrounding this recording are vague, to say the least. Although the session was presumedly underwritten by the Sinatra or Barbato family coffers, Sinatra is accompanied by a large-sounding orchestra with a full contingent of strings. It seems a tad on the expensive side for such a home-grown project. The conducting for the orchestra has been credited to one Frank Manne, who might have been a local leader or musician's contractor. Sinatra was restricted primarily to a one-chorus vocal refrain followed by a long instrumental section. That would sound dance band-y enough, and the piece is taken in a medium-slow foxtrot, but the strings give the ensemble a different sound altogether. Surprising, Sinatra returns for a brief outchorus reprise near the end. (Coincidentally, Sinatra's first genuine record, "From the Bottom of My Heart" with Harry James, also affords him an extra half-chorus return—all but unheard of in the band era, especially among unestablished newcomers.) Sinatra sounds mature and polished (although perhaps a trifle self-conscious in this classical adaption), giving us a fair idea of why so many leaders would soon be interested in him.

Yet even here, if Sinatra is striving for a sound beyond the reach of his youthful imagination, at least he's striving for something. He's well on the way to his development of the custom-tailored vocal arrangement— even "Our Love" rates as more interesting than the cut-and-dried charts other singers were recording in 1939. In everything he was doing, even at this early stage, Sinatra had a plan, an outline of his career, a destination. In the words of Mitch Miller, "He had a direction. He knew where he was going, come hell or high water."

The two most amazing discoveries of the swing era were made listening to local radio. The first occurred when John Hammond heard Count Basie broadcasting from the Reno Club in Kansas City in the spring of 1936. (Coincidentally, Lester Young had recently discovered the Basie Reno Club band in the same fashion.) In June 1939, Harry James, who had just left Benny Goodman's orchestra to try his luck with his own band, was taking a nap in his room at the Lincoln Hotel. The radio was on, and James's wife, singer Louise Tobin, was getting dressed to leave for Boston where she had a gig with Bobby Hackett's band. "I heard this boy singing, and I thought, 'There's a fair singer!' Now I didn't think he was fantastic, I just thought, 'Well, now that's a good singer.' So I woke Harry and said, 'Honey, you might want to hear this kid on the radio. The boy singer on this show sounds pretty good.' That was the end of it as far as I was concerned."

Apparently concurring with his wife's judgment, the next night James drove out to Route 9W in Englewood Cliffs. "I asked the manager where I could find the singer," James related to George Simon, "and he told me, 'We don't have a singer. But we do have an emcee who sings a little bit.'" As Sinatra recalled, the Cabin was "where Harry James heard me. He actually heard me on the radio. They used to have a dance band pickup on WNEW five nights a week, for different clubs around the metropolitan area including Jersey and Connecticut. When he left Benny Goodman and started his own band and came over to see me, I almost broke his arm so he wouldn't get away 'cause I was dying to get out of that place!"

Although James and Sinatra have corroborated each other's stories, theirs is not the only account of the "discovery." Manie Sachs, who in 1939 was "in charge of artists" (in his words) at the MCA talent agency, maintained that he had actually first heard of "the singer at the Rustic Cabin roadhouse" by reputation. After hearing Sinatra (who, Sachs also recalled, was waiting tables) for himself, Sachs recommended him to James. "He wasn't the most beautiful guy in the world," Sachs said in 1955, "but something about his face was appealing—and he could sing." Within a few months Sachs would switch jobs from MCA to the newly reorganized Columbia Records, where he would be the first to record the new singer commercially.

Several executives of station WNEW also claimed credit as Sinatra discoverers. But one thing seems certain: James happened to be at the Rustic Cabin, the leader was impressed and invited Sinatra to audition for him. "Harry was auditioning singers at the Lincoln Hotel," said Skeets Herfurt, who heard this story shortly afterward, "and Frank walked in with no arrangements. The other guys who were auditioning for Harry had charts and everything. But Frank just walked in, walked over to the piano player, told him what he wanted to sing, what key he wanted to sing in, and stood up and sang—and knocked everybody out. They were auditioning a lot of people that day, but the musicians said that when they heard Sinatra, that was it. There was no doubt about it."

As far as Sinatra was concerned, however, James was only the front-runner; a number of other fledgling units were also interested. The second most likely to sign Sinatra was Bob Chester, who was just organizing his first band—heavily influenced by Glenn Miller—in the spring of 1939. Although Chester had come from a Detroit family rich with auto-industry money, he made up his mind to succeed without benefit of his parents' bankroll, and he had convinced a considerably more established bandleader, Tommy Dorsey, to buy a piece of his action.

Coincidentally, Miller himself had already passed up the chance to hire Sinatra. "I first heard the Miller band sometime between '38 and '39," Sinatra told Dave Garroway in an interview conducted not long after Miller's death in 1945. "I was segueing between Jersey and New York, trying to make a buck here and there. Glenn was starting that new-sounding band that he had, and I believe at the time he was at the Grand Island Casino. The first time I heard the Glenn Miller Band, I walked up to him and said, 'Glenn, I want a job!' I really did! But he was busy hiring Ray Eberle at the time, and he said to me, in essence, 'Don't call me, I'll call you.' But I did get to meet Glenn quite early in my career, and we became great friends, as a matter of fact. Every time I heard the band I got a big boot out of it, and I still do when I hear some of the records that they made in those days."

Sometime in early 1939, Chester and seventeen-year-old trumpeter Alec Fila (who had just left Jack Teagarden's band) visited the Rustic Cabin. Fifty-five years later, Fila couldn't recollect why they were there, whether by coincidence or if they had gone expressly to catch Sinatra, but Chester was taken enough by the singer to offer him a job with his embryonic orchestra. Fila also recalled that Sinatra did sing with the band at the New Yorker Hotel. "They had a year-round ice show there, with a retracting floor," said Fila. "I have a very vivid [mental] picture of Sinatra at the mike and the ice skaters on the floor. But I couldn't say whether it was a rehearsal or if it was one of the evening shows, or how long he was with the band. That might have been his only night."

Other accounts depict Sinatra as rehearsing with Chester's men in late May 1939, even helping to tote their library up to the fourth floor of New York's Steinway Hall. Saxist Ed Scalzi told Herb Kurtin that Sinatra actually cut two test sides with Chester, "My Love for You," which he would keep singing into his tenure with James (and record ten years later for Columbia), and the Mexican novelty "Alla en Rancho Grande."

The Chester episode indirectly brought him to the attention of Tommy Dorsey, who by the end of the year would deem him ready for his organization's number one "A" band. (He also used Chester on his resume: a late 1942 solo radio program stated that the newly liberated Sinatra had sung with Harry James, Tommy Dorsey, and Bob Chester.)

Xylophonist Red Norvo, long admired by Sinatra, had a better shot at planting Sinatra on his bandstand. Unlike the James and Chester orchestras, however, the Red Norvo–Mildred Bailey Orchestra had already passed its peak in 1939, although this would conclude only the second phase in Norvo's long career as one of jazz's most thoughtful soloists and innovative ensemble leaders.

"When I was married to Mildred," Norvo recalled in 1994, "her brother, [former Rhythm Boy] Al Rinker, lived up in the Nyack area. To get there we used to go over the George Washington Bridge and through Jersey. We went up there one Sunday, and coming back we stopped at the Cabin for a drink. That's when we first heard Frank. I hadn't paid much attention to him, singing with this little band. But Mildred remarked right away, 'That kid can sing!' She picked him out right away. It was just like when we heard Billie Holiday for the first time with John [Hammond], Mildred said, 'She's great,' and then John went and 'discovered' her.

"There were so many great songs coming out at that time," Norvo continued, "and we needed a male singer to help Mildred out. We called Frank, but he had just accepted a job with Harry James." Sinatra joined Harry James and his orchestra, then barely three months old, at the Hippodrome Theatre in late June 1939.

Sinatra most often names Tommy Dorsey as his major inspiration. The Voice should know, but clearly James, whom he called "a dear friend and a great teacher," resounds as an equally important influence on the technique as well as the emotional content of Sinatra's music. "In six months with Harry," Louise Tobin explained, "Frank learned more about music than he'd ever known in his life up to that point." Certainly Dorsey's long-breath method of extending notes became extremely useful to Sinatra, but the restrained Dorsey could get neither as blisteringly hot nor as swaggeringly sentimental as James, and Sinatra later could and did. If Dorsey suggested methods of carrying or phrasing a tune, James provided a working model of how to pack an emotional wallop.

From James, too, Sinatra could have learned how to intermingle pop-song tenderness with blueslike invective, how to swing and how to give and take with an orchestra, how to personalize a melody, and how to mesmerize an audience. James' big band, one press pundit wrote in 1943, "features ten strings and turns out a good deal of the sweet stuff which narcotizes teenagers." No one quite handles a note like Harry James. He pushes them and pinches them, squeezes them and caresses them, tempers each iota of sound in every possible way. Even when he's being delicate, James swings and swaggers with such force that his lines threaten to jump right out of the groove. And there's a brave voice in his head, which would in time speak to Sinatra as well, telling him not to be afraid of schmaltz. It's okay when it's honest, and especially when, as with jazz's greatest sentimentalist, Johnny Hodges, it's leavened by a touch of the blues.

James and Sinatra took their first crack at achieving big-name status together, then split up, but, coincidentally, both reached the higher echelon of celebrity at the Paramount Theatre in 1943. The world had already witnessed throngs of post-Depression and repression youth working themselves into a lather over Benny Goodman, Glenn Miller, and a few others, yet no one had ever seen anything like the James phenomenon. Even more restrained commentators were comparing him to Dionysus and Gabriel, paralleling the Sinatra phenomenon to a remarkable degree.

While the Paramount Theatre was an impressive place for a band to make its local debut, the Paramount Hotel, where James' band hung their hats in between shows, was far from equally respected. Says Tobin, "If you were doing pretty good, you stayed at the Picadilly. If you were doing fair you stayed at the Forest. And if you were doing terrible you stayed at the Paramount. Needless to say, at that point we were at the Paramount."

The few recorded James-Sinatra songs, while constituting a declaration of their compatibility and the possibilities of their relationship, sadly also amounted to a musical coitus interruptus since the two performers were separated before the inevitable climax could be achieved. Still, they made a telling case that The Voice and The Horn could have made beautiful music together indeed.

Of the ten songs commercially recorded, eight are believed to have been arranged by Andy Gibson, who also wrote for Duke Ellington, Count Basie, Charlie Barnet, and Cab Calloway, and later received credit for the rhythm and blues hit "The Hucklebuck" (which Sinatra recorded for Columbia). The remaining two, "It's Funny to Everyone but Me" and "My Buddy," are believed to be by Jack Mathias, who had written for Jerry Blaine's orchestra in 1937 and who attracted more attention at the time for such instrumental specialties as James' "Night Special" and "Trumpet Rhapsody." Several of the ten also exist in alternate takes, and an additional ten tunes have surfaced in the form of live airchecks.[3] The first Sinatra-James item, "From the Bottom of My Heart" (which both Gibson and James got their names on as composers), opens with James stating the melody and then Sinatra doing the same (and, naturally, the lyrics besides). Perhaps inspired by the vote of confidence in having been awarded that extra "tag" chorus, Sinatra sounds leagues more assured than on the more pompous "Our Love," flowing smoothly over both refrains in two takes.

"Melancholy Mood," the other Sinatra vocal out of the four tunes

3. Airchecks supposedly exist of two more songs, taken down during the Baltimore Hippodrome gig—Sinatra singing "Wishing" and "My Love for You." He recorded neither one with James (although the second tune was supposedly on his Bob Chester acetate).

James recorded on July 13 at the first session with the new singer (made after the band returned to New York to play the Roseland Ballroom), changes texture completely. As the title indicates, Sinatra explores a self-pitying state of mind that serves as a twenty-year forerunner of the *Only the Lonely* atmosphere. The leader states the tune, by Walter Schumann (who later wrote the theme to *Dragnet*), growling like Duke Ellington's plunger specialist Cootie Williams, trumpeting the tune in a succession of "jungle style" wah-wahs. Similarly, a tenor break later in the chart, identified by Phil Schaap as being by the great future Ellington star Al Sears (whose only pop hit, "Castle Rock," was much later recorded by the Sinatra-James combination), anticipates Ben Webster, then still with Cab Calloway's band.

If the first two Sinatra records seem forward-pointing triumphs, others come off like odd glimpses backward; Sinatra and James are sitting side by side in the back of the caboose, looking to see where they have been. Gibson's arrangement of Walter Donaldson's 1922 "My Buddy," Sinatra's first "oldie" (not counting "Shine" and "Curse of an Aching Heart" with the Hoboken Four), utilizes a schottische tempo of the sort Crosby and Dorsey were independently bouncing along around 1937. Sinatra sounds uncomfortable in the first eight lines and then tries to cover it up by playing with the time in the second, but his rushing and lagging the beat nearly make it; newly added trombonist Dalton Rizzotto and leader James come off better, using their mutes not to growl but to turn in a peppy middle-register chorus reminiscent of James' predecessor with Goodman, Bunny Berigan.

Still, the James-Sinatra sessions began with an edge over the Dorsey ones in that leader, arranger, and singer tried at the outset to create a style of their own; contrastingly, the Sinatra-Dorsey collaborations would start with an attempt to squeeze the new singer into a mold that had already been established. "It's Funny to Everyone but Me" looks for a new band-vocal trick in a variation of the Tommy Dorsey "Marie" routine; instead of the sidemen chanting a steady stream of song titles behind the crooner, they just sing one title at the end of the first ("It's the Talk of the Town") and the last eight bar phrases ("I Gotta Right to Sing the Blues"). The longer lines of the bridge bring out a little more oomph from Sinatra, but the band-chant routine falls flat.[4]

4. Composer Jack Lawrence, who originally wrote this song for the Ink Spots, feels the James band's recitations were inspired by that vocal group. (Coincidentally, Lawrence wrote four of the James-Sinatra items. James would later more directly borrow the "Marie" format, and on an Irving Berlin tune yet, for his 1944 version of "Always.")

"All or Nothing at All" experiments more successfully with unconventional band-vocal structures. "It's Funny to Everyone but Me" and "From the Bottom of My Heart" use brief vocal reprises, and "Ciribiribin" even opens with Sinatra singing the verse, but in contrast to the usual band-vocal-band format, Sinatra dominates all of "All or Nothing at All." Assisted by a brief intro and an instrumental interlude saturated with James' distinctive lead horn, this might as well be a vocal-with-accompaniment side as a dance disc, looking forward to future sides in both men's careers: James' largely all-vocal epics with Helen Forrest and Sinatra's purely vocal sides released under Dorsey's banner and direction (not to mention his entire subsequent career as a headliner).

Although lyricist Jack Lawrence and composer Arthur Altman knew James, they didn't write "All or Nothing at All" specifically for Sinatra. This is something you could never tell from listening to it, with its long-meter format, set in 64 bars, and the same kind of "All the Way" attitude the mature Sinatra would incorporate in his performance persona. "He's recorded 'All or Nothing at All' many times over the years," commissioning at least three subsequent arrangements by Stordahl, Costa, and Riddle, Lawrence pointed out in 1995, "but it's interesting to listen to that young voice when he first started and the way he attacked that song and what he did with the breath control, with all of the wonderful phrasing that he did even in those early days. Later as he went along he learned a lot more and added a lot more interpretation. Every time he rerecorded it, there would be another great lush arrangement, but I still prefer to listen to that young voice singing that song."

"All or Nothing at All" was not released until the summer of 1940 and did not hit the charts until Sinatra's *Hit Parade* phase three years later. Nonetheless, the song seems to have been Sinatra's biggest number with James—at least three live versions of it exist, including one from the band's best-remembered gig, at the 1939 World's Fair. Appropriately, the minor-mooded "All or Nothing" also harkens to both past and future vocally, as Sinatra suggests the long lines that would comprise his most radical break with tradition. Yet traces linger of some '30s square-jawed "popera" baritone like Nelson Eddy, ending on a Romburg-type high note that could wear a Viking helmet or a Mountie hat. Sinatra clearly wanted to expand jazz-pop singing's rhythmic base, but for the time being was only eliminating possibilities and learning what he *didn't* want to do. And although it alluded to the Italo-American machismo we associate with Sinatra, the disc's heavy-footed melodrama lacks the tenderness he would later bring out in similar though subtler performances. All in all, it justifies James' later remark that Sinatra was "a very serious singer [even] then. There was no kidding. When he sang, he sang."

Other James sides peer into directions Sinatra would never explore again. One in a long line of intercultural, interracial-romances-that-can-never-be, "On a Little Street in Singapore" comes out of the pop song equivalent of what black film historian Donald Vogle calls "the tragic mulatto syndrome." From *Madame Butterfly* onward (as heard in such '20s pop pieces as "Poor Butterfly" and the classic "Japanese Mammy"), East and West may meet, but in terms of a long-term relationship, they don't stand a Chinaman's chance.

"On a Little Street in Singapore" finds Sinatra and James making like two American sailors in a Far East opium den. The trumpeter, anticipating Gene Kelly's wolf act from *Anchors Away,* brags audaciously through his horn that he intends to take on every trollop from Tokyo Rose to Shanghai Lil. The timid young crooner seems confused by the place's elegantly exotic trappings. Perhaps fearing that that underpinning bolero beat will throw him off, Sinatra plays it cautiously, sticking very close to the melody and the beat. Sinatra would never seriously return to this genre. The only way he could take on texts on similar subjects, such as "South of the Border" and "Isle of Capri," was to de-melodrama-tize them into rhythm numbers with near-nonsense lyrics.

"Ciribiribin" was adapted by James and Lawrence from an Italian song, but it's the swinging beat that both the leader and crooner latch on to. Bing Crosby, flanked by opposing bastions of hipness (Joe Venuti) and squareness (the Andrews Sisters), which cancel each other out, recorded in an even zingier version of this Italian air, but Sinatra also turns in a respectable showing. James had already selected "Ciribiribin" as his theme song and recorded it in January as an instrumental, in an extended treatment of the way it would open all Harry James sets over the next forty years. On Sinatra's final session with the band, James rerecorded the 1898 aria with the departing singer, thereby making it the closing theme for the James-Sinatra saga.

Though they were making progress musically, not much was happening for the band at the box office. After leaving the Paramount Theatre in June, it got little attention at the Roseland Ballroom in July. Despite valuable exposure in broadcasts from the Steel Pier in Atlantic City in August and the 1939 World's Fair in late August and early September, this extremely spirited first James band failed to make an impression on the public.

Business was bad in Chicago in late September, and then business was bad in Denver. Trumpeter Chris Griffin recalled first meeting Sinatra in Chicago during this westward swing and confirmed, "There was nobody there!" The James men were collectively enthusiastic about their upcoming engagement at the Los Angeles Palomar, where many other hot bands had made good. Unfortunately, their hopes were burned to the ground along with that ballroom on October 4, when Charlie Barnet's band apparently got too hot.

James considered himself lucky to find a substitute gig at a restaurant called Victor Hugo's in Beverly Hills, but he got an early indication of what a disaster that would be when the band's salaries were immediately attached. James' faith in Sinatra was such that when he realized he couldn't afford both of his singers, he did without a femme vocalist, and this in an age when bandleaders considered canaries a necessity and crooners could be easily replaced by some guy from the sections—the way Bob Chester did it. Sinatra later said, modestly, that the starving sidemen valued and depended on his wife's cooking as much as they did his singing.

The band was so demoralized at Victor Hugo's that when a drunk shoved Sinatra's mike into his face, according to a *Time* reporter, "Sinatra took it without comment." Sinatra was already developing other aspects of his personality by this time: as he reflected in his scripted commentary to the 1965 *Man and His Music* album, "I was young and full of zip, zap, and zing, and I was also full of myself." "I thought he was a good singer," said Billy May, who first met Sinatra around this time (while he himself played in Charlie Barnet's great band). "But the musicians in Harry's band, and later in Tommy's band, had the opinion that he was a smart-ass Italian kid. He kind of bugged all the guys in the band [at first]. But he soon learned how to get along with them." However, other observers closer to the source feel differently. "Offstage, Frank was a very quiet kid, not at all a braggart," clarinetist Drew Page later put it. "I never noticed any cockiness in his attitude. Mostly a loner on the bus, he dozed, read magazines, and seldom said anything. But he readily responded to humor—he was easy to break up, especially on stage."

Heading back east again, while playing Chicago's Hotel Sherman, the James band shared a benefit for the musician's union with Tommy Dorsey and other, more established bands; it was there that Dorsey, in search of a replacement for the recently departed Jack Leonard, hired Sinatra away from James. The singer and the trumpeter, several months his junior, were more like brothers than leader and sideman; besides, Sinatra had faith in James and his band, and felt like a rat deserting a sinking ship. In a much quoted line, the singer said he would have been happier opening a vein. Still, he knew he was making the right move for his career and his forthcoming family; Nancy, Jr., was due to arrive in June 1940. As James later told radio interviewer Fred Hall, "Nancy was pregnant, and we weren't even making enough money to pay Frank the $75 he was supposed to get. So he went with Tommy Dorsey, and I said, 'Well, if we don't do any better in the next six months or so, try to get me on, too.'"

As a barometer of their individual fortunes, the team's most memorable collaboration, "All or Nothing at All," in its original release sold a mediocre eight thousand or so copies over many months of gathering dust in stores (at the time, ten thousand was acceptable and fifteen thousand was news). At Victor Hugo's, when Sinatra was halfway through the number, the manager decided it was going to be nothing at all and sacked the entire band on the spot. But four years later, when both James and Sinatra were considerably hotter, publisher Lou Levy convinced Columbia to rerelease "All or Nothing at All" as a means of sidestepping the musician's union's ban on recordings. They moved a million pieces in no time. Because of its vocal-dominated structure, younger fans never even questioned that the disc was anything but an all-star pairing of a great band with the number one singer in the country (the Sinatra-James tenure being generally forgotten even by Sinatra fan club members by that time).

Sinatra eventually summarized his time with James as "a wonderful six-month experience," describing his former boss as "a real nice guy with real know-how as a musician." Louise Tobin elaborated, "Sinatra learned a lot from Harry. He learned a lot about conducting and a lot about phrasing. And I know they had a lot of mutual admiration for each other. Harry always knew he was going to be a star because of his great ability. There was never any question about that in his mind. And that's also true about Frank. I remember Frank as a very young boy always exuded that confidence. He didn't have to say, 'I'm a great singer,' but you just knew he was. And I think Frank's little comments along the way were helpful to Harry. They had a good relationship until Harry died."

The Sinatra-James story had one particularly happy postscript. The two made a wartime propaganda two-reeler in 1945 and occasionally played concerts together over the years, including a show at Caesar's Palace, Las Vegas, in November 1968, and another in 1979. In 1976, Sinatra and James both guested with Count Basie on a TV special hosted by John Denver, an event that would have been consigned to the realm of the ludicrous were it not for a fiery, inspired run-through of the original 1939 chart to "All or Nothing at All."

Yet their most remarkable reunion occurred in 1951. They were both still under contract to Columbia, and Mitch Miller reteamed them for three sides. (Although Miller doesn't take credit for the idea, the juxta-position of this combination with these songs could have come from no one else.) Ray Conniff, a former swing band trombonist and later a mid-dle-of-the-road superstar on Columbia, arranged and conducted on all three pieces in his role as James' main writer. The previous year Sinatra had recorded his first LP, *Sing and Dance with Frank Sinatra*, using a process known then as "tracking" and today as overdubbing. Perhaps because of a scheduling conflict, the 1951 Sinatra-James session, Con-niff recalls, was done in the same fashion. The overdubbing isn't the only factor that links these cuts to the *Sing and Dance* sessions of the previous year; Sinatra's rhythmic energy also made these three cuts worthy sequels to that extraordinary LP. James is also a veritable dynamo here, giving out gloriously as if to show Sinatra what he had been missing the previous twelve years.

Sinatra's former boss was having problems with his own current one. "Mitch wanted me to do some real corny things—gimmicks and all of this stuff—and I refused to do them," James told deejay Fred Hall, "so I left the company. It was that simple." James added that he considered the "Castle Rock," from that session with Sinatra "the worst thing that either one of us ever recorded. You ask Sinatra, and he'll tell you the same thing." Yet Sinatra absolutely nailed down the mood of Sears' and Conniff's superfast dance extravaganza. At the conclusion of his first vocal on "Castle Rock," Sinatra exhorts his former boss, "Go get 'em, Harry—for old times' sake!"

"Deep Night" is the closest to a romantic number here. James ends teasingly with a seductive muted solo. Earlier in the piece, James blasts wide open with a sixteen-bar statement that climaxes in a crescendo that sounds like five gloriously schmaltzy Harry Jameses exploding at once. Here and on "Farewell, Farewell to Love" (written by either George Siravo or Conniff, but in any case based closely on the former's instru-mental "Barbecue Riffs" version) the old torch becomes a bonfire.

When he knew he was dying of lymphatic cancer (and he worked until a week before he died), James composed a statement that summed up all the schmaltz, soul, humor, and chutzpah of both his art and Frank Sinatra's: "May it be simply said of me," Harry James said on his deathbed, "'He's on the road to do one-nighters with Gabriel.'"

CHAPTER THREE

"OF LOVE AND YOUTH AND SPRING": WITH TOMMY DORSEY, 1940–1942

Have we not all about us forms of a musical expression which we can take and purify and raise to the level of great art?

—RALPH VAUGHAN WILLIAMS

In 1951, Frank Sinatra could sing "Hello, Young Lovers" and mean it. It's about offering one's own experiences as example to budding romances. Later in the '50s, Sinatra would expand on that idea as the connecting peg for his pivotal "concept" albums *Songs for Young Lovers* and *Songs for Swingin' Lovers!*

In 1940, however, Sinatra was too much the naive young lover himself to offer such advice. The sound of Sinatra in his three years with Tommy Dorsey is that of a sage-to-be experiencing the thrills of first romance. He cannot yet step back and watch the action from a broader perspective; the Sinatra of the Dorsey years is a virginal Sinatra, if such a thing is imaginable.

The way Sinatra could get through the many ephemeral tunes that Dorsey presented to him was to take them at face value; they didn't need the deeper meanings he would find a few years later. This Sinatra may not yet be able to extract all the wry ironies from "How About You"; and, similarly, in Jimmy Van Heusen's "Looking for Yesterday," he leaves us unconvinced that he has all that many yesterdays to look for. However, the Sinatra of 1944 onward never could have put over such delightfully naive texts as "Pale Moon (an Indian Love Song)" or "Our Love Affair" so earnestly. The Sinatra of 1940 to 1942 is a completely different animal from the Sinatra who later conquered the world several times over (even, as we shall see, very different from the Sinatra of 1939), but he's no less worth listening to. Though he quickly became the Dorsey band's biggest drawing card, he was still, after all, only one of many attractions that the leader presented in an evening's entertainment.

The band would rise up out of the pit on a moving platform, as Sammy Cahn described them in action at their most famous stomping ground, the New York Paramount Theatre, "and Dorsey would be playing his theme song, 'Getting Sentimental over You.' When the pit went up, he went into 'Marie,' and he would stop the show with that. Then he would introduce Connie Haines. Big hit. Then he would introduce Jo Stafford with the Pied Pipers. Big hit. Then he'd introduce Ziggy Elman on the trumpet. Big hit. Then he would introduce Buddy Rich, who would really shatter the theater.

"When all this was finished, out came a thin, frail human being. And I mean the word *thin* in its purest sense, thinner than my pinky. He sang, I'll never forget it, 'South of the Border.' And he just topped the whole show." Within a few years, Sinatra would be filling all these functions by himself—singing love songs, uptempos, novelties, and theater-shatterers—but for now his task was to master the craft of ballad singing.

The last extant item of the Dorsey-Sinatra relationship is "The Song Is You" (a major mantra of Sinatra's career), performed live on the radio as part of Sinatra's farewell appearance with the Dorsey orchestra on September 3, 1942. The Jerome Kern anthem had marked the most striking performance of Sinatra's first session under his own billing (and without Dorsey), done on January 14 of that year. Eight months later he reprised it on the air with the Dorsey band itself for this special concluding broadcast.

The amazing growth between the two versions, the confidence and cool assurance of the September version as measured against the tenuousness of the January reading, is striking. In fact, it could serve as an emblem of Sinatra's remarkable artistic development during his three years with Dorsey. And much of that, all evidence indicates, was directly attributable to the fortitude and personality of Tommy Dorsey, as both a man and a musician, as well as to the young Sinatra's ability to take full advantage of one of the most remarkable opportunities for artistic growth ever afforded a popular performer.

Ten years older than Sinatra, Tommy Dorsey (who at thirty-five was known to his employees as "The Old Man") struck Sinatra as a role model, in both a musical and a personal sense. In spite of a fiery temperament and a fondness for the bottle, Dorsey inspired awe throughout the industry for his incredible personal and professional discipline. Internally, Dorsey was strong enough not only to suppress any urges that might come between himself and the advancement of his fortunes, but, more important, to ignore any obstacle that might get in the way of his making the best music possible. As those who have been close to both men testify, all these characteristics would eventually also become part of Sinatra's own personality. "Frank is like Tommy," said drummer Alvin Stoller, "very demanding."

On any Tommy Dorsey record, including the eighty-three with vocals by Frank Sinatra (a series bookended by two of its least spectacular titles, "The Sky Fell Down" and "Light a Candle in the Chapel"), inevitably the first noise that catches one's ear is the sound of the leader himself; the first thing you always heard was the trombone. The way Dorsey played it, and the way his arrangers molded the band's music around it, had far more to do with the fashion and form of popular singing than anything the jazz tradition would lead you to expect. Dorsey's trombone always occupied the center of attention. It didn't matter whether the number was a business-as-usual dance arrangement of a current ballad, a hot jazz uptempo instrumental (then known as a "flagwaver"), or one of the band's movie-style production numbers—three-ring circuses that involved several spotlighted singers, a vocal group, and any number of instrumental soloists. Dorsey's mesmerizing horn pulled at you, pleaded with you, entranced and entreated you into listening to the story it told. Dorsey stands as one of the greatest virtuoso players of all time. Not exclusively a jazzman in his own playing—although his band recorded acres of the finest big-band jazz numbers ever conceived—in the nearly forty years since his death, Dorsey continues to reign as pop music's supreme instrumentalist.

In Dorsey's day, big-band swing was so intrinsically close to pure jazz that the major jazz and pop instrumentalists barely bothered to keep a scorecard of which was which. The public couldn't necessarily distinguish between Dorsey or Charlie Barnet, who could swing but didn't necessarily improvise, and Benny Goodman or Harry James, who did both. The difference was purely academic. Dorsey's own enjoyment of jazz, like Sinatra's, was surpassed by no one's, but improvisation was probably the least of his abilities as a player. He continually denigrated his own soloing abilities in deference to his contemporary Jack Teagarden (and even, as he told friend Walter Scott, to Les Jenkins and other trombonists in his own band).

Dorsey can best be appreciated as one appreciates a singer: he leaves the substance of the original melodies intact but remolds it to his own image. He doesn't dramatically reshape a tune the way an all-out jazzman like Dexter Gordon would—as if he were spontaneously composing the song or rewriting it. Instead, the tune is a friend of his that he wants you to meet, and to make a good impression he's dressed it up in one of his good suits. In the words of ex-sideman Buddy Rich, who couldn't stand Dorsey personally, "He was the greatest melodic trombone player that ever lived. Absolutely." Since Dorsey essentially sang with his trombone, it's easy to see how someone who sang with his own vocal instrument would have much to learn from him.

Dorsey's legato style, through which he divided melodies into increasingly longer phrases, had obvious ramifications on the future of music in other ways. To a certain extent Dorsey anticipated some of the mind-set of modern jazz circa Charlie Parker (which is ironic when you consider Dorsey's opinion of that music: "Bopsters! They're musical communists!"). Parker also thought in terms of lines longer than the human voice was achieving in the '30s. Dorsey's style, both in itself and through his influence on Sinatra, would encourage singers to use longer and smoother phrases.

Dorsey's tone is no less remarkable. "Just beautiful!" said contemporary trombonist Steve Turre; like Louis Armstrong or Sonny Rollins, Dorsey could alter it to stomp on one solo and moan on the next, and still no one would ever confuse him with anyone else. That tone could be supersmooth on the ballads, then increasingly buzzier as the tempo picked up, and then downright smeary on "Well, All Right." His uptempo features, in the main Teagarden-like paraphrases, deserve no less attention.

Dorsey was too often unfairly compared to Teagarden, most of all by himself, and to the major improvising swing trombonists who had worked with Count Basie, such as Dicky Wells, Benny Morton, and Vic Dickenson. Dorsey would gladly sacrifice his soloist's ego for the greater glorification of the tune or orchestration. On exotic works like "Dawn on the Desert" or the more famous "Song of India," Dorsey proved himself capable of competing with Duke Ellington's entire trombone "pep" section. All three major members of that greatest 'bone grouping of all time—Lawrence Brown, Tricky Sam Nanton, and Juan Tizol—idolized TD; Brown often described himself as a "Tommy Dorsey man."

The trombone man may be the best man in the band, but with Dorsey it was as much a matter of concept as technique. In June 1939, several months before Sinatra came on board, Dorsey recorded his major leader-era extended solo on trumpet on Irving Berlin's "Back to Back." Dorsey hereby made the point that his development as a melody-oriented trombonist was deliberate and not due to any deficiencies as an improvisor, since, it turned out, as a trumpeter, Dorsey sounded more spontaneous but was a less interesting musician (he had doubled on the instrument at the start of his career and made his first records as a leader playing it).

At various points in his career, Dorsey's demeanor received more press attention than his music. When he and his wife clubbed a lesser-known film actor with a chair in a barroom brawl, all three of them under the influence, the event and the trial that followed were covered in far more papers than had ever reviewed Dorsey's records or even reported on the boffo box office his band always did. But in other kinds of fights, as in many kinds of music, Dorsey knew when to play it cool. I'm not enough of an armchair psychologist to offer an analysis of the love-hate relationship between Tommy Dorsey and his brother Jimmy. Let's just say that by the time Jimmy was thirty-one and Tommy a few months away from turning thirty, it had festered to the point where either brother could instantaneously piss the other off merely by looking at him in the wrong way.

Which was what happened several nights after the Dorsey Brothers Orchestra debuted at the Glen Island Casino on May 23, 1935. Tommy was conducting, Jimmy let slip a minor crack about the tempo he had set, and that was it. Without even looking at his brother, Tommy packed up his trombone and walked off the stand. (The younger Dorsey wasn't merely upset over the tempo: guitarist Roc Hillman told researcher Raymond Hair that Jimmy D. had shown up soused.) The gig that was to be the band's big break turned out to be their big breakup. It was as much a landmark event for the swing era as Benny Goodman's tumultuous opening at the Los Angeles Palomar three months later.

In the early years, between 1935 and 1939, Dorsey consistently had room for improvement in the vocal department. The band's first resident crooner and canary were Jack Leonard and Edythe Wright, neither of whom had much to offer in the way of style. After years of getting Wright as a side you hadn't ordered on her dozens of discs with Dorsey, it's possible, with effort, to gradually warm up to her sound and personality.

Leonard, for his part, anticipated Sinatra in two key respects. Even as local girls were beginning to swoon over Sinatra when he was with the Hoboken Four, Leonard's own smooth-styled singing was upsetting delicate distaff nervous systems at Dorsey dances and theater gigs. And that was because, as Leonard rightfully claimed long after he had stopped performing, he, and not Sinatra, had been the first vocalist to absorb Dorsey's musical influence. "Tommy didn't tell me to do it," Leonard later said. "It was an automatic thing. Sitting there on the bandstand night after night, you had to be influenced. It rubbed off on you whenever you sang." Yet ultimately Leonard only hinted at the long-breath style that did so much to elevate Sinatra to superstardom.

If the shrill texture of Leonard's piercing pipes didn't turn you right off, his blasé attitude would. "Josephine," Leonard and Dorsey's campy retro hit from 1937, features the singer at his most obnoxious, but it's one of the few records where Leonard displays any personality of any kind. The one well-remembered Dorsey-Leonard record, "Marie," succeeds by revealing the singer as an unknowing buffoon, and Sinatra would later turn the "Marie" formula completely around. Dorsey and Leonard may have made "Our Love" a number one hit in 1939, but Sinatra, even on his demo disc of the Clinton-Tschaikovsky piece, puts the number over much more convincingly than his Dorsey precursor, who even had the benefit of an Axel Stordahl arrangement.

Leonard's and Sinatra's emulation of Dorsey was hardly unique at this time. "All the band singers with the bands would listen to these great musicians play all night long, and they were all very affected by jazz musicians," as arranger Quincy Jones remembers the big-band era. "Peggy Lee, Ella Fitzgerald, Sarah Vaughan—they were all very jazz-oriented because they were playing with these great jazz instrumental-ists, and the instrumentalists were the focal point. In those years the players were the ones getting all of the attention, so naturally the singers emulated them, and that's why their phrasing is so good and so instru-mental-like."

Dorsey's radio producer and confidant Herb Sanford thinks that the first time Dorsey may have heard the name Frank Sinatra occurred when Jack Leonard asked Dorsey if he had heard the Harry James ver-sion of "All or Nothing at All." It's unimportant that through the Bob Chester association and a possible earlier audition for TD himself, Dorsey doubtlessly already knew who Sinatra was long before the James-Sinatra discs were released. What's worth noting is Leonard's own first reaction to Sinatra. Leonard was in some sense speaking for the entire profession of bandsingers in 1939. "There's a guy on 'All or Noth-ing at All' who does the vocal, and he scares the hell out of me," Leonard is said to have told Dorsey. "He's that good."

"The first time I heard him," recalled Dorsey's star clarinetist Johnny Mince, "we were standing in front of a hotel before going in for a one-nighter. Tommy said, 'Come here, Johnny, I want you to hear something.' Sinatra was singing 'All or Nothing at All' with Harry James on the radio, and Tommy asked me, 'What do you think?' I said, 'Boy! He really sings well. He really does.' Even though I used to like Jack Leonard, Frank Sinatra had it all over him." (While most accounts agree that the James record of "All or Nothing at All" convinced Dorsey to hire Sinatra, the catalogue number of that disc indicates that this side would not be released until approximately June 1940. However, the James band broadcast the number frequently in the summer and fall of 1939, and Dorsey doubtless heard Sinatra sing it live on the radio.)

Sinatra joined Tommy Dorsey and his orchestra sometime in January 1940, after Dorsey realized that his initial replacement for Jack Leonard, baritone Allan DeWitt, wasn't going to work out. Dorsey press agent Jack Egan later reported that Sinatra had to wait in the wings while DeWitt worked out his two weeks' notice with TD.

Clarinetist Mahlon Clark, then still in high school in Portsmouth, Virginia, was invited to a prom at the University of Virginia in December 1939 or January 1940. Dean Hudson and his orchestra played the first night, and Dorsey was to play the second; Sinatra arrived a day early and sat in with Hudson's band. "And Dean got up and made an announcement that we had in the audience the new singer with the Tommy Dorsey band, and it was Frank. He came up and sang 'South of the Border.' I remember it very well because it knocked us all out. We thought, 'Who is this?' It sounded beautiful."

Mince and his wife, the former Betty Williams (herself a Dorseyphile), recalled that Sinatra joined while the band was on the road in Sheboygan, Wisconsin. Still, they might not have mentioned his name in Sheboygan; Jack Egan insists that Sinatra first sang with Dorsey at the Lyric Theatre in Indianapolis. In 1955, Sinatra himself said it was in Baltimore, Maryland. Jo Stafford, who had joined the band only about a month previously as one of Dorsey's new vocal group, the Pied Pipers, remembers "very vividly" that Sinatra came on board in either Minneapolis or Milwaukee. "We left the Palmer House in Chicago and went to play a theater in one of those towns just a couple of hours' train ride from Chicago." The earliest documented aircheck of Sinatra with Dorsey comes from Rockford, Illinois, on January 25, 1940; the new combination made its first commercial recordings for Victor on February 1.

Ms. Stafford's memories are more musical than geographical, however. "We had not met him," she said. "We didn't have to rehearse that morning because our stuff was already rehearsed. We knew the new boy singer was coming with the band, but we didn't go to the rehearsal." Stafford also summarized her initial reaction to the sight, and not the sound, of Sinatra as "kinda thin." Sinatra later recalled his first date with the band only by the embarrassing fact that his hands were covered with blisters, the result of twenty-seven innings of softball played with his fellow Dorseyites a few hours earlier.

"So the first time I saw him was on stage during the show, and Tommy introduced him as the new boy singer," Stafford continued. "He walked out and started singing, and it didn't take more than eight or ten bars to know that you were listening to something entirely unique and different. You know, nobody had ever sounded like that before. And you knew that it was something very, very good. I was terribly impressed." When Deane Kincaide, Dorsey's chief jazz arranger at that time, was recently asked if they were worried that the newcomer wouldn't be able to fill Leonard's shoes, he answered that from the very beginning, Sinatra "was far and away the top guy as far as that's concerned."

In March 1940, Sinatra came into his home territory for the first time with the Dorsey group when the band played the New York Paramount. At the time, Pee Wee Erwin, a jazz trumpeter who had worked for many years with Dorsey, and pianist Joel Herron, who would later compose "I'm a Fool to Want You," were playing in Johnny Green's radio orchestra. "One day Pee Wee asked me, 'Do you wanna go to the Paramount?' I asked what for, and he said, 'Jack Leonard's outside. He's in his soldier's suit. He's been hauled into the army, and he wants to go over and hear the new kid with Dorsey.'" Herron remembered, "We went backstage at the Paramount where they knew Pee Wee and Leonard, and we sat down in front with [me in the middle]. We went there essentially to see this kid get killed. The band came on and did 'Sentimental over You,' the theme, and Dorsey came forward and said, 'Without any further ado we'd like to introduce our new boy singer, Frank Sinatra, singing our hit record "Who,"' which Leonard had recorded [in 1937]. When this new kid came running out, we all were sure that he was gonna fall on his ass. But when he started to sing, I sunk down in my seat. I felt humiliated for the guy who was sitting next to me [Leonard], who had just become the oldest kind of news that there was in the world."

Inspired by this initial success, Sinatra later said, "I began to work harder than ever. The audience reaction meant they liked me. I didn't know what was causing the reaction exactly. I was experimenting with singing and different forms of phrasing and picking songs better." Still, on many of Sinatra's earliest appearances with Dorsey, the singer sounds as if he has actually gone backward since the best of the James sides, particularly "All or Nothing at All." (The live version from the 1939 World's Fair was even more spectacular than the studio version.)

Some of the first extant Dorsey-Sinatra broadcasts are notable mainly because Sinatra does not steal the show from the rest of the band. The earliest show that commonly circulates among collectors, from the Meadowbrook on February 2, 1940, has Sinatra doing three tunes. Here, our ears are primed to pick up the trombone man first, and then Babe Russin attracts more attention with his lengthy clarinet solo on "So

What" (not to be confused with the later Miles Davis composition). To a certain extent this could have been because with James, Sinatra and arranger Andy Gibson were starting from scratch. With Dorsey, Sinatra first had to worry about fitting into the molds that had previously been set for Leonard before he could think about starting anything of his own.

What did Sinatra hear in Dorsey? If Harry James instilled in Sinatra a greater feeling for jazz, Dorsey imparted to the young singer something even more meaningful than his own prodigious technique: the concept of stating a melody so that it could instantly be recognized, yet at the same time personalizing it so that it sounded like a creation completely by or for the performer.

Dorsey billed himself as "The Sentimental Gentleman of Swing," taking the name from Mitchell Parrish's 1932 song, "That Sentimental Gentleman from Georgia."[1] Yet Dorsey was probably the least sentimental of all bandleaders. There's nothing the least bit maudlin or mawkishly cloying in any of Dorsey's hundreds upon hundreds of records. The trombonist specialized in what are better classified as intimate and eternally danceable ballads. The vast majority of swing-band leaders, like Bob Crosby, who played as hot as they could get away with and indulged in the love songs only begrudgingly, were far more prone to excess sentiment than Dorsey. With his trombone and his band, Dorsey preached to Sinatra that if you get into a tune so that you really feel it when you tell its story to an audience, you needn't get sentimental over it. As Sinatra sings in "This Is the Beginning of the End," all you need to do is read the writing in your heart.

Evidence that Sinatra was learning this lesson well can be found as early as the third or fourth TD–FS session. The first specific cue Sinatra picked up from Dorsey involved extending individual phrases so that he could express the whole idea of an eight-bar line in a single breath. "You see, any brass instrument player has the same breathing and lung-power problem as a vocalist," Sinatra told Sidney Zion. "They have it a little easier because they blow through a small aperture, and they can cover their mouth with their hands, while a singer couldn't possibly sing like that all the time. You have to get up and sing but still have enough wind down here to make your phrases much more understandable and elongated so that the entire thought of the song is there."

"Dorsey was my teacher, and he was Frank Sinatra's teacher, too. He

---

1. That fact really peeved lyricist Parrish because Dorsey never even used Parrish's tune but instead commissioned his own to hawk the "sentimental" idea, the lovely "I'm Getting Sentimental over You."

taught me how to phrase," remembers Arthur "Skeets" Herfurt. "Frank mentions the same thing—that Tommy is the one who taught him to phrase. Tommy sometimes used to make the whole orchestra (not just the trombones) play from the top of a page clear down to the bottom without taking a breath. It was way too many bars! But I sure developed lung power, which I still have at the age of eighty. Everybody in the band would learn to play like Tommy did."

Dorsey-style phrasing seems to have been exactly what popular music needed in the early '40s. Remember that the mainstream of pop singing had received little fresh input since Bing Crosby and Louis Armstrong a decade earlier: Ella Fitzgerald was years away from her prime, and Billie Holiday was still largely an esoteric influence. The male singers in the big bands had assumed Crosby's rich baritone register (Ray Eberle and Leonard are exceptions) but by and large continued to put a song over in a stuffy, unreal way. Crosby's jazz influences were beyond them, and Armstrong was not taken nearly as seriously as a vocalist as he would be in the '50s, his greatest era of pop success.

Sinatra sought to discover how technique and interpretation could work together to reach a higher level of artistic credibility. The belter-crooners would blast through a song, taking a breath, gasping right in the middle of a line, shattering both the rhythmic momentum and the mood. By extending the line, Sinatra could put over both the lyrical idea and the melody that much more convincingly. Naturally, he developed the chops to hit high notes without blinking—even a toughie like the one that comes out of nowhere at the end of "I'll Be Seeing You" (1940). But more important than hitting them, Sinatra managed to hold them, developing both the physical lung power and the dramatic ability to set up a line of lyrics so that it made sense.

"So I began using the pool at Stevens Institute of Technology whenever I had a chance, and I would swim underwater," Sinatra continued to Sidney Zion. "The guys there would say to me, 'Don't you ever swim on top of the water?' I said, 'No. There's a reason for it. I don't want to explain it.' But it did help me develop. I was very small. I weighed about 130 pounds, and I just had to grow a little more. I did lots of exercises. I did running and that kind of stuff.

"And then when I joined Tommy's band, and even prior to that, I wondered what it was that enabled him to execute sixteen measures of a song. If you count fairly slowly and you count four to a bar, that's a long time. It took me a year and a half to figure out that he was breathing in the corner of his mouth because, the fink, he had his mouth covered, you see, and I couldn't see him doing that most of the time. But he could [extend a phrase] for eight measures or maybe ten full measures without breathing, actually without breathing. And I watched him for two years, and I realized that I was learning a great deal, I was growing again."

Dorsey's desire for perfection affected not only Sinatra but the entire band. Dorsey pushed everybody "all the way" to the limit, as Alvin Stoller (who replaced Buddy Rich) recalls. "He was a very demanding man. It wasn't a matter of *can* you do it, or *should* you try it, it was just *do* it! I learned a lot just by following him and watching how he worked. When I got in the band, Tommy wanted this and he wanted that. Eventually you find yourself capable of doing things that you didn't know you could do. If you don't try, you won't make it—talking about it isn't going to make it happen. Tommy would just force you to do it. It hardened me as far as playing is concerned, it gave me an assurance that I didn't know I had."

As Sinatra elaborated for Arlene Francis: "I began listening to musicians, both jazz and classical musicians; for instance, I was fascinated by Jascha Heifetz, who could make a change of his bow in phrase and get to the end of the bow and continue without a perceptible missing beat in the motion. I thought if that could be done on an instrument—and the violin and the flute are two good examples—why not do it with the human voice? It was very tough to do it. It took a lot of calisthenics and physical work to get the bellows—the breathing apparatus—built up."

If "The Sky Fell Down," the first Dorsey-Sinatra item (heard extensively in the recent film *Used People*), and "Moments in the Moonlight" are on the choppy side, "Say It" shows Sinatra beginning to connect notes into long, virtually seamless breaths. Here he also achieves a singular unity with Dorsey's trombone, Dorsey, in this case and others, further accommodating the new singer by muting his bell to produce a sound even closer to a human voice than usual. "The Call of the Canyon," composed by Billy "The Last Roundup" Hill, sets the long-breath sounds of both Dorsey and Sinatra against a contrasting background, as out-of-tempo brass play a countermelody depicting the clip-clop of a canyon pack mule in the fashion of Ferde Grofé's "Grand Canyon Suite," all supported by a waddling arco bull fiddle.

"The Beginning of the End," "Where Do You Keep Your Heart?," and "The World Is in My Arms" (from Al Jolson's comeback show, *Hold Onto Your Hats*) find Sinatra extending phrases over a shuffle rhythm in three charts wherein Sy Oliver (or possibly Jimmy Mundy) revives his patented Luncefordian two-beat, a perfect accompaniment for a John Bubbles sand dance. These three numbers are also rare examples of drummer Buddy Rich's evoking the more traditional style of predecessor Davey Tough.

In later years, when Sinatra mostly recorded standard songs, the singer enjoyed the advantage of having lived with much of his repertoire for decades before committing or recommiting it to shellac. During the Dorsey days, Sinatra's longtime personal manager, Hank Sanicola, who doubled as capable if unspectacular pianist, would run over tunes with the singer before a date. In later years that role was largely assumed by composer Jimmy Van Heusen, probably Sinatra's closest friend, and occasionally by his more accomplished regular accompanist, Bill Miller.

If Sinatra was prepared, the band usually wasn't—which wasn't necessarily a bad thing. "Whenever we went to a recording studio, we'd almost always get new arrangements that we had never played before," explained pianist Joe Bushkin, "so the guys would get really on top of it. We would put more energy into getting it to sound tight. Tommy didn't do it purposely, but that's what made the hit records. The listeners could pick up on the enthusiasm of the band. We never got anywhere with the goddamn stuff that we were already familiar with. It just so happened that whatever we played on the road had already been recorded. Then we could play our record numbers on the job. Which made sense because if you're traveling three hundred miles a night and just barely making the gig, you sure can't call a rehearsal."

Further, both Dorsey and later Sinatra placed jazz skills at a premium when hiring musicians. "If the band sounded a little bit off," said Bushkin, "Tommy might give a little heat to any lead player who was strictly a technical player. But he never bothered any of the guys who could improvise, like Bunny Berigan or Don Lodice."

"Tommy became almost a father to me," Sinatra often said, and he selected TD as the godfather of his first child, Nancy, Jr. Many of Sinatra's friends claimed that the iron-fisted Mr. Dorsey supplied a stronger, paternal image than the singer's own father, the very passive Marty Sinatra. As with any familial relationship, the course was not always smooth. During the entire first year of their relationship, Dorsey held Bob Allen, a talented crooner then working with Hal Kemp's orchestra, over Sinatra's head; when Sinatra would act up, Dorsey would threaten to call Allen. Once Sinatra walked into the band's dressing room (as Allen later told researcher Bob Conrad) and discovered the other singer's tuxedo draped over the chair. After another session of pleading and shouting with Dorsey, Sinatra went on that night. (Years later, Allen and his wife bumped into Sinatra in a bar. Obviously pie-eyed, he growled to Allen, "So you're the fucker who thought he could replace me!" Eventually Allen did take Sinatra's place as Dorsey's star vocalist, in 1944–45.) On another occasion, Connie Haines recalled, Dorsey canned Sinatra and replaced him with Milburn Stone (later of "Gunsmoke" fame) until Sinatra came crying back to him.

Listening only to the Dorsey-Sinatra numbers, especially the earlier, 1940 titles, does Dorsey a disservice. You have to hear the band's entire output, the instrumentals, and the other vocalists, the radio show banter, and "Memory Medley"s, to appreciate the full range and versatility of the Dorsey orchestra. Apart from the sentimentalist sessions, which we'll come to shortly, Sinatra was initially assigned only the basic bread-and-butter fox-trots. And listening only to these tends to paint an unbalanced picture of this band whose leader was dedicated, he claimed in radio announcements, "to the proposition that every tune deserves its own style." "No two arrangements are alike. Each one is tailored to fit the mood of the tune," Dorsey said, tying the individual numbers together only with the sound of his own trombone and his standards of excellence.

More than half of the Dorsey-Sinatra recordings use the same three-chorus format and medium-slow fox-trot tempo: a chorus by Dorsey, a chorus by Sinatra, then a jazzier, slightly louder and faster chorus by the ensemble, which could be deemed a "dancer's chorus." Dorsey always dominates the first chorus, although he rarely plays all thirty-two bars of it. Occasionally he divides the responsibility, as do most band charts looking for variety, by assigning the bridge to another horn soloist or, more frequently, the entire ensemble. Most often, however, Dorsey plays the bridge himself but leaves the final eight-bar "A" section to serve as a transitional passage wherein the main melody gets restated immediately prior to the entrance of the vocalist. On virtually every record Dorsey claims the first sixteen bars, the "AA" of the first chorus, for himself, making sure the trombone playing the major strain of the melody is the first thing that hits you, which explains why it was so crucial that Dorsey play sixteen bars without stopping for a breath.

The third chorus often includes brief solo statements from various horns, Dorsey wisely not saving his hot men exclusively for the more jazz-oriented instrumentals. Clarinetist Johnny Mince supplies greater warmth than the young Sinatra on some of the earlier tunes, especially "I'll Be Seeing You," "Moments in the Moonlight," and "April Played the Fiddle." Bunny Berigan, the major trumpet legend and epic lush of the '30s who reassumed his old chair in the Dorsey band after his own unit went belly-up, gets to blast a bit in the third chorus of "I Haven't Time to Be a Millionaire" and elsewhere. Berigan also reassumes his old role in several Sinatra-Dorsey readings of "Marie," a classic solo that sounds even better following Sinatra than it did Leonard, and reprises this role in the live and studio versions of the tune's sequel, "East of the Sun." In the '80s, when Sinatra performed Berigan's theme song, "I Can't Get Started," he often introduced it as a dedication to Berigan, his onetime roommate on the Dorsey tours. "He was the greatest trumpet player in the world," Sinatra would announce with complete and total earnestness. "Then one day we couldn't find him."

The standard three-chorus format applies to most of the major Dorsey-Sinatra numbers; as we'll see, the leader jettisoned it mainly for "Sentimentalist" and production number excursions. Although by 1942 it seemed silly to confine Sinatra, the band's most popular attraction by far, to these single chorus refrains, that point was far in the future in early 1940. Even the arrangement of "Polka Dots and Moonbeams," the earliest Sinatra-Dorsey number to drop the third chorus, was dictated by the limits of recording technology rather than in deference to Sinatra. Live aircheck versions of the tune, done with the arrangement not yet finalized (one running nearly four and a half minutes or roughly a minute longer than a conventional single), do contain a third chorus, which offers more superwarm Mince.

By May 1940 everything was coming together. In March and April, Sinatra and the band had already recorded a number of their greatest pieces, such as "The Beginning of the End," "The World Is in My Arms," "East of the Sun," and the blockbuster, "I'll Never Smile Again." Dorsey's widely anticipated engagement at the Astor Roof in May was set to be a big deal, marking the band's New York nightclub debut with their new vocalist as well as the grand reopening of a once and future after-theater hotspot. On opening night numerous luminaries, such as Benny Goodman and Oscar Levant, could be spotted in the audience.

Pianist Joe Bushkin, who had joined the band five or six weeks earlier, recalled that Sinatra's first vocal on that premiere night called for him to sing with the Pied Pipers, while his second, "Begin the Beguine," was strictly a solo feature for him. According to Bushkin, "Beguine" (which unfortunately wasn't preserved in either a live or a studio recording) marked the first Dorsey piece to feature Sinatra throughout, with just a brief eight-bar instrumental interlude for the band. "He wound it up with a nice big finish," said Bushkin, "and the place went bananas!" The singer had stopped the show, something that rarely happened during a program of dance music. It was a bonus that Dorsey was immediately keen to take advantage of. The crowd wouldn't let Sinatra off without an encore, and Dorsey wanted to oblige. But "Beguine" represented the total of Sinatra features that Dorsey had in his band book.

Dorsey instructed the band to play "Polka Dots and Moonbeams," but because it wasn't a vocal feature, he took the four-bar transitional passage that precedes the vocal and from there went right into Sinatra's "middle" chorus. After "Polka Dots," "the people were still going nuts," Bushkin continued, so rather than force a dance number into a vocal feature, Dorsey told Sinatra, "Just sing whatever you want with Joe." The two began an impromptu voice and piano duo. Bushkin remembered that Sinatra's confidence was unshakable. He simply went on singing to the wild delight of the now no-longer-dancing crowd. The twenty-three-year-old pianist, however, was completely taken aback. "As we were playing, I was trying to figure out his range," said Bushkin. "I was thinking quickly, 'Where is his top note?' If I can get to the top note, the bottom will take care of itself."

Three or four tunes (including "All the Things You Are") later, a much-ruffled Bushkin was still trying to follow Sinatra as best he could. "Then he turned around and said, 'Smoke Gets in Your Eyes.' Well, if you know that tune, man, you know that you can really get lost in the middle part [the bridge]. Unless you really know what you're doing, that chord change will just lose you. I'm right out there without bread and water, man! Next thing I know, Frank was out there singing it all by himself. He was singing the bridge, a capella. I was so embarrassed. I mean, Jesus, all the guys were looking at me, so I just turned around and walked away from the piano! I went to the side and then ran back to the piano and finished up the tune. And that was the last song we did. I thought Tommy was going to kill me, but he thought it was so funny!

"And that," Bushkin concluded, "is the night that Frank Sinatra happened." Other attendees concurred. When radio's leading couple, announcer Andre Baruch and singer Bea Wain, came down to dance to the band, Dorsey asked them what they thought of the new vocalist. Baruch was less than enthusiastic ("It [his career] will never happen"), but Wain spoke for most of those present when she told TD, "He's wonderful. He's just electric!"

On the aforementioned "Polka Dots," Sinatra's early uneasiness effectively conveys the Sturm und Drang of a nervous young wallflower at a prom. The song itself is one of the first of many by Jimmy Van Heusen that Sinatra was to record. Van Heusen at this time was beginning his long association with Crosby, and in fact the Dorsey-Sinatra discography contains many more songs associated with Crosby than with Sinatra. In the three years of Sinatra's tenure with the band, Victor assigned Dorsey the task of devising dance band versions of songs from four Crosby pictures, and the results of those assignments offer an accurate barometer of Sinatra's progress. On April 10, 1940, Dorsey recorded the two "plug" songs from Crosby's current release, *If I Had My Way:* "April Played the Fiddle" and "I Haven't Time to Be a Millionaire." "Polka Dots," with its references to an Irish-American "pug-nosed dream," perfectly suited Mr. Crosby and Mr. Burke. But the typical metaphoric conceits and allusions that made Burke and Crosby so perfect for each other are lost on Sinatra at this early stage; Sinatra would have looked equally silly in Crosby's hat, pipe, and Hawaiian shirt.

Burke's optimism, ironic but devoid of all sarcasm, was too specific a target for Sinatra to hit in 1940. He got around the problem on Burke's "Too Romantic," from *Road to Singapore,* the first of Crosby and Bob Hope's *Road* movies, but that song portrays an exasperatedly nervous would-be Romeo. Dorsey, who had been a sideman on Crosby sessions in the '20s and '30s, enthusiastically encouraged Sinatra to study the singer, exhorting Sinatra that there was "only one singer, and his name is Crosby."

The Dorsey period afforded Sinatra ample opportunity to study Crosby—on screen, when the Dorsey band played the same bill at the New York Paramount with that premier *Road* picture in March 1940 and, unexpectedly, in person when the Dorsey band arrived in Hollywood in November 1940. At the time Dorsey made his first feature film appearance in Paramount's *Las Vegas Nights,* musical director Victor Young also used some of Dorsey's sidemen, including Joe Bushkin and Buddy Rich, to record some music for the second Hope-Crosby classic, *Road to Zanzibar.*

Sinatra's and Crosby's personal paths crossed again a year later when the band returned to Hollywood, this time to participate in what MGM later released as *Ship Ahoy.* "Frank had never met Bing," recalled trumpeter Yank Lawson, who had recently returned to the Bob Crosby band after a season with Dorsey. "We were doing the music for a picture called *Holiday Inn,* and he asked me if he could go out and see the filming. He wanted to watch Bing work because Bing was his idol. Crosby was the big star of that time, and Sinatra was still just the singer with the band. Frank met me out at the Paramount lot, and I took him in. He just loved it, watching Bing."

Several months after "Too Romantic," Sinatra pulled off the real thing in Dorsey's January 1941 versions of the songs from *Road to Zanzibar.* That second *Road* show opened with Crosby's rapturous baritone bouncing through one of Burke's all-time greatest moonbeams-and-metaphors opuses, "You Lucky People, You," over the main titles. Dorsey similarly commenced his version of "You Lucky People, You" with Sinatra singing, making it one of the earliest Dorsey sides to start with Sinatra in the first chorus rather than the second, and also giving the singer an extra outchorus at the end. Sinatra more than justified the temporary promotion, coming on with such contagious cockiness and charisma that he vividly brings Burke's wraparound skies and green velvet landscapes to life.

He did just as well with the romantic, yet not too romantic, "It's Always You" (later revived, like many other early Sinatra numbers, by Chet Baker) and made one wish that Dorsey had given the other two *Zanzibar* songs, "Birds of a Feather" and "You're Dangerous," to Sinatra instead of Connie Haines, good as she was in this period. By the time of his next reworking of a Crosby song, Irving Berlin's "Be Careful It's My Heart" from the final season of his Dorsey tenure, in June 1942, Sinatra hadn't exactly caught up with Crosby, but he had considerably narrowed the gap between them.

Dorsey's two chief arrangers on the Sinatra numbers, Axel Stordahl and Sy Oliver, dispensed with the three-chorus mold more frequently after "You Lucky People, You." Though the standard dance band formats suited Dorsey most of the time, he still got his biggest personal kicks by experimenting with looser, small-group sounds, as he had with the Dixieland-styled Clambake Seven from December 1935 to August 1939. By the end of 1939, when Dorsey wanted to branch back into settings smaller than the full orchestra, he again stressed vocals but dispensed with the dogged Dixie rhythms.

The first sessions with the new small unit, "The Sentimentalists," took place in April and May 1940, and immediately gave Dorsey and Sinatra their biggest hit together, "I'll Never Smile Again," thus ensuring that Dorsey would maintain the Sentimentalist format for the rest of Sinatra's stay with the band and beyond. The Sentimentalists presented more intimate music for listening (or dancing very slowly) in contrast to the standard three-chorus foxtrot. In the beginning Dorsey also applied the Sentimentalist handle to several instrumental jazz numbers recorded by the full orchestra; as with "I'll Never Smile Again," they're intended more for listening than dancing purposes.

The first two Sinatra Sentimentalist titles, "East of the Sun" and "Head on My Pillow," boast enough jazz solo space to suggest a direct extension of the Clambake Seven series. In format and quality, "Pillow" comes very close to the Teddy Wilson–Billie Holiday sides. Trumpeter Bunny Berigan, who played on many Lady Day sessions, here underscores that feeling, as does Sinatra himself, fashioning his most relaxed, Holidayesque chorus yet. (*Down Beat* magazine had recently published a photo of the young Sinatra digging Miss Holiday like everyone else at Chicago's Off-Beat club, taken the previous September.)

After the unprecedented success of "I'll Never Smile Again," the Sentimentalist label was reserved for further slow vocals by Sinatra, with the Pied Pipers weaving in and out, and backed by the band's rhythm section with Dorsey himself and one or two other horns.

"We were rehearsing on a Saturday afternoon, up at the roof of the Astor Hotel," Sinatra recalled, "and Tommy asked Joe Bushkin to play the song. I noticed that everybody suddenly was very quiet, the whole orchestra sat quietly when he played it. There was a feeling of a kind of eeriness that took place, as though we all knew that this would be a big, big hit, and that it was a lovely song."

Dorsey was impressed enough with the song's effect to commission an arrangement by Stordahl and alto and baritone saxophonist Freddie Stulce, and Sinatra took it upon himself to learn it. Stordahl had earlier written some charts that anticipate the Sentimentalist sound for the band's earlier vocal group, "The Three Esquires," in which the arranger himself served as one of the singers, including the original hit version of the standard "Once in a While" (a number redone on the radio with Sinatra and the Pipers).

On April, 23, 1940, Joe Bushkin remembers, "we were in the studio, and we had already done our sides. We still had about twenty minutes left, so Freddie said, 'Well, I wrote that chart for that gal in Canada [the composer Ruth Lowe], and Tommy said, 'Let's give it a try.' So we do a take, and it was kind of empty. Then, Frank sees a celesta in the studio and has them shove it over by me at the piano. He says, 'Just fill it in.' When they finally orchestrated it, my ad lib became part of the arrangement." Sinatra adds, "We made the song with the Pied Pipers and myself, and it was not a very good record. So [a month later, on May 23] we remade it, we did it a second time, still with Tommy. It was strange that it had to be made three times [once by Glenn Miller and twice by Dorsey] before we got it right."

"Smile Again" is heartbreakingly languid, some of the un-fastest music ever recorded, tepidly crawling through the super-slow tempos pioneered, again, by Billie Holiday. Sinatra and the Pied Pipers function as equals, neither side of the equation attracting more attention than the others. Sinatra only occasionally arises out of the ensemble to stress key lines in solo, including virtually all of the bridge, almost like the leader of the vocal group rather than a featured star.

No less than Sinatra, the Pipers themselves had collectively absorbed much of Dorsey's legato style, and all five voices harmonize exquisitely with Dorsey-esque extended notes that amplify the sense of loss in the narrative. Bushkin's celesta provides the only instrumental sound we are conscious of behind the singing, although there's a small and barely noticeable horn ensemble audible here and there. Dorsey himself plays an indescribably mournful eight bars of the main theme before Sinatra and the Pipers cap the piece with a brief outchorus.

"There was practically no band," recalled Jo Stafford. "It was very, very sparse. It was a very tough idea. It was hard to hold the pitch because there was so little background from the band. You really had to mind your p's and q's keeping it in tune." Perhaps because it was such a toughie or perhaps because it featured so little of the band, Dorsey rarely featured "I'll Never Smile Again" in his live broadcasts.

Two months later, not long before the fast-rising "Smile Again" reached the number one spot, Sinatra and the Sentimentalists recorded the first sequel to it. This time they tried the idea with a standard rather than a new song and reused the danceable tempo and Bunny Berigan interlude from "East of the Sun" and "Pillow." How better to showcase the intensely intimate sound of the Sinatra-Pipers combination than with "Whispering," an old-timer Sinatra had previously sung solo with Dorsey as part of a radio "Memory Medley"?

Another standard, "Stardust" (which Sinatra had previously performed on broadcasts with Harry James), returns to "Smile Again"'s crawl-tempo. Although it is generally attributed to Paul Weston (who had written a very different arrangement of the tune for Dorsey back in 1936), today the arranger refuses the credit, explaining that he had left Dorsey's employment shortly before Sinatra joined and never had the chance to write anything for the singer. The 1940 "Stardust" is strictly the "Smile Again" layout applied to another tune. And most effectively, too, judging by its effect on Buddy Rich, who was hardly the band's sensitivity specialist. Rich, who prided himself on being hypermasculine and downright antisentimental, later confided to friend Mel Tormé that Sinatra's rendition of "Stardust" had him hiding his face so that no one would catch a glimpse of his tears.

"Do I Worry?" (which should have been called "What, Me Worry?") also comes very close tempo-wise, although it's by the full band with Sinatra in solo, sans Pipers. A hit for the Ink Spots, "Worry" would have been better off left to them, what with Sinatra trying to suggest one of the formulaic musical monologues routinely perpetrated by "Spot" falsetto Bill Kenny.

More imaginatively, the 1924 "The One I Love Belongs to Somebody Else" and the newer "Dolores" effectively de-sentimentalize the Sinatra-Pied Pipers combination, opening up new possibilities for the five voices in the realm of groovier tempos. Upon coming to work for Dorsey,

arranger Sy Oliver immediately cast the combination as Dorsey's equiv-
alent of the natty three- and four-voice groups he used with Jimmie
Lunceford's band (particularly in familiar favorites like "My Blue
Heaven"). The arranger would later perfect a distinctively Oliver-
Dorsey style, but this early effort sounds more like his previous band
than his current one, though it certainly doesn't suffer because of it.

Proving that turnabout is fair play, Sinatra hums behind the Pied
Pipers, rather than the other way around, on the first part of the bridge
on "The One I Love." "Dolores," with its super-catchy internal
rhyming scheme, is a perfect period piece, which not only reestab-
lishes the Sinatra-Piper hierarchy but boosts his billing, since he's
clearly the star and they're the back-up. That role amounts to a show of
faith on Dorsey's part since Sinatra had not yet established himself on
rhythmic novelties. Sinatra proves he's just as adroit at putting over
one of these snappy, catchy ones as any love lament, as does Dorsey in
a sprightly spot propelled by Buddy Rich's chinka-chinka cymbals.
Both restore the damage done to the song by comic Bert Wheeler in
Paramount's *Las Vegas Nights,* which marked not only Sinatra's first
feature film appearance but, surprisingly, also Dorsey's. The record is
too short: we could go on listening to Sinatra, the Pipers, and TD serenade "Dolores" chorus after chorus. It gave the Sinatra-Pipers series its
sole up-tempo number one hit. "I Guess I'll Have to Dream the Rest"
from June 1941 again goes after "Smile Again"'s buyers, but with the
full orchestra and Sinatra securely in the spotlight. The lyric has more
of a sense of humor than "Smile Again," and the melody merits a live-
lier bounce.

What it took to revive the original "Smile Again" sound was strings.
Sinatra has said in several interviews that he might never have left James
for Dorsey if the latter didn't have a string section. If that was the case,
Dorsey probably told Sinatra that he was thinking of adding violins in
order to entice the singer to jump ship, since the Sentimental Gentleman employed no such section until 1942, by which time Sinatra was
already preparing to go out on his own. As it happened, Sinatra's first
date with strings (since his 1939 demo of "Our Love") turned out to be
his own premiere solo session, the Bluebird date of January 1942. In
fact, according to a *Down Beat* clipping from early 1942 ("Dorsey Will
Sweeten Brass with Fiddles"), the results of the Sinatra-Stordahl session
put the idea in Dorsey's mind, and when Artie Shaw broke up his band
to join the service, Dorsey seized the opportunity to annex his former
rival's violin section en masse. In any case, the strings support the Sinatra-Pipers combo suitably on their last four outings, "Just As Though You

Were Here," "Street of Dreams," "It Started All Over Again," and what was to be both their last number one hit[2] as well as Tommy Dorsey's, "There Are Such Things."

The strings, at last, give the Sentimentalists a sound that is truly Sentimental; those who know the normally snappy "It Started All Over Again" will be surprised by the stateliness of this ballad reading. Dorsey was taking the fiddles very seriously, even bringing in light classicist David Rose to score "By the Sleepy Lagoon" and "Melody in A" for the enlarged band. The sound of the strings dominates much more than Dorsey's trombone, heard only in brief instrumental breaks between the vocal choruses. Still, the lightness the strings and voices apply behind Sinatra on "Just as Though You Were Here" is appropriate, considering how that song was to be treated with increasing dramatics as the war went on. On the other hand, the strings may treat the melody of "Street of Dreams" grandly, but the orchestration makes the text seem naively light-headed.

In ballrooms and on remote broadcasts the band played fairly exclusively for dancers, and virtually everything Sinatra did with the Pipers could be danced to. Dorsey and all the major bands worked just as much in theaters, however, playing stage shows up to an hour long between movies, where dancing was not encouraged. Helping them to compete for theater work, the band had become, like that of Dorsey's friend Glenn Miller and innumerable sweet bands, a jazz-tinged variety show. As Sinatra later observed, "Every band had a million singers back then." In addition, to keep the flow of variety going, the Dorsey entourage occasionally introduced its own "in-house" novelty acts, such as dancing saxist and comic singer Skeets Herfurt.

Sinatra's three central duets with Connie Haines, "Oh, Look at Me Now," "You Might Have Belonged to Another," and "Snooty Little Cutie," which also utilized the Pied Pipers, seem to be strictly aimed at radio and theater audiences. Haines, whose tenures with both James and Dorsey paralleled Sinatra's almost exactly (although she has since revealed that she and he couldn't stand each other personally), is something of an enigma. Her work from both before and after her Dorsey period can be so sugary cute it threatens to leave audiences begging for insulin. But apparently the un-Sentimental Gentleman helped Haines restrain her refrains, since her

2. The poop on chart hits comes from the recognized authority on such matters, Joel Whitburn, in his *Pop Music Memories, 1895–1955* (Record Research). While Whitburn's "charts" before 1940 are largely speculative, it's generally agreed that his information on the '40s and '50s accurately reflects what was published at the time in *Billboard*.

three years with Dorsey resulted in some irresistibly perky and personable bandchirping. Several months before the first commercial Dorsey side to combine Sinatra, Haines, and the Pipers, the band tried the threesome on a radio-only ballad, "That's How It Goes."

Sinatra and Haines come on like spunky siblings rather than singing sweethearts à la Nelson Eddy and Jeanette MacDonald, giving each other as many elbows to the ribs as adoring glances, landing somewhere in the long stretch between Burns & Allen and Regis & Cathy Lee. Their pinnacle, "Oh, Look at Me Now," has the two of them trading lines for the first chorus, with the Pied Pipers predominating in the second. The less spectacular "You Might Have Belonged to Another" has Sinatra singing the entire first chorus in solo, and Haines and the Pipers getting more to do in the second. Bobby Troup's "Snooty Little Cutie" opens with the Pipers, and in the second chorus the decision goes to Ms. Haines, who comes off like an updated swing-era Betty Boop; Sinatra sounds slightly uncomfortable. "Snooty" sounds better, however, on an August 1942 aircheck with (in addition to a second half-chorus of Dorsey trombone) Stafford replacing the departed Haines.

Although, as it happened, Dorsey and Sinatra recorded more songs by Jimmy Van Heusen than any other composer (a track record Sinatra would maintain for the rest of his career), the four songs that the singer-bandleader team did by Matt Dennis and Tom Adair, who were hired by Dorsey to write songs for the bandleader's publishing company, are virtually the leitmotifs of The Voice's early career. In fact, Sinatra considered "Violets for Your Furs," "Everything Happens to Me," "Let's Get Away from It All," and "The Night We Called It a Day" such essential career milestones that he remade all four within a few years of going to Capitol Records in the mid-1950s. Dorsey also recorded four other Dennis-Adair tunes, including "Let's Just Pretend," and a dance arrangement of "The Night We Called It a Day" with Jo Stafford. Sinatra and Dorsey scored their last major hit together with "In the Blue of Evening," Tom Adair's lyric to a theme by New York bandleader Alfred A. D'Artega.

The Dennis and Adair story essentially begins one evening in late 1940 or early 1941 when Dennis, an accomplished (and later widely recorded) pianist and singer, was performing in a Hollywood nightclub. "Tom came in one night to hear me play and sing some of my things," Dennis remembered, "and he said to me, 'I'd like to write a song with you.' And I said, 'Let me see what you have.'" And the first thing he showed me was the lyric to 'Will You Still Be Mine?' It was a hell of a lyric, you know. That kind of thrilled me, so I wrote the music to that very shortly. And a few days later, working over the phone, we wrote 'Let's Get Away from It All' in one afternoon, and then we did 'Everything Happens to Me' a couple of days after that. All in all, it was a hell of a week."

"I was instrumental in bringing Dennis and Adair into the organization," recalls Stafford. "I had known Matt since 1936 or 1937. He used to work clubs out here [in Los Angeles], and I was a big fan. Then the band came out here. At that time, Tommy had a publishing company also. And when I came out here we were having a record date, and I asked him to hear Matt and Tom, and let them do some of their songs. And he hired them then and there as part of his organization. Their stuff was awfully good." Her good turn was rewarded in kind: originally hired as a member of the Pied Pipers, Stafford had sung a few solo vocals with the band on radio only before Dorsey had brought in Connie Haines as a longer-term replacement for Edythe Wright. When Dorsey finally decided to let Stafford take a hack at a solo vocal on a record, the tune was Dennis and Adair's "Little Man with a Candy Cigar."

Dorsey then proceeded to have his other two star singers further the team's tunes, Connie Haines on "Will You Still Be Mine" and Sinatra, as we'll see, on deluxe, extended vocal features of "Everything Happens to Me" and "Violets for Your Furs." "I'd play my new songs for Tommy," says Dennis, "and I'd say 'This might be good for Connie,' or Frank or whoever, and usually Tommy would agree." But what Dorsey did for Dennis and Adair's "Let's Get Away from It All" would have been better than a month of *Chanukahs* for any songwriter: an extra long two-sided extravaganza featuring not only every singer in the unit—all seven of 'em—plus a gaggle of the band's best horn soloists. "Tommy thought it would be very entertaining to do it as a [musical comedy-style] production number," says Dennis. "Tom wrote two sets of lyrics which gave them a little more material, so that everybody could join in. And, of course, the instrumentalists played some wonderful solos."

Sidestepping the possibility that just repeating a 32-bar AABA number for two sides might get repetitious, the Dorsey staff beefed it up with extended transitions and other additional material. The record opens with an instrumental chorus of the tune heavily featuring TD. Next, Jo Stafford and the Pied Pipers sing the verse and refrain once through. A reed passage bridges the gap between the two sides of the disc, and then Sinatra and Haines appear with another chorus's worth of additional lyrics, bantering and one-upping each other more perkily than ever, making the most of the text's snappy attitude and witty rhyme combinations. The instrumental ensemble, spotlighting an enthusiastic Ziggy Elman, and the vocal septet, heavy on the Sinatra, divide the last chorus.

They don't have to drive it in with a spike, after just one hearing, the tune will stay in your head for the rest of your life.

"It was almost like a production number," says Stafford. "We did quite a few of those things after that." Oliver's "I'll Take Tallulah" didn't get as much attention, as it seemed too tied to its movie origin, MGM's *Ship Ahoy* (working title: *I'll Take Manila*), a lamentable script redeemed primarily by the generous amount of footage devoted to the Dorsey troop, although Red Skelton, Eleanor Powell, and Bert Lahr also have plenty of moments. The song's title combined a familiar radio comedy tagline, "I'll Take Vanilla," with the name of the picture's protagonist, Miss Powell as Tallulah Winters.

Where the film arrangement excludes Sinatra entirely, the record version makes him its lead voice. It remains one of the most ingenious works in the Dorsey-Sinatra canon, for it's a genuine butt-kicker with a truly humorous text. Not just another rhythm tune with nonsense lyrics to be quickly sung and gotten over with (the sort of thing that the Dorsey-Oliver "Opus One" makes fun of), it incorporates solo and group voices with considerable humor and swing into the true spirit of the big-band flagwaver.

"Tallulah" contains all the witty rhymes and puns of "Get Away from It All" and adds two elements, leader Dorsey's harsh but friendly squawking, long familiar to radio listeners, and a Latinate rhythm base ground out by percussion master Rich. Starting with a clave beat, the piece puts a rhumba beat behind vocal gags, exchanges between star Sinatra and various guest vocalists—Dorsey, Stafford, and Haines, backed by the Pipers as a swingin' Greek chorus.

By the time the vocal is done, the conga bit has been forgotten and the piece is straight swing uptempo instrumental; to enforce this, Oliver sets up a shouting match between Dorsey and Ziggy Elman that looks backward to the two-trumpet battle of Ellington's "Tootin' Through the Roof" and forward to Oliver's most heralded use of the device in the Dorsey classic "Well, Git It." "Tallulah" ends with blaring, nearly dissonant brass, making you wonder what is Oliver's greater achievement—making the five-minute "Get Away from It All" seem like half that length or cramming more stuff into "Tallulah" than you would ever believe could fit into three minutes.

"Tallulah" had come from E. Y. Harburg and Burton Lane, two songwriters bigger than Dorsey could bag for his publishing concerns. However, the bulk of the band's remaining "production numbers" had been generated specifically by the trombone man's publishing machinations. Around May or June of 1940, Dorsey began a new series of commercial radio shows, sponsored, for once, not by one of the cigarette companies that bought and sold popular music, but by "Nature's Remedy," a laxative firm. Joe Bushkin, expressing the sentiments of the sidemen as a whole, says, "That was a great idea for an advertiser, to take a band that appeals to young people and have them try and sell a laxative! It was pretty stupid."

Dorsey's broadcasts of the Sinatra years and afterward utilized several different kinds of radio programming gimmicks. Sinatra participated in several extant examples of one of these, the "Memory Medley," which operated as the equivalent of the "Something Old, Something New" medley hook that rival Glenn Miller had been using for over a year. After concentrating on college songs (of all things) in the spring of 1940, Dorsey settled on a format of three songs per medley; the first and last would use different vocalists, while the middle would be an instrumental, often featuring Dorsey, Ziggy Elman, or (from 1942 on) the string section. Sinatra seems to have starred as the opening act of each of the medleys that featured him.

The very existence of the "Memory Medley" idea underscores how the idea of doing old tunes was little more than a novelty in the early '40s. There was still more money in the present than in the past. Inspired by the boffo business Dorsey was doing as both publisher and recording artist on "I'll Never Smile Again," the "N.R." ad agency concocted a gimmick to bring its radio program both promotional attention and material. Each week on what came to be called the *Fame and Fortune* show, Dorsey encouraged amateur songwriters to send in their wares. Dorsey would choose a first-, second-, and third-place winner every week, the top prize being a publishing contract and an advance royalty check for $100. Dorsey didn't mention it on the air, but although the sponsor ponied up the prize loot, the copyrights went into Dorsey's "pubberies."

The Dorsey staff "gussied up" the avocational product considerably. While the two runners-up (songs such as "At Least a Little in Love" and "It Came to Me") would receive only rudimentary orchestrations, just one chorus by one of the singers accompanied by a plain vanilla background, the week's winner received deluxe treatment. First-placers, such as "You're Part of My Heart," "One Red Rose," "When Daylight Dawns," and "When Sleepy Stars Begin to Fall," all featured first choruses sung solo by Sinatra—in itself enough of a prize for any songwriter. The second chorus consisted of a mixture of Connie Haines and the Pied Pipers, with Jo Stafford heard in occasional solo spots and Sinatra always returning for the coda. While occasional *Fame and Fortune* songs, like "You Got the Best of Me," showed Sinatra struggling with obviously inferior material, most of the songs were at least competent. Two songs even made it onto the Dorsey-Sinatra recording schedule, and one, "Oh Look at Me Now"—written by Joe Bushkin, with Johnny DeVries— became a standard.

The best remembered of the Sinatra-Haines duets (along with the more epic "Let's Get Away from It All"), "Oh Look at Me Now" also represents Sinatra's first real uptempo performance. Not to worry, Francis takes to swinging the way King Kong takes to climbing skyscrapers. Following his example, the Pied Pipers are also immediately in the groove, making this about the snazziest band and vocal group outing since arranger Oliver's great days with Lunceford.

Bushkin and DeVries wrote one other song recorded by Dorsey and Sinatra, "How Do You Do Without Me?" While the mood of that jaunty little number is mock-egotistical, the atmosphere of Frank Loesser's "Love Me as I Am" is vaguely self-deprecating, anticipating "Why Try to Change Me Now." Burke and Van Heusen's very hip and subtle "Do You Know Why" also calls for some extremely accurate pin-pointings of attitude. At twenty-five, Sinatra can already hit these very precise and distinct emotional targets with astonishing accuracy. It's hard to imagine anybody else who was singing with a band in 1940–42 or even later doing that—not Ray Eberle, or Herb Jeffries, or Dick Haymes, or Johnny Desmond, or Cab Calloway, or Ella Fitzgerald, or Helen Humes, or Jack Leonard, or anybody. Only Bing Crosby or Billie Holiday could have come close.

Sy Oliver deserves a great deal of the credit for Sinatra's early success as a swinger. "Sy was the man who had made Jimmie Lunceford," said Sammy Cahn, "and Sy was a true genius. I don't use the word lightly. And Tommy Dorsey, who was always an incredibly wise musician, knew that that band was Sy Oliver, and he wouldn't rest until he got Sy." Oliver also made the connection between Dorsey and Cahn, who had written Lunceford's theme, "Rhythm Is Our Business," with the arranger.

Melvin James "Sy" Oliver was born in Michigan in 1910. Like Stordahl, Oliver started as a trumpeter in a series of territory bands. By the time he made the national scene in Jimmy Lunceford's band, his horn work had taken a backseat to arranging. Between 1933 and 1939, Oliver served as the central architect behind the sound and style of Lunceford, one of the greatest and most individual big bands of all time.

Dorsey didn't steal Oliver away from Lunceford, as some have claimed, but rather gave the arranger the chance he wanted to leave behind the low pay and other indignities foisted on the black bands of that racist era. While under Dorsey's employ he could escape the tribulations of the road altogether: no longer obliged to sit in the section, he could do his writing in New York. Still, when Dorsey, a longtime Lunceford admirer, gave Oliver the call, he initially hesitated. "Sy was very ambivalent about joining the band," says Paul Weston. "Tommy wanted him, and made him a nice deal. But he didn't know if he'd be comfortable, being the only black guy around." Oliver wrote most of the band's uptempo numbers from that point on, a responsibility he shared first with Deane Kincaide and later with Bill Finegan.

Oliver also presided over the most enjoyable subseries of the Dorsey-Sinatra sessions, the extension of what one 1939 radio announcer referred to as "The 'Marie' Cycle." With supreme cheekiness, the arranger and vocalist took an idea that had been firmly established by their predecessors and proceeded to do it so well that folks all but forgot it had ever been done before. History generally credits the original idea behind "Marie" to pioneer swing arranger Don Redman, and from him it trickled sideways to a lesser known and as yet unrecorded band, Doc Wheeler and the Sunset Royals. Dorsey, as the trombonist himself later wrote, heard the Royals doing it and acquired the chart and the idea from them.

The concept was simple enough: if an instrumental ensemble could riff behind a horn soloist, why not have a vocal group sing a countermelody in the background while the solo vocalist in front sang the main tune and lyrics? Along the way someone decided it should be the members of the band chanting behind a solo singer. It had the rough-and-ready sound of a barful of would-be crooners rather than a professional choir. Background lyrics consisted primarily of titles of other songs (a rule no longer in force by the 1940 "East of the Sun"). The main song itself was an older standard rather than a new number.

Irving Berlin's obscure 1928 waltz "Marie" provided a perfect vehicle for the device, with its ambiguous lack of traditional distinction between the main (A) sections and the bridge (B), as well as its breathless, single-sentence lyric. Dorsey's 1937 Victor recording of "Marie," with an arrangement credited to Fred Stulce, and its flip side, "Song of India," gave Dorsey his two best-remembered numbers. While Dorsey continued to keep "Marie" alive in the band book, he also extended the pattern by fitting other old, generally better known standards to it. After "Marie" came "Who?" (1937), "Yearning" (1938), "Sweet Sue" (1938), "How Am I to Know" (1939), and, Leonard's final disc with Dorsey, "Deep Night" (1939).

Sinatra's earliest documented appearances with the band include readings of the by-now-classic original recipe "Marie" itself as well the band's then-current "Marie" sequel, "Deep Night." In the Dorsey years

Sinatra would eventually get around to "Yearning," "Who?," and "How Am I to Know."[3] With Leonard, much of the amusement derived from the way the chanting band seemed to be putting him down, making musical rabbit ears, as it were, behind the singer for the camera. The idea was that he was square and they were hip. But when Sinatra moved up to the mike, he wasn't just hip, he was immediately hipper than all of them put together. At once the band was having fun with him rather than making fun of him. He comes on strong with the first utterance of the word "Marie," which opens the song. Then when he gets to the next "Marie" at the start of the second line, he glides into it. Throughout all sixteen bars Sinatra is relaxed and affable, going with the grain of the surroundings rather than against it, as Leonard did. With Leonard we quickly want the crooner to shut up so we can hear the cool counterchorus, but with Sinatra it's the other way around.

"I was trying to get Frank to fall in with the lazy sort of two-beat feeling—the Lunceford beat," Oliver later explained to George Simon. "All kid singers tend to push too hard, and so one day I suggested, 'Lay back on it, Frank.' And you know what? He literally laid back with his body. Then I explained to him what I really meant, to lay back on the beat, not to push but to let the beat sort of carry him along. I must say he caught on right away."

Dorsey's record label, RCA Victor, later acquired two live Sinatra performances of "Marie," one from the Hollywood Palladium on October 17, 1940 (issued in the '50s on the *Sentimental Gentleman* double album), and the other, done at the Hotel Astor a few months earlier on June 12 (so far unissued), that spotlighted a "mother" (as Sinatra would say) of a spectacular tenor sax solo by Don Lodice which brings the piece up to over four minutes and makes this the "Marie" to end all "Marie"s.

The two "Marie" clones that Oliver conceived specifically for Sinatra were both "stellar" numbers—"East of the Sun" and "Blue Skies." On the small-group Victor version of "East of the Sun," Sinatra sounds a bit tentative throughout, although he really grooves on the last repeat of the title phrase at the end. Sinatra also had the difficult task of filling the gap between one of TD's exquisite cup-mute choruses and a particularly excellent Berigan bit, the trumpeter's entrance heralded by the band chanting, "Take it, Bunny!"

---

3. Dorsey later revived "Marie" on the radio with guest vocalist Rudy Vallee, one of the few singers who had sung the Berlin opus before Dorsey had gotten to it. Vallee has an even more nasal sound than Leonard and weaker rhythm, but his reading is more enjoyable because of his warm, self-mocking sense of humor.

Zeke Zarchy later remembered, "Frank made a great splash when he sang 'East of the Sun' at the Riverside Theatre in Milwaukee when he first joined the band. When you sing 'East of the Sun,' normally you would sing it like very straight (à la Jack Leonard), well Frank would swing it, just like a horn player would do. Everybody in the band got a big kick out of that. Instead of singing it like a ballad, he really swung it."

For "Blue Skies," Oliver creats a slyly minor key mood for this Berlin ballad, opening with a riff that suggests his later "Swingin' on Nothin'," Dorsey piercing through the ensemble with his trombone like a sunbeam searing through the clouds. Sinatra has never been looser, and is looser still on several aircheck versions; he's not even competing with the background chanters anymore. He fearlessly sits out most of the bridge and gleefully plays with words like "bluebirds." Sinatra also teasingly extends the final "from . . . now on" before the band declaims, "Mr. Elman, go ahead, go ahead." Oliver brings the thing home with crashing brass, and Elman zigs even higher over them, with Bushkin's piano solo providing a brief breather. Never before or since would Sinatra so completely capture the essence of a Dorsey trombone solo, absolutely nailing down TD's phrasing, tone, and conception. He comes even closer than the singing of Louis Armstrong or Jack Teagarden do to their own horn work.

The very best of the Sinatra-Dorsey sides, among them "Pale Moon" and Oliver's "The One I Love," "Oh Look at Me Now," and "Blue Skies," have a perfection to them that makes them as valid as any of Sinatra's later recordings. By 1941, especially, Sinatra, Stordahl, and Oliver were able to take the ingredients of a no-frills, three-chorus bread-and-butter chart and cook them into a special dish indeed. "Without a Song," widely regarded as a major achievement in both Sinatra's and Oliver's careers, shows Sinatra tempering storytelling with swing in a way that points directly to *Songs for Swingin' Lovers!*

Similarly, "Love Me as I Am," "Where Do You Keep Your Heart," and many others have Sinatra finding nuances in texts that other vocalists might write off as grade-B Tin Pan Alley material and turning them into moving, thoroughly felt experiences. He would later describe his singing to Arlene Francis as "a combination of [elements from] musicians and singers that I had heard and was influenced by. Certain nuances that Billie Holiday used to use, and shortly after that it was Sarah Vaughan and Ella Fitzgerald and Louis Armstrong had a great deal to do with it."

He had also risen in Dorsey's trust and, with Ziggy Elman and Bunny Berigan, was that rare deputy Dorsey trusted to conduct the band at rehearsals; when Dorsey missed a broadcast on July 13, 1942, to attend his father's funeral, Sinatra conducted the band and also took over the leader's role as radio host. But he was beginning to feel cramped by Dorsey personally and by the limits of the dance-band format. "Tommy wanted him to be a little more strict with the beat," trombonist Dick Nash explained. "Tommy was always straight up and down, and with that quick vibrato and underneath that good sound. So when Frank sang, he always wanted to be more expressive and bend things around, and maybe delay the beat a little bit and phrase a little more. And of course Tommy would come up behind Frank: 'Hey! Get on the beat, kid. Come on.'"

Sinatra had become, along with supercanary Helen Forrest (of the Artie Shaw, Benny Goodman, and Harry James bands) and the blues-based Jimmy Rushing (Count Basie's sidekick for many years), one of the recognized masters of the thirty-two-bar vocal refrain. But by the summer of 1942 the time had come to grow again. As the girls started swooning around Dorsey's star crooner, the Sentimental Gentleman was less jealous of Sinatra's position as the band's *voce numero uno* than he was ecstatic to have such a popular attraction under contract. "Tommy knew he had something hot," said lead trumpeter Zeke Zarchy, "because Frank was far and away the best band vocalist of the day when he was singing in bands." On a July 1942 broadcast Dorsey even emitted a sarcastic pseudo-swoon as he introduced Sinatra on "Just as Though You Were Here." Dorsey did not feature Sinatra on a greater number of discs than Leonard—he had to divide up space among at least four separate vocal acts in 1940–42—but he gradually allocated more space per disc to Sinatra. A significant portion of the Dorsey sides from 1941 on feature at least a chorus and a half of the singer, often opening with him, something unheard of for a boy singer–bandleader relationship of the time. (Sinatra said that James had started to do this, but unfortunately only "All or Nothing at All" made it onto vinyl.)

Unlike the many band singers who failed to make the transition from dance-band cog to center-spotlight attraction, Sinatra was a dramatist as well as a musician and instantly knew how to use his additional time. "Shadows on the Sand," a narrative that would still seem stupid even if it didn't turn out to be a dream in the end, offers an early example of a Dorsey record that opened with Sinatra and then had him return for an outchorus at the end, but the disc is notable only for that reason. The more conventional love song "This Love of Mine," written by Sinatra, Hank Sanicola, and song-plugger Sol Parker, is a thoroughly effective side that applies the Sentimentalist "Never Smile Again" sound to Sinatra in solo, minus the Pipers and customary celesta. Unlike many stars at the time who claimed cowriter status on various songs, Sinatra apparently actually did participate in the writing of this tune rather than being "cut in," as they used to say, for a piece of the royalty action.

"Frank asked me if I wouldn't mind checking out the melody and lyrics [of 'This Love of Mine']," Matt Dennis remembered, "so I got a hold of Tom [Adair] one day and we sat down, and in a couple of hours, we made some minor, minor changes. I remember changing the melody for two or three measures, and Tom did make some minor alterations to the lyric. Anyhow, Frank liked what we did, and that's how they recorded it. Frank was so proud. And the strangest thing happened, for all these years, everytime I hear 'This Love of Mine' I feel like I'm hearing one of my own songs. And all I did was change a little bit of it, as a favor to Tommy and Frank."

"Pale Moon (an Indian Love Song)" also affords the vocalist more space than was customary in 1941. Along with "Neaini" and "Trade Winds," "Pale Moon" constitutes his major Dorsey-era voyage into the realm of the exotic. This 1920 opus refers not to genuine American (or even Indian) Indians, but to the stereotypical depiction of Native Americans in literature and poetry. In the tradition of Longfellow, as later parodied by the Shakesperian savage in Huxley's *Brave New World,* "Pale Moon" ascribes King Jamesian "thee"s and "thou"s to its honest injuns. Further, the ensemble plays a brief instrumental passage between all the sung lines, to make the whole thing seem even more like a musical setting for a poetry recitation; the spacing gives the number an unusual structural feel, even though it uses the standard AABA format. Note that when white Americans reflect on the romances of exotic races within their own borders, generally these relationships are intraracial as opposed to interracial; it wouldn't do to suggest that the protagonist could enjoy any liaison—even a doomed one—with someone of another skin color so close to home. The idea is the same in the Island flirtations of "Trade Winds," or the Hawaiian guitar tinged "Neiani" (coauthored by Stordahl and Oliver).

Two Dennis and Adair standards, Stordahl's treatment of "Everything Happens to Me" and reedman Heinie Beau's chart on "Violets for Your Furs," presented Sinatra with two of his earliest opportunities to sing a verse. "That was interesting because that was not the practice at that time," observed Matt Dennis. "Verses were common in the '20s and early '30s, with famous standards and show tunes. Today also, everybody sings those kind of verses. But nobody ever sang them in the big-band era because they were only interested in the melody of the chorus. But I enjoyed writing verses, and I told Tom, 'Let's write a verse whether anybody does it or not.'"

From start to finish, "Everything Happens to Me" features not one hint of Dorsey's presence. It opens with sympathetically sighing brass and tongue-in-cheek ominous baritone, an application Stordahl apparently gleaned from Oliver, before Sinatra does a full verse and chorus and a half, and tag. "Violets" opens with a brief trombone teaser before Sinatra's plaintive verse and has one of Dorsey's finest trombone solos yet between Sinatra's two plaintive choruses. Both songs have very specific stories that need to be told precisely and Sinatra later took the opportunity to take another hack at each with Nelson Riddle at Capitol.

Certainly the 1956 "Everything Happens to Me" is a more moving experience. Sinatra is now able to delineate the full ironic range of the text. Sinatra takes the *Close to You* album version considerably slower: the two readings are equally long, but the original still has time for an extra outchorus worth of lyrics ("I've never won a sweepstakes . . ."). Yet Sinatra would never quite improve on the original "Violets for Your Furs," which requires a certain amount of wide-eyed prom-date youthfulness. This the prewar Sinatra has in abundance.

Paradoxically, after Dorsey added the strings in March 1942, he wanted to feature the new section as much as he could, and, perhaps to Sinatra's chagrin, the singer found himself both backed by and competing for space with the fiddles. In fact, Dorsey was more likely to give Sinatra almost a whole disc to himself, as on the otherwise unspecial "I Think of You" in late 1941 or early 1942 than after March of that year. Tracks such as "Take Me," "Be Careful It's My Heart," and "In the Blue of Evening" make it clear that it was becoming impossible even to consider confining Sinatra to a humble thirty-two bars. The Dorsey orchestra with Sinatra by now represented a flagrant and excessive abundance of riches.

Before Dorsey added strings, however, Sinatra had found exactly the right orchestral style, which made sure that he would never have to worry about interference from lush excesses. In contrast to the crammed and overbusy goings-on of the final Dorsey-Sinatra numbers in which the violins, far from being content to remain in the background, try to compete with Sinatra for center stage, as in "Daybreak," there are the four solo sides from January 19, 1942. Victor had already established a precedent of recording the best-known band singers, including Lena Horne, Maxine Sullivan, and Bea Wain, in featured roles without their bands and issuing the results on Bluebird, its thirty-five-cent budget label. As Connie Haines later remembered, "Frank rehearsed day and night for that project."

The numbers were arranged and conducted by Axel Stordahl, who had already established himself as Sinatra's musical director within the

Dorsey ranks (although nearly as many of the FS-TD triumphs had been masterminded by Sy Oliver), and the personnel consisted of an amalgam of studio players—mostly the seven strings and woodwinds, including Charles Strickfadden, who had played the same role fifteen years earlier on Crosby's first records with Paul Whiteman—and Dorsey men. Stordahl and A&R man Harry Meyerson brought in most of Dorsey's reed section but, except for guitarist Clark Yocum, not its rhythm crew; conspicuously absent were pianist Joe Bushkin, replaced by newcomer Skitch Henderson, and Buddy Rich—as the date went drummerless.

Henderson, who had worked with the Sinatra-Stordahl-Dorsey axis and was also on staff at Victor, was a natural substitute for Bushkin on the Victor date. Henderson recalled that although Dorsey knew Sinatra was going to do a solo session, the participants were careful not to throw this fact in the boss's face: "When I had become part of that fraternity with Axel and everything, they [only] talked undercover about how they were going to do this record. It was said that we should keep our mouths shut about the date because the Old Man, as we called him, wasn't too happy about it."

Far from being nervous at this critical, first solo session, Sinatra, Henderson adds, "was always very confident of his skill." Stordahl has his act together no less than Sinatra at this point; one can see the basic evolution from these fairly concrete sketches to the masterpiece Stordahl-Sinatra charts of the mid- to late-1940s. In fact, this orchestration of "The Song Is You" has only a few additional strings between it and the classic "Song Is You" of 1944 and '45 airchecks, recorded definitively for Columbia in '47.

Though the 1942 "The Night We Called It a Day" lacks the vocal majesty of the Capitol remake, the original rings truer. Dorsey had intended to record the song, another of his own publications, with Sinatra and the Pied Pipers, and asked composer Matt Dennis to prepare an arrangement similar to "Never Smile Again." When Sinatra cut the song sans Dorsey, the leader retaliated by recording it with Jo Stafford, but Victor didn't issue the Dorsey-Stafford version for several seasons. Stordahl's string arrangement of "The Night We Called It a Day" thereby became the property of Dorsey and Sinatra simultaneously. Dorsey kept it in his book with Skip Nelson and other crooners in Sinatra's spot, and Sinatra and Stordahl also kept it in their repertoire.

The song that impresses most is the one Sinatra never remade and no one else ever bothered with after 1942, "The Lamplighter's Serenade." One of many obscure almost-gems by the great Hoagy Carmichael, the tune was also done by Bing Crosby, whose well-established paternal identity it suits better. Reflecting Carmichael's and Crosby's compatible backgrounds, the melody has a Bingish device written right into it, a trill on the last word of the line "he sprinkles their hearts with his ma-agic" that Sinatra was duty-bound to honor. It's almost as if some Warner Bros. screenwriter had done a story with Jimmy Cagney in mind but at the last minute the role went to Humphrey Bogart. Still, upon hearing the results, Sinatra was convinced that he needed to be on his own, with Stordahl crafting his arrangements. Sammy Cahn remembered meeting with Sinatra a short time later. "I was sitting with Sinatra, and we were talking, and he says, 'I'm going to be the world's greatest singer.' And I looked at him, and I'll never forget it, I said, 'There's no doubt in my mind. You are the world's greatest singer.' He said, 'Do you mean it?' I said, 'What do you mean, do I mean it? You're the best. You're the *best*. There's nobody better than you. You're the best.'"

Sy Oliver remembered telling Sinatra, "Well, maybe you're not ready yet." Sinatra then contended, "Look at Crosby, look at how he just went out on his own." Oliver insisted, "Well, I think maybe it'd be better if you stayed a little while longer, get more experience." But Sinatra was firm: "No, I'm ready." Oliver concluded the anecdote: "I was wrong! He was ready!"

Sinatra later claimed that as early as the fall of 1941 he realized the time to strike was at hand. (Bea Wain recalled that she supported Sinatra in this decision as early as December 1941, shortly after the outbreak of the war.) Around that time, Sinatra met with CBS's Manie Sachs on the West Coast. The A&R head found Sinatra "impatient to get out on his own, and I said I would take him for Columbia."

Rather than anticipating the postwar boom in pop singing (which he himself would ignite), Sinatra figured that any spots at all for solo croon-ers would be few and far between. "The reason I wanted to leave Tommy's band was that Crosby was number one, way up on top of the pile," Sinatra told Sidney Zion. "In the open field, you might say, were some awfully good singers with the orchestras. Bob Eberly (with Jimmy Dorsey) was a fabulous vocalist. Mr. Como (with Ted Weems) is still such a wonderful singer. I thought, if I don't make a move out of this band and try to do it on my own soon, one of those guys will do it, and I'll have to fight all three of them to get a position." He had reason to get going as fast as he could: in the spring of 1942, Dick Haymes (who had earlier replaced Sinatra with Harry James) was doing solo spots in nightclubs as well as serving as Benny Goodman's boy singer. "So I took a shot and I gave Mr. Dorsey one year's notice. It was in September

[1941]. I told him, 'Tom, I'm gonna leave the band one year from today.' Beyond that year I had another six months in the contract. [That contract was probably from January 1940 to January 1943.] Tommy said, 'Sure.' That's all."

"Now, when I had left Harry James," Sinatra said, "I told Harry that I had heard a boy named Dick Haymes. I said, 'He's a hell of a singer, he's great!' Sure enough, Dick Haymes went over with the James Band.[4] Well, time went by, and finally it got to be about three more months left in the year, and I said, 'Tom, do you want me to find a vocalist?'" Sinatra again recommended Haymes as an obvious replacement, but Dorsey responded, "No, no, no, you're not gonna leave this band, not as easy as you think you are."

When Sinatra eventually left Dorsey, Haymes stepped into his immaculately buffed shoes. The singer and the bandleader parted company on a famous farewell broadcast (September 3, 1942) on which Sinatra introduced Dick Haymes[5] to the Dorsey audience, after which he and Dorsey dropped the newcomer so quickly you'd think he had fallen through a trap door. Sinatra then performed an absolutely riveting run-through of the Stordahl arrangement of "The Song Is You" (from the January Bluebird session). This great orchestration never sounded better than when played by the Dorsey band proper; it's a perfect time capsule that at once captures the past and future of Sinatra.

"I remember Frank left the band at the Circle Theater in Indianapolis," recalled Skitch Henderson. "I was with Jimmy Van Heusen when the phone rang one night, and it was Frank saying, 'The Old Man goosed me with his trombone the last time. I'm leaving the band.'" Getting out of Dorsey's band didn't necessarily mean the end of his business entanglements with Dorsey, as he learned when the bandleader enforced a stipulation that would mean turning over his management and a third of his salary for the rest of his life to his former boss.

4. Sinatra's version of how Haymes joined the James band is at odds with most accounts. The standard tale is that Haymes, who doubled as songwriter, initially approached James only to demonstrate his tunes for the bandleader, who wound up "buying" the singer, not the songs.

5. Haymes lasted only six months with Dorsey before he, too, went permanently solo. Just as Sinatra reprised many of Jack Leonard's biggest numbers, so Haymes kept alive a few of Sinatra's, including "Daybreak." Thanks to the musicians' ban on commercial recordings, this aircheck remains the only Dorsey-Haymes item to have been officially issued. A few other broadcasts are known to exist, however, and Haymes also participated as part of Dorsey's band in the MGM musical *DuBarry Was a Lady*, filmed at the end of 1942.

For the next year the theme song of the Sinatra-Dorsey relationship was "I'll Be Suing You." Skeets Herfurt remembered that Sinatra quickly began referring to his ex-employer as "Boss Tweed," explaining that if you were in Tommy's band you were his "fair-haired boy," but once you left, "you were on his blacklist." Drummer Alvin Stoller recalled one of the more humorous examples of Dorsey's temper: "One day Tommy was mad, and he was firing everybody again. He said, 'You don't like it, get your tail out!' So I said, 'Well, I quit.' He said, 'You can't quit!' Then he said, 'There's three SOB's in this world—you, Buddy Rich, and Hitler! And I had to be stuck with two out of the three [in my band].' I told that to Buddy, and he just fell over laughing. He said, 'How'd we get to Hitler?' I don't think Hitler could play drums, but if he could, I still don't think he would have worked for Tommy!"

For about a year Dorsey continued to collect a share of Sinatra's earnings—a fact that Sinatra's radio writers turned into a running gag on his early solo shows. On a 1943 *Broadway Bandbox* sketch, when Sinatra and resident comic Bert Wheeler, expecting to hear a hunting call, instead get an out-of-tune trombone moaning "Sentimental over You," Wheeler yells, "It's Dorsey, coming to collect his commission!" Sinatra responds, "Again?" When, a few months later on a *Vimms* show, guest Alan Ladd offers to take "Frankie" to a Philharmonic concert, Wheeler wonders if Dorsey will be there since "he owns ten percent of Beethoven." Sinatra continued to rib his would-be owner as late as January 1945 when he appeared on the Edgar Bergen and Charlie McCarthy program. When the wooden one offered to become Sinatra's manager, The Voice responded, "Why shouldn't you be? Everybody else is!"

Publicizing the situation encouraged Sinatra's young fans to start a mail campaign against Dorsey. After George Evans started handling Sinatra's public relations, in early 1943, the press agent organized Sinatra's fan club in Philadelphia into picketing Dorsey's opening at the Earle Theatre. Evans's assistant, Bud Granoff, remembered: "They picketed the theater with signs like 'Dorsey unfair to our boy Frankie!' and 'Dorsey cutting up Frankie!' And George got pictures of this all over the Philly papers. I think that made Tommy change his mind more than anything."

It ultimately took months and months of expensive negotations involving two of the country's top talent agencies, but Sinatra was finally extricated from the contract; he received fatherly advice from Bing Crosby, who warned him it would be smarter to buy off all claims on him as early as he could, and the counsel of lawyer Sol Jaffe, who also represented the American Federation of Radio Artists. AFRA gave permission for sustaining radio broadcasts, which were done without a sponsor, usually from ballrooms and for which musicians would be paid only their normal weekly salary and not the extra cash they would receive on a sponsored show. When Jaffe threatened to have AFRA revoke the permission Dorsey needed to do these sustaining remotes, Dorsey knew he was licked.

At times Sinatra has acted as if they never spoke again. When Dorsey died in his sleep in 1956, Sinatra turned down two old friends, Jackie Gleason and George Simon, assembling a television tribute to Dorsey. He stated frankly that in saying anything nice about Dorsey he would "feel like a hypocrite." Still, evidence suggests that Sinatra and Dorsey were friendly again by the mid-1940s. In 1958 he turned a whole episode of his ABC TV series into a tribute to Dorsey, recruiting Jo Stafford for an entire evening of remembering Tommy. Much earlier, Sinatra guest-starred on Dorsey's program, *Your All-Time Hit Parade*, in September 1944, and then in October 1945 played host to Dorsey on his own *Old Gold* spot.

Around this time Sinatra described Dorsey to George Simon as "a guy who was a real education to me in every possible way. I learned about dynamics and phrasing and style from the way he played his horn, and I enjoyed my work because he saw to it that a singer is always given a perfect setting." In 1955 he elaborated: "Tommy set me up beautifully in the band—the arrangements featured me. Tommy's tempo was always right for singing, never too fast or too slow."

In an interview with disc jockey Ben Heller in 1950, Heller told Sinatra of a recent chat he had had with Dorsey in which the trombonist said of Sinatra, "'What is there to say about Frank? It's been done innumerable times—anything I could say would be superfluous.' And he went on for an hour and a half, and all he did was talk about you." Sinatra replied, "I really think that there'll never be a trombone player or a musician who knows his instrument like Dorsey knows that horn. He's just the end of the world."

Sometime between 1953 and 1956 Dorsey visited two of his illustrious alumni, Sinatra and Nelson Riddle, at one of their Capitol sessions. The event was captured by a photographer, though unfortunately not by a recording engineer. Sinatra related to Heller in 1950 that "I went to see [Dorsey] at the Astor [hotel in New York] a couple of weeks ago, and he just knocked me out. I went up and sang a few songs with the band; I sat next to the brass like I used to. It was a big kick, but listen, I ran right away when I heard him call for the bus!" Sinatra helped TD celebrate his tenth anniversary as a bandleader in 1945, and ten years later took part in his twentieth, rejoining the band for three numbers (which survive via a broadcast).

Sinatra kept a great many of the songs associated with his Dorsey tenure in his act and on his recording schedule. With the Dorsey originals still green in memory, Sinatra rerecorded "Fools Rush In," "Blue Skies," and "When You Awake" in new arrangements. He also kept "I'll Be Seeing You," "There Are Such Things," his own "This Love of Mine," and others alive on the radio, and "Without a Song" in concerts up through the late '80s. In 1951, Sinatra also waxed a beautiful reading of "I Guess I'll Have to Dream the Rest" that comes fairly close to the original of ten years earlier, with a new, otherwise unknown group, the Whippoorwills, replacing the Pied Pipers. The star appropriately amplifies his own role here, and his singing, so much more emotionally aware, reaches both heights and depths of feeling he could only aspire to in the Dorsey days. In 1941, Sinatra fans had to dream the rest; in 1950, he does it for them.

Over the years Sinatra also revived "How About You?," "Oh Look at Me Now," "Violets for Your Furs," "Everything Happens to Me," "Stardust," "Let's Get Away from It All," "Street of Dreams," "Just as Though You Were Here," and "Be Careful It's My Heart" in new Capitol and Reprise arrangements. The ground-breaking "I'll Never Smile Again" came to life in many guises: a duet with former bandmate Jo Stafford on their joint TV tribute to TD in 1958, with the Hi-Los (in the most appealing performance ever by that frequently banal vocal group) on a 1959 Sinatra show, in a full-blown Gordon Jenkins treatment on *No One Cares* in that same year, in a medley with Dean Martin on the latter's program in 1960, in an exact Sentimentalist-style remake for the *Man and His Music* album in 1965, and in a 1971 concert. Sinatra further employed echoes of the Dorsey sound throughout the '40s, primarily in his radio closing theme, "Put Your Dreams Away," another song by Ruth Lowe, which was about as close as one could come in melody and mood (and even trombone solo) to her "Smile Again."

For his part, Dorsey kept something of the Sinatra-Dorsey legacy alive in occasional revivals of some of their biggest hits, such as "Smile Again." In 1952, Dorsey also rerecorded "There Are Such Things" as a trombone solo with Gordon Jenkins' orchestra and choir. That same year Dorsey also came up with the most obvious "Smile Again" plagiarism in a tune titled "You Could Make Me Smile Again."

From "Put Your Dreams Away" onward, the celesta and superslow phrasing were to be keynotes of Sinatra's later Dorsey-style numbers, including the series of "chamber" recordings he made beginning in

1945. That same year, Sinatra renewed his acquaintance with the Pied Pipers, within whose ranks June Hutton, later to marry Axel Stordahl, had replaced Jo Stafford. The former Dorseyites became regulars on the *Old Gold Songs by Sinatra* show, and also occasionally appeared on some of his Columbia sides, most sentimentally on Stordahl's tune "Ain'tcha Ever Comin' Back" (1947). The 1949 "If I Ever Love Again" uses a celesta background and super-close harmony between Sinatra and the vocal group the Double Daters. As late as 1954's "Don't Change Your Mind About Me," Sinatra's last recorded meeting with the Pied Pipers, he was still singing variations on "Smile Again."

Perhaps the best tribute Sinatra could pay to Dorsey was in the number of veterans of that band who eventually went to work for their former fellow sideman, starting with both of his most important musical directors, Axel Stordahl and Nelson Riddle. Sinatra maintained multidecade relations with arrangers Sy Oliver, Heinie Beau, and Richard Jones, who said "Sinatra's musical taste was developed at Tommy's elbow," as well as with Buddy Rich, Johnny Mince, Jo Stafford, Joe Bushkin, Zeke Zarchy, Lee Castle, Don Lodice, Ziggy Elman, and the Pied Pipers (as well as vocalist-guitarist Clark Yocum's brother Verne, who for many years worked as Sinatra's music librarian).

If there's one major disappointment regarding Sinatra's later work with his fellow ex-Dorseyites, it's that his post-1942 collaborations with Sy Oliver were neither as frequent nor as rewarding as they should have been. Oliver continued to write occasionally for Sinatra even while in the service, turning in a treatment of the spiritual "Swing Low, Sweet Chariot" for him to sing on the 1944 *Vimms* show as well as a remake of his equally gospelly Dorsey classic "Yes Indeed." But he seems to have arranged only three commercial sides for Sinatra between 1942 and 1961: "Sweet Lorraine," the minor hit "Don't Cry Joe," and the less successful "A Little Learnin' Is a Dangerous Thing" (Lillian Oliver-Clarke feels that there are more, but these have not yet been identified). The 1946 "Sweet Lorraine" positioned Sinatra with "The Metronome All Stars," consisting of pianist Nat King Cole and an undisputably stellar group drawn largely from the Dorsey (Charlie Shavers and Buddy Rich) and Ellington bands. Sinatra's vocal is just one of many virtuoso solos, and this Billie Holiday–like chart showcases Sinatra at the height of his Columbia-era jazz-singing abilities.

The 1947 "A Little Learnin'. . ." with Pearl Bailey, a none-too-funny comedy blues song by Oliver and fellow arranger Dick Jacobs, also published by Sinatra, is notable only as an early interracial duet. The material, thin to begin with, gets stretched beyond the snapping point when the two-sided performance lingers on into the six-minute range. Thankfully, "Don't Cry Joe" (1949), a blue-tinged lament by clarinetist Marsala, represents a significant improvement. As Sinatra said at the time, "'Don't Cry Joe' is a great song and should be a big hit." The hit went to future Sinatra cohort Gordon Jenkins, but Sinatra's version successfully combines the strengths of both blues and ballad singing, and the Pastels vocal group again blend in superbly. Even the odd way Sinatra bends the note on "'Don't Cry *Joe*'" kind of works, and Oliver cleverly borrows the Dixieland coda from Duke Ellington's "I Ain't Got Nothin' But the Blues" as a tag. Sinatra attributed the spirit of the disc to "the fact that we were in a new studio and it was a wonderful Sy Oliver arrangement. Everybody was kind of all excited about it, that may be the answer too. But I will say that because of the song being so good, we couldn't miss with it last night."

Three years after staging a tribute to Dorsey for ABC television, he decided the time was right to do the same for his own new label, Reprise Records. In a sense, the first three Sinatra Reprise albums directly prefigure the 1979 *Trilogy*, although in reverse order, *Ring-a-Ding-Ding* with modernist arranger Johnny Mandel suggesting the future, and *Sinatra Swings* with Billy May being very much in the present.[6] Sinatra then invited Sy Oliver to join him in a joint exploration of their collective past with *I Remember Tommy*. As Sinatra did with most of his '60s albums, he gave Oliver freedom to do what he wanted with the charts—although unusually on this album he sought the arranger's suggestions on repertory as well. "So many singers worry an orchestra to death," Oliver told Simon, "but never Frank. We picked the tunes together, and then he just let me go. He and Tommy Dorsey were two of the few people who've hired me and never told me what to do."

Sinatra and Oliver attempted the recording of *I Remember Tommy* in two sessions from March 1961, which transpired on the same days that Sinatra recorded his penultimate Capitol album, *Come Swing with Me* with Billy May. "Frank had been working very hard before [those dates]," Oliver recalled, "and after he listened to the tapes, he realized it wasn't what he wanted." Oliver later told Frank fan Ed O'Brien that they had come too close to the original Dorsey sound—a dance band with a small string section. At forty-five, Sinatra was afraid that his voice was thinning as fast as his hair and that he required the crutch of a lush violin section to cover up any technical shortcomings. "He did sound kind of

---

6. In early 1961, Sinatra also announced his intentions to produce and star in a film (never made) about the big-band era which would feature all the surviving Dorsey vets.

hoarse," Oliver said to Simon, "and he also decided we should use more strings."

Whether or not Sinatra sounded rough on the original dates, Oliver added considerably more fiddles on the remake sessions. In May, Sinatra and Oliver redid seven of the eight March titles (adding another five charts), and the eighth, unremade title, "In the Blue of Evening," eventually found its way onto the expanded CD edition of *I Remember Tommy* in 1992. Far from sounding frail, "Blue of Evening" constitutes the best ballad performance on the disc. In fact, one wishes that Sinatra and Oliver had stuck with that original, more authentically Dorsey sound and the lighter twelve-man string team rather than the more imposing fiddlers twenty. Opening with a vaguely Dorsey-like cadenza played by James Decker on French horn, "Blue of Evening" evidences a persuasive sense of economy that TD himself would have been proud of.

Although it contains four or five killer-strong tracks, the completed *I Remember Tommy* does not amount to a classic Sinatra album. By and large, Oliver, the teacher, had been surpassed by his pupils—particularly Riddle and May. Much of the album's texture resembles lesser Riddle; add a few more flutes, bass trombones, and Sweets Edison, and it would sound exactly like Riddle. In fact, Oliver does employ Kenny Shroyer's bass trombone on "Without a Song" and unfortunately illustrates why Riddle used the instrument only for color here and there. Oliver has the thing grunting throughout, and it quickly becomes repetitious.

But not even factoring in the disc's two top-heavy dramatic pieces, "Daybreak" and the hugely overdone "Take Me," nothing on *I Remember Tommy* succeeds as an improvement over the classic Dorsey-Sinatra recordings. Much of the disc seems redundant, not only in comparison to the originals ("Polka Dots and Moonbeams" is decidedly inferior to Axel Stordahl's 1940 arrangment), but in light of the excellent remakes Riddle had done of "Oh Look at Me Now," "How About You," "Violets for Your Furs," and "Everything Happens to Me."

It's sad to report that Sy Oliver actually sounds square in spots. And it's not the Gordon Jenkins kind of old-fashionedness that works because it matches the mood. It sounds doubly out of place in comparison to the high-powered hipness of "The One I Love Belongs to Somebody Else." Further, when Sinatra chooses material like the forgettable "Take Me" over unremade Dorsey-Sinatra masterpieces like "This Is the Beginning of the End" and "The World Is in My Arms," we must question his judgment.

Still, the good tracks on *I Remember Tommy*—the ones included in *The Reprise Collection* especially—are about as good as it gets. "East of the Sun" has an instrumental choir following the same lines that the band chorus sang in the original and excitingly builds to a series of multiple false endings patterned on Glenn Miller's "In the Mood." The very danceable "Imagination" has Sinatra offering another variation on the mock closer idea, repeatedly uttering the penultimate phrase before thrillingly resolving it with the final two notes. "Without a Song" doesn't quite come up to the 1941 Victor or the 1965 reading that opened the first *Man and His Music* TV special but remains majestic just the same; the patented Sinatra-Dorsey celesta tinkles against a monstrous brass crescendo and concludes on a haunting and unexpected final chord in the manner of the Nat Cole–Billy May "You'll Never Know."

"It Started All Over Again," boasting a Bushkiny break by Bill Miller, sounds as good as ever in a suitably simple chart that parallels the original. In contrast, Burke and Van Heusen's "It's Always You" finds new life as a Luncefordian bouncer in a two-beat chart that challenges the original. "I'll Be Seeing You" similarly revamps that hit World War II ballad into a rollicking rocker, following Dorsey's own 1943 rearrangement of the piece with that jivey group vocal, the Sentimentalists.

Sinatra would follow *I Remember Tommy* with two subsequent tributes—the *Man and His Music* album version of "I'll Never Smile Again" (unaccountably left off *I Remember Tommy*) and, for the 1979 *Trilogy*, the Gershwin standard "But Not for Me," stunningly reimagined by Sinatra and Billy May as a Sentimentalist number in the "Never Smile Again" format; Sinatra called upon trombonist Dick Nash (as he had in 1961) to do, as Sinatra put it, "his Tommy Dorsey shit."

Sinatra's most frequent remembrances of Tommy, however, were more personal than professional. It seems as if half of every Sinatra interview was devoted to Dorsey. Saxophonist Jery Dodgion has said that when he played Australia in 1959 with Red Norvo and Sinatra, the singer spent a lot of time with the musicians and that he "talked mainly about Tommy Dorsey." On Irv Cottler's birthday (circa 1977), the drummer happened to mention that he had also spent some months with the Dorsey band, a fact that Sinatra had forgotten. "We stayed up talking from one A.M. to about seven in the morning," said Cottler, "all about Tommy." Recently, Sinatra's press agent, Susan Reynolds, was asked if Sinatra ever reminisces about the old days. "Yes, he does all the time," she responded. "He especially likes to talk about Tommy Dorsey."

The Voice That Is Thrilling Millions and the Sentimental Gentleman of Swing worked together for the last time in the summer of 1956, a few months before Dorsey died, on the same bill with Sinatra's film *Johnny Concho* at the New York Paramount. Although the picture was forgettable (the star himself incessantly put it down in the stage show), the engagement marked a triumphant reunion of the bandleader and singer at the venue of their greatest triumphs. For the trombonist, the gig also extended the short-lived reunification of the Dorsey Brothers Orchestra. Far from holding a grudge against Dorsey, Frank Military recalled, "Frank insisted on using Tommy and his band. They were very close."

That engagement also marked the last occasion that Sinatra's musical director, Nelson Riddle, would work with Dorsey. Since Riddle had written most of the charts that the Dorseys were playing behind Sinatra, the singer flew him out to New York to run over them with TD, who invited Riddle to come to Connecticut as his guest for the weekend. "The reason I went was that I had never seen him other than as an employee," Riddle told Robert Windeler. "I wanted to see what he was like just as a fella. I went up there and found that things were not too swell between him and his wife—things were very tense. We had dinner in this formal dining room, and there were just the three of us. And Tommy said, 'I like the things that you've been doing with Frank very much.' I said, 'To tell you the truth, much of the skill and ability to do these came from you.' And you know, that touched him. He started to cry. Maybe it was the rather jagged emotional times he was going through, but that touched him. I went over and put my arm around him and said, 'That's true, you're the one that steered me.' At that moment the very romantic Mrs. Dorsey piped up and said, 'I hope you mean it.' I said, 'Yeah, I mean it.'"

The gentleman, it seems, was sentimental after all.

It was September 1942. Sinatra had won his freedom, but now that he was out, where would he go? He was young but already quite experienced and with something of a name for himself, and, as it happened, lousy with talent. A million possibilities for growth lay ahead of him, but also a million chances to fail. For better or worse, his career was now entirely his. The apprenticeship was over.

CHAPTER FOUR

WITH AXEL STORDAHL, 1943–1948

The true revolutionary is guided by love.

—CHE GUEVARA

For all of Dorsey's protestations, Sinatra's departure from the fold hardly sent shock waves through the music industry; it's almost as if only Sinatra and Dorsey realized the implications of the event. Dorsey replaced Sinatra with Haymes, and that was the end of it. Sinatra had merely been one voice among many in the Dorsey entourage. In the fall of 1942, Sinatra might well have seemed to be heading for the purgatory of ex-band singers (Jack Leonard, Edythe Wright, Ginny Simms, Ray Eberle) who had gone nowhere. The Dorsey-Sinatra split drew little attention, even in the biweekly bible of the band biz, *Down Beat*—and this in an era when Dorsey's decision to add strings rated a headline.

Columbia Records' Manie Sachs arranged for Sinatra to be one of the vocalists featured on their sustaining (nonsponsored) Thursday night show, *Reflections*. Sinatra appears to have done the program from October 1 to December 31, 1942. Also in October, Sinatra sang a single number ("A Touch of Texas," of all things!) with Walter Gross' orchestra on a CBS show called *Your Broadway and Mine*. More important, later that month Sinatra landed a fifteen-minute nonsponsored show of his own, the first of three CBS series entitled *Songs by Sinatra*. (Although it ran on Tuesday nights from October 20, 1942, to February 25, 1943, like *Reflections*, no airchecks of the program or even a list of songs he performed on it survive.) But while this may seem like a lot of radio activity for a relatively unknown singer, it's doubtful that anyone was listening in 1942. Sinatra was hardly better off than he was before he joined Harry James.

Down Beat, in its October 15 issue, mentioned that "Sinatra, rumored set to make a capella recordings, said that he has no plans along that line." Manie Sachs had been in charge of artists and repertory for Columbia since the label's rejuvenation under William Paley and CBS broadcasting in 1939 (the year he and Sinatra first met). More than an A&R man, Sachs was an indefatigable acquirer of top talent who almost single-handedly put Columbia Records on top—primarily by recognizing the potential of Harry James, Dinah Shore, Doris Day, and many others, particularly Sinatra.

Sinatra and Sachs signed their first agreement in 1942, but the recording contract was merely icing on the cake.[1] Sachs was far more helpful to Sinatra by finding him a berth in the CBS radio empire. Radio was the dominant medium of popular culture before and during the war; the entire record industry was, comparatively, a weak sister. When Glenn Miller's "Chattanooga Choo Choo" reached sales of a million copies in 1942, it marked the first disc to ring in those numbers in fifteen years; even the mighty Crosby hadn't hit the million mark in all of the '30s. Besides which, the question of records was a moot point; the musicians' strike, which had begun in August, prevented everyone from recording.

In short, Sinatra's prospects were not terrific in the fall of 1942. The last time he had been on his own he didn't have a family to support. Now he not only had a wife and child but also the beginnings of the infamous Sinatra professional-personal "entourage" depending on him. To pay the bills he was accepting money on his still-valid Dorsey contract, knowing that his ex-boss intended to collect for the rest of his days. His biggest expenditure at this point was his commitment to Axel Stordahl; he had persuaded the arranger to leave Dorsey, offering considerably more money in exchange for—in the beginning—considerably less security.

"When I left Tommy, things were quiet for about six months," Sinatra told Arlene Francis in 1977. "I had an agent. I decided maybe the action was in California, and I packed up my family and we came out." The only significance of this premature Hollywood sojourn was, as Sinatra put it, "I got a little role in a movie at Columbia Pictures"—*Reveille with Beverly,* Sinatra's first post-Dorsey cinematic appearance. Around this time, "for a very brief period," Skitch Henderson recalled, "he was a sustaining singer on the local NBC station in Hollywood, and I was the house pianist there."

Upon returning to New Jersey, Sinatra said, "we began playing weekend theater dates at different small towns." Since the Dorsey days, the man and his two Nancies had been living in an apartment on Bergen

---

1. Ironically, Sachs almost signed the whole Dorsey band—including the boy singers—to Columbia when Tommy Dorsey's RCA contract expired in 1942.

Street, Jersey City, and, in Sinatra's words, he "happened" to get a week's work at a local vaudeville theater, either in that town or Passaic (or probably both at different times).

The girls were already swooning, and, as Sinatra remembered, the grapevine of theater managers started buzzing in an attempt to learn "what all the noise was about. Why were the kids screaming and yelling and running up and down the aisles?" His representatives at G.A.C. kept bringing over bookers from ever more important venues; finally he made it to a major theater—the Newark Mosque, in New Jersey's most important city (meaning the one closest to New York). His agent then dragged over Bob Weitman, manager of the New York Paramount, which was to '40s pop music what the Palace had been to vaudeville.

As Sinatra told Sidney Zion, "One day they told me that Bob, . . . whom I knew, was coming in to catch the last show. This was on my birthday, December 12. He came in and caught the show, but I didn't see him. I went home, and he rang me at the house and said—it was a famous phrase—'What are you doing New Year's Eve?' I said, 'Not a thing. I can't even get booked anywhere. I can't find anywhere to work.' He said, 'I mean the morning of December 31 and for a couple of weeks after that?' I said nothing. He said, 'I'd like you to open at the joint.' He used to call the Paramount 'the joint.' I said, 'You mean on New Year's Eve?' He said, 'That's right. That morning. You got Benny Goodman's orchestra and a Crosby picture.' And I fell right on my butt! I couldn't believe what he said to me, to be put in a position like that. In those days they called you an extra added attraction. I went to rehearsal at 7:30 in the morning. I looked at the marquee on Broadway, and it said, 'Extra Added Attraction: Frank Sinatra,' and I said, 'Wow!'"

That Sinatra received only tiny billing as an "extra added attraction" is verified by copies of contemporary newspaper ads, which ballyhooed the film, *Star Spangled Rhythm* (actually an all-star production with Crosby as top-billed guest star), and not the stage show. The Goodman aggregation got next highest billing, including the acts within the band—the Goodman small group (BG was sporting a sextet that fall) and budding singer Peggy Lee. Next, two nonmusical novelty acts were billed, the Radio Rogues and Moke and Poke; finally, way down on the bottom of the ad, Frank Sinatra was billed as the marquee equivalent of a bonus track.

In spite of his years of experience with the band and several months of Jersey gigs, Sinatra was mind-numbingly stage-frightened at the opening night at the Paramount, which he must have realized could make or break him. His tension was unexpectedly broken by Goodman himself, who was never thrilled about sharing his spotlight with a star singer;

according to Yank Lawson, trumpet soloist in that particularly great BG band, "Benny didn't know who Sinatra was" (although he had partially subsidized the first James band). Goodman, with his characteristic combination of absentmindedness and total tact, took one look at the shaking, sweating crooner (who weighed about 120 pounds soaking wet—20 of which was hair, he later quipped), heard the deafening ovation from the audience, and demanded, "What the hell was that?"

Goodman's exclamation served to send both Sinatra and the band into hysterics even as the swoons and screams from the audience overwhelmed the music as well as Mr. Goodman's unmiked asides. What they were witnessing was the first important explosion of the phenomenon that pressmen of the day were quick to label "Sinatrauma." "I didn't know why the hell they were doing it," the singer said later of the swooners and bobby-soxers, "but they were doing it."

And they kept doing it. By the next day, January 1, 1943, Sinatra was the hottest act in the country. Not only were trade magazines like *Down Beat, Metronome,* and *Variety* heralding his supremacy, but, more important, lines of kids, mostly girls, stretched around the block. "I was very confused. I had never seen it. . . . Nobody had ever heard that kind of reaction before," Sinatra said later. Inside the theater, massive crowds of teenagers screamed at the top of their lungs; outside, an even bigger mob of girls launched an epidemic of mass truancy and motionless traffic that transformed Times Square into the world's largest parking lot.

As Lawson described it, "Frank stopped the show every time. The lines were four deep clear around the block with people trying to get in the theater." He also recalled that the overworked BG bandsmen, who were doing nine shows at the Paramount every day besides playing for dancers at the Hotel New Yorker each night, found Sinatra and the initial reaction to his music exhilarating: "The applause was so great, and all those kids were dancing in the aisles. We thought it was great!" "What he was doing at the Paramount was by itself beyond belief, and he was doing it for six shows a day," remembered Sammy Cahn. "And the bobby-soxers, the screaming and the hysteria—it was not to be believed!" Sinatra added, "I was also confused because it was very difficult working in the theaters in those days. If I moved, everybody would scream or squeal . . . and I was afraid to move after a while."

One architectural historian, discussing the Brooklyn Bridge, observed that great art creates a need for itself. With World War II expanding, nobody realized the world wanted a new singing star or a new vocal style. Inspired by the female swooning that he had been causing to some degree since the '30s, however, Sinatra understood that what showbiz needed most was a strong new romantic sound. He had also concluded that Stordahl was best equipped to help him develop it. By way of example, Billy May (who served as one of Stordahl's deputies for several years) pointed out that Bing Crosby, then by far the biggest singer in the country, used only four strings; Sinatra insisted on employing twelve. The heavy reliance on "strads" (in *Down Beat*'s parlance) helped Sinatra create a strongly sensual and deliberately non–dance band atmosphere.

It was time for a new singer: by vacating his steady spot with Dorsey, Sinatra was gambling his entire future on that long shot of an idea. No earth-shattering new voice had captured the public's imagination since the Bing Crosby–Russ Columbo–Rudy Vallee triumvirate of a decade earlier. Columbo was long dead, the victim of an accidental gunshot wound in 1934, and Vallee had slowly slid from heartthrob to second banana. Crosby had experienced comparable swoons from female fans at the time he arrived at the top; in fact, both his and Sinatra's first starring feature films (*The Big Broadcast* and *Higher and Higher*, respectively) cast the crooners in identical roles; playing themselves under their actual names (with fictitious love interests) as radio stars dodging femme fans. Once at the top, however, Crosby downplayed the swooning angle, gradually cultivating a patriarchal image, as familiar as your next-door neighbor and as comfortable as a pipe and pair of slippers.

Then Sinatra came on singing about love, marketing his musical romance initially to teenagers, that new demographic group which the swing era and the war had created. "I think that he just had a very appealing, very personal sound," recalled Rosemary Clooney, who was fourteen in 1943, "that young girls my age certainly adored." If his image was cultivated to attract bobby-soxers, his music was directed at the highest possible mind-set. The first major teen idol was also the last one not to pander to his audience.

His very newness made him attractive, and the kids who had grown up listening to big bands in the Depression considered him one of their own—an idea stressed in Sinatra's official publicity biographies of the '40s, which inevitably made him two years younger than he was. "I think it was a time period that was important for them to have somebody to root for during the war years," Sinatra observed in a 1977 interview. "I always felt that I was, in their minds, one of the kids from the neighborhood who grew up and became a success."

The whole of that first Sinatra film, *Higher and Higher*, functions as a paean to his very newness. The freshness of his approach and his sound still seem astonishing fifty years later. Most of Sinatra's successors, the baritones who followed him out of the bands and into solo spots, were still basing their styles on Crosby (similar to the way most of Crosby's competitors in the '30s, such as Dick Powell and Rudy Vallee, had come from the previous generation, stylistically speaking). Sinatra imitators— the now-obscure Ronnie Deauville was the first—would not come along until the first phase of his mass popularity had passed. Dick Haymes, Perry Como, Buddy Clark[2] (and even those like Bob Eberly whose solo careers never quite got off the ground) were all men who would be Bing.

That use of long notes, which established Sinatra from "All or Nothing at All" onward as the first major pop voice to build something new on Crosby's foundation, was also what turned the bobby-soxers on so strongly. As he put it, "If I did what they call bending a note, if I just kind of looped the note, well, they would wail."

Sinatra also usually sang slowly, with a patience and a willingness to take his time as well as a sensuality that must have sounded like forbidden fruit to the repressed postdepressed generation. Compared to Crosby, explained Rosemary Clooney, Sinatra invested much more in his emotional interpretation, "at a deeper level. And I also think Frank showed a vulnerability that perhaps was not in Bing's makeup. Bing wasn't able to come out and sing 'I love you' in a song, that it had to be 'if I loved you' or 'if I say I love you' or something like that. Whereas Sinatra would be more vulnerable and feel very comfortable showing that vulnerability. Therefore, you, as a listener, are more comfortable hearing it." On a piece like "What'll I Do," Sinatra saturates his performance with the strength required to show vulnerability. Never in a hurry, yet always in a tempo you could dance or pat your foot to, Sinatra exuded an erotic warmth that implied slow lovemaking.

It's in that most romantic use of time that Axel Stordahl played a key role in the Sinatra success story. In the Dorsey period, it had largely been up to Stordahl to develop the slow-ballad side of the band—and Sinatra in particular—at the same time the Oliver rhythm numbers turned TD's band into one of the great jazz organizations of all time. Alternating between the two men, Sinatra, like the band itself, could go either way; by the end of his Dorsey tenure he was as adroit a rhythm singer as he was a balladeer. On Oliver's "Without a Song," he was both at the same time. Sina-

---

2. "Crosby, Columbo and Vallee" was a popular song (and was even made into a Merrie Melodies cartoon) in 1932. On a 1944 *For the Record* radio show, Sinatra sang a parody of his hit "Sunday, Monday or Always" with special material lyrics depicting his competition with "Dick Todd, Dick Haymes and Como," which concludes with the aside, "There's just one Crosby." In a 1949 Looney Tunes cartoon, *Curtain Razor*, the trio of competing crooners is identified as "Bingo, Frankie and Al," the latter being the recently resurrected Jolson.

tra realized that Stordahl could help him develop the strong, new romantic sound he was looking for. Even in the Dorsey period, clarinetist Mahlon Clark expounded, Stordahl was known for "writing *beautiful* countermelodies and using the right pretty notes. Frank immediately saw that, so when he went on his own, he took Axel with him."

As the first singer to break out of the dance orchestras into an all-media career, Sinatra released the pivotal stone that caused the avalanche that buried the big bands. "Frank wouldn't want to hear this," said Ted Nash (Sinatra's primary tenor sax soloist in the '50s), referring to the irony that Sinatra was the catalyst for the demise of his favorite kind of music, but he "put the kibosh on the big bands. Before, people went to see the band, and then they'd listen to a solo now and then or a singer here and there. The singers were strictly secondary. But when Frank hit that screaming bunch of kids, the big bands just went right into the background. From then on, [the idea] was to feature the singer completely, and then everyone else jumped into it. So the bands just died after that." As Mel Tormé put it in 1950, "Just as Benny Goodman's 1935–36 band made the public orchestra conscious, so did Frank's rise to fame usher in a new era in popular music, a vocalist's era."

The time had come for Sinatra to graduate to a more substantial radio vehicle. His success at the Paramount naturally increased his stature at CBS, landing him the star spot in the network's flagship program, Lucky Strike's *Your Hit Parade*. Since its inception in 1935 (coincidentally, Sinatra's cousin, Ray Sinatra, had conducted in 1936), the program presented ultrageneric versions of the ten most popular songs of the week, "as determined by *Your Hit Parade*, which checks the best sellers in sheet music and phonograph records, the songs most heard on the air and most played in the automatic coin machines, an accurate, authentic tabulation of America's taste in popular music."

The orchestrations on *Your Hit Parade* were so devoid of personality that, although it drew ratings in the same league as Bing Crosby's *Kraft Music Hall*, the most popular musical show in the country, it did almost nothing for the careers of its stars. Sinatra's immediate predecessor, Barry Wood,[3] all but disappeared after leaving the show despite his visi-

3. Later an industry executive, Barry Wood had an interesting voice, gray and appropriately woody, with a tinge of a raspy sound somewhere in the area of Al Bowlly and Jack Teagarden. While he had sort of a robust charm like one of movieland's stocky baritones (Dick Foran, anybody?), his super-stiff rhythm makes him tough to listen to today. Although Wood had his own NBC series in the summer of 1943, costarring with Benny Goodman, none of his records have ever been reissued, to my knowledge, and he remains but a Trivial Pursuit question as the singer who preceded Sinatra on *Your Hit Parade*.

bility as RCA Victor's number one male vocalist in the pre-Como period. The same fate befell Joan Edwards, a talented vocalist who was never permitted to display any glimmer of personality that might distract from the songs themselves.

Sinatra could not escape the agency's dictatorship of taste even after he became the program's number one ratings asset. Nor did traveling several thousand miles away help: when Hollywood beckoned to Sinatra beginning in the summer of 1943, he petitioned the producing agency, Batten, Barton, Durstine and Osborn, to let him broadcast his portion of the program from the coast. Lucky Strike's dictatorial president, George Washington Hill (labeled a "tyrannical mastermind" by *Newsweek* after his death in 1947), who called the shots down to the smallest harp glissando, agreed to the arrangement if the cost of the requisite wirings and extra orchestra were deducted from Sinatra's salary.

The "West Coast–Frank Sinatra–*Hit Parade* Orchestra," included Billy May as section trumpeter (Zeke Zarchey played lead) and assistant arranger, marking his earliest professional association with Sinatra; Stordahl also commissioned occasional uptempo arrangements from George Siravo. The Hollywood portions also afforded Axel Stordahl his first important, albeit unbilled, chance to conduct, since everything emanating out of the New York end fell under the baton of Mark Warnow (although Stordahl penned at least 90 percent of Sinatra's arrangements, even in cases when he didn't conduct).

Sinatra began on the series in February 1943, and the earliest extant Sinatra vocal from *Your Hit Parade* (which actually comes from a rehearsal, not a broadcast), "I've Heard That Song Before," dates from the twenty-seventh of that month. Again, the notion of the solo singer seems so alien that even after the uproar at the Paramount, Sinatra was hardly treated as a "star" but was still singing a brief thirty-two-bar vocal refrain, big-band-style (there's even a vaguely Dorseyesque trombone passage near the end). The audience seems to resent the three-chorus formality and applauds after the vocal, right over the "dancers' chorus." Within a short time, however, the announcer was saving Sinatra's name for last in the weekly lineup, as in "And starring Frank Sinatra!" Within six months he was given the top spot—the number one song.

When Bea Wain replaced Joan Edwards for four months beginning in July, she quickly realized that Sinatra was at war with the sponsors: G. W. Hill wanted every song delivered with the romance and tenderness of machine-gun fire, and Sinatra, understandably, wanted to employ some of the more sensual sounds that were making him a star. "On that show," Miss Wain recalled, "the tempos were the format. No matter what the ballad was, it had to stay in a certain tempo. And I must say that Frank broke that whole format because when he sang a ballad, it was a ballad. And then I was able to get away with it because he got away with it. We were able to sing slowly and with feeling, instead of just knocking it out."

In spite of the changes he brought, Sinatra seems never to have thought of *Your Hit Parade* as "his" show. When the V-Disc program, which supplied special records to servicemen, began "requisitioning" Sinatra performances, he offered them selections from all his other shows, but never *Your Hit Parade*.

Having proved himself on *Your Hit Parade*, Sinatra was given the opportunity to be more broadly featured in his own costarring series. Titled the *Broadway Bandbox*, the program was again not sponsored but national. It debuted on May 14, 1943, and sporadic airchecks exist from the first show on.[4] For almost two years Sinatra was featured on two programs concurrently, the Friday night *Broadway Bandbox* (and its successors) and the Saturday night *Hit Parade*. Sinatra even made the show's announcements over harp background in the "Lucky Strike Means Fine Tobacco" tradition.

The entire format of *Broadway Bandbox* seemed like a Lucky Strike Extra, one of those rare moments treasured by Sinatra but loathed by the agency when *Your Hit Parade* actually aired a classic song not in the current top ten. Essentially, Sinatra vocals were to alternate with instrumentals by Raymond Scott's orchestra. "The show was a combination," reedman Artie Baker explained. "We would do a Raymond Scott thing, and then when it was time for Frankie to sing, Axel took over because Axel was writing for him all the time."

Guitarist Tony Mottola recalled that initially Scott was expected to conduct the entire program. The producers soon saw the wisdom of bringing in Stordahl to conduct on Sinatra's numbers. "Quite frankly," Mottola elaborated, "in those days Raymond didn't much care for anything but his band. He wasn't too enthralled with being an accompanist for a singer or anything like that, so there wasn't much rapport between Frank and Raymond. That didn't last long because in a couple of weeks Axel was brought in."

In July, Sinatra and Scott parted company; in the fall the singer would shift from the *Broadway Bandbox* to the second series of *Songs by Sina-*

---

4. Seven *Broadway Bandbox* songs have been released on the limited-edition British LP *Sinatra for the Sinatraphile* (Apex AX-6); however, they're way off pitch, putting Sinatra somewhere in the Tony Martin range.

tra, again fifteen minutes and unsponsored, while Scott remained in the same time slot but with a new program title.

While his radio career was burgeoning, Sinatra's "personal appearance" career was making similar strides. In April, a few weeks prior to the start of *Broadway Bandbox*, Sinatra made his nightclub debut at the Copacabana-styled Riobamba, as Joel Herron, who occasionally played piano there, described it: "This management wanted whatever the Copacabana had, with an imitation Copa (chorus) line and imitation of the whole Copa idea." It was a gamble for Sinatra: he had to accept less money than he could have gotten for a movie theater gig and, as Sammy Cahn (who was in attendance on opening night) recalled, "the audience was not [a bunch of] bobby-soxers. This was an *adult*, mature, *sophisticated*, two-o'clock-in-the-morning Manhattan audience."

Herron remembered that Sinatra was quite scared on opening night, but this had the effect of actually quieting the audience. Before he could get any words out of his mouth, he began to back up slowly into the curve of bandleader Nat Brandwynne's piano. As soon as Sinatra emitted the first notes of "Night and Day," he heard feminine sighs and knew that he was in the right place. Long before the first set was over, press agent George Evans had phoned the news of Sinatra's latest triumph to every columnist who wasn't already present.

As at the Paramount, Sinatra had begun as an "extra added attraction" after monologist Walter O'Keefe, comic "songstress" Sheila Barrett, and a dance team, as well as the chorus line. The next week, Herron recalled, the management wanted to bill Sinatra over Barrett, and she decided to leave. The week after, while it would have broken a nightclub taboo to put Sinatra's name above the headliner, the club billed them equally, and O'Keefe left shortly after that.

By May, Sinatra's confidence had soared, together with the club's profits. "A voice would announce, 'And now, *brrr,* the Riobamba prrroudly prrresents, Frrank Sinatrra,'" Sammy Cahn recalled. "Instead of coming out from behind the band, he came walking through the tables. And when he got to the center of the club, he had to do his number. And I say to you again, he was thinner than my finger. And he had them in the grip of his hand. One of my vivid memories is, while he was singing, some gorilla coughed. A giant guy, like 250 pounds. He turned and looked at this guy, and the guy didn't know what to do with himself. Do you understand what I'm trying to say? Frank had power, menace. . . . It was an incredible experience."

Cahn also remembered that Sinatra was simultaneously working the Paramount at the time, which means that the Riobamba engagement may have lasted until the end of May. The gig was also significant in that it may have marked the first of a scant few times when Sinatra crossed paths with Leonard Bernstein. Not yet established as a conductor or composer, Bernstein wrote incidental music for at least one of the club's shows, including a song called "Riobamba" (which Sinatra may well have sung), which the composer later "cannibalized" as one of the themes in his ballet *Fancy Free* (which led to the show *On the Town*, which in turn became one of Sinatra's most memorable films).

The Paramount kept Sinatra busy for most of June. He then spent the summer conquering two more mediums: Hollywood, with his first starring feature picture, *Higher and Higher* (shot mainly in September), and the concert stage. The former was an obvious career goal for any entertainer; the second was entirely unprecedented. No pop singer had ever concertized before, and once again Sinatra sneaked in as a "guest attraction." He took part in a concert series billed as "Music for the Movies," in which classically styled film composers conducted their works. The most notable stops on the tour were at Lewisohn Stadium, New York (August 3), with Max Steiner and the New York Philharmonic, and the Hollywood Bowl (August 14), with Vladimir Bakaleinikoff, Morris Stoloff, and the Los Angeles Philharmonic. Both the classical critics and the popular press (including a particularly sneery write-up in *Life*, which deemed it deplorable that Sinatra actually had the nerve to tell the great classical musicians what tempo he wanted his numbers in) resoundingly disapproved. In turn, Sinatra's uneasiness can be detected at the Hollywood Bowl (the only one of the four concerts known to have been recorded); he stayed fairly conservative for most of his eleven numbers, avoiding dramatic high notes. Still, there's little doubt that the concerts represented a big step for Sinatra personally and a giant leap forward for the respectability of pop singing. He would play the Hollywood Bowl three or four more times in the '40s and eventually make such "big rooms" his regular gigs from the '70s onward.

By the time Sinatra returned back east in the fall of 1943, he had established his pattern for the rest of the '40s: he would do two radio shows each week, *Your Hit Parade* and his own starring show, until the start of 1945 when he temporarily quit *YHP* to concentrate on *Max Factor Presents Frank Sinatra* and then (for two seasons beginning in September 1945) *Old Gold Presents Songs by Sinatra*. His primary focus would continue to be movie theaters like the New York Paramount; during November and December 1943 he played up and down the East Coast as headliner of a package that also included Jan Savitt's orchestra.

After singing for his core audience of bobby-soxers in the daytime, most evenings he would play for their better-heeled parents in night-clubs. Beginning in October 1943, his most notable nitery conquest was the pricey Wedgewood Room at the Waldorf-Astoria, so named, as Sinatra quipped in a 1945 radio gag, because if they could *wedge* one more person in, they *would.* For really big charity occasions he played the concert stages, and he also made at least one film every year. In 1943 the Sinatras bought their first home, in New Jersey, and in 1945 they resettled in Hollywood.

Since leaving Dorsey, Sinatra had left only one entertainment medium unconquered—commercial recordings—and this was due to circumstances beyond his control. The American Federation of Musicians had been on strike against the record companies since the last six weeks of the Sinatra-Dorsey association. While the two younger and scrappier labels, Capitol and Decca, came to terms with the union in 1943, Sinatra's company, Columbia (along with Victor), had been wrongly convinced that Congress would declare the strike unconstitutional during a time of war, and thus waited another year before they finally settled.

All sorts of dodges were attempted to get around the musicians' union between 1942 and 1944. Some labels, particularly independents in far-flung Los Angeles, went ahead and recorded anyway, resulting in some of Nat King Cole's best sides as a jazz pianist. Rising musicomedienne and future Sinatra costar Vivian Blaine introduced the oddest record in or out of the ban, "The Air Battle," in which an accordionist depicts the sounds of a bombing raid, complete with screams of death and destruction, on his squeeze box.

As we have seen, Columbia, following the suggestion of publisher Lou Levy, came up with the lucrative idea of reissuing the Harry James–Sinatra disc of "All or Nothing at All," which, fortunately, so heavily featured the boy singer that it was easily passed off as a genuine Sinatra record. The four-year-old master climbed to the top of the *Billboard* best-selling record charts and was treated like a contemporary Sinatra hit. Sinatra commissioned a new arrangement of the song from Stordahl, which he introduced on the premiere episode of the *Broadway Bandbox* show. Utilizing strings and a soft and subtle long note instead of the belting, dramatic closer of the 1939 chart, "All or Nothing at All" became the first of his own hits that Sinatra sang on *Your Hit Parade.*

Apparently the labels were collectively considering resorting to a capella recordings as early as October 1942 (as *Down Beat* had implied). Bing Crosby, still very much the industry leader throughout World War II, attempted four a capella sides in July and August of 1943, but was not happy with the results and decided to wait until live musicians were available. However, the contenders and would-be contenders to Bing's throne couldn't afford to wait. By 1943 these included Ginny Simms, the former Kay Kyser thrush whom Sachs had signed to Columbia even before Sinatra, as well as Dick Haymes (who had succeeded Sinatra with both James and Dorsey) and Perry Como (late of Ted Weems). Following Sinatra's example, they had struck out on their own.

Neither Sinatra nor Sachs wanted Sinatra's first releases on Columbia to be anything less than the best, and thus they were determined to wait for the end of the ban. "I was a holdout," Sinatra reminisced in 1970. "I really held out. I think the strike went on for a couple of years, and I came in at the end of it with these things. I got a lot of pressure from the people at Columbia Records to do [a capella discs]. I didn't want to cross the lines in a sense."

Jack Kapp, Sach's equivalent at Decca Records, forced him to change his mind. In May and July 1943, Decca had produced a capella sessions with Dick Haymes. The newly liberated Haymes posed a potential threat to Sachs' own star attraction, so "in desperation," as Mitch Miller put it, Sachs turned to Alec Wilder for a capella arrangements for Sinatra and the Bobby Tucker Singers (Sinatra's radio backup choir), nine of which would be recorded between June and November 1943.

As choral singer Ray Charles (who would later bill himself as "The Other Ray Charles") remembered, Axel Stordahl contributed several of these all-vocal charts, although as a member of the AFM he could not be credited at that time. "It was like a vocal orchestra," Charles explained. "You wrote it the way that you would for a band: the bass voices would keep time like a bass would, and you would write sections on top of that. The girls could be the equivalent of either the trumpets or strings, depending on what your orchestration was."

Charles made the comparison to Ray Conniff's early choral record-ings. "He doubles everything the orchestra does in the voices. Only [in 1943] there wasn't a band. You don't have a drum sound and you don't have a guitar sound, but it's written so that you have an equivalent of a rhythm section. Then you have what the brass would play, what the strings would play, what the saxes would play." Despite how some charts had to be tried and retried on session after session, Charles maintained that recording them "wasn't at all difficult." He added, however, "When I listen to them now, I think they're terribly out of tune."

There's a sense of urgency to the a capella sessions made by the three big upstarts of 1943, Sinatra, Haymes, and Como, that's missing in Crosby's four musicianless titles. It seems more fitting that these three newcomers should show their mettle by contending with such unmusical circumstances. On the other hand, it was damned annoying for Crosby to be subjected to them; he had already proven himself time and again. Haymes, Como, and Sinatra worked as hard on these dates as new stand-up comics do on their first *Tonight Show* spot, their enthusiasm often compensating for the lopsided accompaniment.

In getting the dozen background voices strong enough to approximate an orchestra, Sinatra and Sachs apparently decided the important thing was to sound credible even at the cost of excitement. To put it over, they had made an unusual choice of an arranger. Even then acquiring a rep as pop music's in-house intellectual, Wilder had probably first come to Sinatra's attention through the experimental chamber music backings he assembled for Mildred Bailey, then as always one of Sinatra's favorite singers. "The Professor," as Sinatra referred to Wilder, had already recorded several sessions' worth of his singularly individual chamber music for Columbia.

The energy it took to record those a capella charts (fourteen takes have survived of nine separate songs) was only worth expending on surefire material, the much-plugged tunes from three current hit films, among them Sinatra's first starrer (*Higher and Higher*), and the Broadway sensation *Oklahoma!* Only the very first Sinatra Columbia item, "Close to You," was an unaffiliated song, and Sinatra had a special reason for recording it. Earlier that season, "Close to You" (the first of many Sinatra Columbias that he would remake for Capitol) had initiated the multidecade personal and business relationship between Sinatra and Ben Barton. An ex-vaudevillian determined to get into music publishing, Barton had brought the newly written "Close to You" backstage to Sinatra at the Paramount. The singer took to both Barton and the song so much that he decided to publish it as the first copyrighted work for Barton Music.

Sachs recorded "Close to You" and the other eight a capella titles primarily to have something to offer Frank's millions of female fans. Unfortunately, the nature of the a capella beast cornered Sinatra into curtailing the finely carressed notes that made the teeny-boppers swoon so. Manie Sachs once suggested another reason why he temporarily abandoned this device: "The only thing that he minded was the squealing," Sachs recalled in 1955. "They'd do that when he bent his notes. If you follow Frank's history, you'll see that he stopped bending notes for a while."

The a capella Columbias, beautiful as Sinatra's singing is, sometimes seem but faint echoes of the orchestral versions that fortunately survive from Sinatra's radio appearances. For instance, Sinatra's *Hit Parade* rendition of "Oh, What a Beautiful Morning" is so convincing that even the ludicrous image of Sinatra as a bronco-busting, ten-gallon-hatted cow-boy—less Okie than Hobokie—doesn't detract from it. A season later, on a March 1, 1945, broadcast, Sinatra revived "Beautiful Morning" and improved it with a lightly swinging uptempo version that moves deftly. On the commercial Columbia, however, the high-pitched voices are aggravating. All in all, you may find the twelve-voice pseudo-orchestra numbing, but Sinatra sings even more precociously than he did with a genuine string section.

Sinatra would return to only one of the nine numbers, "The Music Stopped," the original a capella version of which had not yet been released. The 1947 "The Music Stopped" contains one of his most mov-ing glissandi (in the first line of the outchorus) and is a tour de force of pauses and fermatas, with Sinatra alternately deciding to either extend or cut short the crucial note on "stopped." The lovely way he goes up on "lights" and down on "low" in the same phrase is also particularly com-pelling; the effectiveness of these effects is severely curtailed on the 1943 reading.

Likewise, the 1943 live orchestral versions of "Close to You" (includ-ing one very different treatment in which Sinatra not only includes the verse but also scats for a few bars) as well as the 1956 Nelson Riddle remake paint a similar picture. Here, Sinatra underscores that the title of the song which launched his solo recording career could have served as a perfect metaphor for his developing style.

Sinatra did more a capella records than any other artist, while Perry Como came in a close second with eight. Still, Sachs gave up before the end of 1943. It's fully a year from "Music Stopped," the last a capella number, to "If You Are but a Dream," the first true Sinatra-Stordahl recording. If you listen to the Columbia sessions chronologically, the transition is overwhelming; done only three days after Columbia made peace with the union, the song seems to be Stordahl's attempt to make up for lost time. He employs a full chamber symphony orchestra on this adaptation of Rubinstein's "Romance," including strings and wood-winds, not to mention eight Bobby Tucker Singers for good measure.

The Sinatra-Stordahl sound is so totally perfected by the time of those November 1944 sessions that it's difficult to trace its development. The 1942–44 AFM ban, apart from lighting the long fuse leading to the explosion that would obliterate quality pop music, thwarts historians in divining the origins of stylistic evolutions in both the jazz and pop worlds. For years there were no known Charlie Parker recordings between the altoist's incubatory debut with Jay McShann and his 1944 groundbreaker "Red Cross." Sinatra's final band vocals with Dorsey and his first Columbia sides with Stordahl suggest a similar gap.

Many jazz fans who had served in World War II were astonished to find out how much that music had changed during the duration. Yet those same music-conscious servicemen had been the only ones able to follow, via records, the equally startling developments in pop music. The sole records released during the ban were V-Discs, made for Armed Forces consumption only, and they offer a fascinating sideways glance into Sinatra's evolution. These document full orchestral versions of many of the songs he otherwise recorded only a capella, live versions of songs he recorded (after November 1944), and many numbers and arrangements that he never otherwise documented. For instance, the earliest Sinatra original V-Disc contained "I Only Have Eyes for You," "Kiss Me Again," and "(There'll Be) A Hot Time in the Town of Berlin," of which only the second title has a close commercial equivalent. The first would be broadly truncated on the 1945 Columbia version, and the third, a wildly jingoistic war anthem by fellow former Dorseyite Joe Bushkin, wouldn't be recorded at all.

The Sinatra V-Discs were at last legally issued for commercial consumption in 1994; one thing they make clear is that by the fall of 1943, at the absolute latest, the Sinatra-Stordahl style was perfected. The classic, early Sinatra ballad sound is unmistakable there in such early V-Disc–only arrangements (none recorded commercially) as "She's Funny That Way," "The Way You Look Tonight," "Speak Low," and Alec Wilder's "I'll Be Around." The only thing that could have improved "The Way You Look" would have been to have Sinatra himself—not the choir—fill in composer Jerome Kern's very erotic, interstitial humming. Otherwise, no one else before or since could make a smile seem so warm or a cheek so soft. A big chunk of the credit for that sound has to go to Axel Stordahl. In fact, it's impossible to overestimate his contribution.

"Axel and Frank were really pioneers," Billy May put it. "Axel was really ahead. They were really going in the right direction and doing something new, and finally the industry caught up with them." Of Sinatra's four major collaborators we know the least about Stordahl. Unlike Nelson Riddle, Billy May, and Gordon Jenkins, he rarely received cover billing on a Sinatra album, primarily because his Sinatra sessions found their way onto LPs years after the fact. Stordahl also had far less of a career apart from Sinatra than the others.

Sinatra himself once illustrated the awe with which musicians regarded Stordahl. When the young Don Costa first met Stordahl, as

Sinatra later related to Sid Mark, he was actually terrified at the prospect of meeting his idol. "In those days I must say that Axel was writing things. . . . Nobody wrote ballads as pretty as he did until many years later when Nelson came along. I think that Axel Stordahl was the daddy that people began to learn from in the sense of writing orchestrations. He was the most prolific of his time."

The one fact that comes through overwhelmingly from those who worked with Stordahl was that he was the ultimate pussycat, perhaps the most beloved man ever to work in Sinatra's circle. Riddle, May, and Jenkins were all adored by their former sidemen, but Stordahl is spoken of as if he qualified for sainthood. "He was one of the single most beautiful men I ever met," said Sammy Cahn. "I tell people that the trouble with Christianity is that I meet so few Christians. When I call a man like Axel a Christian, it's a great compliment. And I don't give out too many compliments."

This is truly remarkable when you consider the responsibilities on Stordahl's shoulders—the pressure of handling all the music for the number one personality in films and recordings as well as, for a long time, two radio shows simultaneously. Somehow, Stordahl managed to please everybody. "Axel was the consummate craftsman," said Mitch Miller, who worked both under Stordahl as a sideman and later above him as a producer. "He came in with no temperament, no nothing. He just brought [his work] in and did it."

"Axel was a wonderful guy," said Billy May. "He had a very low fuse, which is unheard of in the music business. People would explode, and Axel would just stand there, lighting and then smoking his pipe [generally upside down, in the best Norwegian sailor tradition]. Then, after everybody got their egos out of the way, Axel would go ahead and do his job."

Perhaps the most surprising personal tribute to Stordahl came from cellist Eleanor Slatkin. Although both she and her violinist husband, Felix, appear on several Stordahl-Sinatra sessions, Mrs. Slatkin recalled that the conductor exhibited what today would be classified as a "sexist bias" against female musicians. As she put it, "Stordahl wouldn't have women" in the orchestra. Nonetheless, Slatkin describes Stordahl as "a wonderful, *wonderful* person."

Two years older than Sinatra and also apparently a first-generation American, Stordahl was born in Staten Island on August 8, 1913. Originally the youngster sported the more formal old-world Scandinavian name "Odd Stordahl" and just as briefly a head of wavy blond hair, this being long before his most capital dome became one of the more familiar images to the studio audiences of *Songs by Sinatra*.

Stordahl joined his first band of note around 1933 or 1934 as trumpeter and arranger in Bert Block's orchestra. There he shared the brass section at different times with the two key trumpeters who would play lead on both his East Coast and West Coast orchestras a decade later, Ruben "Zeke" Zarchy and then Gordon "Chris" Griffin. He also met the first star vocalist he would write for, Jack Leonard.

Stordahl, Zarchy remembered, "wrote the whole book for Bert Block, the whole library, and he also played trumpet in the band, although he was never much of a player." Griffin remembered that "Axel was writing things for Jack Leonard at the time, [and even then] his arrangements were always simple and melodious and in good taste." While Zarchy or Griffin played lead, Joe Bauer served as second, and Stordahl sat in the third trumpet chair. Block recorded six titles for the American Recording Corporation in October 1935, and while it's not known if Stordahl was still in the band at that time, they were certainly his arrangements.

Thanks to Stordahl, Zarchy pointed out, "Bert's band was not a high-note band. It was a very musical, melodic, 'soft-type' band, swinging. [It was] a perfect band for a restaurant, not with loud brass playing high. [And it wasn't] really a sweet band per se because the sweet bands in those days had three tenor saxes and fiddles, so it wasn't Mickey Mouse. All of Block's music was Axel's, and it was a very hip band. Axel wrote the whole book [without first making] a score. He wrote each part individually and kept them all in his head."

As Dorseyite Paul Weston recalled, national-level bandleaders routinely raided local groups for talent, and Tommy Dorsey, who had recently swooped up the Joe Haymes band en masse, hired three of Block's key personnel in a similar coup in late 1935: Bauer, Leonard, and Stordahl as arranger and fill-in trumpeter. "Joe, Axel, and Jack Leonard were also a singing trio," said Zarchy, "so Tommy got a big package: two trumpet players, an arranger, a vocalist, and a singing group, all out of the same three guys." Stordahl, Griffin remembered, "had a terrible lip!" He knew his limitations as a brassman and did everything he could to avoid playing. Stordahl soon became Dorsey's number two arranger (Weston being number one) and also occasionally doubled, Zarchy said, as one of the voices in the band's vocal trio, "The Three Esquires."

"But when Tommy got mad at somebody or somebody did something and got fired or quit, then sometimes Axel would have to play [third trumpet] for a couple of nights," said Weston. The first trumpeter played the lead that the whole brass section had to follow, the second normally took the jazz solos, while "the third trumpet really doesn't do anything, he just fills out the section," said drummer Johnny Blowers. Even so,

Stordahl detested fighting his way through those third-trumpet parts because, or so he claimed, playing made him abnormally hungry. "That was the big joke in the band," recalled section mate Yank Lawson. "Somebody always had to send Axel a sandwich." "He was a hypochondriac," said Griffin. "He used to get weak when he played the trumpet. They had to feed him every fifteen minutes to keep him from fainting."

Dorsey encouraged Stordahl's ambition to arrange full-time, and in 1938 the leader described Stordahl as his principal writer of "sweet arrangements." A ballad man at heart, Stordahl was never at home working on flagwavers or even danceable fox-trots. Leonard-era items such as "I Hadn't Anyone till You" and "I Can Dream, Can't I" reveal Stordahl working toward what would become familiar as the Dorsey-Sinatra-Stordahl sound, although hampered by a lesser vocalist. "Axel," said saxist and writer Sid Cooper, "was a revolutionary. He taught a lot of people that strings and harp, and so forth, could be used very nicely in a dance band. And he knew how to do it. Looking back, I think I can still hear a lot of things that Axel wrote that were unique."

In 1939 and 1940, Stordahl's stock rose substantially in the Dorsey band thanks to the departure of Paul Weston, which promoted Stordahl a notch and increased his responsibilities to the band book. Soon after, the arrival of Sinatra sparked his imagination and gave him a supreme ballad instrument to work with. Within a short time, the Sinatra-Stordahl combination became a formidable commercial-artistic force even within the confines of the Dorsey aggregation.

"Axel had a gift for making beautiful arrangements," said Zarchy. "That's why Frank wanted him to go with him when he left Dorsey." Sinatra himself later quipped that he took a great pride in offering Stordahl $600 a week to come with him when he had been making $150 with Dorsey (although at this point Dorsey was actually underwriting both Sinatra's and Stordahl's salaries). The first sixteen songs that Sinatra recorded for the *Treasury Song Parade* show (believed to be from January 1943), which were not orchestrated by Stordahl, reveal what it was that made the arranger's work so special. Here, Sinatra is accompanied by a small and uninspired accordion-led combo that would have been at home at any bar mitzvah. It isn't just that Sinatra, as a star attraction, depended on a good band to put him over; rather, hearing Sinatra with just a generic group like this is tantamount to experiencing half of a musical vision. Sinatra was never just a voice or even The Voice, he was always a musical auteur, and here he is without his tools.

Sinatra and Stordahl had introduced an embryonic version of their "sound" at the January 1942 Bluebird date, and perfected their approach through various radio shows in 1943 and 1944. They kept at it through the *Broadway Bandbox* and *Songs by Sinatra*. Finally, in 1944, the Sinatra-Stordahl style landed a half-hour forum of its own, *Frank Sinatra in Person*; it was sponsored by Vimms Vitamins through 1944 and then by Max Factor in the spring of 1945. Virtually all the Sinatra-Stordahl charts recorded by Columbia, especially the pivotal 1944–45 titles, were initially premiered, tested, and polished on this show.

We associate the term "Sinatra-Stordahl period" with all of Sinatra's work after leaving Dorsey in 1942 to the end of his contract with Columbia Records in 1953. The name Stordahl has always been synonymous with Sinatra's Columbia tenure, although the singer and arranger reunited for two post-CBS sessions that comprise the singer's first and last major projects for Capitol Records. The Columbia period itself is marked by the two AFM recording bans; the first strike, 1942–44, begins it, while the second, in 1948, signified the half-time point. From 1944 to the end of 1947, Sinatra worked exclusively with Stordahl on records and radio (not counting one date with Mitch Miller and several all-star and small-group collaborations). From the end of the 1948 strike onward, especially in 1949 (when Stordahl ceased conducting on Sinatra's radio shows), Sinatra worked more frequently with other musical directors. In 1950, Mitch Miller replaced Manie Sachs as CBS's head A&R man, creating a further distinction between Sinatra's early-Columbia and late-Columbia periods.

The Stordahl association certainly represents the most fruitful or, in Sinatra's phrase, "prolific" period of the singer's career. Where Stordahl and Nelson Riddle each wrote approximately the same number of *recorded* orchestrations for Sinatra, roughly three hundred, Stordahl wrote at least that many more that weren't done on records but only played live on Sinatra's weekly shows. In terms of the total number of performances documented, there's nearly as much extant Sinatra material from the '40s as there is from all the other decades combined, even factoring in the abundance of unauthorized concert tapes from the '70s on.

Although the actual record labels only credit "orchestra under the direction of Axel Stordahl," Stordahl was responsible for, at the very least, ninety percent of the arrangements Sinatra performed in all mediums during the years of their collaboration. As Paul Weston pointed out, the heavy workload required of musical directors in this period forced them occasionally to hire other arrangers, especially "when you're doing two and three record dates a week and a radio or a television show at the same time."

But Stordahl's need to use other writers, as we'll see, was fed by his lack of faith in his own ability to score an uptempo assignment. The orchestrator Sinatra and Stordahl employed most regularly, George Siravo, concentrated on swingers almost exclusively. Occasionally other writers were also assigned jazz-flavored charts, including Sy Oliver, Heinie Beau, and Billy May, who is quick to point out that he did only a couple of charts for Sinatra to sing on *Your Hit Parade* and nothing commercially recorded. Another Dorsey vet, Richard Jones, also took care of at least one Broadway-style orchestration. But this amounted only to occasional pinch-hitting: Stordahl really arranged and conducted nearly everything by himself. Small wonder he lost his hair so early.

One can obtain a clearer picture of Stordahl and Sinatra's symbiotic relationship at this point not only by listening to Sinatra without Stordahl, as on the *Treasury Song Parade* (which is slightly unfair to Sinatra in that most of Stordahl's work without Sinatra is also undistinguished), but also by listening to most vocal records of the period. Without question, the best vocal records of the '30s are heavily jazz-oriented, from Eddie Sauter's stylish charts for Mildred Bailey in Red Norvo's orchestra to the informal, ad-lib swing backings heard behind Lee Wiley and Billie Holiday. But most pop vocal orchestrations from the '30s and early '40s are, to put it kindly, tedious. Few vocal records from that era by, for instance, Victor's Barry Wood, Dinah Shore, or Dick Todd are collected, listened to, or reissued today—even though these are good singers who usually did good songs, they're defeated by lifeless accompaniments. Two of the greatest singers of the period, Bing Crosby and Connee Boswell, recorded in both jazz and straight pop settings, and it's small wonder that the greatest interest in these two artists today centers around their "hot" sessions. We listen to Crosby records exclusively for the star singer; the backgrounds on Sinatra discs, while never distracting from the singer, offer as much to listen to (if one cares to) as the foreground does. As a Crosby fan, I'm pained to admit that there's no comparison between the often merely workmanlike writing of his musical director, John Scott Trotter, and Stordahl, who became the decade's leading exponent of the fine-tuned vocal arrangement.

In 1940, two hit records appeared which pointed to the future of pop vocals. The first was the Sinatra-Dorsey "I'll Never Smile Again," arranged by Fred Stulce and Axel Stordahl. While not typical of the mature Sinatra-Stordahl sound, it certainly signified a major step in the right direction. The second was "Flamingo" by Duke Ellington's orchestra, sung by Herb Jeffries and arranged by Billy Strayhorn. Stordahl and Strayhorn here jointly trumpeted the news that vocal accompaniments no longer had to consist of a routine cycle-of-chords and choruses knocked out in cookie-cutter fashion. "Flamingo," in particular, was the most spectacular full and through-composed score (in the classical sense) ever created for a solo voice in pop. No longer were vocal charts interchangeable, meant to suit any voice or any piece of material; Stordahl and Strayhorn began to tailor charts around the soloist and the selection. The orchestra could now follow the singer with passages intended expressly to complement both the musical and dramatic angles of the number, using flourishes and instrumental combinations that illustrated phrases with what Renaissance musicians called "word-painting."

As early as 1938, the trade paper *Orchestra World* noted that Stordahl's "creative work is especially evident in his construction of intros and codas, which are rich harmonically and melodically." Those openings and closings became even more important since, in his mature work, they illustrate how the accompaniment continually complements the singer, even in the moments of the work that are completely instrumental.

"Nancy (with the Laughin' Face)," released in 1945, is one of the definitive Stordahl arrangements. The song originated in Sinatra's relationship with Phil Silvers and Jimmy Van Heusen, who, Sinatra recalled, "hung around my house a great deal in those days." At a party given in the spring of 1944 at lyricist Johnny Burke's house, Silvers cracked a joke that gave a case of the giggles to Burke's wife, Bessie. This prompted Silvers to characterize her as "Bessie with the Laughin' Face." Van Heusen, Burke's longtime composing partner, thought that would make a good title for a song. Since Burke had resolved not to work that day, Silvers took twenty minutes and wrote the words himself. The two substituted "Nancy" for "Bessie" when Silvers got the idea of making a present of the song to Sinatra's daughter at her fourth birthday party a few weeks later.

Sinatra introduced "Nancy" on a broadcast of his *Vimms* radio series around April 1944. In July 1944 he recorded two takes of the song as part of his only completely "original" session for the V-Disc program (which usually utilized performances from his radio shows). That December, Sinatra attempted a take for Columbia, which the company didn't release until fifty years later. Then, according to Silvers, everyone forgot all about it. However, when Sinatra and Silvers toured Europe for the USO in June 1945, Sinatra asked for requests, and "the first scream from two thousand men was for 'Nancy with the Laughing Face,'" as Silvers later wrote. The GI's had fallen in love with the song through the V-Disc, which utilized a longer and slower chart than the commercial take, and when Sinatra rerecorded "Nancy" for Columbia in August, it became, as Silvers said, "one of his perennial hits."

"For the first couple of years people thought I wrote the song," Sinatra has said. "So I had to explain to them that it was Jimmy Van Heusen, and when I mentioned Phil Silvers, everybody giggled. Still, whenever I announce that I'm going to do 'Nancy,' there's a kind of a deep breath from the audience." If "White Christmas" and "Homesick, That's All" and other numbers that Sinatra also recorded in this period made servicemen nostalgic, Sinatra's song to his little girl made them think about their own wives and daughters back home.

Between the two V-Disc takes, the two issued Columbia takes, and various radio readings, there are quite a few lyric variations to the song, which are probably better diagrammed than described. Incidentally, the printed music, copyrighted 1944, naturally includes the now-familiar second set of lyrics for the last four lines, which compare "Nancy" to "Grable, Lamour, and Turner." And the printed music also includes a second libretto for the bridge ("What a wonderful treat to come home to . . .") which neither Sinatra nor apparently anyone else has ever recorded.

Stordahl opens and closes "Nancy" with a five-note figure. One is tempted to call it a riff, but it's played slowly, almost ad-lib, by the full string section and not intended to swing. Sinatra glides in headfirst, carrying the main melody. When backing any sort of solo, instrumental or vocal, arrangers always assign the melody to the soloist in the foreground and restrict the background to harmonic accompaniment patterns, which makes musical sense as well as focusing audience attention. Stordahl rightfully showcases Sinatra's melodic capacity so completely that one can almost never tell what song is being played without the vocal up front.

The strings, playing passages that seem to metamorphose from violins to woodwinds with no audible segue, make up the basic texture, with the brass mainly coming in for punctuation, as on the end of the second A right before the bridge. The bridge itself contrasts the diverse textures of pizzicato and arco string playing in a subtle call-and-response pattern similar to the way most big-band arrangers contrast brass against reeds. When the lyric refers to "mission bells," the fiddlers pluck slightly agitatedly. Then, in the next line, Stordahl resolves this agitation as Sinatra returns lyrically to "Nancy" herself and the "glow" she gives you. On this line Stordahl's strings ease, legato-like, into a warm, calmer, and more relaxedly "glowing" sound.

"Axel was a *very* good string writer, and he also wrote with a very good harmonic sense," explained Weston. Stordahl was also heavily classically oriented. "Axel and I listened to Wagner and Rachmaninoff and Tchaikovsky," said Weston. And Skeets Herfurt remembered, "Debussy was one of his favorite composers. And he got a lot of ideas from Delius, too." Appropriately, on Harry Warren's "I Only Have Eyes for You," Stordahl emphasizes the coincidental melodic similarity to Debussy's "Afternoon of a Faun." Stordahl relied on the strings and woodwinds as his main mode of expression; the rest of the orchestra, including the sax-based dance band, served mainly as a buffer for the strings. "Nelson [Riddle], for example, never really cared much about writing for strings. He would just use the strings as a pad," explained Weston, whereas "both Axel and I were more inclined to write countermelodies against the singer than a lot of the other guys." Stordahl's interest in the European classics led to what Chris Griffin characterized as the "long, lovely lines that Ax had in everything he did, including smoking his pipe." Voyle Gilmore of Capitol Records characterized the Stordahl-Sinatra sound as a "first-rustle-of-spring approach."

That classical sense helped Stordahl develop into the most capable conductor of all Sinatra's collaborators, as virtually all the musicians who worked under them concur (although the competition in that area is pretty meager). Stordahl went as far as hiring David Frisina, the concertmaster of the Los Angeles Philharmonic, as his own first violinist. "Axel was a good arranger for anything," says Frisina, "but with strings especially, he was really something."

Stordahl continually supported the narrative with bonus ideas that weren't in the original composition. He concocted a grand, sweeping chart on "How Deep Is the Ocean," which was highly appropriate for a song that measures love in quantities of the infinite and on which Sinatra sings more dramatically straight than usual. To build to a climax in the outchorus, while Sinatra maintains the same tempo, the background switches from the big symphonic sounds to staccato string plucks that even someone who was not paying attention to the accompaniment would be forced to notice. In effect, Stordahl moves the background closer to the foreground to attract attention and increase tension.

Every single Sinatra-Stordahl record consists of more than a highly potent combination of a great voice and (usually) substantial material. Just about every Stordahl chart also includes what we might call a Lucky Strike Extra: a device, an angle, something additional to make the arrangement function not as just two choruses but as a start-to-finish through-composition.

"Tommy encouraged that," said Weston. "He liked an arrangement to have some form rather than just playing the song and letting somebody sing it—maybe an introduction that might be repeated in the middle."

Weston says of Stordahl's trademark intros and codas: "Axel used to have what we referred to as an 'Axel ending.' On the end of some of the ballads, like 'I Can Dream, Can't I?' [for Dorsey] and others, he would use sort of a complicated tag where he would change key a couple of times in the last four bars."

Very occasionally an idea doesn't work, like the inane choir that intrudes in fast waltz time, like chaperones at a petting party, on "My Romance." More often the simplest ideas work best, such as the ironic holiday chimes at the end of Sinatra's movingly melancholy "Have Yourself a Merry Little Christmas" or the rhythm section dropping out for eight bars to suspend the tempo on the bridge to "The Nearness of You" or the atmospheric tinkly saloon piano and whistling in the fade-out of "One for My Baby."

"Was it a vision," Keats asks in "Ode to a Nightingale," "or a waking dream?" Stordahl decorates "Laura," a *noir* song about a dream girl, imagined but nonexistent, with surreal, dreamlike motifs. Pizzicato fiddlers suggest "footsteps that you hear down the hall," and the muffled French horns together with a flute distant enough to be several blocks away enhance the quality of the scenario. For a closer, Sinatra seems to dissolve into the ether, like the end of a movie flashback where everybody's faces get all mushy and wavy. Likewise, Sinatra's melodic descent at the end of "Autumn in New York" functions like a slow, graceful elevator ride down the Empire State Building.

"Stella by Starlight," from the Ray Milland ghost story *The Uninvited*, showcases Stordahl's ability to create the moody presence of otherworldly entities via spooky one-finger piano passages and bass lines that go bump in the night. On "You'll Never Walk Alone" a similar keyboard figure (played by Mark McIntyre) symbolizes being alone while the background choir represents the concept of communal solidarity.

Sometimes Sinatra and Stordahl take a song far away from what the composer intended. Cole Porter's "Begin the Beguine" began as a Latinate bulldozer, yet S. and S. transform it into an uptempo swing dance piece that builds to a well-deserved climax. Contrastingly, they borrow the customary south-of-the-border beat of the "Beguine" and apply it to "What Makes the Sun Rise," and thereby give what might have been just another love song an entirely new dimension. (In this case, that particular beat was probably written into the original tune by composer Jule Styne, since Sinatra introduced it in the locale of a Mexican restaurant in his 1945 film *Anchors Aweigh*.)

Which illustrates how Stordahl and Sinatra have the good sense to use what the composer gave them to work with when it indeed works for them—or at least meets them halfway. When, on the penultimate line of "Lost in the Stars," Sinatra pauses after singing of little and then big stars, Stordahl fills the break with accordingly little and big orchestral responses, thereby helping to put over the story that much more effectively (Nelson Riddle makes the little littler and the big even bigger in the 1963 remake). In fact, Stordahl and Sinatra spoil us so much that when the team tackled "There's No Business Like Show Business" and came up with that rarity, a Sinatra-Stordahl chart with no extra angle, it's a distinctive letdown. We're disappointed with these two when they're only as good as the next greatest singer-arranger team.

"Axel wrote with great transparency," as his lieutenant, George Siravo, explains. "In other words, if you look at the score, the blacker it looks on the paper, the more depressed a layperson would be. The denser it looks, the heavier it sounds." Stordahl, he expounds, knew how not to overcomplicate. "You might look at his string scores and see only two or three different notes, but the results he got speak for themselves. It didn't take me long to catch on to how to do that in my own writing."

But as important a contribution as Stordahl made to the Columbia sessions, the major musical mind at work was still Sinatra's. By 1944, Sinatra was both a master orchestrator and a supreme instrument, and the interban years (1944–47) represent his first of several artistic pinnacles. Sinatra's primary goal, like Stordahl's, was to, as they used to say, put a song over, to communicate what the words and music really mean. During Sinatra's Dorsey tenure, the leader constantly exhorted him to study Bing Crosby, especially the way Crosby made lyrics, in Mel Tormé's phrase, "ninety-nine percent" of what a singer does.

Sinatra essentially built on the natural, as initially expounded by Crosby, Fred Astaire, Benny Goodman, and Louis Armstrong, exploiting the idea that popular music—singing, dancing, or playing—should be an extension of conversation. He differs primarily from Crosby in that he favors the smooth, even lines of dance music from the mid-1930s, as opposed to the choppier, syncopated sound that Crosby grew up in and forever kept to some degree in his work. Sinatra was born in the same year as Billie Holiday, and both came to the same conclusions concerning how their individual musical advances could help them to put a lyric across that much more convincingly.

Sinatra used longer phrases to achieve greater scope, a broader palette with which to communicate the dramatic underpinnings of a text. In conversationally singing the words of whatever song he was working on, Sinatra now had greater leeway to stress the words that were the most important in the context of the story. He could now emphasize key words or notes through a combination of choices related to dynamics (loud or soft) and rhythm (short versus long notes). And if the songwriters did their homework, especially those writing for Sinatra, like Cahn and Styne on "Time After Time," they already made sure to attach important words to notes distinctive in terms of pitch and duration. As many a songwriter has testified, no singer was more successful in taking advantage of these musical and dramatic opportunities than Sinatra. From "If You Are but a Dream," the first Sinatra-Stordahl Columbia side, onward, it's clear that Sinatra intended to extend this idea further than anyone ever had, choosing the appropriate words, in this case "long" (meaning "want" rather than the opposite of "short"), and stretching it, well, long. He was always the quickest to look for contextually crucial words to hold: "feel" and "lonely" on "There's No You"; "alone" on "When Your Lover Has Gone"; "surrender" on "Body and Soul"; "melts away" on "All Through the Day."

The technique works in reverse, too. Sinatra can get you to pay attention to a particular word by ironically deemphasizing it for emphasis. On that most perfect Sinatra performance of "Nancy," when he arrives at the payoff at the end of the bridge (the word "hello"), he puts less stress on that crucial word than on any other one in the sentence. Here, understating the key word serves to illustrate the lovely gentleness of Nancy as well as underscoring it with a completely unaffected, wide-eyed childlike cadence; both are precisely what the song is all about.

In everything Sinatra does, he has faith in the idea that if you make telling the story your first priority, then musical values can't help but follow. This thinking affords a naturalness to his art that defies explanation; for instance, on the phrase "lengthen in" in the 1944 *Vimms* aircheck of "I'll Remember April," he holds "in" but not "lengthen." And early in his career Sinatra apparently decided that he liked to stress the first note of the final A section, coming immediately out of the bridge, and he stresses this note in at least one out of every four songs he does. It doesn't matter that this word often turns out to be as unimportant as something like "and" in "Where or When" or "I Only Have Eyes for You," or "soon" in "If I Loved You." It just *sounds* right.

Often there's a musical basis for this. Jim Maher recalled a conversation with Harold Arlen in which he asked the composer, "'What songwriter would ever use a fermata on the first note of an eighth-note triplet?' Harold thought about it and said, 'No one. It wouldn't work.' I said, 'Well, you did, in "Last Night When We Were Young." And you know, Frank Sinatra is the only singer who ever picked up on that.'" But whether justified in the score or not, whatever notes Sinatra chooses to extend always sound exactly right.

Sinatra unfailingly triumphs in the development of devices that move the song forward on both the musical and dramatic planes. What we can call the "unclimax," as opposed to the "anticlimax," may be the most effective of these. Apart from exceptions like "Where or When" (on the first of three arrangements that Sinatra has recorded), "Over the Rainbow," and "All the Things You Are," the most intense moment of a Sinatra performance is rarely the last line or note. Sinatra prefers to hit the big notes in the previous rhyme or line before the end, wherever it makes sense to him, and then bring it home on a surprisingly quiet note. He often ends on a long note, but then it's almost never loud, just subtly and quietly extended. Even when the final note is of comparatively brief duration, he almost always diminuendos on it very slowly. On several summer 1944 radio performances of "The Song Is You" and "I'll Be Seeing You," he chooses to fade away by going up through the roof into a superhigh falsetto note that dissolves into the stratosphere. By the time the ban ended that fall, he seems to have decided that this device focused too much attention on the singing medium itself and distracted from the message. He therefore switched to ending most numbers on his usual, more unobtrusive low note, which is the way he ends his 1946 commercial recording of "The Song Is You."

Even on "Time After Time," conceived by Cahn and Styne as a concerto for long breaths à la Sinatra, he ends on a contrastingly quiet note. As with many another closer, he holds it long but softly, so that as the orchestra swells around him you're not supposed to notice exactly where Sinatra stops singing (although CD technology makes this point more discernible than 78-era surface rumble). On "You'll Never Walk Alone," the singer's fading into the ensemble (here a vocal choir as well as the orchestra) becomes part of the message of the Rodgers and Hammerstein anthem: the individual becomes one with the community; no longer will he walk alone.

On a certain level, Sinatra and Stordahl are creating a new wrinkle on the naturalism idea, saying that these songs are so good you don't need to do anything with them. There's certainly nothing like Mel Tormé's or Betty Carter's total reworkings of songs or Sinatra's own later transformation of ballads like "Dancing in the Dark" into hard-swing flagwavers. Yet even a cursory listen will reveal that these gentle and easy-sounding ideas are every bit as inventive, with substituted harmonies and paraphrased melodies, as the most far-out improvisation, and are much more musically substantial than the biggest bravura windup.

In fact, these carefully considered codas can often upgrade B songs to the A level, as happens with "This Is the Night," "So They Tell Me," and "I Want to Thank Your Folks," among many others. It's no surprise that "Angel Eyes," written years later, in 1953, would quickly become one of Sinatra's pivotal numbers and for many years his final song at many a concert. Sinatra loves to end not just a show but almost each song by quietly announcing, "'Scuse me while I disappear." But these unique endings are only part of the story. Sinatra also used dramatic endings where appropriate: on "The Moon Was Yellow," "Falling in Love with Love," and, less convincingly, on "That Old Black Magic." He has no one way of doing things. He lets the material determine the approach.

And different kinds of selections engender different tactics. Sinatra is a straight-down-the-middle pop singer, influenced by pop's two next-door neighbors, academic music and jazz, although certainly more by the latter than the former. In the '40s you will occasionally hear him adopt what could be classified as a vaguely classical stance, not only in the occasional bravura, operatic coda but also in melodies taken from European art music. During the Columbia years he went through enough of these "watered-down" classics to fill an album, which would have been called, obviously, *The Symphonic Sinatra.* These included "Strange Music" and another Grieg-orian ditty from the Broadway show *Song of Norway,* "I Love You, Dear"; "If You Are but a Dream," which was written "after," as they say, Anton Rubinstein; "Till the End of Time," derived from Chopin (and done by Sinatra on his 1945 *Old Gold* series); that best-selling sample of Rachmaninoff-and-roll, "Full Moon and Empty Arms"; and three Russian-inspired tunes that prove what Band of Renown leader Les Brown declared in a 1941 record, namely that "Everybody's Making Money but Tchaikovsky": "Our Love" (Sinatra's 1939 demo), "None but the Lonely Heart," and "Moon Love" (done live with Harry James but not recorded until 1965).

Just as the songwriters have adapted the melodies, Sinatra adopts their stylistic devices to his own needs—the long, surging notes, the high, dramatic style—just because it suits these songs. He affords these tunes the melodic richness they deserve, and he does equally well with international folk and pop songs, such as the German-derived "Here Comes the Night" from the James era and the Neapolitan "Luna Rossa," "(On the Island of) Stromboli," and young rival Vic Damone's number one hit, "I Have but One Heart (O Marenariello)." He rises and surges similarly on what we could call "American opera" arias, "Bess, Oh Where's My Bess" from *Porgy and Bess,* "Ol' Man River" from *Show-boat,* the "Soliloquy" from *Carousel* (particularly the ending), and occasional other collar-poppers done with far more subtlety than Mario Lanza.

The 1944 "I Dream of You" also has the feeling of a quasi-classical opus, although it is a Cahn-Styne song that may have been written for *Anchors Aweigh* (though never filmed or recorded for that production). Yet even amid the stately settings of all these numbers, Sinatra remains primarily a jazz-derived vocalist. He throws in all sorts of subtle rhythmic variations, particularly in the way he alternately accelerates and ritards the pace in the last few lines of the song, which owe far more to jazz than to opera. Likewise, the aesthetic success of "None but the Lonely Heart," the best of his Tchaikovsky pieces, has nothing to do with any classical roots that Sinatra was supposed to have. Rather, it illustrates Sinatra's continuing connection to Tommy Dorsey, who had included this adaptation in his book as a vehicle for his own trombone since 1941.

When classical melodies have already been imported to mainstream pop or when Broadway ballads borrow a soupçon of old-world grandeur, Sinatra can more than handle them. It's only when he tries to sing an unadapted aria that he falters. One *Old Gold* show found him attempting a gag version of "Largo al Factotum" even funnier than Alfalfa Switzer's "I'm the Barber of Seville," and a fragment from the "Miserere" from *Il Trovatore* to rival even the hilarity of the Marx Brothers' monumental night at that opera. To hear Sinatra's straight-ahead hack at "La Ci Darem" from *Don Giovanni,* in duet with soprano Kathryn Grayson in *It Happened in Brooklyn,* is to wince. Likewise, Sinatra's dealings with blues, another musical idiom as removed from mainstream pop as opera, are about on the same level; he can use blues effects or classical effects, but when he dives in too deep, he gets in over his head.

Sinatra's knowledge of both blues and classical styles, so unlike his work in swing-style uptempos and ballads, seems secondhand. The joint influence of Bing Crosby, the man he called the father of his career, and Louis Armstrong can be felt much more directly. Armstrong utilized significantly more classical mannerisms than Sinatra, and almost all the ones you hear in Sinatra's work can be traced back to Armstrong's trumpet solos. The Crosby influence resounds most strongly in the '30s and '40s pop stars who sounded the most like him (Como, Clark, Haymes), but it can also be found in stylists as distinct as Sinatra, Eckstine, and Nat Cole. In fact, two of Sinatra's earliest albums, *The Voice* (1945) and *Frankly Sentimental* (1947), refer both to Crosby and the classical tradition. (It's not generally known that Sinatra even made original "concept albums" for Columbia.[5] Although these late '40s sets, such as *Christmas Songs by Sinatra,* were done as multiple 78 packages, he did plan and release them as bona fide thematic album programs long before the invention of long-playing record technology.)

As in later Sinatra albums, the ensemble texture and resulting mood are consistently uniform; Sinatra and Stordahl devised a kind of chamber group sound in order to further distinguish the album cuts from his regular singles. Although Stordahl had already written more traditional orchestrations of "She's Funny That Way" and "Someone to Watch Over Me," which Sinatra had broadcast in recent months, the team completely rethought those songs for *The Voice.* The accompaniment for both this album and *Frankly Sentimental* derives from a classical small group, employing a core group of four strings and four rhythm plus one or two horns (a format Sinatra would reprise a decade later on *Close to You*).

The emphasis on the violin as solo instrument in this "double quartet" ensemble accentuates the chamber music feel, especially during the violin-guitar duo halfway through "Someone to Watch over Me." A solo guitar stresses the Italianate side of the Sinatra coin, especially throughout the opening of "I Don't Know Why," which begins with just guitarist George Van Eps playing an introductory figure. A very naked-sounding Sinatra soon joins him, and the two duet for ten bars or so before the strings slide in subtly around them. "Axel used the guitar as the prime instrument in the rhythm section," said Van Eps, who played much the same role ten years later on Sinatra's *Wee Small Hours* album. "I don't mean that it takes the place of the drums, but it adds a tonality, a sonority to the sound of the rhythm section. The rhythm is played gently, not bang-bang."

Throughout both these albums Sinatra's singing is even warmer and more tender than usual: in his hands, "Someone to Watch Over Me" becomes a moving expression of vulnerability, explaining why bobby-soxers wanted to mother him as well as wrestle with him in the back of a DeSoto. On "These Foolish Things" Sinatra plays two roles at once, the swain at the romantic height of an affair as well as the sadder-but-wiser ex-Romeo reflecting on the liaison from a critical distance sometime later. He takes "Spring Is Here" straighter and less jazzy than the more playful "You Go to My Head," in order to make the most of the lyricist's

---

5. It should be noted that Columbia Records has done little to keep the public mindful of Sinatra's accomplishments in the area of albums because they haven't kept any of his original album packages in print in the same program that Sinatra planned them. Two additional 78-era albums, *Songs by Sinatra* and *Dedicated to You,* seem mainly to be catch-up collections of mid-1940s tracks that had not yet been issued up to that time.

Hart-felt wordplay: When Sinatra sings "spring is *here,* I *hear,*" he actually pronounces those two homonyms as if they were audibly different sounds. Elsewhere, on the orchestral "I Should Care," the most *yiddishe* title Sinatra ever recorded, he finds several dozen different ways to phrase the three-note "hook," and each time he sings it the shading of its implications changes subtly.

He does the same on the 1947 "Always." When asked a few years ago to talk about why Irving Berlin was such a great songwriter, Sinatra responded, "When a man writes a song and he says, 'Not for just an *hour,* not for just a *day,* not for just a *year,* but always,' that's as simple and as pure as anybody can write a piece of prose or a pop song." Sinatra makes you feel the difference between each, fully milking the value of Berlin's parallel—yet, as he stresses, exceedingly simple—construction by ever so slightly varying the amount of weight given to each of those temporal increments.

"That Old Feeling," another chamber item, utilizes a Proustian trigger of emotion to set in motion a remembrance of an intrigue past. Sinatra's voice conveys quivery nervousness throughout, only relaxing into a swing feel when the words call for it, on "there'll be no new romance for me." "Fools Rush In" on *The Voice* contains a stunning Sinatraism in the way he lets the word "care" diminuendo out into the beginning of the next line, in a perfect, subdued example of emotion suggested rather than overtly expressed.

All through *The Voice* and *Frankly Sentimental,* Sinatra is resolved not just to "Try a Little Tenderness," as one of the songs is titled, but quite a lot. These may qualify as his most tender vocalizing ever. On "Why Shouldn't I," Sinatra turns Cole Porter's wiseguy laundry-list lyric into as sincere a portrayal of passion as the Peruvian ever wrote; he does even more for the normally patronizingly patriarchal "Tenderness." After his atypical sensual humming in "Paradise," we feel we've been there.

Sinatra's "Try a Little Tenderness" and "Ghost of a Chance" use those songs' offbeat verses the same way that Crosby had (taking Crosby's rubato a step further); the layout of "Paradise" also owes much to the classic Crosby Brunswick record. But, as with everything else, although we can trace the lines of influence, all the songs here have been thoroughly Sinatrafied. Here and elsewhere, the concept of Crosby as competitor directly inspires Sinatra to sound more like himself. (Around the same time, Sinatra recorded the 1873 "Home on the Range," undoubtedly inspired by Crosby's 1933 version. Abetted by Dave Barbour's graceful guitar, Sinatra actually sounds as if his home on the range, with all the deer and antelope, actually means something to him. Ironically, until 1993 this sterling sample of Americana had been issued only in England.)

On "I've Got a Crush on You" and "Body and Soul," Bobby Hackett plays trumpet intros (heart-stopping cadenzas à la his idol Louis Armstrong's "West End Blues"), obligatos, and solos that immediately whisk these tracks to the pinnacle of Mount Olympus even before Sinatra's entrance. "It Never Entered My Mind" and "Crush" also signify the apogee of Sinatra's romantic style and the rarefied level of his source material, the first song laced with wry melancholia and the second with coy innocence. And both are imbued with musicality (even considering a mildly flat note in the coda of the original masters of "Crush"). Alec Wilder later wrote that even with the written music in front of him, he invariably heard "Crush on You" with the variations that Sinatra worked into it. And, said Wilder, any artist who had ever heard Sinatra's record could never be tempted to return to the way Gershwin wrote it. Wilder surely also refers to the ingenious harmonic substitutions of George Siravo in the first of only a handful of ballad orchestrations (albeit a rhythmic one with a great jazz trumpeter) that this arranger wrote for Sinatra.[6] Siravo revived this format with Billy Butterfield on "Nevertheless," a 1950 track that serves as a sequel to the earlier chamber sessions.

When *The Voice* was released in 1946, it became both a number one selling album and a major influence on other singers. "I was working in a record store, and Dean Martin came in every day to see me," Frank Military remembered. "And one day *The Voice* album came in, and it sold like hotcakes. I didn't know Frank, and Dean didn't know Frank, but the two of us just sat there listening to all four 78s over and over."

Sinatra learned to create a new character with each song. He shifts from attitude to attitude with every new text the way singers normally use different keys for each tune. Although he's always warm and tender and vulnerable, it's the gradations of and variations on these qualities that make him, in Wodehouse's words, "one of the godlike kind of men." "Homesick, That's All," for instance, finds Sinatra becoming the very picture of a nostalgic GI at war's end. He also perfectly captures the sense of delightfully bemused befuddlement that Al Dubin's lyric to "I Only Have Eyes for You" describes. He's glowingly wide-eyed like a young parent who is still practically a child himself on "Mighty Lak' a Rose" and

6. Lee Wiley reused both Hackett and Siravo's arrangements for her Columbia version three years later. Similarly, Doris Day reprised Sinatra's 1945 outline for "You Go to My Head."

"Cradle Song" (from Brahms's "Lullaby," which he actually croons to sleeping *kinder* in *Anchors Aweigh*) and "The Charm of You." On both he transforms ancient warhorses into intimate experiences. On "Could 'Ja" and the underappreciated "Dum Dot Song" (a swingingly swell record of an inane song), as well as an entire album of Christmas songs, he sings to children on their own level without talking down to them.

In contrast, he communicates rich, multilayered emotional states in "It Never Entered My Mind," one of the most subtle torch songs ever written, and "Guess I'll Hang My Tears out to Dry." Even a "simple" Christmas song becomes a vehicle for emotional depth: he elevates "Have Yourself a Merry Little Christmas" into an enticingly complex happy-sad ode that can stand beside Judy Garland's famous version from *Meet Me in St. Louis*.

In "Guess I'll Hang My Tears . . . ," lyricist Cahn presents us with a protagonist who is determined not to show the world his pain. He feebly attempts to distract us from it with a series of deliberately cheap-shot jokes, beginning with a title that equates love with laundry, employing humor—as a Woody Allen character might—as a defense mechanism. Does it work? The ruse only magnifies the intensity of his anguish. Sinatra would do better by "Tears" on the *Only the Lonely* album (with Al Viola's guitar taking the place of the harp), but even in 1946 Sinatra is a master.

On "Someone to Watch Over Me" and "I Don't Know Why," he sets himself up more as a forlorn, lost dog than the predatory wolf he would play a decade later. "I Begged Her" piles dimension on top of dimension: as in the film *Anchors Aweigh,* he becomes a sheep in wolf's clothing, a bashful bookworm feigning the part of a sly lothario. On "These Foolish Things," he lands halfway between the poles of the Dorsey era virgin of "Our Love Affair" and the sagacious old stud of the '50s, now himself qualified to offer advice to younger lovers.

On some of the uptempos of the period, usually written by George Siravo (about which more later), he's brash and extroverted: "Blue Skies" marks one of Sinatra's fiercest swingers ever, with vital contributions from the soloing sidemen, including his favorite tenor of the time, Herbie Haymer. Yet on the same session in 1946, he and Stordahl also produced one of their most hauntingly introspective works, "Among My Souvenirs" (by coincidence, like "Blue Skies," written in 1927). Sinatra transforms it into an even more personal soliloquy than Rodgers and Hammerstein's "Soliloquy," in which Sinatra recites the text almost as if he were thinking out loud.

Often the more conceptually spare the libretto—"Embraceable You," for one—the more Sinatra dreams up to do with it. Here, as on the slightly fuller "All Through the Day," he passes through several emotional levels within the same text.

The Columbia period certainly constitutes a far more naive era than the Capitol and later recordings. On "Something Old, Something New," playing a horny young bridegroom turned on by the contents of his blushing bride's overnight bag, he even utters, "Golly gee!" Yet Sinatra delineates the difference in the naïveté of a Rodgers and Hammerstein cornfest and a bone-simple Irving Berlin text like "Always." The Voice can always pinpoint that exact shade of difference.

Artie Shaw, with whom Sinatra always has a lot more in common than marriage to Ava Gardner (if not for their understandable rivalry over that most desirable lady, one could imagine them collaborating), may well have been the first popular musician to conceive of a standard repertory of classic American popular songs. Shaw represents the earliest exponent of a generation of musical artists who realized that there was more to pop music than this year's crop of kisses. As Shaw put it, the idea was to take the best possible songs and orchestrate them in the best possible way, a modus operandi that Sinatra quickly adopted. Before Shaw, only marginalized music—cabaret and traditional jazz, not unlike folk music and the blues—acknowledged that there was any kind of song other than the latest chart toppers on *Your Hit Parade.*

Shaw got rich recording five- and ten-year-old masterpiece tunes by the likes of the Gershwin brothers, Rodgers and Hart, and Irving Berlin in a string of hits that began with Cole Porter's then-forgotten 1935 "Begin the Beguine." Even so, no fellow leader picked up the idea; it's almost as if the idea of "good songs" was regarded as Shaw's exclusive gimmick, his equivalent of Kay Kyser's collegiate shtick. It took the coming of Sinatra to establish what became the Great American Songbook, not least because Sinatra's rise entailed the new supremacy of the singer as the dominant force of mass market music. The Voice announced to art-conscious vocalists that if they didn't take a serious look at the classic show tunes of the previous two generations, then they were stuck with whatever happened to be on the *Lucky Strike* show that week.

Ironically, in his first starring feature movie, *Higher and Higher,* Sinatra participated in a typical Hollywood demolition job of a Broadway musical with a super-sophisticated score by Rodgers and Hart. The moguls applied their "leave a little, remove a lot" treatment even more stupidly than usual, retaining only a single and singularly undistinguished tune from the 1940 show: they kept "Disgustingly Rich" and cut "It Never Entered My Mind." In this case they also held on to the show's rather trivial plot peg; they ate the wrapper and threw away the candy. But even if RKO had retained the whole score, within a few years the movie would probably have been forgotten anyway. Sinatra did music the greater service when he revived "It Never Entered My Mind" in 1947, along with seven other Rodgers and Hart songs over the course of his Columbia contract[7] and Lord knows how many more for Capitol and Reprise.

Likewise, in countless concerts Sinatra has introduced "When Your Lover Has Gone" with a sense of wonder that its composer, E. A. Swan, could come out of nowhere, write such a beautiful love song, and then disappear into oblivion. Had it not been for Sinatra, the song—introduced on the soundtrack of Jimmy Cagney's 1931 *Blonde Crazy*, recorded by several contemporary dance bands, and then promptly forgotten—might have vanished as speedily as its one-shot author.

"I take great pride in the fact that I introduced Frank to a lot of the great, great songs," Sammy Cahn said proudly. "I introduced him to songs such as 'You Are Too Beautiful.' I [would say] 'Frank, there's a song . . . ' Because he's got a good sense of music, you can lay a good song on him, [and he'll say], 'Oh, geez, that's good. Let me have that!'" (During the run-throughs prior to the recording of "I've Got a Crush on You," Stordahl reminded Sinatra, "Sammy Cahn taught you this song, Frank.") "That was our love, all of us," Cahn said. "We loved the great standards. How are you not going to love them? Whenever we'd be around someplace, we'd always play the great songs." Sinatra used a divining rod for talent to discover what would become the pop mainstream.

There are virtually no second-rate Sinatra-Stordahl records from the 1944–47 period. The only sides that threaten to bring down the average are a series of blues-inspired small-group novelty items done at the same time as the Stordahl sessions. That's not to say "That's How Much I Love You" and "You Can Take My Word for It, Baby" with the Page Cavanaugh Trio, and "It All Came True" with Alvy West and The Little Band, are bad, they're simply secondary items, which don't measure up to the extremely high standards of the Sinatra-Stordahl material. These combo sides illustrate, as we'll see, the beginnings of Sinatra developing a new uptempo style for himself. Here he finds his initial inspiration in

7. You didn't ask, but here's the answer department: "Lover," "My Romance," "Spring Is Here," "You Are Too Beautiful," "Falling in Love with Love," "I Could Write a Book," "Where or When?" as well as "It Never Entered My Mind."

both the instrumental textures and jivey novelty numbers popularized by the King Cole Trio. Eventually, he would re-invent himself as a swing singer by following a different path. The repertory patterns of those two great artists would continue long beyond the '40s: Nat Cole specialized in finding offbeat, even esoteric, airs and working wonders with them.

Sinatra's influence in determining what singers after him sang is immeasurable. By way of example, another artist could come along and do an album-length homage to, say, Nat King Cole (as has his own pop star daughter) that would naturally contain Cole's best-known songs. A singer or an instrumentalist could also do an album of the songs associated with Billie Holiday, Lee Wiley, or even Bart Simpson. Likewise, one conceivably could pay tribute to Sinatra by reprising his hits, such as "All the Way" and "Strangers in the Night," but it would be pointless to do a set called *The Frank Sinatra Songbook*. It would be redundant. The songs we identify with Sinatra are "Someone to Watch Over Me," "Lost in the Stars," "You'll Never Walk Alone," "Where or When," "Ol' Man River," "Embraceable You" (thanks to the recording ban, actually recorded first by Cole), "I'll Be Seeing You," "Night and Day," and, most of all, "The Song Is You." In other words, songs that are so firmly embedded in our collective consciousness that one hardly requires the pretext of a Sinatra tribute to hear them.

It's true that no one introduced more standards than Fred Astaire, who had all the major Broadway legends almost simultaneously penning film scores for him. But no performer turned more songs into standards than Sinatra, including a great many of the numbers written for Astaire. "If you look at songs like 'Glad to Be Unhappy,'" Frank Military points out, "they were just songs done in little cabarets by chi-chi kind of singers" until Sinatra brought them into the mainstream. "He even took songs out of flop shows, like 'Guess I'll Hang My Tears out to Dry' [from *Glad to See You*] and made them into important standards." (Another example would be "All the Things You Are" from *Very Warm for May*.)

Sinatra's influences in this area even bounced back to the artists who had originally influenced him. In the 1930s, Billie Holiday, Bing Crosby, and Louis Armstrong were content to take whatever tune the pluggers pushed down the pike at them and transform it into something special, whereas a great deal of their 1950s albums constituted what amounted to *The Frank Sinatra Songbook*, since that decade marked their mutually deepest delvings into the standard repertory.

The '40s was Sinatra's most commercially successful era as far as big-selling singles were concerned, and by the time of the 1948 ban he had racked up sixty-three chart hits, including four number ones. Of these

Billboard-listed items, only five or so can be described as standard selections, yet Sinatra continued to devote at least half of his recording energies to time-tested material. He probably could have had almost twice as many hits and made twice as much money had he done nothing but new songs. One has to marvel not only at his own taste but also that of his record rabbi, Manie Sachs. Even in that less aggressive era, Sachs had to compete with Jack Kapp to the left of him and Mitch Miller right behind him, yet here was a man in the record business—the pop-record business, no less—who actually was aware that there was more to making music than the fast buck.

"We talked things over," bandleader Les Brown said recently about his musical relationship with Sachs, one probably similar to Sinatra's. "I picked tunes and talked them all over with Manie. If he gave me tunes that I didn't like, I didn't do them. He was very nice about that; he wasn't a dictator. If I didn't feel it, he didn't want me to do it." It's rather staggering to imagine either Miller or Kapp treating their artists like that. "Manie was one of the nicest men in this business," Brown continued. "A complete doll compared to some of them I've been around."

"Manie was the most unlikely best friend to a man like Frank Sinatra that I could think of," mused Rosemary Clooney. "He was very quiet, very correct, very soft-spoken, smart. He was close to his family and went home every weekend to Philadelphia. But Manie adored Frank from the very beginning, and I think it was mutual. I think that there was a fatherly feeling, although I don't know how much difference there was in their ages—but I think that Manie felt that way toward Frank."

Sachs was born in Philadelphia on January 30, 1902, and he attended Pennsylvania Military College. In the early days of radio, Sachs served as head of public relations and of the "Artists Bureau" at local station WCAU. Around 1932 or 1933 he went to work for the talent agency MCA, where he stayed for the remainder of the '30s. At some point he connected with CBS radio magnate Bill Paley and helped him in his bid to take over the Columbia Records label from the American Recording Company. Partly as a reward, Paley made him head of Artists and Repertoire, a position for which he was eminently suited, despite a lack of technical knowledge about music or recording. He soon became vice-president and director of the label.

Sachs first met Sinatra in 1939, and the two were inseparable for nearly twenty years until his death from leukemia on February 9, 1958. Sachs' departure from the label in January 1950 proved to be one of the key factors in Sinatra's eventual downfall at Columbia.

A *Time* reporter once described Sachs as looking "so much like Sinatra that he is constantly mistaken for him." In 1944, when Sinatra's son was born, the proud papa selected Sachs as his godfather, to the displeasure of the priest who presided at the christening. When the good Father insisted that someone more Catholic fulfill the godfather's obligations at the ceremony (Sachs was president of the Beth Israel Synagogue in Philadelphia), Sinatra refused to participate and stormed out of the church.

Sachs wasn't only Sinatra's rabbi, "he was everybody's rabbi," as his successor, Mitch Miller, recalled. "I always used to say that if Manie Sachs were a woman, he'd always be pregnant because he couldn't say no. There are many instances. One time he was on a plane with [publisher] Howie Richmond, and Howie says, 'Jesus, Manie, I forgot to take out insurance.' So Manie says, 'I'll give you some of mine.' And he meant it! Manie was a malaprop, too. He'd say, 'The bridges crossed a lot of water.'"

As a long-term investment, recording good music actually made money. These were the tunes that Columbia would reissue time after time, beginning in the 78 era and continuing long into the digital age, while most of Miller's Sinatra productions wouldn't see the light of day again until the 1993 *Complete Columbia Recordings* box. There was also a feeling shared by Sinatra, Stordahl, Sachs, and his producers, Morty Palitz, Joe Higgins, Mitchell Ayers, and George Avakian, and other record men such as Norman Granz and Milt Gabler as they stood on the forefront of the LP era in the late '40s, that these were the songs that would become the basic staple of the new technology, and that the long-playing record itself would in turn be the medium for quality music in all areas—jazz, pop, and classical.

The coming of the LP was only one reason Sinatra had to look forward to the future even as the union announced another disastrous musicians' ban in the fall of 1947. When the A&R men of the various labels realized that a strike was unavoidable, remembered Stan Freeman, who played piano on several sessions when Sinatra didn't use his regular accompanist of the '40s, Mark McIntyre, "we started doing eight or nine sessions a day just to get those things in."

The previous June, Sinatra had wound up the second and final year of the *Old Gold Songs by Sinatra* program. In direct opposition to *Your Hit Parade*, which he had left at the end of 1944,[8] *Songs by Sinatra* repre-

8. It's obvious in retrospect why Sinatra would want out once his career was established and his own series, the Max Factor half-hour, was about to start. Sinatra explained at the time that he was leaving because it was too expensive for him to do the show. The cost of the sidemen and the remote phone lines, Sinatra claimed, left him digging into his pocket beyond his own weekly paycheck of $2,000 per show.

sented perhaps the highest-minded commercial radio series in pop music: Sinatra featured songs for the ages as often as he did the best new numbers and his own hits, and even devoted whole programs to the works of Jerome Kern, Johnny Mercer, Irving Berlin, and their peers.

His personal fortunes had risen to almost unfathomable proportions. No one ever thought that he could ever top Columbus Day Riot of 1944 when he returned to the New York Paramount to an audience of thirty thousand fans.[9] Still, he soared higher the following year when he moved from the fading RKO to Metro-Goldwyn-Mayer. Beginning with the phenomenally successful *Anchors Aweigh,* one of the major hits of 1945 (the year the singer bought his first house in Los Angeles), Sinatra launched a string of major musicals for Metro. In 1948, the Sinatras—now four, with Frank, Jr.—relocated to even more spectacular digs in the Holmby Hills section of L.A.

No one could yet see any dark clouds on the horizon. The proof was at the Paramount. "When we played the Paramount in 1947," remembered Johnny Blowers, "the stage would go up about eighteen feet, from way down at the bottom, and he'd look down [at the bobby-soxers] and go, 'Have you been here all day?' Because they'd brown-bag it; they'd bring their lunch and everything else. God almighty, we'd go on the stage at ten o'clock at night, and he'd look down and say, 'You're still here!' Because they stayed all day long!"

Sinatra was by now a multimillionaire, earning, for instance, $41,000 for a single week in a Chicago theater in the spring of 1946. As raconteur Billy Rose wrote, "Only the Internal Revenue Service knows what this moon-kissed stripling with the bedroom in his voice nets from the records which are being passionately clutched to millions of just-budding bosoms." By 1945, Sinatra caricatures were sharing the scene with such notable figures as Daffy Duck and Lil' Abner. Even his bow ties were a national institution. Nelson Algren, in his novel *The Man with the Golden Arm,* describes his hero, "Frankie Machine," as wearing a "Sina-

---

9. The holiday was in those years observed by Italian-Americans as their equivalent of Saint Patrick's Day (surely you've heard of "Clancy with the Laughing Face"), and the previous year's had been no less of a victory since it provided an official opportunity to celebrate the fall of Mussolini. That the Paramount appearance served to block traffic all day and occupy the services of 421 patrolmen and 20 patrolwomen did not endear Sinatra to city officials. However, the Board of Education did not complain too loudly about the mass truancy he inspired since he had already begun his public school lecture series on racial and religious tolerance. Furthermore, *paisano* Mayor Fiorello LaGuardia (in his last year in office) wasn't about to get upset, since Sinatra's campaigning for Franklin D. Roosevelt had been a much-appreciated boost for the Democratic Party.

tra"—not even a "Sinatra tie" (as in the pop song "Tabby the Cat"), just a "Sinatra"—years before that movie role would go to The Voice.

Today, a faint echo of the mountainous swooning, screaming, and gnashing of teeth perpetrated in Sinatra's name remains on transcriptions of his radio appearances (especially before Sinatra attempted to bar teenagers from his broadcasts in December 1946[10]). Now that the skinny jokes as well as the rationalizations by noted psychoanalysts explaining the bobby-soxer phenomenon have faded, the Sinatra of the '40s can reemerge as a major artist, to be appreciated not for the hysteria he inspired but for the music he created.

10. Both the *Hit Parade* and the *Songs by Sinatra* series were transcribed for rebroadcast to servicemen via the Armed Forces Radio Network (which is the only reason many of them have survived), and Sinatra pointed out that the constant screaming from the peanut gallery was a turnoff to the men in uniform. "They don't like all the noise, and I don't blame them. It sounds like a Chinese hand laundry with everybody clapping."

CHAPTER FIVE

ALL THE IN-BETWEEN YEARS, 1948–1953

No matter how low you fall, there's always an unexplored basement.

—F. SCOTT FITZGERALD

Do not mess with Mister Inbetween.

—JOHNNY MERCER

In the late fall of 1939, at about the same time that Frank Sinatra left Harry James' band for Tommy Dorsey's, the trumpeter suffered another damaging defection. Around November, Buddy Rich left Artie Shaw's orchestra to work for Dorsey, and James' drummer, Ralph Hawkins, left the trumpeter to replace Rich with Shaw. However, a very short time after Hawkins went to work for Shaw, the clarinetist stormed off the bandstand, abandoning the money-making machine it had taken him years to build up. Shaw claimed he was fed up with the dehumanizing pressures of show business and commercial music, and that he would never play again. To most observers in that late-Depression year, it seemed as if Shaw was tossing a monkey wrench in the works of the American dream: to be willing to throw away hundreds of thousands of dollars in pursuit of what was then an obscure concept called artistic integrity.

Frank Sinatra's fall-and-rise, the seeds of which can be detected as early as 1947, and which didn't completely end until early 1954, is usually discussed purely in terms of Sinatra's personal life. The singer's career downs-and-ups are generally rationalized away as being the exclusive product of his passionate yet tortuous romance with his second wife, movie star Ava Gardner. It would be naive to think that an artist as emotionally driven as Sinatra could participate in such a situation and have it not affect his work. Still, when we take the long view, the Gardner factor amounts to only one of many elements.

The major issue was that Sinatra had to wrestle with the same question of artistry versus business that vexed Shaw. Sinatra was just as much of an artistic rebel as Shaw, campaigning for class against a business that was increasingly discovering the commercial possibilities of mediocrity. Shaw's "cure" was more immediate—he was back in the saddle within a matter of weeks, while it took Sinatra nearly five years to get back to where he had been before. Yet the singer's solution was more permanent: at roughly the same time as Sinatra's "comeback," Shaw concluded that the only way to preserve his sanity was to pack up his marbles and go home for good, an irreparable loss to music.

Sinatra unknowingly took the first baby step toward disaster in September, 1947, when he rejoined *Your Hit Parade*, the excessively commercial radio series which he had left less than three years earlier. During his original stint on that show in 1943 and 1944, Sinatra had been able to stay true to himself by simultaneously doing his own series of starring shows. He did *Your Hit Parade* for the exposure and the money, but it was never a real Sinatra product—that honor went to *The Broadway Bandbox, Vimms, Songs by Sinatra*, etc. Now in 1947, when he returned to the Lucky Strike fold, the idea was that *Your Hit Parade* would take the place of his own show. For the only time in the twenty-four-year-run of the program, the *Parade* would pivot around a single star singer, who would also announce most of the tunes and do many of the commercials. It was an advertising agency's dream—the combination of the top-ten format and perhaps the most popular singer on the air. But what loused it up was an element no agent could negotiate: quality, or, rather, the lack of it.

Luckily for Sinatra, his first stretch on *Your Hit Parade* coincided with the end of the golden era of American songwriting. On a single show in May, 1944, for instance, Sinatra sang two well-known standards-to-be, Jerome Kern's "Long Ago and Far Away" and Cole Porter's "I Love You." The same episode also included two other top-drawer songs that would also remain, to a lesser degree, in the collective repertory: "I'll Be Seeing You," a 1938 number that took on new meaning at the start of World War II, and the Cuban ballad "Poinciana."

At the start of the new series in 1947 it seemed there was hope, especially since, in his first two months back on the show, *Your Hit Parade*'s second-billed singer was none other than the great Doris Day herself. In fact, their duet on "It's No Business Like Show Business" turned out better than Sinatra's solo Columbia waxing. But even though the new *Hit Parade* spotlighted Sinatra more than any other performer in the program's history, and Sinatra's own musical director, Axel Stordahl, had taken over Mark Warnow's spot as arranger-conductor, it still wasn't Sinatra's show. This was still the *Hit Parade*, and Sinatra, for all of his ideas about the deeper responsibilities of pop music, had to toe the line—the bottom line.

It's not that Sinatra didn't get to sing some first rate tunes in his second run on *Your Hit Parade* (which lasted until May 1949). "Haunted Heart," "Ballerina," "It's Magic," "Now Is the Hour," and lots of other swell songs that Sinatra never got the chance to record[1] turned up on the charts in those two years, while the older "Over the Rainbow," "Great Day," "Zing! Went the Strings of My Heart," and others occasionally tiptoed in through the backdoor.

But Sinatra should have been wary when the very first song on his very first show was "Feudin', Fussin' and a Fightin'"—not necessarily a bad song in the pea-pickin' hands of the right comic vocalist, a Judy Canova or a Cinderella G. Stump, but singularly unsuited to Sinatra. And there's the rub, bub—Sinatra could take his pick of the top ten, but was obligated to do the number one song each week, no matter what it was. And, unfortunately, in the late '40s, that number one hit was often a novelty of the most inane sort—the postwar years witnessed some of pop music's most trite and banal hits. In January 1948 Sinatra ventured as far afield from the path of the righteous as to treat us to the conceptually lean "Too Fat Polka" (done in a special-material arrangement tailored to get the most mileage out of his own absence of too-fat-ness). That spring, Sinatra watched with horror as "The Woody Woodpecker Song" flew up the charts: on the June 26 show, he can barely bring himself to introduce the vocal group's rendition—one can even hear him exclaim, "I just couldn't do it!" under the music as it starts. But on July 10, when "Woody Wookpecker" reached number one, he no longer had any choice—he *had* to do it.

In a 1948 interview with George Simon, Sinatra told the readers of

---

1. He also got to do "So in Love," from Cole Porter's *Kiss Me Kate*, on two *Hit Parade* installments from February and April of 1949. A major song superbly suited to FS that Manie Sachs, in a rare questionable move, instead assigned to Buddy Clark, Columbia's second star male singer, and which Sinatra never returned to except for a later duet reading with Keely Smith.

Metronome magazine exactly "What's Wrong with Music": "About the popular songs of the day," he began, "they're so lifeless, they're bloodless. As a singer of popular songs, I've been looking for wonderful pieces of music in the popular vein, what they call Tin Pan Alley songs. Outside of show tunes, you can't find a thing." He continued, "The music business . . . must give people things that move them emotionally and make them laugh, too. But we're not doing it, and there's something wrong someplace."

"Nature Boy," which Sinatra performed frequently on *YHP* in the spring and summer of 1948, illustrates Sinatra's point. The top song of the year (along with "Buttons and Bows") and forever associated with Nat King Cole, "Nature Boy" was released by Capitol out of desperation caused by the AFM ban of that year; they had nothing else in the can by the King Cole Trio with strings to go on the B-side of the promising "Lost April." "Nature Boy" then became what every record man dreams of: a freak hit, released at a time when all the other labels' hands were tied. Thanks to the 1948 ban, rival companies could only trot out meager a capella covers, by Dick Haymes, Sarah Vaughan, and others (only Perry Como demurred).

Sinatra made his own musicianless stab at "Nature Boy"—it was his sole commercial recording during the eleven-month ban. But it had been the startlingly fresh combination of Nat Cole's voice with strings that made the original disc a hit. Sinatra's own singing is tender and sympathetic, but the stark choir backing gives the record as much warmth as a Gregorian chant. (On *Your Hit Parade*, Sinatra performed the song with both the choir treatment and conventional orchestral accompaniment.) And even as the heavyweight crooners battled one another to steal Cole's thunder, its composer, Eden Ahbez, and a publisher of Yiddish music were crying plagiarism as they sparred over the publishing royalties. It struck no one as ironic that a song with a message of love and peace should come to symbolize how cutthroat the pop music business was becoming.

In the *Metronome* interview, Sinatra went on to complain about how most songwriters had to "prostitute" their talents if they wanted "to make a buck" because "not enough publishers are buying the better kind of music," and then he detailed how record companies were also in on this unending search for the fastest buck possible. Even though quality songs are available, he pointed out that both publishers ("usually fly-by-night") and record men would "rather take an easy song, one that's a novelty. It's a very short shot that will click right away, but that doesn't last over the years. Most publishers don't think that far ahead."

All of which helped to put Sinatra on the short end of the stick. At this time, in the words of Al Capp (as well as Betty Comden and Adolph Green in *On the Town*), his troubles were multiplying like shmoos. Much of the trouble was strictly due to spin-doctoring. Sinatra's extra-musical image had been solidified in 1945, the year of his USO tour and of his first spectacularly successful film, *Anchors Aweigh*. He could never have made a hit with G.I.s—had he come on like Charlie Holly-wood, a smooth and polished singing star who was irresistible to women and knew it. As Phil "Glad to See You" Silvers, Sinatra's partner in the tour, later said, "The soldiers had been underdogs so long, I figured they would love [Sinatra as an] underdog." The singer had already begun taking that tack on his radio shows, developing it steadily, particularly on the *Old Gold* series.

Where the initial impulse might have been to present Sinatra as a romantic Romeo, Sinatra instead endeared himself to greater numbers by incessantly undercutting that image. He constantly cracked jokes at his own expense, usually involving his weight and his alleged puniness. On one show, to select a single example, Sinatra purports to recall exactly what his father said when he first saw him as an infant in his incu-bator, and then goes into "There's No You."

Yet Sinatra could hardly convince anyone of his frailness after he flat-tened columnist Lee Mortimer on April 8, 1947, the first and by far the most damaging of his altercations with the fourth estate. Let it be said that virtually everyone wanted to punch Lee Mortimer, most of all his fellow newspapermen. Ed Sullivan almost never said a bad word about anybody (even when he himself was later engaged in a feud with Sina-tra), referred to his fellow columnist as a specialist in "mean needle work." "I've been accused constantly of getting in scuffles with people in the press," Sinatra claimed in 1977, "and I actually only had one physical bout in my lifetime with anybody in the press. That was Lee Mortimer, and if he [were] alive today, I'd knock him down again."

Before this incident, the papers had been inclined to go along with whatever setup the newsworthy crooner and his ingenious press agent, George Evans, had dreamed up (with the exception of the Hearst papers and other Republican-slanted journals which took exception to Sinatra's support of Roosevelt). But after this upset with one of their profession— even the unmourned Mortimer—the reporters took off their kid gloves. From that point on, Sinatra would always be viewed with suspicion. This was hardly reconcilable with the Sinatra of radio and pictures who had said in one show, regarding his role in *Anchors Aweigh*, "I felt pretty much at home as Clarence Doolittle, the shy little violet from Brooklyn."

But Clarence Doolittle wouldn't belt Lee Mortimer, nor would Clarence Doolittle be seen with Lucky Luciano. Again and again, those out-of-the-know will insist that mob support made Sinatra's career. Yet one is finally left with the impression that Sinatra's persistence in being photographed with hoodlums like Sam Giancana and Spiro Agnew has only held him back. Clarence Doolittle would never leave his wife and three kiddies and thereby invoke the unspeakable D-word, a move that undoubtedly turned the public off him more than anything else. "People forget the climate in those days when Frank started running around with Ava," as Mitch Miller pointed out. "Ingrid Bergman had a child out of wedlock. Hell, everybody in Hollywood has a child out of wedlock today, and they brag about it. In those days she was banned from movies in America. When Sinatra left his wife, the priests told the kids, 'Don't buy his records.'"

Nor was Clarence Doolittle the two-fisted, high-living, skirt-chasing swinger that it was becoming clearer and clearer Sinatra was. The "hat" years differ from the late "skinny" years in that Sinatra had yet to learn how to turn the high-rolling, ring-a-ding-ding image to his advantage.

Not all of Sinatra's departures from "character" were negative. George Evans, who rates as at least a co-creator of the Doolittle image, threatened to provoke controversy—in a most un-Doolittle-like fashion—by encouraging Sinatra to push his liberal political agenda. To the dismay of the predominantly right-wing media, Sinatra actively campaigned for the cause of tolerance to high school assemblies and radio audience alike (and Doolittle-esque spiels such as "Get the big box of tolerance, it comes in the red, white, and blue package" did little to soften the impact). Sinatra, who went as far as to have a letter published in *The New Republic,* was even branded a communist by Senator Allen Tinney, whose brand of red-baiting paved the way for Senator Joseph McCarthy.

Yet Sinatra continued to try to pass himself off as Clarence Doolittle, and it's a credit to his acting talents that he could make the character seem so believable as late as 1949's *On the Town,* especially after the tepid *Take Me Out to the Ball Game.* The Sinatra persona had to become more in sync with the Sinatra of the newspapers because the public just wasn't buying it anymore—literally.

On the Town constituted his farewell to MGM.[2] Studio boss Louis B. Mayer was friendly enough with Sinatra to make a public appearance on

2. His adios to MGM may actually be "Farewell Amanda," which Cole Porter wrote and Sinatra recorded for *Adam's Rib,* possibly done after *On the Town,* although only a few seconds of Sinatra's vocal can be heard in the film.

Songs by Sinatra on October 8, 1946, yet Sinatra was fired by Mayer a season or two prior to the end of Mayer's own career at MGM. As Sinatra has told the story in many interviews, it's one of those Hollywood morality plays that's so wacky it has to be true. Sinatra remembers that he was frequently summoned to Mayer's office for father-son-style chats in which the legendary mogul would ramble on with rhetorical questions along the lines of "Why does Katharine Hepburn have to be seen in public with that goddamned communist Henry Wallace?"

Then one day while Sinatra and a number of other contract players were eating at the MGM commisary, one unnamed soul happened to mention that old man Mayer was in an all-body cast because of a riding accident. It seems he fell off his horse. Up pipes Sinatra: "Nah, he fell off Ginny Simms," referring to the latest of Mr. Mayer's liaisons. The rest of the table was shocked that he had the effrontery to actually utter such a crack while on the Metro lot. Sure enough, Sinatra was soon summoned once again to LBM's office, and was there handed his walking papers.

But, Sinatra has acknowledged, he had seen it coming. The success of *Anchors,* among many other honors, allowed him to topple Van Johnson as *Modern Screen* magazine's most popular film personality for 1946, but not one of his post-*Anchors* efforts displayed the same box-office magic. *Till the Clouds Roll By* afforded him a guest shot, and *It Happened in Brooklyn* is today a sleeper favorite among Sinatraphiles only. Then came a parade of the pathetic, starting with the truly terrible *The Miracle of the Bells* (a loan to RKO), the at-least-laughably-lame *Kissing Bandit,* and the merely meager *Take Me Out to the Ball Game.* In fact, it's surprising that he was able to leave the studio on such a high note with *On the Town; Ball Game,* it would have seemed, had killed the idea of teaming Frank Sinatra and Gene Kelly.

Some of the nastier stuff that you can read about Sinatra goes into lurid detail on the subject of his flagrant nose-thumbing at Hollywood, his refusal to show up on time or at all, his resistance to multiple takes, and his general failure to take movie-making seriously, which runs diametrically counter to his hyper-professional approach toward making music. In that respect, he was the opposite of Crosby, who did his best work, especially as a singer, on the soundstages and became increasingly casual about his recordings. Once Sinatra had conquered picturedom with *Anchors Aweigh,* he doesn't seem to have given a damn about his films. He wasn't even willing to use his records to plug his pictures, recording only one song from *Ball Game* and none of the score to *On the Town.* Yet all he contributed to music meant little at the box office, though, with Crosby and Doris Day, he was one of the few great singers (from the jazz and band world) to make it as a leading player.

As he tumbled from the priciest lot in Hollywood, making only two pictures from 1950 to 1952 (and those for the comparatively underfinanced studios of RKO and Universal), theater attendance for his live shows similarly tumbled, and he was fast being categorized as a B-level radio performer. He left *Your Hit Parade* for another program sponsored by the Lucky Strike people, *Light Up Time*, which began in September 1949. The show costarred Metropolitan Opera star Dorothy Kirsten, filling a function originated by Jane Powell, a semi-regular in the final months of *Songs by Sinatra*.

Light Up Time appropriated both the time slot and the format of Lucky Strike's competitor, the *Chesterfield Supper Club*; both were on for fifteen minutes every weeknight at seven. Due to the increased demand for material, Axel Stordahl no longer had time to conduct for Sinatra on the new program. While Stordahl scrambled to keep up with the demand for new arrangements, Jeff Alexander, previously known as a choral director (on Sinatra's "Nature Boy" and elsewhere), came in to conduct. After a two-year hiatus, Sinatra resumed doing movie theater tours in December 1949, occasionally using trumpet great Ziggy Elman as his conductor. Elman also frequently stood on the podium in early 1950 on the *Light Up Time* series. Toward the end of the series, in March 1950, Sinatra returned to New York for a nightclub engagement while Alexander remained in Hollywood to complete a film assignment. Lucky Strike then passed the baton to Skitch Henderson, who had played piano on the 1942 Bluebird session and had accompanied Sinatra at the Waldorf in 1945 and on several occasions since. One of the last big-talent, high-profile radio programs, *Light Up Time*, Henderson explained, marked "the end of so-called rich radio."

The main problem with *Light Up Time* was that the show ran only fifteen minutes, just time to squeeze in two solo spots for the star, one solo by Kirsten, and a duet in between the commercials. "We'd do thirty-two bars with the orchestra, which was a minute-thirty, and then I would do something pianistically, which we could maybe squeeze to a minute-fifteen, and then we'd do a closer with the orchestra," Henderson has said. "So we could do a medley of three tunes—to get the song pluggers off our backs—sometimes in as little as four minutes or four minutes and twenty seconds. What everybody forgets, and I can't even believe it when I hear the tapes, is that we had a two-minute commercial to open the show. Two minutes! Unbelievable. Extolling the virtues of Lucky Strike. Oh, it was a grind."

In an established radio tradition, *Light Up Time* opened nightly with a bright fast number, almost always orchestrated by George Siravo. "It was like one chorus and a half with a couple of bars intro," said Siravo. "I think I even got [the intro] down to a bar and a half because there was a three-beat pickup vocally. Wow! That's like doing the hundred-yard dash in about a second and a half."

Sinatra actually did the 108-bar "Begin the Beguine" on a March 1950 show and it took up practically the entire program. On the March 13 episode, Sinatra and Kirsten do "A Fine Romance," and then Sinatra announces, "We'll buy a minute from NBC and do another chorus!" Apart from the time factor, Lucky Strike's budget did not allow for the use of a full string section every night, so the fiddles became a luxury that Sinatra was allowed to indulge in only occasionally. Between the lack of strings and the rush, the show lost the deep-focus sound, the extended, sensual romanticism that had distinguished the Sinatra-Stordahl collaboration.

Besides which, Sinatra was understandably depressed by the turn of his personal and professional fortunes. Although it would be difficult for him to sing badly, it became harder for him to live up to his own high standards. On the December 27 show, Sinatra misses the first note on "A Man Wrote a Song" and has to start it again, and then completely fluffs the lyric on "You're the Cream in My Coffee." Henderson felt that Sinatra's heart was only really in it maybe two nights out of the five a week the show was on. "That was the beginning of Frank's problems," he said. "I think he was concerned, as anybody would be, with his life and what was going to happen. And the publicity was so negative at that time. You know, the media was pounding him."

Sinatra's personal and professional problems were leading to the tandem breakups of two relationships, his musical marriage to Axel Stordahl and his relationship with the mother of his children. Much of the blame for the downward spin in Sinatra's recording career has traditionally been pinned to Mitch Miller, by Blue Eyes himself and most of his biographers. But Sinatra's spiritual recession became apparent on his recordings long before Mitch Miller entered the picture and the infamous disasters of the Miller era. "The Hucklebuck," for instance, as adapted by Andy Gibson (who arranged for Sinatra with Harry James) from Charlie Parker's "Now's the Time," and arranged by George Siravo, wasn't necessarily a bad record. It was one with almost no Sinatra presence, however; in much the same way that Gibson dictated the melody to Siravo via Ma Bell, Sinatra could have phoned in his meager vocal part.

Despite the armistice between the musicians' union and the record companies in December 1948, 1949 was a strange year for Sinatra records. The first post-ban item is a piece of country-western nonsense called "Sunflower," recorded with an unidentified hillbilly band (the song was later appropriated for the title song of *Hello, Dolly*, recorded by Sinatra in 1964). Sinatra would make virtually no major classic sides in this season, very little from which was ever reissued until forty-five years later in the *Complete Columbia* package.

Sinatra's immediate post-ban recordings were notable only for their lack of distinction. The first new session with Stordahl's orchestra began with a European import called "Comme Çi, Comme Ça," whose title characterized the blasé recordings Sinatra churned out that season. Even when given strong material, he never quite flies. In 1947, three of Sinatra's best 78s had been pairings from three new musicals, yet in 1949, Sinatra can't even get off the ground with the two big numbers from *South Pacific*. Of the two, "Some Enchanted Evening" is merely disappointing, particularly in light of what Sinatra had led us to expect with his earlier, ace renditions of Rodgers and Hammerstein's "You'll Never Walk Alone" and "Soliloquy." In any other year Sinatra would have been able to interpret "Bali Ha'i" as the anthem of hope and distant dreams that it is. Unfortunately, his sole recording of the piece finds him all but choking on poi and steel guitars.

Still, even this comparatively weak year had a couple of worthwhile sessions: a further show-tunes pairing, this one from *Miss Liberty*, yielded a yummy, "bubbly" (in Sinatra's phrase) duet with Doris Day. On "Let's Take an Old Fashioned Walk," his partner's sunshiny attitude helps reawaken his own, while the Disneyesque "The Old Master Painter" is also cute and peppy. One of the great Victor Young's finest works, "Mad About You," is the first new Sinatra-Stordahl masterpiece since 1947, replete with sweeping strings, soaring horns, and one of those precious voice-fading-into-ensemble endings.

Stordahl had nothing to do, however, with Sinatra's best all-around session of the year. On one July day in New York, the singer turned out three classics, all off the familiar ballad path but with excellently handled orchestrations by George Siravo and Sy Oliver which he makes the most of. On "It All Depends on You," Sinatra fairly brims with excitement, leaping into the fray after one of Siravo's catchy introductory vamps. After a sixteen-bar instrumental break (originally written for a full chorus, half of which had to be deleted on the spot for space), Sinatra reenters, digging engagingly against the grain of the ground beat, jazzily expanding his contractions, and adding extra notes ("I can be very lonely . . .").

When he shoots up to a high climax on "it all dee-*pends* . . ." in the last line, it has the effect of a man racing up a mountain.

"'Bye Bye Baby' was written by Jule Styne; he's just a wonderful songwriter," Sinatra said in a contemporary interview. Not only is Sinatra himself swinging on this movingly rhythmical show tune (from *Gentleman Prefer Blondes*, which would open that December), but for once even the choral group—including Lillian Oliver (Mrs. Sy)—gets groovy. During the session, Sinatra, who was, as always, more responsible for both the sound and the performances of the others involved than any producer, coached the backup singers (replaced on one radio reading with a Ziggy Elman trumpet solo) in catching the rhythmic cadences of the tune.

In addition to "Mad About You," Sinatra and Stordahl turned out one other classic ballad in their best tradition in the fall of 1949, "(On the Island of) Stromboli." The song itself, at the time of the recording, seemed perfectly innocent, being Sinatra's second partially Italian record and simply the theme from a forthcoming Ingrid Bergman movie. A few months later the title seemed incredibly nervy, as both the film and the actual island became synonymous with one of the most notorious scandals in Hollywood history when Bergman left her husband and family for director Roberto Rossellini. Soon Sinatra's record became doubly infamous when he in turn became entangled in a home-wrecking relationship of the same career-breaking consequences.

Even without those extramusical attachments, however, "Stromboli" is a devastatingly powerful performance. Being faux Italian, it should have been completely bogus, yet it's far more moving than the three genuinely Neapolitan pop tunes Sinatra waxed ("I Have but One Heart" and the more overdone "Sorrento" and "Luna Rossa"). Sinatra and Stordahl, in effect, transform "Stromboli" into what "Bali Ha'i" should have been: the island of forbidden dreams. In this case the ornaments of local color, the mandolins, zithers, and concertinas, help both singer and arranger pull it off. Stordahl's standard closing devices—fades, dissolves, and last-second modulations—have never been so captivating.

If Sinatra found himself in a slump in 1949, he was by no means alone; all of Columbia Records seemed to be slipping. Sinatra was in a rut, Buddy Clark (their biggest crooner after The Voice) had been killed in a plane crash, and Dinah Shore left the label for Victor. Even worse, Shore was part of a general exodus to RCA that also included producer and arranger Mitchell Ayers and, the most serious loss of all, Manie Sachs.

In January 1950, when Sachs left, the label's prospects were slim, but by the end of 1951 Columbia had been reborn yet again and was now by far the most profitable label in the business, dominating nearly every top ten list in *Billboard*. The transformation was due entirely to one man: Mitch Miller. "He was really the first 'record producer,'" in the modern sense of the term, said Tony Bennett. "After Mitch made it, a million other guys tried to copy Mitch's cigar and his beard."

Although Miller was later cast as the number-one villain in the Sinatra saga, in actuality he's too complicated a character to fit into any simple stereotypical role. Described by *The New York Times* as "the bearded connoisseur of the echo chamber," William Mitchell Miller was a prophet, producer, factotum, instrumentalist, conductor, A&R man, guru, TV star, mover and shaker, patriarch, businessman, and professorial intellectual who had an uncanny knack for pleasing the man on the street. Miller had so many facets that his soul must resemble one of his productions; only by multitracking could he superimpose all these identities on top of each other. How else could he collaborate so successfully with Sinatra, Charlie Parker, Igor Stravinsky, and David Seville of *Alvin & the Chipmunks* fame? For better or worse, Mitch Miller had much to do with the genesis of modern popular music. Said Bennett: "He was the one who showed everybody how to be a producer."

Miller established the primacy of the producer, proving that even more than the artist, the accompaniment, or the material, it was the responsibility of the man in the recording booth whether a record flew or flopped. Miller also conceived of the idea of the pop record "sound" per se: not so much an arrangement or a tune, but an aural texture (usually replete with extramusical gimmicks) that could be created in the studio and then replicated in live performance, instead of the other way around. Miller was hardly a rock 'n' roller, yet without these ideas there could never have been rock 'n' roll. "Mule Train," Miller's first major hit (for Frankie Laine) and the foundation of his career, set the pattern for virtually the entire first decade of rock. The similarities between it and, say, "Leader of the Pack," need hardly be outlined here.

Born on July 4, 1911, in Rochester, New York, Miller was a prodigy who could play Bach's two-part inventions on piano at age six. After he switched to oboe, his facility on the instrument made him, at fifteen, by far the youngest member of the Rochester School Symphony Orchestra, the Syracuse Symphony, the Eastman Symphony, and the Rochester Philharmonic. Granted a scholarship to the prestigious Eastman School of Music, Miller received his diploma in 1932. At his graduation recital, Miller performed an early work written for the occasion by Alec Wilder, his fellow student and lifelong alter ego.

Although you might never know it from his work, Miller, no less than

Wilder, claims to keenly appreciate the best jazz and pop music of the '30s and '40s. "I listened to everything. Oh, God, yes! During the Eastman days, you could get three records [for] a dollar, Blue Deccas and Bluebirds," he said recently. "Hell, I was listening to Louis Armstrong, Jimmie Lunceford, Jan Savitt, and the Hi-Hatters. I was interested in all kinds of music. I went to hear all the bands, starting with Benny Goodman, then Artie Shaw and Charlie Barnet, because each of these guys had something to say."

After arriving in New York—where, he later said, there were "never enough oboists to go around"—Miller had his pick of the most coveted oboe gigs in town. These included Andre Kostelanetz's top-rated radio orchestra, the pit band for Gershwin's *Porgy and Bess,* as well as a touring symphony that accompanied Gershwin himself; from 1936 to 1947, Miller served as oboist with the CBS house symphony orchestra. In these years Miller continued to consort with the major philosophers of jazz and pop music, most notably Wilder and John Hammond (who had met Miller through a mutual friend, Alexander Schneider of the Budapest String Quartet). Miller also played under guest conductor Stravinsky, who later described Miller as having impressed him "by his finest musicianship combined with technical perfection together with the rare human qualities of sensibility, dignity, and modesty—uncommon phenomena in our tumultuous time."

Miller and Wilder were closest at this time, Miller acting as Wilder's first of many better-connected boosters, introducing him to A&R executives, musicians, and singers wherever he could. Although Sinatra and John Hammond never had any use for each other, Sinatra soon became part of this circle of musical intelligentsia. Wilder, who with the help of James Maher later wrote the serious musicalogical study *American Popular Songs,* would help support Sinatra philosophically in his advocacy of the works of Porter, Gershwin, Arlen, and others, as music that would last even as would Schubert and Liszt. Sinatra called Wilder "The Professor," and while his private nickname for Sinatra was "Thin Lou," Wilder officially referred to Sinatra as "The Master."

The Sinatra-Wilder-Miller discussions left the realm of the theoretical and became concrete over several sessions in November and December 1945, resulting in two groups of work, one vocal and the other instrumental. In November the threesome persuaded Sachs to invest his star-power in two "experimental" songs so far removed from the *Hit Parade* that Columbia didn't want to release them at all.

"Alec never pushed himself," said Miller. "I would push him. Other people would push him. But Alec had a lot of feel for the offbeat. Willard Robison wrote this song ['Old School Teacher'], and it was unusual. So

Alec brought it [along with his own 'Just An Old Stone House'] to Frank and said, 'This is your type of song,' even though the subject matter was certainly different from what Sinatra had done. So Alec did the arrangement, and I did the conducting."

Both tunes have a feeling of rural archaicness, with the word "old" in their titles, which was typical for Robison, the godfather of rustic American *lieder*, but unusual for Wilder, resulting in one of his most beautiful songs. Although the two are similar enough in theme and style to make a perfect coupling, "Old School Teacher" came out only uncommercially as a V-Disc. The other piece, Wilder's own "Just an Old Stone House," lay totally unissued until five years later when Miller, who by that time had taken over Manie Sachs's job, put it on the back of the more likely hit "American Beauty Rose." Apart from several star collaborations, these two lovely and introspective, if somewhat meandering and arid airs, comprise Sinatra's only orchestral date without Stordahl from the beginning of the post-Dorsey period until 1949.

Around this time, Sinatra heard a number of Wilder's classical compositions and said, "They should be recorded." With Miller's encouragement, Sinatra began pulling Manie Sachs's coattails. Sachs could rarely say no to Sinatra, but in this case he declined. "He said, 'We can't because we don't have enough shellac to even press the stuff from our own artists,'" said Miller. "And Sinatra gave us the bad news. So I came up with an idea. I said, 'Why don't *you* conduct them? Then he can't refuse you—if your name is on it.' That's because Sinatra was so hot then. And Frank agreed, although he had never conducted. You can't fake conducting. I'm not being a bit bitter, saying Sinatra's no conductor. How can you conduct if you can't read a score, if you don't know what to tell the musicians? But, on the other hand, he had a feel for music.

"So I would prepare the orchestra. Sinatra was then at the Waldorf, and he would finish at one in the morning. All the top musicians were there with us at the old Liederkranz Hall on Fifty-eighth Street. And I rehearsed all the stuff and got it ready, and Frank came in and he waved the stick. And he didn't get in the way." Wilder later related to Maher how Sinatra stared down a roomful of the hardest-boiled studio musicians in that hardest of hard towns and told them, "Listen, I don't know the first thing about conducting, but I know this music and I love it, and if you'll work with me, I think we can get it down." Said Maher, "They would have given hell to any less-than-astute so-called leader who tried to pass himself off as a conductor."

Milt Bernhart remembered the effect that the album had on many young musicians. In 1946, while the Stan Kenton band was doing six or seven shows at the Paramount, "I bought myself a record player, and I'd buy records. And in those days there weren't that many records to buy that were really going to be interesting to a musician. One of [the few] was *Frank Sinatra Conducts the Music of Alec Wilder.* I bought that album and I wore it out. But I played it backstage in a dark room, sleeping between shows. To me, that music was gorgeous."

Had "Old School Teacher" and "Old Stone House" been issued in 1945, they would have probably marked the first pop record with Miller's credit. Miller began making the transition from musician to businessman in 1947 when John Hammond became vice president of Keynote Records and brought in Miller initially to head the company's classical division. By the time Mercury bought out Keynote, Miller had taken over the company's popular recordings.

In 1947 and 1948, Miller filled in several times as conductor on *Your Hit Parade* with Sinatra, on occasions when Sinatra would be in New York and Stordahl and the rest of the company remained in California. Still New York's key studio oboist as late as 1950, he appeared as a sideman in a modern jazz context with Charlie Parker, Buddy Rich, and Ray Brown on Mercury's *Bird with Strings* album. He also continued to serve as Sinatra's and Stordahl's favorite oboe man, particularly on their high-minded chamber group dates.

Miller and George Siravo remembered one date, November 5, 1947, especially keenly. At the end of one song (they don't agree which), Sinatra felt he had laid down a perfect take. The engineer reluctantly informed him that unfortunately it was several seconds too long to fit on a conventional ten-inch 78. Sinatra and Stordahl felt that either of their alternatives—editing the arrangement or picking up the tempo—would, Sinatra said, "kill the feeling." While they were deliberating, a gruff, cigar-toned voice spoke up from the back of the ensemble: "We could fit the whole thing in over at Mercury!"

Sinatra looked around and spied the goateed face of Mitch Miller, who was at that time running pop A&R at the fledgling Mercury Records label where they apparently had more up-to-date cutting equipment. Now angry, Sinatra charged into Manie Sachs's office. "When Frank told the story to Manie," Siravo recalled, "he was really hotter than a pistol. 'You mean a big fuckin' outfit like Columbia can't do what a nickel record company like Mercury can do? I don't believe this shit.'" Sinatra ultimately stormed off, leaving it to Sachs and the engineers to contend with the problem of fitting the track on the disc. Perhaps this is what inspired Columbia to invent microgroove.

"I don't think Manie had a nerve in his body. I had never once seen him get angry," Siravo continued, "but this time he was pissed! 'That fuckin' Mitch Miller! You take my word! I take an oath, this guy will never again set foot at Columbia Records as long I'm here!'" "Manie tried to have me banned from doing any more sessions," Miller confirmed, with no hard feelings, "but arrangers would come in and say, 'I want Mitch,' so he couldn't do that." Siravo, not missing the irony of Sachs trying to bar the man who would eventually succeed him, concluded that no one would ever have thought at that time that, as he put it, "Mitch would go on to become the great white father."

"Mule Train" proved a career-establishing coup for both belter Frankie Laine and producer-promoter Miller, who smuggled it from under the noses of potential competitors and moved a million units in five weeks. When Goddard Lieberson, another fellow Eastmanite, took over all matters musical at Columbia, he persuaded Miller and Laine to switch rather than fight. Lieberson appointed Miller head of CBS's pop singles operation in February 1950, replacing Sachs (while George Avakian continued to run the long-playing pop department).

Miller instantly became the most powerful man in the music business and by far the most successful record producer up to that time. He achieved this through his combination of marketing acumen and musical knowledge in perfecting the lowest common denominator mentality in pop music. "What makes you want to dig in your pocket and buy a record? It's got to be something you want to play over and over again," said Miller. "You look for qualities to make somebody buy it. I was trying to put stuff in records that would tighten the picture for the listener."

Pop music before Miller was largely swing-band based. Sinatra, who used a more swinging sound both earlier and later than his Stordahl decade, was a rebel at the time in that his textures were primarily string-oriented. Though Miller continued to use singers with big-band backgrounds (Rosemary Clooney and Guy Mitchell) or orientations (Tony Bennett), he eschewed Goodman-Ellington-Lombardo–style brass, reeds, and rhythm. He put harpsichords behind Clooney, bagpipes with Dinah Shore (as she finished out her CBS contract), and French horns foursquare around Guy Mitchell.

Miller completely revolutionized the concept of what record making was, using the latest techniques made possible mainly by the invention of recording tape: multitracking, reverberation, and overdubbing. "I think Mitch Miller set the business back thirty or forty years," opined master orchestrator Johnny Mandel, "which is inexcusable for somebody who was as great a musician as he was. He was a marvelous oboe player. But then he started hiring all these bad singers, people such as Guy Mitchell and Champ Butler—Rosemary Clooney is an exception. The singers would fuck up. And the musicians loved it because they were getting all this great overtime. Finally, the labels looked at the budgets and asked the tape companies, 'Hey, isn't there some way we can do the background, let the band go, and have the singer on his own track?'"

"Mitch had a very good commercial sense and a sophisticated sense, too," recalled Stan Freeman, keyboard soloist on two of Miller's best-remembered sides ("You're the One" by Sinatra and "Come on-a My House" by Rosemary Clooney). "For instance, Cy Walter and I did two albums with Lee Wiley. I always loved Lee, she was one of my favorites, but Lee was never a big commercial success. But Mitch said we owe it to the people to record her, knowing full well it was not going to be a big seller."

Miller felt an especially keen push to make money with Sinatra product. "Sinatra had to pay the IRS a big fee for back taxes," Miller elucidated. "He had gone to Manie Sachs, who got Columbia to lend him the money as an advance against royalties. Then Manie left to go to RCA. Now, I get to Columbia. Ted Wallerstein, who was then president, says, 'Mitch, we've got to make this money back.'"

The Miller-Sinatra relationship began with the best of all possible intentions and considerable optimism from both men. Wallerstein had initially instructed Miller to move Sinatra product by "getting him the best things." The producer recalled, "Of course! That was my whole point. So people don't understand that. I made 'Azure Te,' 'Why Try to Change Me Now,' all marvelous, fabulous records! But you couldn't give them away *at that time.*"

Thus, Sinatra and Miller, who had campaigned together together for the cause of art music and Alec Wilder in 1945, became unlikely bedfellows in 1950. The new Sinatra-Miller collaboration started very fruitfully indeed with "American Beauty Rose," from their very first session together in March. Up to 1950, Miller explains, "Frank made very few rhythm songs. 'Saturday Night' was one and another one was 'It All Depends on You' and 'Five Minutes More.' I thought he should do more." When Miller heard Redd Evans' "American Beauty Rose," he suggested it to Sinatra as a Bobcats-style follow-up to "Five Minutes More," and even subtitled the song "Dixieland with a Beat" on the original 78.

Sinatra and arranger Norman Leyden, who had won his wings with Glenn Miller's AAF Orchestra (and Tex Beneke's no less marvelous postwar Miller band), bounce through this irresistible piece which

seems to be in both 2/4 and 4/4 simultaneously. Another former Miller-
ite, multi-reedman Jimmy Abato, blows clarinet over the top of the het-
erophonic ensemble, along with ex-bandleaders Billy Butterfield and
Will Bradley. Best of all, Sinatra joyously milks a libretto that funnily and
punnily compares girls to flowers. "American Beauty Rose" charted, but
hardly high enough to reverse the trend of steadily worsening sales for
Sinatra discs that had already started.

With "American Beauty Rose" now a minor chart success, Sinatra and
Miller elected to do an extended project predicated upon "rhythm
songs." "When I [started] running Columbia," Miller elaborated, "I
thought Frank should do a whole album of rhythm songs. We got Siravo
to do the arrangements and conduct." The feeling among most of Sinatra's friends and observers was best expressed by Milt Bernhart: "He
never really was given a chance to swing, so he never really took himself
seriously in that area, and at Columbia Records, they didn't, either."
Only about ten percent of Sinatra's Columbia output had been uptempo
material, although he featured faster tunes much more often on the
radio.

The Voice's nonballad material in the years before 1950 reveals how
Sinatra and Nat King Cole experienced a love-hate relationship with
each other's idioms. Cole's transition from pianist and combo leader to
pop singer with orchestra reflected a transition from his own idiom to
that perfected by Sinatra. At the same time, while Sinatra rose to fame as
a balladeer, his attempts to add a swinging dimension to his vocabulary
encompassed an attempt at working through the King Cole Trio style. As
Cole evolved into a pop singer, he learned a lot about how to tell a story
songwise from Sinatra. When Sinatra invaded Cole's kingdom, he still
was his own man vocally, but everything else about his early combo discs
is very much in the Cole Trio format: the bouncy, medium-uptempos,
the instrumental texture (usually piano, bass, and guitar), and the
delightfully ephemeral material. He recorded with four groups in this
fashion between 1946 and 1949: Alvy West and his Little Band, the Page
Cavanaugh Trio (with whom he also worked in person), the Phil Moore
Four, and the Tony Mottola Trio. With the exception of the last (Mottola's
unit consisted of three of Sinatra's regular studio sidemen), all were
working groups that Sinatra had heard in clubs.

The results were generally charming if not first-tier Sinatra. On the
one hand, these sides might have made more of a long-term impact had
he sung the same kind of high-class show tunes he was recording concurrently with Axel Stordahl (almost none of these tracks, for instance,
were reissued in the LP era). "I don't know who picked the songs," plec-

tarist Tony Mottola said. "I'm sure Frank didn't pick them all. You think, why would they have him sing a dumb song like 'My Cousin Louella'?" With a few exceptions the songs selected are indeed insignificant, to say the least, for example "It All Came True" (done with Alvy West's very bar-mitzvahy group) and "You Can Take My Word for It Baby" (written by Dinah Shore aide Ticker Freeman).

On the other hand, most of the charm that these records have may stem from the trivial nature of the tunes. George Avakian, who supervised the Cavanaugh date, feels that Sinatra sounds so wonderfully loose precisely because the songs didn't mean anything to him. He's marvelously off-the-cuff, particularly on the older "S'posin'" and "We Just Couldn't Say Goodbye" and shows he understands what to do with a Louis Jordan–King Cole–style punchline-oriented novelty like Eddy Arnold's "That's How Much I Love You."

The four final selections in the series, from December 1948 and January 1949, are especially Coleish, owing to pianist Phil Moore's reliance on "Royal" block chords (a device popularized by Cole and then George Shearing which Moore claimed to have invented). Guitarist Bob Bain claimed that the foursome, which actually included five men, among them a clarinetist (Marshall Royal) and a drummer (Lee Young), "never really sounded like the King Cole Trio because Phil wasn't a real jazz soloist like Nat. He was more of a 'comp' player, and he would just kind of tinkle around. He let Marshall play all the solos. The drums gave us a different feel in the rhythm; it was more like a Basie thing." Still, no one ever came closer to stealing the Cole Trio's thunder than Sinatra and the Moore foursome do on "If You Stub Your Toe on the Moon." "Why Can't You Behave" (from *Kiss Me Kate*), "Kisses and Tears" (from *Double Dynamite*), and in particular "Bop! Goes My Heart" (on which Sinatra hits, with difficulty, a flatted fifth) are no less charming.

Appropriately, when Sinatra and Mitch Miller decided to do an entire album of uptempo dance numbers, which eventually became *Sing and Dance with Frank Sinatra* (1950), George Siravo was the choice for the role of arranger-conductor. As Sinatra said in a 1949 interview, "'It All Depends on You' is a George Siravo arrangement. He's one of the untapped arrangers, I feel. He's a very fresh style guy, he's just fine."

The very first Columbia Stordahl session (which produced "If You Are but a Dream") yielded one of Sinatra's best-remembered swing hits, the perennial "Saturday Night (Is the Loneliest Night of the Week)." While clarinetist Artie Baker and drummer Johnny Blowers add considerably to the proceedings, most of the credit for the success of "Saturday Night" (after Sinatra) should go to Siravo. The arranger cited the disc as an example of an arranger "taking liberties with the foundation of a song," implying that his substitute harmonic pattern improves upon composer Jule Styne's original. Siravo had gone on Sinatra's payroll just in time for the end of the 1942–44 AFM ban and the start of the Sinatra story on Columbia. He began writing for Sinatra on the *Vimms* show in the first week of October, 1944, beginning with "Sunday" (Jule Styne's first major copyright, coincidentally). By that time, Siravo was a veteran of the reed sections of (to name just a few) Harry Reser, Glenn Miller, Jan Savitt, Gene Krupa, and Will Hudson, and would continue to write pro- lifically for Krupa, Shaw, and Charlie Barnet.

Siravo was born in 1916 in Staten Island, a few blocks away from the Stordahl family, but Sinatra was the one who brought him to his team. While continuing to write for Sinatra, he also worked for other singers. Sammy Cahn gave him a big chunk of the credit for making Doris Day's disc of "It's Magic" a hit. Returning to New York from the West Coast around 1950, Siravo eventually did singles and albums under his own name for Mercury, Columbia, and Kapp. In his post-Sinatra period he wrote for Tony Bennett (most notably the *Who Can I Turn To?* album and hit single), Jimmy Roselli, Connee Boswell, Vic Damone, and many more.

Siravo's most memorable achievements on record are his orchestra- tions for Sinatra's first two ground-breaking LPs, *Sing and Dance with Frank Sinatra* for Columbia and *Songs for Young Lovers* for Capitol. He was the first arranger to help Sinatra fully explore his swinging side. He also occasionally scored ballads for young Blue Eyes, such as "I've Got a Crush on You," "Nevertheless," and "There's Something Missing," all of which have a jazz component in the person of a prominent obligatist. Unfortunately, the singer recorded only a handful of the bright bouncers that Siravo wrote for *Songs by Sinatra*. The idea of an entire album of fast songs might have made him nervous, especially since there would also be technological tension to add to his troubles—this would be Sinatra's first album in the new long-playing 33-rpm record format. What's more, there were many other pressures gnawing away on both his confidence and his voice. As reedman Sid Cooper expressed it, "Your confidence goes, your voice goes. That's what the name of the game is."

For years Sinatra had turned down offers to work at the Copacabana because he thought the show's policy of multiple shows per night would hurt his throat. As late as December 1949, the Sinatra office informed *Variety* that "he definitely ruled out the Copacabana, where the policy is three shows nightly. He declared his pipes wouldn't take the number of shows along with his radio chores." Yet on March 28, 1950, he opened at the Copa while continuing to do the nightly *Light Up Time* spot, accompanied at both venues by Skitch Henderson. Sinatra brought in so much business (as Rosemary Clooney, Joel Herron, and others have testified) that the club would not let him get out of doing a full three throat-straining sets per night.

Sinatra was fortified for the opening by a reunion with old friend Sammy Cahn, with whom he had been on the outs for about two years. Cahn recalled, "And then, when I heard he was opening at the Copa, the phone rang: 'Sam, Frank.' 'Hey, Frank.' 'Sam,' he said, 'you got a moment? I'm opening at the Copa.' I said, 'Hey, not only did I know that you're opening at the Copa, but I've been thinking, if we were speaking, what would I have written?' 'Will you come into New York?' 'Yes, I will.'" Cahn "trained," as he said, three thousand miles coast to coast and went to work with Sinatra, writing special material and boosting his morale. "And the stuff I wrote," he emphasized, "everything worked."

Sinatra at least began the engagement at full strength. As Herron recalled, the air was already rife with rumors that Sinatra was losing his voice. As soon as Sinatra burst out singing "I Am Loved," however, everybody in the joint thought, "If he can't sing anymore, then what the heck is that?" The Columbia version of the song, recorded that November, accordingly captures an ebullient Sinatra warming himself in the glow of his aura. "Sometimes you could hear that there was just kind of a raspiness or a hoarseness," said Rosemary Clooney, who, like many others who were there, feels that reports of the death of Sinatra's voice at the Copa were greatly exaggerated. "I can't tell you he sounded bad."

But as the weeks went by, Sinatra couldn't sustain that opening-night momentum. "After the opening, he got great reviews. I was so proud, I was so happy," Cahn continued. "I was going back, and I went to the Hampshire House to say good-bye, and he was in bed. I said, 'Frank, I want to talk to you. I don't know why you're doing what you're doing. All I can tell you, if I pick up that phone right now and call a music publisher and say, "Hey, got a song for Sinatra?"—they'll hang up on me. And Frank, you're the best. You are the best, but you're like a horse with three jockeys. Why are you doing this? I promise you, if you say to me, "Hey, Sam, let's go," I'll stop whatever I'm doing and just stay with you, and we'll go.' He kept saying, 'I know, I know, I know.' I said, 'I'm not being a hero. You do what you can do. You'll be sensational.' So that was the low point."

Most of the time, Henderson recalled, "the Copa was wonderful. I consider that one of the tremendous experiences of my life. And the Copa was the end-of-the-line great New York club. *Always* sold out. I mean, wall-to-wall people in that funny room and that funny, archaic line of four girls who danced. Frank did some of the most wonderful shows I have ever known him to do at the Copa." Clooney concurred: "He was doing business. I know he was moving people left, right, and center." Unfortunately, the singer was surrounded by assassins in the guise of the Copa's lackluster house band. "Nicest men in the world," said Henderson, "but they were a terrible orchestra. We always had horrible train wrecks with them."

The Copa's Jack Entratter booked Sinatra for eight weeks—one of the longest bookings in the club's history (fully twice the norm)—and the box office seemed good enough to sustain it, but Sinatra's failing health demanded canceling the last two. "I was doing three shows a night, five radio shows [the exhaustingly overcrowded *Light Up Time*] a week, benefit performances, and recording at the same time," Sinatra later told Arlene Francis. "And then I opened at the Capitol Theater [in the daytime] toward the end of the engagement. I went out to do the third show [at the Copa] at about half-past two or quarter to three in the morning, and I went for a note, and nothing came out. Not a sound came out. And I merely said to the audience, as best I could [whispering], 'Good night.'"

This was the time when Sinatra was biting off his first LP. "When we came to do these records, Frank's voice was in terrible shape," Miller recalled. "Frank would be in an [isolation] booth, and he'd sing a beautiful phrase, and then on the next phrase his voice would crack. But you couldn't edit! So you'd have to throw the whole thing out. I can say this now: I could have been kicked out of the musicians' union because tracking was not allowed. There were a lot of musicians involved. So what I did, to save the session, I just shut off his mike and got good background tracks. Didn't even tell him.

"Then after it was over, I said, 'When your voice is back . . .' We'd come in crazy hours, in a locked building, so no union representative could come in. Then when Frank came in, say, at midnight, we would play the disc. He would put earphones on and he would sing, just the way they do now.[3] And we would remix it. He did them very well after that, and the whole orchestra was perfect on it." Siravo and saxophonist Jerry Jerome remembered the session slightly differently: in their collective recollection, Sinatra wasn't present at all, although they were never informed why.

3. For obvious reasons, Columbia did not keep a record of when Sinatra's vocals were actually recorded. The orchestral parts were recorded in April, shortly before Sinatra's catastrophe at the Copa. The vocal tracks could have been recorded anytime up until October, when *Sing and Dance* was released.

Sinatra played Atlantic City on Labor Day weekend of 1950, a month or so before the *Sing and Dance* album was released, and gave an interview to local disc jockey Ben Heller in which he said, "We've got a lot of jazz things that I'd like you to watch for. . . . I made them with George Siravo some months ago, tunes like 'Lover' and 'Blue Heaven.' [They're] bright [and have] good jump tempos, both to listen to as a vocal and to dance to."

The tracking process (as it had on "Fella with an Umbrella," over-dubbed during the 1948 recording ban) apparently allowed Sinatra to feel freer and looser than he might otherwise have been in trying something so new with fifteen union musicians looking at their watches. He's gloriously loose from the start, dancing in front of Siravo's muted wah-wah brass on "Should I?" (tenor sax solo by Babe Russin), offering a snappy scat sequence in place of the last line of the second bridge, and, in long-breath Sinatra style, stretching the last "I" to make it the climactic point rather than the following two notes, "love you," which taper off. He tackles "You Do Something to Me" (baritone sax break by Ernie Caceres, tenor solo by Russin) as a major-to-minor progression, again getting jazzy in the second chorus, stretching and syncopating "you" over two notes and then doubling the time in the last line, adding extra beats: "which no one else *in the world* can do!"

Throughout, as in "Lover" (piano solo by Ken Lane, trombone solo by George Arus) where he shoots for a super-high climactic note ("mine") at the end of the second bridge, Sinatra constantly takes chances and goes for broke in reaching for notes that, according to showbiz lore, he wasn't supposed to have been able to hit with his overworked, underconfident pipes at this low point in his career. He comes close to cracking at the end of the second chorus bridge on "My Blue Heaven," but he and Miller liked the swingingly spontaneous feel of the take and left it in. Siravo and Sinatra apparently conceived of the track as homage to Sy Oliver, reprising many of the telltale mannerisms of Oliver's arrangement for Jimmy Lunceford. There's the laughing, muted brass and the tremolo-dripping alto à la Willie Smith and the reprise of the interpolated repeat of the line "a nest that nestles where the roses bloom," exactly as the vocal trio had done on the 1935 Decca Lunceford.

Appropriately for a song still associated with Louis Armstrong, who recorded it more than twenty years earlier, "When You're Smiling" marks Sinatra's most Satchel-mouthed vocal ever, as when he pulls back at the start of the second chorus. He fox-trots back and forth with the band on the bridge to "Paper Moon" (an update on a Siravo *Vimms* show chart from 1944) with an idiosyncratically charming sandpaper-soft note on the payoff word "love." The full-but-light beat Sinatra gets going on

"The Continental" (muted trumpet solo by Billy Butterfield) perfectly suspends itself between the hard-swinging and the relaxed; it not only anticipates but very nearly equals anything on the Capitol Sinatra-Siravo *Songs for Young Lovers*.

Alas, Sinatra the swinger was not to be accepted by the record-buying public until the Capitol era, after he died in *From Here to Eternity* and was reborn in "Young at Heart." Although *Sing and Dance* remains one of the best albums of Sinatra's entire career, it never made it to the *Billboard* LP charts. Columbia never rereleased the eight tracks (the eighth being "It All Depends on You," a Siravo chart from July 1949) together on a twelve-inch LP, and Sinatra himself obscured *Sing and Dance* by rerecording six of the eight on his 1959 Capitol album *Sinatra's Swingin' Session*.

But to return to 1950: there was no chance for overdubbing at the Copa. Sinatra made the front page of the May 3 issue of *Variety* when he canceled the rest of his engagement and spent the next few months in the company of Jimmy Van Heusen, resting and tending to other business in Florida, the Mediterranean, Paris, England, and home in Los Angeles. He also made his first TV appearance on May 27, on Bob Hope's *Star Spangled Revue* and, by the end of June, was ready to record again. The only question was what.

Mitch Miller, naturally, had his own answer. For *Sing and Dance*, Miller had functioned as a traditional producer in the Milt Gabler –George Avakian sense, making sure all the technical needs were seen to but letting Sinatra and Siravo make the creative decisions. The musicians themselves rarely had "problems with Mitch," bassist Herman "Trigger" Alpert recalled. "Although, working with him was never as musical as working with Frank, let's face it." But since they weren't selling any records doing it Sinatra's way, Miller felt the need to step in and take over. From this point onward, Sinatra's recorded output begins to reflect the taste of the producer as much as of the singer.

In the Sachs era, Sinatra and Stordahl operated as their own producers, as can be verified in the circulating tapes of Columbia safeties (sixteen-inch 33 1/3 backup recordings of entire sessions, from start to finish), making sure the sound of everything was exactly right and instructing the trombone section to move a fraction of an inch closer to the mike and the bassist (usually Trigger Alpert) to play a little louder in the bridge of the first chorus. When Miller took over, he assumed that he would fill that function as he did for other CBS artists. "Frank never [had to run things himself] with me," Miller insisted, "because how could he complain? The sound was [perfect with] Percy [Faith] and me [in the control booth]."

Not surprisingly, there were times when things got hairy. Blowers recalled that once Sinatra instructed Miller, "'You don't tell the band what to do from the control room. Tell me or tell Axel, and we will tell the guys.' Now, I don't guess Mitch heard him very well because Mitch would forget about that, and the next thing you know, he was telling the band to do this and do that, and this was annoying Frank no end. Then we would sit down and listen to a take.

"With Frank and Axel, you corrected mistakes. You made your own dynamics. Frank didn't want [anyone else] turning dials; leave the damn dials alone. But Mitch did. I guess it was a couple or three times or something. But then all of a sudden one day I guess Frank had as much as he could stand, and finally, quietly, he just looked at the control room and said, 'Mitch, out'—and Frank always pointed his finger—and he said, 'Don't you ever come in. Don't you *ever* come into the studio when I'm recording again.'" Blowers remembered that "Mitch never came again. Frank wouldn't permit it, because he knew what he wanted." Perhaps this incident occurred at one of the very last Columbia dates; Miller certainly seems to have been present at nearly all of Sinatra's later Columbia sessions. And long before *Sing and Dance* failed to become the salvation of The Voice's career, Miller had already proceeded along to plan B.

For the remaining two and a half years of his Columbia tenure, Sinatra's recorded output is stupefyingly schizophrenic, alternating between pinnacles such as "Hello Young Lovers" and "I'm a Fool to Want You" and nadirs such as "One Finger Melody" and "Tennessee Newsboy." As trumpeter Chris Griffin explained, "Frank was kind of mixed up at that time." Yet Miller insisted he resorted to novelties like "Mama Will Bark" only when he and Sinatra realized that people "weren't buying the great records."

Taped immediately after the original *Sing and Dance* dates, "Goodnight Irene" and "Dear Little Boy of Mine" qualify as the first Miller-style Sinatra sides. They derive from two of Miller's predilictions: his dislike of carbon-copy-style "cover" records (note that Sinatra's "Irene" sounds nothing like the Weavers' mega-hit arrangement) and his early belief in the commercial possibilities of folk and country music. While not true Sinatra, they're not bad. Though the idea of Sinatra singing Leadbelly sounds off the wall, the two sides are surprisingly palatable. Sinatra sings them straight, with the same sort of depth and purity that he would later invest in the Kingston Trio's "It Was a Very Good Year." Miller also plays it straight, for once disavowing hooks and gimmicks for a simple, effective arrangement that smoothly combines his choir with a chiming organ. "Irene," which is billed as by "Frank Sinatra with the Mitch Miller Singers," reached number 5 on the charts by early August, giving Sinatra his biggest hit of the entire "nosedive" period.

That this song scored a hit for Sinatra seems to have chagrined the singer as much as it pleased him. When Sinatra played Atlantic City that August, he brought with him his standard rhythm section of the period (Graham Forbes, piano; Matty Golizio, guitar; Frank Carroll, bass; and Johnny Blowers, drums). Blowers has recalled that the very substantial crowds ("It was a madhouse") kept demanding "Irene." "I don't think Frank liked it too much, but it was a big hit for him. I used to think to myself, 'How in the world did [Mitch] ever get him to do this?' That Mitch Miller, what a cornball. But anyway Frank did it—and it was big. It went over."

In Sinatra's Atlantic City interview with Ben Heller, which took place backstage at that same theater, the following dialogue took place:

SINATRA: We've got a new one that's moving pretty good called, you'll excuse the expression, "Goodnight Irene."
HELLER: Hey, that's a nice tune.
SINATRA: You wanna bet? (pauses) Naw, it's really cute.
HELLER: You oughta do a lotta songs like that.
SINATRA: Don't hold your breath!

Miller didn't hold his breath: in November the producer had two similarly faux-folksie pieces arranged for Sinatra, "My Heart Cries for You" and "The Roving Kind." Sinatra was to sing them in a session set up in a brief window of opportunity during a layover in New York while traveling from Los Angeles to Africa (on the trail of Ava Gardner). "We came to the studio right away, and I played these two songs for them. He looked at Sanicola, he looked at Benny Barton, then he said to me, 'I'm not going to do any of that crap.' I had musicians hired, I had the chorus hired. The session was supposed to be that night because he was going away the next morning." When, at the last minute, Sinatra refused to do them, Miller quickly replaced Sinatra with a young singer named Al Cernick. The two mega-hits that Sinatra had turned down launched the career of the recently signed singer, who was now known as Guy Mitchell.

Miller finished the story: "I dare say if Sinatra had done them at that time, I don't think they would have been hits. If he did them perfectly. Because the prejudice against him personally at that time, wrongly, was outrageous."

"One Finger Melody" typifies the kind of Miller-style inanity on which Sinatra was willing to waste his talent. It seems probable that Miller brought Sinatra the song and offered him the publishing rights (which went to Sinatra's firm, Barton Music) as a further inducement to sing it. It's one of the dopiest discs he ever did, replete with an archetypal Miller "Chopsticks"-like piano part, and it's obvious which "one finger" the piece brings to mind.

Still, dogs of this pedigree were hardly the rule. In fact, in direct defiance of the economic climate of this phase in the singer's career, the Sinatra-Stordahl combination continued to turn out some of its finest work deep into the Miller era, and the trilogy of songs from the recently opened Rodgers and Hammerstein milestone *The King and I* represents the collaboration at its Olympian zenith: "Hello Young Lovers," "We Kiss in a Shadow," and "I Whistle a Happy Tune." (A decade later, Sinatra would add a fourth tune from the show to his repertory, "I Have Dreamed" on the *Concert Sinatra* album.)

To give "Hello Young Lovers" a slyly Eastern atmosphere, Stordahl had drummer Blowers obtain a set of miniature cymbals from the Zildjian percussion firm. This proved to be only the first stumbling block in trying to get that particular tune down on wax. "We made twenty-two takes on 'Hello Young Lovers,' [after which] we hated that song!" said Blowers. "Next door to [Columbia's studio on] Thirtieth Street was a bar. And we wanted to get out of that studio so fast, we beat each other to the bar to see who got his drink the fastest. That was a long date, but it had to be done."

"Hello Young Lovers" opens with a minor-key, borderline-dissonant string passage playing under Blowers' chinking Oriental bells. Sinatra sings slowly and deliberately, as if every word weighed a ton and he were pushing them up a mountain like the boulders of Sisyphus. He imbues the bridge with extra heaviness in spite of its references to flying down the street with wings on one's heels. Then, in the final A, he extends the irony by extolling his young-lover listeners not to cry while bringing himself to the very verge of tears. The piece moves into a more conventional European string feeling toward the end, but as Sinatra reaches the dramatically defiant conclusion, the Oriental motif returns behind him, then quickly swells up as if to envelop him, as singer and orchestra dissolve together in a cinematic fadeout.

Constructing the arrangement to suggest lovers meeting illicitly in a Siamese garden, Stordahl fills "We Kiss in a Shadow" with delicately fluttering songbirds, as depicted via a five-note theme that flits about between various flutes and woodwinds. To help the words paint a picture of the lovers set free into the world outside, we no longer hear the caged birds because they have been freed to fly. But "Shadow" ends with the songbird motif, signifying that this episode of liberty was only a fantasy. The motif, established as a symbol of gilded cage repression, is repeated on one, two, three woodwinds (the last a bassoon) capped by Blowers's chimes.

"I Whistle a Happy Tune" may have been the most immediately significant of the three since it suggests that Miller's ingratiating use of extramusical noises can actually make a valid contribution to a Sinatra record. The unidentified whistler who puckers throughout the record is a charming touch, helping the singer to assume the correct little-boy naïveté, especially in contrast to the melancholy, sagacious narrator of "Hello Young Lovers." The song is another triumph of acting as well as singing; Sinatra further conveys a fittingly wide-eyed gaze by singing squarely on the beat and syllabifying big words like de-cep-tion as if he had just learned them. When, at the windup, Sinatra wants to convince us that he has conquered fear itself by whistling the happy tune, he relaxes his grip on the beat and starts to sound more like himself.

Yet even at its apogee, and with the additional hook of a Miller gimmick, the familiar Sinatra-Stordahl balladry was no longer selling in suitable quantities. Neither swing numbers nor pseudo–folk pieces were working commercially, either. Miller's motto was, then and always, "Try something!" In this period the singer and producer found yet another avenue to explore: big-voiced ballads of the sort that were doing boffo business for other singing romeos of the era—Mario Lanza, Frankie Laine, Tony Martin, and the very young Tony Bennett. Throughout the likes of such heavy-sounding (and often classically derived) songs-for-corsetted-crooners as "Take My Love," "You're the One," "Come Back to Sorrento," and "Luna Rossa," Sinatra is trying to come up with something suitable for this increasingly bombastic period of pop music. Even "I Hear a Rhapsody," which he had broadcast as a light and sensual dance piece with Tommy Dorsey a decade earlier, is reborn as anvil-heavy melodrama.

Too many of the post–*Sing and Dance* uptempos have a top-heavy, overdone feeling to them, particularly "Birth of the Blues" and "Bim Bam Baby." Yet Sinatra continues to try to come up with something congruous with his own artistic persona. "There's nothing more pathetic," a character observed of John Barrymore's destitute aristocrat in *Grand Hotel*, "than a nobleman who cannot help but remain noble."

These heavy-handed pieces led to an all-time Sinatra masterpiece, "I'm a Fool to Want You." The song originated largely by accident. Joel Herron, a Sinatra fan since the Dorsey era and a friend since both were employed at the Riobamba in early 1943, was musical director at the Copacabana in the mid-1940s and, not long after, accompanist to Jane Froman. He had been using Brahms' "Third Symphony" as a theme song, and a lyricist friend of his, Jack Wolf, got the idea of using the "Andantino" from the symphony as the basis for a love song. Herron primarily adapted the theme and wrote an eight-bar bridge for it, and Wolf titled it "Take My Love." Wolf then brought it to Barton Music Corp., knowing that if Ben Barton liked it they would not only have a publisher but an important artist to record it in Barton's partner, Sinatra.

Sinatra recorded "Take My Love" in November 1950 and also featured it on his television show, but, like most of his records of the time, it went nowhere. Later, Herron recalled, "Take My Love" "was used in an MGM film called *Undercurrent* with [Katharine] Hepburn and Robert Taylor. That season Herron was conducting for a radio series called *The MGM Theatre of the Air*, which opted to do an adaptation of *Undercurrent.* "But then we couldn't use 'Take My Love' because of some sort of cross-licensing problem," Herron said, "so they asked me to write something else. . . . Trying to compose something similar, I came up with the melody that later became 'I'm A Fool to Want You.'"

Upon realizing that "Fool to Want You" was a better, not to mention more original, song than the number that had inspired it, Wolf again brought it to Barton, and Sinatra recorded it. "When they played us the side, I freaked out when I heard it," remembered Herron. "He changed part of the lyric. When the session was over, we were with Ben Barton and Hank Sanicola, and Jack and I went off by ourselves and said, 'He's gotta be on this song!' We invited him in as a co-writer."

Stordahl, who based his orchestration closely on the original song demo scored by Herron and arranger Joe Gordon, made it even more somber by adding a choir in the final half-chorus. According to legend, Sinatra filtered the song through his faltering relationship with Ava Gardner, which was at once breaking his heart and cremating his career. Reaching the bridge, Sinatra really socks it to us, and when he utters the phrase "time and time again" twice, he skillfully extracts totally different meanings each time, musically and dramatically, following the melody optimistically up on the first and depressingly down on the second. At the end of the release, Stordahl amplifies the singer's angst with a solo crying violin.

After packing an opera's worth of pathos into a single thirty-two-bar chorus, Sinatra supposedly became so overcome with grief that he bolted from the studio in tears. Yet "I'm a Fool to Want You" is more than an aural manifestation of the Frank and Ava soap opera. "That's bullshit!"

said Miller. "Because what he's drawing is the emotion from *your* personal life. He's saying it for you."

Herron considers his own involvement with "Fool" a "historical accident," meaning that the success of this particular record, one of the classics of Sinatra's career, reflects more on the singer than on the songwriter. That success came almost entirely in the future. Initially, "Fool" reached only number 14 in the *Billboard* charts and sold thirty-five-thousand copies, which, Herron said, "was nothing for a Sinatra record [except in those lean years]. We thought we were done for." Undoubtedly, a competing recording by Billy Eckstine, which ironically reached the market first, cut into Sinatra's sales.

What's really amazing about the Miller-era work is that so much of it sounds so good even though Sinatra was having problems with his pipes at the time. "He was under a lot of pressure," Chris Griffin recalled. "That's the only time I ever saw him tight on a few record dates." "We would be on a record session, and we just couldn't get a take in. [His voice] would just crack up," trumpeter Zeke Zarchy confirmed. "We'd take a break for fifteen to twenty minutes. [On one session] we went three hours overtime at double pay. On one of the breaks they sent out for hot tea, and then we waited around for forty-five minutes, and we never completed it. They finally called the session to a halt because his voice wouldn't hold up. These things could happen to anybody. Stress, overwork, it all ties in. It wasn't all of a sudden. He had a very tough schedule—all stars do—and it all just broke down."

These difficulties are testified to only by the memories of his associates. They are not borne out by the recordings. Even on the songs that weren't issued until the '90s, it's rare to find a bad note. The Voice sounds slightly thin on "Faithful" and elsewhere, but you can't find a single example of out-and-out bad singing. It's even harder to find an instance where Sinatra doesn't put all he has into every song, from the stunning "I Could Write a Book" to the inane "Tennessee Newsboy."

And the period abounds with great little-known Sinatra sides, like the jaunty "Walkin' in the Sunshine of Your Love," an exceptionally fine number performed as an industrial-strength swinger arranged by Siravo. On "My Girl," only an okay ballad, Sinatra bends notes in a manner that anticipates his Capitol sound, using microscopic diminuendos and interesting stresses; the line *"when the night is cold"* could be on any song on *Young Lovers*.

Yet when one thinks of the Frank Sinatra–Mitch Miller collaboration, it's the abominations that first come to mind. In the listener's eye, Sinatra can be visualized as the hero of a children's cartoon. On one side,

Mitch Miller materializes as a bearded devil in a puff of cigar smoke, prompting the singer with his pitchfork to compromise his standards with the motto: make millions with medocrities. Sinatra's high-minded halo-wearing artistic conscience perches on the other side, telling him to harken instead to the angel on his shoulder and to stick with the caliber of material he did best.

Despite a proclivity for Mammon-worship, Miller deeply resents the contempt with which Sinatra and his fans have long held him. "You cannot force anyone to do a song. People don't understand this. Sinatra [later] said that I brought him all these shit songs, I forced him to do shit songs." Miller has consistently insisted that he never had to force Sinatra or anybody else to do anything they didn't want to do. His track record did most of the forcing for him. If Miller went to artist A with a song and he turned it down, and then the song became a hit for artist B, "then the next time you bring a song to him, he's going to listen."

Rosemary Clooney said that Miller did, in fact, threaten to terminate her contract unless she recorded "Come on-a My House," but she added that Miller was normally much more "kind and sensitive" than that. Miller and Tony Bennett both admitted that he practically had to pin Bennett's arms behind his back to get him to do most of the numbers that established his career.

"Mitch kept giving Frank this terrible crap to record," says Paul Weston. Weston feels that Miller was so insistent and persistent, and such a good *convincer*, that he was impossible to fluff off, and that Sinatra, who was already terribly in debt to Columbia and not feeling very sure of his own better judgment, was particularly vulnerable to Miller's demands. "Frank was so disgusted and teed off at having to do that, it was ridiculous. You can't believe the crap that he had Jo [Stafford] record, tunes like 'Underneath the Overpass' and 'Chow Willie,' stuff that just died."

In both Clooney's and Bennett's cases, all parties concerned would probably agree that the fact the songs became hits rendered the opinion of the artists rather irrelevant. Sinatra probably wouldn't have been thrilled if any of his Miller-produced novelties had been hits (such as "Goodnight, Irene"), but it made him all the more miserable that they flopped. It's enough to make you agree with Milt Bernhart's contention concerning the later Columbia work: "If the things were uptempo, they were stupid. Those Mitch Miller things were all wrong for him."

The most infamous Sinatra performance of the period is that dog tune to end all dog tunes, "Mama Will Bark." The genesis of the piece is twofold, beginning when Sinatra shared the stage with the entity known as "Dagmar," who looked like the result of some genetic cloning experiment gone awry, resulting in a combination of Steve Reeves and Jayne Mansfield, on his CBS TV show of April 7, 1951. The two also performed together when Sinatra returned to the Paramount Theatre a few weeks later and when the entire company of that stage show, including Joey Bushkin and Eileen Barton, appeared on Sinatra's program on May 5.

At that time Dagmar was famous for revealing more cleavage on Jerry Lester's program than anyone had previously dared to display on TV. "She was just a big, buxom southern gal, that's all," as Eileen Barton put it rather mildly. Mitch Miller was immediately struck by the Sinatra-Dagmar chemistry. "In that show he had this dumb blonde, Dagmar, and they did a bit on the stage," Miller said. "So this song came in—you know, that 'Mama Will Bark' thing. And I thought, '[Let's] try this novelty.' Now, first remember," Miller added, "nobody brings Sinatra in the studio [to do something] that he doesn't want to do. I don't care who it is. Then, he had the right to okay its release. So he could have bombed it all the way."

Miller continued, "I even put 'I'm a Fool to Want You' on the other side to ensure [the sales of] it." Furthermore, Dick Manning, composer of "Bark," who would later have a success with "Fascination," had previously landed a big hit with a similar animalistic aria entitled "The Pussy Cat Song (Nyow! Nyot Nyow!)." So there were many reasons why "Bark" might have scored a hit, but as Miller also said, "With novelties you never know. We made this record as a shot in the dark."

The two major misconceptions concerning "Bark" are that it was a total flop ("The only good it did me," Sinatra said, "was with dogs") and that it was the worst record of Sinatra's entire career. Truth to tell, if "Bark" had just died, no one would ever have heard of it and it wouldn't keep coming back to haunt Miller and Sinatra. It did get on the charts (only to number 21), which didn't make it a mega-hit but meant that a lot more people bought it than *Sing and Dance with Frank Sinatra*.

"Mama Will Bark" is certainly no dumber than "Come on-a My House." (Can you imagine if Sinatra had to reprise it at every concert the way Clooney is obliged to keep doing "My House"?) "Frank probably thought Mitch was kidding when he brought that thing in," said Chris Griffin, who played trumpet on the date, "but that's the kind of song Mitch thought was really great!" While lunging about with the tone-deaf doggy diva, Sinatra throws in references to Joyce Kilmer as well as a Jimmy Durante impression. Like the lyric says, it's the dog-gonedest thing you ever heard.

*   *   *

By now Sinatra's film and broadcasting careers were also on hold, particularly when *Meet Danny Wilson,* which at the time looked as if it would
be his last picture, quickly opened and closed in March 1952. At that
time the *New York World-Telegram* pointed up the differences between
Sinatra audiences of 1942 and 1952—mainly that, ten years earlier, there
had been one. (Forty years later, however, Sinatra was still going strong,
unlike the *World-Telegram.*) Skitch Henderson recalled, "Earl Wilson,
God rest his soul, really pounded the town for two days to get all of
Frank's [old friends] to go down to the Paramount to see him. It was
really a sad night because nothing was working. You're embarrassed for
somebody that you love when things don't work. It happens to all of us at
one time or another." Sinatra appreciated the support but probably
would have preferred not to be seen by old chums at this particular time.
Mel Tormé and Milton Berle went to see him together during this
period, and Tormé remembered, "I thought he couldn't sink any lower
than that. That was the fall that preceded the rise."

In spite of his career doldrums, Sinatra was all over the airwaves in
the early '50s—which wasn't so much an indication of his popularity as a
testament to William Paley's faith in him. As he cracks rhymingly on one
program, "This is Paley's bad guess on CBS." On October 7, 1950, Sinatra launched his first TV program, and despite his faltering popularity
and obvious unease in the new medium, the sixty-minute show made it
through two seasons. For conductor Stordahl the benefits were more
personal: on the January 27, 1951, telecast, Sinatra announced the marriage of the arranger to June Hutton, lead singer with the Pied Pipers
and featured femme vocalist on the program.

While the comedy sketches on the *Frank Sinatra Show* seem embarrassingly primitive today, most of the music on these CBS outings (sponsored the first season by Bulova watches and the second by Ecko
housewares) is astoundingly good. Sinatra commissioned new charts
from his regular writers, particularly Stordahl and Siravo, and at least
one new one, Neal Hefti, who contributed a chart of "Get Happy."
Besides that, and apart from being the last extended project Sinatra and
Stordahl would work on together, the show produced little of professional significance. Sid Cooper, who subbed occasionally, recalled that
from the band's perspective "it seemed like a big mixed-up situation at
that time."

He would also strike out, in both senses of the phrase, with two new
radio programs. Sinatra had initially negotiated, in the summer of 1949,
with the Mutual network to do a celebrity disc jockey show, which
apparently never got off the ground. Around 1950–51, he did make it to

radio with *Meet Frank Sinatra* on CBS. Heard today, the show seems like an unwieldy combination of *Songs by Sinatra* and *Oprah*. In addition to singing with a rhythm section, Sinatra gave members of his studio audience the mike and exchanged snappy *You Bet Your Life*–style dialogue with them as well as with occasional guests, such as Billy Eckstine, Richard "Junko Partner" Hayes, and Jule Styne. The show made so little impact that even hardcore Sinatra aficionados have barely heard of it. Musically speaking, the series, which ran through the spring of 1951, deserves some attention. His subtly swung versions of "S'Wonderful," "One for My Baby," "The Moon Was Yellow" (all from the January 3, 1951, show) recorded with a hip rhythm section only, swing like songs Sinatra would record four or five years later.

By 1952, Sinatra was dropped by his agency (MCA), his movie studio, his network, and his record company. "In my mid-30s I began to see things from a different angle, and I found that I became more tolerant of people," he said in 1977, "maybe because I had been knocked around a little bit. Nancy and I had a separation, and that hurt a great deal. Those things happen, unfortunately. Nobody likes it. I hadn't seen the children for a while, and I was kind of faltering a little bit in my work. I think I began to take stock."

After the humiliating debacle of "Mama Will Bark," relations between Sinatra and Miller disintegrated even further. In November 1951, Sinatra married Ava Gardner—Dick Jones played piano, Axel Stordahl was the best man, and Manie Sachs let them use his brother's house for the occasion. Like loving Ava Gardner, hating Mitch Miller became an emotional centerpiece of Sinatra's life.

Rosemary Clooney remembered working in Vegas at the same time as Sinatra during this period and how he slammed Miller and, in particular, "Come on-a My House" with the same vituperativeness he later reserved for columnists. "He was knocking Mitch, not me," Clooney said. "But nevertheless, a little of the fallout got dropped on me." Shortly after, Sinatra's aide, Hank Sanicola, sent a note of apology.

Also in November 1951, Sinatra informed *Billboard* that he was not planning to renew with CBS when his contract ran out in December the following year. "Chief beef hinges on Sinatra's claim he isn't getting a fair shake on song material," the story said. "Sinatra has waged a long-smoldering feud with Mitch Miller." Sinatra reported that he was negotiating with both RCA Victor and Capitol Records as possible future homes.

It all came to a head on June 3, 1952, a date that captures all the highs and lows of Sinatra's in-between years in a single session. Although it marked the first of several thousand discings with his favorite drummer,

Alvin Stoller (and only the second with pianist Bill Miller), this penultimate Columbia session proved the very epitome of Mitch Miller's
dream and Frank Sinatra's nightmare. Axel Stordahl was supposedly the
musical director, and Paul Weston was officially the producer and A&R
man. Mitch Miller, however, making one of his rare in-person appearances on the Coast, was dominating the proceedings and calling the
shots. It's doubtful that Sinatra had any input whatever, but it is com-
mendable that although he was supposed to have lost his voice by now,
he nonetheless managed to squeak out no less than five very acceptable
commercial masters in a single session.

"Frank was going through a very tough time with his voice," Weston
recalled, "and it was very difficult for him to even get through a three-
minute vocal. Frank was disgusted. It wasn't *his* fault, you know." As for
the material itself, whether Miller-inspired or not, soft ballads were out.
Sinatra first trots out "Luna Rossa," a big, dramatic, semiclassical table-
pounder with a chiming choir, and gets nowhere with it. Then comes
Heinie Beau's brash but beautiful arrangement of "Birth of the Blues," a
chart so down and dirty it could accompany Blaze Starr. Although certainly entertaining and often ranked a Sinatra classic, both this piece and
"Bim Bam Baby" (arranged by either Beau or Siravo) demonstrate how
absolutely essential Nelson Riddle was in inventing a brassy and swinging yet subtle sound that finally worked for Sinatra. Here, even more
than on the three 1951 Harry James numbers, Sinatra goes for an aggres-
sively nasty sound (anticipating his 1966 "That's Life") which is at once
invigorating and a little disturbing.

In trying to sing the blues, Sinatra does better with "Paris Blues" (the
subtitle for "Azure Te") than he does with "The Birth of the Blues."
"Azure Te" (orchestrated, again, either by Siravo or Beau) consciously
touches on that same harsh sound as one of several textures which it juxtaposes to act out a narrative. The piece plays the concepts of "Paris" and
"blues" off each other by alternating between taxicab horns that agitatedly beep a phrase from Gershwin's "An American in Paris" against the
blaring brass characteristic of American swing. More baguette than
beguine, its atmosphere suggests a Louis Jourdan movie, although
"Azure Te" was in fact introduced by Louis Jordan, whose pianist, Wild
Bill Davis, had written it (and would later arrange "April in Paris" for
Count Basie).

At the end of 1952, Sinatra must have felt as if he were staring at a
musical dead end. Jim Conkling, a former top man at Capitol Records,
had recently taken over at Columbia, and his first assignment was to let
Sinatra go. As Conkling's friend Milt Bernhart pointed out, this "was not

a slap in the face or a hardship for Sinatra; he didn't want to be at Columbia anymore." Although Manie Sachs couldn't move Sinatra to RCA—he said he could force the issue but Sinatra was better off where he was wanted—Conkling may well have suggested the outside possibility that Sinatra get in touch with Alan Livingston, who had recently replaced him at Capitol.

The final two Columbia sessions took place in June and September 1952. Bill Miller recalled that not long after the September date he "heard him on the phone saying, 'Hey, I just fired Columbia.'" Sinatra would record only one more tune for the label, on a split session with the long-forgotten Mindy Carson. It's often been printed that Columbia only gave Sinatra a split session as a way of brushing him off. Actually, having two vocalists share a date was a fairly common practice. Tony Bennett did many of his dates that way at that time.

In December 1944, when Sinatra quit *Your Hit Parade* for the first time, the last song he performed on the program was "Don't Fence Me In," which could be taken as a comment on the restrictive nature of that show's format. In his final months at Columbia, Sinatra recorded a number of tunes with allegedly autobiographical titles: "The Birth of the Blues," "There's Something Missing," and "Don't Ever Be Afraid to Go Home," an odd choice for a recently divorced man. And then there's the one about the idol who had "Feet of Clay." Sinatra's parting shot to Miller was "Why Try to Change Me Now?"

The last Sinatra Columbia side, it was the first song of note by the twenty-three-year-old composer Cy Coleman. Coleman reported that, on the date, Sinatra slightly altered the melody of the original opening interval. "I listened to the record and it sounded so natural, the way Frank did it, that I thought to myself, 'He's right!' So I left it that way. So I changed the music! That's the first and only time I've ever done that."

Miraculously tender and sensitive even by Sinatra standards, the song allows him to convey an unapologetic humility rarely heard from him before or since. "Why Try to Change Me Now?" makes for a far more moving piece of self-analysis and, ultimately, affirmation than the comparatively shallow "My Way." The song also receives a beautiful arrangement by Percy Faith, in the best Stordahl flute-and-celesta tradition. Stordahl, as it happened, had recently signed an exclusive contract with Capitol Records and could have done a date with Sinatra only with that label's permission.

The Sinatra-Stordahl sound had by now run its course; Sinatra was working with other writers and Stordahl with other singers. Stordahl conducted for Sinatra on The Voice's first date for Capitol in 1953, and then the collaboration ended abruptly. Milt Bernhart recalled a story, perhaps aprocryphal, that began circulating around the time the "come-back" was getting into gear. "Frank got a call to play a theater in New York, so he called up Axel, who by that time, on the strength of his Frank Sinatra reputation, had started getting shows here in Hollywood. . . . So Frank called him and said, 'We're leaving Sunday for New York.' And Axel said, 'God, Frank, I just began this show with Eddie Fisher.' And Frank said, 'Apparently you didn't hear what I said. We're leaving Sunday for New York, and we're going to be at the Capitol Theatre.' And Axel said, 'I can't do that, Frank. I've got a contract.' Frank said, 'Good-bye,' and hung up—and that's the last time they saw each other until that Capitol date ten years later [the 1961 album, *Point of No Return*]. Period."

Other, closer friends of both men dispute this account. According to Billy May, "Sinatra's career was kind of taking a nosedive then. He was looking for a change of scene. . . . I can't see how it could be a personality conflict, knowing both those people." And Paul Weston, who was close to Stordahl all of his life, recalled that Stordahl never had anything negative to say about Sinatra. "There wasn't any rift or anything like that— as far as I knew."

Talking about his "Year of Mondays" with Sidney Zion, Sinatra would say, "I lost a great deal of faith in human nature because a lot of friends I had in those days disappeared. I don't say it begrudgingly because I [learned] something about human nature after that. I found out, or at least I think I understood, that some people don't know how to help. They want to, but they don't quite know how to do it. They're either shy or afraid they'll louse it up and make it worse than it is, because later on, when things got better for me, I just came back and kept working. I did lay down for a while and had some large bar bills for about a year, I think. But after that I said, 'Holiday's over, Charlie, let's go back to work.'

"And then I began to meet these people who disappeared from my life—almost all of them, except for one or two dear, dear friends. I saw them and I said, 'How are you? How've you been?' And they were astounded, they were absolutely stunned that I even spoke to them. That's when I became aware of the fact that perhaps they didn't know how to handle it, they didn't know how to come to me and say, 'I haven't got much money, but I can lend you X amount of dollars.' Which I didn't want anyway because I was picking up a little job here and there. But at least out of that I learned something about human nature. Even if I fell on my butt, I learned a great deal about that."

At the end of the film *The House I Live In,* Sinatra's Oscar-winning

attack on racial intolerance, the singer admonishes his juvenile congre-
gation, "Don't let 'em make suckers out of you." He wasn't going to let
anybody make a sucker out of him, either. Rather, he was about to be
redeemed, as T. S. Eliot wrote in *Four Quartets*, "from fire, by fire."

So don't count him out yet—the ballet ain't over till the swan dies.

THE HAT YEARS

CHAPTER SIX

WITH NELSON RIDDLE, 1953–1979

"Grant me Paradise in this world; I'm not so sure I'll reach it in the next."

—TINTORETTO
(Jacopo Robusti, 1518–1594)

Was there ever a more perfect, more powerful or goose-bump-raising record than Frank Sinatra and Nelson Riddle's "I've Got You Under My Skin"? After Sinatra's first chorus, swinging and passionate enough for any six crooners, trombonist Milt Bernhart emerges from the ensemble as Sinatra's wordless alter ego. Never was angular dissonance put to such effective use in mainstream popular music, Riddle here displaying a capacity for multistylistic juxtaposition akin to that of Charles Mingus. Bernhart flies out, shrieking like one of Stan Kenton's girdled nails-on-chalkboard brassmen who has somehow quantum-leaped smack into the middle of an otherwise smooth-groove, pat-your-foot Basie chart.

For half a chorus the trombonist plumbs depths of emotion that, at the end of his sixteen bars, we tell ourselves that no mere words could ever reach. But then Sinatra returns for an outchorus to end all outchoruses: he starts by using Bernhart's highest emotional peak as his own lowest note and builds from there to a musical dramatic climax that fully exploits Cole Porter's lyric as meaningfully as his melody, combining pure swing with caveman machismo, capable of grabbing even the most Frank-resistant listener way down at the bottom of the soul.

Earlier, Sinatra's intimate ballads made little girls keel over in their bobby socks. More recently, Sinatra had graduated from simply being the object of romantic attention to an inspiration. The lyrics of "Hello

Young Lovers" purport to offer advice to the lovelorn, but Sinatra is more accurately lending his formidable powers of seduction to millions of budding romances. "Skin" shows the more aggressive Sinatra that men like, the warrior with a conscience who speaks more directly to them than Monday-night football or locker-room boasts of backseat conquests.

But it's not only his perfection of faster tempos that separates the man from the boy when comparing '50s to '40s Sinatra. In ballads, too, Ol' Blue Eyes remains far from The Voice while continuing to "thrill millions." "I've Got You Under My Skin" is only one of sixteen remarkable performances recorded in October 1955 and January 1956 for *Songs for Swingin' Lovers!,* Sinatra's definitive (certainly) and best (probably) collection of uptempo standards. Similarly, *Only the Lonely* resounds as his most moving gathering of downer love songs; and "It's a Lonesome Old Town (When You're Not Around)" may be the unkindest cut of all thirteen songs originally earmarked for that album.

There's irony in everything about the performance. Written in 1930, "Lonesome Old Town" had served its whole life thus far as the theme song of bandleader Ben Bernie, known even at the birth of radio as "The Old Maestro." When people heard the six notes that defined its tune, they had been conditioned to expect a band as corny as Guy Lombardo's combined with ancient vaudeville spieling as schmaltzy as that of Ted Lewis. Sinatra and Riddle could have treated "Lonesome Old Town" as a takeoff on Bernie, as Spike Jones or Dean Martin might have done. To induce audiences into accepting the song on a serious level, however, the singer-arranger team had first to strip "Lonesome" of its sentimental excesses and then reconstruct it as a bona fide exercise in musical drama. As on "Skin," Riddle employs his trademark instrument, the trombone, as Sinatra's foil and second voice, and once again the arranger throws a nod to Kenton writer Bill Russo. Where "Skin" alluded to the polyrhythms of the Kenton-Russo "23 Degrees North, 82 Degrees West," "Lonesome" hints at the twinkling-stars background effect Russo devised for Kenton's "Improvisation" and "Over the Rainbow." Riddle had used modernist and Kenton-vet Bernhart as the instrumental star of "Skin," Sinatra's most traditionally swinging track. Paradoxically, on the space-age "Lonesome" he recruits the warmer-toned and older-fashioned big-band trombone of Ray Sims. On "Skin" the ensemble is swing style and the soloist more modern; on "Lonesome" the arrangement is futuristic, but the soloist is no more beboppy than Jack Teagarden playing the blues.

The progressive textures appropriately expand the context of the lyric. It's no longer just a town that's lonesome and old; our protagonist now confronts an entire universe of despair. The two voices, Sinatra and his shadow, Sims, wander about this godforsaken landscape aimlessly in search of love but finding only an abyss of nothingness. The warmth of the two soloists only serves to underscore the unending vacuum that is creation. All human effort and emotion amount to nothingness. There is no protection from the pain, no safe place. We are all merely Lucky Strike Extras in the vast *Hit Parade* of existence.

The rapture of *Songs for Swingin' Lovers!* and the nihilism of *Only the Lonely,* apart from being Riddle's two favorites of the twenty-one albums he arranged with Sinatra, can be safely described as the highpoints of the collaboration and the zeniths of the careers of both men, individually and as a team. Still, they are hardly singular pinnacles. We could point to *A Swingin' Affair, Swingin' Lovers's* sequel, as perhaps an even more thrilling ode to sensual syncopation, while *In the Wee Small Hours* and *Close to You,* prequels to *Only the Lonely,* are in many ways no less disturbing juxtapositions of romance and anguish.

In truth, virtually all the Sinatra-Riddle albums are masterpieces, their collaboration being sanctified from the first downbeat counted off at the first session onward. The seven essential works of their association—*Songs for Young Lovers* (1953, although not entirely a true Sinatra-Riddle product, as we shall see), *Swing Easy* (1954), *In the Wee Small Hours* (1955), *Songs for Swingin' Lovers!* (1955–56), *Close to You* (1956), *A Swingin' Affair* (1956), and *Only the Lonely* (1958)—have the right to be considered the greatest extended works in all of popular music. These seven are surrounded by only slightly lesser efforts, including five anthologies of independently recorded single cuts, *This Is Sinatra* (1953–55), *This Is Sinatra: Vol. II* (1954–57), *Look to Your Heart* (1953–55), *All the Way* (1957–60), and *Sinatra Sings of Love and Things* (1957–62); two subsequent "real" albums diminished only slightly by extramusical circumstances, *Nice 'n Easy* (1960) and *Sinatra's Swingin' Session* (1960); two soundtrack souvenir sets, *Pal Joey* (1957) and *Can Can* (1960); and five no-less-noteworthy postscripts, *The Concert Sinatra* (1963), *Sinatra's Sinatra* (1963), *The Days of Wine and Roses: Academy Award Winners* (1963–1964), *Strangers in the Night* (1966), and *Moonlight Sinatra* (1966).

Pat Hobby, the has-been hack screenwriter antihero of Scott Fitzgerald's tales of the Hollywood hills, functions as an outlet for ideas that had occurred to writers of his generation but which they didn't want to speak in their own voices. Whereas Jake Barnes, in Ernest Hemingway's *The*

Sun Also Rises, returns from war "half a man," Hobby views war as an opportunity for growth. Hobby's heroes and heroines come marching home with their batteries recharged, their spirit strengthened, their scope expanded.

In 1953, Sinatra "came back" from the depths of his own private armageddon, a personal cataclysm that had involved the woman who later personified Papa Ernie's own Lady Brett. Using a war movie— *From Here to Eternity*—as the vehicle with which to announce his second coming, Sinatra's artistic abilities had indeed undergone Hobby-like renewal. "You have to scrape bottom," he said at the time, "to appreciate life and start living again."

When pianist Bill Miller first went to work for Sinatra in 1952, he joined the singer's aggregation at his all-time lowest point. In the first few months of their association, Miller witnessed The Voice's career slide from bad to worse—Sinatra's split from Columbia Records and the failure of his TV series, not to mention his stalemated movie career. Sinatra was forced to rebuild from the ground up. No longer tied to either coast for broadcasting or picture work, he took to the road for several months and gradually added a new dimension to his work beyond the familiar sound of the Sinatra-Stordahl collaboration. Though he must have continued to use many of his big ballad hits, he concentrated on a new book of smaller-scale uptempo arrangements he had commissioned from George Siravo—arrangements that Sinatra would not get to record for some time because he had no recording affiliation. That would shortly change, due to a lucky call made by his new agency, William Morris.

"Sinatra had hit bottom, and I mean bottom," recalled Alan Livingston, then vice president in charge of A&R and sales at Capitol Records. "It's hard to imagine now, he was so down-and-out. He had been under contract to Columbia Records, and nothing was happening. When his contract was up, Mitch Miller let him go, and he could not get a record deal. He could not get a job in a nightclub, and his buddies couldn't help him—even with his old friend Jilly [Rizzo] in Atlantic City. Manie Sachs, his closest buddy, couldn't give him a job. Manie was at RCA and wanted to sign him, but the A&R department there said, 'Forget it.'"

"So I was sitting in my office one day, and the president of the William Morris Agency called me, a man named Sam Weisbrod, whom I knew well," Livingston continued. "And he said, 'Alan, we've just taken on representation of Sinatra. Would you consider signing him?' And without hesitation, I said 'Yes.' He said, obviously surprised, 'You would?' That's how bad it was. So Sam brought Sinatra in to meet me. I had never met him before. He was meek, a pussycat, humble. He had been through terrible times. He was broke, he was in debt, Ava Gardner had left him. I was told he had tried to kill himself on occasion. He was at the lowest ebb of his life, which I'm sure Frank would acknowledge to you—it's no great secret. Everybody knew it.

"Frank and I talked, and I signed him to a seven-year contract, one year with six options, which is as long as you can sign anybody. I gave him a standard royalty of five percent and gave him a scale advance. He was glad to have a place to make records. And that's how I signed Sinatra."[1] The signing took place on March 14, 1953, at Lucy's Restaurant in Hollywood, with Sinatra aides Hank Sanicola and Frank Military present.

Not long after the ink was dry, Livingston spoke at the company's annual national convention. "We had every salesman in our distributing company there, every branch manager, every district manager, every promotion man. There must have been a couple of hundred people. And I got up at these meetings and talked about future artists and recordings, and I announced that we had just signed Frank Sinatra," said Livingston. The whole staff was so totally underwhelmed that they groaned *en masse*. "My answer to them was, 'Look, I can only judge on talent. I can't judge what people did in the past. I only know talent, and Frank is the best singer in the world. There's nobody who can touch him.' And I feel that way still."

Only two Capital A&R men were even vaguely supportive, Voyle Gilmore and Dave Dexter. Dexter was quite enthusiastic and Gilmore a bit less so, but Sinatra didn't want to work with Dexter (the producer and writer later claimed that this was because he had panned one of Sinatra's Columbia discs in *Down Beat* years earlier), so Livingston appointed Gilmore Sinatra's producer: "I knew Frank would pick his songs," said the VP, "and that he knew what he wanted to do." Choosing a musical director for Sinatra would prove more difficult. "Frank came in and said he wanted to work with Axel Stordahl, whom he'd been working with the better part of his career," said Livingston. Stordahl was under contract to Capitol, but Livingston had a better idea. "I said, 'Do me one favor and yourself a favor. Work with Nelson Riddle.' We were very high on Nelson. He was marvelous. Nelson knew how to back up artists and make them sound great without interfering with their singing. He knew

---

1. Livingston's account of how Sinatra came to Capitol is the most believable; however, there are other versions. Both Axel Stordahl and former label executive Jim Conkling have been given credit, while A&R staffer Dave Dexter later claimed to have instigated the signing entirely on his own.

where to bring the orchestra in, where not to. He was just a marvelous underscorer for a vocalist. So I wanted Frank to have the benefit of that."

It seems likely that Sinatra realized that his music needed an infusion of newness, especially as he had been focusing on George Siravo's more jazz-oriented arrangements for the last few months. As Frank Military put it, "I think what happened was that Sinatra kept growing, and he outgrew [what he had been doing in the '40s]. That's basically what it comes down to. He knew he needed something more, and he got it. I think that's very important to say, that Frank kept moving when everyone else stood still."

At the same time, however, Sinatra probably also felt that there wasn't anyone he could trust as much as the reliable Scandanavian, who had been responsible for almost all his hits. Sinatra told Livingston, "I've worked with Axel Stordahl for practically [my whole career]. I can't leave Axel. I've got to work with him."

Livingston worked out a compromise with Sinatra whereby they agreed to try a new Sinatra-Stordahl session on Capitol. If the records sold, so be it, but if they didn't, Sinatra would try a date with whoever Livingston and Gilmore picked, meaning Riddle. "So we put out the first records with Axel [including 'Don't Make a Beggar of Me' and 'I'm Walking Behind You'], and nothing happened," Livingston continued. "I was determined to get Frank with Nelson Riddle."

"Frank had to be sold Nelson Riddle," said Bill Miller. "It was Capitol's idea to utilize Nelson, and after the first couple of sessions, he thought, 'Well, that's it.' Then when Frank tried Nelson on ballads, he said, 'Whew, we gotta be careful with him,' because Nelson had these harmonics—he used these polytones, G over A, A over G, all that. I said, 'Hey, Frank, it's different. It's working.'"

It's possible that the meeting with Livingston was the first time Sinatra heard the name Nelson Riddle. Riddle had been responsible for several major pop music hits, but circumstances had thus far kept his name from circulating beyond the inner recesses of the industry. In 1953, Riddle was a burgeoning major talent seeking a style he could call his own, while Sinatra was desperately in search of a new sound powerful and fresh enough to reestablish him as pop music's most significant force. It was kismet that they should be forced together.

The most celebrated vocal arranger and musical director in history, Nelson Smock Riddle, Jr., was born on June 1, 1921, in Oradell, New Jersey, a few towns away from the Sinatra home. "Smock is a Dutch family name," his son Christopher recently pointed out, "and it probably should have been allowed to go the way of a lot of unfortunate names, but it was carried on with my father." Riddle never liked the middle name, but with characteristic causticness he passed it on to his firstborn, Nelson Smock Riddle III.

Nelson Smock Riddle, Sr., was one of those musical amateurs who George Bernard Shaw said would probably wind up in hell. Like Irving Berlin, he could pick out a tune on the black keys of the piano, which wasn't so bad if you didn't mind hearing everything in F-sharp (or if you had the ability to write "White Christmas"). "My father owned a trombone, which was mine for the reaching for," Riddle recalled not long before he died, "and he accompanied me in such hit tunes of the day as 'Harbor Lights' and 'Red Sails in the Sunset,' which made my toes curl because they were so boring."[2]

"Nelson was a very bright kid," said Bill Finegan, one of Riddle's earliest professional associates. "He was sardonic in his youth, and on the grim side. He had a sense of humor and we had a lot of laughs together, but he could be very grim." Many of Riddle's friends have described him as having a caustic, self-deprecating sense of humor, which in reminiscing about his family and his boyhood in New Jersey was often turned on his father.

"We didn't feel the Depression at all," Riddle said, because "my father made his own Depression. It was all the same to us because we were already in a depressed state by the time the Depression got there." By way of example, Riddle recalled that after eight weekly lessons on the trombone, his teacher told him to go home and not come back because "your father hasn't paid me for the first lesson, let alone the eighth one." The lessons were a dollar each, and the Riddles didn't have the money. Then, turning the screws on himself, he continued, "Anybody worth his salt would have gone out and sold some papers. I don't know why that didn't occur to me. I guess I was a spoiled brat."

"Nelson played trombone, and he wanted to learn about jazz. He claimed he didn't know anything about it," Bill Finegan recently recalled. "Somebody told him about me." At the time, Finegan, who was four years older than Riddle and lived just a few towns away, had just sold his first arrangement to a name band (Tommy Dorsey's "Lonesome Road"). "So he came, and I started writing out jazz choruses for him on the trombone," Finegan said. "I noticed he was talented, and one thing led to another and I said he ought to be a writer and got him started writing."

2. Almost all of the quotes from Nelson Riddle are taken from several radio interviews conducted by Robert Windeler of KCRW, Santa Monica (1984–85) and Jonathan Schwartz of WNEW, New York (May 29, 1983).

As he later told Jonathan Schwartz, Riddle wrote his first arrangement in 1938; the tune was "I See Your Face Before Me," coincidentally composed by the disc jockey's father, Arthur Schwartz. (He and Sinatra would put their definitive stamp on the tune in 1955 on the *Wee Small Hours* album.) "When I studied arranging with Bill Finegan, inflation had taken over; lessons were now two dollars," Riddle recalled. "Bill came to me one afternoon quietly and diplomatically, and he showed me a piece of paper and said, 'This is a check your father wrote me. It bounced.'" However, Finegan cautioned, "I don't know if that story is true. Nelson liked to tell things like that."

In early 1939, Finegan joined the writing staff of the rapidly rising Glenn Miller Orchestra. Not long after, the eighteen-year-old Riddle landed his first break with a national band in a new outfit led by Tommy Reynolds, a clarinetist who not only played like but also happened to look like Artie Shaw. Primarily a section trombonist, Riddle also wrote some arrangements for the band and went on working closely with Finegan. Riddle had already moved on by the time Reynolds first recorded in December, but it is conceivable that some of the thirty-three titles Reynolds recorded for Vocalion and then Okeh in 1939 and 1940 include arrangements by Nelson Riddle.

"I helped him put some charts together for Reynolds and some other bands, too," some of which he might have also played in, recalled Finegan, who continued to serve as Riddle's mentor until the younger man moved to Los Angeles after the war. "Bill Finegan got me started in the business," Riddle said later. "And some of the sounds you heard [in my work] early on might have emanated from him because I idolized him in those days. I still do, because I think he was one of the front runners of fine arranging." "Nelson was a protégé of Bill Finegan, and he had a lot of talent," remembered Larry Elgart, who worked with them both when all three worked with Elgart's brother Les' first band in 1945. "A lot of Nelson's choices of fourth chords and harmonies and things like that come straight from Bill."

Riddle made his first impact with Charlie Spivak's orchestra, the highly respected trumpeter's second attempt at bandleading. Reed player Harry Klee, who would become Riddle's lifelong friend and co-worker, had joined Spivak's band a few months before Spivak himself did, back when the group worked in a roadhouse called the Nightingale on the highway to Richmond, Virginia, under the direction of local leader Bill Downer. Although Spivak had been a much-respected soloist and lead player with half a dozen major bands, he was unsure of what he wanted in his first band, which stayed together only a few months at the beginning of 1940. By April or May, "somebody recommended that Spivak come and hear [Downer's] band," said Klee. "Spivak came through, and he offered to pick up the whole band. He made Bill a manager, and we went on the road with him."

"They used to call him cheerie, chubby Charlie Spivak," said Riddle, describing his first important boss. "He was very pleasant and an excellent trumpet player. Charlie's control of the instrument and his tone, and so on, were magnificent. He had the control and breathing apparatus on the trumpet that Tommy Dorsey had on the trombone. Tommy became one of the great legends of all time. Charlie didn't." Where Riddle had begun writing arrangements for Reynolds almost immediately, according to Finegan, Spivak was considerably slower to recognize Riddle's abilities in that area; one sideman remembered that "Nelson was not Charlie's idea of a great arranger."

"I think the first arrangement that Nelson wrote for Spivak was 'White Christmas,'" said Harry Klee. "That was a pretty big seller for Spivak." Riddle also recalled scoring Josef Myrow's "Autumn Nocturne," recorded by Spivak several months earlier. "White Christmas" may have made a bigger noise commercially, being the top-selling band vesion of the biggest tune of all time, but the arranger was more proud of "Nocturne," because even though "Claude Thornhill had a great record out on that," said Riddle, "Myrow [said he] liked our arrangement very much."

"When we had a rehearsal of the band," Klee recollected, "Nelson would pass out little slips of paper with, oh, maybe six, eight, or ten bars of music on them, where he was trying a new kind of voicing—you know, for new sounds. And he did this all the time back then, cataloguing what he thought was good and discarding what wasn't." Said Riddle, "I learned quite a bit in that band."

In 1943, at age twenty-two, Riddle was a prime candidate for Uncle Sam, an involuntary career readjustment that he didn't relish. "My dad wasn't particularly patriotic," said Chris Riddle, "and regarded the entire war as a personal inconvenience." Riddle had been told that the Merchant Marines needed musicians for its band and that by serving with that branch for a year he could avoid being drafted in the regular army. He served in a Merchant Marines band stationed at Sheepshead Bay, Brooklyn, and later fondly remembered this service hitch: "It helped me no end, and I learned I loved to write for strings."

After his discharge, Riddle was thrilled to work for eleven months with Tommy Dorsey because, as he put it, "Tommy had even more strings than they did in the Merchant Marines." The band's guitarist, Bob Bain, recollects that "the first time I played one of Nelson's arrange-

ments was with Tommy, a song called 'Havana.' Nelson wrote only ballads, Tommy didn't give him any jazz things. Nelson loved it because [it
meant that] he could write for strings. Bill Finegan and Sy Oliver were
writing a lot of the great jazz things."

After concentrating so hard on writing for a string section, Riddle next
had to learn how not to rely too heavily on one. Dorsey instructed him,
"You're making the strings too important. One day I might want to dump
the whole string section—basically it's a tax deduction. I want to have
that flexibility. When I get rid of them, I want to have an [arrangement] I
can still play." Riddle "was crushed. I felt really badly about that. But I
revised my plans so he could use them without strings. Actually, it wasn't
bad training to be able to write both ways."

In his year with TD, beginning around June 1944, the orchestra's
most lucrative venue was the *All-Time Hit Parade* radio series, which
teamed the band with a different big-name guest star every week. On
the September 17 show the celebrity was Frank Sinatra, although it's
unlikely Riddle and FS actually shook hands at this time.

Riddle reached a traumatic career crossroads with Dorsey. A few
years afterward, when Willie Schwartz first identified Riddle to Mahlon
Clark, Clark asked, "Is he a good arranger?" Schwartz answered "*Great*
arranger. Half-assed trombone player, but he's an excellent arranger."
While with Dorsey, it was Finegan who "talked him out of playing the
trombone. Nelson got to the point where he was a good writer," whereas
on the trombone "he could [solo a little]. He just was nothing special. I
told Nelson, 'When you play in the band and write, the leader treats
your writing like it's a hobby. He'll play the stuff, but you won't get paid
much for it,' which was true in those days. So he spent a couple of days
with me, and I kept talking to him. And after much agonizing, he finally
agreed to give it up."

Then something happened that would prevent Riddle from playing
the trombone professionally again. He had hoped that his hitch with the
Merchant Marines would keep him out of the "real" war, but the military
changed its rules, and in April 1945 he was drafted. He stayed in the regular army until June 1946, leading a band for the officers' club in Fort
Knox, Kentucky. During that time, he was somehow involved in an accident in which a garage door somehow came down on his head and
knocked out his front teeth. Because one high-ranking officer in particular had liked his band, he arranged for the officers' dentist (rather than
that of the enlisted men) to work on Riddle's teeth. "For the rest of his
life he had pivots for front teeth. You couldn't tell," said Chris Riddle,
"but he didn't play after that."

Riddle's new bride, Doreen Moran, whom he had married in South Carolina in October 1945, supported him in his resolve to arrange full-time. Immediately after the war, he wrote for Tommy Dorsey and Spivak (including "Laura"), and he and Finegan both arranged for a new orchestra led by trumpeter Larry Elgart. Although Elgart never claimed to be a swinging soloist himself, he leaned toward the new progressive jazz sounds that bands like Gillespie's, Herman's, and Kenton's were beginning to explore. Not surprisingly, the first Elgart band went bankrupt, and when the trumpeter-leader struck gold eight years later, it would be strictly with a businessman's bounce band that had no pretensions to anything else.

After Elgart's early band folded, Riddle went to the coast, and he and Finegan rarely saw each other, unofficially ending their mentor-protégé relationship. "The difference between Bill and Nelson," as the trumpeter's brother and later coleader, Les Elgart, conjectured, and the reason "Nelson attained a lot more success than Bill is that although Bill was still a genius, Nelson wrote with a lot more abandon. Nelson wrote more freely."

Riddle himself acknowledged as much: "I thought [Finegan's later group, the Sauter-Finegan Orchestra] was magnificent. They had some sounds there that were incredible. [But], and this isn't negative . . . it was so intellectual that perhaps some of the emotion was not present. Both Sauter and Finnegan were internal people, and neither was outgoing or gregarious at all. They were quiet, studious people, and I think some of their work shows that. It shows in the clockwork precision and intricacy of their work, but it also might occasionally show in the lack of fire and drive."

Riddle's activities are harder to trace in his freelance period, although we do know that it was Bob Crosby who brought him out to the West Coast not long after he was mustered out of the service. Crosby later claimed that he first met Riddle by accident in a dentist's waiting room; however, a former fellow Dorseyite, guitarist Bob Bain, then in Crosby's rhythm section, actually introduced Riddle to Crosby. "He was looking for an arranger," said Riddle, "and I sort of foisted myself on him." Riddle wrote a few pieces for Crosby (including "I'll Never Be the Same" and "Night and Day," which he remembered fondly), but the singing bandleader's promise of work was negated by the IRS, which made it economically impossible for Crosby to put a group together at that time.

Although Riddle later depicted himself in this period as being "stuck in a strange town with no union card and back to basics again," he immediately fit into Los Angeles' busy studio recording scene, writing for records and radio. Around 1947 he impressed NBC's West Coast musical director Henry Russell enough to receive frequent assignments, and Bob Bain also remembers Riddle writing for accordionist Ernie Felice. "He was doing anything just to make a few bucks," said Bain. He would write for anybody in those days. It was just work, for $100 to $150 an arrangement."[3] In these years he also studied string orchestration formally with the Italian composer and teacher Mario Castelnuovo-Tedesco. "That was on the G.I. Bill, incidentally," he said in 1983, "so by the time I hit Capitol in 1950, I knew my way around the orchestra fairly well."

The first commercial recording outfit to give Riddle a shot at arranging for pop singers was not Capitol, however, but Decca, where Sonny Burke, who had worked with Riddle in Spivak's band, ran the show. Riddle is believed to have written as many as twenty-five arrangements for Bing Crosby in these years, as well as for other singers at Decca. He also gained his first opportunity to conduct at a record session on a Crosby date. "I remember the date because I had to call his wife," Bain explained. "I had promised Doreen that I would call to let her know that everything went okay."

Around 1949 or 1950, Riddle also started receiving some hand-me-down work from Sinatra's rhythm specialist, George Siravo. They had first met in the middle of a session at Columbia's Hollywood facility. "The first time I ever laid eyes on Nelson, he was on crutches and was so bandaged, he looked like a mummy. He looked like somebody in a war hospital scene. He told me he was driving while he was bombed, and he hit a tree while going through Beverly Hills. He had been laid up in the hospital. He said 'If you're overladen with work, if you have any crumbs, if you could throw me a bone, I would greatly appreciate it.' That's how he got a foothold at Columbia."

Exactly how much or how little Riddle wrote at this time is unknown, since he never received credit. Riddle didn't begin to emerge from anonymity until 1950, when an accident led to "Mona Lisa," the first hit record he was associated with. Sonny Burke, who in addition to his Decca duties had directed some sessions for Mel Tormé and other Capitol artists, apparently brought Riddle to the attention of Capitol Records. At the time, Nat King Cole had reached the halfway point in his

---

3. One manifestation of how prolific he was can be easily documented: he and Doreen had six surviving children—Nelson Smock Riddle III (1947), Rosemary (1948), Christopher (1950), Bettina (1954), Cecily Jean (1962), and Maureen Alicia (1962). A seventh child, Lenora Celeste, was born in 1957 but lived only six months.

transition from pianist and leader of the King Cole Trio to a mainstream pop singer with orchestra, and in his dates for Capitol he alternated between a full big band and his world-famous trio.

Producer Lee Gillette wanted to try another format for Cole, a big Gospel-style choir to back the singer on a pseudoreligious excursion called "The Greatest Inventor of Them All," obviously inspired by Sinatra's "The Old Master Painter." Since the number was primarily choral, Gillette appointed Les Baxter, a former vocal group singer and contractor, to direct the session, and Baxter subcontracted Riddle to write at least one of the strictly orchestral nonchoral tunes on the date.[4]

When "Mona Lisa" became Cole's biggest hit to date, it established him as one of the strongest-selling singers in the industry and also launched the career of Baxter, first as a vocal accompanist and then as an early guru of "easy-listening" and "space-age bachelor-pad" music. About the only one "Mona Lisa" didn't affect immediately was its ghostwriter. Baxter did at least two more sessions with Cole, generally also written by Riddle, the second of which produced another blockbuster in "Too Young." As Riddle recalled, however, Cole soon learned who Riddle was and liked his work "very much, and that was my wedge."

Riddle's long-awaited chance to get his name on a record and begin a relationship with a major singer came through a magnanimous gesture from fellow arranger Pete Rugolo. Although Rugolo had been Cole's first regular musical director, he nonetheless pointed out to Cole's manager, Carlos Gastel, that "Mona Lisa" and "Too Young" were actually Riddle's work. "I told Carlos that Nelson should be given a chance because he was so good," said Rugolo. Riddle soon graduated from ghostwriter to full-time musical director for Cole—for approximately ten years and well over 250 songs. "I was never as commercial as Nelson," Rugolo said, "but once Nat started with Nelson, that's when he really hit, so he just kept Nelson with him."

In August 1951, Riddle began arranging and conducting regularly under his own name for Cole, and within a few months he was writing for as many singers as he could make time for on Capitol, including Mel Tormé, Kate Smith, Jerry Lewis, and, thanks to friend Billy May, Ella Mae Morse (a novelty blues singer for whom he concocted the hits

---

4. Equal Time Department: this is Riddle's story, supported by Billy May, Pete Rugolo, and every musician I spoke with who worked on these dates. For his part, Baxter claims to have done all the arrangements on all his sessions by himself. Alan Livingston believes that Baxter might have given Riddle an oral sketch of what he wanted in each chart.

"Oakie Boogie" and "Blacksmith Blues"). By 1952 he was writing for singers across the whole spectrum of labels, most spectacularly Billy Eckstine on MGM, for whom he crafted a stunning ten-inch album of Rodgers and Hammerstein songs.

Yet at thirty-one, Riddle was still considered a newcomer when Livingston and Gilmore brought him to the attention of Frank Sinatra in 1953. According to several musicians and other observers at the first Sinatra-Riddle session, virtually everyone present had been told that the charts Riddle was about to conduct had been written by Billy May. Sinatra was still reluctant to consider a new musical director but was not averse to doing a guest-star team-up with a name band, as he had done with Xavier Cugat and Harry James, and would do again many times. In 1953, Billy May was a name bandleader. Having landed several hit records for Capitol with his "nonworking" studio orchestra, he decided, with the label's encouragement, to actually take a band on the road.

As it happened, the very period May was out doing one-nighters occurred when it was decided to combine the name value and sounds of Frank Sinatra and Billy May. At his very first Capitol date (conducted by Stordahl), Sinatra had already experimented with a Billy May–style background on one tune: May's own composition, the upwardly modulating, blues-tinged "Lean Baby" (the title signifying a description, not an instruction). "Lean Baby" had been arranged by Heinie Beau, who was at that time both May's and Stordahl's (not to mention Paul Weston's) premier deputy, closely following May's original instrumental hit.

"Lean Baby" charted, if not spectacularly, and from there Sinatra and Gilmore decided to do a Sinatra-May session. Capitol asked May to arrange and conduct, but May was on the road. Gilmore saw this situation as a potential opportunity for Nelson Riddle. May recalled, "They said, 'Would you mind if we got Nelson Riddle to do them in your style?' They would use the same studio guys that I had used. I said, 'No, go ahead.' And we worked out a deal for a royalty."

Riddle was probably not thrilled at the prospect of anonymously aping the distinctive style of another writer, but, as trombonist Milt Bernhart remembered, "he did it for the reason that he wanted to be there." In other words, to get a shot at working with Frank Sinatra. Said May, "It came out where I got all the credit, but Nelson did the work." (May, who had been forced to labor anonymously for too many years, promised he'd return the favor; and he did, several years later when he ghosted for Riddle on a television assignment. "Oh, I helped him on a lot of things like that," May continued. "We worked back and forth. We were good friends.")

"So I went in," said Riddle, remembering the date, "and did two sides like Billy May would do them—'South of the Border' and one other ['I Love You']—and two sides as I would do them, 'World on a String' and 'Don't Worry 'Bout Me.'" All the musicians at the date were told that the charts were by May, and the records were released as "Frank Sinatra with Billy May and His Orchestra." Bernhart remembered, "Those people who were on the date—Sy Zentner, Tommy Peters, Conrad Gozzo, Pete Candoli, and the rest—had worked quite a bit with Billy May. They were definitely fooled and were convinced it was Billy's writing!"

It's conceivable that even Sinatra himself was taken in. Sinatra almost certainly sketched out what he wanted in the orchestrations beforehand. The singer had done "South of the Border" occasionally in the early '40s, and he had based this particular arrangement on one he had performed on the radio in 1944, accompanied then by Spike Jones, who was only slightly more outrageous and slightly less musically hip than May. Sinatra had probably learned "I Love You"—not the Cole Porter classic but a 1923 show tune, from *Little Jessie James*, by Harlan Thompson and Harry Archer—from the great 1939 Jimmie Lunceford–Sy Oliver recording; it pops up occasionally on his 1950–51 broadcasts. He had also been doing "World on a String" at a number of 1952 engagements, even using it as an opener at the Chez Paree in Chicago.

Alan Dell, then a Capitol employee (and later the guru of all good pop music at the BBC), has recalled that Sinatra came in fully expecting to see the full frame of Billy May at the dais on that day, April 30, 1953. "When Frank came in, he saw a strange man on the podium and said, 'Who's this?' I said, 'He's just conducting the band. We've got the Billy May arrangements.' So he sang 'South of the Border' and 'I Love You' and said, 'Great. What happens next?' I said, 'Try this one,' and they went into 'World on a String.' Then he said, 'Hey, who wrote that?' I said, 'This guy, Nelson Riddle.' He said, 'Beautiful!' And from that the partnership started."[5]

The partnership did not get under way immediately after that first date, however. According to Milt Bernhart and several other musicians, the second Sinatra-Riddle session, which was to have been the first non-

5. As further evidence of how memory can screw you after thirty years, the two non-May-style numbers, "World on a String" and "Don't Worry 'Bout Me," were actually recorded *before* the pseudo-May pieces, "I Love You" and "South of the Border." This concurs with Bill Miller's memory of the session: "We did the first two tunes with Nelson, then he made an announcement. He said, 'Now we have to make like Billy May'— because Billy obviously couldn't be there. So Nelson was asked to write à la Billy May, which he did pretty well."

"ghost" date, occurred either soon after or perhaps even before the April 30, 1953, date. Bernhart recalled that this session began with "Wrap Your Troubles in Dreams" (which Sinatra and Riddle would remake a year later on their second album). Riddle called the downbeat, but before singer and orchestra even got the first take down, Sinatra stopped everything cold. "The band stopped, and Frank said to Nelson, 'Call a break.' So the contractor said, 'Take ten.' Sinatra crooked his finger at Nelson, and the two of them walked out of the studio. I don't know why, but I followed them. They went out into the hallway and into a smaller studio."

While the rest of the musicians broke out a deck of cards, Bernhart stood in the hallway and observed Sinatra and Riddle behind a sound-proof glass where he could see them talking but not hear what they were saying. "Nelson was standing frozen, and Frank was doing all the talking. His hands were moving. He wasn't angry, but he was obviously telling him something of importance. I was positive I knew what Frank was saying to him. I could tell by the arrangement. It was very busy. *Very* busy. There were all kinds of things going on behind the vocal. Frank undoubtedly told him that 'When you're writing, write a fill for me when I'm through singing but don't write a concerto behind me.'

"Nelson had a lot of technique as an arranger, he had been studying around town with very legitimate teachers like Castelnuovo-Tedesco. But some people have to be told to take it easy when they're writing for a singer."

Bernhart continued, "When we came back, the date was over. Sinatra could have dumped him. Other singers would have said, 'Well, get another guy,' if they were as important as Frank Sinatra. But he didn't. Which means that he recognized something in Nelson that a lot of people wouldn't."

If the *Billboard* charts are to be believed, Sinatra landed only about as many hits in the first Capitol sessions as he had in the last Columbias. The new label's A&R crew, particularly Livingston and Gilmore, were excited by the sound of the second and third dates, which got him away from the "out-of-tempo, rustle of spring" sound of the Sinatra-Stordahl era. The May-styled "South of the Border" has Sinatra swinging harder and more convincingly than anything he had done in the '40s (even the best of Siravo), and "World on a String," with its magnificent decrescendo opening, displays a newer, more confident Sinatra.

The next date, in May, produced "From Here to Eternity," which offered the first evidence of the long-awaited career turnaround that Sinatra, Gilmore, and Riddle were praying for. In a Tin Pan Alley side-swipe at Rudyard Kipling, songwriters Fred Karger and Bob Wells had borrowed the line "damned from here to Eternity" from "Gentleman Rankers" (which had already been softened into "The Whiffenpoof Song") and used it as the basis for a love song. In itself it was no better or worse than dozens of movie themes (usually with lyrics by Sammy Cahn) that Sinatra would tackle with Riddle. The song had been written to promote *From Here to Eternity*, a movie Sinatra had begun shooting two months earlier in March, his first major film since 1949 and his only screen appearance at all since 1951; it would have considerable ramifications for his career. Milt Bernhart gives Sinatra credit for having the instinct to realize how important *From Here to Eternity* would be: "If you had just read the book, why would that change a person's whole life? Why would that have mattered? Frank knew that it would. He knew where he was going."

Suffice it to say that *Eternity* put Sinatra back on the top of the movie trade and all of showbiz. It wasn't just because it was a major film, his first "serious" role and his only Oscar as an actor, or because it was the major box-office hit of the year. No less an impartial judge of Sinatra's career than Mitch Miller observed, "By getting stomped to death in that movie, [it was like] he did a public penance for all [the wrongs he had done]. You can chart it. From the day that movie came out, his records began to sell." *Eternity* trumpeted: the old Sinatra is dead! Long live the new Sinatra.

If Sinatra records began to sell again with the success of *Eternity*, he did nothing to produce more until the end of the year, continuing to "woodshed" for most of that year on the road. He made his first peacetime tour of continental Europe in the summer, which was an out-and-out disaster, inspiring such *Billboard* headlines as SINATRA LAYS EGG IN NAPLES, NEEDS COP AID and MR. SINATRA, GO HOME. He did a bit better in Britain that July: two BBC appearances on a program called *Show Band Show* find him in surprisingly good voice. But, unfortunately, apart from a stunning "Don't Worry 'Bout Me" (much better than the record, and including the verse), The Voice was in a disappointingly disagreeable mood in his concert at the Opera House in Blackpool.

But from the day that *Eternity* was released, August 17, 1953, Sinatra was touched with that old "comeback" magic. At the end of that month he did a week at the 500 Club in Atlantic City—to what *Variety* labeled a "standing-room-only" crowd. Moving north, he entered one of the truly charmed engagements of his career, at the Riviera in Fort Lee, New Jersey. (One night both Harold Arlen and Manie Sachs were in the house.) The trade papers were close to ecstatic, and the mainstream press was also falling in line. He was also gathering momentum via appearances on *The Buick Show* with Milton Berle, *The Colgate Comedy Hour* with Ethel Merman, and at the Sands in Las Vegas in October.

Sinatra had previously played the Riviera exactly a year earlier. During that 1952 engagement, Frank Military recalled, he had already had something of his "Capitol" sound (this was before "Why Try to Change Me Now?") but had yet to be rediscovered by his audience. "Before *Eternity,* nobody showed up. Nobody even came to the dressing room [to congratulate him]. I said, 'Where are all the people?' He said, 'These people only come out for stars, and I'm through with them!' The following year *Eternity* comes out. We go back to the Riviera, and you can't get into the dressing room! I said, 'Frank, you said you were never talking to these people.' He said, 'There are no other kind of people!'"

One "location recording" of the Riviera engagement does exist, but it has circulated only among collectors and is in horrible sound (the band is all but inaudible). Fortunately, Sinatra wanted to capitalize on the exuberance of this immediate post-*Eternity* mood, and decided to document these "road" arrangements on what would be his first Capitol album, *Songs for Young Lovers.* Sinatra then sold Gilmore on Siravo's work by bringing him to hear the band book in action at his October gig at the Sands in Las Vegas.

The Siravo orchestrations Sinatra used at the 500 Club, the Riviera, and the Sands (among other venues) used eight musicians, although they may have been written for a slightly larger ensemble. When Sinatra and Gilmore decided to record these charts in Los Angeles (Sinatra avoided recording in New York during the entire Capitol era), they again recruited Riddle to conduct. For the album, Sinatra used eleven men, indicating that the orchestrations had either been trimmed for live appearances or perhaps beefed up (by either Siravo or Riddle) for recording. In any case, the sound quality on the Riviera tape is just good enough to confirm that the *Young Lovers* charts are practically identical to the ones Sinatra was using on personal appearances at this time.

"This is something new as far as I'm concerned," Sinatra announced at the Riviera. "We usually have eighteen brass and guys with [all kinds of] saxophones and Freddie Martin–style stuff, but we decided to try something different this time." As clarinetist Mahlon Clark recalled the *Young Lovers* sessions: "Frank used the arrangements he was using on the road then, written for a small band," of two reeds, four strings, guitar, piano (or celesta on "Little Girl Blue"), bass, drums, and harp. "I remember that they were tattered and worn," said Clark, and unlike most arrangements that studio men were called upon to play, "they were not new. Nelson brought in only one new chart of his own, written for that combination, and it was 'Like Someone in Love.'"

Riddle was undoubtedly getting fed up with having to ghost for another arranger, first May and now Siravo, especially since conducting was far from his strong point. Also, the only credit on the album cover read "Accompanied by Nelson Riddle," which probably annoyed Riddle and Siravo equally.[6] Yet if Sinatra was looking to show him a model of what he was looking for in an arranger, however, he could not have picked a better textbook than the seven Siravo charts. Siravo consistently supports the singer without getting in his way, a skill Riddle would soon master.

Young Lovers comes so close in mood and feeling to Siravo's own albums of chamber jazz with strings, such as *Polite Jazz* (Kapp), it's a wonder anyone could have mistaken the charts for Riddle's. (Although the violin intro on "Violets for Your Furs"[7] sounds more typical of later Sinatra, that probably has as much to do with the individual player, Felix Slatkin, than the chart itself, as Slatkin soon became Riddle's preferred fiddler.) These seven tracks also sound much more like earlier Sinatra-Siravo chamber works, like "I've Got a Crush on You" and "Nevertheless," despite the absence of a trumpet soloist, than they do anything by Riddle.

Both Siravo and Riddle often include original introductions and countermelodies, but the older man almost constantly riffs unobtrusively behind the main vocal line in a way that seems much more firmly anchored to the swing era. For instance, Siravo relies heavily on a rhythm guitar (Allan Reuss or Al Hendrickson) playing a solid four, often in unison with Mahlon Clark's clarinet, in a fashion that's very suggestive of the Benny Goodman–Charlie Christian small groups. This comes through on the riff underpinning of "I Get a Kick Out of You" and "They Can't Take That Away from Me," both of which effectively cannibalize the bridge as an ad-lib verse introduction.

6. Siravo occasionally came into the King Karol record shop in New York where Sinatra fan Bob Sherrick was then working and griped that he had been gypped out of his credit on *Young Lovers,* and nobody believed him. Many years later, Tony Bennett happened to be speaking with Riddle and mentioned that he would soon be seeing Siravo. Riddle then told Bennett to pass along to Siravo his apologies—even though he wasn't personally responsible—for Siravo's being cheated out of his credit on *Young Lovers.*

7. While preparing a Carnegie Hall tribute to Sinatra, Jonathan Schwartz had the opportunity to examine some of the actual orchestrations in the Sinatra library. He reported that the chart of "Violets for Your Furs" credits the arrangement to Dick Jones. Skitch Henderson has expressed the opinion that Jones wrote more charts for Sinatra than he is given credit for.

For his part, Sinatra has never sounded more amiably energetic than on his premier Capitol album and, indeed, on the whole first year of sessions for the label. When "Funny Valentine" switches in and out of waltz time in the outchorus, Sinatra seems to levitate from one time signature to the other. He's so rhythmically hip in "A Foggy Day" that he transforms three syllables from an Ira Gershwin line into a stop-time break— "lost its charm" could be "oh! play that thing" in "Dippermouth Blues." And on the same song, when he repeats "shining" four times just because it sounds so good, "shining" is exactly what he's doing.

Although Bill Miller (who plays superlative accompaniment behind Sinatra in the ad-lib verse) dismissed "I Get a Kick out of You" as "too square," it became the sole Siravo arrangement to remain in Sinatra's working "book," and he continued to perform it virtually every time he found himself in a small-group context.

"Like Someone in Love" is immediately identifiable as Riddle's work, not only because it spotlights one of his soon-to-be signature sounds, the flute, but it also employs the quasi-impressionistic harmonies that Riddle would gradually perfect. Riddle plays two reed sounds against each other, Mahlon Clark's clarinet and Skeets Herfurt's flute. "Skeets had some beautiful alto solos, but I remember he was having a hell of a time with the flute part!" said Clark. "As he was struggling, I was sitting there thinking, 'Thank God it's him, not me,' because I didn't play flute at all."

With "Young at Heart," recorded two sessions later, Sinatra at last lands a major record hit to complement the cinematic sensation of *From Here to Eternity*. "Young at Heart" functions as a hymn to recharged batteries. If in *Eternity* Sinatra had said the requisite number of prayers to kiss off his previous life, how better to begin his next one than with a text about starting over? Although soon connected to a moodily melodramatic and overacted flick, the song "Young at Heart" is entirely believable sweetness and light throughout. Riddle douses Sinatra in a large field of strings that never become heavy; the arranger makes sure of this by trimming the tops of their sonic range with a flock of even higher and lighter flutes. Riddle's orchestra shines brightly but never more brilliantly than Sinatra himself. The comeback was now complete.

"Young at Heart" also symbolizes the vocal arrangement Sinatra was looking for when he beckoned Riddle aside a few sessions previously for some friendly pointers. As late as the Riviera gig, when Sinatra introduces his arrangers, the singer mentions Riddle but also refers to "the head man, Axel Stordahl." "Young at Heart" is the disc that finally "consummates" his musical marriage to Riddle. Sinatra had never been completely off the charts, but "Young at Heart" marked the first time he topped them since 1947. Although he and Riddle each collaborated with others in this period, by and large the professional marriage remained intact. For the next and most remarkable phase of both of their lives, they would be a team.

Sinatra and Riddle remained essential to each other because each man pushed the other to heights neither could achieve individually. It remained for Riddle to develop both the ballad side and the swinging side of Sinatra, or rather to extend the legacies of Axel Stordahl and George Siravo (and before him, Sy Oliver). And the Sinatra-Riddle sound has since become what we think of when we think of Sinatra; the pre-Riddle period can be reduced to a prelude, the post-Riddle era to an afterthought.

Anyone with half an ear can hear what Riddle did for Sinatra, but it takes a little more digging to ascertain what Sinatra did for Riddle— apart from making him a national name by letting him ride on the coat- tails of one of the most phenomenal comebacks in showbiz history. The first ten years or so of Riddle arrangements, from the few we know of from his big-band tenures to the early Cole charts, reveal an orchestrator of obvious talent but little recognizable style. Even more than Cole, who was never as involved with his big-band accompaniments as Sinatra, working with Sinatra was the catalyst that inspired what would soon be instantly identifiable as the Nelson Riddle sound.

Lightness shines as the primary ingredient of the Riddle style. Whether he has ten brass swinging heavily or an acre of strings, Riddle always manages to make everything sound light; that way, the weightiest ballad doesn't become oversentimental and insincere, and the fastest swinger doesn't come off as forced. Like his predecessor, Axel Stordahl, Riddle started with early-twentieth-century impressionists like Debussy and Ravel, particularly the second and third pieces in the latter's *Le Tombeau de Couperin* series (orchestrated in 1926). "Sometimes Riddle will throw on a nice dissonant chord at the end of a ballad," composer Joel Herron observed. "It's like holding up a sign saying, 'Speak to Ravel.'"

At the end of "It Never Entered My Mind," the intro and coda of "Gone with the Wind," and throughout "I'll Never Be the Same," Riddle employs a faux Oriental "wind chimes" figure. He once said this motif derived "from my obvious admiration of the French impressionists. They were fascinated by the characteristics of the music of another land, and it was nothing at all to them to bridge the gap and use those charac- teristics for their own purposes. In the *Mother Goose Suite*, there's the 'Empress of the Pagodas,' which is a distinctly Oriental scene seen through the eyes or heard through the ears of a French impressionist."

"I loved how Nelson used Ravel's approach to polytonality," said Quincy Jones, who seemed to be describing "Young at Heart" when he continued, "Nelson was smart because he put the electricity up above Frank. He put it way upstairs and gave Frank the room downstairs for his voice to shine, rather than building big lush parts that were in the same register as his voice. Nelson wrote some of the greatest arrangements for vocalists that I've ever heard."

Like most jazz-oriented writers of his generation, especially his close colleague Billy May, Riddle derives from Ellington and Strayhorn and the great writers of the swing era as much as from the Europeans. "Nelson Riddle's role model was Duke Ellington" was how Milt Bernhart put it. The jazz influence is apparent on the surface; the classical leanings can be detected only in the deep background.

As with Ellington, the instruments and instrumentalists that Riddle composed for were crucial to his emerging style, and even more so were the idiosyncratic sounds of the musicians themselves, especially Sinatra. Both men were products of a big-band background, and Riddle reinforced Sinatra's conviction that the musicians best equipped to support him were not the conservatory-trained studio staff musicians of the '30s and '40s but guys who had cut their teeth as teenagers in the touring swing bands. Riddle leaned strongly toward veterans of the "progressive-minded" Woody Herman and Stan Kenton organizations. "When Nelson started to work at Capitol, he was looking for fresh blood," said Bernhart. "Before Nelson, the studio people were convinced we couldn't read or wouldn't show up. There was a bad reputation." Trumpeter Harry "Sweets" Edison, tenor sax Ted Nash, clarinetist Mahlon Clark, and flute specialist Harry Klee (like trombonist Juan Tizol, Klee was featured as a solo voice for texture and color but rarely as an improvisor) are probably the regulars Riddle featured most extensively as soloists.

Bass trombonist George Roberts was among the closest to Riddle personally and one of the most essential to him musically. Roberts reported that in the early '50s Riddle used him as a sounding board. "He said he needed identification." Riddle had experimented earlier with a variation of the famous George Shearing Quintet sound, using a tightly harmonized blend of piano and vibes for the memorable introduction to Nat Cole's "Unforgettable." The disc proved a success (and was eventually a multigenerational hit), and Riddle worked variations of that intro into Cole's "It Happens to Be Me" and "If Love Is Good to Me." Still, he realized that this kind of gimmick could grow stale if used further—a conclusion eventually arrived at by Shearing himself.

In working and talking with Roberts and his other musicians, Riddle gradually devised a combination of Roberts' bass trombone, flute, muted trumpet, and strings as his signature sound. Roberts had first played professionally in the Navy and attended a Los Angeles conservatory after the war. He eventually worked with Gene Krupa, where he first modulated from the traditional tenor trombone to its big brother, the bass instrument. After a stint in Las Vegas with Ray Herbeck's sweet band, Roberts toured for two and a half years with Stan Kenton, where he was first widely heard. Kenton once introduced a Roberts feature number (the unrecorded "Yesterdays") by claiming that here was the first bass trombonist who used the instrument for more than "blowing roots and tonics at the bottom of big chords." Urbie Green told Roberts, "You're the only guy who plays that thing like a trombone."

On the "Young at Heart" date, the first Sinatra-Riddle session where Roberts is known to be present, Riddle dropped the trumpets and had the trombones, abetted by two French horns, assume most of that section's responsibility (in addition to their own). Roberts would be Riddle's most employed instrumentalist over the years, prominent on, to name just a few, "Makin' Whoopee" on *Swingin' Lovers,* "How Deep Is the Ocean" on *Nice 'n' Easy,* and throughout *Wine and Roses.* Roberts trails Sinatra like Phillip Marlowe on "In the Cool, Cool, Cool of the Evening," and while Ol' Blue Eyes extolls the glories of "Swinging on a Star," Roberts grunts gleefully as if to answer that he'd rather be a pig.

Pianist Stan Freeman, who worked with Riddle and Sinatra separately, points out that "although all the arrangers were good, Riddle was the best of them all. His use of everything in the orchestra I thought was just wonderful, and really complemented Sinatra's singing more than the others. He had an identifiable style—you knew a Nelson Riddle arrangement when you heard it." Not only is a Riddle arrangement immediately distinguishable from a chart by any other writer, but you can instantly tell a score in *Songs for Swingin' Lovers!* from one in *Sinatra's Swingin' Session,* and one in *Nice 'n' Easy* from one in *Moonlight Sinatra.* Although they all share common elements, no other arranger could create so many different universes, each with its own stylistic glossary, for Sinatra to exist in.

The style is still a work in progress on Sinatra's second Capitol LP, *Swing Easy,* arranged entirely by Riddle (with the arguable exception of "All of Me," possibly inspired by a Siravo "Riviera" chart, which Riddle almost completely rewrote, adding, among other things, a brass section). As we've seen, the evolution of the classic Sinatra "concept album" form had a technological imperative. First, there was the advent of microgroove recording, which made slower-spinning and hence longer-playing phonodiscs possible.

Even more important, the perfection of the process of recording on tape and the development of high-fidelity microphones now made it possible to capture the most delicate nuances. One could now explore enough minute details from track to track to fill an entire album of eight to twelve or even sixteen songs in a similar mood. The fuller frequency range made Riddle's whole sound—and therefore his career—workable, dependent as it was on contrasting the strings above with the trombones below. Riddle utilized the new technology to the fullest, making every chart explode in a rainbow of orchestral color.

Not surprisingly, the first theme Sinatra tackles in this brave new era is fast and swinging, uptempos having been one trail he rarely traveled in the Columbian era. "Sinatra in the '40s was the crooner with the bow tie," said guitarist Al Viola, who worked with Sinatra in both eras. "With the Page Cavanaugh Trio [who accompanied Sinatra frequently between 1945 and 1949], we hardly did any uptempo things. When he came back in the '50s, I noticed right away that he was still a crooner with the teenagers and all that, but now he was also *the* swinger. He had a real strong baritone, and he was more into the swinging things, like 'Lady Is a Tramp.'" Soon Sinatra would be declaring "Oh! Look at Me Now" to all who doubted, tellingly reusing that first important fast tune he ever recorded (with Dorsey in 1941) as the climax of *A Swingin' Affair*. And when Sinatra sings "I'm in the groove again" near the end of "Takin' a Chance on Love" on *Swing Easy*, he isn't just whistling "Dixie."

Although not as purely jazz styled as his collaborations with Count Basie a decade later, *Swing Easy* finds Sinatra constantly altering the melodies and reimagining them with far more abandon than anything he dared attempt in the previous decade. On "Just One of Those Things," the tender kiss-off piece that opens *Swing Easy*, Sinatra fashions his equivalent of a twelve-bar blues chorus out of the words "good-bye and amen." Likewise, on "Get Happy" Sinatra repeats the opening line over and over beneath a fade-out coda, like a lick being stated and echoed by a trumpet or saxophone.

Swing Easy also marks the first appearance of trumpeter Harry Edison. Born two months before Sinatra and, like the Old Man himself, still on the road as of this writing, Edison established himself as a jazz giant when he starred as Count Basie's leading brassman from 1937 to about 1950. By then long considered jazz's number one master of the obligato, Edison toured in the early '50s as Josephine Baker's musical director. But in spite of his accomplishments in the jazz world, and also despite his spending all but a decade or so of his eight decades on the road, Edison is best known as a studio player with Riddle and Sinatra. Always preferring to work in front of club audiences, Edison "blames" his Hollywood studio years (roughly from 1952 to 1965) on a particularly status-conscious wife. She "had" to own a house in Hollywood "and go every Saturday to the beauty parlor. I don't know why she had to get her hair done so often," said Edison, adding, "The only happy marriages I ever had were when I was broke."

Lester Young christened Edison "Sweets," and for nearly sixty years the nickname has served as a perfect description of Edison's playing. Rarely as direct a player as, say, Roy Eldridge or Harry James, Edison shares with his frequent costar Benny Carter a unique capacity for playing at you from around the corner. He constructs pithy, angular, yet always swinging phrases that approach the melody from odd angles and often seems to be playing obligatos even when he's flat-out soloing (as in "Jeeper's Creepers" on *Swing Easy*). Edison's skill as a master melodist allows Riddle to play with perceptions of foreground and background; the instrumental section of "We'll Be Together Again" on *Swingin' Lovers* consists of the main ensemble playing a variation on the melody, which is phrased quickly to allow Edison plenty of room for his interline statements. The heckling from the sidelines often becomes more important than the show on center stage.

Equally important for an obligatist, Edison can say an awful lot in a very few notes, and most of his parts on Sinatra records consist of merely a very well placed handful of beeps. Sinatra and Riddle came to value Edison's beeps so highly that he was rarely expected to play with the regular trumpet section. Rather, he would be positioned to the side of the ensemble, wearing headphones and playing into his own mike, waiting for the precisely the right moment to insert his tasty trumpet remarks into the foreground action.

Edison, the only musician to figure prominently in the careers of both Frank Sinatra and Billie Holiday, one of Sinatra's major inspirations, said that it wasn't a question of knowing what to play behind a singer so much as *when*. "You have to wait for them to breathe or something," he said. Or, as Riddle put it, "I think the muted trumpet can make a comment and yet not get in the way of the singer." Edison reported that although he disliked Hollywood and the studio scene, he nonetheless considered working with Sinatra and Riddle, no less than with Holiday, a highlight of his career.

Riddle said of Edison's playing in general that whatever the situation, "he certainly caught the mood." Adding that Edison was responsible for most of the whimsy on his records, particularly *Swing Easy, Swingin' Lovers,* and *Swingin' Affair,* Riddle continued, "The humor is in Harry's head. You show him what you want, you delineate the area that he's going to play in, and he's the one who actually makes the humor of the comment. You just show him where. He can be on my team anytime."

Edison was also celebrated as the studio fraternity's resident character; according to one story, Sinatra once stopped an entire session—thirty men waited around on Capitol's time—so that he and Edison, both rabid baseball fans, could catch a few innings on TV. Riddle recalled an instance when "Harry Edison showed up at a Sinatra date with a policeman on each arm. I think he'd run several red lights, and the cops nailed him. He said, 'I'm on my way to work with Sinatra,' and they said, 'Sure, you are!' He said, 'All right, come on with me, and I'll show you.' So they marched him into the recording session, and there was Frank and everybody. They released him and laughed and walked away."

For *Swing Easy* Sinatra supposedly sought the sound of the Red Norvo–Mildred Bailey "Mr. and Mrs. Swing Band" of the late '30s. While Riddle never goes so far as to mimick Eddie Sauter (Norvo's musical director and later Bill Finegan's partner), he does emphasize Norvo's instrument, the vibes, here played by studio percussion virtuoso Frank Flynn. Today, Flynn recalls that both Sinatra and Riddle were delighted with the way the vibes were used in *Swing Easy* and that he considers it (along with his solo on Riddle's and Ella Fitzgerald's "Midnight Sun") the best thing he ever did. Just the same, Sinatra and Riddle never opted to use the vibes that way again (although the celesta more or less assumes that role in *Songs for Swingin' Lovers!*, particularly on "You're Getting to Be a Habit with Me," "Pennies from Heaven," and "Swingin' Down the Lane," and throughout *In the Wee Small Hours*).

Flynn may have been close to the truth when he said that the charts reminded him more of Ellington than Sauter. The trombones do engage in a hocket passage (playing individual lines that overlap in a disjointed hiccuplike fashion) in "Jeepers Creepers," much the way Ellington had his "pep section" do in the 1938 "Braggin' in Brass." "Wrap Your Troubles in Dreams," with its clean, streamlined swing that must be the diametric opposite of the original, overbusy chart of a year earlier, sports a very hot chase chorus between clarinetist Eddie Miller (of Bob Crosby fame) and trombonist Ray Sims. Sinatra's own vocals have never come closer in jazz feeling to early '40s Billie Holiday. In using a more or less standard fourteen-piece dance band instrumentation, making this one of Sinatra's only sets without strings, Sinatra and Riddle more likely sought to refer to the swing era in general rather than to any specific band or artist.

Still, Sinatra doesn't quite take it all the way. Around the same time as *Swing Easy*, he and Riddle were also developing his swinging side in a series of singles, the material apparently selected by Voyle Gilmore, although subject to Sinatra's approval. Songs like "Take a Chance," "Ya Better Stop" (with its ingenious parody of a "fade-away record" ending), and "Why Should I Cry over You" were obviously not up to the level of the time-tested standards Sinatra was doing on the albums, although "The Tender Trap" became a cornerstone of the new Sinatra iconography. (Further, both "Same Old Saturday Night" and "You'll Get Yours" have become perennial favorites of Sinatra fans, although neither entered his regular repertoire.)

Sinatra also put at least two new tunes from this group on the standard song map at this time: "The Man That Got Away" and "Learnin' the Blues." The latter had been a local hit single in Philadelphia for singer Joe Valino, then known as the Sinatra of the City of Brotherly Love. Valino's disc had been sent to Sinatra by amateur composer Dolores Vicki Silver. Sinatra later recalled that of all the song submissions he received over the years, "only one that was sent to me that ever had any—to use a strange word—professionality. It was called 'Learnin' the Blues,' and it was written by a girl named Silver from Philadelphia. . . . She never wrote another one that I know of." With its infectious riffs (a whole trumpet section beeping like Edison) and vibraphonic backgrounds, it was one of the biggest sellers Sinatra ever had.

On some of the lesser singles Sinatra and Riddle try to compensate by stuffing the arrangements with business to distract from their deficiencies. "Not as a Stranger," a definitely inferior Van Heusen movie theme, rates an intriguingly offbeat Riddle treatment that bears more than a passing similarity to the many quasi-exotic charts he wrote for Nat Cole (particularly "I Am in Love"). "Same Old Saturday Night," a Sammy Cahn text that even down to the title is "Saturday Night (Is the Loneliest Night of the Week)" spelled sideways, is irresistibly bouncy in the classic Sinatra-Riddle mold. On the whole, the uptempo singles require busier orchestrations while the charts on the stringless *Swing Easy*, if anything, err on the side of the ultra-trim, being primarily concerned with staying out of Sinatra's jazzy way.

By 1956's *Songs for Swingin' Lovers!* Sinatra has found the perfect balance between the two extremes. As played by a swing band supplemented by a whole string orchestra, Riddle's arrangements are considerably fuller than those for *Swing Easy*. Yet while it's often considered a compliment that a given orchestrator can make a group sound larger than it actually is, it's to Riddle's credit that he never hits you over the head with the idea that thirty men are actually playing at once. The depth of the larger ensemble is there whenever Sinatra needs it for emotional enhancement, but most of the time Blue Eyes and the band swing economically, not to mention mightily.

And swing is the thing. Where *Swing Easy* can be described as a vocal album that swings, *Lovers* is a swinging vocal album, and the difference is crucial. It's been argued that the absence of a strong trend in dance music after the war facilitated the rise of rock and roll; with the big bands fading, there wasn't much for baby boomers to beat their feet to in the music of either Dinah Shore or Dizzy Gillespie. The mid-1950s found Sinatra striving to make his music relevant to both the old and new generations of dancing disc buyers. The exquisite *Swing* albums took the high road to the feet, but one March 1955 session, which produced a single so tacky it would have offended Mitch Miller, took the low road to defeat. This date yielded Sinatra's sole attempts at doo-wop: "Two Hearts, Two Kisses" and the autobiographically named "From the Bottom to the Top." Although he showed foresight in being the first really big traditonal pop star to dabble in this genre—this being even before RCA brought Elvis Presley out of Nashville—the pairing wasn't even up to his 1952 hack at rhythm and blues, "Bim Bam Baby."[8]

With *Swingin' Lovers*, however, Sinatra tapped into precisely the right mixture, which would allow him to sustain his popularity well beyond the age of Elvis and Aquarius. His uptempo albums could be listened to by music fans, but more often serve as perfectly programmed sets of dance music. What's more, with Sinatra cramming as many as eight songs per side, the party could keep moving for nearly twenty-five minutes without anybody's having to stop shuffling long enough to flip the platter over. The very generous length of *Swingin' Lovers* and *Swingin' Affair* contributes to the euphoric mood of the discs. (In each case, Sinatra originally recorded sixteen songs and dropped one. On the CD edition of *Affair*, the "bonus track," "The Lady Is a Tramp," has been restored, but on *Lovers*, the additional song, "Memories of You," remains a no-show. Both albums also originally concluded with a Dorsey remake, "How About You?" on the first and "Oh! Look at Me Now" on the second.)

8. Although Riddle had presided (barely) over Nat King Cole's first doo-wop date, 1954's "If I May," the more utilitarian producer-arranger Dave Cavanaugh handled Sinatra's foray into that field. The earliest Sinatra-Riddle excursion into kiddie pop came with 1956's "Hey! Jealous Lover," using more conventional Sinatra elements: an overtly commercial Riddle orchestration, a Sammy Cahn lyric, and a '50s *Hit Parade*–style vocal group far whiter than the Nuggets, the group who had doo-wopped behind Sinatra on the 1955 titles.

Though less frisky than on *Easy*, Sinatra remains quite jazzy on *Lovers* and especially on *Affair*, where he begins to cultivate the harsher sound that would dominate his work from the late '60s on. In the great jazz tradition, he gets more playful on the second choruses of these tracks; every one of the numbers on these three albums consists of either two full choruses or a chorus and a half. Many have instrumental breaks of eight or sixteen bars, and Riddle fills most of the blank space, either between lines or choruses, with the most suitably fitting filligrees—Edison beeping, Roberts grunting, Harry Klee's flute, or Mahlon Clark's clarinet. (On "Swinging down the Lane" Riddle has a characteristically plunging Edison chasing after a more straight and open Harry James–style trumpet solo by Conrad Gozzo.) Far from cluttering up the landscape, Riddle's additional bits of business enhance the vocals and the main melodic line; no less than Edison, all the Riddle sidemen could, in Bernhart's words, "make history in three and a half beats."

With each of his initial three all-swing albums with Riddle, the blue-eyed one gets progressively deeper into a feeling of abandon with the lyrics. Always a rhythmic master, the balladeer Sinatra is the master of long legato phrases and the swinging Sinatra conquers short, staccato bursts. When he jumps on these one-note phrases, he often twists them and playfully slaps them, like a Harlem Globetrotter rolling the ball across his shoulders. It's a rhythmic and dramatic exercise, the musical specifics of which derive as much from Sinatra's association with Buddy Rich and his love for Louis Armstrong as from Tommy Dorsey.

It is especially effective when he contrasts the two approaches, as on the steadily modulating "From This Moment On" on *Swingin' Affair*, in which he extends the main phrase but emphasizes key syllables such as "hoop-de-do songs" by delivering them in brief percussive barrages. Likewise, on "Memories of You" he seamlessly integrates a staccatolike stress on syllables in the middle of a long legato line ("*your* face beams *in* my dreams").

He can kid a lyric by interjecting slight alterations, such as "this cat's so willing" in "Makin' Whoopee" on *Lovers*, or "ring-a-ding ding," the pet phrase that grew into a song, first documented in "I Won't Dance" in *A Swingin' Affair*. He instills these with a feeling of spontaneity, and generally they are ad-libbed: three alternate takes to "Stars Fell on Alabama" (probably recorded the week before the final master) reveal Sinatra gradually working out his modifications, such as "stars fractured 'Bama." (Considering that librettist Mitchell Parish already took considerable liberties when he described 'Bama as a fairyland—few of us who have lived there would characterize that state as such—Sinatra's goosing up that text doesn't seem quite so impertinent.) These ad-libs help Sinatra to bounce the text like a toy balloon, but without popping or deflating the intent of the lyric. He makes it bend without breaking.

In his inventive use of ingenious introductions, codas, and counter-melodies, Riddle reminds us of Axel Stordahl. That they have so much in common here underscores how Sinatra chose this element to nurture in his collaborators. Riddle comes up with a descending, flutey phrase at the start of "Stars Fell on Alabama" that depicts falling stars, similar to one that he would expand into the long, dramatic opener to "Lost in the Stars" almost ten years later in *The Concert Sinatra*. Other Riddle "extras" are not nearly as programmatic: rather than alluding to gospel sounds, the mock-spiritual "Lonesome Road" (also on *Affair*) opens with Bill Miller riffing way down low in the bass range, followed by a Latin rhythm pattern played on a shaker.

As with so many other Sinatra albums, *Swingin' Lovers* started with a tentative session that he later scrapped. That date commenced with a Riddle run-through of "I Thought About You," an unusual number both for its A B A B' pattern and because it marked one of the rare works composed by Sinatra's buddy James Van Heusen with a text by Johnny Mercer. Not that this June 1955 attempt was "too busy," it was just different. This original orchestration starts with a big orchestral intro, has Edison playing behind Sinatra for his first sixteen bars, and then features Juan Tizol for most of the sixteen-bar instrumental section. By the time Sinatra and Riddle perfected the outline, in January 1956, it would open very quietly, with a Klee flute introduction; the woodwind passage would then continue behind Sinatra for the first eight bars of the refrain. Sinatra and Riddle then divide the second chorus in a most ingenious manner: Riddle plays the first A with prominent Edison, then Sinatra sings the first B, then Sweets and the ensemble again play the second A instrumentally, and Sinatra takes it out with the final eight bars, the band capping it with a variation on a Basie tag. He doesn't get as hot and exciting as "I've Got You Under My Skin" or "The Lady Is a Tramp" but gives the effect of starting the song as a ballad and finishing as a flagwaver.

From the beginning, the *Swingin' Lovers* project had "hit" written all over it. The opening track, "You Make Me Feel So Young," amounts to "Young at Heart" in swingtime. Sinatra captures that same brand of childlike exuberant inocence, playing up lyricist Mack Gordon's charming schoolkid-awkward isolation of the word "in-div-id-u-al" (as on 1951's "Whistle a Happy Tune"). Perhaps that spirit also served to bless the disc with the same kind of cashbox magic "Young at Heart" acheived.

Swingin' Lovers was such a big hit that the sequel, *A Swingin' Affair,* arrived before the year was out. A still brassier, harder-hitting set than *Lovers, Affair* may be an even more exciting affair all around. *Lovers,* however, has "I've Got You Under My Skin," which still resonates as Sinatra's coup de grace of uptempo masterpieces. At the very last minute he decided to include "Skin" on the session of January 12, 1956, which meant, Riddle recalled, that "it was a work of pressure because I had to stay up quite late one night and finish it."

Riddle wrote it, as usual, according to Frank's specifications. "He said, 'I want a long crescendo.' Long crescendi, like other dynamics in music, whether they be long crescendi or long diminuendi, are another color, and without them music can become unpalatable, tasteless, and uninteresting." The arranger added, "I don't think he was aware of the way I was going to achieve that crescendo, but he wanted an instrumental interlude that would be exciting and carry the orchestra up and then come on down where he would finish out the arrangement vocally."

One of the first things Riddle thought of was Ravel's "Bolero," which he described as having "the most calculatingly orchestrated crescendo" and an "absolutely tantalizing slow addition of instruments to this long, long crescendo, which is really the message of 'Bolero,' and it is excruciating in its deliberately slow addition of pressure. Now that's sex in a piece of music." For the arranger, like Sinatra, sex and music were interchangeable. "I remember [once when] my mother and father were having a screaming match," said Chris Riddle, "and she said to him, 'All you ever think about is music and sex!' I was about sixteen, and the next day I asked him about it. He looked at me with a twinkle in his eye and said, 'After all, what else is there?' Music and sex! I mean, he really saw things that way. That was like a window into his insides."

However, Riddle was stuck for an idea for this particular patch of color. "I was sitting home one day when Nelson called me up and said, 'Frank wants a long crescendo in the middle of "I've Got You Under My Skin,"'" recalled George Roberts. "Nelson said, 'Do you know any Afro-Cuban rhythmical patterns and things like that?' I said, 'Well, why don't you steal the pattern out of Kenton's "23 Degrees North, 82 Degrees West" [from 1952]. He said, 'How did it go?' I gave him the beginning trombone lines for that Afro-Cuban thing, and he expanded that for the long crescendo that Frank wanted." "I remembered a Stan Kenton record," Riddle recollected, "and that trombone back-and-forth thing. I was always fascinated by it. I tried to find an equivalent to use behind singers, and that was my version." Riddle swiped from Russo only conceptually; he does lay several Latin rhythm patterns over each other, but it's hardly the same polyrhythm that Russo employed in designating the coordinates of Cuba.

Like Russo, Riddle uses the passage to lead into a trombone solo, played by former Kentonite Milt Bernhart. Bernhart recalled that both Sinatra and Riddle seemed to know that this would be a special track and they were keen to keep doing take after take until they had it exactly right. Bernhart had conditioned himself to Sinatra's more customary way of working: If you can't get it in four or five takes, tops, drop it and possibly try again later. For that reason he put everything he had into the first few takes of the number and feels he was spent by the time they got to the take Sinatra wound up using.

"Toward the tenth take," Bernhart recalled, "somebody said in the booth, 'Could we get the trombone nearer to a microphone?' I mean, what had they been doing? So they said, 'There's a mike there for the brass.' It was on a very high riser. The engineer asked, 'Can you get up to that one?' And I said, 'Well, no, I'm not that tall.' Somebody said, 'Why don't we get a box?' So they were looking for a box. I don't know why there wasn't a grip, but Frank Sinatra himself went and got a box and brought it over for me to stand on. It was funny."

Bernhart felt silly standing on the box, and while he has claimed he ran "out of gas" at least a dozen takes before the one that got used, his solo has become one of the most widely heard trombone statements ever recorded. Bernhart regrets he didn't realize at the time that Riddle had actually based the whole instrumental sequence, with his solo, on the bridge to "Skin."[9] But it's the very atavistic, off-the-chord energy of the solo that burns it into your brain with such sizzling force. And yet as passionate as Bernhart gets in his twelve bars or so, he pales beside Sinatra, who returns to ram the lyric home with nothing short of orgiastic fury.

Said Riddle, "I remember bringing [the chart] to the recording, and everybody was very impressed." It marked one of the few times the musicians on a Sinatra date actually stood up and applauded the principals: star, writer-director, and supporting player. "I know the evening that we did it," Riddle recalled, "he expressed considerable enthusiasm for the arrangement, and I guess later on, when he took the tape home

9. Bernhart said, "If I had known it was the bridge, I would have used that as a guide. I didn't know exactly what this was supposed to be because it had chords, but it was only really one chord. He just put down all these flats, and it was a flat chord. It's not easy to do on the trombone. The more flats, the harder. So that threw me a curve. What am I supposed to do in those few little beats? Something hysterical, something historical."

and played it, he was even more enthusiastic. As it turned out, it was sort of a cornerstone recording for both him and me."

Swingin' Affair, as issued, doesn't have one individual cut that stands out as much as "Skin" does on *Lovers,* but the set as a whole packs even more wallop. *Affair* is leaner and meaner: there are far fewer filigrees, less of the highly ornamental filling of every space that we find on *Lovers.* On one of the four dates, Sinatra downplayed the string section to accentuate more of a big-band sound, emphasizing "swingin'" over "lovers." On the same date Sinatra and Riddle recruited drummer Irv Cottler. Cottler wasn't as flexible a stylist as their usual first choice, Alvin Stroller (who was much more comfortable with tempo changes, for instance), but he was a powerhouse pounder who solidified the straight-ahead feeling.

Cottler, who had first recorded with Sinatra on the "Skin" session, became his regular "road" percussionist off and on for thirty-three years. "Nelson has a beautiful approach to building a chart," was how Cottler described such archetypical works as "Skin" and "The Lady Is a Tramp." "He starts with a foundation and builds up to the roof. Other writers start from the roof and go down, but where can you go from the roof?"

Where *Lovers* included several slower pieces, such as "We'll Be Together Again," *Affair* is practically all variations on "Skin"; crescendos and bolero patterns abound. Almost every track is directly or indirectly patterned after that chart, starting slow and gradually mounting in dynamics, speed, and intensity. Sinatra had sequenced "Skin" at the start of the second side of *Lovers* for easy spotting with the tonearm, and *Affair* swings further by opening with the strongest "Skin" follow-up, "Night and Day." In redoing the best-remembered song from his premier session as a soloist, Sinatra was again declaring, Oh, look at me now.

"Night and Day" repeats the polyrhythm from "Skin," and leads once more to a trombone feature, this time the valved brother of the instrument as handled by its leading exponent, Juan Tizol. A far calmer player than Bernhart, Tizol also figures prominently on "From This Moment On" and, as Riddle's resident Ellingtonian, on "I Got It Bad (and That Ain't Good)." Riddle used him so much (on Sinatra sessions as well as Nat Cole items like "A Blossom Fell") because, the arranger said, "he had, to me, a very exotic sound on that valve trombone."

Sinatra had planned one number for *Affair* that would rival and possibly even exceed "Skin," namely Rodgers and Hart's "The Lady Is a Tramp." Sinatra already knew that "Tramp" would be a crucial number in his forthcoming film *Pal Joey,* so he decided to save the number for that picture's souvenir "sound track" album. (In its place, Sinatra inserted "No

One Ever Tells You," *Affair*'s one nonstandard, which, although recorded as a single a few months earlier, fits perfectly into the album.) "Lady Is a Tramp" also slowly increases in force as the piece progresses, Sinatra starting with Bill Miller's ever-perfect piano accompaniment, and Riddle adding other elements one at a time—violins, horns, and the now-expected fills from Edison and an unidentified solo flute.

It's almost as if Sinatra and Riddle wanted to summarize—in a single track—everything they had accomplished on the three swing albums, starting with the economical playfulness of *Easy* (Riddle reconceiving the main melody as a groovy riff), moving to the dances-with-strings of *Lovers*, and ending in the hyperhard euphoria of *Affair*. Sinatra had developed a favorite device of singing one phrase (especially the last few words of a bridge) a capella for both dramatic and rhythmic emphasis, as on "Foggy Day." It never worked more effectively than here where the ensemble drops out long enough for Sinatra to utter two and then three syllables: the brass crashes and then rests as Sinatra sings, "She's broke." The brass erupts again and immediately pauses once more as Sinatra goes into "but it's oke!"

No less than "Skin," "Tramp" would be a Sinatra classic, performed thousands of times over succeeding decades. "[Frank] seemed to take a particular delight in [Tramp]," said Riddle. "He always sang that song with a certain amount of salaciousness. He savored it. He had some cute tricks with the lyric, which made it especially his." Many of the live versions, not surprisingly, gather and disperse even more ecstatic energy than the Capitol reading. Sinatra performed what might be the single most exciting version on a Bob Hope TV special around the time that *Pal Joey* was released. Here, instead of intoning the three words "but it's oke," Sinatra merely pauses for three beats, along with the band, shrugging his shoulders and silently registering an expression that's oke as oke can be.

"It was as if you went to Vegas and hit five jackpots in a row," arranger-composer Neal Hefti stated. Indeed, with both *Swingin' Lovers* and *Swingin' Affair* in 1956, Sinatra and Riddle were more than on a roll. "As far as I'm concerned, no one has even come close to what Nelson achieved with Sinatra," said Hefti. "This isn't taking anything away from any of the other people. It's just that the moon and the stars were in the right position at the same time, with Frank and Nelson, plus Capitol Records, plus Frank being so exuberant because he had won the Academy Award. It was all of these things. God! That enthusiasm just keeps going on and on and on! It's just like the Richter scale: each new thing makes the last number ten times higher. It was just unbelievable."

*   *   *

As new and as bold a dimension as the swing albums brought to the Sinatra canon, the singer continued to do his greatest work with ballads. If anything, his newfound confidence in his abilities as a swinger added scope to his interpretations of love songs. Perhaps it was only because he had proved his strength and masculinity by swinging with so much ferocity that Sinatra garnered the fortitude to walk around with his heart as exposed as he does on *Wee Small Hours, Close to You,* and *Only the Lonely.*

On his first Capitol session, the singer proved that the familiar Sinatra-Stordahl ballad style no longer made magic—or money. Sinatra sounds breathless and thin on several patches of "I'm Walking Behind You," while "Don't Make a Beggar of Me" turns out to be a listless waltz—a time signature that never really excited The Voice to begin with. Both seem a million miles away from mid-1940s masterpieces like "Laura" and "Nancy."

One date with Ray Anthony's band, and charts by former trombonist Dick Reynolds (author of "If I Ever Love Again," which Sinatra recorded in 1949), provides another example of how badly he needed Riddle. "I'm Gonna Live till I Die," a kind of *Ed Sullivan Show*-Sammy Davis, Jr.'"belt" number, sounds like a stock chart that could have suited any Broadway leading man graduating to Vegas. The treatment on "Melody of Love," another waltz (that dates back to 1903), overextends the singer's pipes, as if the voice were trying to cover too much harmonic ground, and may be the only Sinatra record completely bereft of anything resembling drama or even a climactic moment.

Almost as if to prove his immediate worth to Sinatra, Riddle rewrote an arrangement Stordahl had done for Sinatra on their 1953 Capitol date, that session's one standard, "Day in, Day Out" (which Sinatra had first sung in 1939 with Harry James). Comparing the Stordahl and Riddle single-chorus treatments of "Day" further illustrates the sharp degree to which Sinatra outlined his arrangements beforehand and how two different arrangers translated that outline into a finished chart. Riddle doesn't entirely smooth out Stordahl's pizzicato patterns or try to dispense with the somewhat grandiose pounding pattern ignited by Sinatra on the word "pounding." But the arranger very subtly softens these devices in a way that renders both structure and song more relevant to the Sinatra of the Capitol era. (As it turned out, neither treatment made it onto commercial vinyl in its day. Sinatra decided he preferred "Day in, Day Out" as a swinger and waited until the end of 1958 for Billy May to provide him with such a version.)

"Sinatra's voice went through range changes," as Sammy Cahn observed. "His sound changed. He went from the violin with Axel, that

pure violin sound, to the sound underneath, the viola, with Nelson."
Along with the deepening range, Sinatra also widened his rhythmic
vocabulary and gained a more vivid emotional palette. But these gifts
had a price tag: with his innocence he lost a chunk of his chops. He no
longer possessed the intonation that was so consistently accurate during
the Stordahl years. Sinatra never sang flat in the '40s, but occasionally, in
the classic Capitol period, The Voice was a little under pitch. At times he
was doing this for emotional effect, but it may be overgenerous to claim
that it was always deliberate. Super-precise pitch was simply no longer
the point: Sinatra and Riddle were creating a way of moving audiences
that depended less on always hitting the right notes and sounding sweet.

The emotional-musical vocabulary has grown so large that Sinatra
had transformed himself into the sole vocal artist capable of sustaining a
single mood for sixteen songs, exploring every variation, every grada-
tion. Despite remarkable consistency, he is never exactly what his album
covers claim. The film noir image that graces *In the Wee Small Hours*
could easily have fronted an early '50s paperback of a hard-boiled crime
novel. Yet the jacket contains Sinatra's jazziest album yet, boasting
wilder deviations from the melody than any of the *Swing* sets.

Wee Small, Sinatra's third Capitol collection, inaugurated his tradition of using a title song to set the mood, something he continued doing
off and on for the rest of his career. Though he generally used either a
known standard or a newly commissioned opus from his "in-house"
tunesmiths, Cahn and Van Heusen, to open *Wee Small* he used a new
number that just happened to come to him. Bill Miller has recalled that
when Dave Mann[10] and Bob Hilliard demonstrated the number for Sinatra, both singer and pianist instantly realized that "In the Wee Small
Hours" was going to be an important number for them. (Sinatra's sole
disappointment was that Mann and Hilliard already had a publisher.)

On both *Wee Small Hours* and *Close to You*, Sinatra and Riddle
worked out the idea of slightly varying the instrumentation from track
to track while still using a core section of musicians on every number.
On *Close* it's a string quartet abetted by a standard four-piece rhythm
section. On *Wee Small* the core unit is a five-piece rhythm section, with
bass, drums, rhythm guitar, and two keyboardists—Bill Miller in his
regular spot at the piano and guest Paul Smith on celesta.

10. A professional pianist himself, Mann had worked with Riddle in Charlie Spivak's
orchestra and played on several Sinatra sessions, most famously taking the Claude
Thornhill–like opening solo on "I Begged Her" (1944).

Riddle generally supplements the five-piece rhythm with a full contingent of strings, generally jettisoning his familiar cast of horn players. Harry Edison only plays here on the two tunes with the strongest jazz associations: Duke Ellington's "Mood Indigo," on which he plays a figure Riddle would expand into the background riff for "Witchcraft," and Harold Arlen's "Ill Wind." The latter contains one of Sweets' longer solos in Sinatraland: he stretches a mere eight bars into thirty gloriously erotic seconds.

"Ill Wind" also has a haunting Benny Carter–like alto obligato by Skeets Herfurt (Skeets and Sweets, together again), while Mahlon Clark's clarinet effectively frames "What Is This Thing Called Love" with a fetching original lick. (An alternate take reveals that Sinatra originally planned a four-minute, two-chorus treatment of the Cole Porter tune, the first half of the second chorus devoted to spotlighting an instrumental section featuring Clark against the strings.) The title opening track sets the pace, with the two textures—rhythm and strings—playing off each other in a perfectly invisible arrangement. One isn't conscious of the music or even Sinatra's voice, just the pure emotion emanating from the speakers.

Indeed, in all contexts and all degrees of either agony or ecstasy, even if Sinatra falls short of the occasional note tonally, he always hits precisely the right tone emotionally. Listening to "Deep in a Dream" on *Wee Small Hours* and "The End of a Love Affair" on *Close to You* makes you think that if Sinatra put the tiniest bit more emotion in his singing he might sound hysterical, and yet if he were to pull the most minuscule bit back, he would come off sounding detached. Somehow, he always finds the perfect balance.

In playing the strads and rhythm off each other in *Wee Small*, the two keyboards afford the rhythm crew greater presence, although neither Miller nor guest celestaist Paul Smith can be described as a heavy-handed player. Sinatra began using the five-piece format independently of Riddle, on his final regular radio series, *To Be Perfectly Frank*. The program had begun in the wake of *Eternity*, in November 1953, and continued for a year as a fifteen-minute sustaining program before a shampoo corporation picked up the tab and rechristened it *The Bobbi Show*. (Luckily, the series was also transcribed by the AFRTS, ensuring that a number of episodes survive today.) A refinement of the anarchic *Meet Frank Sinatra*, Sinatra was reincarnated as a singing disc jockey, spinning his own platters as well as those of other artists, and also usually singing one original number per show (which were probably prerecorded at sessions of at least four tunes or more).

Sinatra was at his all-time jazziest on these shows, done in the same time period and frame of mind as *Swing Easy.* He generally taped the new performances for the series with either Bill Miller or a five-piece group of clarinet and four rhythm, referred to on the air as "The Sinatra Symphonette." On at least a few shows he used the piano-celesta front line, bringing in Paul Smith to play the smaller, more tinkly keyboard. The spirit of the program spilled over into the rhythm-oriented *Swing Easy,* as you'd expect, but also into *Wee Small Hours,* where Miller and Smith again make like a hip Ferrante and Teicher.

As mentioned, Riddle augments the five rhythm with fiddles on three sessions, one of which also uses one trumpet and four reeds. On a fourth date, departing from established Sinatra tradition, the singer recorded four songs using just the five-man unit. Sinatra set up and sequenced "Glad to Be Unhappy," "Can't We Be Friends," "I'll Be Around" (on which a celesta riff spins a punningly circular pattern), and "Dancing on the Ceiling" so seamlessly amid the twelve-string tracks that few listeners even notice the absence of an orchestra. (Along with two tracks on John Graas' album, *French Horn Jazz,* they signify a rare example of Riddle writing for a small jazz group.)

Sinatra and Riddle relied on Bill Miller even more than usual here, counting on the pianist to exploit his background in jazz and conduct the date, and also help to chart the tunes for the rhythm section from Sinatra's verbal sketches. "Frank said, 'I want to pretend you just sat down and you're going to fake a tune behind me,'" Miller recalled. "And I said, 'You want it to sound strictly right now, off the cuff?' He said, 'I want some of the tunes to sound unrehearsed.' I agreed with him, but I still took the liberty of writing out the parts for the bass player and Paul Smith and everybody so that we all played the right chord changes."

"Last Night When We Were Young" rates as the most powerful performance in the set. Perhaps the most dramatic operetta-style work by the normally blues-oriented Harold Arlen, the piece could be one of the better "heavy" ballads by Jerome Kern (à la "Yesterdays") or Sigmund Romberg ("Lover Come Back to Me"). Sinatra does not resort to trying to sing it with a "big" belting voice, the way he might have in 1951 or 1952.[11] Instead, this track anticipates *Only the Lonely* in terms of Riddle's deep, dark colors, and the way Sinatra makes even nihilism an intimate experience.

11. Jonathan Schwartz tells the following story about *popera* star Lawrence Tibbet, who had included "Last Night When We Were Young" in his gut-busting repertoire. Upon hearing Sinatra's rendition, the barrel-voiced baritone responded simply, "Oh, I see," meaning, "So that's how it should be done."

Except for "Last Night . . ." (recorded a year before the remaining fifteen tracks), *Wee Small* may be a less devastingly moving experience than *Only the Lonely,* but it's no less effective. Sinatra and Riddle continually demonstrate, as on the intro, in which the celesta maps out the melody, that the light colors are just as enthusiastically expressive as the dark ones.

This was Sinatra's first twelve-inch album (released as both a twelve-inch set and a double ten-inch; there's no doubt that he planned *Wee Small* as a twelve-inch even though the ten-inch edition happened to come out first). It's also the album that finally ensured the future of the Sinatra-Riddle relationship. "That's what I think hit Sinatra," said Miller. "That's what gave him the inspiration to say, 'Hey, let's do more of that.'"

As with the *Swing* series, "more of that" turned out to be more than just a cloning of a previous album's success. From the cover on—virtually the only Capitol set to show Sinatra in the act of singing, mike in hand and without a hat—*Close to You* was perhaps the least conventional of the Capitol series and the only one not in print continually from the '50s to the CD era.

The album began out of Sinatra's desire to do a set with the Hollywood String Quartet, and as such evolved from Sinatra's long-standing personal and professional relationship with the HSQ's first violin and cello, Felix and Eleanor Slatkin. The Slatkins had founded the Quartet around 1940, not long after they were married, at which time Felix was serving as concertmaster at Twentieth Century-Fox pictures and Eleanor was playing for Warner Bros. All four members of the group were primarily employed by picture studios, and the group was organized as a means of playing something deeper than Max Steiner or the aptly named Erich Korngold. The quartet suspended operations during Slatkin's war service but after 1946 stabilized with Felix's assistant at Fox, Paul Shure, as second violin and Alvin Dinkins on viola. During the '50s, Felix conducted the Hollywood Bowl Symphony Orchestra, which became one of Capitol's major classical music attractions, and the HSQ served as that orchestra's little brother chamber group. (Felix and Eleanor Slatkin, as successful as they were, never achieved quite the renown of their son, Leonard Slatkin, the widely celebrated conductor of the St. Louis Symphony Orchestra.)

Felix Slatkin first appeared on a Sinatra session in 1946; Eleanor initially turns up beginning the following year. The most intense period of their working together began with the Riddle-Capitol era in 1953 and ended with Felix's death in 1963. During that decade, Sinatra and Riddle insisted on using Slatkin not only as their regular concertmaster but as a resident senior conductor to support both Sinatra and Riddle in their baton work.

"We became very, very close friends and saw a lot of him between the recordings in those days, and spent many weekends with Frank at his home in Palm Springs," remembered Eleanor Slatkin. "Frank, as you know, has a tremendous collection of classical records, and he fell in love with the quartet. So he said, 'You know, I think it would be a terrific idea to do an album with a string quartet.'" The potential problem was that the quartet by itself might not be enough to support a pop singer—even one who exceeded many classical voices in artistry and execution. And even if it could, the quartet alone might not sustain the attention of a pop audience. So, inspired by the Sinatra-Stordahl sessions of a decade earlier, as Paul Shure recalled, "Nelson decided to use a string quartet and [four rhythm], and each tune would have another instrument. He'd have string quartet and French horn [Vince DeRosa], string quartet and flute [Harry Klee or James Williamson], string quartet and trumpet [Sweets Edison], string quartet and solo violin [Slatkin]. It was all a core of string quartet writing with different instruments added."

Actually, after Sinatra, the string quartet more than dominates the proceedings almost all the time, the additional instruments appear only occasionally. Clarinetist Mahlon Clark plays on just "I Couldn't Sleep a Wink Last Night" and the originally deleted "If It's the Last Thing I Do," while Edison shows up only once, to telling effect on "The End of a Love Affair," where he leads our hero through the purgatory of a romance gone sour like a trumpet-toting Virgil. Vince DeRosa's French horn assumes the role and register normally filled by George Roberts, grunting low in the background. DeRosa also plays on "Don't Like Goodbyes," "It Could Happen to You," and "I've Had My Moments," but here Riddle uses him more for coloration than as a featured improvisor. In effect, DeRosa solos so low, we're barely conscious of him.

On the first date, Sinatra attempted only one tune, and that he rejected it without trying any further numbers that day indicates he wasn't happy with Riddle's initial attempt to arrange for this unusual "double" ensemble. It took longer to record *Close to You* than any other Sinatra album before *Trilogy:* five sessions stretched over eight months, from March to November 1956.

Even a cursory listen will reveal that it was well worth the effort: it's hard to disagree with Shure's assertion that, "musically speaking, I think it's the greatest album that Sinatra ever did," even considering Shure's understandable bias. This is surely Sinatra's most intimate and delicate singing ever, and he imbues every track with an attention to nuance remarkable even for him. On the *Swing* series as well as the "suicide" albums, such as *Only the Lonely* and *No One Cares*, the singer paints with broadly upbeat or tragic strokes; constrastingly, *Close to You* could have been rendered with an eyebrow pencil.

As Riddle mentioned, he usually counted on Edison and, to a lesser extent, his other regulars for the humor content of his albums, especially the *Swing* sets. *Close to You*, however, jettisons most of the two- and three-beat knick-knacks Riddle typically employs to fill Sinatra's empty spaces (excepting the "guitars" and "trumpets" sounded when Sinatra utters those words in "I've Had My Moments" and "End of a Love Affair"—apparently that was too much for him to resist) for a sound that's dramatically starker yet emotionally more expansive.

Yet *Close to You* has more of a comic quotient than any other Sinatra-Riddle disc, because Sinatra's singing extracts so much irony from the songs themselves. As both programmer and singer, Sinatra has compiled a perfect selection of tunes to fit the requirements of the context, being at once deeply moving and darkly comic. On "P.S. I Love You" and "Everything Happens to Me," Sinatra is careful not to jump too hard on the obvious gag lines, while on the more sullen "Easy to Remember" and "Blame It on My Youth," he furrows out the more optimistic angles buried deep in the texts.

Again, you have to marvel at Sinatra's capacity to find the most appropriate song. Everyone else who saw *Hollywood Party* (1934) could only snicker at the effrontery of a film that missed the boat on the standard "Blue Moon" and cast Jimmy Durante as Tarzan (all right, "Shnarzan"). Certainly no one but Sinatra would have discovered that this box-office disaster contained such a tellingly ironic libretto as Walter Donaldson's "I've Had My Moments." (The 1934 song anticipates the 1937 "A Foggy Day" in its opening half-step movement, which is similar to Gershwin's minor third, as well as its Gershwinesque repetitive rhythmic patterns.) Sinatra conceives of "Moments" as a beautifully schizophrenic battle of inner moods, one overt braggadocio, the other acutely self-conscious humility.

With an irony most appropriate to the *Close to You* collection, Sinatra claimed that "There's a Flaw in My Flue," the single funniest item of the sessions, was not actually intended for the finished LP. During the war, Bing Crosby, in a special soldiers-only broadcast, introduced a music and comedy routine he called "Your All-Time Flop Parade" (itself a parody of Sinatra's first important show, *Lucky Strike Presents Your Hit Parade*, and its brother, the *All-Time Hit Parade*). With songs by fellow funsters Johnny Burke and Jimmy Van Heusen, Crosby and guests like Judy Garland and Ethel Merman offered up such deliberately amateurish airs as "Yachting," "Hammacher-Schlemmer, I Love You," "Silver-

Coated Moon," and others that foreshadowed the marvelously mediocre music of Jonathan and Darlene Edwards. "There's a Flaw in My Flue" had been introduced by Crosby and Merman on der Bingle's *Philco Radio Time* show of March 23, 1949.

Nancy Sinatra, among others, later claimed that her father recorded "Flaw in My Flue" to rib Capitol's A&R department; how long would it take before Voyle Gilmore realized that this tale of fireside pipe dreaming, with lines like "smoke gets in my nose," was a well-calculated piece of leg-pulling? If that was the case, then Sinatra outsmarted himself. The lyric was not much sillier than the next most laughable (unphotographable) song on the album, and Sinatra and Riddle performed it with such sincerity and so little camp that it obviously belonged on *Close to You*. It might have made it, too, had Sinatra not wised them up to his gag at the eleventh hour. He recorded two more songs, "If It's the Last Thing I Do" and "Wait till You See Her," perhaps *Close to You*'s best track, which did not make it onto the album at the time because the basic twelve tracks already totaled more than forty-five minutes, or roughly as long as the sixteen on *Wee Small* and *Swingin' Affair*.[12] Fortunately, all three were added to the CD edition in 1987.

"Nelson was a master at what I guess you'd call 'counterpoint,'" Mahlon Clark observed. "He wrote wonderfully for strings and had a knack for writing things 'fat' so they sounded large." Riddle had found a perfect middle ground between the classical (as in Mozart) and the jazz (as in Benny Goodman) uses of the chamber group. "Everything Happens to Me" seems to be all fiddles, the other instruments barely noticeable, while "Easy to Remember" relies mainly on vibes and flute which update the keyboard textures of the Cole-Riddle "Unforgettable," as the quartet takes it easy. Throughout, the strings sound harmonically rich in the European sense, but the rhythm section keeps things moving, without the static beat that usually prevents anything vaguely classical from working in a jazz or pop context. It sounds neither too long-hair nor too jivey. Considering how full the vocals and the orchestrations are, it's amazing how each track comes off as a marvel of understatement.

Wee Small Hours was hardly all gloom and doom, apart from "Last Night When We Were Young" (and even that bears a pregnant-with-hope pause); it suggests a dark point that we hope will be followed by the dawn. *Close to You* depicts that sunrise, with Sinatra's protagonist refus-

12. The fifteen tracks on *Close to You* total nearly fifty-five minutes, which would have required three LP sides in 1956. *Wee Small* stretched the limit by getting in fifty minutes on two LP sides.

ing to wallow in self-pity but rather taking a self-deprecatingly bitter-sweet look at his own romantic foibles. The singer then painted what many consider his greatest ballad collection, *Frank Sinatra Sings for Only the Lonely*, in colors so pitch black that no light could possibly escape.

As we have seen, "There's a Lonesome Old Town" suggests a barroom ballad of the twenty-first century. The album's title and contrasting opening track, brings to mind the nineteenth. "Only the Lonely" establishes the first of several slightly varying moods that the twelve songs pass through: heavy, though not grandiose, but densely decorated with the trappings of late-romantic-period music, as transmuted into the Sinatra-Riddle idiom. Riddle accentuates the texture of the semisymphonic sound with touches like a Chopinesque piano on "Only the Lonely" (apparently not played by Bill Miller but by the more classically oriented Harry Sukman) which forges ahead of Sinatra.

If *Only the Lonely* sounds more conventionally classical than usual in its texture, it's partly because of the size of the orchestra. "We had so many musicians," guitarist Al Viola has recalled, "that when I got to the first date, I thought it was a union meeting! I thought a whole bunch of guys had gotten together to talk about an election or something. But no, all these musicians were actually there to work." On the title cut as well as "Angel Eyes," "Willow, Weep for Me," "Guess I'll Hang My Tears out to Dry," and elsewhere, Sinatra also specified the use of a far less clearly defined tempo than in anything he had sung up to that time.

As an arranger, only Riddle could take these borderline classical elements and make them relevant to Sinatra's American jazz-pop home base. In wanting some tracks to utilize rubato rhythms in such an overtly European fashion, Sinatra must have realized he was seeking something beyond Riddle's abilities as a conductor. "Nelson never pretended to be a conductor," Milt Bernhart has pointed out. "Conducting is an art unto itself. None of the jazz arrangers had any conducting experience when they began to write. He had never, ever considered himself in line to be a conductor. Suddenly, there he was. Nelson took some lessons, studied with a few people, such as Felix Slatkin, so that he could do better. On motion picture calls, it was all you could do to follow him."

"He made it tough on the musicians in that he wasn't that correct about what he did with his motions," added reedman Ted Nash. "But fortunately, most of his stuff was in tempo, except the endings and things. But he just sort of waved his arms around and kept everybody together informally like that." The musicians got through it because, Skeets Herfurt concluded, "we were used to all sorts of conductors."

On *Only the Lonely*, Riddle would certainly have gotten lost in the ad-lib sections of his own arrangements. Most musicians agree that Sinatra, who conducted three albums for Capitol more than a decade after his Alec Wilder instrumental sesssions, wielded the baton at least as skillfully as Riddle, if not more so. But because he never cared to do what Mel Tormé later pulled off successfully in singing and giving the downbeats to the band at the same time, this didn't help him any while planning *Only the Lonely.* The project initially began life as an album for Sinatra and Gordon Jenkins, a follow-up to their 1956 *Where Are You.* When Jenkins was occupied in Las Vegas, Sinatra decided to go ahead with Riddle (he and Jenkins would instead get together on *No One Cares* the following year).

Sinatra and Riddle attempted three charts for *Only the Lonely* on May 5, 1958, but as often before, ditched the entire session. In addition to making changes in the arrangements, Sinatra had decided that he wanted a different kind of guitar sound in the intro to "Guess I'll Hang My Tears out to Dry." (George Van Eps had played on the May take, presumably using his self-developed seven-string instrument. In the issued version, Al Viola plays the intro on a more conventional gut-string guitar.) In addition, it's possible that Sinatra deliberately wanted to switch conductors when he learned that Riddle was soon leaving town. "I was booked to do a tour of Canada with Nat Cole that summer," the arranger recalled. "I wrote all the arrangements, but Felix Slatkin, a fine violinist and fine conductor, did the [June] session, [while] I was up in Edmonton, Alberta, or one of those places."

As first violinist, "Felix was always available for Frank," said Eleanor Slatkin, and in May 1958, Sinatra "just called and said, 'I want you to do an album with me.' And of course, Felix was thrilled." Viola added that "Felix was top-notch. I mean, that was really conducting because this wasn't in dance tempo. This was almost like a mini-symphony, the way Nelson wrote it."

When Riddle later cited *Only the Lonely* as "the best vocal album I've ever done," he explained to Alan Dell that this was "because I had time to work on the arrangements—a week!" (Riddle claimed to have written as many as three or four orchestrations in a single day.) It's indicative of Riddle's sense of irony that his "favorite" album should be the one most linked in his mind to personal tragedy. He wrote the orchestrations "at a time when my mother was in Sinai Hospital with terminal cancer. I think the somber circumstances of [my] mother dying contributed to the darker colors of the album." She died a few weeks before the sessions began. Riddle added, "And I had also lost a daughter three months earlier"—referring to Lenora, who was six months old when she died of a respiratory problem—"so if one can attach events like that to music, perhaps *Only the Lonely* was the result."

Riddle also implied that it was just an accident Slatkin happened to conduct one of the dates for the album. That Sinatra chose to tackle the charts with out-of-tempo passages on this session suggests, however, that he was being very specific as to the skill levels of his various conductors. Apparently he wanted to commit as many of the more difficult numbers as possible to tape while he still had a tactful excuse to use a conductor other than Riddle; the Slatkin session did indeed include all the tougher, tempoless tunes.

The exquisite remake of "Guess I'll Hang My Tears out to Dry" suspends much of the rhythm during the voice-and-guitar-only verse and all of it during the bridge. Viola explains that "one of the notes [on the verse] was very difficult, so I did a classical tuning for that special note. That way I didn't have to worry about the fingering. It also was a pedal point note, and at that time we were at the key of F-sharp. That's why it came off so good and rang out so clear and sharp."

The 1953 "Angel Eyes" was introduced by its composer, Matt Dennis (in the film *Jennifer*), and was quickly recorded by Herb Jeffries, Ella Fitzgerald (who once named it as her favorite song), and Nat King Cole. But with the release of *Only the Lonely*, it immediately became inseparable from Sinatra. The only thing the Sinatra version lacks is the verse, because Dennis and lyricist Earl Brent wouldn't write that section of the song until the 1970s.

On the minor-mooded "Angel Eyes," the arrangement shadows the James M. Caine-like libretto by having the piece gradually fall ever more out of meter, as if to further convey the protagonist's sense of doom and confusion. The arrangement of "Ebb Tide"[13] follows the same trajectory, only in reverse, using the rising and falling of the orchestra, following the suggestion of Debussy in "La Mer," to depict the sea. Sinatra floats rhythmically as if on a life raft, although for much of the piece he is deliberately out of sync with the aquatic/orchestral motions. He seems to be fighting the ocean, resisting its undertow by rowing in the opposite direction, until at the conclusion of the text when the protagonist and the world, represented by the elemental force of the water, are at last at peace.

13. "Ebb Tide" was originally an English instrumental hit by Robert Maxwell (best known for "Song of the Nairobi Trio") to which lyrics were later added by Carl "It's All in the Game" Sigman. Although the piece has had strong ties to rhythm and blues, with hit versions by Roy Hamilton (1954), Lenny Welch (1964), and the Righteous Brothers (1965), its most profound interpretation after Sinatra's was by Jerry Colonna. Ah, yes!

Sinatra tried to bite off no less than eight tunes on the Slatkin session, seven for *Only the Lonely* and one for a single. This latter item, "Monique," the rather forgettable theme from his upcoming film *Kings Go Forth,* was released as "with Felix Slatkin and His Orchestra" (the chart had been Riddle's), apparently as compensation to the violinist for deferring all credit on *Only the Lonely* to Riddle. Sinatra attempted so many tunes—fully twice the usual four—primarily in an attempt to finish as much of the album as he could before he left to shoot *Kings Go Forth* in the south of France that June.

While Sinatra did decide to drop Billy Strayhorn's "Lush Life," he compensated with two equally sophisticated and moving pieces of material, one a standard, the other the album's sole original. The 1932 "Willow, Weep for Me" finds Sinatra in a grimly expressive mood, while Riddle and trumpeter Pete Candoli make the most of the song's unusual harmonics—though not written in a minor, "Willow" is nonetheless filled with minor and augmented chords. Riddle described it as "sort of a shady, mysterious, sad sound that occurs to me anytime I see a willow tree."

The title song, "Only the Lonely," commissioned and published by Sinatra from Cahn and Van Heusen, required the full talents of a Slatkin to conduct and a Riddle to orchestrate. Paralleling Miles Davis' contemporaneous experiments with modal harmonies, Van Heusen and Riddle have devised a piece similar to "Milestones" or any of the tunes on *Kind of Blue* in which a very minimal melody gets repeated over and over in different registers and varying degrees of musical-emotional intensity. As he does with most of the numbers on the album, Sinatra performs "Only the Lonely," which lays out in a form diagrammable as A A' A A' B A A", in a single devastating chorus.

The Riddle-directed numbers from the remaining two sessions for *Only the Lonely* use more conventional jazz-pop tempi and are no less effective for it. "What's New," which is full of entrances that take so long for Sinatra to come in that you're pulling your hair out in suspense, again casts Ray Sims as trombone-playing company for Sinatra's misery. Paradoxically, the two most old-fashioned pieces, "Blues in the Night" and "Lonesome Old Town," become the furthest out and most Stravinskian, Riddle's treatment of the Arlen tune being particularly reminiscent of *Le Sacre du Printemps.*

"Goodbye," composed by Gordon Jenkins and adapted by Benny Goodman as a closing theme, concludes the A side of the original album. The song itself features a one-measure, six-note instrumental "response" to the central melody line that seems typical of the "moaning" passages in Jenkins' arrangements, originally expressed as G G F, G G F, but also repeated as G G F$^{\#}$, G G F$^{\#}$.[14] Riddle first states it Jenkins-style, arco on the deep bull fiddles, but then transforms the phrase into something deeper than Jenkins could ever have conceived. "The idea of that [phrase] being a mandatory thing bothered me, although I'm crazy about the song, I always have been," Riddle recalled. "You just find another way to do something that might add a little touch of freshness." Riddle has the two-part lick echo throughout the orchestra on all kinds of instrumental textures—as if the universe itself were conspiring against the thwarted lover of the lyric with a resounding, inescapable "good-bye."

Sinatra once said, "There are times if I want to do something that has a lonely effect, we go back to the [solo] piano or an alto saxophone as part of the orchestration." "One for My Baby," apart from serving as a sequel to "Angel Eyes" as the album's other aria of barroom dialogue, is the definitive collaboration between Sinatra and Miller. Done at the end of the first of the two Riddle-led dates, the original take of "One for My Baby" seems to have been sketched by Miller to Sinatra's specifications (perhaps with no input from Riddle) and recorded after the other musicians had adjourned to the nearest establishment of the kind described in the text. At the next date, Sinatra decided to take "Baby" again, this time with the benefit of a Riddle-arranged string background and an alto obligato by Gus Bivona. "We did it in one take," Miller said of the issued version. "We were in the key of E, which puts the alto in C-sharp or D-flat, a dumb key, but it worked." Paradoxically, the light shimmer of violins, which are felt more than heard, makes the emotional content of the performance sound even starker. "One for My Baby" is the finest piece of musical acting Sinatra has ever turned in. He has never sounded closer to the end of his rope, and he makes the lyric come alive, word by painful word, in an intimate reality that's as frightening as it is believable.

When Sinatra and Riddle began work on *Only the Lonely* in the spring of 1958, it was their first album together since *A Swingin' Affair* a year and a half earlier. Because of extramusical circumstances, they would not collaborate on another album until *Nice 'n' Easy* two years later. Sinatra used the gaps before and after *Lonely* productively, mainly to work on albums with other arranger-conductors as well as singles with Riddle.

14. It was a long-standing tradition among ex-Goodman employees that whenever they heard this theme, no matter where they were, they were compelled to sing the following words over the six-note filler riff: "Go to hell, go to hell." Billy May, irrepressible wiseguy that he is, once concocted a mambo version of "Goodbye" in which the band chants "Cha, cha, cha—cha, cha, cha" atop this lick.

Lonely was a high point in the Sinatra-Riddle partnership that the two men would not achieve again. But then again, neither would anyone else.

Between 1957 and 1960, Sinatra redefined his relationship with Capitol Records and also switched producers, from Voyle Gilmore to Dave Cavanaugh, which couldn't help impacting on the way he worked with Riddle. Gilmore doesn't seem to have done anything in particular to have incurred Sinatra's displeasure; he just, in the words of Billy May (who much preferred Cavanaugh), somehow got on "Frank's shit list." Both Bill Miller and Alan Livingston feel that Gilmore "deserves more credit than he got." Miller said, "I wasn't sure of [Gilmore] in the beginning, but occasionally he'd have an idea of his own, like [how to] cut up an arrangement, and some of those things worked." Riddle has recalled that although "Sinatra picked his own things," Gilmore nonetheless "presided as a benign face and presence in the proceedings. Voyle was very easygoing and a very pleasant man."

Frank Military recalled the most remunerative example of Gilmore's ability to pick songs for Sinatra: during the filming of *Pal Joey* in 1957, Capitol got hungry for a new Sinatra single, but the singer had even more on his plate than usual at this particular time. When Sinatra, Sanicola, and Military got to the famous Tower, "Voyle came in with a pile of records maybe a foot high. So Frank said, 'What's that?' Voyle said, 'Songs we're gonna play to see what we're gonna pick.' Frank said, 'No, pick *one* song. That's it.' So Voyle picked one disc, put it on the turntable, put the needle on, and it was a song called 'Witchcraft.' We all sat and listened. As he played it and it finished, Frank looked at us and we looked at him, and Hank shook his head no. And Frank said to Voyle, 'Play it again,' so he put it on again, we went through it again, and he looked at us and Hank again. Then he said, 'This is the song *I* want to record. You guys put whatever songs you like on the rest of the session, but this song I like.' So he had great taste. It was a fabulous song. We went in and recorded it. It took him two and a half hours to get that one song down, but he got it down right."

Introduced by a descending riff that Riddle had first suggested in "Mood Indigo" and laid out over a pattern vaguely like "Bolero," "Witchcraft" became another touchstone in the Sinatra canon. Composer Cy Coleman is justifiably proud of that disc, citing it as an example of a "good marriage" in which "the words belong to the melody. That's when the lyric and music are good, too . . . you can't pull them apart." Lyricist Carolyn Leigh (who had written Sinatra's "Young at Heart" with jazz arranger Johnny Richards) had come up with the phrase "It's Witchcraft," and Coleman had originally devised another, more "exotic" melody to fit it. But when poking around at the piano, he came up with another melodic line that they instantly knew was better suited to the title.

Riddle seems to have felt that his relationship with Sinatra had begun to disintegrate as early as 1956. "Sinatra took good care of Nelson," Alan Livingston explained, and up to that point he "would not work with anybody else. Riddle was his man. And Frank was very protective of him: he took Nelson on the road with him and did everything he could for him. And Nelson was delighted because he emerged far bigger than he had been before that. I mean, [before Frank], Nelson was not really that well known. Sinatra took him with him, really. Sinatra appreciated him, so it was a good relationship."

"And it was that way for a while," Bernhart elaborated. "Almost [like] a marriage. It was day and night. Picture calls, television, records, everything you can think of. Day and night. He wasn't home enough. His wife became jealous of [the time he spent with] Frank."

As Sinatra put it, "Nels is the greatest arranger in the world, a very clever musician, and I have the greatest respect for him." As Riddle put it, "[Sinatra] was very good to me. He opened some doors which, without his intervention, would have remained forever closed to me because the music world in this town was a tight, scared, greedy crew. It was even in those days when work was a lot more plentiful; there were [still] eighty musicians for every job." As Billy May put it, "Frank was good for Nelson. Christ! You make a record with Sinatra, boy, you start getting calls. I started hearing from MGM to do pictures and things like that, just suddenly, out of the blue. And Nelson got that, too."

Although Sinatra continued to think of Riddle as "his man" at least as long as the duration of the Capitol contract—for virtually all his singles and ten out of his sixteen "concept" albums—he began experimenting with other arrangers in 1956. Without intending any slight to Riddle, he had at least two good reasons for turning to Billy May and Gordon Jenkins. First, he didn't want to be "married" to any one particular arranger's sound; he feared that ten years earlier he had relied too heavily on Stordahl and had been chained to one approach when his audiences tired of the Sinatra-Stordahl style. Like Nat King Cole, who wisely switched from a small combo to solo microphone when his trio was at the very height of its popularity, Sinatra knew that the time to switch to something new was before what he was currently doing had worn out its welcome. Second, as early as 1956, Sinatra had begun to think about not only controlling but also owning his recorded performances outright. Whether he could achieve that in conjunction with Capitol or if he needed to go elsewhere, he seems to have anticipated wanting a brand-new sound to distinguish the new venture. Riddle, who would arrange five final albums for Sinatra on Reprise between 1963 and 1966, was still his most frequent partner, but his was no longer the only name on Sinatra's dance card.

"Right at the point that Nelson felt he was Sinatra's boy, just when he had gotten used to the idea, Frank started to look around and try other people," remembered Bernhart, "for no reason in particular, not as a slur, not as a slap in the face—but Nelson took it that way." Riddle, whose ego was but a fraction of those of the Hollywood hotshot arrangers who got rich imitating him, was incapable of taking Sinatra's decision as anything but a slight. "Frank used Nelson for many albums until one day he decided on Gordon Jenkins," recalled Frank Military. "I remember Nelson calling me and saying, 'What did I do? What's the matter?' I said, 'Frank just wants a different sound.' But Nelson was really upset about it. However, Frank knew what he wanted; he needed a change, he needed to get something fresh happening."

Riddle seems to have little reason to be upset that Sinatra was having an occasional fling with other orchestrators since he himself was working with so many singers—even Sinatra's two closest rivals of the early '50s, Cole and Billy Eckstine. Out of necessity, Riddle would write for anyone who would pay him roughly $100 a score. The fee was officially $5 a page, and arrangers did not begin to receive additional royalties for sales of their work until long after the role of orchestrator, as it existed in Riddle's era, had faded from popular music. "It wasn't right. It wasn't fair," said Livingston, "but we obviously weren't going to change the industry." In struggling to support six children, two wives (eventually), and a house in Bel Air, Riddle worked himself into an early grave.

The record business' treatment of the orchestrators who were its life blood may seem a little cold-blooded in retrospect, but nobody besides the bandleader or star whose name was top-billed on the label received royalties then, and often not even him. Billy May was sent statements for the steadily selling series of instrumental albums and singles under his own name (not as an accompanist); Gordon Jenkins raked in considerably more loot as a composer than he did as an orchestrator, even though he had only a handful of hit songs to his credit. But despite the best intentions of Capitol, neither would happen for Riddle. "The company really tried to give Nelson an opportunity to be an artist in his own right and in his own name," Livingston pointed out. "What we were trying to do was give Nelson something of his own that he could make a royalty on." Riddle made instrumental singles as well as albums of dance and then easy-listening music, and penetrated the charts on several occasions, with "Brother John" and "Lisbon Antiqua." According to Livingston, these "were done as a gesture to Nelson," and though they "were of some value" to Riddle, his solo career "never really happened to any extent. He was never *the* record star. He was the accompanist."

What's especially ironic about Riddle's life is his decades-long envy of the success of a musician who could in no way be considered a rival in terms of talent: Henry Mancini. As Bill Finegan pointed out, "Nelson was a better writer than Mancini ever could hope to be." However, it wasn't Mancini's lesser abilities as an artist that Riddle resented, but the younger man's aptitude for self-promotion and creating his own lucky breaks. The gold-thumbed Mancini, along with the other major hit makers of the '60s, was blessed with a remarkable flair for stringing together repetitive, hook-oriented melodies that stood him in good stead with both the countinghouse and the Oscar and Grammy committees. "Nelson said to me once that he would have traded all those arrangements, for which he was paid a flat fee, for one song of Mancini's. Just one song!" Bernhart continued. "But Nelson wasn't a songwriter, he was an arranger. For which you don't get riches—not like Hank Mancini!" Livingston concurred: "Everybody envies Hank Mancini."

The thing that Riddle did earn, however, was the admiration of his peers. "I always loved doing things of Nelson's," said Mahlon Clark. "I told him once. After a date we went over to a bar and were having a drink. I said, 'Every time I do a date with you, I come out feeling like I've accomplished something.' With so many other leaders, it's just making noise, getting it over with and getting the hell out." "It's doubtful Riddle ever felt the same way," said Livingston. "I think he never really appreciated his own talents."

"Nelson was really a genius," claimed Bernhart, "a quiet genius and a troubled one. He really was a big success, but you'd never know it to talk to him. He was a man who figured that he had missed the boat somehow."[15]

15. According to Bernhart, whenever someone told Riddle how much he admired one of his charts, Riddle's response was inevitably, "'Well, for that arrangement I got paid $150.' 'I've Got You Under My Skin' is historic, but he's thinking in terms of the dollar signs. I would say to him, 'Yeah, but it led to a lot more money.' But his comeback was always the same. "I wrote 'Mona Lisa,' and they paid me $75. So what?'" Sure enough, when reminiscing about "Mona Lisa" on his National Public Radio profile, Riddle said, "Les [Baxter] had authorized me to put in a bill for $6 a page. The A&R man at that time [probably Lee Gillette] said, 'I can't okay this. I'm only authorized to pay you scale, which in this case is $3.99 a page.' He said, 'We'll round it off. Let's make it four bucks.' So four times thirteen pages is $52. In my estimation, Nat Cole used that arrangement so many times that he ended up getting it for less than a penny a performance [of Capitol's money]."

"Nelson was a very warm, sensitive guy," Livingston recalled. "We used to sit at lunch, and he'd just bare his heart to me. I mean, tell me how miserably unhappy he was and that he didn't know what to do with his life."

"Nelson was best at telling stories about his life, which were so tragic they were funny," says fellow trombonist and arranger Billy Byers. TV producer Bob Scheerer adds, "Whenever he got a new assignment he would say, 'Here's another telephone pole in the desert of life!'"

When Sinatra went to May or Jenkins, he wanted to draw on what they had achieved on their instrumental recordings and with other singers. With Riddle, however, Sinatra exercised far greater control. He apparently allowed Riddle far less individual freedom than most of his other collaborators, and Riddle seems to have lived in mortal terror of Sinatra's rejecting one of his arrangements. They had to be perfect so that Sinatra could not possibly find anything that had to be changed. Riddle would stay up all night if necessary to make his charts just so, ignoring his wife and family in the process.

Other well-known Hollywood arrangers used assistants and ghost writers without shame when their workloads were too heavy; Stordahl, May, and Paul Weston relied heavily on Heinie Beau, for instance. Riddle's ego and his financial situation prevented him from taking that route very frequently. "I could always tell" when Riddle was presenting the work of another writer, said Rosemary Clooney. "I never questioned it because I knew if he needed to, he needed to. It meant he was really swamped. It happened, but only rarely."

"God knows he was a workaholic. That's all he did," said Clooney. "He got along with very little sleep and smoked too much." Billy May explained, "He got a divorce, and he had a big settlement to pay. Then he got another wife, and she was expensive—and it was a big hassle. So he was always writing. He had to write. He couldn't say no to anything. You would think that after a while it would get to be garbage, but it was *all* quality stuff. With all that trouble and everything, when he sat down to write, he really turned out a good-quality product, whether it was jazz or a ballad or whatever the hell it was. I admire him very much." Other arrangers agree. "We were angry with Nelson because he was so great and he worked so cheap," adds Billy Byers. "When somebody that great is giving it away because of lack of self worth, or whatever, it made us angry. I wasn't envious, but I wish he could've had more, because he deserved it."

And money wasn't his only problem. According to Chris Riddle, "My father unfortunately had a penchant for being swept off his feet by young lady singers. Then he'd feel guilty and come to my mother, and get on his knees and confess—which was the wrong thing because she lacked self-confidence, and that tore her to pieces, to know that he was doing this. She's the last person he should have told." While these were mostly brief encounters, Riddle also experienced a full-fledged affair with Rosemary Clooney that lasted at least six or seven years.

"Music is not only a profession and an art to me," Riddle once said. "Through the years, particularly in trying times, it has been, and still is, a protective wall." Riddle made a perfect partner for Sinatra because of his corresponding capacity for sadness and elation. "Nelson naturally sort of breezed through everything. Nothing upset him," said Ted Nash. "He was more somber than Axel or Billy. Nelson never had much of a personality with the guys. He liked working with us and all that, but he didn't give you a feeling of any warmth." Mahlon Clark remembered that Riddle "hardly ever laughed."

Anyone who has heard "Makin' Whoopee" on *Songs for Swingin' Lovers!* knows he's in the presence of an ironic sense of humor of the highest order. Those close to him, like Clooney, knew that "Nelson had a big streak of bitterness. But I could usually kid him out of it." Because he liked to laugh. He was very funny. Very dry, but very funny." Occasionally Riddle even used his characteristic deadpan puss[16] as a tool for playing practical jokes: Riddle once told Bing Crosby that a certain guitarist had a drinking problem, and Joe Bushkin then spent months trying to convince Crosby that the austere Mr. Riddle had been pulling his leg.

The Sinatra-Riddle relationship fell apart slowly, over nearly thirty years, but in 1960, Riddle, who had made only one album with Sinatra since 1956, seems to have settled for the privilege of being The Voice's most frequent collaborator, if not his only one. Early in the year it looked as if Sinatra's partnership with Riddle, and possibly even his entire recording career, was doomed to become a casualty of his rapidly deteriorating relationship with Capitol Records. By April, after much negotiation, Capitol heads Glenn Wallichs and Alan Livingston agreed to release Sinatra from his long-term contract (renewed for another seven years in 1958), leaving him free to concentrate on his own newly founded label, Reprise Records, once he had completed an agreed-upon number of releases for Capitol.

16. Clooney has also recalled that once when Buster Keaton was a guest on her TV show, Riddle (musical director of the series) composed an especially appropriate instrumental to accompany the great clown's antics. If only Johnny Hodges had been present, it would have been a meeting of the three great stone faces of American popular culture.

Thus, Sinatra began planning his first releases for Reprise while he still had four albums left on his Capitol contract. Even knowing he would be forced to compete with himself, Sinatra never had it in him to turn out less than his best. Unable to compromise his music, Sinatra also agreed not to rerecord any songs he had done on Capitol for Reprise for a certain period. Sinatra then decided to focus on what he had already been leaning toward in his albums with Gordon Jenkins: producing definitive versions of tunes he had previously waxed in his Columbia tenure. Capitol had no objection, feeling that Sinatra's efforts amounted to his equivalent of their *So and So in Hi-Fi* series or to Nat Cole's and June Christy's early 1960s stereo redos of their major recordings (which had even been on Capitol to begin with). Thus, when Sinatra sings "I've Heard That Song Before" on *Come Swing with Me,* he really means it.

The two remaining albums with Riddle contain very few new items— only the out-of-place title track on *Nice 'n' Easy* and three tunes on *Sinatra's Swingin' Session.* Sinatra wasn't about to let that prevent these from being essential sets, however; *Nice 'n' Easy,* in particular, can hold its own against any other Sinatra album. An exquisite collection of ballads that doesn't sound the depths of despair as had previous sets, Sinatra and Riddle painted *Nice 'n' Easy* in stunningly vibrant yet subdued pastel colors. The two men recorded twelve glowingly warm standard love songs over three sessions in March 1960. Nobody remembers what the original title for the project was, although it may well have been *The Nearness of You.* Both the song and the use of it as a title were dropped when Sinatra decided to replace it with "Nice 'n' Easy" as the lead-off track. Although the team of composer Lew Spence and Alan and Marilyn Bergman had already written a number of successful singles for Sinatra (such as "Sleep Warm," "Half as Lovely, Twice as True," and "So Long My Love"), the singer rejected "Nice 'n' Easy" in a flamboyant manner the first time that he heard it.

Then again, Spence himself hadn't thought much of the central melody of the song the first time it occurred to him; he discarded it immediately, and only because he and the Bergmans happened to finish another song early did he bother to demonstrate the unfinished fragment for them. Alan Bergman instantly thought of the title "Nice 'n' Easy," and with that much to work with, the rest of the melody and lyric came quickly. Spence demonstrated the song to Sinatra during a break from the filming of *Ocean's Eleven,* but the singer's initial reaction was to pick up the music with the tips of his fingernails and let it fall to the ground like so much garbage.

Fortunately, Hank Sanicola realized the song's value and over the next

Sinatra described Harry James, with whom he toured for six months in 1939, as "a dear friend and a great teacher." As the great trumpeter's wife, Louise Tobin, has confirmed, "In six months with Harry, Frank learned more about music than he'd ever known in his life up to that point." A master of the blisteringly hot as well as the swaggeringly sentimental, "The Horn" provided his young singer with the best possible model of how to pack an emotional wallop. On the bandstand in the early years (*above*), with Margie Carroll in tow. (Charles L. Granata Collection.) A late 1960s reunion (*left*) in the rehearsal studio. (Wayne Knight Collection.)

The Voice, around the time of his 1944 *Vimms* radio show, with two of his favorite performers—Judy Garland (*right*), an occasional broadcasting co-star deep into the television era (Charles L. Granata Collection), and Bing Crosby (*below*). Often identified by Sinatra as "the father" of his career, Crosby's lyric-driven yet supremely musical approach was indeed a major influence on Sinatra as well as every other vocalist of the '30s onward. In this crooner's summit, Der Bingle is for once the comparatively conservative dresser. (Wayne Knight Collection.)

At Columbia Records in the mid-'40s, Sinatra perfected the exquisitely romantic sound that had already propelled him to national celebrity. He combined the legato, deep breath-based sense of rhythm he had gleaned from Tommy Dorsey with the tenderest and most emotionally vulnerable exposition of a love lyric that any singer had ever mastered. Then he wrapped the whole concoction in the impressionistic string textures (and gently swinging pulse) of longtime orchestrator Axel Stordahl. In the studio (*top*), and in the control booth (*above*) at the 1946 Metronome All-Stars Date with, left to right: George Simon (the *Metronome* writer who produced the date), Columbia executive Mitchell Ayers, drummer Buddy Rich, and occasional artistic conscience Alec Wilder. *Left*: One of the final Columbia dates, February 6, 1952. Note Bill Miller on piano and celeste in the background. (Charles L. Granata Collection).

Two more unusual shots from "The Voice" era of the mid-'40s: At a theater date with Charlie Spivak (*right*), the band-leader who gave Nelson Riddle his first national exposure. The cast of Old Gold's *Songs by Sinatra* (*below*), spring 1946, including Sinatra, Skitch Henderson, June Hutton (who married Axel Stordahl in 1951) and the Pied Pipers, and fellow traveler Sid Caesar, center. (Wayne Knight Collection.)

The passing of the torch: The last date with Axel Stordahl as his regular musical director, and the very first Sinatra session for Capitol Records (*above*), April 2, 1953. A mid-'50s Capitol date with Stordahl's successor, Nelson Riddle (*below*). Although the singer had actually been singing uptempos since his Harry James tenure, the Sinatra of the '50s is more strongly associated with hard-swinging material than The Voice of an earlier era. More than simply singing fast, what Sinatra achieved with Nelson Riddle on Capitol Records was a renaissance of the great swing band tradition, as re-fitted with the harmonic sophistication of contemporary classical style. On a series of classic albums that ranged from 1953 to 1966, Riddle was the only orchestrator Sinatra completely trusted in terms of expressing "sadness as well as elation." (Charles L. Granata Collection.)

Capitol Days, continued: An epiphanous moment at a record date (*above*), capturing the spontaneous, electrifying excitement that has always been Sinatra's unique province. Sinatra with Voyle Gilmore (*below left*), his producer (or, more accurately, coproducer) from 1953 to 1958. This session marked both the first date to be held in Capitol's newly erected stack-of-pancakes–shaped tower, February 1956, as well as Sinatra's most auspicious performance as a nonsinging orchestral conductor. Sinatra's work as a baton-wielder, it should be noted, was no superstar's indulgence. Most of the musicians who played on this and other dates under Sinatra's direction acknowledge that he was a more than competent conductor on pop material, at least as good as most of the arrangers who normally held the stick on Sinatra sessions. *Below right*: Another shot from the first Capitol date. (Charles L. Granata Collection.)

In the '60s (*left*), Sinatra, now working for his own self-owned label, Reprise Records, expanded his horizons while maintaining his long established turf of ballads and swingers. (Wayne Knight Collection.) Collaborating with over a dozen brand new arrangers, Sinatra's projects ranged from sets as bold and brassy as *Ring-A-Ding-Ding* with Johnny Mandel and *Sinatra and Swingin' Brass* and *Sinatra-Basie* (notice the rare shot, *below*, of Mr. Basie *not* at the piano) with Neil Hefti, to projects as soft and **intimate as the two *Francis Albert Sinatra-Antonio Carlos Jobim*** albums. (Charles L. Granata Collection.) Sinatra seemed to be marshaling all the resources of the hip—adult pop and jazz, from Basie and Ellington to the bossa nova—to take a stand against the forces of squareness that were surrounding Reprise's lonely island of musical sanity.

Twentieth-century icon: Sinatra in front of an audience, late '40s (*left*) and early '60s (*below*). (Charles L. Granata Collection.) When a singer brings a lyric to life, we typically call that process "interpretation." Sinatra elevates interpretation into his own personal three-minute slice of reality, the same kind of reality that Jimmy Cagney spoke of when he defined the art of acting as being able to "stand on the balls of your feet and tell the truth." Whether Sinatra is enacting "One for My Baby" so vividly true to the lyrics that you actually see the bartender with the bent ears wiping down glasses, or "throwing away" the lyric to some '20s bauble reinvented as a rhythm song, Sinatra is never less than eminently believable.

few weeks kept playing it whenever Sinatra was within earshot. Sinatra finally asked, "What is that cute little thing you keep playing?" And, as Spence recalled, "Hank told him it was my song and that he was recording it in a couple of weeks. Frank said, 'Well, I better get Nelson and give him a key. I don't remember giving him a key on that one.' Frank not only recorded it but decided that he would make it the title of an album." Sinatra devised his classic coda, which reprises the tag and false ending, from Count Basie's "April in Paris" ("like the man says, one more time," which plays off the last line, "nice and easy does it every time") on the actual date.[17]

With its finger snaps and gentle swing, "Nice 'n' Easy" has little in common with the rest of the album. Riddle coated the set with a soft sheen of brilliantly arranged strings and the most prominently displayed coterie of sidemen he had ever used, spotlighting a different sideman on almost every track—but not making a point of it. Thus we hear Plas Johnson's tenor on "That Old Feeling" and "Nevertheless," George Roberts turning in one of his fullest statements ever on "How Deep Is the Ocean?", Harry Klee on "Fools Rush In," trumpeter Carroll Lewis making like Bobby Hackett on "Nevertheless" and "She's Funny That Way," two stunning Felix Slatkin solos on "Try a Little Tenderness" and "Mam'selle," while Bill Miller delivers a classic coda on "I've Got a Crush on You." (On CD, *Nice 'n' Easy* sounds even better with "The Nearness of You" restored. Deleted from the original album, the track was released initially on the hodgepodge collection *Sinatra Sings of Love and Things*.) For his part, Sinatra has never sounded more convincingly blue and pensive; this is make-out music no less pleasurable than the activity it's designed to accompany.

As an album of ballads lacking a noirish or suicidal feel, *Nice 'n' Easy* might be described as a general update of Sinatra's '40s sound. The final Sinatra-Riddle-Capitol set, *Sinatra's Swingin' Session,* can similarly be characterized as a virtual remake of Sinatra's first LP album, *Sing and Dance with Frank Sinatra. Swingin' Session* reprises six out of the eight songs on that 1950 set (while a seventh, "Lover," appears anew on *Come Swing with Me*).

Riddle had all the arrangements ready to go, but, as he later recalled, when Sinatra arrived at the date the singer surprised him by announcing that he wanted to do all the tunes at tempos twice as fast as he had previ-

17. The session tapes of the tune have Sinatra fooling around with spontaneous and off-color exclamations in the coda, such as "Put your hand on it, baby, that's all," "Yeah, you dirty mother!" and "That quarter rest is murder!" (It could be called "Nice 'n' Sleazy.")

ously planned. Riddle hadn't given him any four- or five-minute epics to begin with, so Sinatra's decision left them with a whole bunch of tracks that were short enough to fit on an answering machine message and a twenty-five-minute album—not much longer than the original ten-inch *Sing and Dance* disc. (Sinatra later performed Riddle's "My Blue Heaven" in the original slower tempo live at an Australian concert in 1961.)

This was by no means typical of the four contractual obligation albums: "You Go to My Head" on *Nice 'n' Easy* and "That Old Black Magic" on *Come Swing with Me* both clock in at four minutes or more, as do three tracks on *Point of No Return.* One is left to wonder if it's mere coincidence that the longest tunes on *Swingin' Session* happen to be the three non-remakes, among them "Blue Moon," which finds Sinatra improvising all sorts of imaginative harmony lines on the melody. That tune, incidentally, marks one of the only items in the Sinatra discography suggested by Bill Miller. The pianist recalled, "He said, 'Pick a tune for me. What would you play if you were going to sit down at the piano right now?' I said, 'Oh, maybe "Blue Moon."' He said, 'Okay. Call Nelson and tell him to make "Blue Moon."'"

Still, it's clear that Sinatra sensed the wisdom of Glenn Miller's dictum: "I don't want those m-f's to dance, I want them to listen!" Sinatra increased the metronomic count only in order to make the *Swingin' Session* justify its extravagant title. It gives the charts a superpunchy feeling, so that on "Should I?" both Sinatra and tenorist Buddy Collette (visible on the cover), who shares the reed solos with Plas Johnson, move so fast they almost sound as if they're hyperventilating. At one point on "My Blue Heaven," Sinatra even eliminates the first syllables of each A section to keep everything moving.

So it's damn the torpedos, full speed ahead. The frenzied pace enforces the frantic feeling of fun, making this Sinatra's most trimly swinging set—less like Lunceford and Oliver and more like Basie or Goodman. Riddle even uses the strings in a rhythmic fashion, which is to say barely at all most of the time, and has them plunk away pizzicato in swing time on his dewaltzed treatment of "Always." For all the relentless energy that Sinatra and Riddle displace, they remain true to the spirit of the songs and themselves. "September in the Rain," with its booming bass coda by Joe Comfort, "Always," and "I Can't Believe That You're in Love with Me" have well-conceived closers combining original lyric and musical variations that Sinatra all but throws directly into the audience, as if in a 3-D movie. Far from being too fast, "When You're Smiling" even gives Sinatra time to detour through an unanticipated Louis Prima impression.

However, with Reprise a reality, Sinatra redoubled his efforts to move into a new post-Riddle sound, employing his once-constant collaborator only for a mere two singles between 1960 and 1963. Riddle had accepted that Sinatra would seek new sounds from such masters as May and Jenkins, and later Johnny Mandel and Sy Oliver, but Sinatra's turning to a relatively unknown quantity named Don Costa rankled him. "When Don Costa showed up and got into the picture, Nelson was very hurt," said Milt Bernhart. "And those around town knew that."

By 1963, Sinatra had sowed enough oats with other writers to renew the partnership with Riddle in earnest; over the next five years they would collaborate frequently, turning out five entire albums. Riddle would also arrange a number of individual Sinatra tracks for other Reprise multiartist album projects as well as singles.

These five Reprise albums are hardly the Sinatra-Riddle equivalent of the post–Frank Baum *Oz* books, meaning a familiar cast of characters achieving a significantly lesser level of magic. Nothing quite reaches the twin peaks of *Swingin' Lovers* and *Only the Lonely*, but these five mid-1960s albums are less concerned with climbing back to familiar heights than they are with marking out new territory. Sinatra and Riddle work with new instruments, such as a prominent guitar background on "Moon River," Brazilian percussion and bossa nova patterns on "I Wished on the Moon," and a Hammond organ throughout the whole *Strangers in the Night* set. Sinatra finds new ways to put over very heavy ballads in *The Concert Sinatra* (1963) and new ways to swing on *Strangers in the Night* (1966). He also explores alternate methods of organizing songs via not only emotional but thematic juxtapositions.

Only *Sinatra's Sinatra* (1963), the least regarded of the final five Sinatra-Riddle albums, attempts to rekindle the old fire with the original pair of sticks. An album inspired by economic rather than artistic necessity, it attempts to compete in record stores with earlier hits still controlled by Columbia and Capitol. Yet *Sinatra's Sinatra* remains true to its concept of presenting new versions of Sinatra's personal favorite songs and not merely regurgitating the twelve titles that happened to sell the biggest for a higher royalty rate on his own label. The two newest charts, the two new Riddle scores for songs originally recorded with Stordahl, fare the worst: "Nancy" has lost the bloom of her youth and Sinatra can't summon the same spark he had infused her with in 1945. Likewise, the singer has simply outgrown the naive "Oh What It Seemed to Be."[18]

18. FS turned in his best version of this George Weiss–Bennie Benjamin hit on a 1946 *Old Gold* show, a radio rehearsal that has circulated among collectors. At one point, Sinatra breaks up and starts singing à la Mickey Katz, "Oy, vot it seemed to be."

Riddle's rerecordings of his own charts vary in practice, although all the instrumental backings sound more spectacular in the new stereo setting. "I've Got You Under My Skin" finds trombonist Dick Nash sitting in for Bernhart, who had a film call he couldn't get out of, mixing his own licks in with quotes from Bernhart's classic 1956 solo. "Of course, everyone has to end that solo with the phrase that Milt used," said Nash, "which is Milt's trademark. I felt you *had* to use that, it fits the tune so well."

Sinatra gets "damn well" animatedly aggressive here and on "Witchcraft" and elsewhere, and on "Young at Heart" he sounds a little more knowing for having been around the block a few times in the intervening years. "In the Wee Small Hours" constitutes the most successful remake, deliberately substituting a nicer 'n' easier lightness for the drama of the 1955 original.

On the whole, it's too bad that the 1963 Sinatra doesn't work as hard at wooing these tunes away from his younger self as he does on *Academy Award Winners*—for instance, at winning "Cool, Cool, Cool of the Evening" and "Swinging on a Star" away from Bing Crosby, and "The Continental" and "The Way You Look Tonight" from Fred Astaire. *Sinatra's Sinatra*'s greatest benefactions are the three Cahn and Van Heusen classics that defy the concept of remaking earlier hits, particularly this second-time-around version of "The Second Time Around," which Sinatra had initially recorded in 1960 as the first Reprise single. "Call Me Irresponsible" finds Sinatra riding in like the cavalry to save a swell song from an epic barker of a clambake called *Papa's Delicate Condition.* As for "Pocketful of Miracles," that seems to be "High Hopes" spelled sideways, a spoonful of Frank Capra-corn swallowed with a wordless kiddie choir. Both tunes could be anagrams for "Swinging on a Star" and signify rare instances of the great Sammy Cahn confined to the shadow of Van Heusen's former lyricist, the great Irish blarney salesman, Johnny Burke.

For a "least" album by the team, *Sinatra's Sinatra* is still pretty damn good. As for the remaining '60s sets, *The Concert Sinatra* (1963) derives just as much from Sinatra's career-long quest for extended song forms as it does from his partnership with Riddle. Likewise, *Strangers in the Night* (1966) comes out of his attempts to be contemporary with the psychedelic '60s. The two sets signify the widest extremes of the collaboration: *Strangers* works on the most minimal and easiest to digest tunes of both the classic and contemporary pop traditions; *Concert* goes for the most high-browed works they can transform into ambitious "concert" arrangements. *Concert* also represents the closest Sinatra would come to a composer "songbook" album. Celebrating the twin titans of the integrated story musical, all but one (Kurt Weill's "Lost in the Stars") of its eight extended selections derive from Richard Rodgers and/or Oscar Hammerstein.

If the 1956 *Close to You* represented Sinatra and Riddle at their most intimate, *Concert Sinatra* finds them at their most epic. Where *Close* utilizes a chamber group, *Concert* deploys a complete symphonic contingent. Riddle's orchestrations are particularly adept at humanizing the largest backup group any pop star would ever sing in front of. The arranger commences the first track, "I Have Dreamed," with the lightest possible sound—his familiar flutes—and has his enormous contingent of string players enter so slowly, almost imperceptibly, as if to suggest an engineer gradually turning up the volume.

Sadly, Riddle had been deprived of one of his most crucial voices not long before the album: Felix Slatkin had died shortly before the session, and, as Eleanor Slatkin recalled, Sinatra insisted that she participate as a kind of work therapy to keep her from being overcome with grief. "Unless she agrees to play," Sinatra said, "I won't do the album." In spite of the absence of Felix's familiar violin sound, by the outchorus of "Dream" the excitement has snowballed to the point where, although Sinatra never sounds as if he's straining, he has taken his chops to the very outer limits of where they can go.

Riddle is almost invisible on "Soliloquy" and "Ol' Man River," two songs that don't leave much room for, say, moving the bridge to where the verse is supposed to be. The arranger does insert a characteristic Riddleism on "My Heart Stood Still" (which Sinatra had performed occasionally on the radio in 1943–44 and on TV with Riddle in the '50s but never previously on records). As Sinatra begins a modulation from the verse to the chorus, just when the lyric mentions castles that "rise in Spain," Riddle dangles a few castenets to distract attention from Sinatra's key change. Likewise, the pronounciation of the words "my heart's do-main," is classic Sinatra phrasing. In contrast, "Lost in the Stars" is a showcase as much for the arranger as the singer, a chart with an original and strikingly Stravinskian forty-five-second intro. Riddle depicts heavenly bodies skittering about the cosmos before our aural "eyes" focus on one lonely being on one little star.

Where "Lost in the Stars" nihilistically illustrates how man is ultimately alone in the universe, "You'll Never Walk Alone" argues that the solidarity of humankind counts for more than the existence of any suprahuman being. On this track and throughout *Concert Sinatra*, Riddle's charts are especially supportive of the swelling and surging that Sinatra is aiming for and that he accomplishes here even more effectively than with Stordahl. The one-finger piano solo on this quasi-spiritual, used so effectively by Stordahl, sounds even better in Riddle's big, big, big-band orchestration. And for all the big-voiced singing that goes on in this *Concert* setting, the two still get in some tenderly sensitive balladeering before the very big ending of "Bewitched."

Days of Wine and Roses: Academy Award Winners (1964) and *Moonlight Sinatra* (1965) amount to the only actual Sinatra-Riddle "theme" albums. That means, in this case, that the individual songs of each are united by related conceptual material. In the first, it's the supremely irrelevant fact that each song happened to win an Oscar for best song introduced in a motion picture; the second contains ten out of the approximately ten thousand great popular songs that refer to the Earth's satellite in their titles and lyrics. The nine classic Capitol sets are more musically linked by similarities of tempo and mood, but Riddle keeps the colors no less delightfully consistent on *Award Winners* and *Moonlight*, and this in spite of how each set incorporates both swingers and heart-wrenchers.

Academy Award Winners' full title (if you believe the back cover) reads, *"Frank Sinatra sings* Days of Wine and Roses, Moon River, *and Other Academy Award Winners."* While it doubtlessly peeved Riddle to invest so much energy into making Henry Mancini's melodies sound better than ever, Sinatra obviously relished the chance to sink his teeth into two of Johnny Mercer's finest latter-day lyrics. Indeed, apart from Mercer's contributions the two songs were so overexposed at the time that they started sounding hackneyed long before the composer took home his consecutive Oscars. Still, Sinatra and Riddle infuse them with a feeling of freshness, thanks to an almost perverse originality.

The abstract lyrics of "Days of Wine and Roses" declare it a definite downer, while those of "Moon River" enhance its psuedofolk attitude, making it more blandly optimistic. Sinatra and Riddle invert "Wine and Roses" into a medium-bounce swinger, with George Roberts grunting all over the place. Contrastingly, Vince DeRosa's French horn moans low on "Moon River," expressing a Tom Sawyer–like yearning for faraway places with strange-sounding names. In the foreground, Sinatra and Riddle's melancholy mood negates the lyric's huckleberry friendliness.

Some musicians who play on *Academy Award Winners* claim that the set was put together even more quickly than usual, and some of the charts may be the work of one of Riddle's deputies, like Gil Grau. Yet it can't be said that any of this haste made waste of any of the finished product. "The Way You Look Tonight," in the tradition of "Goodbye" and "Blues in the Night," finds the two men making particularly effective use of the extralyrical four-note "humming" phrase that Dorothy Fields and

Jerome Kern incorporated in the melody. The strings play it in a slightly different register at the end of each A section until the end of the track. At that point, Sinatra, who has rarely exuded so much energy, warmth, and vitality, splits the phrase with the ensemble as if they were breaking open a bottle of Chianti Classico together.

As mentioned above, both *Academy Award Winners* and *Moonlight Sinatra* seamlessly intermingle fast and slow tempos as well as moods that go up and down. The ballads in *Academy Awards* include the only reading of "Secret Love" that makes the song work with a mature attitude rather than the younger-than-springtime idealism Doris Day originally bagged the Oscar with. Similarly, Sinatra's "It Might As Well Be Spring" brings a more relaxed, second-time-around sensibility to a piece previously associated with Dick Haymes' more virginally anxious "busy as a spider spinning daydreams" interpretation. Sinatra would have done better to swing or at least radically rethink "Love Is a Many-Splendored Thing"; this barrel of corn is nearly too heavy for even the mighty Sinatra-Riddle weightlifting team to hoist off the ground.

Reflecting cover artist George Bartell's illustration, Sinatra and Riddle render *Moonlight Sinatra* in a marvelously expressive palette of blue and purple tints. *Wee Small Hours* and *Only the Lonely* take place in a night without stars, but the nocturnal setting of *Moonlight* is almost as bright as day. This is the difference that C. S. Lewis articulated between mere empty "space" and the magnificent richness of "the heavens"— particularly on "Moon Song." An album for snuggling rather than wristslashing, *Moonlight* ranges from the flagwavingly up "Oh, You Crazy Moon" to the grandly Tchaikovskian "Moon Love." "I Wished on the Moon" constitutes a study in contrasts all by itself, opening with a somberly heavy out-of-tempo verse, itself one of Dorothy Parker's most poignant pieces of poetry, then moving to a gently Brazilian-flavored refrain. All of these moonlight moods are depicted in their blue hues as deep purple dreams.

Repertorially speaking, *Moonlight* also amounts to Sinatra's most ambitious homage to his original inspiration, Bing Crosby. Fully half the album's tunes had been introduced on the screen or on wax by Crosby: "Moonlight Becomes You," "I Wished on the Moon," "The Moon Got in My Eyes," and "The Moon Was Yellow." Though never sung by Crosby, "Reaching for the Moon" had served as the title song of his first solo feature-film appearance in 1931.

Papa Bing had originally recorded "The Moon Was Yellow" in 1934, and Sinatra had first sunk his teeth into it in 1945, in a heavily dramatic reading that edged toward the style of Allan Jones and Tony Martin.

Returning to the tune in 1958, Sinatra and Riddle restructured it along the basis of the previous year's "April in Paris" with Billy May, reemploying the bridge as a sort of in-tempo verse. (This treatment of the song was convincingly scaled down for a sextet during Sinatra's 1962 world tour, from which it survives in several performances.) Sinatra's third "Moon Was Yellow," for the 1965 *Moonlight* album, keeps a glimmer of the original's lightly Latin feeling, opening with a flute and guitar and shadowing the singer with maracas. But it's a much mellower south-of-the-border groove than the roses-in-the-teeth of his earlier renditions, relaxing from a torrid tango into a gentler bossa beat. And what of the bridge-as-verse device? Sinatra has found a more welcome home for it, using the idea to open the entire album at the intro of track one, "Moonlight Becomes You."

In his 1948 interview with George Simon, Sinatra, talking about his favorite kinds of music, referred to "all the great Glenn Miller things"; several Miller sidemen later worked extensively with Sinatra, including Zeke Zarchy, Trigger Alpert, reed-doubler Willie Schwartz, and Billy May. Miller, whose theme song was his own "Moonlight Serenade," was inclined to include as much moony material in his book as he could. In 1965, Sinatra used Miller as his secondary source for lunar laments, among them "Moonlight Mood," "Moon Love," and "Oh, You Crazy Moon" (also recorded by Tommy Dorsey), in addition to the original "Serenade."

Although at least three separate sets of lyrics were written for "Moonlight Serenade," the late bandleader used his own piece strictly instrumentally and only as an opening and closing theme. Sinatra infuses it with a double shot of romance while keeping it no less danceable than when under its composer's baton. "Moonlight Mood" opens with a particularly successful reading, accompanied by Bill Miller's piano only, of a little-known verse to a very-little-known Peter DeRose song Sinatra had previously transcribed in late 1942 for the war effort. "Moon Love," based on Tchaikovsky's Fifth Symphony, proceeds at a stately yet down-to-earth tempo and becomes especially convincing at the conclusion, where Sinatra diminuendos out, disappearing in the style of "Angel Eyes" on the word "disappear." The only number on the disc not derived from Crosby or Miller was "Moon Song," which had been introduced by the moon-shaped Kate Smith, who had considerable experience with hauling moons over mountains.

Riddle's use of the strings affords *Moonlight* its particular shade of stariness, and he brings them down in order to accentuate the rhythm section on "Oh, You Crazy Moon," along with a swaggering trumpet obligato, probably Conrad Gozzo or Pete Candoli. "Crazy Moon" is the most Basie-like piece on the album; you could almost swear you're hearing that unmistakable Marshall Royal–led reed section. In 1967, Sinatra would mastermind a three-way collaboration—himself, Billy May, and the stylistic tradition of the Duke Ellington orchestra, employing none other than Ellington and crew themselves. A rumor has long circulated that in the same period Sinatra was also considering a triumverate teaming of himself, one of his heavy-duty writers, and a legendary American orchestra, this time meaning Nelson Riddle and Count Basie.

He never did get around to a Sinatra-Basie-Riddle album because, one suspects, he channeled his expression of that energy into the 1966 album *Strangers in the Night.* Two years earlier, when "Softly, As I Leave You," Sinatra's cover of a British hit by Matt Monro (long billed as the Blue Eyes of Britain), began climbing the *Billboard* charts, Reprise assembled an instant album around it with miscellaneous singles. In 1966 Sinatra landed another surprise hit with a song about which he has been especially vocal in expressing his dislike, "Strangers in the Night," by the old Muzak master Bert Kaempfert. This time, however, Sinatra and producer Sonny Burke decided to take the high road in using "Strangers in the Night" for an album of material that immediately overshadowed its title track.

Subtitled "Sinatra Sings for Moderns," the disc is diminished only twice by the singer's attempts to "go modern." These are the non-Riddle title cut and the dismal "Downtown," a Petula Clark hit so beyond saving that Sinatra can only verbally grimace (à la Jackie Gleason) in what comes off as an attempt to win sympathy for having to perform it. Those two tracks aside, the remaining eight selections, including two covers of contemporary hits, "Call Me" and "On a Clear Day," are the last fully realized, top-drawer examples of the Sinatra-Riddle collaboration.

Of the total ten, only Richard Rodgers' "The Most Beautiful Girl in the World" comes from one of the more highly respected composers of the great show-music tradition that Sinatra's albums more typically celebrate. Sinatra had included one waltz on *Moonlight,* "Reaching for the Moon," an archaic Irving Berlin piece that could also have fit snugly on the Sinatra-Jenkins *All Alone.* By contrast, Sinatra thoroughly dewaltzifies "Most Beautiful Girl." Not only does he even out the three-quarter piece into straight four-four time, he revs it up from the romantic to the rhythmic, overloading the chart with so many flying organ licks and bongo beatings that it explodes, zooming on a roller-coaster ride fast enough to give the old girl heart palpitations.

The use of the organ was obviously inspired by the way Basie played it and worked it into his big- and small-band settings. "You're Driving

Me Crazy" had been a Basie perennial, using both the original title and head melody as well as a familiar variation on its chord changes entitled "Moten Swing." Sinatra and Riddle may also have been influenced by *Let's Face the Music and Dance,* a 1961 Nat King Cole–Billy May album in which Cole himself played several organ solos within a post-Sinatra *Swingin' Lovers* context.

Tenor sax star Jimmy Forrest, who certainly knew about playing with electric organs, once told Joe Goldberg that as accompaniment the organ "gives you more scope. You feel as if you have a big band behind you." Riddle and Sinatra use the organ as if it were a whole other orchestra; most often the instrument and the orchestra don't play at the same time but trade phrases back and forth like two warring big bands in a Savoy Ballroom battle. The string section, present but playing a far less prominent role on these two sessions, also functions as yet another band; appropriately, only two of the three "orchestras" present can be sensed in the same sentence. Whenever the electric instrument is heard behind the band, the unknown keyboardist was instructed to play softly so that the electronic strains can take the place of the strings; when the fiddles appear, the organist sits out that chorus or part of a chorus.

Although the blues are hardly Sinatra's forte, the Basie-organ feeling gives Sinatra the support he needs to make this his bluesiest excursion. Riddle's trimly blue arrangements suggest a bridge between the patented idiosyncratic swing of the Sinatra-Riddle tradition and the more mainstream swing that Basie used to back Joe Williams. Comfortable with neither the blues nor rock, Sinatra here brings the blues-rock "Call Me" into his own idiom by meeting it halfway. Conversely, he pushes his own earliest hit, "All or Nothing at All," into a domain where the kiddie-pop and Sinatra-Riddle traditions are consistent with each other, Riddle reprising an off-the-chord trombone section episode that sounds like three rhineroci mating to the tune of Milt Bernhart's interlude on "I've Got You Under My Skin."

The Count's influence also helps bring a touch of the blues to three roaring-twenties goodies by Walter Donaldson: "My Baby Just Cares for Me," in which Sinatra is bulwarked by more grunting Roberts; "Yes, Sir, That's My Baby," where he lets the ensemble "sing" the first two notes for him; and "You're Driving Me Crazy." On "My Baby Just Cares for Me" Sinatra had kidded his tri-state roots by choosing to pronounce the word "choices" as "cherces." On "Crazy" he sounds like it's his "cherce" to pronounce the line "would hurt me"as "would hoit me" but that instead he changes his mind at the last second, and then reiterates the last two words correctly. Yet the momentum he achieves on this particular take (number three) so pleased Sinatra that he chose it over another take (number one, issued on a private foreign LP) in which he got the three notes right the first time but didn't swing as hard.

The most Basie-like track is not one of the standards but the contem-pop cover "On a Clear Day,"[19] on which Sinatra offers the instruction, "Let it lay back now. Don't push any phrases, let 'em linger." "Clear Day" uses some of Riddle's familiar textures, along with structural and tempo-ral devices associated with Basie's stylists, such as Thad Jones, Eric Dixon, and Neal Hefti. Riddle is particularly keen to pick up on the great Basie tradition of stop time and rests, having the whole enchilada simply pause before Sinatra's entrances for both dynamic and rhythmic effect and then having the ensemble surge in at twice the volume. The coda, too, in which Sinatra repeats "on a clear day" over and over like a broken record, pays such successful tribute to Wild Bill Davis' arrangement of "April in Paris" that one fully expects to hear the Count's stentorial tones piping out, "One more once!"

However, there would be no "one more time" for the Sinatra-Riddle partnership, not really. "Toward the end, Nelson didn't particularly like Frank," said Bill Miller. "He felt as if he was being fluffed off." In the years immediately before and after his retirement, easily the least inter-esting of his career, Sinatra would rely heavily on Don Costa to try to translate top 40 hits into the Sinatra idiom, with mixed results. Between 1967 and 1977, Sinatra called Riddle only on a handful of occasions: for several TV shows and concerts, one minor album (*The Sinatra Family Wish You a Merry Christmas*, 1968), and two singles, ("Blue Lace" and "Star" from 1968), plus the chintzy, unreleased "Evergreen" and the charmingly touching "I Love My Wife" in 1976.

It shouldn't be inferred that Riddle and his two wives and six kids were going hungry during these years. Although the adult pop-record business was drying up, Riddle found more lucrative work writing tele-vision and then film scores, an avenue opened to him by Nat Cole and Sinatra; his first full-length scores were for their films *St. Louis Blues* and *Johnny Concho*, both in 1956. Although he won an Oscar for his work on *The Great Gatsby* in 1974, neither his film music nor his own recordings made him a household name. Further, as Chris Riddle

19. Riddle would have more experience with the song: in 1970, conspiring with Vin-cent Minnelli, who was to movies what Riddle was to music, he achieved the impossible by making Barbra Streisand come off like a human being in the film version of *On a Clear Day*.

pointed out, the Oscar somehow became the "kiss of death" for Riddle's career; potential clients perhaps feared that the award would put him out of their price range. He was also no further along in the happiness department, divorcing Doreen to marry his longtime secretary, a marriage that all who spoke to me described as a disaster.

In 1977, Sinatra and Riddle began work on a "concept album" follow-up to *Academy Award Winners* and *Moonlight Sinatra,* a set of songs based on women's names. It's not known how many arrangements Riddle actually put on paper, but Sinatra laid down vocal tracks on six known numbers while Riddle recorded orchestral parts on at least another four. These include a remake of "Nancy" considerably warmer than the 1963 reading, a swinging treatment of Buddy Clark's hit "Linda" that annexes an electric piano to the mix, and a fine performance of a disappointingly subpar Van Heusen song dedicated to "Barbara," who had recently become the fourth Mrs. Sinatra. All the tracks that have been officially released and privately circulated (three came out on *The Reprise Collection* in 1990) make one wonder why Sinatra decided not to complete the project, exalting the glories of the fair sex and using the wonderful "I Love My Wife" as the topper.

Sinatra did complete another three-LP set in the late '70s for which he contracted only a single arrangement from Riddle. Perhaps still hoping to finish the *Ladies* project, the arranger submitted only one song for *Trilogy.* Although the title referred to the past, the present, and the future, its underlying meaning, to Sinatra fans at least, implied the three arrangers most closely associated with the mature Sinatra: Riddle, May, and Jenkins.

Unfortunately, that wasn't what Sinatra and Sonny Burke had in mind; Sinatra long since had operated under the impression that Don Costa would be his Stordahl-Riddle of the soft-rock era, and nobody but Costa would be considered for the "Present" portion of the album. Anyone who has heard Riddle's treatments of contemporary ditties on *Strangers in the Night* or, for that matter, Beatle George Harrison's "Something" on *Trilogy,* which uses a Slatkinesque violin to make the thing resemble a real song, must acknowledge that Riddle leaves Costa in the dust (with no disrespect to the younger writer) even on this godforsaken continent.

Sinatra had initially intended Riddle to handle the "Past" section of *Trilogy,* but by the time recording began, the two men had already passed the point of their final breakup. Billy May has recalled that around the time the set was being planned, he was having dinner with Riddle and a German record producer for whom both were making albums. "So in the course of the conversation, the German guy started asking Nelson about Sinatra, and Nelson got very angry. I'd never heard him talk that way before. He got very vehement about how he didn't like Sinatra anymore and how he felt that he had been taken advantage of."

Milt Bernhart, who was closer to Riddle on a personal basis at this time, recalls that a testimonial dinner, a fund-raiser, was to be given in Riddle's honor at the Century Plaza Hotel. "So they figured they ought to try to get Frank Sinatra. Nelson said, 'Sure, you can try. I don't know him. I haven't worked with him for a while. But go ahead and try.' They got hold of Frank somehow, and his office said okay. On that basis they sold out the house at a thousand dollars a plate."

All would have been fine except that, as conductor Vincent Falcone remembers, Sinatra's business manager, for whatever reason, went ahead and booked the singer on that same date. "So they called Nelson and asked him to postpone the date, which he did. It was an incredible feat, to postpone this date with all these celebrities, and so forth. I mean, who could imagine a tribute to Nelson Riddle without Frank Sinatra? They rescheduled it, and I think the same thing happened again. And I don't know why Sinatra didn't overrule him. I just don't have any idea. I never discussed it with Frank. It was a touchy spot."

Bernhart remembers that on the day of the dinner "Nelson almost died then and there. They had to find somebody else, and they ended up with Sid Caesar. But that was a far cry from Frank Sinatra. And the audience, I'm afraid, wasn't thrilled. So Nelson went around mumbling about that for several years: 'He let me down.' It was a big blow." Most of his friends simply chalked it up to Riddle's paranoia and poor self-image. "I'm sure Sinatra has his side of the story," said Billy May. "I think it's basically just a misunderstanding that got out of hand. But it's too bad because they worked together so well."

Bill Miller felt that both parties acted childishly: "I think Nelson got an assignment from Frank, and he turned it down. So Frank [grumbled], 'Who needs you?'" Falcone added, "One time Frank and I were in the dressing room in the suite at Caesar's Palace. We were talking about Nelson, and I was shouting his praises. Frank turned to me and said, 'Call Nelson on the phone and ask him if he'll write a chart for me.' And I said, 'Wow, man. I'm going to be a part of history here.' I was a casual friend of Nelson's, so I picked up the phone and I called him. 'Nelson, Mr. Sinatra asked me to call you. He would like to know if you would write an arrangement on . . .' whatever the song was. I don't remember. And there was just dead silence on the other end of the phone for a good ten, fifteen seconds, and Nelson said, 'Tell him I'm busy.' And he hung up."

When *Trilogy* became a reality, the "Past" part of the project went to May instead of Riddle. "I saw Nelson around that time," said May, "and he said, 'Did they call you to do the *Trilogy* album?' I said, 'Yeah, I'm going to do it.' He said, 'Good, because that's what I was supposed to do. You're getting it on account of me.' I said, 'Well, then, I owe you one.' But we had been doing that for a long time, you know." (Chris Riddle believes that his father turned down *Trilogy* because he wanted to do all three sections himself—that or nothing.)

Riddle's mother had died of liver cancer, and when he himself underwent a liver operation in 1980, most of his friends were surprised to learn his liver was shot. "I like a glass of vodka, but I never drank so that I was inebriated," he said. "I had a weak liver, and I suppose I was one of those guys who should never have anything to drink." Chris Riddle added, "At that time the doctors told me that ninety-five percent of these operations were successful and that people who undergo this procedure normally have at least five more years. Well, that's exactly what Dad had, five years."

In those last five years the orchestrator caught the first glimmer of the Riddle renaissance when Linda Ronstadt hired him to remake a number of his Sinatra charts for what developed into a series of retro-camp albums. The formula: a rock voice wearing '50s outfits on the cover and struggling through songs and arrangements she naively associated with the '50s but which were actually timeless. Journalist Pete Hamill accepted the blame for turning Ronstadt onto the classic Sinatra-Riddle sound, and when Ronstadt was advised to hire Riddle for such a project, with characteristic acumen she commented, "I didn't know if he was still alive or if he was like seventy or something."

Discussing the difference between the '50s and the '80s, Riddle observed, "We were in there editing the tapes from the things we'd done, and she was doing a few bars here and there. She asked, 'Nelson, how did they do those thirty years ago?' I said, 'We did 'em in one piece. We did four sides in three hours. Try that!' It takes her a whole goddamned week to do four sides, and she thinks she's going fast!" In a photograph with Ronstadt in *People* magazine, Riddle comes off looking like a middle-aged banker cajoled into chaperoning his addlebrained daughter to her senior prom.

"For once, Nelson made a sweet deal on those Ronstadt things," states Billy Byers. "The record company didn't want to pay for the arrangements, so Nelson took a percentage. And he made a killing!" It's immaterial that the arrangements he wrote for Ronstadt represented the soggiest and least inspired of his forty-plus years of writing, or that the singer hadn't the faintest idea what to do with the lyrics or tunes that she was attempting, the discs sold well enough to justify three entire albums:

What's New (1983), *For Sentimental Reasons* (1984), and *Lush Life,* released in 1986, the year after Riddle's death.

The sole positive aspect of the association, as well as a similar "crossover" project with opera diva Dame Kiri Te Kanawa (*Blue Skies*), was the renewed attention it brought to Riddle. As Rosemary Clooney testifies, "What Linda did for Nelson was courageous and beautiful," and, she says between the lines, it brought him a little closer to happy— even if he would never express that feeling in public. "Some friend of mine ran into Nelson in a supermarket," remembers Byers. "He said, 'Nobody likes my stuff anymore and I'm getting phased out of the business.' But this was *after* the Ronstadt records came out!"

But the oddest event of Riddle's final months was his "absolution" of Frank Sinatra. In January 1985, Sinatra, a former liberal turned Grand Old Party animal, asked Riddle to accompany him to a dinner given in celebration of the reelection of Ronald Reagan. "Frank spent the whole evening hanging out with my dad," Chris Riddle recalled, "even when Barbara [Mrs. Sinatra] brought this or that Republican bigwig to shake his hand. Frank fluffed them off so he could give all his attention to Dad. When we got home, I asked him what they were talking about all that time, and Dad said, 'We were talking about old times. Frank wants to make some more albums. He wants to record all the great songs that he missed over the years.'" The younger Riddle added, "I could tell that the fence was mended."

A few days after Riddle died, at sixty-four on October 6, 1985,[20] his daughter Rosemary entered his office to pick up a couple of pictures of her father and family. She noticed an unfinished chart on the piano, and though she didn't take note of what song it was, she saw that it was from the proposed Sinatra-Riddle album. With an irony that would have amused the arranger himself, Riddle—unlike Billy May (*Trilogy: The Past*), Gordon Jenkins (*She Shot Me Down*), and his "favorite," Axel Stordahl (*Point of No Return*)—would never have his "last hurrah."

"Nelson, from what I understood from him, was not crazy about the Linda Rondstadt project," said one associate who wishes to remain unidentified. "He did it, but from my standpoint it wasn't his greatest writing. . . . There was a generation gap. But were he to have done one more album for Frank, I'm sure it would have been the absolute pinnacle of his career. And I think the world has lost something because of that."

Not long before his death, Riddle told National Public Radio inter-

---

20. Chris Riddle believes there's a strong possibility that his father died of AIDS, which he could have contracted through a transfusion in 1980 when the disease was already spreading but long before the blood supply was being adequately screened.

viewer Robert Windeler, "There is no particular story, and if there is one, I don't know it. [Sinatra] is not inhibited by any particular loyalty. He did not feel that that was an application of loyalty, and perhaps he was right. He had to think of Frank. I was hurt by it, I felt bad, but I think I was dimly aware that nothing is forever. A different wave of music had come in, and I was closely associated with him in a certain [other] type of music. He would have been putting added weights around his neck to try to pry me loose from that identity which we shared. So he moved into other areas. It's almost like one changes one's clothes. I saw him do it with Axel Stordahl, my favorite; I should have realized that it would be my turn. He just moved on."

"All the good things that happened just didn't matter as much as they should have," Bernhart observed. Reiterating that Sinatra's desire to add the colors of other writers to his tonal palette was never intended as an affront to Riddle, Bernhart concluded, "Mr. Sinatra needs new worlds to conquer. That's a true artist."

In his lifetime, Riddle so completely represented the definitive sound of great American pop that he was taken for granted. All of his classic albums with Sinatra and Nat King Cole were routinely ignored by the Grammy people, for instance, who preferred to wait until the dread Ronstadt projects before honoring our greatest vocal arranger. Critic Gary Giddins reported that he failed to take Riddle seriously until jazz-tenor champ and arranger Al Cohn pointed out to him how highly musicians and other writers thought of Riddle. In the mid-1990s, not only are all the albums he arranged for Sinatra, Ella Fitzgerald, and Cole seeing the light of day in the digital disc format, but companies are reissuing albums by far more obscure vocalists simply because they feature arrangements by Nelson Riddle.

"He was a good musician all the way around," said Billy May. "Since he's gone, I've heard a lot more stuff that I had no idea he did. Things are coming out now of his that I was completely unaware of. And every once in a while I'll hear something that just knocks me right off my feet. It makes me think about what a good musician he was."

"Summer Wind," from Sinatra and Riddle's final album, *Strangers in the Night,* is the greatest triumph of the collaboration in its '60s phase. The song reached only number 25 on the pop singles chart, but it undoubtedly rates as the most keenly appreciated "inside" favorite of many regular Sinatra customers. The grass roots popularity of "Summer Wind" is confirmed by its being constantly in demand on jukeboxes and being requested at Sinatra concerts, a position consolidated by its placement in the film *The Pope of Greenwich Village.*

Although lyricist Johnny Mercer generally receives all credit for "Summer Wind," the melody was written by Henry Mayer (with an original German text), otherwise known in this country only for "My Melody of Love" (earlier recorded by Sinatra), a hit for the more ethnically compatible Bobby Vinton. Published in West Gemany in 1965, "Summer Wind" was recorded that year by Perry Como in a deadly dull, teutonic hillbilly treatment whose only plus is that the touching second chorus (unsung by Sinatra) is included. Despite the origins of "Summer Wind," the phenomenon described is more Italian than German in nature. In southern Italy, the *sirocco* breeze from northern Africa arrives every year, signifying the end of summer. Its coming and going, like that of the "Ebb Tide" on *Only the Lonely,* can be used as a dipstick to compare romantic and personal happiness with the passing of seasons.

As usual, Sinatra plays the unrequited lover, while the *Strangers* album's two orchestras—the organ and the big band—share the role of the wind itself. Riddle has constructed a remarkably catchy *leitmotif* to represent the breeze, which makes one question his oft-confessed inability to compose melodies. This figure is first stated on the organ and then repeated by various voices in the band—the high reeds, the low reeds, the baritone sax in solo—and then becomes a countermelody and background riff to Sinatra's exposition of the central melody. The summer wind, as depicted by this figure, is a symbol of loss. At first the breeze blows in gently, illustrating to the protagonist the difference between what has been and what is. As Sinatra's emotions mount, the wind and the music waft upward into a crescendo of hurricanelike intensity with the help of two modulations. Like a tornado, it reduces the hero's happiness to rubble and then softly drifts away, as tenderly and as cruelly as it entered.

Even if the Sinatra-Riddle relationship was about to blow away in the same fashion, they had already completed an uncountable number of classic singles tracks, television shows, motion pictures, and miraculous albums. Together, they transmuted a technological breakthrough into an artistic triumph, creating a new art form and producing its greatest works. When Théophile Gautier uttered his theory that "the work comes out more beautiful from a material that resists the process—verse, marble, onyx, or enamel," he could have added twelve-inch vinyl pancakes to the list.

Woody Allen once said that he wanted to achieve immortality through "not dying." Sinatra and Riddle achieved it by creating, in fourteen albums, one of the greatest bodies of music in all of American popular culture.

CHAPTER SEVEN

WITH BILLY MAY, 1953–1979

> *Spare me from drunkards and soldiers in love.*
> —RUMER GODDEN,
> *Enchantment*

"Billy May is always driving," Frank Sinatra once said, and then he elaborated: "Recording with Billy is like having a bucket of cold water thrown in your face." Billy May's life and music are nothing short of Rabelaisian in their tendency toward outrageous extremes. The mottos of Gargantua, "I drink for the thirst to come" and "Appetite comes with eating," could be lyrics to a Billy May instrumental. May, who spent several years as arranger-composer for Daffy Duck and Tweety and Sylvester, could be portrayed far more accurately in a Tex Avery cartoon than in a print profile.

Rosemary Clooney tells one of the great May stories:[1] "Billy didn't like [one Hollywood arranger] and said that this guy copied everything. He would even go to the point that he'd hire the same musicians that Nelson Riddle had worked with and say, 'How would Nelson phrase this?'" The last straw broke May's back when he learned that this arranger, then an executive at Verve Records, had the ego to order a conductor's chair with his name on the back on a brass plaque; the chair was stored in the Capitol Tower, whose recording facilities Verve often rented.

"Billy got drunk and started yelling, 'I built this building,' and then went roaring into Capitol," Clooney continued. "He was looking for that chair. And he was going from floor to floor. . . . The security guards were after him. They said, 'Please, Billy, you can't . . .' He said, 'I want the chair.' He was like a bull, you know. When he finally found the chair, he

1. Billy objects to this story and insists that it never happened this way, and that it was just a minor incident which got blown out of proportion. It is, however, typical of the Paul Bunyanesque tall tales that musicians tell each other about May.

just threw it right out a window!" May eventually learned to restrict his awesome intake with the assistance of Alcoholics Anonymous; fortunately, he never attempted to curtail the brilliant audacity of his music.

May's primary weapon is contrast: each sound that comes must be radically different from the sound that preceded it; a high string passage that's already a stalactite more chilling than you'd expect must be followed by a reed ensemble that oozes enough slurping vibrato to out-reverberate an entire section of Ben Websters.

Like Sinatra himself, May became a hero to the members of the musicians' union local 47, not only for his supreme musicality but for his warmth and clown prince personality. "I always felt that most people who wanted to be musicians probably got stuck working in a garage or something," May explained, "so those of us who were lucky enough to do what we loved should at least have some fun with it."

"Billy was about my favorite guy to work with," said saxist Ted Nash, "because everything was so loose, and his stuff was so playable. Everything was right, and he appreciated the guys so much. It was a very exciting kick to do all that stuff with him, like the *Sorta May* album and the Sinatra sessions. We really looked forward to going to work on those nights when we knew what we were going to be in for."

May was no more skilled a conductor than Nelson Riddle; in fact, Bill Miller identified May as the worst stick-wielder he and Sinatra worked with, "with all due respect to his musicianship." As Dick Nash described it, "Billy's beat was a big sweep. He would start up by his ear and come down by his hip with his right arm, and then he'd go back up to his ear again, down to his hip, one-two-*three*-four, and the four was at the ear again. But then, Stravinsky wasn't a great conductor, either."

"He would give a cutoff, and it would look like he was chopping down a tree," said Harry Klee, "but everybody knew that they had to cut off with that." As Eleanor Slatkin put it, "Billy was certainly not what one would call a conductor. But somehow he inspired you in a way that Nelson couldn't."

Skeets Herfurt offered a somewhat more basic depiction of May's conduct as a conductor: "Billy used to stick his finger up his nose and then point it at somebody, and then flip it—and that would be our downbeat! That's pretty raw, but he always did it that way." Another typical May stunt that Herfurt remembered was to announce sternly at the beginning of a date, "There'll be no drinking *off* the job!"

Percussionist Emil Richards recalled still another novel method that May employed to count off a tempo. "In his drinking days he would [be holding] a fifth of 100-proof vodka, and he'd go, 'One, two,' and then on three and four he'd chugalug maybe the whole fifth! Meanwhile, he was beating out three and four with his hand, the red lights were on, and the band was to come in after four—and we were all trying not to laugh. All the while Frank was going, 'I don't believe this guy. I just don't believe this guy!'"

May was also universally regarded as the fastest orchestrator to work in Hollywood. When doing an album with George Shearing, the pianist, who is blind and doesn't use written music, once dictated a tune to the arranger. Richards remembered, "George told Billy, 'I want to play you this tune that I'd like to do, and then I'll go back and tell you where I want the strings and everything else.' Shearing played the melody once through and then announced, 'Okay, now we'll go back to the beginning, and I'll show where the brass should be.' And Billy said, 'Well, take it from after the bridge because I've got that much orchestrated already.'"

While continuing to utilize Nelson Riddle as the main dish on his musical menu, Sinatra turned to Gordon Jenkins and then Billy May— with whom he already shared quite a history—when he was hungry for other flavors. Sinatra also conceived of his "concept" albums with May along different lines. The Sinatra-May partnership began in earnest with *Come Fly with Me* (1957), which also marked Sinatra's first "topic" album which linked songs together through similarities in their titles and texts rather than their music. On *Come Dance with Me* (1959), Sinatra sustained the highest energy and the most uniform set of tempos he would ever attempt. *Come Swing with Me* (1961) serves as Sinatra's unsentimental paean to the swing era by reprising familiar favorites of the '40s in a spectacularly unconventional orchestral setting. The three major Sinatra-May albums of the Reprise period, *Swing Along with Me* (1961), *Francis A. & Edward K.* (1967), and *Trilogy: The Past* (1979) also have singularly individual approaches.

Sinatra and May met in 1939 when the singer was with Tommy Dorsey and the budding arranger was playing trumpet and writing for Charlie Barnet (whose band also included Sinatra's future pianist, Bill Miller). Barnet was not exactly famous for keeping his sidemen well disciplined; in fact, his own high-living, hard-drinking, skirt-chasing life-style set an example for the rest of the band.

May had been arranging and playing trumpet and other horns with Pittsburgh's leading dance orchestra and was already somewhat more sophisticated than the legends portray him. Born on November 10, 1916, May took up the tuba in high school and learned how to write a band arrangement because, he said, of his ego: "I got to be such a good tuba player that the tuba parts were pretty dull. I sat in the rear of the stand

and thought, 'The world's never gonna hear me sitting in the back of this band playing woomph, woomph.' So I started looking at the other instruments and tried to figure out how they worked. I didn't realize it at the time, but I was intrigued with becoming an arranger and an orchestrator." He had switched to trombone by age seventeen, the year he began working professionally with Gene Olsen's Polish-American Orchestra.

By 1938, May had worked his way up from Olsen through the bands of Al Howard and Lee River, and finally landed a spot with Baron Elliott, who led what was essentially a local-level clone of Guy Lombardo's orchestra. Although it was considered, in May's recollection, "the most successful band in Pittsburgh," the group's innate lack of musicality threatened to drive May nuts, and he taught himself to play trumpet essentially to relieve his boredom. He gradually worked himself up to becoming the band's first trumpeter; the section's original leader had more technique and more of a traditional sweet-band trumpet tone, but May had more "balls" in his playing—which suited the vaudeville shows that the Elliott band frequently accompanied.

One night in June or July of that year, "Barnet came into town and I heard his band on the radio. Boy! I went out and asked him if I could make an arrangement for him. And he said, 'Yeah, we're gonna rehearse tomorrow.' So I stayed up all night and wrote a chart, and I went into the business with Barnet." Remaining in Pittsburgh, May wrote half a dozen or so charts for Barnet, but their relationship was interrupted by the leader's sudden decision to spend a few months in Bermuda with the latest in a long succession of Mrs. Barnets.

When Barnet re-formed around the end of 1938 or the beginning of 1939, he invited May to join him in New York, initially as a writer. When one of the band's trumpeters fell ill, "we pressed Billy into service at the last minute," Barnet recollected. "He did such a tremendous job that from then on he became part of our trumpet section as well as our writer."

Barnet and May were off to a flaming start with "Cherokee," a classic of the big-band era which May had consolidated from ideas that originated when playing the Indian-inspired tune impromptu on the stand. "Cherokee" had previously been recorded by composer Ray Noble as part of a suite of Native American–inspired melodies (most eventually recorded by Barnet) and by Count Basie as a jam session vehicle. Nonetheless, the hit went to May and Barnet's brilliantly swinging arrangement, the leader citing "Cherokee" as "the biggest hit of my career." The team followed it with a number of harmonically daring sequels, including Noble's "Commanche War Dance," the themeless "Redskin Rhumba," and "Pow Wow." May and Barnet, who would remain close friends for the next fifty years, reunited in 1954 for a 12-inch LP of Indian love calls.

In the summer of 1939, Barnet took a cue from Basie and decided to add a fourth trumpeter; he demanded that May rewrite the entire book to accommodate the extra brassman. Barnet also encouraged May to write as many jazz instrumentals as he liked, including "Lumby" (named after the barrel-chested, lumberjack-like individuals who comprised the band's trumpet section), among them "In a Jam" and the masterpiece soprano-trumpet battle "Pompton Turnpike," as well as pop tunes that ran the gamut from Rodgers and Hart to "He's a Latin from Staten Island." Like Jimmie Lunceford's band, the Barnet crew combined rock-hard swing with a sense of humor. They paid homages to the bands they liked—with titles such as "The Duke's Idea" and "The Count's Idea"—while taking potshots at the Mickey Mouse units they abhorred: "The Wrong Idea," May's most notable effort as a vocalist (not to mention trumpeter, arranger, and composer) savaged the hell out of Kay Kyser, Sammy Kaye, and Guy Lombardo in one fell swoop.

On October 4, 1939, while the band played at the Palomar in Los Angeles (a day after they had done a remote broadcast from that venue), the ballroom burned to the ground, along with the band's entire library and instruments. (In October 1979, a pickled Charlie Barnet called up Billy May and asked, "Do you realize it was forty years ago tonight that we burned the Palomar down?") Although May and Barnet humorously commemorated the disaster with an original novelty called "Oh What You Said (Are We Burnt Up!)," in which the band chants "Oh Palomar!," the fire forced May and the Barnet arranging crew to recreate the book from their collective memory.

"I was with Charlie for two years, and it was quite an experience, quite an education to work in that band," said May. "Glenn Miller was aware that Barnet was getting popular, and he found out that I was doing most of the charts. Miller was kind of power-hungry, so he offered me a job." May joined the Miller band at the Café Rouge at the Hotel Pennsylvania (as in Pennsylvania 6-5000), New York, on the night that Roosevelt won his third presidential term in 1940. His main incentive at the time was financial: the base pay was $150 a week, nearly twice what Barnet was paying. With additional checks for playing broadcasts, recordings, and films, as well as his arrangements, May was bringing home $300 a week, a stupendous sum in the early post-Depression era and one that eventually subsidized his first home in California. Although May initially compared the switch from Barnet to Miller as "like moving from going to work in an amusement park to working in a factory," he eventually conceded that his Glenn Miller experience "helped me immensely. I learned a lot from Glenn. He was a good musician and an excellent arranger."

Miller and May were hardly fast friends or drinking buddies. May disliked Miller's military-style taskmastering as well as the one-style nature of the band and characterized the leader as "a mountain of resentments." For his part, Miller didn't appreciate May's refusal to place his tunes with Miller's publishing company or his reluctance to use the patented Miller clarinet-led-reeds sound in his charts. Miller also had two full-time arrangers in Bill Finegan and Jerry Gray, so although May served with Miller for two years, he arranged only about twenty charts for that band in that time—a fraction of what he had done for Barnet. Today, May points out that he was not responsible for any of the band's signature hits, but he did write the beautiful left-field introduction to Finegan's "Serenade in Blue." Further, Miller didn't bother to record nearly half of May's numbers.[2]

Their differences were such that by the spring of 1942 Miller and May wanted to call it quits. May had run into pianist Buddy Cole, who was then playing for his brother-in-law, steel guitarist and bandleader Alvino Rey (both men were married to members of Rey's main attraction, the King Sisters), and Cole extended an invitation to May to arrange whatever he wanted for Rey. When Miller found out, he at first threatened to fire May but instead asked him to stay a few months longer because Miller was planning to fold his civilian band as soon as he landed a commission to form a Glenn Miller Army Orchestra. But Rey couldn't offer May a permanent spot, because the war situation was gradually forcing him to disband. While working for Rey, May decided to move to Los Angeles, the band's home base and also the home of his first wife, Arletta; he knew she could move in with her parents in the event that his number came up in the draft (which, fortunately, didn't happen).

In later years, it became commonplace to deprecate May's prowess as a brassman. Frank Sinatra once (at a 1979 concert) described him as being "of the days of the dance bands, when he was a third trumpet

2. May and all the other Miller men were surprised to learn later that with the continuing interest in the band, even their "minor" numbers were restored to print by RCA, along with many charts that Miller had performed only on airchecks. As part of a divorce suit in 1954, May let his ex-wife keep the royalties for his tunes and then found out that Universal Pictures was about to make The Glenn Miller Story with Jimmy Stewart. As a result, his ex's first royalty check amounted to about $12,000.

player, a very bad third trumpet player. He had an embouchure like a guy sucking a Popsicle! But he became a brilliant arranger, and he still is, and always will be." Yet Glenn Miller thought enough of May's playing to feature him on at least as many records as Bobby Hackett—and that's really saying something.

Even so, by the end of his Miller tenure May realized that his future lay more in writing. "He was never that great [as a player,]" says Dick Nash. "He would admit to you himself that he was never a real soloist. And that's why he got into writing." Shortly after going out on his own, May participated in his one major session as a jazz trumpeter with a small group. This was with Jack Teagarden and the Capitol Jazzmen, and May later claimed he was only called because their first-choice trumpeter, Charlie Teagarden, never showed up.

More important for his career, May gained a toehold as a trumpeter-arranger-composer in the still-burgeoning radio industry. A brief gig with Bob Crosby led to steady work for five years with the bandleader's brother, Bing, and his musical director, John Scott Trotter (arranging "Atchison, Topeka and the Sante Fe" among other numbers for the older Crosby). Similarly, a stint with the Ozzie Nelson band developed into his first position as a leader when he replaced Nelson as the in-house bandleader on the Red Skelton show.

While continuing to work for Skelton and Crosby, May also played and occasionally wrote for the Hollywood *Your Hit Parade* orchestra, conducted by Axel Stordahl to back Frank Sinatra. "When Axel got stuck and needed some help, I did a couple of things for Sinatra," said May; however, he is unable to recall any of the tunes he arranged for Sinatra at this time, except for Cole Porter's "Don't Fence Me In." (They probably all were uptempos, a chore he shared with George Siravo and Heinie Beau, and none were recorded commercially.)

Around 1945 or 1946, May began to ghost-write occasionally for Paul Weston, then musical director for Capitol Records. He gained another ally at the fledgling label when he encouraged an old friend, Jim Conkling (who was married to still another King sister), to take a staff position there. Conkling went on to become president of Capitol and, later, two other major labels as well, Columbia and Warner Bros. Capitol eventually began using May as a second-string house director for the assignments Weston didn't have time to take, including such B-level singers as Clark Dennis and Ella Mae Morse.

His star rose again when a newcomer to the A&R department, Alan Livingston, began to develop a line of children's records. May, who by then had considerable experience underscoring the cartoonish capers of

Red Skelton's "mean wittle kid" on the radio, was a natural to do the music. Beginning with "Sparky's Magic Piano" and "Bozo the Clown" and moving on to the familiar Warner Bros., Walt Disney, and Walter Lantz characters, May and Livingston soon dominated the newborn market. "Jesus, every grandparent in the world bought those things!" remembered May, who recorded approximately sixty children's albums for the label and landed his biggest hit as a composer with "I Tawt I Taw a Puddy Tat." With their storybook packages, the Capitol kiddie records cornered the market on children's audio-visual entertainment until, as May has recollected, "TV came in and knocked the bottom right out." Fortunately, by that time both Livingston and May had used their success in the kiddie-music field as a springboard out of it, Livingston becoming president of Capitol when Conkling and Weston moved to Columbia.

Until the early '50s, May was still working at hand-me-down projects for Capitol, such as the music-minus-one style *Join the Band* ("sit in with these big band backgrounds") and a brilliant series of Latin American dance records released under the pseudonym "The Rico Mambo Orchestra." May graduated from the B list to the A list completely by accident in 1952: he had made an album of dance music, and although it was done in his own style, May's name was overshadowed by that baron of ballrooms and bouncing businessmen, Arthur Murray. However, said May, the label "liked those sides so well, they put them out as singles," including "All of Me" and "Charmaine," and were astonished to find they had a series of hits on their hands. As May put it, "That's what put me in the band business." Around the same time, May started backing the label's more prestigious artists in a "guest star" capacity, most notably its number one singer, Nat King Cole.

May, who had criticized Glenn Miller for sticking to an immediately identifiable formula ten years earlier, at once became Hollywood's most-talked-about arranger-bandleader because he had created a reed-and-brass sound that no one could forget. "That's when I started writing the slurping saxophones," he said. "It was a sound that had been around a long time, a lot of guys had done it. A lot of saxophone players were doing it individually, and I thought it would be interesting to have the whole section do it." "One time Billy asked me," recalled Skeets Herfurt, 'Skeets, can we do that just like Willie Smith does in the Lunceford band? Can we do that with a sax section, with all those smears and those big glissandos?' I said, 'Sure, why not?'"

Herfurt elaborated: "He always voiced the reed section in thirds, and then he would double the two: he would have an alto and a tenor and an alto and a tenor. They would be playing in thirds, and we had lots of slurs and things, and that's the way he got that sound." Eventually, Willie Smith, who with Duke Ellington's Johnny Hodges and Ben Webster had inspired the "slurping" sound to begin with, joined the ranks of Hollywood studio musicians and was May's first choice. When Smith was on the road with Ellington (as Hodges' replacement) or Harry James, May employed the more-than-capable Herfurt as lead slurper. "It was an easy enough sound. Pretty soon everybody started doing it, and it lost its distinctiveness," May said. "But I had it first. I made some money on it." If May had originally conjured up the slurping sound as a gimmick to attract attention, it nevertheless became a very musical device in his capable hands.

As Larry Clinton had done fifteen years earlier, after the success of a series of recordings with an all-star studio orchestra, May decided, with Capitol's encouragement, to launch an actual working and touring dance band. "Billy had a rush of blood to the head that he wanted to have a band, and he certainly had the talent," Nelson Riddle recalled. "And he had what at least passed for a new sound, which was the hardest thing of all, those slurping saxophones." It was every musician's dream to be presented as a star leading his own orchestra, and even though May couldn't get the top-echelon players he used in the studios to leave their families for the road life, he was especially proud of the mainly younger men he did use, including future studio star Dick Nash and ex-Miller trumpeter Johnny Best.

"Billy would just come out and beat the band off and do his thing," Nash has said. "He'd talk, maybe introduce somebody, the singer or whatever, but he wasn't a big, flamboyant kind of flagwaver as a bandleader. He just wasn't the Sammy Kaye type. And though he played trumpet well, he wasn't a Doc Severinson, who would get out there and flash it up." May added, "I never have enjoyed being a bandleader in the sense of a Ray Anthony–type person. When someone would come up to me and say, 'Would you please play happy birthday to Myrtle?' I was just as apt to tell him what Myrtle could do with her birthday. If you're gonna be in that position, you gotta be like Lawrence Welk."

In addition, May insisted on playing his trumpet solos on standard tunes in weird keys, such as "Embraceble You" in B-natural (commonly regarded as a hillbilly key). Nash continued, "So I asked him one time, 'Why do you do that?' He said, 'Oh, just to keep my mind from going stale.' He'd have to think about what note came"—to keep from going nuts at having to play the same tunes the same way night after night.

"So," May concluded, "I sold the Billy May band's personal appearance rights to Ray Anthony," who appointed once and future leader Sam Donohue its conductor. "I preferred to be an arranger and to live in California, doing the work that I had been doing prior to that. So after a year and a half on the road, I came back."

During that year and a half, Frank Sinatra came to Capitol Records. In his first sessions for the label, Sinatra tackled a "cover" of Billy May's bluesy original "Lean Baby," and a deliberately May-styled hit single of "South of the Border" and "I Love You," arranged à la May by Nelson Riddle. May at that time was shouting "ah-one and ah-two" for dancers somewhere south of Savannah.

Milt Bernhart, who played on the date, has speculated that "Billy was on the road with a band that was breaking his bank account—which is very funny, sadly funny. But if he had been in town instead of on the road, who knows what history would have produced? If Billy had been here, then Nelson would not have had the opportunity, not a chance."

May and Sinatra next crossed paths when the singer commissioned the arranger to compose and orchestrate an original concert work for *Tone Poems of Color*, a semisymphonic instrumental album Sinatra conducted in 1956. Billy May's "Purple" comes right after Gordon Jenkins' string-heavy "Green" and starts out somberly, although not as overtly sentimentally as its predecessor. As befitting one of the gayer colors, "Purple" also has lighter episodes in which the tempo changes drastically with the aid of a Latin percussion section—hardly standard equipment for a symphony. "Some of the pieces got more complicated than others," May has recalled. "Some changed tempos and things like that—and some of them got a little over Sinatra's head as a conductor. So Felix Slatkin, who was playing first violin, stepped in and helped him."

In the fall of 1957, a few months after completing his first two albums with Jenkins, Sinatra at last decided on the perfect project for May's capabilities, *Come Fly with Me.* Up until 1957, Sinatra had always shown considerable humor in his music, particularly when he sang Sammy Cahn's bon mots or Nelson Riddle's generally witty orchestrations. But only with Billy May does Sinatra feel comfortable injecting a distinctly comedic note into the proceedings. With Stordahl and Riddle, Sinatra has no reason to sing a song other than that he thinks it's good or, in a few cases, when one of the coproducers thought it was good. With Billy May, however, Sinatra began recording numbers that hadn't much value in and of themselves ("Isle of Capri," for instance) but that the team could just plain have fun with.

With May, Sinatra explores his latent fascination for songs that represent the antithesis of the top-drawer Broadway songs he typically favored. For every "Embraceable You" written in the 1920s there were ten songs like "Give Me My Mammy" or "I Got a Bimbo Down on the Bamboo Isle." May and Sinatra developed a knack for parodying these songs at the same time they were performing them. Only with May, for instance, does Sinatra really delve into the realm of exotica. These cheap and potent songs of the 1920s and '30s invariably depict affairs between American (read: Caucasian) men and the variously colored women of faraway places with strange-sounding names, romances that invariably end not with benefit of clergy but with tomorrows that never come. In other words, "Let's go 'South of the Border' and get laid."

Sinatra hadn't recorded a genuine piece of exotica since "On a Little Street in Singapore" with Harry James and "Pale Moon" and "Neani" with Dorsey. When he finally decided he wanted to record "South of the Border," which he had been singing since it was new in 1939, he wanted Billy May. Sinatra realized that with May he could make great expressive music without necessarily taking the song he was singing seriously— sort of a hard-swinging, heterosexual approach to what might be called "camp" in other circles.

May had first alluded to non-Western life-styles in the "Cherokee" Indian cycle with Barnet back in 1938. He claims he was reattracted to exotic effects by his favorite postwar big band, the Eddie Sauter–Bill Finegan Orchestra. "They had outstanding musicianship and a wild combination, and they carried the dance band business to a wonderful extreme, the way I would have liked to have seen it go. In the '50s, when hi-fi and stereo first started coming around, Eddie and Bill started mon- keying around with all those exotic percussion sounds. Before that, you really couldn't get a decent sound on the orchestra bells or the glocken- spiel, the big tam-tam, the big gong, and things like that. They were pio- neers in that, and I just followed up on it."

As fascinating as their music was, Sauter and Finegan lacked the knee-slapping humor and driving danceability of Billy May. In his whimsical voyages south, east and west of the border, May kept finding himself "In a Persian Market," playing either "The Desert Song" or a "Song of India." By 1956, May was already, in pianist Paul Smith's words, "the guru of arrangers—the daddy of 'em all!" That Sinatra should appoint May as his fellow traveler on an album revolving around the theme of international shlepping, the first side climaxing in "Mandalay," was a foregone conclusion. After *Come Fly with Me* flew to number one on the *Billboard* pop album charts, the master learned a thing or two from the pupil when Bing Crosby put May at the helm of not one but two "so nice to go traveling" world trip packages of duets with Rosemary Clooney (*Fancy Meeting You Here* for RCA and *That Travellin' Two Beat* for Capitol).

In programming this latest "concept album," Sinatra went even further than he had gone in his thematic sets with Riddle. For four concept albums in a row from 1957 to 1959, Sinatra started by commissioning (and then publishing) original title songs by Sammy Cahn and Jimmy Van Heusen. In the case of the first two Sinatra-May albums, the team wrote closing as well as opening songs. When Cahn submitted the original lyric to Sinatra on the title track, "Come Fly with Me," one line originally went, "If you could use / some exotic views / there's a bar in far Bombay." According to Cahn, Sinatra originally recorded it as such. Then, at the end of the date, Cahn informed Sinatra that he had additionally written a slightly racier alternative lyric. Cahn considered that text—which substituted "booze" for "views"—suitable for Vegas but not for a family-oriented Capitol Records release. Upon learning this, Sinatra immediately recoralled the musicians, who were then heading for some exotic booze of their own, and rerecorded the song with this somewhat more colorful line.

The Sinatra concept album with the widest emotional palette, *Come Fly* alternates between stone-hard swingers and lovely and lush romantic pieces, all tied together by the idea of sighing for exotic lands. Sinatra may not be quite so schizophrenic as he claims, however; the four loveliest love songs (with the most similar titles)—"Autumn in New York," "April in Paris," "Moonlight in Vermont," and "London by Night"— were all done at the same session. The three wackiest rhythm numbers—"Isle of Capri," "Let's Get Away from It All" (not an expansion of a Sinatra-Dorsey classic, like Riddle's "How About You?", but an effectively concise cutdown) and "Mandalay"—none of which required strings, also rated a date all to themselves. ("Blue Hawaii," the only indistinct chart on the set, would have been better served if May had indulged in some raucous, mock-island effects.)

For one who got "in the band business" with brash uptempos, May turned out to be an amazingly sensitive writer of romance. He led Sinatra through the singer's most effective straight-ahead waltz ever, "Around the World." May later described this as "the best ballad in the album. Victor Young won an Academy Award for that [film's score]. That's a beautiful tune, and Frank sang the shit out of it, too. Boy! He's really a good singer." No one but Sinatra and May could so seamlessly juxtapose "Isle of Capri," which they treat as a send-up of Tin Pan Alley conventions, with such a wistfully nostalgic treatment of the rhyme- and cliché-free "Moonlight in Vermont." In "Autumn in New York," May finds nuances of almost dire melancholia undreamed of even by the great Axel Stordahl.

"Billy is so diversified," is how pianist Lou Levy put it. "He's probably the greatest all around in terms of humor as well as seriousness, and different modes like the Mexican Mel Tormé album (*Olé Tormé*), which is another great album." As Peggy Lee said, "If I had to pick someone for a desert island arranger, it would be Billy because he can write every style for brass or strings or for large or for small, and he writes with such humor as well as beauty." May is most frequently applauded for his explosive sense of dynamics, color, and humor. "Brazil" uses a marimba (although otherwise the chart explores the song's longtime big-band association rather than its South American roots), while "Isle of Capri," which double-times into a pasodoble, brings a mandolin into the picture in its instrumental break. The latter tune, sung by wags as "'Twas on a pile of debris that I found her . . . ," also marks the return of May's trademark slurping saxes. The arranger had largely abandoned these grandiose glissandi by 1957, omitting the reeds altogether for his Grammy-winning *Big Fat Brass* album of 1958. In fact, Nelson Riddle usurped the slurps on "South of the Border" (included on the CD issue of *Come Fly with Me*). One suspects May revived the sound partly in response to its effectiveness on "Border," because "Isle of Capri" is in every way a follow-up to that 1953 single.

Come Fly with Me's masterpiece, an adaptation of Rudyard Kipling's "Mandalay," resounds as Sinatra's and May's most outrageous piece of persuasive percussion. English Sinatraphiles consider the track a rarity because it was dropped from U.K. pressings due to Rudyard Kipling's un-Kipling-ly stodgy estate (this being only twenty years after the poet's passing). "Kipling's daughter had the nerve to ban that in England! How *dare* she?" Sinatra sarcastically complained at a June 1958 concert in Monte Carlo. "Of course, she drinks a little bit, so we'll forgive her."[3]

After the success of the film *From Here to Eternity*, with its Kipling-inspired title, Sinatra seems to have nurtured a spiritual kinship with Kipling's recurring hero, the warrior with a conscience. In 1962, he

---

3. Sinatra took special delight performing "Mandalay" before an audience of mostly British descent in Melbourne, Australia, in 1959: "This particular song was written from the poem by Rudyard Kipling. Now it seems that we have done a rather different version of 'Road to Mandalay,' so that his family has objected, and anywhere in the British Empire it's not to be played on the record. So they took it off the long-playing record of *Come Fly with Me* and replaced it with 'Chicago.' But this is an unusual version of 'Road to Mandalay,' it's comedic, but it swings, it jumps. I think that Rudyard Kipling's sister [*sic*] was chicken not to let us put it on the record."

made a film called *Sergeants 3*, which borrowed the title of "Soldiers Three" and the plot, in a bizarre cowboy transmutation, of "Gunga Din"—they're still fightin' Indians! Accordingly, *Sergeants* marked the first of several Sinatra films to be scored by Billy May. In what amounts to Sinatra's only "spoken word" recording, in 1966 he attempted a bizarre, disappointing radio-style adaptation of "Din," which remains released only privately. Sinatra also skirted the edges of "If," the most popular Kipling work of the poet's lifetime; "Pick Yourself Up," which Sinatra recorded in 1962, alludes to "If" at the end of its bridge ("you'll be a man, my son"), and, on Sinatra's 1951 TV series he sang a 1934 British pop offering called "If" (then a hit for Perry Como) that amounted to a somewhat less witty swipe from the composer's country-man. In 1974, he recorded yet another "If"—and if only he hadn't, as this was a dreary rock and roll ballad by David Gates.

Kipling published "Mandalay" (along with "Gunga Din") as part of his 1892 collection, *Barrack-Room Ballads*. The poem was set to music in 1907 by Oley Speakes, and it became a staple of the standard British baritone's art-song repertoire; in the '20s, several dance bands began playing the tune instrumentally and in fox-trot tempo.[4] The May arrangement begins by trimming the libretto into song form, omitting entire sections (including one that includes the line "I've a neater, sweeter maiden in a cleaner, greener land"). The singer swings the famous opening lines on top of an undulating bass vamp in order to thor-oughly Sinatrafy Kipling's old "Burma Broad." While Sinatra sasses her with his ring-a-ding-ding attitude (throwing in "come you back, you mother soldier!" at Monte Carlo), May does the same with percussive bumps and beeps aplenty. When the piece threatens to go into a march in the instrumental, like a British (not French) foreign legion of Bengal lancers, May quickly dragoons it back into swing time.

But the pièce de résistance is the delightfully baffling ending—or lack of same—which never ceases to surprise listeners no matter how many times they've heard it. "Billy had the arrangement written," recalled percussionist Frank Flynn, so that "Frank sings, 'And the dawn comes up like thunder,' and I had this thirty-two-inch gong which really "spoke" when I hit it, and then the arrangement went on for another half chorus."

"We had a very difficult ending on the thing, and finally we made one

---

4. Coincidentally, another song called "Mandalay," unrelated to Kipling, was pub-lished in 1924 and recorded by, among others, Al Jolson and Paul Whiteman's orchestra. The Kipling piece is sometimes referred to as "Road to Mandalay" or "On the Road to Mandalay" to avoid confusion.

take, and there was a pause there after the gong," Skeets Herfurt said. "However, when we got to the gong, Billy just kind of waved his hands to signal 'Don't say anything.' And instead of going on, Frank put on his hat and threw his coat over his shoulder, like he does, and walked out of the studio!" Herfert continued, "We all laughed like mad. We said, 'What's happening? Is Frank going to come back and do it again?' No, that was the way they put it out." May much preferred Sinatra's spontaneous ending, using it as if to acknowledge, "You're a better man than I am, Francis A." Drummer Alvin Stoller offered another explanation as to why "Mandalay" ends so abruptly—not corroborated by others at the session—namely that May might not have actually had time to finish the ending.

"I tended to procrastinate," May said in a characteristic understatement. Paul Weston once joked that May was a very conscientious worker; he would always be sure to *start* working on his arrangements at least three hours before every session. "Then he'd take whatever he had to the session and start recording, start the band, and continue to score from the podium. Meanwhile, these little people would be scrambling up the stairs to the copyist with two score pages at a time. But he always finished, and the arrangements were always great."

"If the session was at eight," Alan Livingston elaborated, "a few minutes after eight, Billy would come in with copyist behind him, still copying, literally, at the session. If we had four sides to do, as usual, the first three would be done, but the copyist was still doing the last one." Sinatra amplified, "With Billy, you don't get the copies of the next number until you've finished the one before." Ted Nash elaborated, "We'd get through one tune and bring out the next one. It wouldn't be finished, but we had to get it down. So he'd have to half-arrange the thing out of his head. He'd start assigning notes. 'All right, third alto take this note and go up half a tone.' And he'd assign notes to all the guys in the band. And sure enough, he'd get the date done somehow, but it got pretty hairy!"

As if recording so much weren't enough, at the time of *Come Fly with Me,* May was also handling the "cues and bridges" every week for the last great original radio comedy series, *The Stan Freberg Show.* "Billy May's the only man I ever knew who could conduct a full orchestra and chorus while he was stone drunk," claimed Freberg collaborator (and cartoon voice) Daws Butler. "He could hardly stand up, but he never missed a beat." Said Frank Flynn, "I remember one afternoon when we were rehearsing with Stan and we were going to work with Frank that night." Recalling the circumstances under which May arranged the title track, "Come Fly with Me," with its remarkable taxiing-down-the-run-way intro, Flynn continued, "I can remember Billy saying, 'Geez, I still have to write two arrangements for the date tonight!' This was at four in the afternoon, and we were going to work at eight that night." But tales of May's antics should not detract from his musicianship; it's to his credit that he could behave so extravagantly and still be regarded as a consumate professional. "Billy May was the most *meticulous* of arrangers," stressed Eleanor Slatkin. "When you looked at his manuscripts, it was as if they were *printed,* they was so gorgeous. He might have acted sort of, well, carefree, but when it came to the music, he was a perfectionist."

Sinatra never called May, as he did Riddle, to handle any of his '50s singles releases, with the exception of a sole 45 that contained his only non-soundtrack duets for Capitol, "Nothing in Common" and "How Are Ya Fixed For Love," done with Keely Smith. May already had a reputation as a witty accompanist for duos and would also orchestrate them for the teams of Nat King Cole and Dean Martin, Bobby Darin and Johnny Mercer, Frank Sinatra and Sammy Davis, Jr. (later on Reprise), Bing Crosby with both Rosemary Clooney and Louis Armstrong, as well as the summit duets of the *Reprise Repertory Theatre* series.

"That first album [*Come Fly with Me*] was so successful, we did a second one," said May. Returning to Sinatra's metaphor of the Billy May style as the equivalent of a faceful of ice water, *Come Dance with Me* resounds as their splashiest effort ever. A far more streamlined set than the comparatively frivolous *Fly, Dance* jettisons the mock-exotica and Cecil B. DeMille percussion (which they would reprise in 1962 with "Moonlight on the Ganges") for Sinatra's most straight-ahead collection of, as the back cover copy promises, "vocals that dance." The first completely stringless Sinatra set since *Swing Easy, Come Dance* is so intense in its devotion to hardcore superswing that it practically becomes ascetic.

Once Sinatra gave Cahn and Van Heusen the titles for the opening tracks, "Come Fly with Me" and "Come Dance with Me," the songs practically wrote themselves. Said Cahn, "'Come Fly with Me,' easy. 'It's Nice to Go Traveling' [the closer on *Come Fly*], easy. 'Come Dance with Me,' easy. We get to the closing song of *Come Dance with Me,* and Van Heusen and I couldn't think of a song about dancing that Irving Berlin hadn't already thought of. He covered all the bases of dancing [in five songs written for Fred Astaire]: 'Cheek to Cheek' [also in *Come Dance with Me*], 'Change Partners (and Dance with Me),' 'Let's Face the Music and Dance' [not to mention "It Only Happens When I Dance with You," recorded by Sinatra in 1948, and "You're Easy to Dance With"]. Sinatra is used to me coming back the next day with whatever song he asks for. When he doesn't hear from us, he's on the phone: 'Hey, where's that last song?'

"I remember, I turned to Van Heusen and said, 'Hey, let me ask you a question. Has there ever been a "Last Dance?"'" Van Heusen says, 'Gee, I don't know.' We call ASCAP. There's a 'Save the Last Dance for Me' [a 1931 waltz] but no 'Last Dance.' Well, we wrote that song as fast as you can speak." Cahn also recalled that at the date he suggested a memorable Sinatraism, encouraging the singer to stress "when *will* we leave / but *till* we leave" in the last chorus. It marks one of those occasional cases when Sinatra accentuates a syllable that doesn't necessarily mean anything to the lyric but does wonders for the melody, and thereby further sparks the whole piece.

At once taut with tension and swingingly relaxed, *Come Dance* includes a couple of other dance-directed ditties, such as Arthur Schwartz's masterful "Dancing in the Dark" (Sinatra even swings the verse) and "I Could Have Danced All Night." The nineteen-piece orchestra suggests any one of the powerhouse big bands that roamed and gored in the 1940s, with May's sidemen focusing all their energies on spotlighting the singer. Sinatra strikes a perfect balance between his kinder, gentler approach of the '40s and his more hostile, antisocial sound of the '60s onward. As any credible big-band musician or actor knows, making your entrance properly is half the battle. Sinatra is never more exhilarating than when he returns for his outchoruses, especially on "Too Close for Comfort" and "Baubles, Bangles and [Cool, Cool] Beads" where he reenters during a rest just a microbeat before the orchestra.

As if to prove that there's more to jazz than soloing, the only notable individual excursion is a brief break for Bill Miller in "Day In, Day Out" (Sinatra's third recording of the tune for Capitol). The one musician whose presence can be heard and felt throughout *Come Dance* is Alvin Stoller, who enjoyed the distinction of being not only Sinatra's and May's preferred percussionist but the most in-demand drummer of the great years of the Hollywood pop and jazz recording boom. Born in 1925, Stoller pounded tubs for at least a dozen major bands in the late swing era, earning his early rep with Benny Goodman and Charlie Spivak (where he first worked with Nelson Riddle). One of Buddy Rich's closest friends and disciples, Stoller proved himself a contender in 1945 when he credibly stepped into Rich's unfillable shoes in Tommy Dorsey's orchestra.

Leaving TD in 1947, Stoller freelanced around New York with big bands at the city's movie- and vaudeville theaters and with dozens of variously sized units on Fifty-second Street. He first played for Sinatra (as well as for the supporting act, the Will Mastin Trio with Sammy Davis, Jr.) at the Capitol Theatre, circa 1948, and first recorded with him at the infamous penultimate Columbia date of June 1952. By that time Stoller had moved to Los Angeles, where he found more work than he could handle in the studios. Initially, both Sinatra and jazz producer Norman Granz seem to have cast Stoller in the same role that Dorsey assigned him—as a more available and less pugnacious Buddy Rich. "Alvin even looked like Buddy for a while," affirmed Mel Tormé. In fact, when Rich himself was in need of a drummer to play behind him on *Buddy Rich Sings,* Stoller was the one who got the call.

Within a short time, however, Stoller had amply proved he had a style of his own, a way of propelling a big band with terrific power yet with a beat that was always flexible and loose. Considering himself more of a studio player than a jazz musician, Stoller practically lived in the studios for several decades, playing for everyone from Billie Holiday and Bing Crosby to the soundtrack for *West Side Story.* Stoller was inevitably the first drummer Sinatra, May, and Riddle called when they had a date coming; May in particular all but refused to record if Stoller wasn't available. Early on, May also cast Stoller as an anemic vocalist on "The Dixieland Band" and "Fat Man Boogie" (where he sarcastically squeaks, "Eddie Condon?"). In 1957, May paid tribute to Stoller by writing a "Hawk Talks"–style orchestral showcase for the drummer, entitled "Brushed Off."

Unfortunately for Sinatra, Stroller was making too much money to leave the studios to tour with the singer, who at time needed a drummer for the road. When Stoller was called back East to attend his father's funeral during the *Swingin' Lovers* sessions, he recommended Irv Cottler as his substitute. May and Riddle also used Cottler when they couldn't get Stoller. "Irv was a fine time drummer, but he really had no technique," Bill Miller explained. "He could do a two-bar fill great, maybe four. Beyond that, forget about it. He just didn't have the chops. Not like Alvin. That's why Frank used Al on almost all of the albums."

In *Come Dance with Me,* Stoller decorates Sinatra's and May's work with brilliant splashes of rhythmic color throughout and no end of rimshots on precisely apropros afterbeats (as on the triple repeat of "Something's Gotta Give"). The drummer rated both May and Riddle as masters of writing for percussion. Riddle was smart enough to write "just a very passive type of drum part," Stoller recalled, because Riddle trusted Stoller to come up with something better than anything he could think of. "Billy was just the opposite," fully annotating a percussion part with every last little figure he wanted, all of which were flawless. "Billy has in his head what he wants on paper, and you just play that," Richards elaborated. "In fact, Billy would start yelling, 'That's not in there! What're you doing?' I learned real early not to mess with Billy's music."

Stoller shines particularly brightly on *Come Dance*'s "Saturday Night," a tune that offered Sinatra a chance to improve on his 1944 hit; and in the process he switched arrangers from one Stordahl deputy, George Siravo, to another, Heinie Beau. By 1958, Beau had become May's and Paul Weston's most reliable aide-de-camp, writing three of the charts on *Come Dance*. Unlike Riddle, May (a competent trumpeter), or Jenkins (the world's squarest piano player), Beau was as capable an instrumentalist as he was an arranger, and he typically exploited both skills by including spots for his solo clarinet in many a Sinatra chart of the '40s. Beau is probably the only arranger to work continually with Sinatra from the Dorsey days through the Reprise era. "Whenever Paul or I would get stuck, Heinie would help us out," said May. "Heinie Beau was a very gifted man—and fast," recalled trumpeter Zeke Zarchy. "You needed something done quick, and he'd have it." May added that "Heinie worked for both Paul and myself, so he could imitate either one of us. He wrote like me because that's what I wanted."

Beau was also responsible for much of Sinatra's final two Capitol albums, both from 1961—*Come Swing with Me* (conducted by Billy May), on which he wrote seven of the twelve charts, and *Point of No Return* (conducted by Axel Stordahl), for which he wrote three. May was in particular need of Beau's services in 1961 because, in addition to his usual full schedule of vocal and instrumental albums, he was also serving as musical director (and Doc Severinson- or Phil Harris-like verbal sparring partner) on Milton Berle's weekly variety series.

The last of the three Sinatra-May albums for Capitol, *Come Swing with Me* relaxes from the almost tyranically tight tempi of *Come Dance*, giving May a chance to draw on his roots in the Sy Oliver–Jimmie Lunceford sound. Sinatra and May not only include Oliver's original "Yes, Indeed!" but directly quote from the Oliver treatment of "On the Sunny Side of the Street" for Tommy Dorsey. (Coincidentally, on the very same days that Sinatra was recording *Come Swing* for Capitol, he was also taping *I Remember Tommy* for Reprise with Oliver himself.)

In *Come Swing*, Sinatra and May combine *Dance*'s compressed terpsichoric textures with *Fly*'s warmth and humor. May arranged *Swing* sans strings and also sans saxes, basing the orchestral style on his *Big Fat Brass* album. He recalled that "Frank heard the *Brass* album and mentioned that he'd like to do an album using that sound." *Big Fat Brass* had been particularly effective because, particularly in titles like "Ping Pong," May was the first heavyweight jazz arranger to fully utilize the sonic possibilities of stereo separation. Although both *Fly* and *Dance* had used the new technique effectively, May was instructed to take it to the max for *Swing*. "That's one of the things that Frank and Capitol agreed on," said May.

Sinatra and the label agreed on few other things at the time, because he had initially wanted to make this all-brass album for his own company, Reprise. But he still owed two albums to Capitol, who had made the original *Big Fat* set and insisted they wanted this Sinatra and May brass pairing for themselves. As with the two final Sinatra-Riddle LPs for Capitol, both sides agreed to stack the deck with tunes Sinatra had previously recorded for Columbia, only five of the twelve offerings being virgins at Sinatra sessions.

"We went through [the repertory] together, and Frank said, 'These bastards want me to do these standards.'" May reports, "He said, 'I don't know what to do with "Sunny Side of the Street." I don't know how to make it.' He realized that I had the same problems he did, and he was right. What are you going to do with 'Black Magic'? Frank had been singing that son of a bitch for twenty years. What more could we do with it? That was the attitude he and I both had with that album."

Sinatra was careful not to let his disdain for Capitol bring down either his relationship with May or the quality of the album. "He just wanted to get the sides in," said May. "He didn't spend any extra time on them, but we just ran everything down and got them in as fast as we could. He sang everything at least twice, and there were no deliberate problems one way or the other. I mean, we were aware that he was pissed off at Capitol, and everybody in the studio was trying to be nice to him."

Far from being an angst-ridden product of precarious artist-label relations, *Come Swing with Me* amounts to one of the happiest productions of the entire Sinatra canon. May essentially limits himself to two textures, brass and rhythm, and, naturally, two channels, left and right, but he beefs up both sections, using no less than nine trumpets (including such brass athletes as Mannie Klein, Conrad Gozzo, John Best, and Zeke Zarchy), seven trombones, and a quartet of French horns. This latter foursome is usually in the deep background but is audibly prominent as a section on "American Beauty Rose."

"Those albums became a kind of a tour de force among brass players," French hornist John Cave has recalled, referring to *Big Fat Brass* and *Come Swing with Me*. "Considering the type of music and the way it was aimed for the ceiling, it was amazing that you could get four horn players who could play it! And do it in unison. I don't think the horns missed a thing in the whole album, and that's very unusual, too."

Turning to the rhythm section, May throws in a harp, used strictly as a big guitar for timekeeping purposes, as well as three members of the vibe family and a harpischord for a one-bar break on "American Beauty Rose." In addition to using the reliable Joe Comfort's bull fiddle, May employs a tuba as a brass bass, so even the rhythmic functions of each orchestration seem to brag in brass.

May was not necessarily interested in dividing his sounds by section for the stereo separation, although the trumpets and trombones do battle beautifully in the intro to "Sunny Side of the Street." More often, he breaks the trumpets all by themselves into high and low subsections and has those two teams challenge each other, as in "Paper Doll." Although his distinctive saxes, slurping or otherwise, are gone, his patented device of punctuating brass bleats with xylophone plinks has rarely been more effective. "Having the vibes play the lead with the brass section really put the cutting, percussive edge on the brass," said Emil Richards. In addition to making the brass sound brassier, "it also punctuates the staccatoness of the rhythm and brings out the top line of everything much better. Billy utilized that a lot, and I used to love it because it gave me nice lines to play with the brass." This is heavy metal for real.

One runs out of superlatives for Sinatra's singing as he continues to use his signature vocal devices beautifully, as well as inventing new ones. There's the pause between the dehyphenated "you" and "are the lover" on this definitive four-minute "Old Black Magic," and his unexpected swoop downward on "I would die" in "Lover," as well as that song's amazingly easy sounding final three notes. *Come Swing with Me* is one of the few Sinatra albums on which Cole Porter is not represented, but we might describe it as a breathtaking display of a "glorious technicolor and stereophonic sound," to quote from *Silk Stockings*.

Although Sinatra couldn't land the May brass project for his own label, he decided to split the difference into two subsequent albums for Reprise: an all-new May set, taped only two months later, in May 1961, and *Sinatra and Swingin' Brass* with Neil Hefti in 1962. The Sinatra-May Reprise album—actually only the second Sinatra LP for the new company—bears a photo on its cover of the blue-eyed one popping through a pair of double doors which suggests swinging both as in saloon doors and as in Billy May. Even the album's title is as baffling as the ending of Mandalay." Originally issued as *Swing Along with Me* (FS-1002), that title was first bannered on the front and the back covers (next to a shot of Sinatra making like Arnold Palmer—yet another kind of swinging). Then Capitol complained to a judge that this title came too close for comfort to their own recently released *Come Swing with Me,* and as a result, on later pressings of FS-1002, the title was changed to *Sinatra Swings*. The current CD, which, like the original stereo LP, features a mix of "Granada" with forty seconds edited[5] (the song appeared complete on only original mono pressings), is identified as *Swing Along with Me* on the front and *Sinatra Swings* on the back, both spines, and disc label.

Whatever you want to call it, chronologically and in terms of repertory and orchestral texture, the set belongs with the Capitol threesome of *Come with Me* LPs, especially the original *Come Fly*. Sinatra uses another twelve songs that he must have heard growing up in the '20s and '30s, none from later than the swing era. "The Curse of an Aching Heart," for instance, is the kind of tune Sinatra might have yelped atop his father's bar as a toddler (and which he sang in a 1935 aircheck with The Hoboken Four). The disc consists primarily of medium ("Have You Met Miss Jones") and up (I Never Knew") swingers. However, Sinatra and May lay out "It's a Wonderful World," which May had first arranged for Charlie Barnet in 1939, in the "shuffle rhythm" of Jan Savitt and Bon-Bon Tunnell, who had originally popularized the piece.

Although the saxes return for a full big-band sound, Sinatra uses only strings on the third and last session, a date that included a ballad, "Don't Cry Joe," and two samples of loopy exotica: "Granada," the latest cucaracha conquest, and "Moonlight on the Ganges," which takes him back to the pagoda in "Mandalay." On the same note, "Don't Be That Way" attempts a twist on the un-ending of "Mandalay." Two camp classics, "Aching Heart" and "Please Don't Talk About Me When I'm Gone," which had already been saved, as Bing Crosby would say, from "tired tenors at tea parties" by Fats Waller and Billie Holiday, herewith become veritable declarations of "I Got Rhythm!" Once again swimming against the rhythmic currents, Sinatra jumps on and off the beat with uncommon vigor in the second chorus of "Please Don't Talk . . ."

The two new "travel" pieces, "Ganges" and "Granada," are Sinatra spectaculars. "Moonlight on the Ganges," like "Limehouse Blues," originated as a Limey tune of the '20s that Yank jazz bandleaders adopted and raised as their own, including Glenn Miller in 1935, Benny Goodman and Eddie Sauter in 1940, and Tommy Dorsey and Sy Oliver in 1942, where Sinatra most likely encountered it. Another tale of loving and leaving a non-Western babe, this one a "little Hindu" (a word no one can pronounce quite as effectively as Crosby in his 1939 aircheck),

---

5. Not confused enough yet? The booklet for the current CD of FS-1002 gives a timing of 3:38 for "Granada," which is in fact the length of the complete version; however, the actual track on the disc plays only to 2:49.

"Sahib" Sinatra, lacking only pith helmet and jodhpurs, guides us through an extravaganza of Far Eastern percussion.

As Sinatra observed in 1981, "Billy May almost always uses the extra percussion, like vibraphones, xylophones, bells, and chimes and all that jazz." For "Ganges," contractor Bill Miller must have put the call out to every tub-thumper in the L.A. union to handle an entire Sun Ra–style section of gongs, chimes, vibes, xylophones, kettle drums, woodblocks, and fine Oriental bric-a-brac. May makes the brass and strings dance around these various *tchotchkas* with a seven-veiled sense of mystery and intrigue: Marlene Dietrich in a gorilla suit. Never has Sinatra's technique of soaring over the ground beat of his accompaniment taken him so far aloft, nor has it seemed so necessary for him to stay in the sky above rather than the polyrhythmic Persian market below.

Both pieces are as much showcases for Sinatra's still-evolving vocal techniques as for May's bag of tricks. Sinatra is surrounded with Latin percussion on "Granada," as once again the hard-swinging and frivolously exotic components of the performance alternately complement and compete with one another, even as the soft strings chase around the blaring trumpets and clamoring castenets. Written in 1932, this piece by Augustine Lara (author of the somewhat softer "You Belong to My Heart") served as a vehicle for everyone from Deanna Durbin to Bing Crosby but was mainly identified with quasi-operatic Latin belters like Carlos Ramirez. Even Frankie Laine snarled it out, in a rendition so corny it wasn't even funny, vehemently spitting consonants as if he were whipping a galley slave; later, in the 1960s, "Granada" became a swing exercise for Stan Kenton, courtesy of Bill Holman.

Only Sinatra and May realized that only by treating "Granada" with an arch sense of humor did its dramatic aspects become palatable. Sinatra enters theatrically, but at the end of the bridge, just when the pot of chili threatens to explode, May releases a little steam heat with smooth and swinging string passages: from toreador to cuspidor. Sinatra puts just the right extra emphasis on the "d" sound in "snow-clad" so that it resonates warmly in our ear, and then lightly and musically syncopates the musical term *habanera* with a gentle, Crosbyesque trill. May had cha-cha's on his brain thanks to a recent Capitol album he had done of big-band themes played in mock-mambo style. So, to spin a fresh variation on the climactic choir in "South of the Border," May closes "Granada" with the sidemen trolling "cha cha cha!"

Swing Along with Me reaches a boil with "You're Nobody Till Somebody Loves You." Although from the string session, this number, written and introduced by sweet bandleader Russ Morgan in 1944 and more convincingly put over by the King Cole Trio the following year, strikes the listener—almost literally—as the hardest hitting tune on the set. "You're Nobody" starts excitingly, with a left-field string introduction and Sinatra delivering a straight, swinging chorus, loping almost tenderly behind the beat and backed by a light string shimmer. Bill Miller eases into the turnaround (change of choruses) with gentle, Basie-style tinkling.

The second thirty-two bars get louder, forsaking the fiddles, although where the traditional second chorus of a number like "I Never Knew" is wilder and jazzier, pregnant with unexpected pauses, here the second time around is sharper and more clearly focused. Sinatra concludes this chorus by repeating the penultimate phrase twice, as if he were going to end it here, but surprises us by swinging into what might be the earliest full third chorus of a full thirty-two-bar tune of his career. He reaches for a long note in the last "A" section ("above") and then winds up and throws as if he were Dizzy Dean, the strings adding to the intensity by jumping back in a reaffirming choir in the last few bars. This is what one Sinatra sideman meant when he characterized The Voice's voice as "a big, strong swinging horn."

Swing Along with Me/Sinatra Swings worked out so well that it outfoxed itself. It was so good, there was no topping it, leaving Reprise content with one Sinatra-May album in the catalogue while Sinatra concentrated on projects with Sy Oliver, Neil Hefti, Robert Farnon, and others. Sinatra, as head of Reprise, kept May busy with, among other things, an album with Ethel Merman, and while there never was a subsequent Sinatra-May set, the two men worked on numerous odds and ends together. Sinatra also kept the classic May charts, particularly those from *Come Fly with Me* and *Swing Along with Me,* alive in his concerts and television performances right up to the present day; he rerecorded "Come Fly with Me" for his musical autobiography, the 1965 *A Man and His Music* set, live at the Sands with Count Basie, and again in 1993 for *Duets II*.

In 1962, Sinatra and May undertook two new Cahn and Van Heusen numbers, "Boy's Night Out" (a very '60s sounding movie-title theme which had been a hit for Patti Page) and "Cathy," which the singer decided did not amount to the team's best work and never released. In 1964, May arranged two more singles sides (conducted by others at the actual sessions), one, unissued, an amiably dopey piece of French pastry called "Since Marie Has Left Paree" and one, released, that did little for the team's reputation, "Pass Me By." Written by Coleman and Leigh, authors of "Witchcraft," Sinatra and May conceived of this corny-as-Kansas-in-August item in a circus setting; Peggy Lee and Lou Levy did better by it as a swinging jazz march.

May also scored a number of Rat Pack pairings in 1962 and 1963, beginning with the single "Me and My Shadow" by Sinatra and Sammy Davis. Although the number was buttressed by some amiably Vegas-type special lyrics (presumably by Sammy Cahn), had it not been for the real affection between Sinatra and Davis, and May's rampant wit, it would have taken nerve to sing this politically incorrect soft-shoe show-piece in the era of "We shall overcome." For two of the *Reprise Repertory Theatre* show, anthology albums, May arranged two monu-mental trios, "We Open in Venice" from *Kiss Me, Kate*, with Sinatra, Dean Martin, and Davis, and "The Oldest Established" from *Guys and Dolls*, with Sinatra, Martin, and Bing Crosby.

The May-Sinatra solo from *Guys and Dolls*, "Luck Be a Lady," became legendary, due to Sinatra's swaggeringly jocular combination of a gambler's flamboyance and the tight, even swing of May's streamlined aggregation. May had originally arranged the piece at a pace closer to the breakneck speed that Robert Alda and Marlon Brando took it in the Broadway and Hollywood productions, but Sinatra suggested that they take it a bit more leisurely. Their reading of "Luck Be a Lady" has since become so definitive that all the original-cast versions now seem ridicu-lously fast. Frank Loesser wrote the piece to depict smarmy Forty-sec-ond Streeters bereft of necks shooting craps in a sewer; Sinatra and May transform these Damon Runyan types into smooth-groove Vegas high rollers, complete with glitzy, brightness-at-midnight lighting and gold Visa cards.

In the fall of 1967, either Bill Miller or producer Sonny Burke notified May that Reprise wanted him to do another album with Sinatra. This one was to use the orchestra of Duke Ellington and would eventually be released as *Francis A. & Edward K.* May was selected not only for his familiarity with the idiosyncratic voices of both halves of the proposed equation but because of his reputation as a musical mimic. "Billy May can write any way, like anyone," claimed trumpeter Zeke Zarchy. "If you say you want a Duke Ellington arrangement or a this-guy arrangement, Billy can write like that. But he also can write like himself." (May had previously recreated the sounds of Jimmie Lunceford and Kay Kyser for Capitol and would later rerecord virtually the entire swing era for Time-Life Records.)

The idea of May writing for Ellington was as much a surprise for Sinatra as it was for May. On some level he had been considering a col-laboration with Ellington for at least twenty years, but when he began planning the Ellington album in earnest in the early Reprise years, he

assumed that Billy Strayhorn, Ellington's composing and arranging partner of twenty-eight years, would handle the orchestrations. But after
years of illness, Strayhorn, who was only a month older than Sinatra,
died on May 31, 1967. (Supposedly, Sinatra paid part of his medical
expenses.) Plans for the album continued, however, and Sinatra and
Burke switched from one Billy to another. Far from resenting being second choice, May remembered, "I felt very flattered that they asked me
after Billy died."

May's relationship with Strayhorn, who had also grown up in
Pittsburgh, went back even before Strayhorn went to work with
Ellington. "I started my professional career at a little place on Station
Street in Pittsburgh called Charlie Ray's," Strayhorn once reminisced.
"They had a little place upstairs, and the bandstand was about a flight
and a half up. Billy May used to come to this place and play trumpet and
trombone. He would come up and sit with us in our little nest. We were
up above the room in a little bandstand, above the steps. They used to
throw people down the steps every night, unruly people."

When May went to work for Charlie Barnet at the end of 1938, he discovered that the leader was such an obsessive Ellington devotee, he
could not have learned more about Ellington's music had he apprenticed
with the Duke himself. In his two years with Barnet, he scored a number
of Ellington items, including "In a Mizz," "Rockin' in Rhythm," "The
Sergeant Was Shy," "Ring Dem Bells," and "Merry Go Round," that
were faithful both to their sources and Barnet's burgeoning style. While
with Glenn Miller, May conceived of a brilliantly Millerized treatment
of "Take the A Train" that wrapped Strayhorn's melody in Miller's
patented clarinet-led reeds. (May's later "Say It Isn't So" detours unexpectedly through "A Train"'s piano solo and countermelody.)

"Duke was a big influence on me since the days I was with Barnet,"
said May. "He was such a pioneer, you know. He really did amazing
things. I have records of Duke's from the '30s, and God! They're doing
things that some of these modern bop guys are just doing now." In the
early '50s when he launched the Billy May Orchestra, first in the studios
and then on the road, May's primary inspirations were Ellington and the
two-beat sound of the then-defunct Jimmie Lunceford band, as masterminded for Lunceford by future Dorsey-Sinatra arranger Sy Oliver.
When May later related to Oliver how influential he had been, "Sy told
me that Duke was a big influence on him and that he actually got that
[Lunceford] sound from Duke. There are some two-beat things that
Duke did, and he just didn't follow up on it. But Sy told me that's where
he got the idea." The two-beat "All I Need Is the Girl" on *Francis A. &*

Edward K. illustrates the myriad connections between the sounds of Ellington, Oliver, and May.

Sinatra first met Ellington in about the spring or summer of 1942. "He was with Tommy Dorsey," Ellington later wrote. "They all came down to the College Inn at the Sherman Hotel in Chicago where we were playing, and I think it was just about the time he was ready to split the Dorsey gig. I could tell that by the way Tommy said good night to him!" Always one for fancy handles, Ellington seems to have perpetually referred to the singer as "Francis." Sinatra had also already become friends with Al Hibbler, who in May 1943 became the major male vocalist of the Ellington band.

In the fall of '42, Sinatra and Ellington crossed paths again when Sinatra, by that time playing as a single, shared a movie theater bill with the Ellington band at the State in Hartford, Connecticut. "I played three days at a theater in Hartford when Ellington was there," Sinatra later recalled, "and believe me, it was one of the biggest kicks of my life." Both were to enjoy major triumphs within a few months, Sinatra at his breakthrough New York Paramount booking that December, and Ellington at his premier Carnegie Hall concert a few weeks later.

Ellington and Sinatra couldn't have spent much time together off-stage during the Hartford engagement because the composer was furiously struggling between shows to finish the forty-five-minute *Black, Brown and Beige* in time for Carnegie Hall. The film was the noir classic *The Cat People,* and Ellington later quipped to aide Stanley Dance that he wasn't sure which had the greater impact on his muse while he wrote this pivotal piece, Sinatra or *The Cat People.* When Ellington guested on Sinatra's *Broadway Bandbox* program later in 1943,[6] *BB&B* was a subject of their banter. However, Sinatra and Ellington possibly did work together informally later that year; as Billy Strayhorn remembered in 1962, Sinatra would occasionally sit in with the Ducal aggregation during their stay at New York's Hurricane Club.

Sinatra's love for Ellington's music was well known, although he rarely attempted to combine the Duke's ideas with his own. Sinatra recorded far fewer songs by Ellington than he did, say, by Walter Donaldson. Only two Ellington tunes appear on the classic Sinatra Capitol albums, "Mood Indigo" on *In the Wee Small Hours* and "I Got It Bad" on *A Swingin' Affair.* In the Reprise period, only "I'm Beginning to

6. Ellington did not play behind Sinatra on that early meeting; he hadn't brought his band along and performed instead as a featured soloist accompanied by the Raymond Scott–Axel Stordahl orchestra.

See the Light" (like "I Didn't Know About You," done on an aircheck in the mid-1940s) turns up, on the 1962 *Sinatra and Swingin' Brass*. In 1955, Sinatra and Nelson Riddle also recorded a Capitol single of "How Could You Do a Thing Like That to Me?," a pop tune by Ellingtonian Tyree Glenn based on the melody of the 1947 "Sultry Serenade," which the trombonist had written and performed with Ellington.[7]

Sinatra's attempt at Strayhorn's best-known vocal ballad, "Lush Life," which he bit off at the overloaded Felix Slatkin session for *Only the Lonely*, was at once marked for greatness and failure. The first came in Nelson Riddle's masterful arrangement, which juxtaposes a deliberately out-of-tune piano against a Coplandesque string section. The second in that, as Bill Miller recalled, Sinatra "didn't take the trouble to learn it" correctly and tried it at an already overbooked date.

Although he turned in a stunning tune number eight, "Willow, Weep for Me," he didn't have the physical fortitude to make it through number seven, Strayhorn's ambitious air. "It's a rather complicated song, and I think Frank would have been momentarily put off by all the changes that had to go on," said Riddle. "Not that he couldn't have sung it with ease and beautifully had he tried a couple more times." On the sole circulating partial take of the three allegedly recorded, Sinatra gets through the out-of-tempo "verse" section but breaks down in the refrain. After a characteristic Kingfish impression, he resolves to "put it aside for about a year." Sinatra later told Miller that he had decided to "leave that one for Nat Cole."

Sinatra had expressed interest in recording with Duke Ellington as early as 1947. At the conclusion of the "Body and Soul"/"I'm Glad There Is You" session of November 9 of that year, Sinatra and CBS producer George Avakian were making small talk when Avakian informed Sinatra that Ellington would be recording in the same studio two days later. Sinatra then said something to the effect of "You know, I've always wanted to make a record with Duke." Avakian, a keen fan of both men, summarily brought Sinatra's idea to Manie Sachs, but the A&R chief wasn't particularly interested. "As great as Duke was, he wasn't selling a lot of records for us at that time," said Avakian. "Manie realized that Ellington was important and that he should be on the label, but he didn't give him a lot of attention."

Sinatra and Ellington formally began doing business together in 1962, when the Maestro switched from a contract with Columbia to a handshake agreement with Sinatra and Reprise. Ellington recorded almost as prolifically for the company as Sinatra did in the next three years (a fact that only a discographer might be aware of, since the Ellington Reprise albums have been reissued only on other labels, primarily Atlantic and

7. On a 1966 TV medley with Sammy Davis, Jr., Sinatra also performed snatches of "Don't Get Around Much Anymore" and "Take the A-Train."

Discovery). As early as 1964, the label announced a forthcoming Sinatra-Ellington album.

Sinatra had already recorded with a number of Ellingtonians, including Juan Tizol, Willie Smith, and Al Sears. Three of Duke's men appear with Sinatra on the 1946 Metronome All-Stars date: Johnny Hodges, Lawrence Brown, and Harry Carney. In 1960, tenor great Ben Webster recorded the first ever Reprise album, and in 1962 he solos on "Beginning to See the Light," on *Sinatra and Swinging Brass.*

Sinatra made a point of giving Ellington the same creative autonomy he sought for himself in founding the label, and he also granted Ellington license to produce sessions by other artists whose work he deemed worthy, resulting in the first American release by the South African piano great Dollar Brand. The output of Sinatra and Ellington ran along parallel lines when *The Concert Sinatra* and *The Symphonic Ellington* were recorded on two different continents in February 1963. Commercial considerations impacted equally on both artists, as could be witnessed on releases such as *Sinatra '65* and *Ellington '65,* and on occasions when both were importuned to record Beatles songs. In 1966, Sinatra arranged for Ellington to write the score to his film *Assault on a Queen.*

Adding Ellington to his label was one way in which Sinatra could, eventually, incorporate the Ellington sound into his own work. Another was by hiring Strayhorn himself. According to David Hajdu, author of the forthcoming first biography of Strayhorn, one of the arranger-composer's roommates recalls that Sinatra called Strayhorn several times in the early '60s, offering him the chance to do some work for Reprise, both for Sinatra and, presumably, to make records under his own name. However, Ellington himself was always overly protective of his most crucial collaborator, sometimes in ways that could be construed as furthering his own interests over Strayhorn's. He soon got wind of Sinatra's offer and squelched it, not by ordering Strayhorn not to accept, but by overloading him with so much work that he could never consider outside offers.

Sinatra also attempted to get Strayhorn on his team through Al Hibbler, who had left the Ellington organization in 1951 for a successful solo career. After a series of hit singles and excellent albums for Decca, Hibbler's career was gradually running out of steam by 1960, thanks partially to his breaking from his former manager and partially to his involvement with the civil rights movement. However, Sinatra realized that a new Hibbler album, with state-of-the-art production and ace arrangements (by Gerald Wilson), could have financial as well as musical merit, and personally called Hibbler to suggest such a project in 1961.

And he still wanted Strayhorn. Hibbler remembers, "When I went with Sinatra to Reprise, Frank asked me, 'Can you get Strayhorn?' I said, 'I doubt it, man!' I asked Strayhorn, and Strayhorn went and told Duke." Hibbler continued, "Duke came to me and said, 'Man I don't appreciate you trying to take my arranger! You took what you could get from me, and now you're tryin' to break up my band!' I said, 'No, I wouldn't do that.'"

This might have been the incident that provoked Ellington into leaving Reprise in 1965. "They weren't too close, because Duke always accused Frank of trying to take Billy Strayhorn from him," says Hibbler, "and he accused me of trying to help him." For the remaining nine years of his life, Ellington became a free agent contractually, producing his own sessions, as in effect he always had, and selling the masters to whatever outfit was interested. He would record only one more album for Reprise, and that was *Francis A. & Edward K.*

All this was in the background when Billy May began working on the arrangements for the album in 1967, beginning as always by setting the keys with Bill Miller for the eight tunes already selected by Sinatra and Sonny Burke. In addition to a series of singles with guest vocalists as worthy as Bing Crosby in 1932 and as bizarre as Johnnie Ray in 1958, Ellington had done two ground-breaking albums with Rosemary Clooney and Ella Fitzgerald. Both the Clooney and Fitzgerald projects had been Songbook albums of all Ellington-Strayhorn compositions, and Sinatra might have gone that route had Strayhorn been alive. But just as Sinatra wanted May to provide a bridge between the Ellington universe and his own, he chose a mixture of old and new (largely non-Ellington) songs that fit a middle ground. Sinatra rarely chose to duplicate what other singers had done before him and wasn't a believer in the Songbook concept to begin with.

Sinatra and May restricted the song selections to eight extra-long tracks, leaving plenty of room for the imaginations of both May and his soloists—Johnny Hodges, Cootie Williams, Paul Gonsalves, Lawrence Brown, and the rest—to stretch out. Sinatra and Burke selected only one overtly commercial number, the Bobby Neff hit "Sunny," graced primarily by Harry Carney's endlessly resonant baritone sax lines.

Around the third week of November, May and Miller flew up to Seattle, where Ellington was working to try out the charts in a rehearsal without Sinatra. "We rehearsed them all afternoon and, Jesus, the rehearsal was terrible," said May. "They were all terrible sight readers in that band. The drummer, Sam Woodyard, couldn't read music at all. But they had a trick where he had to watch one of the saxophone player's feet for when he'd stop playing and when he'd start. So the second time through, the saxophone player would mark his part, and he'd move his foot or something, and that would be the cue for the drummer. It was all shit like that."

Most of the studio men whom Sinatra, May, and Riddle were used to working with had all spent time with the touring swing bands. Still, in the studios it was just as important to be able to read a piece of music as if it were a newspaper as it was to be able to play with a strong swing feeling, for a Sinatra sideman anyway. However, Ellington's sidemen didn't learn Ellington's music by reading it, said May, "they got it by playing every night, and when they got it, it was fine." Many of the finest improvisors couldn't have made the studio grade, reading-wise. Harry Edison was an exception, and he has noted that in the beginning Riddle was especially generous in helping him with his sight reading.

"We went through the whole album, we rehearsed it all," May continued. "Duke made a big issue out of saying to me, 'Oh, get the music ready and we'll rehearse it. We'll play these on the job. I'll play Frank's vocal part on the piano.'" May and Miller attended the band's performance that night, and when Ellington began calling May's charts, they assumed he was going to keep his word. "Well, they have two weeks before the session," May has recalled thinking as he and Miller flew back to Los Angeles that night. "If they keep playing them every night like that, they're bound to nail 'em, and everything'll be all right."

However, the Ellington organization was not only the greatest amalgamation of soloing and composing talent the jazz world has known, it was also a band of prima donnas who could only be held together by the biggest ego of them all. Each of Ellington's major players had the talent, the star power, and the reputation to be a leader in his own right. Cootie Williams and Johnny Hodges had been leading groups of their own for years, and many must have felt that only the color of their skins was keeping them sidemen, virtually anonymous. As Mel Tormé had learned in a disastrous tandem billing at New York's Basin Street East, the Duke and his men typically invested energy only in playing Ellington and Strayhorn's own music. Tormé's and May's accounts agree that the band just didn't care to put any effort into the work of outside arrangers; they just didn't care. As May put it, "The older Duke got, the more full of [himself] he became."

The session began on December 11. "I guess it was kind of in doubt as to whether all of the band would show up," engineer Lee Hirschberg recalled. "The guys would have been playing the night before, and maybe having a few drinks, or whatever. So the first day was kind of up in the air as to whether we would get anything done or not. I don't think the guys in the band started arriving until about forty-five minutes after the session started."

At the podium, from the first downbeat on, May realized that "they never touched the charts again; they never even looked at 'em after that day." He reflected, "The best big band that Duke ever had, in my estimation, was about 1940 to 1942 when he had just added the fifth saxophone and got Ben Webster. That's what I tried to write for, to go for that sound. But by 1967 it was completely gone, they had started to go to pot although they still had that distinctive sound."

May's solution was to add a couple of "ringers" to the band, reading studio men who could follow the charts and play in the Ellington style. With one good reader playing lead for each of the sections, the others could gradually follow and get it right. In addition to Al Porcino on trumpet, that also involved replacing "The Piano Player," as Ellington referred to himself. While Ellington did perform on several numbers, so did Jimmy Jones, who was both a great accompanist and an amazing Ellington impersonator. Milt Raksin, a Hollywood pianist best remembered for his work with the bands of Gene Krupa and Tommy Dorsey, also filled in on different numbers.

"You never saw such completely disconnected people in your life," observed Milt Bernhart, who happened to be playing a date in the adjoining studio. "There was Johnny Hodges and Paul Gonsalves, and they were thinking about what they were going to have for dinner that night—everything else but this. It had reached Frank, too. He wasn't really thrilled. At that point somebody wheeled in his birthday cake. It turned out it was his birthday."

Part of the problem was also Sinatra himself. He was not in his best voice that week and sounds too thin in some spots and overly heavy in others, and he occasionally comes up short in the pitch department (like the plaintively whining last note on "Come Back to Me".) Sinatra doubtless realized he wasn't operating up to his usual technical standards, and probably, if this had been any other occasion, he would have postponed the dates. But realizing the impossible logistics of getting both himself and the Ellington band in the same studio at the same time, he decided to go through with it. He also had the option of recording orchestral tracks for himself to overdub vocals at a later date, but he might have been aware that both the Clooney and Fitzgerald albums with Ellington had been overdubbed, and realized that they suffered because of it.

Besides, what makes *Francis A. & Edward K.* a success is how Sinatra works with the Ellingtonians, in a way that could have been captured only with them all in the same room at the same time. Once the sessions began in earnest, Sinatra, May, Ellington, and the studio and regular band members put their egos behind them and got to work. It finally didn't matter that their collective sight-reading skills weren't up to snuff. As engineer Lee Hirschberg stated, "They were just such an incredible band, it was like they were joined at the base of the skull by some invisible thing. They just locked into everything. It was an amazing session, really."

"That was a hard album, and there's some disastrous shit in there," May put it, "but some of it's awful good." The disc starts with "Follow Me," from *Camelot,* the musical fable that titled a political era in which Sinatra had played no small part. Years earlier, Sinatra and Riddle had heralded the coming of this "brief shining moment" with "High Hopes," for which the singer had commissioned a new, pro-Kennedy libretto from the original lyricist, Sammy Cahn, as an election jingle. In 1961, to commemorate the coronation of "the wisest, most heroic, most splendid king who ever sat on any throne," Sinatra sang "That Old *Jack* Magic" around the same time that he and May rerecorded Johnny Mercer's original text for *Come Swing with Me.* The assassinations of Bobby Kennedy and Martin Luther King in 1968 announced the end of that "fleeting wisp of glory known as Camelot," and Sinatra and Ellington anticipated that, too, with the melancholy "Follow Me."

That chart's languid pace and bluish mood set the tone for the album. The Clooney and Fitzgerald sets had proffered a mixture of fast and slow numbers, but Sinatra, who prefers a more consistent tone, decided to concentrate on torpid tempi. That this is one of Sinatra's few slow sets not put together entirely of suicide songs makes it the most erotic of all Sinatra albums; like *Ellington Indigos,* here is the perfect inspiration for really close slow dancing. Yet at this hardly horserace speed, as May said, "'Follow Me' swings like hell!"

And, apart from being the rare Sinatra LP to mix new and old tunes, *Francis A.* contains what might be his most concentrated singing. Whether it was the newness of the setting or because he was afraid of missing notes, Sinatra bears down with a supertight intensity. Instead of sounding unrelaxed—in fact, he's quite loose on "All I Need Is the Girl"—he sounds more keenly centered than ever. For the first time since the '40s he abstains from familiar Frankisms such as "baby" and "jack" and throws in hardly any of his ad hoc lyric alterations.

The only Ellington original out of the eight, "I Like the Sunrise," had been written for Al Hibbler to sing at the start of the composer's 1947 *The Liberian Suite,* which he had composed in celebration of the hundredth anniversary of the first African republic founded by freed slaves. With its allusions to emancipation, "I Like the Sunrise" was an appropriate aria for a fading Camelot, and Sinatra sings it with reverential majesty, although he supposedly phoned Hibbler after the session and told him, "You're the only guy in the world who can sing that goddamned thing!"

Francis A. & Edward K. features other examples of the kind of pieces that Sinatra and May and Ellington liked to dabble with, as in the exotic contemporary Latin American "Yellow Days" and "Poor Butterfly." May captures the Ellington sound to a "T" throughout, but despite his intentions it's the great 1967 band's texture he pinpoints rather than the more widely celebrated edition of 1942. He really gets it down on "Yellow Days," which contains an instrumental chorus that, after a stunning Johnny Hodges solo, seems to take the band off on a tangent resembling one of the original D or E sections Ellington frequently wrote into his pieces (thereby transcending standard song form) but which is actually based on composer Alvaro Carillo's melody and harmony. "Butterfly," a more directly Puccini-inspired 1916 forerunner to "South of the Border," tells yet another tale of an American Pinkerton loving and leaving a femme foreigner, with Sinatra leaping into a higher and more powerful second chorus.

The track most frequently cited as the album's masterpiece bears another quasi-exotic reference in its title, "Indian Summer"—a cut May described as "just outstanding." When asked to name his favorite arrangement for Sinatra, Nelson Riddle selected "Indian Summer," citing it as the only chart he wished he had written. The beauty of the piece is its simplicity; it never attracts attention to itself or the ensemble but functions as a velvety background for Sinatra and Johnny Hodges, who contributes one of the most sensual solos of his life. Milt Bernhart remembers it as "the only thing really good that happened" on the date: "Hodges played that alto solo in the middle, and it's really quintessential Johnny Hodges."

Bernhart has explained that Sinatra and his musicians usually had an unspoken empathy, preferring not to blow their cools; only if a soloist played something really extraordinary would Sinatra offer more than one or two complimentary words. The most enthusiastic Bernhart ever saw Sinatra get was after the playback of "Indian Summer": "He said, 'My God! That's unbelievable, John.'" Hodges, as usual, said nothing.

Sinatra bookends *Francis A.* with key songs from consecutive Alan Jay Lerner shows, concluding with the set's one out-and-out uptempo, "Come Back to Me" (he had already recorded "On a Clear Day" from the same score). For this hard and fast number, May turned for inspiration to Ellington's famous "Diminuendo and Crescendo in Blue," first written and recorded in 1937 and spectacularly revived at the 1956 Newport Jazz Festival. Although May has insisted that he likes "the old version better because there's some really nice clarinet things," he features Paul Gonsalves here, remembering the tenorist who drove the crowd wild at Newport with twenty-seven spontaneous choruses as, to say the least, "an exciting player."

Apart from Gonsalves' soaring statement, "Come Back to Me" has Sinatra and the band racing and roaring and rocking in rhythm, the muted trumpets wa-wa-ing in double time and the brass skyrocketing into proto-Kenton dissonances. May concludes with a stuttering stop-and-start finish reminiscent of Ellingtonian train portraits like "Daybreak Express" and "Happy Go Lucky Local," thus ending a generally blue-tinged album on an upbeat note. By the time the train winds to a halt, you know you've been on a breathtaking ride, and you walk away convinced that, for all the *mishegoss* that went into it, you've just listened to a great album.

The overall experience clearly was not a magical one for either Ellington or Sinatra; neither, to the best of my knowledge, ever cited it as a career highlight. In his 1973 collection of reminiscences, *Music Is My Mistress*, Ellington praised Sinatra for his '40s campaign against racial intolerance and also for rallying to his support once in the '50s when several of his bandsmen were caught in a gambling raid that the papers threatened to blow into a big scandal. He also mentioned a "recent" occasion on which he had again surprised Sinatra on his birthday by showing up at his party and bringing his band with him. But he didn't mention *Francis A. & Edward K.*

Over the next twelve years Sinatra and May worked on only one single side together, the aptly titled 1976 "The Best I Ever Had." In 1979 Sinatra again called on May as his second choice to arrange another whole album. Once more May didn't mind at all. As already discussed, the singer initially wanted Nelson Riddle to orchestrate "The Past," the first disc of *Trilogy*. Though evidence suggests that Sinatra turned to May because he had had a falling out with Riddle, a comparison of the work of the two writers suggests that May was better suited to the job. Sinatra wanted a sound very closely based on '40s big-band-style orchestrations, a genre that May was much more firmly grounded in than Riddle. "I felt badly Nelson and Frank had had a little difficulty between them," said May, "but I was very happy that I got the assignment."

For once, the arranger was consulted in the choice of repertory. Not only did May and Sinatra convene at the singer's compound, along with Sonny Burke, general factotum "Sarge" Weiss, and longtime crony Jimmy Van Heusen, but Gordon Jenkins, who was involved in a whole other part of the album, also came along to offer his two cents' worth. Unfortunately, Sinatra had neglected to summon a pianist. "I don't know where Vinnie was that day," said May, referring to Vincent Falcone, who had temporarily replaced Bill Miller as Sinatra's accompanist. Jenkins, whom May tactfully described as "not the world's greatest piano player," was forced to serve in that capacity.

The copy on the album of *Trilogy* describes the criteria for "The Past" as "songs generally written before the rock era," but nine out of the ten come from the big-band years or earlier. "The approach for 'The Past' was that they went by composer," May recalled. "They had a stack of songs, all kinds of 'em, that Frank was considering. What were Irving Berlin's big hits in this period? What were Richard Rodgers'? Sarge had complete catalogues of their songs!" May also remembered that many of Van Heusen's earlier songs were discussed, including the possibility of a remake of "Deep in a Dream" from the *Wee Small Hours* album (none made it onto the finished disc).

Sinatra and May also discussed the possibility of paying tribute to various band sounds of "The Past" by orchestrating various numbers in the style of, say, Benny Goodman or Woody Herman. Again, they decided against it. "The minute you start fooling around and start trying to use the Glenn Miller sound, for instance," explained May, "you realize that's an instrumental sound; it doesn't work in the background behind a vocal. Frank was smart enough to know that after he brought it up. So it was more a matter of just getting a feeling of that era rather than being specific about any particular band."

Still, since "The Past," like several Sinatra sets before it, referred in part to the singer's own, he decided to include tributes to the two band-leaders who had sired him, Harry James and Tommy Dorsey. Neither homage, however, would be a remake of a number he had sung with those bands. "I Had the Craziest Dream," with a vocal by the Queen of the Canaries, Helen Forrest, had been one of James' biggest hits in 1943. "In fact, Frank was talking about bringing Harry in on the session," said May, "and then he said, 'Aw, God knows what kind of a record deal he's got, and we'll have to get clearance from some son of a bitch. Fuck it. Charlie'll play the shit out of it anyway.'" Charlie Turner, at this time Sinatra's lead and solo trumpeter on the road and in the studios, indeed captures James' soaring brilliance and bravura.

Dorsey had never recorded "But Not for Me," although Judy Garland had sung it in *Girl Crazy*, a film in which the Smiling Irishman's band also appeared. Rather than use a specific performance as a starting point, Sinatra and May conceived the piece along the lines of "what if it had been recorded by Tommy Dorsey and his Sentimentalists?" With a trimmed-down vocal chorus emulating the Pied Pipers, Sinatra recreates the feeling of his Dorsey-era "I'll Never Smile Again" and "Stardust": he and the faux Pieds phrase very slowly in superclose harmony, The Voice rising at first only from the vocal ensemble for key lines and the entire bridge, accompanied by a celesta. As in "Smile Again," the two vocal choruses are divided by an instrumental bridge consisting of a strictly-from-Dorsey trombone solo, played by Dick Nash. "I didn't have any idea what we were going to do until I bumped into Billy on the way into the studio," recalled Nash. "He said, 'Oh good, Frank told me that he wanted you to do your Tommy Dorsey shit.'"

"It was a lucky coincidence that the tune of 'But Not for Me' happened to perfectly fit that category," said May, "so Frank said we could do it that way." While May also wrote a reed section passage behind Nash that could have been written by Sy Oliver in 1941, he brings in the strings in a deliberately un–Axel Stordahl–like way. Further, Sinatra sings the verse—not completely unheard of in the Dorsey days, but a rarity—divided into two sections, the first backed by strings, the second, effectively, by a spare solo piano. And though Sinatra and May had perfected the bridge-as-verse structure in "April in Paris," here they revert to a favorite Crosby construction of the '30s, the verse-in-the-middle model.

"Street of Dreams," Sinatra's third commercial version of the Victor Young opus (and one of four remakes in *Trilogy*), was inspired less by any previous Sinatra version than by an earlier Sinatra-May treatment of another song. "Frank likes the arrangement I made for him of 'You're Nobody Till Somebody Loves You' [from *Swing Along with Me*], and this was the same idea: I wrote a counter-line that swings pretty good," May commented. "So he said, 'Do it the same way.' But unfortunately I had to call him in New York and tell him, 'Hey, man, "Street of Dreams" is only sixteen bars, and we're gonna have a short record.'" Sinatra suggested using the song's verse, which he wasn't familiar with, so May sang it to him in Young's original march tempo. While the refrain itself can be construed as surreal and even upbeat, the very dramatic verse, performed convincingly by Bing Crosby (1932) and Tony Bennett (1959), anchors the song to a despondent tale of drug addiciton. "Oh, fuck it," Sinatra responded. "We'll just make a short record."

They expanded "Street of Dreams" after the fashion of "You're

Nobody Till Somebody Loves You" by adding a juicy intro, a full third chorus, and, unexpectedly, a superlong *outro:* an instrumental of forty seconds that continues long after The Voice has stopped singing. "He liked the way the thing was swinging on the end there," May explained, "so that's why we extended the ending so long, to a fade." Sinatra had originally intended to use "Street of Dreams," with its three key changes, as his concert closer; the long coda would provide him with plenty of time to take a bow and beat it. But after *Trilogy* was released and "New York, New York" became the Sinatra superhit of the decade, there was no way he could end his concerts with anything other than that ode to the Apple. Shortly thereafter May prepared a more concise and conclusive closer for "Street of Dreams."

Sinatra and May recorded nine of the ten songs (all but "All of You") over three sessions in July 1979. "Then by September, Frank said his chops were in better shape and he could sing higher," said May. "It was a pretty complete overhaul." Some tracks were taken, unaltered, from the original July dates ("It Had to Be You" and "Craziest Dream"), and some were strictly retakes using the same charts ("More Than You Know"). But for some, May raised the key half a step ("They All Laughed" and "My Shining Hour"), added or removed the verse, and generally revised or rewrote most of the orchestrations.

One tune recorded in July, "Surrey with the Fringe on Top"—which would have been the only Richard Rodgers piece on the set—was discarded entirely because Sinatra and May decided "it was a buncha shit! I don't know why he picked it. He didn't like what he did on it vocally, although he did like the arrangement." They replaced it with Cole Porter's "All of You," from the 1954 *Silk Stockings* and by far the most recent tune in "The Past." Though Sinatra uses the cleaner lyric ("sweet and pure of you" as opposed to "take a tour of you") in this fast and snappy run-through (two thirty-two-bar choruses in less than a minute and a half), there's no shortage of charismatic Sinatra virility.

"The Past" prevails as a Sinatra-May mixed-mood package in the great tradition of *Come Fly with Me.* Sinatra is marvelously wistful and forlorn in "Craziest Dream" and close to his all-time tenderest in "More Than You Know" and "My Shining Hour," even if some of the notes seem beyond the reach of his pipes—as the orchestra and strings swell behind him like Hulk Hogan flexing his muscles. Conversely, he's agreeably aggressive on "Let's Face the Music and Dance," all but snarling—"Har! Har! Har!"—as he lets the past laugh on "They All Laughed," and he gets more animated with each consecutively punchier chorus of "All of You" and "Street of Dreams."

May's style is generally lush, romantic, and relaxed, full of splendidly simple and effectual charts like "It Had to Be You" that leave little to suggest the work of the technicolorful whimsy of "Granada" or "Mandalay." Only the first track, "The Song Is You," and the last, "They All Laughed," betray May's distinctive earmarks; "More Than You Know" concludes with a string figure that suggests certain Riddle-Slatkin passages. "Laughed" and "Street of Dreams" at times suggest May's always-welcome post-Lunceford two-beat, the first in particular wobbling warmly.

Even the large vocal chorus, something Sinatra rarely used since the Stordahl days (it generally spells sudden death in a non-Muzak context), by and large fits the mood and only occasionally comes off as pasty. Further evoking the '40s, Sinatra and May chose a big-band texture that never conceals the imperfections in Ol' Blue Eyes' equipment, making him sound more vulnerable and more believable, as opposed to "You and Me" on "The Present," on which Don Costa protects The (thinning) Voice with more cover-ups than Richard Nixon ever dreamed of.

May was particularly impressed with Sinatra's outline of "My Shining Hour." Describing the number's shining moment where Sinatra connects the last note of one section to the first of the next, May said, "He knows what he wants. He said, 'When we get to the bridge there, I'm gonna pull the long breath bit.' That was the Tommy Dorsey thing in which you take a lot of breath in, and when everybody thinks you're gonna have to stop and breathe, you fox 'em and carry over the phrase. He's a master at that. He deliberately made sure that I knew he was gonna do that, so I enhanced it by making the fucking band come up there. I put some chromatic harmony under it, and it really paid off. I have to say that it wouldn't work with every singer. Frank really knows what he's doing."

The team's familiar irreverent humor dominates the endings of "They All Laughed" and "Face the Music." At Sinatra's suggestion, the first concludes with the entire ensemble collapsing in a series of guffaws. In a way particularly fitting for a tune about paying the fiddlers, May winds up "Face the Music," after the vocal, with a very brief Latin brass fanfare. "All the mariachi bands in Los Angeles used that as their sign-off at the end of the set, and Frank was aware of that," May pointed out. "Verne Yocum [Sinatra's copyist and brother of Pied Piper Clark Yocum] made Frank a very complete part with lyrics and a little sketch about what was happening. It was written in three-quarter time, and Frank looked at it and said, 'What the fuck is that on the end there?' I said, 'Ah, you'll see. You'll like it.' And he did." The unexpected tag figures as an instrumental counterpart to "Aye! Aye! Aye!" in "South of the Border" or "Cha!

Cha! Cha!" in "Granada," as if to announce to the audience, "We who are about to get plastered salute you!" (May had thrown in a similar mariachi tag at the end of his classic instrumental of "It Happened in Monterey.")

"Billy did an incredible job," pianist Vincent Falcone said. "I mean, he did 'The Past' as well as it could be done. He captured everything." When *Trilogy* was finally released, "The Past" was resoundingly hailed by critics and collectors alike as more than just the best of the three discs but justification enough for purchasing the entire package. "I did mine first," he said, modestly ascribing his success to factors other than his talent. "And everybody tells me that mine is the best of the three—only because they know the songs better, although Don Costa did a wonderful job on his." *Trilogy* would have been a better buy had it consisted of three entire discs of Sinatra and May working on worthwhile material, as even the chicks and ducks and geese scurrying from the "Surrey with the Fringe" suit Sinatra a lot better than the nauseating "That's What God Looks Like." In the end, "The Past" is much less nostalgic or saccharinely sentimental than either "The Present" or "The Future."

"And that," said May, "was the last really major thing I did for Frank, other than a couple of odds and ends." Few of these bits and pieces were released until the 1995 *The Complete Reprise Recordings* suitcase. In 1982 and again in 1983 they attempted a new Sammy Cahn and Jule Styne piece called "Love Makes Us Whatever We Want to Be." October 1986 saw them recording "Only One to a Customer" by Styne and Carolyn Leigh, an affably snappy number that he also performed in concert earlier that month; the singer introduces it as his first attempt at the tune, which he announces was "arranged by Billy May when he was sober." From the same session, "The Girls I've Never Kissed," an amateurish aria by rocksters Jerry Lieber and Mike Stoller, saw Sinatra trying to land a pop charter along the lines of their hit for Peggy Lee, "Is That All There Is?"

Most recently and most promisingly, in 1988 May scored two standards that Sinatra had not previously tackled, a terrific, rocking "My Foolish Heart" and "Cry Me a River." Sinatra supposedly never laid down a vocal on the latter, but a tape exists of a rehearsal. Though The Voice is so off-mike it's impossible to assess his contribution, the arrangement is so on the money that one wishes Sinatra and May had done a whole new album entitled *Come Cry with Me*.

In 1991 a Japanese film concern opened negotiations with the Sinatra office to get the Old Man to sing a new number over the main titles of a picture they were producing. Sinatra supposedly deemed the proposed song, written by French film composer Maurice Jarre, unperformable, saying he would consider singing it only if Sammy Cahn would punch up the lyrics and Billy May would handle the orchestration. The melody was so minimal, however, that there was nothing to arrange, meaning that May would practically have to start from scratch, for which he deserved a co-composer credit and a share of the royalties. May told Cahn, "Look, I'll make the arrangement, but I'm not into the business of changing other people's songs."

According to May, the producers had gone as far as commisioning the chart from May, hiring all the necessary musicians and booking studio time, before they even had a firm commitment from Sinatra. When the singer finally decided not to go through with it, the filmmakers next considered contacting Ella Fitzgerald. The only good thing to come out of the whole megillah was May's classification of Jarre as a "Godzilla-eats-the-Steel-Pier type of composer!"

"I used to have a house in Palm Springs, and I'd see Frank socially once in a while," said May. "We had a lot of fun down there, but I never got that close to him. We'd have a ball some night, and then maybe I didn't see him for a couple of years." May feels that their professional relationship has lasted so long because neither was ever dependent on or beholden to the other. They just happened to work together on some very happy occasions when a particular project had Billy May's name written all over it. Comparing his Sinatra experience to that of his close friend Nelson Riddle, May remarked, "Nelson felt that Sinatra uses people and things like that, and for all I know maybe he does. But, see, some people allow themselves to be used. That's why I say I like it the way it is."

Tenor sax player Ted Nash felt they worked together so well "because Billy never was in awe of Sinatra. He was just another singer, and he'd come on the date. 'Okay, how's it going, Frank? Here we go, let's make a tune.' Where the other guys sometimes would be uptight, knowing Sinatra's reputation. Because he could come on pretty strong if he didn't like something. So they were always concerned that something would happen. But Billy didn't care. If you didn't like what he did, he'd change it to suit you. What's the difference?"

Sinatra never expected May to be subservient to him. "Sinatra treated him differently" than he did, say, Don Costa, said Vince Falcone. "He respected his time, he respected Billy's right to say no. If Don ever said no to the Old Man, the Old Man wouldn't speak to him for two weeks. But Billy was different because Billy kept his distance." Nash added, "Frank sometimes has uptight people around him, but Billy was so loose. He would go, 'Let's go, Frank. Let's make one of these turkeys.' And

Frank would break up, because he dug Billy's style with that type of thing."

As Sinatra himself told Robin Douglas-Home, "Billy handles the band quite differently from Gordon or Nelson. With Nelson, for instance, if someone plays a wrong note, he'll hold up his hand and say quietly, 'Now in bar sixteen, you'll see that it says the brass comes in half a note after the woodwinds' or something like that. But Billy—there he'll be in his old pants and sweatshirt, and he'll stop them and say, 'Cats, this bar sixteen, you gotta go oomp-de-da-da-che-ow! Okay? Let's go then, cats!' And the band will go."

Emulating one of his role models, Axel Stordahl, May doesn't let much get to him. "I know what I like, I know what I like to write, and I know what has influenced me and what's successful. I know where I can steal money, and I know where I can make it. If you're in any kind of business, you know that sometime you're going to have to do something that's junk, and you do it anyway. But I know if I'm gonna do an album with Frank, then it's gonna be an important album, and I'm gonna try harder."

We should be grateful for any attitude that kept these two masters working together so productively and for so long.

CHAPTER EIGHT

GORDON JENKINS AND THE SEARCH
FOR LONG FORMS, 1956–1981

> *It was longer than a whore's dream.*
> —BEN HECHT
> on *Gone with the Wind*

A simple man stands out on the edge of a cliff, peering into the heavens, trying to fathom the ways of God and the universe.

In earlier and more naive, that is to say more racist, generations, dramatists often colored this man black; even such forward-thinking sages as Oscar Hammerstein considered that perfectly natural casting, and Paul Robeson felt no compunction about playing such a character. Hammerstein and Jerome Kern wrote "Ol' Man River" for Robeson to sing in 1927, and it became the original Broadway ode to the mysteries of both human existence and intolerance. The librettist once described the text as "a song sung by a character who is a rugged and untutored philosopher. It is a song of resignation with a protest implied."

In 1931, Buddy DeSylva, one of the future founders of Capitol Records, copublished "That's Why Darkies Were Born," which raised the same idea, this time with a less poetically abstract racial angle. Its choice of language was unfortunate, needless to say, but then, too, the first word of the verse of "River" in the original, unexpurgated libretto (and as recorded by Al Jolson) had been "niggers." "That's Why Darkies Were Born" further presented the black man in a way that the multiethnic Tin Pan Alley could relate to—casting the "colored" race in the same role as Jews in the Old Testament. To take up the black man's burden meant to shoulder both the suffering and the moral and religious obligations of the rest of the world.

In the next generation's attempt to address the same issues, still another "big" song from the largely liberal theatrical community implies that man's inhumanity to man is more the fault of an absentee deity than man himself. Kurt Weill and Maxwell Anderson's "Lost in the Stars," also the title of a musical drama about apartheid, is almost the equivalent of Cassius' declaration that "the fault, dear Brutus, is not in our stars but in our selves."

Sinatra felt the need to confront these concerns in his music for the same reasons as Kern, Hammerstein, Weill, and Anderson; he went as far as to tell Alec Wilder that he considered "Ol' Man River" the essential song in his repertoire. If Sinatra's renditions of "River" and "Lost in the Stars" help those texts to transcend the time in which they were first staged, it's partly because he has divorced them from the specifically racial angles they were originally written to comment on. When Sinatra sings them, they no longer deal with the specific problems of one particular people, they confront the entire human condition. Sinatra transports these songs away from levee riverboats and Johannesburg prisons and universalizes them.

"He was always looking ahead," as Zeke Zarchy, who in 1946 was the lead trumpeter with the Sinatra radio orchestra on the West Coast, recalled. "I remember once I was at his house for dinner. There were half a dozen people there, and we all walked into his den where he had his hi-fi set up. He played us some things from *Carousel*, which had just come out. We heard the big 'Soliloquy' that the main character sings, and we were all impressed with it. Frank said, 'These are the kinds of things that I want to do.' At that time he was just doing his regular ballad stuff. And sure enough, he went into that field."

Sinatra's career-long quest for big texts and big issues runs parallel to and eventually joins a similar search by composer and orchestrator Gordon Jenkins. The two men would first unite to extend Sinatra's series of saloon-song sets. Gradually, they would join forces in a crusade for the ultimate musical depiction of the plight of mankind, something like Don Quixote and Sancho Panza riding off in search of the Impossible Song.

Like so many other threads of the Sinatra career, the singer's earliest attempts at addressing large issues in expanded song forms were made in conjunction with Tommy Dorsey. Dorsey gave the concert treatment to many a standard, the only one involving Sinatra being their 1941 treatment of "Without a Song." Although Sy Oliver fashioned a very full six-minute treatment of the piece, he nonetheless treated Vincent Youmans' melody simply and eloquently. The leader himself opens "Without a Song" with a full first chorus of trombone—this at a time when he rarely played more than sixteen bars on a typical opening. Sinatra then sings the full refrain, backed by the now familiar "I'll Never Smile Again"–style celesta played by Joe Bushkin.

Again, "Without a Song"'s pseudo-spiritual lyric reflects on man's dealings with the deity, and the reference to "darkies" seems out of place in relation both to Sinatra's developing stand on civil rights and arranger Oliver's racial background. Subsequent Sinatra performances, as on the 1961 *I Remember Tommy* album and the 1965 *Man and His Music* TV special, would omit the reference. Even though Victor opted to record "Without a Song" as a twelve-inch release, they still couldn't get more than four and a half minutes of music on one 78 rpm side; the commercial record ends not long after the vocal with a brief trombone coda. However, one surviving radio performance of the complete six-minute arrangement goes on to include both a full chorus of tenor from Don Lodice and a more elaborate, Luncefordesque closing cadenza by Oliver.

By 1943, "Ol' Man River" had become a part of The Voice's permanent repertoire; the musical *Showboat* had doubtless formed a part of his musical background, all of its songs were much-heard hits during Sinatra's formative early teens. When the show was new, in 1927, Bing Crosby, then still in the midst of his own big-band apprenticeship (with Paul Whiteman), recorded the first jazzy, uptempo version of "Ol' Man River." Taking his cue from the Young Groaner, throughout most of the '30s the Old Man remained in swingtime, in snappy versions by Duke Ellington, Martha Raye, and the Harry James–Dick Haymes combination that must have made composer Kern cringe.

Sinatra is first known to have addressed the song deep in the middle of the first recording ban on the occasion of his first concert tour (one evening of which, the August 14 Hollywood Bowl performance, survives).[1] He then brought the Kern anthem to his radio audience on the October 10, 1943, broadcast of his *Broadway Bandbox* program. Sinatra's idea was to restore the song's tempo as well as its dramatic and philosophical implications, which seemed even more relevant in the era of the war against fascism. The piece had been written for and later was performed by Paul Robeson and was introduced by Jules Bledsoe, yet

---

1. That performance of the piece constitutes the only other time Sinatra publicly uttered the most distasteful word "darkies." Sinatra was, in fact, the first singer to make a point of avoiding such expressions, even though they were then considered acceptable by Hollywood and Tin Pan Alley then. However, I'm sure the ever-perverse Sinatra would balk at being labeled the first "politically correct" pop star.

Sinatra didn't have to sing like Bledsoe (you can tell the world I said so). While not sacrificing any of the piece's power, he raises the level of the tune from a blustering basso to his own lighter and more beautiful baritone, making the message of the piece more believable and true.

Perhaps not quite trusting his own better judgment, or more likely to satisfy the time constraints of network radio, Sinatra's earliest known broadcast of "River" trims the verse and limits him to a single two-minutes chorus. By the time he had graduated to his own *Vimms* show in 1944, he felt secure enough to reattach the rest (on a May installment). In October of that year, Sinatra broadcast "River" again, this time accompanied by former Bing boss Paul Whiteman, and two months later he finally committed the piece to four minutes of shellac, shortly after the settling of the musicians' strike.

The Stordahl-Sinatra treatment of the Kern anthem is so staggeringly definitive, it makes even Robeson's powerful production seem almost as dated as Jolson. Even the faux "colored" slang doesn't get in Sinatra's way; he actually seems to "bend" and "bow" with his voice when he comes to those words in the verse, and there are two stunning early examples of The Voice's high-wire acts. First, there's the Dorsey-style long-breath joining of the last note of the bridge to the first note of the final A section. Stordahl supports this with underlying harmony that's both chromatic and dramatic. In contrast, the accompanist turns up the tension on Sinatra's second vocal superfeat, the agonizingly long note at the climactic "a-long" by suspending both the orchestra and the beat entirely. (Needless to say, this orchestration does not sport one of Sinatra's and Stordahl's characteristic small endings.)

"Ol' Man River" would remain a Sinatra showpiece for the remainder of the CBS and Stordahl era. He stretched it to four and a half minutes for an August 1945 Hollywood Bowl tribute to Kern (then still living), and MGM made it the high point of their 1946 Kern biopic, *Till the Clouds Roll By*. "My idea with that song," composer Kern once commented to the crooner, "was to have a rabbity little fellow do it—somebody who made you believe he was tired of livin' and scared of dyin'. That's how you do it, Frankie." Still, the composer would have had to admit that an aura of majesty permeates the many Sinatra readings, even the visually overdecorated MGM version. Though the studio tried like blazes to muffle the message of the song by draping Young Blue Eyes in what could be one of Liberace's cast-off white tuxedos and then perching him atop a white Roman column out of an Andy Warhol nightmare, they couldn't keep the pure power of its plea for a more just God from coming through.

In search of something to fit on the flip side of "River," which required a twelve-inch 78, Sinatra and Stordahl came up with a fascinating miscalculation. It's hard to label "Stormy Weather" a flop, since both the singing and the orchestration are so beautiful in themselves, even if they're not right for the song. Sinatra would perform this chart only once more, on a V-Disc issued in 1947. On that occasion he would introduce "Stormy Weather" as "a song that tells of the blues." Yet the Sinatra-Stordahl treatment, with its upbeat sound and optimistic attitude, thoroughly nullifies the blues base of the tune, a defeat unfortunately underscored by the presence of an especially pallid vocal group.

No one else had so deliberately called attention to the fact of Harold Arlen's writing this 1933 classic in a major key. Further, Sinatra's very original reharmonization of the title phrase makes it sound even more major—even like a different song, one that could be called "Sunny Weather."[2] Only growling trumpeter Yank Lawson effectively catches Arlen's stormy blue mood; unfortunately for the V-Disc, the pair retained the vocal group and dropped the trumpet solo to trim the chart from four to three minutes and change. The 1959 remake, with Gordon Jenkins replacing Stordahl, found Sinatra probing more convincingly darker colors.

"Stormy Weather" also amounts to one of the only standards that Sinatra and Stordahl recorded for Columbia without "auditioning" it first on the radio. "Begin the Beguine," their next "concert" work, underwent extensive overhauling before the team deemed it ready to commit to shellac. Nine years old in 1944, "Beguine" had first been heard in Cole Porter's 1935 *Jubilee*, which didn't become one of the big hits of that Broadway season (although it was far from the flop it's supposed to have been). Although other numbers from the show made *Your Hit Parade*, "Beguine" itself went unnoticed, being a rhumba that was taken seriously only by Xavier Cugat at the time. As a Latin American specialty, "Beguine" was thought of neither as a ballad nor as an uptempo until Artie Shaw put the song and himself on the map in 1938.

Although Fred Astaire and Eleanor Powell danced to "Beguine" in the *Broadway Melody of 1940* and although Bing Crosby sang it for Decca in 1944, the song remained the property of the swing groups, this status being confirmed by pianist Eddie Heywood's hit recording for Commodore in 1944. Containing more melody and lyrics than any three

2. Actually, there was such a song, and Lita Grey Chaplin (ex-wife of Charlie and mother of Sid) sang it in a 1934 Warner Bros. minimusical two-reeler costarring future rat-packer, nine-year-old Sammy Davis, Jr.

other songs, its 108 measures were used by pianists and vocal coaches to scare off more aspiring and perspiring singers than any song before "Lush Life"—even Astaire never attempted to sing it. Sinatra's earliest performance is believed to be an undated aircheck circa 1943 or early 1944; it's a medium-tempo (or, as Louis Armstrong used to say, "half-fast") arrangement that's closer to a ballad than a swinger, and at that pace the piece lasts four minutes and starts to drag. The texture of the orchestration is even stranger than the tempo because it contains Stordahlesque string figures as well as Dorsey-Stordahl–style celesta and, of all things, a Hawaiian guitar plucking out an annoying arpeggio in the coda.

By the summer of 1944, Sinatra had come up with the perfect treatment. Using Porter's superlong melody and dramatic narrative for a series of marvelously subtle tempo changes, Sinatra turns the "Beguine" into a tour de force of developing dynamics as he switches from soft crooning to agitated belting. At three and a half minutes, this fast-and-slow, loud-and-soft "Beguine," which Sinatra performed both on Armed Forces Radio Service's *Mail Call* and his own *Vimms* show, seems just perfect. He revived the Porter tune for at least three more airings beginning in the fall of 1945 and then at last recorded it for Columbia in February 1946.

Unfortunately, perhaps because "Ol' Man River" and "Stormy Weather" never made the charts, Columbia elected not to let Sinatra attempt another twelve-incher at this time and had "Beguine" rearranged to fit snugly within the confines of the standard ten-inch 78. Although either George Siravo or Heinie Beau wrote the shorter (2:54), faster commercial chart, the "Beguine" never quite begins at this over-rushed pace, and the piece never has an opportunity to build to the same plateau of excitement as the 1944 radio interpretation. Nonetheless, Sinatra's single made the charts, and, despite Tony Martin's hit version of 1939, he remains the singer most identified with "Begin the Beguine," which he continued to perform almost more than any other number. It turns up at least eleven times on *Songs by Sinatra* and even on the cramped *Light Up Time*.

At a time when most radio sponsors choked on their Chesterfields at the thought of a number that ran over two minutes, Sinatra was frequently turning in three-and-a-half or four-minute epics, even on the hyper-reactionary *Hit Parade*. Inevitably, he also turned to standard works of heavy musical, though not necessarily political stature, such as "Dancing in the Dark" and "Long Ago and Far Away." And though Sinatra never performed Earl Robinson's left-leaning cantata *Ballad for*

Americans, he soon became identified with "The House I Live In," Robinson's impassioned plea for ethnic and religious equality.

The film short, *The House I Live In,* resulted from the labors of three writers long associated with humanist (which in those days meant leftist) concerns: lyricist Lewis Allen, best known for "Strange Fruit" (with Billie Holiday); composer Earl Robinson, who would later write "Black and White" and other odes to equality; and screenwriter Albert Maltz, who would suffer the dubious distinction of being one of the original Hollywood Ten—the most celebrated victims of the McCarthy-era blacklist.

In 1940, Robinson had collaborated with librettist John Latouche on *Ballad for Americans,* a one-act oratorio celebrating freedom as one of the principal U.S. values. Thanks to four-sided recordings by Paul Robeson and, more important mass-market-wise, Bing Crosby, the fifteen-minute work reached a wide audience in the Roosevelt era. Two years later, Robinson and Lewis Allen teamed up to write a song called "The House I Live In," which expressed many of the same ideals as the "Ballad" but in more concise song form. The song was perfectly in keeping with the progressive politics of the Roosevelt era as well as the world war that was at least serving to make racism unpopular. Thanks to the AFM ban, "The House I Live In" went unrecorded until after the strike, but the popular black gospel group the Golden Gate Quartet sang it in the Universal feature *Follow the Boys.* Their version included a chorus apparently never used again ("the little church at Concord / Where freedom's fight began . . .").

Frank Sinatra's crusade against intolerance was at its zenith throughout 1945. "George [Evans, Sinatra's press agent and philosophical mentor] was very political and so was Frank, and in that period he was very liberal in his politics," Evans's assistant Bud Granoff has said. "George was always trying to create the image that Frank was more than just a pop singer, and he had a friend who was a principal at a high school in the Bronx. It was George's idea to get Frank to go and address this high school auditorium and talk to the kids about juvenile delinquency. But Frank said he didn't feel qualified, he didn't feel he could handle it. But George pressured him and pressured him and pressured him, and finally Frank did it, and it wound up on the front page of the *Daily News.*

"It was a big front-page story with a picture of Frank talking to these kids. Well, Frank saw the response this brought, so they embarked on a nationwide tour. Frank started to address groups of kids in different cities. I think he did about ten cities, and this got a whirlwind of publicity and sort of changed the image of Frank from being an ordinary record performer, a record star, into a public figure of some importance. In those days performers weren't political activists, but he was one of the first ones."

It should be stressed that although Sinatra was keen to benefit from the positive publicity of these efforts, there were other things he could have done if he and Evans were interested solely in obtaining good press. In those days a large part of the media was controlled by ultraconservative barons of industry, such as William "Rosebud" Hearst, and Sinatra left himself wide open to attack from all manner of pro-Republican, anti-Roosevelt columnists (the worst being the dreaded Westbrook Pegler, the Rush Limbaugh of the '40s). As columnist Billy Rose observed in 1947, "Taking potshots at Sinatra in print is a good way [for newspapermen] to butter up the publisher who's paying [their] salary." Perhaps it seemed to Sinatra that espousing the best politics, no less than singing the best songs, would be beneficial to his career in both the long and short run. Or perhaps he was just doing what he believed in.

In 1945, the National Conference of Christians and Jews, the Bureau of Inter-Cultural Education, and other such organizations bestowed commendations on Sinatra for his work against prejudice. In that year Sinatra selected "The House I Live In" as the musical cornerstone for this multimedia crusade, envisioning the three-year-old tune as the subject of a movie one-reeler as well as a Columbia Records release. When producer Frank Ross suggested making a film out of one of these tolerance speeches, along with a song to the same effect, the singer phoned the prestigous director Mervyn LeRoy,[3] whom he had met by chance on a train trip several months earlier. They recorded and shot the film in two days in May 1945; then in August, several special broadcasts aired to celebrate the Allied victory in Europe provided Sinatra with the perfect occasion to introduce the song in public, and he recorded it later in the month for Columbia.

Sinatra featured the song many times on his *Old Gold* show, particularly between the autumns of 1945 and 1947; in the Academy Awards ceremony of March 1946, both Sinatra and LeRoy received special Oscars for the film—the first for both men. Seen today, the film is charmingly naive, especially in light of Sinatra's future associations. But it does have a undeniable potency thanks to Sinatra's ability to make anything

---

3. Mervyn LeRoy later claimed that Sinatra approached him with the idea, and "after I played the record a few times, I became very excited about it." This must have been a test transcription, because Sinatra's Columbia disc of "The House I Live In" was waxed several months after the picture was finished.

believable when he sings, especially ideas that we know to be true. It isn't so much the speech that Sinatra gives that's so effective but rather the fact of his giving it. The ideas Maltz touched upon in his screenplay anticipate Edward R. Murrow's famous report on Senator Joseph McCarthy in 1954: "We cannot defend freedom abroad by deserting it at home." Coincidentally, Sinatra later told Murrow in a CBS TV interview that his Oscar for *The House I Live In* meant even more to him than the one he subsequently won for *From Here to Eternity*.

By the time the "150 years" mentioned in the song had grown to "200 years," Sinatra had returned to the song on numerous occasions, most famously in his *Main Event* concert of 1974. However, the two most interesting revivals of "House" correspond to subsequent periods of political activity: during the early '60s era of Kennedy and Camelot for his patriotic LP *America, I Hear You Singing* and, understatedly, in support of the Reagan regime at a concert to commemorate the centennial of the Statue of Liberty ("the lady in the harbor") in 1986. In these later renditions, the "House" has grown a bit out of proportion, and Sinatra has perhaps gotten too far away from the simple sincerity of the 1945 readings.

The original Sinatra-Stordahl treatment of "The House I Live In," as documented by Columbia and RKO, remains a powerful piece of singing. It is a model of drama and timing, with Sinatra intimately involved with the big things and the small, the laughter and the tears; even the pauses carry precisely the proper amounts of weight and wait. The piece ends, fittingly, with a suggestion of "America the Beautiful" in the coda and remains an ardent entreaty for ethnic and religious equality. "The House I Live In" exemplifies that momentary instant of postwar optimism when the world thought that both good music and good politics might actually be in the cards.

Sinatra recorded another comment on racial politics in August 1946, "Lost in the Stars," which Tony Bennett has since pegged as "a song about apartheid." It's not known how he came upon this number from a show that didn't open until three years later. According to Weill's biographer, Ronald Sanders, Weill and Anderson didn't even conceive of the song or the show *Lost in the Stars* (which opened in 1949) until the end of 1947.

However Sinatra happened upon the tune, "Stars" immediately became another cornerstone of his platform of progressive social and musical ideology. Drawing on metaphors alluding to African folklore, Anderson's text amounts to a prayer to a god who is less omnipotent than impotent. Musically it amounts to a most unassuming concert piece: it clocks in safely at 3:13 (although an AFRS radio version from three months later adds another twenty-five seconds), and Sinatra's vocal, which follows a fourteen-second intro, is altogether gentle (belt-free) and even danceable.

The 1963 *Concert Sinatra* version has considerably more teeth to it, proclaiming a more compelling sense of the frustration alluded to in the libretto, which again seems perfectly appropriate to the political background of the '60s. Not only is Sinatra himself more enraged and less forgiving in the remake, but Nelson Riddle's orchestration retains all the strengths of Stordahl's original while at the same time improving on them. The superlong introduction portrays outerspace activity more vividly, while the soft, then loud flutey fanfare at the finish more spectacularly animates "little stars" and then "big stars." Anderson and Sinatra depict inhumanity and persecution in another place in order to show that it can happen here. The text may refer to the mythological vocabulary of another continent even as the music uses interstellar imagery, but the shock value of "Lost in the Stars" hits us right at home.

And then there's the granddaddy of all Sinatra concert works, Rodgers and Hammerstein's 1945 "Soliloquy." Supposedly introduced late in the rehearsals of *Carousel*, it took Hammerstein two weeks to perfect the poem, which was summarily set to music by Rodgers within two hours. In 1989, Sinatra said of the piece, "I just [wish] more performers would do it. If they [only] had the guts, they've got the talent [and] big voices, but nobody does that." Manie Sachs indulged Sinatra in giving him two sessions in April and May 1946 to attempt the eight-minute work, which they broke into two halves for the A and B sides of a twelve-inch 78—dividing it conveniently after the line, "My kid ain't even been born yet!" The two dates resulted in two complete, issuable masters on "Soliloquy," the first of which came out only on an armed forces V-Disc release at the time, and the other pressed commercially as part of Columbia's higher-toned green label Masterworks series. Since then, CBS has reissued only the V-Disc version on LPs, waiting until 1993 to come out with the 78 version (on their *Complete Sinatra* box) again. Although both sanitize the term "virgin" from the show libretto into "wench," the somewhat gutsier April master refers to a "fat-bottomed bully" while the May take renders the bully "flat-footed"; the second reading also softens the last line from "by God" to "by gosh." (Both versions were severely edited for release on Columbia EPs.)

As everyone knows, "Soliloquy" ranks as the definitive hymn to fatherhood and paternal responsibility, although listening to lines like "You can have fun with a son / But you've got to be a father to a girl," one hopes that Hammerstein is inside the head of this one particular character rather than trumpeting a truism to all mankind, as he was wont to do. The work also exemplifies an aspect of Sinatra reveled in by his legions of followers if not as openly celebrated: after we've gotten off on Sinatra the carouser and Sinatra the tender romantic, we also want to see his serious and stoic side. No matter how many babes he beds or bottles he belts down, we tell ourselves, he's still thinking about his kids and family.

Whether or not personal growth and change are at the root of all drama, "Soliloquy" may represent virtually the only instance in musical theater or opera where the evolution actually occurs in the middle of a song. And Sinatra and Stordahl take full advantage of Rodgers' brilliant device for illustrating this idea: at the very moment where our hero postulates, "What if he . . . is a girl?" (saying the word "girl" as if it were "drug addict"), then how strange is the change from major to minor. All the musical and textual ideas of the first half are thereupon echoed, coming back in a distorted form as if to haunt us, much like the way Ellington uses recurring themes in his extended instrumental "Reminiscing in Tempo." On the 1946 record, the second half also extends the antihero's premature reverie on the subject of his girl child by adding a passage ("when I have a daughter . . .") that appears on the original cast album and on Sinatra versions early and late; he omitted it from the otherwise definitive *Concert Sinatra* version.

Between 1946 and 1963, Sinatra is said to have made at least two further attempts at "Soliloquy" (apart from two known radio readings), neither of which got off the ground. In 1955, Sinatra was cast as the lead in the movie version of *Carousel*, and devoted at least several documented sessions to pre-recording the score in both Los Angeles and Boothbay Maine, where the picture was to be shot on location. According to legend, Sinatra walked off the set when he learned that Twentieth Century Fox expected him to film each scene twice (for different screen ratios, i.e., Cinemascope). Another version claims Sinatra beat it rather than being holed up in Maine for a whole summer. But it seems more likely that the singer left because of Rodgers and Hammerstein themselves, who doubtlessly considered Sinatra too hip and too real to fit into one of their productions.

A reading of the score's biggest ballad, "If I Loved You," with Sinatra singing the verse as a patter duet with Shirley Jones and the chorus in solo, survives. Several takes at "Soliloquy" have been listed in at least one discography, although no one seems to have heard any of them. It was a shame, because Sinatra would have made the perfect good-bad guy lead that the story demands, with far greater depth than the cardboard Gordon MacRae, who wound up with the part and the song.

Earlier that same year, Sinatra took another hack at "Soliloquy" for Capitol Records in the company of Richard Jones, the former Dorsey arranger who had ghosted on several occasions for Stordahl. Jones had also played piano at Sinatra's second wedding and had since graduated to the head of classical A&R (and producer-arranger for Jackie Gleason) for Capitol. "Frank wanted to give him a job," said Bill Miller, "and he [let Jones arrange] 'Soliloquy.'" Rather than biting it off in big four-minute chunks, Sinatra used modern tape techniques to tackle the piece in segments, to be spliced and edited together, movie-style. He wasn't able to finish it in one session, and before he could return to the thing, the movie deal fell through, losing him his interest in the piece at the time. It was no great loss, as Miller explained, because Jones merely "wrote a stock arrangement of 'Soliloquy.'"

"Finally," Miller concluded, "Nelson did the right one." As with the other remakes on *Concert Sinatra*, the new "Soliloquy" is slower (clocking in at about the same time but with one segment deleted), stronger, and definitive. The Reprise version is about balances: Sinatra striking the right mix of aggressiveness and tenderness, Riddle finding the border between Broadway bravura and his own, less earthbound imagination. Although the piece has been attempted by Mel Tormé, Sammy Davis, Jr. (in a surprisingly touching rendition for Decca), and Jack Nicholson (in the film *Heartburn*), Sinatra's "Soliloquy" remains the only time the work has been completely successful outside of the show that spawned it. (Sinatra put "Soliloquy" back into his "book" again beginning in the mid-'80s, and a slow, almost grandfatherly rendition from 1988 was included in the *Sinatra 80th Live In Concert*.)

Sinatra would have done well with the Earl Robinson–influenced "You've Got to Be Taught" from Rodgers and Hammerstein's *South Pacific*, especially compared to the two lackluster readings of songs he did record from that hit show. The Voice's then-diminishing "audience base," as Ross Perot would say, in the light of the nation's tightening of the noose around any ideas that did not march to the extreme right, perhaps contributed to Sinatra's decision to avoid further big-concept songs in the late '40s and '50s. His two best-known uncompleted Capitol projects were and are his attempts at two more capacious works, the above-mentioned "Soliloquy" and "Lush Life."

The most ambitious Sinatra work of the '50s that did get released was his all-instrumental album *Tone Poems of Color*. Most musicians agree that Sinatra, who conducted three albums for Capitol more than a decade after his 1945 Alec Wilder instrumental sessions, wielded the baton at least as skillfully as any of his arrangers (with the exception of Stordahl), if not more so. Sinatra had recorded this symphonic, if not strictly classical, set to cut the ribbon officially on Capitol's own recording studios in their new pancake-shaped skyscraper on Vine Street in February and March 1956.

Inspired by the poetry of Norman Sickel, a radio writer who had worked on the *Perfectly Frank* series, Sinatra commissioned original works for full orchestra from a talent pool that began with his Capitol cronies Nelson Riddle and Billy May. He also invited old friend Alec Wilder and three movie orchestrators he had worked with, Jeff Alexander, André Previn, and Elmer Bernstein. (The only Sinatra collaborator conspicuous by his absence was Axel Stordahl.) Sinatra assigned each writer a different "tonal color" and text, and then amassed nearly sixty musicians in the new Capitol facility.

"One thing that I really enjoyed was when Sinatra conducted," reminisced reedman Ted Nash. "He was so serious about that. It wasn't a throwaway thing. Everybody wants to be something they're not. A singer wants to be an arranger, and a comedian wants to be a singer, and Sinatra really wanted to do a good job conducting on that. He was just real serious and wanted that thing to turn out great." About a year before his next and last instrumental album, Sinatra concurred: "Do you know what I really am? A frustrated conductor!" (He said at that time that he wanted to commission Riddle to compose "a complete concerto for Spanish guitar" for himself to conduct, but that set apparently became his 1962 *Frank Sinatra Conducts Music from Pictures and Plays*.)

Eleanor Slatkin remembers that on two of the four sessions for *Tone Poems*, concertmaster Felix Slatkin "was damn near conducting [the strings] from his chair, but Frank was so gifted musically that he could bring it all off. Felix kept his group in shape very well." Nash added, "But in the woodwinds we were really concentrating with Frank and working hard to get everything just right." Said Harry Klee, "Frank was a wonderful conductor. That's the first I ever knew that he could conduct." "He surprised everybody," added Bill Miller. "We knew he couldn't read, but he knows when the notes go up or down. He knows about 'pianissimo,' 'piano-F,' he knows what all that means. He's pretty fearless. He did all right!"

Most of the writers, particularly the swing-oriented Riddle and May, stepped outside of their characteristic styles to tackle their *Tone Poems* colors. However, the somber strings and heavy mood of "Green" automatically announced the presence of Gordon Jenkins. Even the one-finger piano solo that opens the piece—actually played by Miller—simulates Jenkins' own hunt-and-peck keyboard style. Although Sinatra had previously sung several of the arranger-composer's pop song hits, such as "San Fernando Valley," on the *Vimms* show, the uneasy "Green" represented the first time Sinatra ordered an orchestration specifically from Jenkins.

"Billy May is driving, while Nelson has depth," Sinatra once said, "and with Gordon Jenkins, it's all so beautiful and simple that to me it's like being back in the womb." Sinatra had a place in his toolbox for all three, as Billy May humbly elaborated: "Frank would more or less pick Gordon Jenkins if he wanted to do something sentimental with strings, and then he would get either myself or Nelson—mostly Nelson—to do just the nuts and bolts stuff."

Although all three of Sinatra's central Capitol collaborators had established themselves with Nat King Cole before starting to work with Ol' Blue Eyes, each took a different route to attracting his attention. Riddle would spend a lifetime making other artists look good, Billy May proved himself a hit-making bandleader in his own name, and Gordon Jenkins was that rara avis, an equally successful songwriter and arranger—and, in another guise, an administrator and executive. Sinatra had first met Jenkins during one of his early visits to the West Coast with Tommy Dorsey and later said that after hearing the six sides Jenkins had scored for Judy Garland in 1946, "I always dreamed about him doing some work for me."

Jenkins was born in Webster Groves, Missouri, a small town near St. Louis, on May 12, 1910, the son of a church organist who also played piano for local movie theaters, and the younger brother of a local bandleader. A Decca sleeve note later claimed that Jenkins became "a master of orchestration" because "he had learned to play practically every instrument." In 1925, Jenkins won an amateur contest in St. Louis playing his ukelele, a competition hosted and judged by Cliff "Ukelele Ike" Edwards himself. Still in his teens, Jenkins played banjo in his brother's band at a nearby summer resort. Twenty years later, while directing music for bazooka-blowing Bob Burns' radio show, Jenkins surprised his studio musicians by playing vibraphone with a small group he drew out of the main orchestra which he called "The Suitcase Six."

Jenkins was eventually replaced in this Dixieland-style unit by the more practiced Frank Flynn, who remembered, "Hell, anybody's going to sound better because Gordon was hardly a vibes player." Likewise, he never quite become a virtuoso pianist in the traditional sense. In fact, it was the very rudimentariness of Jenkins' Muzaky, post–Eddy Duchin piano style that would later generate a series of instrumental chart hits for him. He played professionally from the age of ten, when he subbed for his father, and gigged around small-time speakeasies and saloons (including Joe Gill's band at the Hotel Chase) until he worked his way up to a spot at local radio station KMOX.

Jenkins left Missouri for the first time in 1930, with Henry Santry's orchestra. "It didn't work out," Jenkins recalled a decade later. "He didn't like me and I didn't like him, so we called it off. I was pretty close to New York, so I decided to go there. Out of seven million people I knew just one, and he didn't seem to be able to get me a job." The composer would later reflect on this first New York experience in his 1945 *Manhattan Tower*. When Jenkins came down with influenza, he decided to return home to Webster Groves. There, the young man took a job at the local Fox Theatre and got the opportunity to write original material for the acts that played, along with the talking pictures. He married Nancy Harkey, his high school sweetheart, in 1931.

The following year Jenkins landed a major break when he got the chance to fill in for Isham Jones' ailing pianist while the famed band-leader was playing the Coronado Hotel in St. Louis. Not long after the band had returned to New York, Jones sent for Jenkins. A legendary arranger and pioneer of the modern dance band format, Jones was a milestone man in serious popular music and a worthy role model not only for Jenkins but for protégés as diverse as Woody Herman and Victor Young. A fantastically successful songwriter, Jones would write at least three songs that would be recorded by Sinatra—"Swinging Down the Lane" (on *Swingin' Lovers*), "It Had to Be You" (on *Trilogy: The Past*), and "The One I Love" in the company of Gordon Jenkins (as well as with Dorsey and Sy Oliver). Jenkins seems to have only played briefly with Jones, never turning up on any of the band's hundreds of Victor record-ings; it's not known how many numbers he arranged for the band at this time.

In later years, Jenkins credited both Jones and Victor Young, who had already left Jones' sphere to begin his own series of dance-band record-ings in 1931, as his primary inspirations. "I was fortunate enough to meet Victor when I was twenty-two years old," he recalled, explaining that Young attended a Jones recording session and "heard something" in one of the younger man's orchestrations "that attracted him. . . . Well, he asked me if I would take a walk with him, so we went for a three-hour walk in Lincoln Park in Chicago, and he talked to me about music and what a chance I had to be a success—and some of the things I'd done wrong on the record date, some of the things I'd done right. He'd never seen me before, and he took three hours to teach me things that you don't know when you're twenty-two: when to let the singer sing, when to fill in, and so forth. I think I learned more in that afternoon than you could learn at college about practical writing. Something like that keeps you going a long time. When I got home, I was ten feet off the ground." For his part, Isham Jones gave many of the younger man's early songs their all-important first hearings.

In 1936, around the time that Jones was ready to retire and disband, Jenkins was surprised to receive an unlikely offer to direct the pit orchestra for a Broadway revue, *On with the Show,* starring Bea Lillie. He grew bored with conducting the same music the same way every night ("I even offered to rearrange the music free of charge") and jumped at the chance to join the music staff at Paramount Pictures. However, after anonymously scoring *The Big Broadcast of 1937, Artists and Models, Blossoms on Broadway* ("which I've been living down for several years," he later said), *College Swing,* and others, he discovered he liked Hollywood even less than Broadway. "There are always five relatives doing a job one could do," he complained, "and you have to please a bunch of guys who don't know *Madame Butterfly* from 'Chopsticks.'" After an altercation with an ego-tripping mogul, Jenkins departed.

He finally came into his own in radio and then recordings. Gogo Delys, a singer he had worked with in New York, married one of the heads of NBC's West Coast operation and recommended Jenkins. Within a short while he was in charge of all musical direction on all Los Angeles broadcasts, giving Skitch Henderson, among others, his first spot as a conductor. In the early '40s, he began working as sort of a second-string John Scott Trotter for Decca—or, as Billy May would say, "a nuts and bolts" arranger. In 1945 he officially joined the label's staff as a full-time conductor and, eventually, musical director.

Throughout the '40s, Jenkins' stock steadily rose as a songwriter, record producer, arranger-conductor for vocalists (on records and radio), and a recording name in his own right, all four careers being heavily interrelated. Jenkins first established himself as a distinctive orchestral stylist while serving as musical director for crooner Dick Haymes in his glory years, both at Decca and on the radio. With Sy Oliver, Jenkins was also the only arranger to work with Billie Holiday, Ella Fitzgerald, Louis Armstrong, and Sinatra. (Oliver also worked with Crosby; Jenkins with Jolson and Judy Garland.) At one point in the late '40s, between recordings by Gordon Jenkins and his orchestra (including the mega-hits "Maybe You'll Be There"—later remade with Sinatra—"Again," and "Don't Cry Joe") and backings for various Decca pop singers, no less than five of the nation's top ten singles were Jenkins productions.

As a composer, Jenkins cracked the *Hit Parade* with two early winners for both himself and lyricist Johnny Mercer: "You Have Taken My

Heart" (1933) and "When a Woman Loves a Man" (1934), as well as Benny Goodman's and Woody Herman's theme songs, "Goodbye" (1935) and "Blue Prelude" (1933). Jenkins was also well known for a number of Americana pieces that reflected various moods of the country at war and after—both nostalgic, as in "Homesick, That's All" (1945) and "P. S. I Love You" (written in 1934 but more successfully revived in 1946, also with a killer lyric by Mercer), and upbeat, as in "San Fernando Valley" (1943), the latter inspired by the area where he and his wife raised their three children. Over the years, Sinatra recorded at least six Jenkins pieces (not even counting "San Fernando Valley," done on the radio, and *The Future*) both with and without their creator at the podium, including "Homesick," "P. S. I Love You," "Goodbye," "This Is All I Ask," "How Old Am I?," and "I Loved Her."

In terms of his relationship with his musicians, Jenkins was entirely different from Sinatra's other primary musical directors. They did not consider him one of their own like Riddle, a cutup like May, or a saint like Stordahl. Most sidemen remember Jenkins as being at least a little bit uptight, although engineer Lee Hirschberg, who saw a different side of Jenkins from his seat in the engineering booth, felt that this was because Jenkins, even after all those years and all those hits, tended to get "a little bit nervous about being in the studio. . . .But he was a really incredible guy. I mean, just an amazing guy!" Skeets Herfurt described him as being "not at all outgoing. He was a very quiet man, but very talented."

Jenkins may well have developed the mask he wore in public—serious, sophisticated, and slightly sour—as a way of covering his homespun Midwest background. Joel Herron, composer of "I'm a Fool to Want You," which Sinatra remade with Jenkins, said that the conductor was about as merry as "Oxford dons walking around in England, with caps and gowns" and long faces. Even Skitch Henderson, who was both a fan and a friend of Jenkins, characterized him with the single word "dour" and said, "I was always apprehensive of him," adding for emphasis, "Always. Always!" The nicest compliment that most musicians care to pay Jenkins was that he was, as Frank Flynn put it, "a real gentleman."

Yet there were other circumstances in which Jenkins' co-workers saw quite a different side of him. "I always saw Gordie as like a small-town kid," recalled dancer Dante DiPaolo, referring to Jenkins' zeal for his hobbies—carpentry and photography. "He had those kinds of qualities." DiPaolo worked with Jenkins extensively in Las Vegas, where Jenkins composed and conducted the music for a series of big casino nightclub revues, most notably at the Tropicana (boomtown's answer to the

Copacabana; their shows were staged by the same Monte Proser). DiPaolo added, "I knew him as a very fun guy. He just wanted to hang out with the younger people and have fun!"

And Vegas wasn't the only place where Jenkins let his hair down.[4] Few of his professional associates realize that he was an enormous fan of traditional jazz (he even worked a Dixieland blues into his otherwise distinctly unbluesy opus *The Letter*), and Louis Armstrong in particular. According to drummer and friend Johnny Blowers, "Gordon was a real jazz-crazy guy. He insisted on using jazz guys on all his dates." For example, his favorite drummers on the West and East coasts, Nick Fatool and Blowers, respectively, both had very solid groundings in Dixie and swing.

Jenkins and his longtime colleague Milt Gabler conceived the idea of presenting Armstrong like a mainstream pop singer, complete with full orchestra and choir. "Gordon stood up on his little podium," as Gabler recalled the session, "so that all the performers could see him conduct. But before he gave a downbeat, Gordon made a speech about how much he loved Louis and how this was the greatest moment in his life. And then he cried."

Just as with his personality, opinions vary so widely regarding Jenkins' talent as an orchestrator that it's almost impossible to get a consensus. Bill Miller named Jenkins his least favorite arranger: "I didn't like his writing at all; his stuff was so dull and boring. The piano parts were so simple that they were terrible!" "He was a little more old-fashioned" than Riddle and May, Dick Nash explained. "He didn't have the knowledge of the newer harmonies that would work and fit, like the flat ninths and raised ninths, and flat fives, and so forth. He didn't utilize a lot of the new technology, so therefore it was kind of old hat and boring."

Milt Bernhart elaborated: "I'm not a big fan of Gordon Jenkins, and everybody who ever wrote an arrangement felt the same way. Nelson wouldn't bum-rap him, and neither would Billy May, but if they were pressed, they would say, 'Well, Gordon doesn't really know an awful lot about harmonies and orchestration'—and he didn't. When he took somebody else's song, the harmony was right out of the lead sheet. He couldn't expand on it; he couldn't alter changes to make them prettier.

---

4. Jenkins also let his hair down as a songwriter in Vegas, as opposed to his usual high-minded musical dramas. The Capitol album *Gordon Jenkins Conducts Monte Proser's Tropicana Holiday* boasts a bevy of busty backstage babes on its cover, while the disc itself collates high points of three such revues. Jenkins's original tunes include "Sex" and "I Feel Like a New Man," which features the line, "With his head on my shoulder/He can leer at my brassiere."

Axel took everything and made it into a better piece of music! And Nelson could also do that, and so could Don Costa."

And in fact, while Riddle and May have both spoken admiringly of Jenkins, they, perhaps unintentionally, limit their praise to his many successes as a songwriter. "He was a good friend of mine and a great guy," said May. "He was a good songwriter and wrote some beautiful songs, especially 'This Is All I Ask.' I've been a fan of Gordon's for a long time. I was admiring him in the days when I was just starting out, when he was writing for Isham Jones." Riddle said he was "crazy about" the song "Goodbye," which he orchestrated for Sinatra when the composer was unavailable, and he added that he "admired Gordon so much for having written it." Composer Joel Herron, although critical of the Sinatra-Jenkins albums, also said, "I think the most important thing that he wrote was 'Goodbye.' I played it at my wife's funeral, and better than that I can't say."

Miller found Jenkins' technical inadequacies extremely frustrating, to say the least. "He would write, for example, a D-minor-seventh, but he would have an F chord written or play an F triad and put a D in the bass. Why not just write 'D-minor-seventh'? He would never just voice it the way it's supposed to be voiced. And some of his voicings in the reeds were militaristic sometimes, with oboe and bassoon. Why? They just didn't mesh."

Opinion is similarly divided as to Jenkins' prowess as a conductor. In his baton-waving, he had a big strike against him even before he made it onto the podium in that he was left-handed. (In the end of his libretto for *The Future*, Jenkins refers to himself as "Lefty.") "He was very hard to follow," said violinist Paul Shure, "because he wasn't a lefty who beat [time] the correct way—he beat backwards! So if you were on the wrong side of him and you weren't prepared for it, it was very hard to follow."

Yet Lee Hirschberg feels that Jenkins' musical smarts more than compensated for his southpaw status. He could "always conduct. I've never seen anybody command as much respect on a podium as Gordon did. He had an incredible sense of pitch. He could sit there with an orchestra of thirty or forty people and look at someone and say, 'You're out of tune. You better tune up.' He was amazing that way." Nick Fatool agrees: when asked if Jenkins was difficult to follow, the drummer answered, "No, I never found that. Not for me. But maybe the violins or somebody [would feel differently], but hell, [I thought] Gordon was a great conductor." Vincent Falcone added, "[Frank] told me that even though Gordon conducted with his left hand, he always said, 'Pay attention to this guy!'"

The musicians who complained about Jenkins' technical shortcomings have been too busy being trees to get a proper perspective on the forest. What attracted both Sinatra and the public at large to Jenkins was his song-writer's sense of both melody and drama. And though Jenkins' writing may be shallow and his harmonic abilities pale in comparison with Riddle's, his surfaces are inevitably precisely pertinent to what Sinatra is singing over them—and often quite beautiful in themselves.

Sinatra's fondness for Jenkins' work—and as Nick Fatool and others have testified, "Frank sure loved Gordon"—proves Raymond Chandler's observation that "all us tough guys are hopeless sentimentalists at heart." When pressed to explain why Sinatra seemed to think so highly of Jenkins, even Bill Miller finally admitted, "There's a certain square-ness about Frank; I say that affectionately. He has an old-fashioned side, and Gordon Jenkins represents that. As a singer he doesn't hear the har-monies the way we would. He hears those high singing strings—that was Gordon's gimmick." Indeed, Jenkins depends so heavily on the strings that his orchestrations sound like nothing without them—as Sinatra learned when he misguidedly attempted "September of My Years" and, even worse, "It Was a Very Good Year" with the stradless Basie band in *At the Sands* in 1966.

Paradoxically, Jenkins' biggest booster is the youngest and most mod-ern musician ever to work in Sinatra's inner circle, pianist and conductor Vinnie Falcone. Another piano player, Lou Levy, said Jenkins' style "was emotional more than it was harmonic," and in response Falcone asked, "And isn't that what it's about?" He elaborated: "Gordon attacked the strings dif-ferently from the way many arrangers do in that he would double certain voices and stack them. So when he did one of those sweeping things, you had several octaves of the same sound coming down.

"It's always been a dream for me to develop a style so that no matter what you do, it's always identifiable," Falcone continued. "And I have to say that Gordon achieved that. When you hear George Shearing, you know it's George Shearing; it's the same for Art Tatum or Miles Davis. You can't say that for everybody, only for very, very, very few people. You really can't say that unequivocally for Don Costa, who was one of the greatest that ever lived. Not that this diminishes Don's talent, but it cer-tainly is a credit to Gordon that he developed those little signature things so that when you hear his arrangements, you just know it's Gordon Jenkins."

As we shall see, Sinatra's work with Jenkins runs to two opposite extremes, both contingent on Lefty's work as a songwriter and as an orchestrator. On one level, Sinatra saw in Jenkins a potential partner in highbrow experiments, not only in a lofty Europeanization of barroom ballads but eventually in extended structures that transcend conventional song forms. On another level, Jenkins could take material from folk and even rock sources and render it relevant to Sinatra. In the immediate pre- and postretirement periods, when Sinatra was most concerned with appealing to a generation that thought Irving Berlin was a city with a wall in it, he turned to Jenkins fully as frequently as to his more loudly appointed partner in cradle-invading, Don Costa. "No one could deny," as Bernhart has confessed, "that Jenkins had a knack for getting to the heart of a certain kind of a song, especially 'It Was a Very Good Year.'"

Old-fashionedness was exactly what Sinatra and Voyle Gilmore were looking for when they assigned Jenkins the task of orchestrating *A Jolly Christmas with Frank Sinatra.* The twelve tracks on this seasonal set fairly hang from the chimney with simplicity. That's because Jenkins has chosen to wait before letting his cat of high, moaning strings out of his Santa sack. "I'll Be Home for Christmas" contains the sole discernible glimmer of the patented Jenkins string section sound, and even there it's audible only for a brief instrumental passage.

On this particular set, Jenkins employs a choir, in place of his more customary string figures, as the basic element of the background behind Sinatra. The orchestrator rarely if ever used a chorus on his vocal accompaniments, but these large vocal groups were *de rigueur* on his own records (usually the Ralph Brewster singers, who in fact perform here on *A Jolly Christmas*). All of this would indicate that Jenkins assumed that the perfect chart consisted of two major elements, either solo voice and strings or choir and strings, or, here, solo voice and choir. To use all three elements, star voice, choir, *and* strings, Jenkins seems to feel, would be too much. (Sinatra and Riddle apply the same principle in balancing the organ, strings, and orchestra on the *Strangers in the Night* album.)

Intriguingly, the most distinctive chart is the least Jenkinsy of them all: the opening "Jingle Bells" commences with the chorus cooing a jivey "Rag Mop" version of the ancient tune, over which Sinatra swings lightly and politely. But if the backings aren't as automatically, recognizably idiosyncratic, they help us focus all the more on how well the star singer does even without a supporting cast. On "The Christmas Song," "Mistletoe and Holly," "The First Noel," and others, Sinatra seems to be reaching back to the innocent sound he used on his first Christmas concept set, done a decade earlier with Axel Stordahl. On others, such as the sacred works "Hark the Herald Angels Sing," "Adeste Fidelis" (earlier he had even attempted "The Lord's Prayer" and Schubert's "Ave Maria" on

various broadcasts), Sinatra sounds much more authoritative and majestic in his maturity.

Whether he's tossing off references to "baby" or "Jack" with Billy
May or ever so sincerely intoning "Merry Christmas" at the end of
Sammy Cahn's "Christmas Waltz," Sinatra is never less than convincing.
He even seems to have talked himself into believing that it was really
Christmas—after the third and final date, Sinatra traded in his "ring-a-
ding ding" for a "ho! ho! ho!" when he threw a Christmas party for the
musicians, chorus, and engineers in the middle of July.

Jenkins later recalled that there was some trepidation about whether
or not the atmosphere would be quite so jovial. The conductor was a
taskmaster who liked to have things go his way. As Nick Fatool put it, "All
he wanted you to do was just play what he wrote, and don't add anything
to it." And the singer was well known for not liking to be bossed around,
to put it mildly. "The first time we worked together, a hundred people
showed up because they thought it was going to be a free-for-all,"
Jenkins reminisced.[5] "He had a reputation of being tough to work with,
and I also have a reputation for not holding back. So the studio was just
jammed [with people] waiting for the fight to start. And we never did
have any fight, not ever. We have never had a cross word."

Not that everything was a Doris Day movie: Jenkins exchanged several cross words with Felix and Eleanor Slatkin. Like most conductors,
Jenkins had his own concertmasters whom he liked to use—usually
Dave Frisina—and relented only reluctantly when Sinatra insisted on
using his own preferred first violin and first cello. "He was told he *had* to
use me, and he didn't like it at all," said Eleanor Slatkin, who feels that
Jenkins, like Stordahl, "didn't like women in the orchestra."

If Jenkins, no less than Sinatra, toned down his trademarks for *Jolly
Christmas*, they appear in spades on *Where Are You*, released around the
same time as the *Christmas* set, although actually recorded several
months previously, and even more promisingly on the 1959 *No One
Cares*. "Just Friends" contains Jenkins' famous spiraling strings motif,
which aurally suggests a carpet being rolled open *up* a flight of stairs.
The device is well known to anyone familiar with either of Sinatra and
Jenkins' two 1965 meetings, the *September of My Years* album and
Jenkins' segment of the *Man and His Music* TV special.

On all four of his classic downbeat ballad albums from 1955 to 1959
(not counting the more optimistic *Close to You*), Sinatra included one

5. Most of the quotes from Gordon Jenkins in this chapter are from a radio interview
with deejay (and game show host) Wink Martindale, probably done in the late '70s.

blues-tinged song: "Mood Indigo" on *Wee Small Hours*, "Blues in the Night" on *Only the Lonely*, "Baby, Won't You Please Come Home?" on *Where Are You*, and "Stormy Weather" on *No One Cares*. On each of the Jenkins Capitol sets he also made a point of doing at least one classically derived number: "I Think of You" (via Rachmaninoff) on *Where Are You* and "None but the Lonely Heart" (from Tchaikovsky) on *No One Cares*. The twenty-four tracks on the two sets—among them Isham Jones' "The One I Love (Belongs to Somebody Else)," originally dropped from *No One Cares* because early stereo albums had considerably shorter playing times, but restored to the 1991 CD edition—also encompass material from such lofty sources as Alec Wilder (two four-word "where" question songs, "Where Is the One?" and the dirge "Where Do You Go?"), Leonard Bernstein ("Lonely Town"), and "Autumn Leaves," a French *chanson* describing dead plants.

Indeed, Sinatra seems to have considered Jenkins the perfect partner with whom to reexamine the European string textures of his work with Axel Stordahl, and at least half of the songs on these two sets are remakes from the Columbia period. "If you're going to make comparisons, which are always dangerous, you could compare Gordon to Axel," Skitch Henderson observed. "Because it was that kind of wonderfully romantic style of writing which fitted Frank's voice, I felt, a great deal." The depressing "Where Do You Go?" immediately moves beyond the romantic and into the funereal; a hymn for the spiritually bankrupt, it would make a perfect soundtrack for a public-service film designed to document the plight of the homeless.

Where are You and *No One Cares* were clearly inspired by the success of *Love Is the Thing* (and, to a lesser extent, the Jenkins–Judy Garland collaboration, *Alone*), wherein Jenkins wrapped Nat Cole with a heavy blanket of violins in a program of vaguely upbeat (in mood if not tempo) love songs. Recorded in October 1956 in the new stereo process, *Love Is the Thing* zoomed to number one on the pop album charts, becoming Cole's biggest selling LP in his lifetime. "Ghost of a Chance" contains a passage where the strings seem to verbalize the words "I know I must," which Sinatra finishes with "I'm dreaming," much the same way Jenkins had the strings "sing" the humming phrases of "Paradise" on the second Cole-Jenkins album, *The Very Thought of You* (1958). ("Don't Wait Too Long" on *September of My Years* similarly contains a chorus in which a one-finger piano solo takes the words out of Sinatra's mouth.) The opening title track, "Where Are You," boasts Sinatra's purest and most relaxed Cole-style singing ever.

But if Sinatra wanted Jenkins' sumptuous strings for his first foray into stereo, the resemblances to the Cole albums end there. Sinatra-Jenkins was automatically a deeper, more personal experience than Cole-Jenkins, Sinatra insisting on offering more than love songs; these were ballads with a grabbing angle and a story to them. And Cole paid attention. The King's final album with Jenkins, *Where Did Every One Go?* in 1961, had one hell of a more interesting tale to tell.

Jenkins relies on strings so heavily that he disavows brass and reeds entirely, offering only three low-blowing French horns (heard to great effect on "There's No You"), a handful of woodwinds, and a barely audible rhythm section (with Fatool usually playing brushes) to counteract the fiddles. "Jenkins did do some good writing for woodwinds," said reedman Harry Klee, "but he actually just used the woodwinds as a cushion under the strings."

Jenkins almost never does anything to attract attention to his arrangements. The French horns that function as foghorns at the start of "I Cover the Waterfront" and the countermelody behind The Voice on "Where Is the One?" are exceptions. Dave Frisina, concertmaster for the Los Angeles Philharmonic and Jenkins' preferred first violinist for many years, said of the arranger, "Gordon wrote beautifully for strings. He wrote very simply, and he couldn't get complicated. He liked to have a lot of violins playing the melody, and when he did, I tell you, it sounded oh so beautiful."

If he's not as technically interesting as Riddle or May, Jenkins brings out some of Sinatra's most compassionate performances ever, both on the slightly more varied *Where Are You* and the all-downer *No One Cares*, both of which use Billie Holiday–style crawl tempos. Sinatra continues to sing very tightly behind the beat, temporarily relaxing his grip on it as he comes out of the bridge on "Waterfront" as if to suggest even greater resignation.

On "Laura," he uses a much fuller, juicier voice that fills both stereo channels. Many of the other twenty-three tracks on these two sets find him employing a much thinner, more emotionally charged vocal palette, signifying extremes he could not have reached in the Stordahl era. He could never have made the shadows steal across a lonely room, as in "I Think of You," so vividly before, and throughout much of *No One Cares*, in particular, Sinatra seems to be on the verge of real tears.

Even Jenkins' detractors are forced to admit that the two albums have undeniable highlights. "I Can't Get Started" and the remake of "Why Try to Change Me Now" make for perfect Sinatra anthems (no less than "My Way"), in particular the former, with its theme of brash bravura chopped down to size. "Started" also anticipates the 1981 Jenkins-

Sinatra "Thanks for the Memory" with its new set of lyrics (probably by Sammy Cahn), Sinatra being the only singer truly capable of singing (from the 1936 original), "All the papers, where I led the news / With my capers . . ." and really meaning it.

Both collaborators seem to have considered Leonard Bernstein's "Lonely Town" the high point of *Where Are You*. By 1956, Sinatra had wanted to do the song for more than ten years; in fact, that was how Metro-Goldwyn-Mayer was able to entice him (along with Gene Kelly) back into sailor suits for the 1949 film *On the Town*. According to lyricist Betty Comden, it was decided to cut the number from the picture because Sinatra's role was considered the second-string love story, and it wouldn't do to assign him the most powerful ballad. "The last day of shooting came, and they said, 'That's a wrap!' He said, 'Well, where's my song? When do I do "Lonely Town?"' And they just said to him, 'It's out. You're not doing it.' And he was very, very angry."

The *Where Are You* reading more than makes up for the injustices done to both Sinatra and Bernstein by MGM (namely, denying one the chance to sing the other). Most of "Lonely Town" uses especially minimal backing to—for once—call attention to Sinatra's tremolo, making him sound all the more nervous and lonely as well as illustrating emptiness, until the fitting phrase "unless there's love," at which the full string section enters to underscore the alternative to loneliness. Asked to name his favorite Sinatra performance, Jenkins responded, "For many years, [Frank's] and my favorite were the same. He thought that 'Lonely Town' was the best record he ever made, and I did, too. Now I think it would be a toss-up for me between 'Lonely Town,' 'Laura,' and 'Send in the Clowns.' 'Lonely Town' has such a feel to it: the orchestration, the way he sings it . . . so well!"

When Jenkins complimented "the orchestration" of "Lonely Town," he wasn't merely patting himself on the back: one of the key components of this particular chart, its distinctive French horn introduction (probably played by Vince DeRosa), had been devised by the singer himself. "I had a recording of a piece of symphonic music, I can't think of the name of it," Sinatra told Sid Mark in 1984, which started him thinking about "the beginning of 'New York, New York'"—the opening number of *On the Town*, which is briefly reprised in the intro to "Lonely Town"—"and Gordon liked [the idea], obviously, and used it, and it worked out very well, too." Mr. Maestro enthusiastically endorsed Sinatra's idea for the opening, not least because, as French hornist John Cave recalled, "Gordon Jenkins was a horn maniac. He just loved horn! He had [us] wall to wall all the time. He always used it almost like a solo instrument: he always had lots of solos."

Other elements of the "Lonely Town" orchestration came exclusively from the arranger's own machinations. As he put it, "I got carried away and put in a few free bars of 'Never Leave Me' from his extended work *Manhattan Tower* at the end." While Jenkins speaks of inserting a royalty-free excerpt from this tune in "Lonely Town," the quote is heard for less than two seconds here. "Never Leave Me" turns up much more prominently in Jenkins' arrangement of "Chloe" for Louis Armstrong and is so similar to his basic, much-used major-minor "moaning" motif that we can say it's used extensively in the *September of My Years* and *She Shot Me Down* albums.

Sinatra's only full-orchestra reading of "I'll Never Smile Again" (the only commercial version not to use the 1940 vocal group and celesta treatment) nearly became a major train wreck at the *No One Cares* sessions. One passage "goes from B-flat to D," recalls Bill Miller. "But Gord went right up to an F-seventh, real high. It was *terrible!* It had to be a D chord in there. It *had* to be. I played it down. I asked Frank what to do, and he said, 'Oh, well, shit, have Nelson change it.' I called Nelson, and he rewrote the four bars. And of course he didn't sound like Gordon Jenkins. When you hear that arrangement, when it comes to going up to the D chord, you can tell it's Nelson, that it was an insert. I remember that vividly."

"Cottage for Sale" builds down to a beautifully conceived un-climax of Jolsonesque basement-low pedal notes. And this is a minority opinion, not shared by fellow Frankophiles or the song's composer, but Sinatra turns in a much more moving "I'm a Fool to Want You" (originally recorded six years earlier) the second time around, dropping the melodramatic choir and adding more real drama with an especially poignant extra outchorus. Lastly, Clarence Williams' blues song "Baby, Won't You Please Come Home," with the Chairman *kvelling* as if unable to resist basking in his own radiance, makes for a wonderfully warm and witty way to end a Sinatra album.

Sinatra had first turned to Jenkins, as we have seen, because he was afraid of relying too much on Riddle—or any single arranger. This also led him to feel, as Frank Military recalled, that "something was happening to his voice. So we did the sessions for *Where Are You,* and they were magnificent. When we finished the last cut on the album, Frank said, 'Let's get a copy, we'll take it up to the house.' So we went up to his place and played the acetate. It was absolutely fabulous. We listened to the whole thing. He turned to me and said, 'I thought for a minute I was losing my voice.' I said, 'God, there's no indication of that here. It's the most magnificent album I've heard for a long time.'"

Sinatra was also delighted with the sales of *Where Are You*, which reached number three in *Billboard*, not far behind *Love Is the Thing*, and began planning an even heavier downer set as a follow-up. This eventually became the 1958 *Only the Lonely*, and even after Jenkins informed Sinatra that he was too busy in Las Vegas to undertake the project, Sinatra retained Jenkins' most celebrated composition, "Goodbye." In 1959, Sinatra and Jenkins reteamed for the above-discussed *No One Cares*, and then in January 1962, Sinatra had a whole other idea in mind when he planned his first set with Jenkins on Reprise.

In analyzing Sinatra's career in hindsight, like a team of Monday morning quarterbacks, we can fairly accurately reconstruct his decisions to do certain records. The Billy May albums, *I Remember Tommy*, the Basie series, for instance, all seem like natural and obvious ideas that Sinatra almost could not have helped thinking of. In a million years, however, we'll never be able to figure out—and the Old Man himself has doubtless forgotten—how he conceived of the *Come Waltz with Me* album, which was released as *All Alone*, a set of archaic ballads, primarily from the teens and twenties, rendered in waltz time.

Come Fly with Me and *Swing Along with Me / Sinatra Swings* contain the kind of loopy exotica that appealed to Sinatra's and May's senses of rhythm and humor. Likewise, one senses that *All Alone* gave Sinatra and Jenkins a chance to address the stoic sides of their natures through a genre of music that had been a crucial part of each man's early artistic evolution. The Sinatra-Jenkins combination began on *Where Are You* and *No One Cares* with the works of largely eclectic highbrows, like Bernstein, Wilder, and Vernon Duke. It's key, then, that none of the nine antiquities on *All Alone* were written by the intelligentsia of Tin Pan Alley who were writing waltzes at the time: no Kern, no Youmans, no Rodgers. Rather, Sinatra and Jenkins have chosen to confront a more basic, even atavistic kind of ur-pop tune[6]—such as "Are You Lonesome Tonight?," which, although in 1960 it provided the Pelvis with his most memorable ballad, is actually so old it was originally published as "Are You Lonesome To-night?" The set also includes no less than five numbers from that master of playing a simple melody, Irving Berlin (including "What'll I Do," "When I Lost You," and "Remember").

6. The list includes "Charmaine," which, in 1926, American songwriter Lew Pollack based on a 1913 waltz by Hungarian composer Erno Rapee. The piece was popularized in the film *What Price Glory* and then revived and re-revived over the years in pop recordings by Harry James, Billy May (one of the big hits that made him a reluctant bandleader), Mantovani, and, in 1951, Gordon Jenkins and his orchestra, with a vocal by the Bingish Bob Carroll.

Given the circumstances behind *Swing Along with Me,* one would assume that similar legal entanglements with Capitol Records—or fear of them—would have pressured the singer to retitle *Come Waltz with Me,* as yet unreleased, as *All Alone,* even after he had gone to the trouble of commissioning a new title track from Cahn and Van Heusen. Yet it could just as easily be that when Sinatra heard the playbacks on "Come Waltz with Me," he decided that the track—with its comparatively bright intro and slightly faster tempo—just didn't fit in with the rest of the album. He also may have felt that using the word "waltz" in the title gives away the whole show, whereas the less musically descriptive "All Alone" affords more of an air of mystery and romance to the interconnecting factor among these (now) eleven songs.

Far from being stillborn, the song "Come Waltz with Me" (the only time Sinatra actually deleted a specially written title track) was eventually introduced by Steve Lawrence. "[Arranger] Sid Feller and I were doing an album of waltzes at the time," said Lawrence, "and Sid evidently met with Sammy [Cahn] and told him we were doing some waltzes. So Sammy said, 'I got a great song.'" Taking the cue, Lawrence and Feller appropriately titled their album *Come Waltz with Me* (which, like Jo Stafford's more swinging *Do I Hear a Waltz?,* isn't nearly as magisterial as the Sinatra-Jenkins album). When the 1992 CD of *All Alone,* following an earlier Japanese LP edition, at last restored the missing track, it underscored the correctness of Sinatra's original decision to omit it. Although we're glad to hear it, it just doesn't fit: the original album begins superbly with "All Alone" and concludes with "The Song Is Ended," a perfect closer if ever there was one.

Another appropriate title might have been *Ruminations at Dusk,* for all of the songs are painted in the reds and yellows of a sunset. You feel as though you're rifling though faded song sheets in an old-time small-town music shop at closing time. Further, each of the nine "oldies" tunes concerns itself with an absence, so that even apart from the fact of their age, each song has a built-in factor of nostalgia and longing for a happier past. To make this concept even more real on "All Alone" and "The Song Is Ended," the deceptively uncomplicated Berlin ballads Sinatra uses to begin and end the set, Jenkins conjures up an ethereal "air" voice. Portrayed vocally by Loulie Jean Norman, Hollywood's number one "vapor voice," this incorporeal entity serves to illustrate the fantasized presence of a departed other. Which explains why the comparatively recent songs on *All Alone* don't quite fit. Sinatra had included them perhaps to show that the waltz lives on, yet the more optimistic "Girl Next Door," from 1943, cheerfully looks forward to a love affair, while Cahn and Van

Heusen's disappointingly minimal movie theme, "Indiscreet," from 1958, describes one in progress.

Still, for all the emotional unrestraint of Jenkins' "sobbing and throbbing" strings, we can't approach his work without sensing the kind of decorum that goes with buttoned shoes—a sort of starched collar correctness. Sinatra has no such reservations, however, and on many levels the central drama of the album emerges from the tension between the singer's impassioned pleading and the quaint parlor setting of the backgrounds. The third key element, the waltz factor, affects the other two, making the backdrops seem more formal and the singing even more fervent. This album appeals to Sinatra's sense of rhythm and brings out the most in him, no less than any of the swing albums. He responds to the 1-2-3, 1-2-3 time signature by remaining even further behind the beat than usual, and this, combined with the heaviest sounding voice he had yet brought to a recording session,[7] results in some of his most powerfully passionate singing. The set illustrates an observation that Jenkins once shared with Nick Fatool: "We were drinking after a record date, and Gordon said, 'Frank puts himself in the mood to sing a [particular] song.'" The drummer feels that Sinatra did an especially good job of putting himself in the mood to do these waltzes, particularly "Do You Miss Me Tonight."

One imagines that Sinatra considered *All Alone*, like the later *Francis A. & Edward K.*, at once a personal triumph and a professional disappointment. Both were great albums that racked up his smallest sales of their periods, consisting as they did of especially idiosyncratic song choices and arrangements which he almost never sang again in either concerts or television appearances. *Where Are You* and *No One Cares* charted at numbers three and two, respectively, but *All Alone* made it only to twenty-five. Apparently this was not the serious side of Sinatra that moved product.

When he returned to his comparatively more traditional "big song," as in "Ol' Man River" and "Soliloquy," a year later on *The Concert Sinatra*, the quality of the music and the quantity of the sales figures were more in check. Although Jenkins had the greater reputation for dealing with extended song structures, Riddle was by far the superior choice to handle the *Concert* set. He characteristically plays off Sinatra's gift for economy, while Jenkins elaborates on Sinatra's penchant for spectacle. Works like "Lost in the Stars" and "I Have Dreamed" are

---

7. Writer Peter Levinson, who attended the sessions for *All Alone*, recalls that "Frank looked like hell when he came in. It was if he'd just been to nine orgies. Nobody could believe that he sang as beautifully as he did on that album."

already big enough, and the last thing they need is for Jenkins to inflate them further with his emblematic grandiosity.

Jenkins and Sinatra take a simple song like "Remember" and elevate it to a concert work; Riddle and Sinatra start with an epic like "Ol' Man River" and make it intimate. The *Concert Sinatra* album succeeded as forty minutes of relatively light, albeit emotionally deep, orchestrations of very heavy songs; meanwhile, the Sinatra-Jenkins collaboration continued on its course of weighty treatments of increasingly more rudimentary material.

The next step was for Sinatra to begin taking advantage of Jenkins' sympathy for folk songs. Although Jenkins had been the most commercially successful composer of the more imposing multisong cycle format, he still was an old softie for the most basic kind of nonprofessional tune. As an A&R man for Decca, Jenkins, even before Mitch Miller, was promoting the mass-market possibilities of folk music way back when such performers meant more to readers of *The Daily Worker* than they did to those of *Variety*. When Jenkins wanted to bring the Weavers to Decca in 1949 and the top brass turned him down, he so believed in their commercial potential that he signed them to a personal contract. In other words, if the group's records didn't sell, he would have to pay them out of his own "San Fernando Valley" money. That the Weavers-Jenkins "Goodnight, Irene" sold so well that an artist as unlikely as Frank Sinatra was importuned to "cover" it,[8] offers evidence enough of what an astute judge of the market Jenkins was.

The 1965 *September of My Years* represented the fifteen-years-later union of the two top-selling purveyors of "Goodnight, Irene," Jenkins and Sinatra. Not that all of *September* qualifies as fake folkie; among the thirteen tracks you'll find three remakes of standards that Sinatra had recorded previously. Jenkins' charts of "Hello, Young Lovers" and "September Song" aren't up to Stordahl's, although the Weill song is actually more effective here than the 1946 version. That's because Sinatra now has more playing time for two of the song's very moving verses and greater capacity emotionally for conveying the meaning of the text. Besides which, as the last track on the album the 1965 version benefits from the listener's snowballing response to the previous twelve selections. For once, Jenkins compares surprisingly well with Riddle, on

8. Mitch Miller covered "Goodnight, Irene" with Sinatra, and then Jenkins turned around and did the same with the Weavers to Guy Mitchell's and Mitch Miller's "The Roving Kind." Incidentally, the original "Irene" was released as "by Gordon Jenkins with the Weavers."

a new treatment of "Last Night When We Were Young," which neither he nor The Voice has to fear will be judged harshly in comparison with the better remembered *Wee Small Hours* reading.

September signifies another double-edged conceptual musical "theme" album in both senses of the term, being a collection of songs about getting older which Sinatra has effectively cast in the simple and repetitious mode of the folk song. Each song is also atypical in its setup of the performer-audience relationship. Not one is a conventional love song sung by the protagonist to his object of desire; instead, each is a meditation on life and love as intoned inwardly by an old stud to himself. Even "September Song," originally written to be sung by the hero of *Knickerbocker Holiday* to his leading lady, has had a few pronouns altered so that Sinatra can direct it internally.

Apart from the three familiar faces mentioned above, most of the rest of the album consists of numbers that came in over Sinatra's transom when he put the word out that he was looking for September songs. Naturally, Cahn and Van Heusen had first dibs, and they supplied the track that titled the finished album, as well as "It Gets Lonely Early." Had Cahn not come up with the song "September of My Years," one wonders if Sinatra might have titled the album either *September Songs, The September Sinatra,* or perhaps *Songs for Somber Seniors,* or even *Hello, Old Lovers.* Jenkins himself was next in line, and he also got two songs in, "How Old Am I?" and "This Is All I Ask," marking the first time Sinatra recorded any of the conductor's own compositions in his company.

The rest consists of relatively new material by some of the more off-beat characters from the fringes of the songwriting community, who either submitted trunk tunes that fit the theme or hastily penned new ones they hoped Sinatra would deem suitable. These include: "The Man in the Looking Glass" by Bart "Fly Me to the Moon" Howard; "Don't Wait Too Long" by ex-bandsinger Sonny Skylar (best known for his vocals with George Hall and "Laughing Boy Blues" with Woody Herman), who had earlier written the folk-style hit "Hair of Gold, Eyes of Blue" (sung by Sinatra on *Your Hit Parade* in 1948); "I See It Now" by Alec Wilder; and the album's masterpiece, "It Was a Very Good Year," by Ervin Drake, best known for Billie Holiday's "Good Morning Heartache" and his not exactly deathless lyrics to "Castle Rock," a Louis Jordan hit also recorded by Sinatra. The Old Man was also putting the accent on youth for inspiration in that three of the pieces had been introduced or previously recorded by Tony Bennett: "Don't Wait Too Long," Jenkins' "This Is All I Ask," and the stunning, neglected "Once Upon a Time" (from the show *All American*).

The whole setup hinged on Sinatra's impending fiftieth birthday (the point when he began publicly acknowledging his year of birth as 1915, incidentally), although quintagenarianhood may not seem to be an adequate excuse to cry the blues about getting on in years. Considering that 1965 marked a mere twenty-five years since Sinatra had left Harry James, one wonders if he would have gone through with this rather premature contemplation of his old age had he known he had not even begun the second half of his solo performing career. Don't forget, however, that many of Sinatra's closest associates bought the farm while they were in their fifties—men like Tommy Dorsey, Axel Stordahl, Manie Sachs, Felix Slatkin, and, later, Don Costa. (Plenty of jazz greats whom Sinatra adored had died considerably younger.) Besides, we should be grateful that Sinatra had the foresight to assemble this musical "last will and testament" while he was young enough to be of sound mind and voice. "The songs all had a thing about age and growing older," said Jenkins, "and I was exactly the right age to do it, as he was. We were talking about it on the date, that neither one of us could have made that album at any other time in our lives."

The alliance of The Voice with the material and the orchestrations, a combination that makes the music seem at once simple and sophisticated, makes for another nearly perfect Sinatra album. Jenkins relied on the most uniform textures of any Sinatra arranger, and as with *All Alone*, not only do all the orchestrations seem to be cut from the same cloth but so do the songs themselves. And despite the eventual predictability of the recurring images—the falling leaves, graying hairs, technicolor breezes, a preoccupation with gazing forlornly at children, and the strange click-clacks in the back of one's sacroiliac (everything but hanging out at McDonald's)—the concept itself almost never seems forced. Only Wilder's "I See It Now" comes off as thin and redundant; he would have done better to attempt the *Fantasticks*-ly folky "Try to Remember."

The album's acknowledged masterpiece is "It Was a Very Good Year," a performance that came to symbolize the ne plus ultra of Sinatra and Jenkins. The folkiest piece on the platter, "Very Good Year," was actually introduced in 1961 by the Kingston Trio, a far cry from the King Cole Trio or the Benny Goodman Trio.

In the same way that Sinatra's presence elevates Jenkins' near-kitsch (it's often brilliant kitsch, but it's kitsch nonetheless) into high art, the singer turns this simple metaphor of life as a series of wine vintages into poetry. Sinatra gets the most out of the lyric's use of liquor lingo and transmutes "Very Good Year" to very near the level of "You Go to My Head" and "One for My Baby," the ultimate saloon songs. Drake's opus is divided into four choruses, each a reminiscence set up as a parallel narrative that we experience along with the singer, which he indulges himself in as if he were sampling fine old wines in a cellar.

Between each of these episodes, Jenkins supplies a wailing string-and-oboe passage that grows increasingly severe with each segment until, by the end, the whole section sobs and throbs to the nth power. This is also a quintessential example of Jenkins' "wailing, moaning strings." As Bill Miller said, "And then he had that little thing where we used to kid, when he'd go from minor to major or major to minor. And right after the record date we'd all walk out singing, 'Gor-don Jen-kins.'" Pianist Lou Levy added, "Gordon had his identity and his sound. Everything was sort of a wail and a moan. He had a way of getting that kind of sound. I could take only so much of it, but with Sinatra, it worked. And I know Frank liked it. How can you knock an arrangement like 'Very Good Year'? That's really sort of a masterpiece."

It worked even better seven months later, with the long-dreaded big five-oh birthday getting nearer, when Jenkins conducted a segment of Sinatra's first spectacular series of TV specials, titled *A Man and His Music*. Here they use "Very Good Year" as the premise for a medley, thoughtfully exploiting its episodic structure as a means to incorporate other songs, including Riddle's "Young at Heart," and two from the *September* set, "Last Night When We Were Young" and "Hello, Young Lovers"; they also work in "The Girl Next Door" from *All Alone*, this time more clearly defining the singer's viewpoint as that of one looking back longingly at a time when he had the hots for his neighbor's daughter. Jenkins' charts are so uniform, it made more sense to have the whole segment run continuously with no breaks between numbers. One almost wishes that they had used "Very Good Year" this way on the *September* album, perhaps turning one whole side of the LP into an uninterrupted song suite. Then again, it already is that in everything but the trivial fact that there happen to be pauses between the tracks. (A year later, Sinatra and Jenkins devised an equally moving ballad medley segment for the 1966 special *A Man and His Music, Part 2*. This one used a new Jenkins treatment of "Just One of Those Things" to frame "My Heart Stood Still," "But Beautiful," and "When Your Lover Has Gone.")

And then it came to pass that Sinatra and Jenkins moved in a direction that, if graphed, would resemble the printed music to one of the arranger's sweeping descending phrases. The team gradually moved from highbrow to middlebrow Tin Pan Alley, and then swooped another step down to quasi-folk music and then to quasi-rock, each level going for a simpler order of composition.

From 1956's *A Jolly Christmas* to 1965's *September of My Years,* Sinatra had thought of Jenkins entirely in terms of full-length albums, while he used Riddle and occasionally May for his bread-and-butter singles. The first sign that Sinatra had appointed Jenkins as his number-two man (behind Costa) for soft rock was that Jenkins' name started showing up on Sinatra 45s. That stage of their relationship began with three tracks from 1967 that were collected on *The World We Knew* LP: "This Is My Love" (which Sinatra had cut eight years earlier as "This *Was* My Love") and two movie themes, "Born Free" (which was re-born free a decade later as the title music to *Star Wars*) and "You Are There," from Sinatra's own film *The Naked Runner.* All three of these fairly meager melodies benefit immensely from Jenkins' inflationary tactics; one might go so far as to say that Sinatra and Jenkins actually make them sound good.

But most of the sides that Sinatra recorded with Jenkins after returning from retirement make "meager" look good. Jenkins and Costa divided up conducting and arranging chores on Sinatra's two albums from 1973 and 1974, *Ol' Blue Eyes Is Back* and *Some Nice Things I've Missed.* Although the songs were nothing on *The World We Know,* at least Jenkins was free to treat them with his "house" sound and no external elements, and could touch them with an air of his familiar dour dignity. However, while tunes like Joe Raposo's "You Will Be My Music" and "Noah" have beautiful intros, Jenkins' strings and oboes are compelled to compete with components of kiddie pop as soon as the main melody commences. "You Will Be My Music" contrasts the arranger's moaning violins with horrid whining, nasal electric guitar and a brutally out-of-place rock drum underpinning. Kris Kristofferson's "Nobody Wins" (an apropos title) finds the cowboy from Hoboken affecting a country twang as Nashville rhythm mixes with gloomsville fiddles. The epically awful "Noah," a contender for the worst thing Sinatra ever recorded, decorates an abysmal hook and flauntingly garish idea with a full rock-gospel choir.

Most of the other tracks Jenkins arranged for Sinatra between *September of My Years* and *Trilogy*—enough to fill a CD of their own—can be dismissed as simply nondescript and are more an indictment of Sinatra's song selection process than of his singing and choice of collaborators. This group includes a number of tracks recorded on the same dates as *Ol' Blue Eyes* and *Nice Things* which wound up being issued only as singles, as well as two tunes that came closer to standard quality, Stephen Sondheim's overrated "Send in the Clowns" (which the arranger described as "the best song [written] in the last twenty-five or thirty years") and Johnny Mercer's underrated "Empty Tables." Milt Bernhart recalled, "That arrangement of 'Send in the Clowns' was easy to play, but it didn't do much for the song. It had some sort of a fanfare going on that just didn't do much, and I don't think Sinatra cared either. Eventually Frank gave up on the arrangement. It's still a great song, I think, if it's done the right way." Sinatra remade both "Clowns" and "Tables" with superior, piano-only backings that amount to some of his finest moments with Bill Miller.

But Sinatra buried two genuine gems in the midst of this mostly forgettable stage of his collaboration with Jenkins, both coming to him from unexpected sources. "Just as Though You Were Here" had been one of the last tunes Sinatra recorded with Tommy Dorsey and the Pied Pipers back in the summer of 1942; thirty-two years later he recorded his only solo version, one of the only standards he attempted in the entire pre-*Trilogy* decade. He and Jenkins rethink it even more thoroughly than they had "I'll Never Smile Again" on *No One Cares,* beginning with a lovely and lavish intro—which for once doesn't give way to ersatz rock—and an orchestration full of fitful stops and starts. The Voice sounds leaner than usual for the period, which again contributes to the exceedingly well communicated pain of the performance but perhaps also explains Sinatra's decision not to issue this very moving rendition at the time.

"There Used to Be a Ballpark" (done on *Ol' Blue Eyes* and live at Carnegie Hall in 1974) comes out of left field. Joe Raposo was one of the most performed songwriters of the '70s and may have seemed like an odd choice for Sinatra, since his work was so emphatically youth-oriented. A generation of Gerbers dribblers grew up with Raposo's songs on *Sesame Street,* and most of his tunes apart from that show are fittingly infantile, including his soft-rock works and the score for the animated flop *Raggedy Ann and Andy.* Sinatra apparently thought that Raposo was going to be the next big thing and that his songs might provide a suitable bridge between Richard Rodgers and the Jackson Five. Ol' Blue Eyes recorded no less than six of the young songwriter's pieces, including "Bein' Green" on *Sinatra and Company,* "Noah," "You Will Be My Music" (which Sinatra introduced as his "protest song" in contemporaneous concerts), "Winners," and "Ballpark" on *Ol' Blue Eyes,* and "The Hurt Doesn't Go Away" from the same sessions but never included as part of the album.

At first, "Ballpark" seems to be an old-time sports fan's recollections of an extinct baseball field. Raposo astutely makes the first word "And" so as to commence with the concept that we've caught some old codger rambling on in midsentence. As it happens, Sinatra, like his one-time boss Harry James, has been a lifelong Dodgers fan. It's been alleged that he loused up two important documents—the 1961 album with Basie and the 1981 *Man and His Music* TV special (coincidentally, also with Basie)—because he ruined his voice rooting for Dem Bums. Yet his personal involvement with the national pastime (or even his friendship with that delicate master of tact, Leo Durocher) is immaterial. Within a few lines it becomes clear that Sinatra is talking about something much broader than baseball or sports. As with the movie *Field of Dreams,* singer and songwriter use the game as a symbol for bigger issues, and lines like "The old team isn't playing / And the new team hardly tries" make this as stinging an indictment of the decline of American culture as anyone has ever sung.

"I think people didn't understand the significance of it, the idea about the Dodgers and the ballpark," said Lou Levy, who served as Sinatra's pianist on various occasions when he sang the number. "It's great if you know what it means, but a lot of people just sat and wondered what the song was all about. Likewise, I know kids who go to see the *JFK* movie who have no idea what the Bay of Pigs was. Lots of times nobody knew what the song was talking about, and it just didn't come across." Still, one hopes that even people who only know Durocher for his urbane, Noel Coward–like *bon mots* would react like the thousands of Brooklyn boys in the '60s and '70s who looked at the housing tract erected on Ebbets Field and wondered what it all meant. "There Used to Be a Ballpark" has an air of mystery and mystique that speaks to millions who never so much as threw a pop bottle at an umpire.

Trilogy, Part Three: The Future, the next and most ambitious phase of the Sinatra-Jenkins team-up, sprang more from recurring motifs in each of their individual careers than from anything they had thus far achieved jointly. As we have seen, Sinatra had a predilection for "big songs" of the "Ol' Man River" and "Soliloquy" variety which he had developed steadily from the Dorsey era up to *The Concert Sinatra.* Jenkins, too, had a yen to speak to big topics, not just with big tunes but with big bunches of songs, joined together in a format that amounted to a pop song cycle in the Schubertian sense of the term. "Gordon's whole thing was the story," Dick Nash pointed out. "I mean, that was his forte."

Jenkins began developing ways to use music as a form of extended audio drama when he was a staff conductor for NBC in the early '40s. He had worked with, among others, Arch Oboler, a suspense-oriented dramatist who was to radio more or less what Rod Serling later was to televison. As musical director for Dick Haymes' Autolite show in the mid-1940s, Jenkins somehow persuaded the singer and his sponsor to let him indulge himself in a series of "Autolite Operas"—ten-minute pastiches utilizing the talents of Haymes, occasional costar Helen Forrest, and the NBC orchestra and chorus. The "operas" amounted to a combination of protracted medleys of familiar songs with new lyrics as well as original material, constructed in the form of a musical narrative with connecting dialogue. Although the Autolite Operas apparently were seen as especially creative thinking in those days, today they seem dreadfully hokey and impossible to sit through.

Over the course of two years in the early '40s (in addition to his other work) Jenkins composed *Manhattan Tower*, which he recorded for the first time in 1945 for Decca. This multipart pop song fantasia, narrated by radio actor Elliot Lewis, contains a vague story line (which Jenkins stressed much more strongly in his later "updates" of the work) but is primarily a series of orchestral and choral impressions of New York. The frightful kitschiness of the Autolite pieces becomes a positive aspect of the wonderfully corny *Tower* suite. Its ridiculously stoic narration[9] and concept are emblematic of the good kind of camp that still works fifty years later. *Manhattan Tower*, originally a twelve-inch 78 album (four extended sides) and later a twelve-inch LP, was an immediate best-seller. Decca later claimed that it sold over half a million units, a remarkable statistic considering that it contained no well-known songs and no big-name stars or Broadway or Hollywood tie-ins.

In 1956 when Jenkins went to Capitol, the new label contracted him to rerecord and enlarge *Manhattan Tower* (besides adding new songs, Jenkins also recorded the recently expanded "Never Leave Me" as a single with Haymes). By this time, *Manhattan Tower* had become one of the signature works of the LP era, and various labels recorded at least two subsequent full-length versions, with star singers Patti Page (Mercury) and Robert Goulet (Columbia). "New York's My Home" was sung by cultural icons as disparate as Milton Berle (on his Buick TV show) and Ray Charles (on *Genius Hits the Road*).

Through *Manhattan Tower*, Jenkins became a star composer-conductor on a level that his comrades in both the songwriting and orchestrating professions envied. The popularity of the work enabled him to perform it three times in New York, once taking his own orchestra into the Capitol Theatre, in 1949. He also presented it on three occasions in

9. Just a sample: "As I entered the tower for the first time, I knew that I had found contentment, a home that I would leave many times yet never really leave . . . and on the street were the people who built that fire and kept it alive, seven million keepers of the flame."

Las Vegas, once in 1953 at the Thunderbird as *Gordon Jenkins'*
Manhattan Tower, with a full cast of singers, dancers, comics, and
impressionists. Two of the songs for later editions of the *Tower* even
became hits on their own, "Married I Can Always Get" and "Repeat
After Me." He conducted selections from this really big suite on Ed
Sullivan's really big show and even incarnated it as a television special in
1956 featuring Ethel Waters, Cesar Romero, Phil Harris, Hans Conried,
and Helen O'Connell.

It also led to other *Towers*, beginning with the considerably cornier
California, only remembered, deservedly, as the rarely played B side of
the twelve-inch Decca *Tower* LP. Although the generally hip Tom Adair,
who had written the extended "Let's Get Away from It All" for Dorsey
and Sinatra, wrote lyrics for both the Autolite Operas and *California*, it
took Mel Tormé to compose a savvy and swinging song suite on the same
theme, with his 1949 *California Suite*. In 1948, Broadway producer
Arthur Lesser commissioned Jenkins and Adair to write a dozen songs,
or roughly two-thirds of the score, for his revue *Along Fifth Avenue*, in
which Jackie Gleason took over for Willie Howard, who died before the
production reached New York. Since the songs (which included one of
Jenkins' best in "Skyscraper Blues") and the show were again highly
New York oriented, the production could have been titled *Manhattan
Tower II* or *Son of Manhattan Tower*.

Throughout the '50s, Jenkins alternated between sets of mood music
that merge preexisting songs into "concept" albums (*Hawaiian Wedding
Song* and *France*, which intercuts dialogue vignettes of Americans in
Paris with froggy, froggy tunes) and his own song suites like the descriptive though surreal *Seven Dreams* (best line: "Livin' in a houseboat ain't
like livin' in sin"), a piece that approximates what Berlioz's *Symphonie
Fantastique* might sound like if it had been written by Meredith Wilson.
Jenkins also concocted a number of more plot-oriented oratorios for star
singers, such as the legendarily atrocious *The Letter* with Judy Garland,
and the providentially lighter and looser *What It Was, Was Love*, an
"AlbuMusical" (LP and TV special) for Steve Lawrence and Eydie
Gorme.

None of these subsequent works had the charm of the original
Manhattan Tower, although Jenkins was not about to admit that he was
the master of a genre that was doomed to be limited to only one completely successful piece. With the decline of the grown-up LP market,
Jenkins received fewer and fewer offers and did not supplement his
recording income with movie and television assignments, as did Riddle
and May, although he worked for NBC again in the '50s and scored the

films *Strange Music* (1946) and *B'wana Devil* (the first three-dimensional feature, in 1953). He also made an album with rock star Nilsson in 1973 that anticipated the Ronstadt-Riddle collaboration by a decade. Jenkins' first attempt at an extended piece in perhaps fifteen years came when he and Sonny Burke, a close colleague and fellow arranger-producer from their mutual Decca days, collectively conceived the idea for *The Future*.

"I was working in Vegas when Gordon came up with Sonny Burke," as Sinatra recollected in 1984, "and they said, 'We want to talk to you about a piece of material that Gordon is thinking about.' And he told me about it, and I said, 'Boy! That's a lot of music. That's a lot of work.' He said, 'Yeah, I know, but I think I could do it. I think I know exactly what I want to do.' Then, at the next visit to Vegas two or three months later, they came up again and brought up a reel-to-reel tape. We put it on the machine, and I tell you, it put me away the first time I heard it. It really knocked me out."

"The Future" was the third and final part of *Trilogy* to be taped as well as in the album sequence. "I worked on it for many months before we did it because I wanted to be sure it was all right," Sinatra said. "It was all brand new. Everything was brand new." Vincent Falcone elaborated; "We spent weeks [going over it], and not only on the road. I spent a great deal of time with him up at the house in Beverly Hills. We used to go down to the projection room where the piano was. It was a separate building down by the pool, and we spent hours down there! I had to teach him all of that material because it was all original."

It required even more personnel than *The Concert Sinatra*. Not only was there a full symphony orchestra, but vocal contractor Marlene Ver Planck (who herself has a career as a singer-pianist) hired a full chorus of backup singers—nearly a hundred performers in all. As recording engineer Lee Hirschberg has recalled, no studio in Los Angeles was big enough to hold that many people, so he and producer Burke had to set up a remote recording operation at Hollywood's Shrine Auditorium.

"Sure it was difficult," Falcone continued, "It was difficult [even] for me to learn it! I had to remember it all, too. Because when we went to the recording session, backstage at the Shrine, there was a lot of stuff where there was no piano part written. And it was my job to make sure that [Sinatra] toed the line, so to speak. And I used to go to him after several takes and tell him, 'You'd better do that over again' or 'You'd better listen to this because you're not going to be happy with it.' I would do things that other people were afraid to do."

In the long run, there's no apologizing for *The Future*. Talk about trying to predict the future; no one who's ever heard Sinatra's low-brow misfires—"Mama Will Bark," "Noah," or "Bad, Bad Leroy Brown"— could have guessed that he would undertake the most spectacular disaster of his recording career in trying to take the high road. In the past he had stumbled only in futile, uncharacteristic attempts to talk down to his audiences, but "The Future" blew it by addressing ideas that were at once too grandiloquent and too stupid.

This third disc of *Trilogy* almost resists description. The first track, titled "What Time Does the Next Miracle Leave," opens with an extended prelude in which Sinatra introduces himself while the orchestra tunes up. Then, for nearly ten minutes he sings about visiting various planets. The composer intended this trip to symbolize an inward voyage as well, since each interstellar location carries with it a more earthbound recollection of the protagonist's own life—a clever idea that doesn't come off. The second cut, "World War None," is a comparatively short (four and a half minutes) metaphoric hymn to the end of war. The whole segment is sort of like Jenkins attempting to orchestrate one of the mumbo-jumbo spiels of Sun Ra.

The next three cuts on the disc actually comprise *The Future* per se, described on the jacket as "A Musical Fantasy in Three Tenses for Frank Sinatra, Philharmonic Symphony Orchestra and Mixed Chorus." The selections, or "tenses," are titled "The Future," "The Future (continued) 'I've Been There'" and "The Future (conclusion) 'Song Without Words.'" "The Future" opens with a simple and effective prelude, a twelve-bar blues song by Jenkins' wife, "blues singer" Beverly Mahr. The piece seems to be taken directly from "The Conductor" episode of *Seven Dreams*, where it was also sung by Mahr. The two had met while working on the Haymes show in the mid-1940s; at that time, Mahr was the "Miss" in that show's vocal group, the Six Hits and a Miss. An accomplished studio singer on *Manhattan Tower* (she was the original soloist on "New York's My Home") and *California* long before she became the second Mrs. Jenkins, Mahr participated in almost all of Jenkins' dates that required a chorus. She also collaborated with her husband on the album *My Wife the Blues Singer,* one of the few truly frivolous releases in the history of the Impulse! record label.

Between the star singer and the choir's would-be clairvoyant meditations on the future, Jenkins has worked in two subsongs that could stand on their own, "I've Been There" and the ensemble vocalese "Song Without Words." As the central section of the project, this trio of tracks is particularly notable in that it says even less than the preceding items, "What Time Does the Next Miracle Leave" and "World War None"—

indeed, Jenkins seems to be telling us that in the future there will be boredom, since almost nothing happens here.

The disc concludes with "Before the Music Ends," which has enough material in it for at least one good thirty-two-bar pop song, but as it stands, it sounds more like one of Sinatra's rambling Vegas monologues set to music, complete with insider references to Dino, Sarge (Sinatra lieutenant Irving Weiss), Chester (Jimmy Van Heusen's real name), and Lefty (the southpaw maestro from Missouri himself)—and that's not to mention Schubert, Beethoven, Verdi, and Puccini. "Frank sort of liked that type of thing because he felt it gave him a wider scope," said session singer Loulie Jean Norman, who chirps about building a house on a star in "The Future (conclusion)." "But I couldn't make heads or tails of it."[10]

Once again Vince Falcone volunteers as the strongest defender of *The Future*: "I cannot understand anybody criticizing that work. The criticisms were that it was too much ego from Sinatra, but they missed the whole point entirely! The point was the past, the present, and the future! *Trilogy* was conceived as the culmination of an incredible career. Yet he wasn't old enough to hang it up, so there was a future. And the future, as Gordon saw it, meant saying thank-you to his friends and reminiscing while he was still in the business. It's a retirement without being retired"—sort of like a testimonial. "It may not have been classic Sinatra, but it wasn't intended to be." As Billy May put it, "You gotta look at it this way. If Frank liked it and Frank commissioned it, then Gordon did a good job. I was down there when they recorded it, and, Jesus, it was sensational!"

The entire third disc of *Trilogy* was obviously conceived after Burke and Sinatra had decided to do "The Past" and "The Present." As a concept it almost works—songs that everyone remembered from thirty years ago or more, followed by songs on the radio in more recent seasons. Then why not cap it with an album of brand-new material? However, instead of orchestrating such an overblown oratorio, Sinatra, Jenkins, and Burke should have considered *The Future* a follow-up to *September of My Years*. Sinatra would have done better to just call up his dream team of songwriters: Jenkins, certainly, but also Cahn, Van Heusen, Wilder, Bart Howard, even Joe Raposo, or whoever else had a good idea. Just ask them for philosophical songs that Sinatra could sing

10. Loulie Jean Norman had participated on dozens of sessions with Sinatra and Jenkins going back to the '40s (including the Capitol and Decca *Manhattan Towers*). Still, *The Future* must have reminded her less of her work with Francis and Lefty than it did of her most widely heard performance, the wordless vocal heard over the main titles of *Star Trek* (the first generation, that is).

with his standard thirty- or forty-piece orchestra and strings, with Jenkins arranging and conducting. It would have been hokey and a little pretentious, slightly more so than *September*, but as Billy Bigelow would say, that'd be all right, too: it would have been the kind of hoke that suited the stoic Sinatra.

Even the most disastrous of Jenkins' cantata works have their moments: *The Letter* contains one of the composer's most moving arias, "That's All There Is," a piece he later recorded with Nat Cole, and one of the Tropicana shows yielded "I Live Alone," another great suicide song that Sinatra, Cole, or Garland should have done. "I've Been There" from "The Future" would have worked perfectly on a less high-faluting, more doable album, as would "Before the Music Ends," with a little trimming and rewriting by Cahn or Tom Adair, and "There Used to Be a Ballpark."

Unfortunately, all concerned had to learn the hard way that Sinatra's voice and personality couldn't help but overpower the delicate premise of these cantata works, and there was no way he could just assume the naïveté required of the hero of *Manhattan Tower*. Jenkins' best works are based on the old idea of the suspension of disbelief; in contrast, Sinatra always has to be explicitly believable—it's in his contract.

Sinatra defended *Trilogy: Part Three, The Future* by claiming that the critics and others who rapped it "just didn't understand it at all." Nevertheless, with the next and last project that he worked on with Jenkins, Sinatra made a point of returning to their roots: saloon songs. "Gordon was getting old and sick, and Frank wanted to do one last album with him before he died," said Falcone. "He wanted it to be Gordy's last stand, if you will. And I think a lot of that came from the fact that Gordon received such criticism for the *Trilogy* album." (Around the same time, Jenkins wrote a whole new band book for Benny Goodman. Although the King of Swing had long used Jenkins' "Goodbye" as a closing theme, the new charts he concocted at this time turned out to be another fiasco.)

She Shot Me Down (1981) was the album that got away, arriving all but unnoticed between the very successful *Trilogy* and the more heavily hyped *L. A. Is My Lady*. *She Shot Me Down* is the (almost) all-new album that "The Future" should have been; its nine tracks include two standards, two "found" pieces, and five items largely written with Sinatra in mind.

Like most of *Trilogy: The Present*, *She Shot Me Down* would be taped in New York, where Sinatra had the benefit of recording with the same supertight orchestra he had long been touring with. Even though Jenkins had never worked with this particular reed section, he quickly came to appreciate its facility. When he counted off the first tune, lead alto player Sid Cooper, who solos on "South to a Warmer Place," reported, "There

were little touchy things [in the chart], and he wasn't used to the saxophone section. And after we played the first tune—and we played it
very well—he called [contractor] Joe Malin over and whispered in his ear:
'Whatever we do in this album, give Sid Cooper double scale.' And
when Joe came over and told me that, well, I was really flabbergasted.
And I mean, I did nothing for it except what I always did, which was to
make everything the best I could under the circumstances." (Cooper also
reported that the band was still teasing Lefty by moaning "*Gord*-on
Jenk-ins" atop one of his major-minor moaning motifs.)

The two non-Jenkins charts that begin and end the set mark its
extremes: "Good Thing Going" by Don Costa (who replaced the late
Sonny Burke as the set's overall producer) is a namby-pamby opener
that leads one to fear this will be another '70s-type set of soft rock;
Nelson Riddle's medley of "The Gal That Got Away" and "It Never
Entered My Mind" is an act that nothing could follow. Jenkins' seven
arrangements come closer to the latter than to the former. Though none
of these new compositions reached a for-the-ages level of quality, Sinatra
and Jenkins accentuated the asset of their very newness; how much better to help the master singer-actor unfold his tale if the audience isn't as
familiar with the outcome as they are with "My Funny Valentine." Don
Costa's tune "Monday Morning Quarterback" and Jenkins' own "I
Loved Her" (a great song that's better than all of *The Future* put
together, containing a characteristic one-finger piano part) come off
especially poignantly when you don't anticipate the punch lines.

If the rock movement and *The Future* had derailed Sinatra and
Jenkins from their familiar path, the high-strung *She Shot Me Down* gets
them back on track: Jenkins' moaning strings swarming around and supporting the impassioned performance of the star singer. The album's
monicker comes from the subtitle of "Bang Bang," an opus by Sinatra's
Palm Springs *paisano* and kiddie pop savant Sonny Bono, which the
team has formatted as a follow-up to "A Very Good Year." Again they've
taken a ludicrously simple melody and made an orchestral spectacular
out of it; again they maximize the dramatic value of the text's repetitive
parallel construction.[11]

11. The original, unissued 1973 version of "Bang, Bang" is just as powerful and
moving, as is the unedited master on Jule Styne's "Hey Look No Crying," which is also
two minutes longer and more disturbing than the one released. One Jenkins work that
didn't make it to the album at all was a deep, dark, and radically rewritten (by the original lyricist, Tom Adair) treatment of Sinatra's old fave, "Everything Happens to Me."
Sinatra laid down stunning versions of that chart in both '74 and '81, and all four of
these "bonus" items deserve to be widely heard.

She Shot Me Down marked another farewell in that it was the last time Sinatra would work with his friend of forty years, Alec Wilder, who died in 1980. (Several years earlier, the composer-author had written two instrumental pieces for Sinatra to conduct in concert, but they never became part of his regular act.) Said Falcone, "The only disappointment to me on that album was the fact that, although Alec Wilder was a great writer, he was on his way out also. [Frank] wanted to do those songs of Alec's, 'A Long Night' and 'South to a Warmer Place.' They were written for him. Again, they weren't exactly classic Sinatra, but he got the right arranger because they were right up Gordon's alley."

Alec Wilder's witty, if a wee bit underpolished, "South to a Warmer Place" and a de-Bob Hope-ed "Thanks for the Memory" with completely new lyrics (written for Sinatra by the original librettist, Leo Robin) and surprising harmony lines from Sinatra amount to comic relief in one of the saddest sets Sinatra produced in the thirty-five years since he had perfected the concept album. Though he sounds stronger on some numbers than he did on much of *Trilogy* two years earlier, the occasionally shakiness of his pipes only adds to the passion of his performance. "I Loved Her," "Monday Morning Quarterback," and, most of all, Wilder's morbid lament "A Long Night" (a follow-up, in a sense, to "Where Do You Go?") amount to the most painful readings Sinatra has ever given any material.

In reminiscing about his years of working with Frank Sinatra, Jenkins explained that a kind of magic took place between him and Frank. "It's as close as you're gonna get without being [of the] opposite sex. Because I like to have him right in front of me, and I just never take my eyes off him. It's kind of a hard thing to describe, but [there's] a definite mental connection between the two of us when it's going down well. He lets it loose. He's all over the place when he's going. He doesn't hold anything back.

"But the excitement with [Frank] is following him because he likes to wander around. He doesn't necessarily do a song the way he rehearsed it. So you have to never take your eyes off him. I wouldn't dare. You have to just never let up or relax for a minute. He'll leave you; he'll stop in the middle of a bar and talk to somebody [ringside]. Then you've got to figure where he's gonna start again or whether he's gonna start at the beginning. He might give you a little hint, but he might not, and he assumes you'll be there.

"Frank is withdrawn. He's the charmer of all time when he feels like being charming. Nobody comes close to him. But when he quits laughing, you're not any closer to him than you were before. You talk about high standards—he's the inventor! The things that he's gotten into, scrapes and bad publicity, in my opinion are only because he expected more of people than they ever delivered. If he hires you to do something, he expects it to be the absolute world's best, whether it's cutting the grass or playing the piano. He never questions how much money—he pays whatever you want, really—but he expects it to be absolutely perfect. And it depresses him when it isn't.

"Also, I stay away from him as much as I can when we're not working. It's a temptation to hang around him because he has so much to offer, but I figure that we've gotten along fine by not being buddies. So when we get through at night, if he goes out the left door, I go out the right door. I think it's worked out fine."

Sinatra eulogized Jenkins [to Sid Mark] as "one of the modern geniuses of good pop music." *She Shot Me Down* would be Jenkins' last triumph, and in a sense it would also be Sinatra's—his last unequivocably great record. Jenkins died of a disease named after another left-handed legend, Lou Gehrig, at seventy-three on May 1, 1984.

"There was something about Gordon that Frank liked," said Loulie Jean Norman. "I know Gordon just adored Frank Sinatra. It was a real love affair, musically, between those two." Certainly no other singer-arranger team had so completely mastered the art of emotional exhibitionism—the art of hanging one's tears out to dry.

THE TUX YEARS

CHAPTER NINE

LOOKING FOR THE HOOK, 1960–1971

Go on being uncommercial. There's a lot of money in it.
—JEROME KERN

The central conflict in the history of popular culture in America is not, as many assume, a simple question of art versus commerce. Rather, it's a fight on two fronts: popular artists gradually wresting control of their work and at the same time trying to convince the public that the word "artist" is as relevant to them as "popular." On the whole, it has been a fairly useless struggle. As the artists gradually won more and more power, the qualities that made American mass-market entertainments so special gradually vanished. Clarinetist Artie Baker, who worked with Sinatra in the mid-1940s, has correctly observed that "when the companies started paying musicians royalties, that's when they stopped making music."

Sinatra had spent the first twenty years or so of his career gradually building up to the point where he could claim that he both controlled and owned what he produced. Control was comparatively easy: after leaving Dorsey, Sinatra always had the willpower to go with his own judgment (except in one brief period when circumstances pressured him to abide by the decisions of Mitch Miller). Still, only the first five years or so of the existence of Reprise Records were nirvana to Sinatra; by the mid-1960s, circumstances once again compelled the singer to work with material outside his own personal taste.

That Sinatra did so well at the cashbox with the likes of "That's Life" and "Goin' out of My Head" must have delighted him and ticked him off in equal parts. By the time of his retirement in 1971, when Sinatra was recording mediocre material almost exclusively, the notions of ownership and control had become irrelevant. Apart from their economic worth, these were not works of art worth fighting over compared with the classic Sinatra recordings of the early '60s and earlier.

Still, it was a long way between *Tone Poems of Color,* Sinatra's first "officially" self-produced album, and *Ol' Blue Eyes Is Back,* the release that heralded the end of Sinatra's retirement. Only three years after the "Young at Heart"/*From Here to Eternity* "comeback," Sinatra began making moves toward total ownership of his output. This was happening gradually throughout the film industry, with the demise of the Hollywood studio system and the rise of television (where new power figures like Desi Arnaz and Sheldon Leonard were establishing the role of the performer-mogul) but was still unknown in the record business. It was just at this time, with the simultaneous explosion of long-playing discs for adults and rock singles for kids, that the record industry as a whole began making enough money to fight over.

By 1956, Sinatra had formed both Bristol Corp. and Essex Productions, the former to handle his film work and the latter for recordings. (When Sinatra signed the contracts to star in *The Joker Is Wild,* the film was produced by Bristol and the soundtrack album—never released—was to have been produced by Essex.) *Tone Poems* represented the turning point; it was the first Sinatra release with the Essex name and the first to be taped at Capitol's new pancake-shaped office building and studio. That a mere record company—which had started as a humble contender in a humble business—now controlled the same kind of high-image real estate that the movie studios did (two years after Decca Records bought Universal Pictures) was in itself telling.

Although not part of a vertical multimedia monopoly like RCA and CBS (with their radio affiliations) or Decca, Capitol had by now become a major power with considerable resources, thanks to its having recently been "acquisitioned" by the multinational EMI corporation. For his part, Sinatra was rising comparably in money and power, and even some months before his current contract was scheduled to run out in 1957, he negotiated a new seven-year pact for considerably more dough. "When we took him on two and a half years ago, Frank couldn't get a record," Alan Livingston of Capitol told *Down Beat* in 1956. "Now, every company in the business is after him, and it would be silly to deny that he has had generous offers from every quarter." Livingston was referring specifically to Victor Records, which was making a bid for Sinatra when dealings with Capitol stalled. To finance his own nonrecord ventures, Sinatra raised capital from Capitol, so to speak, in the form of a sizable advance against future royalties.

Sinatra wanted the entertainment industry to think that his office was now producing and owning all Frank Sinatra recordings. He informed the trade press that Essex was a "full-fledged independent record company" and that he himself remained "only nominally a Capitol artist," claiming that all Sinatra product was merely distributed by Capitol. Essex was even interested in signing other artists and announced it was negotiating with Natalie and the Beachcomers (a group that in December 1956 had opened for Ol' Blue Eyes at the Sands, an establishment in which Sinatra also had a piece of the action).

Livingston pointed out, however, that the Essex arrangement was "purely a paper deal for tax purposes. We still owned every Sinatra record made at Capitol, and in perpetuity." Sinatra's main advantage was to acquire capital and gain status so that his royalties would go into a corporation rather than be taxed as personal income.

The singer was growing increasingly dissatisfied with this arrangement and went so far as to claim that it affected the quality of his work. "Some of my [later] work for Capitol lacked the spark that it might have had," he told Robin Douglas-Home. "You can't give your best when you're not happy with the people you're [working] for. I wasn't happy with Capitol, and I'm afraid some of those later albums show it."

The first manifestation of Sinatra's discontent was his switching producers, from Voyle Gilmore to Dave Cavanaugh. Billy May felt that this was a change for the better. "Dave was a musician's musician. He was a good arranger and everything, plus he had been a saxophone player and Frank knew that. And, to put it subtly, Cavanaugh wasn't on Frank's shit list."

Throughout 1958 and 1959, Sinatra repeatedly insisted to Capitol chairman Glenn Wallichs that Essex had to become what the singer was telling *Variety* it was: a genuine subsidiary label, owned by his office but reaping the benefits of the distribution system Capitol had built up over fifteen years. Wallichs flatly turned him down.

"It isn't that the deal Frank proposed was so terrible," Livingston has said. "It was just totally contrary to everything going on in the record business then. And Glenn said, 'If I give it to you, Frank, I've got to give it to Nat Cole. I've got to give it to so-and-so and so-and-so. You're disrupting our whole business.' But Frank went off in a huff and said, 'Screw you. I won't record anymore. You can't make me sing.'"

Sinatra himself continued: "I said I wanted to quit Capitol even if it meant not recording at all for two years until the contract ran out." Indeed, starting a one-man recording ban was the only bargaining leverage Sinatra had. Between finishing *No One Cares* in May 1959 and starting *Nice 'n' Easy* in March 1960, Sinatra didn't record so much as a single. (He broke his strike only to participate in five tracks for the *Can-Can* sound track album because he had a vested interest in promoting his film.)

Even as Sinatra's proposal to create a subsidiary "imprint" within the Capitol aegis was being rejected, he set about acquiring a label of his own. Around this time he came into contact with Norman Granz, owner and operator of Verve Records, and began negotiating to take over that rapidly growing concern. Sinatra and Granz supposedly had gotten as far as agreeing on a sale price of $2 million. That arrangement did not go through, and Verve was summarily acquired by MGM Records.

At least two stories have been told as to why. According to the first, when MGM heard what was happening, they instantly offered Granz an additional half-million over what Sinatra was offering on the condition that Granz sell immediately—in other words, not take the offer back to Sinatra for a counterbid. Sure enough, the first thing Sinatra said when he calmed down was that he would have matched Metro's offer. As a result, Sinatra carried a multidecade grudge against Norman Granz that some claim is the reason he never recorded with Ella Fitzgerald—his own favorite singer and Granz's number-one client.[1]

The other story is that someone in Sinatra's office loused up the deal—perhaps deliberately. He continually postponed appointments to sign the papers and kept asking to examine and reexamine the company's books; when MGM entered the picture, Granz was relieved to go with them. Why would the adviser not want Sinatra to buy Verve? Purchasing a corporation would have provided Sinatra with certain income tax advantages, but perhaps he could have done even better by starting a label of his own.

Which is where Sinatra was by 1959: trying to build his own company and simultaneously extricate himself from his Capitol contract. The sole benefit of the Verve fiasco had been Sinatra's coming into contact with Morris Ostin, the company's young controller and secretary. Known to all simply as "Mo," he soon became Sinatra's aide-de-camp in this new project of organizing a record company. "I helped build that," Sinatra told Ostin one day as he pointed to the Capitol Tower. "Now let's build one of my own."

---

1. Granz did subsequently permit Lady Fitz to appear with Sinatra on three television shows, most notably the 1967 spectacular, *A Man and His Music + Ella + Jobim*, but the single most popular male and female representatives of the great American songbook never made it into a recording studio together.

Around the fall of 1960, Bill Miller began notifying Sinatra's regular sidemen that they could soon expect to receive paychecks from a new client. "We're going to be doing a lot of dates in the near future," he told percussionist Emil Richards. "Don't let it out yet, but Frank's starting his own label." In December 1960, Sinatra and Ostin officially announced to the trade that the new company's name would be "Reprise"—which Sinatra pronounced "Reprize" rather than the more common "Repreese" (which is, in fact, how he pronounces it in "April in Paris"). The name held a double meaning: the first part indicated the company's slogan, "Records you'll want to play again and again," and the second was that Sinatra intended to give his artists the benefit of his experiences at Columbia and Capitol in that the rights to masters would eventually revert back to the performer, who was then free to "reprise" them in whatever fashion he or she wished.

Ostin, the firm's original vice president and general manager, remained top dog at Reprise until he stepped down at the end of 1994. Felix Slatkin was originally named the company's first "artist and repertoire man"; it is not known how long the violinist/conductor actually served in that capacity. In October 1959, the Sinatra office announced that the "operations head" of the new concern would be Morty Palitz, who had been one of Sinatra's producers at Columbia and was currently A&R chief of Jubilee Records. The deal with Palitz apparently never went through, and Sinatra hired arranger and producer Sonny Burke. A onetime bandleader best known for his work with Jimmy Dorsey and Charlie Spivak, as well as for the songs he wrote with Peggy Lee (the *Lady and the Tramp* score) and Lionel Hampton ("Midnight Sun"), Burke was currently head of Decca Records' West Coast recording activities. Burke had become available thanks to a stroke of misfortune that seemed anything but fortuitous at the time. "When Decca was about to be sold to MCA, the company eliminated all contracts with executives, including Sonny's and mine," explained Milt Gabler. "But then Frank grabbed Sonny right away." Joining Reprise in 1960, he became Sinatra's personal producer until his death in 1980.

Reprise Records had been in business since January 1960, when the new label recorded *The Warm Moods*, an album by tenor saxophone colossus Ben Webster, accompanied by a string section directed by "Young at Heart" composer Johnny Richards. Like Verve, the label Sinatra had attempted to buy, Reprise boasted an especially strong line of comedy LPs, but beyond a series of discs by Ellingtonians such as Webster, Al Hibbler, and the Duke himself (as both artist and producer), Reprise never did develop into much of a jazz label. The company's strong suit was pop singers, and any headliner who cared to leave his or her present setup, artists like Rosemary Clooney and fellow rat-packers Dean Martin and Sammy Davis, Jr., were personally invited by Sinatra to come aboard the good ship Reprise[2] for unprecedented artistic freedom and financial participation.

Before Sinatra himself could record for his own label, there was still the matter of his Capitol commitment. Wallichs and Livingston had come to realize that there was no stopping Sinatra now that he wanted out, and their primary concern was to get as much product out of him as they could before he split. They reached the compromise for four "contractual obligation" albums described earlier, three of which finished within a year: *Nice 'n' Easy* (March 1960), *Sinatra's Swingin' Session* (August 1960), and *Come Swing with Me* (March 1961).

Although the music itself does not bear out Sinatra's not exactly unbiased opinion that his later Capitol recordings suffered, these sides were not produced any too easily. On several of these dates, musicians witnessed a rare glimpse of the famous Sinatra temper that the newspapers were so keen to write about but that he had almost never brought to a session. Billy May has recalled attending a date circa 1960 (otherwise undocumented) when Nelson Riddle conducted and Sweets Edison sat in his familiar solo trumpet chair. "In those days Frank was deliberately being his petulant worst because he was pissed off and didn't want to be there," said May. To express his annoyance, Sinatra constantly complained about the microphone setup and kept demanding take after take, finding fault both real and imagined with each run-through.

"They'd get to, like, take twenty-eight, and Frank gets to the end of it. Nelson cuts the band off, and Frank starts looking around trying to figure out what he's going to get mad at this time. Sweets had a high, squeaky kind of voice, and just as the echo [of the take] was dying away, before Frank can think of anything, Sweets says, 'Shit, baby, you can't do it no better than that!' It broke Frank up so bad, he just fell right on the floor. That's become one of the great stories of our industry. We use it all the time. Someone says, 'Are you happy with the record?' And everybody says, 'In the immortal words of Sweets Edison . . .'"

Whereas Sinatra had spent each of the two preceeding decades with

---

2. The artist roster went beyond Sinatra's personal taste. It's impossible to imagine that Sinatra actually enjoyed the work of Andy Williams, yet he made several bids for that top-selling crooner's contract. On the other hand, the Chairman was very vocal in his appreciation of Tony Bennett, yet never approached him with the idea of switching affiliations.

one dominant arranger apiece, exploring variations on a sound that remained consistent from project to project, in the early to mid-1960s he sought endless variety. Sinatra was again adhering to Bing Crosby's pronouncement that it was wise for a pop singer to work with "a lot of different arrangers." Crosby wrote in his autobiography, "Whenever a good arranger or a good band was free and without previous contractual obligations [as head of his own company, Sinatra could even work around those], we grabbed them for a few dates."

"He wasn't missing anything, he just felt that he needed a change," explained Frank Military. "He just wanted to get a different sound, which he did." Between 1960 and 1967, Sinatra recorded an exceptional series of nine "one-shot" albums with that many different arrangers and bands: *Ring-a-Ding Ding* with Johnny Mandel (1960), *I Remember Tommy* with Sy Oliver, *Point of No Return* with Axel Stordahl, *Sinatra and Strings* with Don Costa (all 1961), *Sinatra and Swingin' Brass* with Neal Hefti, *Great Songs from Great Britain* with Robert Farnon, *Sinatra-Basie* arranged by Neal Hefti (all 1962), *It Might As Well Be Swing* with Count Basie's Orchestra and arrangements by Quincy Jones (1963), and *Francis Albert Sinatra & Antonio Carlos Jobim* with arrangements by Claus Ogerman (1967).

All these writers succeeded in helping Sinatra expand his musical palette while remaining true to his own heritage, to go forward by building on what he had already achieved. Remember also that these were done in addition to the classic sets Sinatra continued to turn out in the '60s with his three long-standing collaborators from the Capitol era, Nelson Riddle (five new albums for Reprise), Billy May (three between 1961 and 1967), and Gordon Jenkins (two albums, one in 1962 and the other in 1965).

In December 1960, Sinatra finally taped his first album for Reprise, *Ring-a-Ding Ding*, arranged and conducted by Johnny Mandel. Sinatra had decided that with the new venture he wanted to get even further away from the classic Sinatra-Riddle sound that he had "come back" with ten years earlier. The collaborator he chose was Johnny Mandel. The arranger, born in New York in 1925, had played trumpet with Joe Venuti and other bands before coming into his own as a modernist orchestrator and composer with Boyd Raeburn's progressive-jazz aggregate in the late '40s. In 1948, Sinatra had said of Raeburn, "I don't understand his stuff. Maybe it's a little too far ahead for me. I don't think, though, that as a national liking it has much of a future."

Sinatra would have come across Mandel's name several times in other contexts: when he played bass trumpet in Count Basie's brass section in 1953, when he orchestrated *Hoagy Sings Carmichael*, the "Stardust" composer's most successful venture as a vocalist, in 1956, and when he wrote part of *Come Rain or Come Shine,* an album for a considerably stronger singer, Dick Haymes, in 1955. Sinatra was also "a big admirer," as Mandel said, of David Allyn, a Haymes-influenced crooner who had worked with Mandel in the Raeburn band. Sinatra was particularly fond of *Sure Thing,* a classic album of Jerome Kern songs by Allyn and Mandel. Allyn and Sinatra, the former recalled, had been friends since 1939 when each got his first important job with a fledgling band, Allyn with Jack Teagarden and Sinatra with Harry James.[3]

Thus, if Sinatra had heard of Mandel before 1960 it was as a writer of either progressive jazz or straight ballads. "I didn't get to make many records at that time," said Mandel, "because even though I'd been in the business for quite a while, I hadn't gotten enough of a name that they'd use me on records. So I wrote a lot of club acts, and one of them was for Vic Damone. Vic used to play the Sands, and we had a real dynamite act at the time. I'd written a lot of hard-swinging things. And Sinatra came in and heard it, and he came up to Vic and asked him, 'Who did those?" And Vic told him. So I think that's where he got the idea for the swinging things."

Having decided to do a disc with Mandel, Sinatra arranged to get together with the arranger and Bill Miller. "I'd known Bill for quite a long time, so he had Bill bring me out to the Columbia ranch where he was shooting *The Devil at Four O'Clock.* And he started telling me about how he was finished with Capitol and was starting this new company. Everything was going to be different, he was even going to press the records in different colored vinyl, and all that sort of thing. He had a lot of ideas.

"I remember just watching his eyes as he was talking about the company, and they were sparkling. You know, he had the most striking kind of blue eyes. Man! They drill right right through you! I mean, when he looks at you, he really looks. And when he's telling you something, you see this great animation and conviction there. I think they probably ran into some snags in manufacturing, because the records did come out looking pretty much like other records, although they had his picture on the label. But he made sure they had very good quality vinyl. You could tell he was very, very proud of this thing."

3. Proving that what goes around comes around, when Allyn started his own big band in the late '80s, he asked Sinatra to lend him some charts, and Sinatra responded by giving Allyn use of, among others, some of the Mandel orchestrations from *Ring-a-Ding Ding,* including "In the Still of the Night."

"Ring-a-Ding Ding" had been one of Sinatra's personal pet expressions, appearing most famously as a throwaway substitute for the original lyrics of "I Won't Dance" in *Swingin' Affair*. (It's also heard in "C'est Magnifique" in *Can-Can* and in the special-material lyrics to the Sinatra–Sammy Davis duo "Me and My Shadow.") In a comedy sketch on a Red Skelton show from this period, Sinatra used the phrase as the replacement punch line of a joke, the original of which, he implied, was too risqué for television. Sinatra apparently brought the phrase to Sammy Cahn and Jimmy Van Heusen with the idea of making it into the title song of what would be his first Reprise album, and the songwriters turned it into a clone of their own enormously successful "The Tender Trap" from 1955. Hell, everyone else was using that song as a template (including Bobby Darin in "That's the Way Love Is")—it perfectly summarized America's courting rituals—so why not the guys who wrote it?

Although more complicated structurally, using a central melodic section (A) of six lines instead of four, Cahn's third-person lyric to "Ring" perfectly parallels "Trap." The first half of the song sets up two familiar character types, the husband-hunting barracuda and the swinging single bachelor. By the end of the bridge, the hero finds himself contemplating matrimony and the last A section rhapsodizes over the wedding and the happy-ever-after. (The only line that requires any explanation is "And presto! You do a skull!" As explained in Sinatra's film *The Joker Is Wild*, that refers to a specific variety of vaudeville "take" or surprised reaction.)

The "Ring-a-Ding Ding" title and its repeated references to bells suggested carillon effects to Sinatra, who asked Mandel to "put some bell sounds in there." This led to a field day for percussionist Emil Richards and his celebrated collection of unusual chimes and bells (much as Billy May's chart on "Moonlight on the Ganges" gave Richards the chance to use his exotic percussion implements). "We all loved Mandel," said Richards. "The thing about Johnny is that normally when you pick up a chart to play, you want to change a couple of the chords to make it sound a little more interesting. But with Johnny's music, all you have to do is play what's on the paper, and he does all the substitutions for you. Everything is already there; there's nothing you have to fill in."

Mandel and Richards use tubular bells for orchestral color in several spots, and also contrast these deeper chimes with tiny plinks from triangles and xylophones, most notably in the very elaborate introduction to "Ring-a-Ding Ding." Mandel uses church bells to illustrate the line "the village bell will sound in the steeple," while other bells portray London's Big Ben in "A Foggy Day" and enhance the nightness by suggesting the passage of time in "In the Still of the Night." For the prolonged climax, in which Sinatra repeats "ring-a-ding ding" three times before the final "ding," Mandel reprises Billy May's device of muted trumpets tightly harmonizing with the xylophone.

Mandel remains a big admirer of both May and Nelson Riddle. "You'd Be So Easy to Love" is reminiscent of another Cole Porter tune bearing the same first three words of the title, "You'd Be So Nice to Come Home To" (on *Swingin' Affair*), with trumpeter Don Fagerquist essaying a muted intro and coda, à la Sweets Edison. Likewise, "In the Still of the Night" builds to a diminuendo at the end of the first chorus, surging like yet a fourth Cole Porter tune, "I've Got You Under My Skin," and also breaking into a trombone solo, this time by Frank Rosolino.

But though the tempos on *Ring-a-Ding Ding* move at roughly the same speed as the classic May and Riddle uptempo albums, Sinatra and Mandel achieve a whole new kind of swinging feeling. "A Fine Romance" swings in spite of the hoity-toitiness Sinatra brings to it in his sarcastically proper pronounciation of "tom-ah-toe" and "po-tah-toe" (rather than calling the whole thing off), offering an aural parallel to the cover painting in which Ol' Blue suavely adjusts his bow tie while sticking his pinky out, as if he were taking his sugar to tea.

"Nelson had a lot more of Tommy Dorsey in him, and Dorsey had Sy Oliver writing for him," said Mandel. "Sy had created the Lunceford sound, of course, which used more of a two-four concept than four-four. But Billy always thought more in four. He came out of the Charlie Barnet band, which had more of an Ellington influence, whereas I came out of the Count Basie band. And that's where I was thinking, and that's the way I wrote in terms of a rhythmic approach. It's not a question of saying one is better than the other."

In the first of this series of "one-shot" pairings, Sinatra achieves, in both the rhythm and the overall orchestral textures, the perfect balance of sounds we expect from both the singer and the accompanying orchestra. "Frank always insisted that you use his rhythm section," said Mandel, adding that Mel Lewis probably would have been his own drummer of choice. But the home team rhythm section, especially Bill Miller's elegant comping and Irv Cottler's rich (as in Buddy) percussion foundation, lets you know this is going to be a Sinatra record even as the curtain is still going up.

It's in the solos that we most clearly hear Mandel's work; he was free to use more modern-oriented players, such as Bud Shank on alto, Fagerquist, and Rosolino. Mandel also makes his presence felt in the voicings of the brass and reeds, the latter led by the sax giant Joe Maini. "I used him on everything," Mandel explained. "He was probably the best lead saxophone player I've ever known. Listen to the way the saxes sound on that album—they don't sound like that on anything else Frank ever did."

Ring opens with the two strongest tracks in the set, the title and "Let's Fall in Love." Both casual listeners and serious fans generally like to hear songs they're already familiar with, and when an artist goes into a tune they know, they'll often start applauding. Realizing that this moment of recognition constitutes a dramatic epiphany, Sinatra often delays it as long as possible. Sometimes he uses the verse, but if he doesn't feel the verse is strong enough, he often utilizes the bridge as an introductory verse.

On "Let's Fall in Love," Sinatra does both: He starts with the bridge, which is well known enough that listeners will find it vaguely familiar, yet strange enough that it won't tip everybody off. He then moves on to the verse, which hadn't been sung at all since Harold Arlen wrote it for the 1933 film of the same name. We then come to the one significant alteration of a chart made by Sinatra on the date itself: both singer and ensemble rest for an entire measure before leaping into the refrain. "He stuck an empty bar in there," said Mandel, "which was a very good change." It heightens the tension "because nobody's ever heard this verse before, and it makes you wonder what's coming next. What made him think of it, I'll never know, because I wouldn't have thought of it. But then after you hear that you say, 'Well, of course!'" "Be Careful It's My Heart" finds Sinatra similarly rushing the initial phrases of each A section so he can luxuriate in comparably pregnant pauses.

Mandel characterizes himself as a slow worker, especially compared to someone both incredibly fast and a workaholic like Riddle. Where Riddle could turn out an album's worth of charts in a week, Mandel requires at least a month to do his best work. "If somebody has to have a club arrangement overnight, I can do that," he said, "but it's going to sound as if I wrote it too fast." Sinatra originally assigned Mandel fourteen charts, which he did not have enough time to do (among other things, the orchestrator began taping a full-length album of Ellington and Basie material with Mel Tormé a week before *Ring-a-Ding Ding*).

Time forced Mandel to farm out one entire arrangement and sections of two others. He wrote the intros, codas, and instrumental portions of "When I Take My Sugar to Tea" and "Easy to Love," while Dick Reynolds, who had arranged the disappointing Sinatra–Ray Anthony session of 1954, wrote the actual backgrounds behind the vocal. Even so, an impartial lay listener would have to disagree with Mandel's contention that the Skip Martin-ghosted chart on "Be Careful It's My Heart" "doesn't even sound like me," especially since, between choruses, Martin cleverly reuses the trumpet-xylophone plinks from the title track.

It must have been frustrating for Mandel that he did finish two whole arrangements by himself which never made it to the album—"Have You Met Miss Jones" because it was too slow, and "Zing! Went the Strings of My Heart" because it wound up too fast. Actually, neither goes too far, but they're not exactly danceable and therefore not exactly right for the terpsichoric mood of the album. They don't succeed, in the way that "Let's Face the Music and Dance" does, in building in intensity without sacrificing the dancing beat. And unlike the aptly named "I've Got My Love to Keep Me Warm," they fail to generate the proper amount of emotional-musical heat.

Both of the deleted songs start with their infrequently heard verses, although neither works anywhere near as well as "Let's Fall in Love." "Zing" commences comparatively sluggishly in the verse and rather awkwardly revs up for the refrain. "I guess for some reason he wanted to do the verse slow," said Mandel, who hadn't heard "Zing" at all until 1990.[4] Sinatra had initially informed Mandel that he wanted to use "Miss Jones" as the one near-ballad on *Ring,* but when he heard the chart on the session, he exclaimed, "This sounds like a different album" and then added (off-mike), "This doesn't belong on an album called *Ring-a-Ding Ding.*" After a complete run-through and a half, both singer and arranger decided to shelve the tune. Sinatra revived the Rodgers and Hart number as a straight ahead swinger à la Billy May in 1962 but never attempted "Miss Jones" again as a ballad with verse.

It's easy to see why "The Coffee Song" (first recorded by Sinatra in 1946) would have taken Mandel so much time to orchestrate: the chart has more things going on than there are coffee beans in Brazil. Working with two completely different choruses' worth of lyrics (albeit with the same bridge), Sinatra and Mandel wend their way through a relentlessly rhythmic rhumba pattern, the arranger's very adroit use of the string section (on the bridges), a series of countermelodies—including one that ascends chromatically (behind "a politician's daughter")—and several unexpected modulations.

---

4. "Zing! Went the Strings of My Heart" was the Maltese falcon of Sinatra rarities for thirty years, until collector Ed O'Brien turned up a copy, which he presented to producer Joe McEwen for use in the four-CD set *Frank Sinatra: The Reprise Years* (issued in 1990). The following year the track was finally restored to the twelve issued tracks of *Ring.* The Mandel-Sinatra reading of "Have You Met Miss Jones," which is only a rough run-through and not a finished reading, has so far been issued privately on a collectors-only CD.

Mandel said "You and the Night and the Music" has his favorite introduction, and here Sinatra does not choose to include Arthur Schwartz
and Howard Dietz's decadently moving verse. At the end of the second
chorus, he makes the melody more dramatic and brilliantly drives home
the writers' original intention on the phrase "if we could live for the
moment" by singing "if" and "live" on notes a fourth higher than the first
time around. "In the Still of the Night," which Mandel names as his
overall favorite item from the set, also rises gradually in pitch and
increases in power. Mandel added, "I would have loved to have done a
ballad album with Sinatra." The two talked about reuniting in the early
'80s, during a season when Mandel unfortunately was already all booked
up. Sinatra also got around to recording two of Mandel's superlative
movie theme songs, "Emily" and "The Shadow of Your Smile" (the latter
with Mandel's former leader, Count Basie), but *Ring-a-Ding Ding*
remains a superlative once-in-a-lifetime collaboration.

Reprise released its first package of five albums in February 1961: *Ring-
a-Ding Ding*, Webster's *Warm Moods*, Sammy Davis, Jr.'s *The Wham of
Sam*, *Mavis* (Rivers, that is), and *It Is Now Post Time* by Joe E. Lewis (the
comic whom Sinatra had portrayed in the 1957 film *The Joker Is Wild*).
Both sales and reviews were as strong as Sinatra had hoped. When
advance orders on *I Remember Tommy* from later in 1961 totalled
200,000 units, Sinatra said (to Robin Douglas-Home), "The order was
something of a record figure in my experience. It makes me laugh when
I think back to when we started Reprise. The buyers all thought it was a
joke, you know—the boys getting together for a laugh. They treated us
pretty carefully at first, but now we're well under way." Before 1960 had
ended, Sinatra recorded three single charts by Riddle at a date conducted by Slatkin, and in March he started work on another album with
another arranger.

In 1961 or early 1962, Sinatra hired arranger, trumpeter, and former
bandleader Neal Hefti, initially as a producer. Like Mandel and most of
the other younger writers Sinatra worked with in the Reprise period,
Hefti had long been a fan of Sinatra and his arrangers, particularly Riddle and May. "Tommy Dorsey had one of my favorite bands when I was
in high school," Hefti pointed out, "because he had Axel to write the ballads and Sy Oliver for the swing tunes. That combination has yet to be
equaled." Hefti added that while Ax and Sy divided the responsibilities
of supplying Sinatra with arrangements in different moods, "Nelson did
both—and he was the best."

It's particularly revealing, then, that when Sinatra began a three-year stretch of not recording any albums with Riddle, his first move was to harken back to Riddle's predecessors, Sy Oliver and Axel Stordahl. While *Ring-a-Ding Ding* and the albums with Hefti and Count Basie take a more forward-looking stance, *I Remember Tommy* with Oliver and *Point of No Return* with Stordahl show that Sinatra wisely intended to keep the past as part of his future. (As a double tie-in to the Dorsey days, Sinatra made new versions of "I'll Be Seeing You," first recorded with TD in 1940, with both ex-Dorseyites within a few months of each other.)

After winding up the *Tommy* project and the two albums with May, Sinatra finally got around to the project he had long been putting off: the final contractual obligation album for Capitol. "Just before Sinatra finished at Capitol, he did an album called *Point of No Return* with Axel Stordahl," recalled guitarist Al Viola. "It was a little heartbreaking to make because Axel was suffering from cancer."

"I'm sure his lawyers had to do a lot of talking to get him to do it," Milt Bernhart suggested. "I have a feeling he said, 'Let them sue me.' But [Sinatra's main attorney] must have said, 'Frank, don't be a fool. What do you need being sued? Do the album!'"

Either Capitol producer Dave Cavanaugh or Sinatra himself remembered that Axel Stordahl had directed Sinatra's first Capitol session eight years earlier, and from there came the idea of using him for Sinatra's last Capitol date. Viola recalls that Mrs. Stordahl, former Pied Piper June Hutton, had gone to Cavanaugh to lobby on her husband's behalf. "She knew that Frank was leaving Capitol, and she also knew that Axel wanted to get in one last album with Frank because he might not be around much longer," said Viola. Because the project was put together so quickly, Stordahl was importuned to recruit the services of ghostwriter Heinie Beau for three tunes (the arranger-reedman had just served in the same role on the Sinatra–Billy May *Come Swing with Me*).

Sinatra was of two minds, and remained so throughout the taping. On some level he continued to be indifferent. "Frank didn't care," Milt Bernhart felt. "It didn't mean a thing to him. Somebody from Capitol must have said, 'Would Axel Stordahl be okay?' and he probably said, 'I don't care who you get!'" At the same time, Sinatra somewhat welcomed the opportunity to say "*Hasta la vista*, baby!" to the man who had played such an important role in his success story from 1940 to 1953. "Frank couldn't wait to leave, but he decided to do the album as a favor for Axel," Al Viola clarified. "If it wasn't for Axel, he wouldn't have done that album." Bill Miller felt that Frank wanted Axel there as a parting gesture—"You know, 'my old buddy.'"

"I got a call to do the two sessions, and I was really thrilled," recalled

Bernhart, who said that for nearly twenty years he and his wife had referred to the 1942 Sinatra-Stordahl "Night We Called It a Day" as "their song." "I couldn't believe I was going to be there, because this was a reunion of those two people. When we went in to do those dates, Frank didn't show up right away, so we had time to rehearse and run the charts through with Axel.

"When Frank came in, he walked right to the microphone and said, 'What's up!' There were quite a few people there [in the "audience"] and a big orchestra. There was electricity in the air for everybody but Sinatra. So he took the first tune and said, 'Okay.' I'm not even sure we ran it through because pretty soon we were doing one take on everything, and that's the way it went. After an hour he was through with six numbers, and he said good-bye and was out the door—and he did that two nights in a row. We got no more than one or, tops, two takes on everything. On several, Cavanaugh came out of the booth and said, 'Frank, we had a little trouble with the bass on that last take,' but by that time Frank had torn up the sheet. 'I'm sorry,' was the way he put it. 'Next number.' You had to be there to see it."

The most notorious instance of Sinatra's indifference would have to be "These Foolish Things." On the master take, the last note was somehow unsatisfactory, so on the issued version, before we hear the final "you" we are subjected to an obnoxious tape splice on the level of those in Charles Mingus' *Tijuana Moods*. "I don't think he gave them a second chance," Bernhart has speculated. "They might even have had to bring in another singer. It's conceivable that he may not even be singing on that." More likely, Cavanaugh had his engineer splice in the concluding "you" from the first chorus or possibly from the previous take—if there was one—and the vocal tone changes completely between the "of" and the "you."

While *Point of No Return* doesn't boast an original title song (what Sammy and Jimmy could have done with that one!), it still has a lot going for it. With another arranger Sinatra might have done more remakes of CBS sides, but he could see little point in asking Stordahl to redo his own charts. They therefore settled on an almost all new program, remaking only "I'll Be Seeing You" from their mutual Dorsey days plus "September Song" (the least but not the last of his three commercial versions) and "These Foolish Things" from the Columbia period.

Having written almost nothing of interest for nearly ten years, Axel Stordahl could still not only make mincemeat out of most arrangers but give even the champions, Riddle and May, a run for their money. Sinatra, for his part, couldn't force himself to sing badly: he may sound a trifle out of it on "It's a Blue World" but compensates with "I'll See You Again," reusing his old standby, the bridge-as-verse structure. "I still think the album is one of the best things I ever heard," said Bernhart. "If you listen to 'I'll See You Again,' it's hard to believe that it was done in a single take. But it was." Bill Miller added, "I remember Axel even throwing some Nelson Riddle–style polytones in there."

Stordahl's string writing is as formidable as ever, while his work with brass and reeds has actually improved—especially the horn crescendi on "I'll Be Seeing You" and "Memories of You." "You talk about classics," said Bernhart. "To me, 'When the World Was Young' is a classic." Throughout, Stordahl also makes prominent use of the rhythm section, which seemed almost superfluous on many '40s dates; now the bass and drums really have something to do.

We can be greatful for *Point of No Return* at the very least because it gave Sinatra the opportunity to sing "There Will Never Be Another You." Stordahl and Beau also achieve superlative results with the reed section: Beau's "Memories of You" contains a beautiful coda built on give-and-take between Sinatra and Ted Nash on soprano sax. Stordahl stunningly juxtaposes The Voice against Ted Nash's tenor on *Point's* most romantic side, "A Million Dreams." Up until then the property of corn bandleader and singer team Dick Jurgens and Eddy Howard, Sinatra's tight harmony with the reeds reinvents "Million Dreams" here in the Dorsey "Sentimentalist" mode (à la "I'll Never Smile Again"), with saxes subbing for the Pied Pipers.

More than any of his other albums, *Point of No Return* can be viewed as a microcosm of Sinatra's entire Capitol decade. Yet vocally he has so much of his '60s sound—especially his stretching "sweet" for several measures on the waltz "I'll See You Again"—it's difficult to believe this is a Capitol recording. Stordahl's presence accentuates how the simultaneous conclusion of the Capitol years and commencement of the Reprise period finds a great American artist at the perfect midway point— between the best of what he had done in his youth and the most amazing things he would accomplish in maturity.

"I remember after we did the first tune," said Viola, "I went over to June, and she had tears in her eyes. She said, 'Al, you have no idea what this means to Axel. He so wanted to do this album with Frank, he wanted to have this last hurrah.'" Sinatra seems to have intended the line "Goodbye, good luck, old friend" in "A Million Dreams" as a respectful adieu to both the man and the label, especially since the album represented far more of a *Point of No Return* for Stordahl than Sinatra. The gentle Swede ("Axel said about two words per session," said Miller, "whether he needed to or not") would be dead of cancer within two years, at age fifty. He must have been proud of his final project with his greatest collaborator and of its wonderful twilight feeling, so appropriate for a farewell album. Stordahl's presence allowed Sinatra to say good-bye to both the Columbia and the Capitol periods in a single gesture—the *Point of No Return* indeed.

Sinatra had yet one more album to make in 1961: in Reprise's first twelve months, the Chairman had made two full-length sets with Billy May, done two albums with collaborators so old that they were spanking new, and done one uptempo set with a younger arranger with whom he'd never worked before. The only gap left to fill was to do the same with a ballad album. This would be *Sinatra and Strings*, his first of many projects with Don Costa, a fast-rising and extremely talented orchestrator and producer. Costa's first foray into Sinatra's world would, unfortunately, be completely different in character from everything else they would work on together. *Sinatra and Strings* was every bit as brilliant as the rest of his 1961 output, but then beginning at the end of the decade and going up until the arranger's untimely death in 1983, the two men turned out a string of far less spectacular singles and a few generally forgettable albums—for reasons that are not Costa's fault.

With the *Strings* album, Sinatra wasn't just looking for a new arranger, he wanted in a string-ballad set a *feel* completely different from anything else he had previously done. This is precisely what he achieves beginning with the opener "I Hadn't Anyone Till You," with its combination of high drama and relaxed sensuality. In fact, *Strings* owes even less to previous Sinatra ballad albums than *Ring-a-Ding Ding* does to preceding swing sets. Everything on *Strings* tells us we are in the presence of a new and worthy string writer. This is not a set of a saloon songs; while the performances are always moody and occasionally bluesy—particularly "Come Rain or Come Shine"—they're never torchy like those on *Only the Lonely* or *No One Cares*, or darkly comic like *Close to You*, or squirmy like *Where Are You*.

"Do you know who Don Costa really was all the time to Frank?" Sammy Cahn asked. "Don Costa was Axel all over again, with those deeper, fuller strings." *Sinatra and Strings* makes a perfect follow-up to *Point of No Return* in that Costa, as Cahn observed, taps into the legacy of Stordahl, the romantic sound he had perfected in the '40s, as opposed to the shadowy, sharply nihlistic edge of *Only the Lonely* and *No One Cares*.

Like Stordahl's, Costa's work illustrates the theory espoused by Einstein that light (in both sense of the word) has weight, in the way that this ocean of fiddles seems at once ethereal and somber, perfectly suiting Sinatra's mood, which is neither sanguine nor melancholy. Even when

Costa dips his paintbrush of strings into the darker hues, drummer John Markham's brushes keep the proceedings from becoming maudlin. Sinatra's singing is even more larger-than-life than usual as he uncharacteristically relies on more big endings. And yet "All or Nothing at All," his bravura, big-note number from the Harry James years, becomes withdrawn and almost shy, emphasizing the "nothing at all" rather than the "all," and when he sings of "the kiss in your eyes" and "the touch in your hand" in the bridge, you can really feel it.

Sinatra intones "That's All" with equal tenderness, treating the first eight measures (A) as if they were a verse, yet he doesn't take them rubato—not exactly. Rather, by backing himself with only Miller's piano, he deemphasizes the rhythm, and when the orchestra enters on the second eight bars (A1), Sinatra never actually changes tempo but simply makes the beat come front and center. This also affords the opening section the feeling of a nursery rhyme, perfectly underscoring the innocence and vulnerability of the character Sinatra portrays in the lyric. The bridge, relying heavily on octave leaps, has a much more mature attitude, and Sinatra gets the most out of this, too.

"That's All" was written by Bob Haymes, and *Strings* also includes a tip of the fedora to the composer's crooner brother, forever associated with "It Might As Well Be Spring" (which Sinatra would record again three years later on *Academy Award Winners*). Whereas this song is normally the epitome of Rodgers and Hammerstein's antiseptic piety, Sinatra here makes it one of the darker items on the disc, particularly when he slows down on "feel" and then rushes to compensate on "in a melancholy way." When he repeats the expression "spinning daydreams," as if to himself, he gives the impression that he really is.

While *Strings* includes Sinatra's fourth and probably all-time smoothest "Night and Day," most of the album's repertoire consists of first-time attempts at standards. These include an extremely heartfelt "Misty" and "Prisoner of Love," the latter being the theme song of the first Italo-American singing heartthrob, Russ Columbo, as well as a huge 1946 hit for another *paisano*, Perry Como. *Strings* also contains Sinatra's sole mature "Stardust," which he had sung twenty years earlier with Harry James on an aircheck and with Tommy Dorsey as a "Never Smile Again" sequel on which he was only one voice in a chorus.

"Stardust" plays on the idea of delaying the instant of recognition, which you might think he had already taken to its furthest extreme in "Let's Fall in Love" (on *Ring-a-Ding Ding*). Here he puts it off for so long that the record's over even before we reach this epiphanous moment—which is a fancy way of saying that Sinatra's "Stardust" contains only the verse, a decision that supposedly teed off Hoagy Carmichael no end. ("I wrote a whole song, not just a verse!" he allegedly exclaimed on hearing the track.) Sinatra was not only trying to find a new approach to this most recorded of all pop classics but also was telling us that the verse is unduly neglected. It's a very stately opener for a song originally conceived as a jazz instrumental, and no sixteen bars of music had been treated so rhapsodically since Nat King Cole's "Nature Boy."

To beef it up, Costa penned an elaborate introduction, proving he wasn't averse to writing a verse to a verse for the Voice. This intro was a key reason why Sinatra guitarist Tony Mottola cited "Stardust" as his favorite Sinatra performance. "Don sets it up like almost a tone poem in the beginning," he said, "and it could stand by itself as a classical piece. Then Frank just sings this lovely verse, and then Don ends it, as he does in the beginning. Whoever thought of that idea—whether it was Frank or Don or whoever—it's completely original and absolutely beautiful."

"Yesterdays" contains a similarly celestial intro, suggesting that the singer is reflecting on his "happy, sweet sequestered days" from a vantage point in outer space. In this only reading of the Kern classic to compare with Billie Holiday's, Sinatra twists the word "then" à la Lady Day, and has you believing that expressions like "forsooth" and "gay youth" can be uttered without inciting attacks of the giggles.

Sinatra and Costa follow "Stardust" appropriately with "Come Rain or Come Shine," in which Harold Arlen borrows the harmonic pattern from Carmichael's "Georgia on My Mind" for the first few lines. Though hardly as earthy as Ray Charles (although Sinatra alludes to Charles' version in the use of horn obligatists over the strings in the intro), Sinatra can get at least as blue as Arlen and makes the most out of all the gospel feeling the composer wrote into the song. Like a Joe Turner or Jimmy Rushing, Sinatra never tries to instill in listeners the idea that he's actually creating music right now; rather, he's simply allowing it to come out of him—like molasses leaking slowly out of a crack in a barrel. The Sinatra-Costa "Come Rain or Come Shine" may well be the collaboration's masterpiece, effectively combining the high drama of grand opera (as suggested by the strings) with the pure power of the blues.

While *Sinatra and Strings*, as originally released, consists exclusively of standards, two lesser-known titles were recorded for the set but not widely issued until the CD era. There would have been nothing wrong with a couple of new faces in this roomful of old friends, yet the bonus tracks, "As You Desire Me" and "Don't Take Your Love from Me" (which Sinatra had recorded earlier that year with Billy May), don't work on the same level as the rest of the disc.

"As You Desire Me" suggests a sequel to "Gone with the Wind" on *Only the Lonely,* being another song by Allie Wrubel that bears the name of a movie in which it was not heard. The song's slight melody buckles under the weight of Costa's atypically portentous chart, particularly in a Chopinesque piano part which, fortunately, lightens up shortly into the piece. Both "Desire" and the lighter "Don't Take," the latter being an homage both to songwriter Henry Nemo and the singer he wrote it for, Mildred Bailey, benefit from prominent and sensitive rhythm guitar work by Al Viola.

Sammy Cahn, who was not represented on this album, expressed the opinion that "Don Costa was a *genius.*" If everything Sinatra and Costa did together had been on the same level as *Sinatra and Strings,* one might consider Cahn's compliment more than mere songwriter's hyperbole.

It would be difficult to imagine that the output of any artist in any period could be any more charmed than Sinatra's was in the first full year of Reprise's existence, especially when one factors in the remaining contractual obligations for Capitol. These concluded, much to Sinatra's pleasure, with "I've Got a Right to Sing the Blues," a single arranged by veteran writer Skip Martin. Most famous for Les Brown's "I've Got My Love to Keep Me Warm" and the stunning orchestration of "Shine on Your Shoes" that Fred Astaire sings in *The Band Wagon,* Martin occasionally pinch-hit for Sinatra around this time on dates conducted by Johnny Mandel (*Ring-a-Ding Ding*) and Neal Hefti (the Reprise single "Nothing but the Best"). Sinatra recorded "Right to Sing the Blues" at his own expense at the Reprise session of March 6, 1962, on which he also attempted a wacky Billy May chart of "Boys' Night Out" (which is scheduled to be released at last in 1995).

Much of 1962 would be devoted to a venture that remains unique in Sinatra's career. Although the singer has spent a lot of time abroad, his 1962 series of concerts on several continents is invariably referred to as the "World Tour." It is distinguished by the remarkably high caliber of the music produced as well as the surprisingly low profile the tour itself and the documents of it have kept for the following thirty years.

The tour, on which Sinatra and six musicians wound steadily westward (from Mexico to Japan to Europe), had ramifications on three levels for Sinatra: political, personal, and musical. Giving an example of how the good that the man does is overlooked by the press, Sinatra's one-time sparring partner Buddy Rich touched on the first in a talk show interview several years later. "He took [six] of the best musicians in Los Angeles," said the drummer. "He chartered an airplane, went to Japan, went to London [to raise money] for the orphanages. He paid the transportation of the entire technical crew, plus the musicians, plus the entertainers. He gave every musician a set price plus their expenses for hotels and food. And nobody ever knew about it. He just went over and did this out of the goodness of his heart. You gotta be some kind of a beautiful man to do this."

The tour was the largest humanitarian gesture of Sinatra's career. Describing himself as an "overprivileged adult," he set out to raise money and goodwill on behalf of the world's underprivileged children. "Jack Kennedy asked Frank to do this world tour to help needy children of the free world," recalled Emil Richards, who played vibes on the tour. "Kennedy asked him to do it under the auspices of the State Department, but Frank, who had recently bought his own jet, said, 'No, I'd like to do it on my own—I'd like to sponsor it.'" (In the '90s, Mr. and Mrs. Sinatra continue to advocate children's causes through the Barbara Sinatra Children's Center in Rancho Mirage, California.)

As one who fully comprehended the positive and negative power of the media, Sinatra had to decide whether or not to inform the American press about this undertaking, and he chose to exclude them. If it was ever construed that he was doing it for a tax write-off or for the publicity (neither of which would have been as valuable to him as two months of paid work), it would have undercut the whole purpose of the project. Additionally, neither of the two official recordings of these performances, one a live concert and the other a studio album, was released in the United States until the early '90s.

Apart from his personal stake in the Kennedy administration, Sinatra's decision to make the tour was prompted by other, more private reasons. Sinatra had been engaged to marry the dancer Juliet Prowse, and after they broke up, he wanted to immerse himself in some kind of a project that would, according to one musician on the trip, "get his mind off what happened." As one of the added percs of the voyage, Sinatra also looked forward to a tête-à-tête with his much-missed second wife, Ava Gardner, who was living at the time in Madrid.

The World Tour had roots in a less ambitious concert series Sinatra had done three years earlier. In 1959, he had performed in Australia with vibraphonist Red Norvo's quintet (and also visited with the former Mrs. Sinatra, who was then Down Under on location for the picture On the Beach). "The higher up you get in this business," Sinatra said at one of these 1959 concerts, "the more opportunity you have to work with the people you want." Introducing Norvo to the crowd, he continued, "This is a man I have tremendous respect for, musically and personally. I've always wanted to work with his band." The music for the 1959 and 1962 tours grew out of Sinatra's long-standing admiration for the small groups of Norvo and Benny Goodman—particularly the occasions when the vibraphonist and the clarinetist worked together.

Norvo had been friendly with Sinatra since early 1939, when he tried to hire him as a second singer for his orchestra, Mildred Bailey having been the first to alert him to the young crooner's obvious talent. Although Sinatra had recently committed himself to Harry James and never regretted it, his admiration for Norvo's great band of the late '30s knew no bounds. Speaking of how Sinatra, Dinah Shore, Mel Tormé, and other singers have all named the Norvo-Bailey "Mr. and Mrs. Swing Band" as one of their favorites, Norvo recently said, "The arrangements that Eddie [Sauter] made for Mildred were just perfect vocal arrangements, I mean, absolutely perfect. I'm sure Frank realized that."

Then Norvo added, without a note of egotism, "That band had a lot of character that 'stage' [music industry] people at the time appreciated. But it was a soft band, and it was much too early. It might have been a big commercial success ten years later. I felt that it was way ahead of its time." Not coincidentally, Sinatra eventually latched onto three of Norvo's sidemen as part of his permanent entourage: pianist Bill Miller, drummer Irv Cottler, and saxist Herbie Haymer (until he was killed in 1949).

At around the time of the vibes-heavy *Swing Easy,* in 1954, Sinatra was hearing quite a bit of Norvo and his trio, as were Bing Crosby and the other denizens of Palm Springs who frequented the Desert Inn. (Said Norvo, "It was actually the only jazz you could hear in Palm Springs.") In the fall of 1957, when Sinatra needed musicians for a sequence in his war movie *Kings Go Forth,* he hired Norvo's group. Norvo had previously played with his trio at the Tropicana in Las Vegas, but in 1958 Sinatra helped him secure a better deal with the Sands; Norvo opened at Easter, performing primarily in the lounges. The move enabled him to add a drummer and a doubling reedman, and expand from his trio of bass (Red Wooten), guitar (Jimmy Wyble), and vibes to a more conventional quintet. In addition to Wyble and Wooten, Norvo brought in a drummer (eventually Johnny Markham), and another San Franciscan, saxophonist Jerry Dodgion, whose playing had impressed Shorty Rodgers, Norvo's brother-in-law. Norvo's initial gig at the Sands was scheduled to last six weeks, but the quintet wound up staying six months. "Frank liked the band. He listened to jazz all the time," Norvo reported. "And that's the kind of music he wanted in the lounge."

While listening to Norvo's group in Las Vegas, Sinatra hatched the idea of using them in the same fashion that he'd employed the Page Cavanaugh Trio for several seasons a decade earlier. In some cases, especially in far-flung locales, the group would serve as a core rhythm section for the "house" orchestra and a supplement for regular accompanist Bill Miller. In the case of benefits, when there was no budget for a full orchestra, the quintet would be the whole show behind Sinatra.

Around February of that year, the group spent a week learning the singer's repertory and working out small-group arrangements. Although the rehearsals took place at Sinatra's house, the star joined them only occasionally; after all, he already knew the charts. The six men performed together for the first time at a benefit for cancer research in late February at Los Angeles' Shrine Auditorium, and then the combination did their first "paying" engagement at the Fountainbleau in Miami. "From now on," Sinatra announced to the capacity crowd at the Shrine, "in our personal appearances we're going to work together."

After the Shrine (and after Sinatra taped the *No One Cares* album that same month), the Sinatra-Norvo combination flew to Australia for two concerts in Sydney and Melbourne. Fortunately, someone in the sound booth turned on a tape recorder each night, and these two concerts, though not officially released, are by far the most important live recording of Sinatra from the Capitol era.

To use Sinatra's own lingo, he swings like a *mother* (technically, that's only half a word) on the April 1 (Melbourne) concert. As loose and unfettered as he was throughout the '50s, Sinatra offers a more aggressive brand of jazz singing here that points to his Basie albums of the '60s. He's never sounded more inspired and animated, generating so much happy energy, it's a wonder that the continent could contain him. "The smaller group did give him more freedom," explained Jerry Dodgion, elaborating that the informal format also encouraged Sinatra to vary the program and the arrangements from show to show whenever he toured with a small band. "He could be different every night, which is more in keeping with a jazz group."

The ballads are felt more keenly than ever, particularly "Angel Eyes" and "One for My Baby" by Sinatra and Miller, with the rest of the ensemble taking five. The swingers are even swingier than usual, especially "The Lady Is a Tramp" and "At Long Last Love." Sinatra must have been particularly pleased to sing the Riddle *Swing Easy* treatment of "All of Me" with the man who inspired it. And it's particularly thrilling here and on the other two final numbers, "Mandalay" and "Night and Day," when a local Aussie orchestra joins the quintet.

"I don't think he ever sang any better in his life than on that tape," said

Norvo. "I loved the way he sang with the small band. It was very free, and he was right on top of everything we were doing. He just melted into it, I thought. He took responsibility, he beat off the group and everything, he did his own thing. And the band played great for him, they loved working with him." Norvo felt that Sinatra came off so well because in these shows he never presented himself as a star in front of a backup band but was one of the musicians, down in the trenches with the rest of the unit. Norvo added, "He gave us the feeling he was part of the group."

Sinatra remained "part of the group" for some months to come. He and Norvo spent the last two weeks of April treating the paying customers at the Sands to the same program of hard-driving jazz that they'd done Down Under. On another occasion, the Quintet served as a last-minute substitute at the Sands for Dean Martin when that entertainer was apparently too deep in his cups (even by his own capacious standards) to appear. From July 25 to August 1, Sinatra and Norvo did an eight-day, eighteen-show stand at the 500 Club in Atlantic City. This time the singer broke the house attendance record that he'd set three years previously, bringing an estimated ten thousand people into the nightclub and $150,000 into the hands of happy owner Skinny D'Amato. The Norvo unit also played for Sinatra at the opening of his own little place in the sun, the Cal-Neva Lodge, at about this time.

Apart from other undated benefits (including a JFK rally at the home of actor Tony Curtis for a group called "Women for Kennedy," at which Sinatra experienced another altercation with a reporter), that may have marked the last time Sinatra worked with Norvo. That fall, following Sinatra's example, Benny Goodman hired the whole Norvo quintet as the center of his current ten-piece unit and toured Europe in October and November 1959.

Sinatra had announced that he intended to cut an album with Norvo, but at this time he wasn't about to bring any new and exciting ideas to the despised Capitol Records. However, Dinah Shore, who had already had Norvo on her TV show, went ahead and recorded *Dinah Sings Some Blues with Red*. While Shore is no Frank Sinatra, this Capitol set is a delightful disc that employs a cleverly arranged combination of the Norvo combo with a studio orchestra.

Sinatra apparently wanted Norvo to rejoin him for his next summer's string of personal appearances, but during that season Norvo had again gone out on tour with Goodman. So for the first time, Sinatra and Bill Miller assembled what the pianist called the "Red Norvo idea" sans Norvo. They hired the ace vibraharpist Emil Richards, only recently off the road with George Shearing, as the harmonic-rhythmic nexus of the unit. Miller also called in rising reed doubler Paul Horn, drummer Sol

Gubin, and representatives of two small classic '40s groups who had since become Sinatra mainstays, Page Cavanaugh's guitarist, Al Viola, and the King Cole Trio's former bassist, Joe Comfort. "Frank Sinatra and the Bill Miller Sextet," as the combination was billed, opened at the 500 Club in July 1960.

Sinatra gave Norvo the first call for the World Tour early in 1962, but plans for the reunion again fell through. "I think we were working at the Wagon Wheel up in Lake Tahoe," recalled Norvo, "when I got a call from Frank's attorney, Mickey Rudin, and he said, 'You wanna go? There was some mixup there. I don't know what it was. I understood that they just wanted me not the band, and I couldn't just disregard my whole band." Sinatra and Miller reassembled the Bill Miller Sextet, bringing the talented Mexican-American jazz bassist Ralph Pena and reedman Harry Klee, who had been Nelson Riddle's number one flautist throughout the Capitol years, along with Miller, Richards, Viola, and Cottler.

Again, the six men rehearsed extensively at Sinatra's own house, with the singer occasionally joining them. This time several of the arrangers who had written the full orchestrations of Sinatra's current repertory participated in scaling them down to sextet size. Neal Hefti wrote some sketches based on his own arrangements (including "Goody, Goody"), as did Johnny Mandel ("In the Still of the Night") and Billy May ("You're Nobody Till Somebody Loves You"). Miller took care of the rest himself: "I just kind of condensed everything down to size from the original charts, so that was really no problem. They were sketches more than full arrangements." Despite using only six men, the voicings are thick and rich. "So we basically sounded like the big bands in all of his recordings," said Klee.

Leaving the States on April 15, 1962, the entourage gave its first concert at Mexico City's International Theater and then played two televised shows in Tokyo. After appearances in Hong Kong and Korea, they spent the longest part of the trip in Israel, giving seven concerts in six cities over the course of nine days. Following several days off in the middle of May (at which time Sinatra paid a call on his ex[5]), the party hit Athens. Then in Italy they performed in three different theaters as well

5. In the first half of the tour, while looking forward like a schoolboy to this amorous encounter with the former Mrs. Sinatra, when the singer reached the line "Some like the perfume in Spain" he would interject a lusty "Yeah!" However, his planned reunion with Ms. Gardner resulted only in a tremendously ugly spat. Thereafter, when Sinatra got to the line about "the perfume from Spain," he would cry "Blecch!"—as indeed he did at the Paris Concert.

as a TV studio where they filmed six songs for local television. Following three shows in London, Sinatra and company gave what has become the sole widely known performance of the tour, at the Lido in Paris. Only two shows followed, at the Olympia Theatre (also in Paris) and at a gala benefit hosted by Princess Grace at the Sporting Club in Monaco.

Although Sinatra brought along a camera and sound crew, the only documents officially produced at the time were two twenty-minute film featurettes, *Frank Sinatra and All God's Children* and *Sinatra in Israel,* neither of which was ever shown theatrically or on television.[6] Since then, a number of complete concerts have also come into collectors' hands, including two from Japan, one from Milan, and one from The Royal Festival Hall—the Tokyo and London concerts also existing in video form. The one concert to have been officially issued, said to be the June 5 show at the Lido—although some Sinatra scholars believe this performance may have actually been taped on the 6th or 7th at the Olympia Theatre—was obviously selected for its superior sound quality rather than for the value of the performance. While Sinatra is giving it his all, that all wasn't very much this deep into the exhausting voyage. This was long before pop stars were able to junket from country to country in luxury, and the strain of the concerts as well as the impromptu appearances Sinatra made almost every day in local orphanages were taking their toll on him. While the *Melody Maker's* Ray Coleman, in reviewing the Gaumont Hammersmith concert (June 3), described Sinatra as evincing the "height of professionalism," even he felt obliged to add, "At times he sounded coarse, even nasal, and he certainly found it tough to sustain the note on certain occasions—notably on 'My Funny Valentine.'"

"Near the end there his voice was getting pretty roughed up," confirmed Al Viola, who rarely criticized Sinatra. "In fact, Monte Carlo [June 9] was pretty rough." By the time they made Paris (June 5 and 6), Sinatra had little voice left. When he recorded in London a week later (June 12–14), he had next to nothing that he could sing with. Discussing the complete itinerary at the Jerusalem show, Sinatra told the audience, "When I arrive home, I'm going to check into a hospital!"

6. Gary Giddins wrote of *Trilogy: Part Three: The Future,* "The temptation to quote directly from the text must be resisted." However, the narration of *All God's Children* is too entertaining not to reprise here: "The pretty one is Princess Margaret—only thirty-two years old and already the sister of the Queen. Shows you what a child can do with help." "These [blind children] are all tapped out in the seeing department—no sight, just high hopes." "Grownups are kids with their dreams removed." And when the scene shifts (in reverse of the itinerary, actually) from London to Jerusalem, the narrator describes the transition as one "from Cheerio to Shalom."

Still, the tour should not be judged only by its most prominent document. The unofficially circulated concerts from Italy (from the last week of May—thus far heard only in inferior sound) and earlier are so wonderful as to rival the excitement of the 1959 Norvo/Melbourne show. Better still is the June 1 Royal Festival Hall concert, where an ebullient Chairman overflows with the energy that's completely gone by the Paris concert of a few nights later. You can tell just by the statistics: in London he sang twenty-nine songs and stayed on stage for over an hour and a half; in Paris, he did twenty-three songs in a little over seventy minutes, part of which he successfully killed with a long, rambling monologue. "Frank worked especially well with the small group," said Viola. "If you listen to those tapes, you'll hear that he was kickin' our [collective] ass! I mean, he was loose! He would turn around to us as if to say, 'Hey you guys come on. This is a concert!' He didn't want us to sound like we were hanging out at some bar." Or, as Sinatra threatens the band in Melbourne in 1959, "Nobody sleeps in this act, Freddie!"

Apart from the hard swingers, which naturally proliferated throughout the tour, some of the most remarkable performances Sinatra created consisted of a series of low-key duets with Viola's guitar. While "I Concentrate on You" and "Try a Little Tenderness" do not seem to have been recorded on any of the taped concerts, "Night and Day" is far and away the highlight for the Paris show, at which, despite his obvious weariness at this point, Sinatra turns out an overpoweringly sensitive reading of the Porter classic.

The 1962 World Tour was a remarkable event, in which Sinatra continuously pushed himself to swingier, jazzier heights. The thirty concerts given in ten weeks amount to the World Series of Sinatra. The only disappointment, apart from the unfortunate fact that the true highlights of the event have yet to be released, is that Sinatra never followed up on what he had achieved in this extraordinary musical pilgrimage. The group was remarkably together after two and a half months on the road, and given a week or two of rest, Sinatra's chops were doubtless back to peak form. It remains a mystery why he never recorded a fresh album with the sextet in the Los Angeles studios or why Reprise waited more than thirty years to release a live album from the many tapes it had accumulated during the tour.

"I got the feeling," said Richards, "that [this jazz sextet] was going to be the kind of bag Frank was going to stay in, and in a sense he did, because he tried to keep as much of the group together as possible." The group worked with Sinatra at the Cal-Neva not long after returning, according to Viola, and they also returned to the 500 Club; at the Athens concert, Sinatra announced that he intended to do a similar World Tour every year from then on. But it was an anomaly that those six top studio men had ever left the lucrative Los Angeles locale to begin with; and while Miller, Cottler, and Viola would devote their careers to Sinatra, Pena, Richards, and Klee once again renounced the road. There continued to be talk of recording a studio album with the sextet as late as 1969, but that year the band's library of written music was destroyed when Bill Miller lost his house in a Los Angeles mudslide.

The 1962 tour did fuel the sharp interest in jazz that Sinatra had been cultivating in the early Reprise period, which was manifested not in small group recordings but in a series of meetings with the Count Basie Orchestra which began the same year. Yet before Sinatra returned home, he followed through on plans that had been worked out to immerse himself in the indigenous musical culture of one of the places he had visited. At the start of one track in the Paris concert, Sinatra announces that he's about to do a song about his favorite city. After a wisecrack about Helsinki, he goes into the Mandel arrangement of George and Ira Gershwin's "A Foggy Day." However, the *Great Songs from Great Britain* album would concentrate on songs actually written in the British Isles rather than simply being about them.

The song "Garden in the Rain" refers to "a touch of color 'neath skies of gray." The finished *Great Songs from Great Britian* is an album of similarly conflicting textures: the unending pastoral richness of Robert Farnon's orchestral backgrounds contrasts sharply with the startling thinness of Sinatra's voice. What's worse, both arranger Farnon and singer Sinatra had no forewarning that they should be planning the album for a vocal artist proceeding at half-steam, and the extremely slow tempos of these romantic ballads leave Sinatra with no place to hide.

Sinatra knew how he was sounding and doubtless would have canceled the three dates had forty-two musicians and at least that many of his English associates not set their hearts on attending. Trumpeter Stan Roderick, who described the sessions as "the biggest record date of the year," had given up other, better-paying work just to be there, explaining, "I turned it down for the honor of playing with such a singer." Sinatra was also loath to cancel sessions that had been set up so far in advance. As early as 1959, the British *Melody Maker* magazine reported that Sinatra had "big disc plans" for recording in London, and in December 1961 he began to assemble the repertory. Around Christmas, Alan Freeman, a producer at Reprise's GB affiliate, Pye Records, received an assignment from boss Louis Benjamin with the warning that "if you take it, you're raving mad." Freeman was soon in touch with Mo Ostin regarding a set of Sinatra songs not only *from* but to be recorded *in* Great Britain.[7]

"Oh, I was thrilled to pieces!" said Freeman. He immediately set about gathering the music for nearly seventy home-grown songs that he considered "suitable." Sinatra sifted through these and eventually boiled them down to the eleven that he ultimately recorded; of these, at least two had been selected by Sinatra before he even received Freeman's package. Coincidentally, these were the only two to stretch the boundaries of the concept: "Now Is the Hour," also known as "Maori Farewell Song," came from New Zealand, and "Garden in the Rain," whose author, Carroll Gibbons, had been born in America but made his reputation as leader of the house band at London's Savoy Hotel.

Eventually, Sinatra narrowed it down to one song apiece from each of the major U.K. writers, including "We'll Gather Lilacs" by Ivor Novello[8] and Ray Noble's "The Very Thought of You." (Sinatra had done Noble's "Love Locked Out" on the *Close to You* album and "The Very Thought of You" on several '40s broadcasts.) "I'll Follow My Secret Heart" marked the second Noël Coward tune Sinatra had recorded in nine months— the only two of his career (the other being "I'll See You Again" on *Point of No Return*). Sir Noël himself would have attended the dates had he not been in France at the time.

The selection process led to Sinatra's third recording of Jimmy Campbell's and Reg Connolly's "If I Had You" (the alternative would have been their "Try a Little Tenderness," which he had also done on both Columbia and Capitol) and of Carroll Coates' "London by Night."

7. *Great Songs* marked the first of two times old friend Mel Tormé brought an album concept to Sinatra: Tormé's *Swingin' on the Moon* had preceded *Moonlight Sinatra*, while *Great Songs* had been anticipated by *Mel Tormé Meets the British*, also recorded "on-location." Sinatra made an attempt to make the *Great Songs* project even more British by trying to commission a painting from Sir Winston Churchill for the front cover. The former prime minister, perhaps sensing that this would not be Sinatra's finest hour, respectfully declined.

8. Sinatra had previously recorded one tune by this highly regarded composer of British musical scores and stage idol: "If Only She'd Look My Way," which was backed by Sinatra's first recording of "London by Night." In many respects, this 1950 single amounts to the blueprint for *Great Songs for Great Britain* in that it consists solely of British songs, was manufactured and sold only in the United Kingdom, and was philanthropically motivated— all proceeds went to a children's fund chaired by the Duke of Edinburgh (who provided a spoken introduction). The major difference between the two discs, apart from the length (two songs verses ten on *Great Songs*), was that the 1962 project was actually recorded in Great Britain.

Coates had also written "No One Ever Tells You" on *A Swingin' Affair* and the considerably less Anglocentric "Sunday in New York," but the premise of "London by Night" (which Sinatra's firm, Barton Music, had published in the United States) was too perfectly suited to the album's theme to pass up.

Likewise, Sinatra doubtless considered Eric Maschwitz's "These Foolish Things" the best known of all British ballads. In its place, he opted for the same composer's more thematically appropriate "A Nightingale Sang in Berkeley Square" (which Nat Cole had recorded eighteen months previously). According to Freeman, "When the story got out that this session was going to happen, Eric called me up and nearly drove me mad! He said, 'For God's sake, make sure this song gets in. It would be the crowning of my career to have Sinatra record one of my songs!' [Maschwitz neglected to tell Freeman about Sinatra's Columbia and Capitol readings of "Foolish Things."] I told him, 'Obviously I'll send it over, and I think it would stand a great chance.' And personally I think that's the one that came out best on the album."

From the beginning, there was no question as to who the arranger would be. Robert Farnon and Sinatra had first met casually back in the Dorsey era when the former played trumpet for orchestrator and conductor Percy Faith, a friend of the Sentimental Gentleman. "I thought he was marvelous, absolutely wonderful," said Farnon. "Up to that point I was a Crosby fan, but not anymore. There wasn't anyone else, really. I became one of Frank's biggest fans and admirers."

Sinatra and Farnon didn't cross paths again for another twenty years. In the meantime, fellow Canadians Faith and Farnon achieved international reputations by heading in different directions, but each eventually worked with Sinatra. Farnon settled in London during the war and quickly established himself as England's most imaginative auteur of what they called "light music." In the 1950s, Sinatra became friendly with the arranger's brother, Brian, who worked as a musical director in Las Vegas. "When Sinatra went through there, Brian used to play some arrangements of mine for him," Farnon recalled. "Don Costa also was a champion of mine with Sinatra. I think it was Don more than anyone who suggested my name when Frank mentioned that he wanted to do an album of British material."

If there's any Sinatra album that *Great Songs* reminds us of, it's *Sinatra and Strings*, with Costa. "Here's a guy who is very influenced by Farnon," explained Tony Bennett. "You hear a lot of Farnon in Don Costa. In fact, so many orchestrators borrow from Farnon, it's what I call 'sweet thievery.' If you want to write string arrangements, only the best of them come up to Farnon. Every orchestra leader in the world knows his name. He writes for 109 men, and it's like silk, it sounds so effortless." Bill Miller can remember the first time Sinatra mentioned the project to him. "As long as we're over there, let's do an album with Farnon," he informed the pianist. "After all, he's one of the best."

Farnon provided a string sound for Sinatra that's as well suited to the singer as those of Stordahl and Jenkins. "That was another reason I listened to all of Frank's records," said Farnon. "Being an arranger, I enjoyed the scores that Axel and also Gordon Jenkins provided for him. Both those arrangers were my cup of tea, as it were. They had a style that I just enjoyed so much." Although Milt Bernhart has never worked with Farnon—and probably never heard the Sinatra-Farnon album—he independently arrived at the same comparison. Citing Stordahl as a masterly arranger for strings, the trombonist added, "Robert Farnon may be the only writer-arranger who's a little bit ahead of Axel."

After Sinatra narrowed down the repertory to eleven selections, he and Miller set the keys with some input from Nelson Riddle. At this point, Freeman, in London, began coordinating with Sinatra in Los Angeles and Farnon, who lived on the isle of Guernsey. The first hitch came when Farnon discovered that the key to "If I Had You" was way off—a full fourth away from where Sinatra could sing it comfortably. Freeman checked over his paperwork and concluded that the cable operator was responsible for the error. "I knew what the key should be because I knew his range," said Farnon. "And so I just took it from there. Frank was very pleased when I told him that I had figured out what key he should actually sing it in. It just happened to be right."

Sinatra passed along few further instructions to Farnon. "They gave me carte blanche and just told me to go ahead and write—which I did," the arranger recalled. "It was a delight to work that way. That was one of the things that was so nice about him. It was lovely to have that freedom." Sinatra and Farnon met again at the time of the Royal Festival Hall concert (June 1) to go over the charts with Miller and make sure the keys and tempos were suitable. The day before the session, Freeman had flown in Bill Putnam, Sinatra's favorite engineer, not so much to supervise the recording but to make sure all was as the Chairman liked it.

On the evening of June 12, Sinatra arrived at the C.T.S. Studio in Bayswater in a Rolls-Royce lent to him by Douglas Fairbanks, Jr., and said to Farnon, "Let's see how it fits, huh?" Four trumpeters, four trombonists, eight saxophonists and woodwind players, five rhythm men (including both Bill Miller and a local pianist, as per union rules), twenty assorted strings, and an uncountable hoard of well-wishers, several dozen in the control room alone, had already arrived. "There were so many people there who had nothing to do with the recording," said Farnon. "There were people all around us, sitting on my podium, under the piano, on the piano. . . . The studio was absolutely crammed with people, and Frank loved it. He didn't mind at all."

The listening crowd held their breath and Sinatra kept his cool when the first number, "If I Had You," turned out to be a double disaster. First, he had difficulty making his initial entrance after Farnon's elaborate, though subtle twenty-five-second introduction (largely taken by the trombones). Then, once that had been worked out, the concert grand piano that Bill Miller was playing became inexplicably incapacitated. Freeman has said that he had a piano tuner "tune it and retune" it all day but that the instrument somehow broke in the middle of Miller's solo. Miller's recollection is that "somebody forgot to tune the goddamn thing, which was unheard of." Freeman somehow had neither a repairman nor a backup piano on the premises, but it occurred to Sinatra to ask if a celesta might be handy.

When one hears the finished "If I Had You," it's difficult to imagine that Farnon had ever intended to use anything but a celesta. Luckily, this was the only number to include a keyboard solo. "I don't use too much piano with orchestra because when we have the guitar," said Farnon. "Both are essentially playing the same thing, and one interferes with the other." (Hence the guitar coda of "Garden in the Rain.") Miller thereafter retired to the sidelines while the local man took over the remaining ten tunes.

One should be glad that they persevered, because "If I Had You" may well be the most-aired track on the set, perhaps because of Farnon's unintentionally Riddlesque references in his use of the bass trombone and an Edisonian trumpet obligato. The somewhat brisk tempo allows Sinatra to sound stronger than on the very slow numbers, while both Sinatra and Farnon make myriad uses of the song's simple melody. Sinatra plays with the rhythm by adding extra syllables in the second chorus ("I could climb the *very* highest mountain" and "*also* cross the burning desert") to aid him in getting around long, sustained notes. When the singer reaches those hot sands, Farnon conjures up a steamy phrase that could have been heard in another of England's major cultural statements of 1962, the film *Lawrence of Arabia*.

Long before "If I Had You" was in the can, Farnon and Freeman realized that their star runner (who, Farnon recalls, was also appearing at Mesmer Hall those same evenings) was hopping on one leg. "He was finding it difficult to sing," said Farnon. "His voice was tired, and it was breaking a lot. He was very angry with himself." The orchestra members were duly sympathetic and supportive. "You're often disappointed when you hear a live session by someone who has only been a name on record," said trumpeter Ray Premru. "With Sinatra, I wasn't." Baritone saxophonist Ronnie Ross added, "Sinatra impressed me enormously. It was a change to hear a good session by a singer who really knew what was up." Farnon recalled an instance when Sinatra "was having great difficulty with 'Roses of Picardy,' and he stopped the orchestra and just looked up at the ceiling, and cried, 'Don't just stand up there. Come down and help me!' And that broke up everybody. Oh, it was a lovely moment."

And so it went. After finishing four tunes in three hours with great difficulty, Sinatra summarily "disappeared" without so much as bidding anyone adieu, most likely because he felt he had let everyone down and couldn't bear to face the disappointed mob. Over the next two nights, thirty-eight musicians (the trumpets were no longer needed), the crowd, and a substandard Sinatra returned, nailing down another four and then three more tracks. On the third night, Nelson Riddle, in London on unrelated business, also put in an appearance. (Both Freeman and Riddle questioned some of Sinatra's phrasing on "The Gypsy," recorded the previous night and, coincidentally, Farnon's least favorite of the eleven tunes. Sinatra listened dutifully to the criticism but maintained that his was the way to go.)

After nearly thirty-five years, the debate regarding *Great Songs from Great Britain* continues. Do Farnon's lush orchestrations and Sinatra's trying so hard compensate for the thinness of his voice? One particularly feels disappointed at "We'll Gather Lilacs." At face value, Sinatra would hardly seem the lilac-gathering type, but for most of the track the singer is expert enough to convince us that he actually does give a hang about sniffing those bloomin' blossoms. When he reaches the end, however, the vocal line gets weak exactly at the point where the arrangement calls for him to surge confidently. Likewise, he is unable to animate "We'll Meet Again," an overly stoic, "no emotions, please, we're British" kind of love song that had no business being revived after the Blitz (except in a deliberately nostalgic context such as here and on Rosemary Clooney's recent *Demi-Centennial* album).

We also come across moments where the singer's fatigue contributes to the melancholia of the material, as in "Now Is the Hour" and the ironically dour "Garden in the Rain." His cracking on both utterances of the phrase "somebody else" on "The Gypsy" (also recorded by Charlie Parker during an epiphany of emotional exhaustion) could be chalked up to part of the interpretation. But the strong moments are very strong. Apart from "If I Had You," Sinatra sounds completely convincing on "A

Nightingale Sang in Berkeley Square," aided by Riddle-like flutes (portraying the ornithological entity referred to in the title) and a sumptuous trombone solo from Ted Heath veteran Harry Roche. During the date Sinatra also seemed delighted that the bearded trombonist hit a clinker, informing him, "I'm afraid you got a little bit of whisker in there, mate," and then hanging over the engineer's shoulder as the nervous techie spliced out the bum notes right then and there. Sinatra also succeeds in phrasing the line "there is magic abroad in the air," which appears in both "Nightingale" and "London by Night," in two such different ways that one almost doesn't notice the coincidence.

It's unlikely that Freeman thought "Roses of Picardy" had any chance at all of making it to the final cut (and originally it didn't). How could anyone have envisioned this World War I artifact as potential Sinatra material? Paradoxically, it's this oldest and most archaic flower in the bouquet that comes off as the hippest. On its own, "Roses" is a singularly undistinguished song, written by "Danny Boy" author Frederick Weatherly and first popularized by John McCormack. In the half-century since "Roses" first sprouted, the number was remembered only dimly in its native country as a rather prissy vehicle for a semiclassical exhibition by alto saxophonist Freddy Gardner.[9]

"Roses" grows around a rather simple metaphor, namely that love blossoms like a flower, but soon, also like a flower, love dies. That's not much to work with, but Sinatra and Farnon contrive to give this paper-thin dramatic hook as much depth as a mystery by Dashiell Hammett. It even starts ominously, with an out-of-tempo verse in a minor key, Sinatra being intriguingly introduced by a subtone clarinet. The lyrics to the verse are tantalizingly vague, the rose simile not becoming clear until the refrain, at which point Sinatra has us hooked. As with his "Where or When," from here the tune builds to a captivating climax in a single powerful chorus. One only notices vocal problems by listening carefully to the last few lines, and it's easy to forgive these in the light of how hard Sinatra is trying and how profound his level of feeling is throughout this moving number.

Freeman, who listened to the complete session tapes again in the 1970s, wonders if Sinatra hadn't decided to junk "Roses" even while he was recording it, much as he did "Miss Jones" during *Ring-a-Ding Ding*. The producer recalls that Sinatra was kidding around and clowning with a vengeance during the recording of "Roses," giving the impression that

9. Rarely if ever heard in the modern era, "Roses" happened to be recorded in the same year as *Great Songs* by two individuals near and dear to Sinatra, Billy May and Bobby Darin, for the latter's Capitol Records album debut, *Oh, Look at Me Now!*

he didn't take it seriously in the least. Which is precisely the opposite of the idea one gets from listening to the cut on the finished disc.

Thirty years later, "Roses" blooms as the most radiant flower of the album. Of the eleven tunes, Sinatra had the most trouble with this song, and for that reason he left if off the original release. At the end of the final session, he and Freeman uncorked another bottle of Jack Daniel's and proceeded to listen to playbacks of all three nights' work. The singer then instructed the producer, "Scrub 'Roses of Picardy.' I don't like it." Freeman argued to have the song remain, but Sinatra remained insistent. "He wasn't holding his notes well," said the producer. "There were notes that should have been held, and he was cutting them off, and it wouldn't have sounded right even [if we covered up the weak spots] with echo." However, Freeman added, "I still think it's a great pity he decided to scrap it because he had so much emotion. It was the most beautiful Bob Farnon arrangement. And he sang it so beautifully, with tremendous *feel*. There was so much feeling in that."

The entire album nearly suffered the same fate as those dying "Roses of Picardy." Sinatra could have rerecorded his vocal parts over the orchestral track at any time he wished, yet instead he elected to make the ten remaining *Great Songs* his only important work never to be released stateside. Over the next thirty years the original British LP became the most sought-after Sinatra item among collectors in the colonies, and the history of the set's foreign issues serves as a microcosmic illustration of the far-reaching ramifications of his music. In the early '80s, Italian Reprise issued it with a new cover and title (*Frank Sinatra in London*); a few years later the Japanese reissued *Great Songs* with the original artwork and "Roses" restored, but with three alternate takes replacing the originals. More recently, an unauthorized German anthology contained a previously unknown alternate to "Roses," while an Italian double CD contains over two hours of alternates, breakdowns, and session chatter. The long-awaited American CD issue apparently uses the Japanese master, including the same alternates as well as "Roses."[10] On the whole, the set has been worth the effort and, for Americans, worth the wait; for all of its faults, *Great Songs from Great Britain*

---

10. The 1992 American Warner Bros. CD also, for whatever reason, parroted the Japanese tradition of printing the text to all the lyrics. Here they simply appropriated the Japanese libretto, which includes such minor errors as "Roses are flowing" (rather than "flowering"). Best of all is in "London by Night": Instead of "Down by the Thames, lights that sparkle like gems," we get "Down by the tennis lights . . ." Oh, well, wait until the Japanese buy all of London, too, and then they'll get it right.

remains one of Sinatra's most compelling musical voyages. As in "Garden in the Rain," surely here is charm beyond compare.

Most of the early Reprise sets used artists' renderings rather than photographs for their covers. The cover of *Sinatra and Swingin' Brass*, recorded four days before the World Tour got under way (and preceded by another set of Sinatra and strings, *All Alone*, with Gordon Jenkins) depicted Blue Eyes in fittingly bright, "brassy" colors. The album inside does not precisely mirror the packaging, however; while the jacket promises no-holds-barred swinging on the level of *Swingin' Affair* or the Billy May albums, *Swingin' Brass* turns out to be a far more controlled, yet no less delightful, forty minutes of rhythmic romping. Not that it doesn't have its free-wheeling moments. The first seven songs accelerate in energy, from the comparatively restrained "Goody, Goody" (which opened nearly all the World Tour concerts), which Sinatra phrases surefootedly on the beat, to the cacophonous "Tangerine," which commences with a dissonant brass crash. (Although Sinatra sings two complete choruses of "Tangerine," he unfortunately does the main lyric twice rather than going for the witty second chorus test associated with Helen O'Connell.)

But "Swing" is indeed the crucial term. Much of the album comes from songs fashioned from band instrumentals ("Don'cha Go Away Mad," originally a hit for Illinois Jacquet as "Black Velvet"), written by jazz composers (Ellington's "I'm Beginning to See the Light"), associated with swing bands ("Goody, Goody" and "Serenade in Blue"), or favorites of swing musicians ("Love Is Just Around the Corner" and "Tangerine"). And when Sinatra and arranger Neal Hefti interject songs by Cole Porter ("I Love You," "At Long Last Love," and "I Get a Kick out of You"), Gershwin ("They Can't Take That Away from Me"), and Kern ("Pick Yourself Up"), they make these classic show tunes sound as if they had originally been conceived as swing-era rhythm novelties.

The one major rhythm writer whom the set overlooks is Hefti himself. Many original instrumentals that Hefti had written for the band books of Woody Herman and Count Basie had become widely accepted as big-band classics, and several eventually attained acceptable lyrics. "Softly with Feeling" and "Plymouth Rock" became, thanks to Steve Allen, "Oh, What a Night for Love" and "Cool Blue," while Bart Howard (whose "Fly Me to the Moon" later became the supreme Sinatra-Basie anthem) made "Li'l Darlin'" into "Don't Dream of Anybody but Me." "Girl Talk" became a Tony Bennett staple without a name change. John Hendricks supplied lyrics to "Little Pony" and "Two for the Blues" (the latter also recorded by Frances Wayne Hefti).

As mentioned earlier, Sinatra had initially hired Hefti both as a general producer for Reprise and as an arranger on such releases as *Dean Martin French Style, Alice Faye Sings Her Famous Movie Hits,* and *Themes from TV's Top 12: A Neal Hefti Spectacular Featuring 40 Guitars and 8 Pianos.* "Somebody from Reprise called [not Sinatra himself in this case] and asked me if I wanted to be a producer," Hefti recalled. "I had never done that before, so I said yes. That was my last exclusive contract. I couldn't work for anybody else but Reprise for about a year."

Like Mandel, Hefti had first become a "name" orchestrator with one of the "progressive" swing orchestras of the '40s, Woody Herman's original Thundering Herd, and then helped revitalize the Basie band of the '50s. But while he never sat in Basie's brass section, he played a far more important role in the band's comeback, contributing such staples of the Count's book as "Splanky," "Cute," and those two little darlings, "Li'l Darlin'" and "Little Pony." On many occasions Basie even contracted Hefti to orchestrate entire albums for him; he would become the most celebrated orchestrator of the Basie "New Testament" Orchestra of the 1950s. As Frank Foster, the Count's lieutenant and eventual successor, recalled, "Even before I joined the band I heard Neal's 'Plymouth Rock,' and I just fell in love with that tune. When I first started writing, Neal and Ernie Wilcox were my two principal influences. The bulk of his stuff was really, really good. I still love to play 'Splanky.'"

Hefti also recorded prodigiously as a house musical director for Coral and Epic (and was responsible for the last hits of both Tommy and Jimmy Dorsey), accompanying singers (including his wife, fellow Herd vet Frances Wayne) and jazz soloists (including Coleman Hawkins and Georgie Auld). At the same time, he made albums as a bandleader under his own banner, ranging from jazz (*Hefti Hot 'n' Hearty, The Band with Young Ideas*) to easy listening that refused to insult its listeners' intelligence (*Singing Instrumentals, Pardon My Doo-Wah*). And, like Billy May, Hefti actually took his own orchestra out on the road for several brave seasons during the band-resistant '50s.

He first worked for Sinatra around 1951. "I did a couple of charts for Frank that Axel didn't have time to do," Hefti recalled. "I was a friend of Axel's, and once in a while he'd call me up and say, 'Can you help me out, I'm really in a jam!' He asked me for a chart on 'Get Happy' [telecasts on February 17 and March 17, 1951], and I had a sort of gimmick going on, a melodic pattern. Then a couple of weeks later Frank said to do one on 'That Old Black Magic' which he was going to use in a picture called *Meet Danny Wilson,* and he said to write it something like the way I had written 'Get Happy.'"

The original liner copy to *Swingin' Brass* constitutes a mass of misinformation: whereas the notes claim that Hefti picked ten of the twelve tunes, like most Sinatra arrangers his input was not solicited in the selection of the songs. They also state that "Sinatra had not been singing in some time" before these two April sessions. Sinatra does sound a little rusty here and there, particularly on the slowest tune, "Serenade in Blue," a composition whose bridge seems designed to exhaust a voice so that it sounds breathless, hoarse, and passionate, yet even here Sinatra finishes on a glorious low tone. Still, he had actually cut no more or no fewer than his usual quota of albums and singles in the previous few months. Lastly, the writer professes that "the two recording sessions were booked six weeks in advance, allowing Neal to get the town's best [side] men." Irv Cottler has recalled, however, that he wasn't able to do the album because the call went out to musicians only two days before the date. Cottler would have been willing to give up an audience with the Pope himself to work with Sinatra, particularly on a swing set with Hefti. Unfortunately, this time the drummer wasn't able to get out of a commitment he already had for that date.

Several tracks recall specific bands: "Don'cha Go 'Way Mad," the most lighthearted lyric on the topic of infidelity imaginable (a swinging "Guess Who I Saw Today"), looks ahead to the first *Sinatra-Basie* album. It points quite specifically to Hefti's work on that record as well as to his dozens of instrumental pieces for Basie both earlier and later, mounting to a marvelous climax in which Sinatra produces even more "baby"'s than Mrs. Dionne.

The brass bass–backed "Love Is Just Around the Corner" suggests the way Benny Goodman phrased the same melody as "A Smo-oo-oth One," particularly the way Sinatra clips the ends of each line in the central (A) sections. Sinatra's second reading of the bridge, after it slows down and gets back to speed, brings to mind Louis Prima, as does the band's unison meatball exclamation. (It's a shame Sinatra didn't also include "Angelina—Zooma Zooma!")

If Jimmie Lunceford hadn't died in 1947 but had lived to follow Basie's example of renewing himself in the early '50s, then "Ain't She Sweet" is the kind of production Hefti would have written for him. A minimal '20s "rhythm novelty," "Ain't She Sweet" bounces along to a two-beat feeling in an atomic-age update of what Lunceford and Sy Oliver achieved in "Margie" and "My Blue Heaven."

"I'm Beginning to See the Light" recalls both credited co-composers, Duke Ellington and Harry James, and in particular points to the trumpeter's evocation of the maestro in his 1944 hit rendition. Having Ben

Webster on hand doesn't hurt; in his only solo on the date (trading fours with the ensemble on the instrumental break), the Ellington band's greatest tenor deputizes as an official representative of "The Guv'nor." Sinatra sings the central strains in harmony with a section of tightly muted trumpets that play the melody with him, violating the number one rule of vocal orchestration but sounding marvelously Ducal-Jamesian. The piece ends unexpectedly on a 1-2-3 Basie tag, played on a celesta.

While Sinatra remakes a number of tunes here from as recently as the Capitol era, the old standbys sound just as fresh as the virgin offerings. "They Can't Take That Away from Me" and "I Get a Kick out of You" aren't substantially different from the Sinatra-Riddle readings, yet the way Sinatra channels his wattage makes them completely new. "Kick" finds Sinatra singing "bop-type refrain" instead of "perfume from Spain" (and "kick from cocaine" in the original *Anything Goes*), and after the familiar "terrifffff," makes a point of sarcastically twisting the "t'would." (This "Kick" also includes a superlative alto solo, possibly by Joe Maini, again leading the reeds.)

Sinatra had sung Cole Porter's "I Love You" frequently in the '40s but never recorded it, even though he found time to wax two other tunes with the same title.[11] The composition finds the great songwriter striving to create a simple, direct lament in the manner of Irving Berlin's "Always" or "What'll I Do?" but has always seemed a little thin to be a real Porter ballad. Therefore, Sinatra instills it with a perfect balance of romance and raucousness, much the way he casually drops the "yourself" syllables throughout the second eight bars of "Pick Yourself Up." On "I Love You," the moment he makes his reentrance for the outchorus is particularly euphoric. Which is as good a description of the entire album as any.

In his official capacity as producer for Reprise, Hefti had cultivated a sturdy business relationship with Sinatra; with *Swingin' Brass*, the two proved that they could make beautiful music together as well. Hefti found Sinatra "easy, very easy" to work with, and Emil Richards recalled that Sinatra really enjoyed working with Hefti: "Frank's got a bunch of peo-

11. All three were from musicals. Robert Wright and George Forrest's tune was based on Grieg's "Ich Liebe Dich" and sometimes listed as "I Love You, Dear," from *Song of Norway*, a 1944 hit that Sinatra recorded for Columbia in 1946. Sinatra cut Harry Archer and Harlan Thompson's "I Love You," which was introduced in the 1923 show *Little Jesse James*, for Capitol in 1953. Porter's song was published in December 1943 but not introduced until *Mexican Hayride* opened on Broadway a month later.

ple he invited to the session [Benny Carter, Papa Jo Jones, Dinah Shore, and two juniors, Sammy Davis and Franklyn Sinatra, among others, were in attendance on the Basie date], and Neil was in the booth listening to a playback. He calls out, 'Frank, come on in! You're gonna cream in your pants when you hear this one!' Frank looks at me and says sarcastically, 'Do you believe this guy? Talking like that in front of all these people?' Frank was digging it!"

As was clear to all concerned, including Richards, Hefti was the logical choice to oversee *Sinatra-Basie: An Historic Musical First.* Hefti described getting an assignment from Sinatra which included only one specific role for him in a "delivered package," and it started with a pile of sheet music and instructions from Sinatra and Bill Miller. Sinatra was no longer providing his writers with as detailed a map as he had in the '50s with Riddle, but still the songs, keys, and tempos had already been determined. All Hefti had to do was work within the parameters of what Sinatra had already worked out. "I really didn't need to talk to him that much. Everything was fairly clear," said Hefti. "I had done enough charts with singers in my life to know what was going on, especially when he would pick the instrumentation or when he would say, 'We're going to do this with Count Basie's band.' If I was told it was going to be Sinatra and Basie, I knew they didn't want it to sound like Carmen Cavallero." As Sinatra announced at the start of the date, "I've waited twenty years for this moment." On another occasion, Sinatra declared the Basie band "the greatest orchestra at any time in the history of the world." He had followed the band since it exploded on the national scene in the late '30s and had known the leader personally since the '40s.

When introducing "Please Be Kind" from the album in Las Vegas that December, Sinatra said, "This is a marvelous Neal Hefti arrangement, and I recently recorded [it in] an album with Count Basie's band. . . . It's most exciting for me because I think most of the singers in the world today would like one shot at singing with the Basie band, and I was fortunate enough to be able to do it." Then, slipping into an "Amos and Andy" dialect, he added, "That's 'cause I'se de president of de record company, that's why I got it done!" And it isn't a stage joke, either, Kingfish. Sinatra continued, "Now Smokey the Bear, that's Sammy Davis. Smokey, he de vice-president, he gonna get the second chance at Basie."

To hear Basieites Earle Warren and Sweets Edison tell it, Basie and Sinatra were constantly hanging out whenever they happened to be in New York at the same time. "He liked to sit there with his arm around Basie," said Edison, to which Warren added, "Which Basie didn't mind because Frank was such a big star and always getting bigger." At some undetermined point, Sinatra also got to know the original Basie band's greatest apostle, the legendary Lester Young. "I knew Lester well. We were close friends, and we had a mutual admiration society," Sinatra told Arlene Francis. "I took from what he did, and he took from what I did." "If I could put together exactly the kind of band I wanted," as Young himself said to Nat Hentoff in 1956, "Frank Sinatra would be the singer." Prez added, "Really, my main man is Frank Sinatra."

As Warren and Edison indicated, Basie didn't consider himself merely a musician but a key player in the show business fraternity. "Basie was fascinated by anybody who had acted in the movies," Frank Foster reminisced. "He loved to be around actors and actresses. And he was totally in awe of talented singers if they had been movies. He was really in awe of them. And of course Frank had been in a few movies."

Where *Swingin' Brass*—"Goody, Goody," in particular—finds Sinatra phrasing more evenly, sacrificing some of his idiosyncratic rhythm accents for greater swing, like Jimmy Rushing or Joe Williams when they take on a fast rhythm number, he goes to even greater extremes on *Sinatra-Basie*. "Nice Work If You Can Get It," for instance, has Sinatra maintaining the hard-swinging, even-toned, unfrivolous lines associated with blues vocal style. This may be partly attributable to an extramusical factor: Alec Wilder later reported that Sinatra had chosen an unfortunate moment to record the disc because that particular October the Dodgers had made it to the World Series. Sinatra yelled his head off at every game, and, said Wilder, "his throat really wasn't in any condition to make the album." (After several takes of "I Won't Dance," Sinatra refers, in the session tapes, to the "frog" in his throat.)

Whatever the reason, Sinatra couches each line in a way that's taut and unfettered, thus tapping into the paradox that is the central strength of the new edition of the Basie band, an aggregation that's at once as tight as the clothes on a floozy and as loose as the lady herself. The band marches with turn-on-a-dime precision to better serve the cause of reckless abandon. Where Riddle and May (other than on *Come Dance with Me*) often color their uptempo ensembles with a dash of humor, Hefti and Basie are serious even when they're being whimsical (as on "Flight of the Foo Birds").

"Basie, as we all know, epitomizes the greatest kind of tempo for swing, in jazz" is how Sinatra described working with the great band (in a 1965 interview with Larry King). "It was a joy because all I had to do was just stay up on the crest of the sound and move along with it. It just carries you right through." Sinatra's appreciation of the nuances of rhythm come through during a run-through of "I Only Have Eyes for

You" on the session tapes, when he asks the pianist (whom he addresses as Bill, which could mean either Miller or William "Bill" Basie), "Can you add a little more rhythm? It sounds like Shep Fields!"

They were able achieve this balance of tension and relaxation thanks to arduous rehearsals. Unlike what happened on the Sinatra-Ellington dates five years later, "the day before the first date, we rehearsed all day, all night," said Bill Miller, officially serving as contractor. "Everybody also came in an hour before so we could go over them again." As Joe Bushkin has pointed out, "The Basie guys could read as well as any studio band," but to help them nail the charts even tighter (as they would with Ellington) Sinatra and Miller brought in ace lead trumpeter Al Porcino. Basie was a capable but not an expert reader, Miller continued, "and he was very slow to learn new tunes, so on a couple of the songs he said, 'You play it.'" It didn't hurt that Miller had already served as "Vice-Count" with Basie-worshiper Charlie Barnet's band, deputizing on such tributes as "The Count's Idea."

Of the ten tracks, only "The Tender Trap," the archetype of Sinatra-Riddle style, fails to work as reimagined in the Basie mold. "Learnin' the Blues," another item from the same idiom, functions more smoothly in the new setting. The two superstrong opening selections, "Pennies from Heaven" and "Please Be Kind," sound even more like the Basie style at its purest than anything on the Count's two contemporaneous instrumental albums for Reprise (*This Time by Basie!*, 1963, and *Pop Goes the Basie*, 1964).

"Pennies from Heaven," on which Miller plays piano, may be the disc's most successful cut. It's certainly a chart Sinatra kept alive for a long time, with various tenor players (like Bob Cooper in 1981) taking the solo originated by Frank Foster. Here Sinatra is firmly entrenched in Basie's rhythmic groove and never deviates from it, to the point of using the last phrase of the bridge ("up—side—down") as a blues stop-time break. This approach also makes the second chorus of "Please Be Kind" swing with strong stresses and firm fermatas to delay the key phrase at the end of each line, giving the second bridge of that refrain over to an instrumental section. Most memorable is the heavenly ending of "Pennies": Sinatra swingingly repeats the penultimate phrase, "For you and, for you and . . ." a mess of times before resolving it with the final note ("me"). Apparently, he concocted this classic coda on the spot; two previous takes have him merely holding the last note while the band plays the phrase over and over instrumentally.

Likewise, "I'm Gonna Sit Right Down and Write Myself a Letter" transforms the whole ensemble into a colossal rhythm section behind soloist

Sinatra, beating out a pattern that suggests a hip Native American rain dance. Working around two booting tenor solos (Frank Wess or Frank Foster or both), the singer expediently drops all articles from the outchorus bridge ("write words . . . sweet . . . knock me off") to show that he's not even going to let the lyric get in the way of his momentum. The comparatively capricious "(Looking at the World Through) Rose-Colored Glasses" comes as close as the album ever gets to capriciousness, recalling "Foo Birds," "Ducky Bumps," and some of Hefti's giddier pieces for Woody Herman. On the other hand, "My Kind of Girl," the one current tune of the ten, becomes the oldest-fashioned stylistically, opening with a closely bridled Sinatra atop sixteen bars of vintage Basie piano and sensitive drumming by Sonny Payne. Both this tune and "I Only Have Eyes for You" recall Basie's classic version of "All of Me" in that after a quietly elegant half-chorus, the entire brass section comes crashing in like thunder on the bridge.

"Nice Work if You Can Get It" delves into Sinatra's own musical past. Of the set's several remakes, it comes the closest to the original (on *Swingin' Affair*) yet is cast in a more frantic mode. Two trumpet solos recall the horn men closely associated with Sinatra, one using a tight mute à la Sweets Edison, the other (probably Sonny Cohn or Porcino) wide open and rich in Harry James–like vibrato. The medium-slow "I Won't Dance," another remake from *Swingin' Affair* (although not reiterating the "ring-a-ding ding" line), effectively caps the program, showing how all the rehearsing paid off. The band works hard to follow the central player closely, and here the individual vernaculars of each of these two master auteurs become indistinguishable.

The finished album was an immediate sensation, ranking with *Ring-a-Ding Ding* and *I Remember Tommy* as about the biggest sellers of the early Reprise era. Still, with two full-length triumphs under their belts (and several singles, all but one of which he conducted but did not arrange[12]), Hefti and Sinatra stopped working together at this point. Sinatraphiles have long circulated the story that Hefti left Reprise because he wanted better billing. The arranger supposedly demanded that his name be part of the title of *Swingin' Brass* (he admitted that *The Thin One and Hefti* and *Hefti Meets the Thin One* were two titles they considered) and that it be prominently displayed on the cover of *Sinatra-Basie*. Nobody who worked with the conductor in 1961 and 1962 described him as any kind of egomaniac, however, and the Neal Hefti of

12. Hefti conducted and scored "Everybody's Twistin' " for Sinatra, a mod remake of Rube Bloom and Ted Koehler's 1935 "Truckin'," with a ragmop (I say ragmop) ending and a countermotive that anticipates the theme song Hefti would later write for the TV show *Batman*. Holy foreshadowing!

the '90s is far more inclined to denigrate his work than tell everybody
how great he is.

Despite his success in the world of popular music, Hefti always felt
uneasy. As he put it, he really didn't like anything he wrote at the time he
was doing it and has even less use for his older works now. "When I
write anything, I try to put it behind me," said Hefti. "I was always a
reluctant writer. I don't really like to write on call like that. I didn't mind
doing a couple of tunes a year when I was with Woody's band, when I
could do whatever I wanted and take as long as I wanted. But when you
tell me, 'Do this and have it tomorrow and that's that,' I never liked that
process. To me, it's like an order." Even though Hefti considered Sinatra
about the best singer around as well as the easiest to work with, he
"never wrote for another singer since that *Sinatra-Basie* album."

Both men did work again with Basie. A month after *Sinatra-Basie*,
Hefti and the Count were at it again in a studio in New York, cutting the
band's latest all-Hefti package, *On My Way and Shoutin' Again!* In 1964,
Sinatra and Basie taped the second of their two studio collaborations, *It
Might As Well Be Swing*, a program of ten charts put together by Quincy
Jones. The sequel has a very different feel from the original. Even considering the absence of any material with prior Basie associations, *Sinatra-Basie* can be described as Sinatra retailoring his approach to fit into
Basie's idiom, whereas *It Might As Well Be Swing* takes it the other way
around, with the Basieites accommodating their guest (even to the point
of adding a string section).

Quincy Delight Jones first worked with Sinatra far from either man's
own home turf. On July 7, 1958, Sinatra gave a special concert in Monte
Carlo, which simultaneously promoted the opening of his film *Kings Go
Forth* and raised money for the United Nations Fund for Refugee
Children, a pet charity of that *High Society* gal, Princess Grace of
Monaco. Coming completely out of left field, Sinatra hired the twenty-
five-year-old trumpeter-arranger-composer to assemble and direct his
accompanying orchestra. "Somebody told me once that Ava Gardner
had told him about me," Jones recalled recently. It seems more likely,
though, that Sinatra had heard of Jones through his early work with
Basie (the title of his first recorded composition, "Kingfish," indicates
that he shared Sinatra's interest in "Amos and Andy"), Dinah Washington, and others.

Before going into the studios, Jones had toured with Lionel Hampton
from 1951 to 1953 and did a lot of freelance dates in New York. In 1956,
he joined Dizzy Gillespie's big band for a continental tour, after which
he elected to remain in Europe to work as the house musical director for

Paris' Barclay Records. (Jones would later serve in the same capacity at various times stateside at ABC-Paramount and Mercury.)

While working at Barclay, Jones presided over a studio orchestra that, thanks to the ensemble playing of the local musicians and the availability of American soloists (both visitors and expatriates), was the equal of any in Hollywood or New York. "We used a regular fifty-five-piece orchestra in Paris," said the conductor. "It was pretty hot, you know. And it had Lucky Thompson, Don Byas, Stéphane Grappelli, Kenny Clark, Zoot Sims—and a lot of people used to come through and play with us. Even the Double Six [of Paris] was the vocal group." Jones claimed that any number of these jazz legends could be present on the Sinatra Monte Carlo concert and recalled specifically that pioneering bebop drummer Kenny Clarke played on that show. (With that knowledge in mind, you can hear that the drum breaks on the Monte Carlo "Come Fly with Me" include a lot more bebop bombs than one would expect from Stoller or Cottler.) "I remember we all went down to Monte Carlo by train," said Jones. "I was scared to death. I was so in awe of him at the time that I hardly said a thing. Our first meeting was really quite brief."

Sinatra next summoned Jones equally unexpectedly six years later in an even farther away place. In the interim, Jones had built up his reputation, writing many individual charts and several entire albums for Basie (*Li'l Ol' Groovemaker* and *This Time by Basie!*, both 1963). Jones also organized his own all-star interracial, intergender, and international jazz orchestra, with which he returned to Europe to accompany both Nat King Cole's and Harold Arlen's "blues opera" *Free and Easy*. On May 27, 1964, Jones, then in New York, received a call from Sinatra in Hawaii, where the singer was on location for another picture, *None but the Brave* (a World War II epic he was producing, directing, and starring in). Sinatra asked Jones to travel to Los Angeles to "pick up" Bill Miller; the two then jetted to Honolulu, where they spent a week working out the details of the second Sinatra-Basie set.

"I went over there, and he had a huge flag up over his bungalow in Hawaii," Jones recalled in 1994. "Only instead of an American flag, he had a flag up with his bottle of Jack Daniel's on it. And that's when we really first met. It was a great, great chemistry. He was finishing up his movie, and when it was wrapped up, we all went to Honolulu and took the top floor of a hotel. He took a bunch of us, I guess about twenty, twenty-five people, and we all had a great time. Then we came back, and when we were flying back home—we were on a commercial flight—we were calling Nancy and Tommy Sands who were down below us in a boat on their honeymoon. I'll never forget that."

Sinatra's modus operandi on this project wasn't exactly the same as it had been with Mandel and Hefti. He and Jones apparently worked out the outline for the arrangements together, and he also welcomed Jones' suggestions in terms of repertory. "We started to talk about the tunes," said Jones, "and it's very funny the way songs come up. You'd suggest one and he'd suggest a couple, and you keep thinking them up and you just come up with a real nice mix."

Working against the clock, Jones became the latest in a long line of Sinatra musical directors who had to bring in additional arranging talent. Jones recruited Billy Byers, a trombonist and composer he'd known for a decade and who'd helped him in the same way on the *This Time by Basie* album. With the exception of "I Wish You Love," Byers doesn't recollect exactly which of *It Might As Well Be Swing's* charts he orchestrated, only that his ghostwriting on these two Jones-Basie productions later led to opportunities to write directly for both Sinatra and Basie. (For instance, Byers arranged one of the band's all-time most performed arrangements, the classic piano feature "All of Me." Originally introduced on *More Hits of the '50s and '60s,* an album originally intended as a Sinatra tribute, Basie also recorded "All of Me" on the *Sinatra at the Sands* set.)

Jones wrote the bulk of his arrangements in Hollywood while Sinatra finished shooting interiors for *None but the Brave.* "I moved in at Warner Bros. in Dean Martin's dressing room while Frank was next door, shooting the picture every day and editing and so forth. So I used to stay there, I locked myself there for a week and just kept writing. I fell asleep late Sunday night, and then on Monday morning I looked up and there's Frank in a military uniform [costume from the film], asking me how I wanted my eggs. He was cooking breakfast!"

As with *Sinatra-Basie,* the band rehearsed prodigiously before the recording, both with and without the star singer present. "I liked Sinatra's lithe, easy manner," Frank Foster has pointed out. "He didn't get ruffled, and he didn't get all excited or anything. The band had been rehearsing with Quincy directing us in the studio and Sinatra walked in. When a star walks in, you think that he or she would [automatically take charge and start barking orders], 'Okay, let's try this or that.' But when Sinatra came in, Quincy asked him, 'What do you want to do, Frank?' Frank says, 'I don't know. What have we got?' And so from that point on, Quincy just said, 'Hey, let's do this.' And Sinatra said, 'Okay.'"

On June 9, 10, and 12, Sinatra and Jones hooked up in the studio with the Basie band, then working in the day at those playgrounds for big kids and little kids, Lake Tahoe and Disneyland. To further guarantee that

Jones' and Byers' new charts would go down easy, they not only brought in Al Porcino again but added a similar ringer on trombone, Kenton and studio vet Kenny Shroyer. Other elements were annexed to the regular band to function as buffers between the styles of Basie and Sinatra, in particular a string section, which appears on half the cuts, and trumpeter Sweets Edison, by now closely associated with both men, playing solos and obligatos on all three dates.

The two most frequently heard tracks on the album are its best, the opener, "Fly Me to the Moon," and its worst, "I Can't Stop Loving You." Although Jones had previously arranged both songs as instrumentals for Basie, the way he and Sinatra transformed the earlier charts into vocal orchestrations is key to an understanding of the album. Sinatra had known composer Bart Howard for over a decade by 1964, having heard him play piano for Mabel Mercer and other cabaret performers at New York's Blue Angel nightclub. Howard wrote "Fly Me to the Moon," originally known as "In Other Words," as a waltz in 1954, and it was quickly picked up by in-the-know singers of varying degrees of celebrity, including June Christy and Peggy Lee (who was the first to suggest changing the title to "Fly Me to the Moon"). Though widely recorded—Howard estimates there were over a hundred versions before Sinatra's—the song's wistful melody and oblique lyric hardly made it *Hit Parade* material.

We don't know whose idea it was to transplant this cabaret ballad into Basieland, but Jones boosted the tempo slightly and put it into an even four/four when he orchestrated it for the Reprise album *This Time by Basie* in 1963. It was hardly one of the more exciting tracks on the album, and when Sinatra decided to address it with the Basie-Jones combination, they recharged it into a straight swinger. "Frank changed the lyrics [and the song] so much," said Howard, "which normally would have annoyed the shit out of me but didn't because it worked so well."

Whereas the instrumental was merely novel, the Sinatra reading all but explodes with energy; the instrumental is a soft-shoe dance, and the vocal version is an out-and-out two-footed stomp. The same elements that sound quaint on the 1963 album—the gentle bass intro and the flute in the first chorus (which harmonizes with the muted trumpets on the instrumental and twitters behind Sinatra on the vocal)—fairly blast on the Sinatra version, which also adds several hyper-dynamic episodes of wildly plunging and soaring brass. Sinatra established the song so firmly as a *swingerlander* (as William B. Williams used to say) that for the last thirty years singers feel that they have to get away from his definitive reading by putting the song back into ballad time. The fast and slow approaches could even be described as two entirely different songs, respectively, "Fly Me to the Moon" and "In Other Words."

The song immediately became one of the anthems of Sinatra's swinging '60s, and though never released as a single, it's been de rigueur at Sinatra concerts and frequently heard on the radio. Further, "Fly Me to the Moon" helped Sinatra become the first musician to gain an audience in outer space: as Buzz Aldrin told Jones, when the astronauts flew to the Earth's satellite for real in 1969, they brought a portable tape player and Sinatra's "Fly Me to the Moon" became the first music ever heard on the moon.

While "Fly Me to the Moon" soars as the most majestic two and a half minutes on *It Might As Well Be Swing*, the set unfortunately includes "I Can't Stop Loving You," another carryover from *This Time by Basie*, which ranks as the most bewildering. Sinatra apparently decided to include this Nashville number, which remains virtually identical to the 1963 instrumental, because a few weeks before calling Jones for the project the instrumental arrangement won Jones his first of nearly two-dozen Grammy awards. Written and introduced by cowboy Don Gibson, the song was popularized by Kitty Wells in 1958 and then hauled into the country-blues domain by Ray Charles on 1962—which is as close to the mainstream as it should have gotten. The Basie instrumental doesn't work for Sinatra but suggests that it might have meant something behind a strong blues voice (Jimmy Witherspoon or Jimmy Forrest).

Which is precisely what it doesn't get. Other than adding strings, Jones barely altered the chart from *This Time by Basie*. Both song and orchestration are entirely unsuited to Sinatra, for all his cowboy contortions, such as a forced twang on "I've made up my mi-ind" and an artificially induced downward thrust on "(those happy) hours." Where fellow Italo-American rat-packer Dean Martin could ride forth unembarrassed as a Gucci cowboy in both Hollywood and Nashville, hearing Sinatra attempt that level of material makes one wince the same way as his movie westerns, like *Johnny Concho* and *Dirty Dingus Magee* do. One is at a loss to explain the consistent popularity of Sinatra's "I Can't Stop Loving You."

Luckily, the remaining eight tracks on *It Might As Well Be Swing* fly closer to "Moon." "I Wanna Be Around" and "The Good Life," for instance, aren't particularly inspired but are the kinds of things that at least could have worked. Although Sinatra was hindered by an indecipherable lyric on the second, he and the band certainly make it work musically, particularly in terms of its tenor break and surprising, sweetly stringy ending.

In 1956, Bing Crosby made an album called *Songs I Wish I Had Sung (the First Time Around)*, a sampling of signature songs of other boy singers, and in 1974, Sinatra would produce *Some Nice Things I've Missed*, which could also have been called *Other People's Money*. *It Might As Well Be Swing* comes closer to Crosby's classy example, containing a surprising (considering that wasn't what he was going for) number of very nice things he had missed but that other male pop stars had hit with.

Thus, in addition to Ray Charles on "I Can't Stop Loving You," Sinatra bumps up against—and generally vanquishes—the lingering phantoms of Jack Jones ("Wives and Lovers"), Steve Lawrence ("More"), Louis Armstrong ("Hello, Dolly"), and Tony Bennett ("I Wanna Be Around," "The Good Life," and "The Best Is Yet to Come").

At the time, "Wives and Lovers" was deemed an "exploitational" song, written to promote—but not heard in—a Van Johnson domestic comedy. That term today would refer to the song's blatant sexism, making "Wives and Lovers" the last openly misogynist song before the heavy metal movement appropriated the idea. (Unlike Betty Carter's version of "Girl Talk," music but not lyrics by Neal Hefti, it has never been reclaimed as a feminist anthem.) Where Jack Jones' hit single was naively sweet in a "young married" kind of way, Sinatra's version is more mature, suggesting that there's more than PTA meetings going on behind closed doors in suburbia. (Sinatra and Basie would have done well to essay another Jack Jones hit, the swingingly agreeable "You Better Love Me.")

He doesn't quite wrest either "Wanna" or "Good Life" away from Bennett, but "Best Is Yet to Come" is second only to "Fly Me to the Moon" as the most winning performance on the album. After a characteristically aphoristic Basie piano intro, Sinatra ecstatically wails the lyrics against an antiphonous choir of muted brass, who throw it back to him like one of Fats Waller's asides to a vocalist ("Tell me about it!"). Sinatra's performance perfectly encapsulates the blend of sensuality and salacious aggression that he epitomized in the decade of the Democrats.

What's ironic is that had things gone according to plan, Sinatra wouldn't have had to compete with Bennett's record of "The Best Is Yet to Come." Composer Cy Coleman had originally earmarked the tune for the Chairman, but when Sinatra sat on it for a year without recording it, the publishers passed it along to Bennett, who had an immediate hit with it. Hit or no hit, one feels that Sinatra was right to wait for the perfect circumstances under which to record it. Like "Fly Me to the Moon," "The Best Is Yet to Come" positively screams Basie-Sinatra from the git-go. Even though Sinatra's wasn't the first version or the biggest selling one, Coleman has said, "The Sinatra version [of any song] is always important . . . no matter what. A Sinatra performance is a wonderful thing, it's a badge of honor."

Other songs on *It Might As Well Be Swing* come from even further away than Nashville, geographically if not stylistically. The Italian "More" has Sinatra phrasing like Harry Edison, knocking out the song's one-note key phrase as if it were a Sweetsian "beep." This track also amounts to the single most successful annexation of strings to the Basie machine. Both "Good Life" and "I Wish You Love" (arranged by Billy Byers) derive from the Gallic, and the latter acknowledges its roots when Edison reprises the muted-trumpet phrase ("all around the mulberry bush") from Basie's "April in Paris." The latter tune begins strictly in Sinatra ballad style with a rubato verse done entirely with strings and then leaps into a full-blooded rocker for the refrain, which Sinatra climaxes with an interjection of "Hot damn!"—if you'll pardon his French.

"I Believe in You" and "Hello, Dolly" come from Broadway (*How to Succeed in Business Without Really Trying* and *Hello, Dolly*), and as early as the mid-1960s it was no longer to be taken for granted that even a successful show tune would provide Sinatra with enough musical meat to chew on. "Dolly" is that rarity, a respectful homage that swings. Sinatra does the first chorus as a rip-roaring romper, with only an exuberant Armstrongian trumpet solo to allude to the eternal presence of Pops. Then with a cry of "Hello, Satch!," Sinatra's second chorus becomes the most gracious piece of noblesse oblige that he has ever offered, beginning with a paraphrase of Satchmo's "This is Louis, Dolly" into "This is Francis, Louis" and bringing it home with a resoundingly Satchel-mouthed, "Oh, yeahhhh!" The only regret is the absence of a camcorder to capture the lighting up of Louis Armstrong's face when he heard the record.

Although not as big a seller on its first release as *Sinatra-Basie*, *It Might As Well Be Swing* has been much more widely heard in the last thirty years. "Fly Me to the Moon," "The Best Is Yet to Come," and "I Can't Stop Loving You" have been omnipresent on every radio programming format oriented toward grown-ups and are being spun many times without mention of the Basie band. And it was remarkable for another reason: it was the first Sinatra concept album comprised entirely of recent songs. Within a few years it would achieve another distinction: Of the several sets of contemporary material that Sinatra would eventually make, the set with Basie remains the only one that rates as a classic. Even the title suggests this. Although these songs were written for the middle of the road (with the exception of the ten-year-old "Fly Me to the Moon"), Sinatra and Basie are telling us that they might as well be swing.

In fact, they are—no less than the big-band oldies that Sinatra reprises on *Swingin' Brass.*

A year after *Swing* was taped, Sinatra and the Basie-ites, with Jones and Edison reprising their studio roles, did several weeks of one-nighters together, climaxing in a concert at the Newport Jazz Festival on the Fourth of July 1965 and a joint appearance on TV's *Hollywood Palace* variety show in October. And two months after that, between January 5 and February 1, 1966, Basie accompanied Sinatra for a full month in Las Vegas, the final week of which Reprise recorded and compiled into the first live Sinatra performance ever released, the incredibly exciting albeit sloppily edited *Sinatra at the Sands.* The bulk of the *Sands* double album consisted of live treatments of Sinatra classics, including Basie-ized treatments of such Sinatra-Riddle classics as "I've Got a Crush on You" (adding Lockjaw Davis on breathy tenor) and "I've Got You Under My Skin" (with Al Grey taking the trombone solo). However, Sinatra and Basie did include a handful of brand new charts, mainly written by Billy Byers, among them the sole Sinatra recordings of "The Shadow of Your Smile" and a polyrhythmic "Get Me to the Church on Time." Another Byers-*Sands* original, his swinging treatment of "Where or When," became a permanent fixture in the Sinatra library. "Basie and Frank always seemed to have a great relationship going on," said Frank Foster. "I know Sinatra always talks about being a saloon singer. [In shows he says things like] 'As soon as this set is over, I'm going to the saloon.' And I imagine Basie hit a few saloons with him."

Between the two Basie albums, the singer made *The Concert Sinatra,* *Sinatra's Sinatra,* and *Academy Award Winners,* his first albums for Reprise with Nelson Riddle, and in 1965 he cut *September of My Years* with Gordon Jenkins. In 1963 he had sold the controlling interest in Reprise. Sinatra and his new company had been considerably weakened by an economic and legal war with Capitol Records, which had "dumped" all his '50s albums on the market at half price. Sinatra's lawyers were not able to get them to stop and had even less luck at convincing the courts that Capitol should be forced to "rescind ownership and restore the masters" to the artist himself.

In a multimedia package deal, Sinatra sold two-thirds of Reprise to Warner Bros. Records and his own services as an actor for a number of films to Warner Bros. pictures, as well as some of his holdings in casinos and other ventures for a reported $3.5 million. That was nearly twice what Sinatra had almost paid Norman Granz for Verve only four years earlier, and Verve's library (extending back to mid-1944) was considerably larger than Reprise's. Essentially, Jack Warner seems to have wanted to buy Sinatra, and the rest of the Reprise organization was so much gravy. Sinatra, for his part, had at last achieved what he had originally set out to do at Capitol in 1959: run his own subsidiary label where he could call the shots and yet let someone else sign the checks. And that's without taking into consideration the millions that went into his pockets.

In 1963 the Chairman also hatched the *Reprise Repertory Theatre*, a series of four discs with which he hoped to give Reprise a stronger label identification than any of its competitors. Using artists from across the label, the series reconstructed four classic Broadway musicals: *Finian's Rainbow, Guys and Dolls, Kiss Me, Kate*, and *South Pacific.* Unlike the painstakingly and sometimes just painfully authentic recreations of the '90s, the Sinatra and Co. versions of these great shows are modernized in a way that falls halfway between the approaches of John McGlinn and Hal Willner.

Although Sinatra produced or coproduced virtually every record he made from 1943 onward, these four volumes were almost the only time he took credit in this capacity—thereby honoring Irving Thalberg's dictum that "credit you give yourself isn't worth having." Not surprisingly, Sinatra makes as good a producer as he does a conductor; in working with Dinah Shore on "I'm Gonna Wash That Man Right out of My Hair," for instance, he elicits from the songstress some of the best work of her career.

In contrast to movie producer Barbra Streisand, whom Isaac Singer has accused of being overly generous toward Barbra Streisand the performer, Sinatra did not excessively feature himself; he rarely appeared on more than two or three cuts per disc, to the disappointment of fans, and often only one of these was a solo (he doesn't take any solos at all on *Kiss Me Kate*). Despite many memorable moments scattered across the four volumes, the problem with the series is that it's too darn democratic. The talent roster, naturally enough, starts with the three major "clan" rodents, Sinatra, Martin, and Davis, and their adopted father figure, Bing Crosby. Yet for every good artist—and there are many, including such class acts as Jo Stafford, Rosemary Clooney, and Keely Smith—we have to endure such lesser lights as Lou Monte, Johnny Prophet, and the McGuire Sisters.[13]

13. There are also several performers who can go either way, like Dinah Shore and straight tenor Clark Dennis, who turn in some of their best work on records here, and Debbie Reynolds, who makes an embarrassingly awful Adelaide on *Guys and Dolls* but redeems herself with a credible duet with Papa Bing on *Finian's*.

The highlights of all these albums are the Sinatra solos (all of which should have been added to the CD edition of the *My Kind of Broadway* collection as bonus tracks, even as "Luck Be a Lady" made it to the original LP). This 1963 "Some Enchanted Evening" was the only one of the three commercial Sinatra versions that amounted to anything, but its success was defeated by the obscurity of the album and the series. Likewise, "Old Devil Moon" with Riddle is a superior remake of the Capitol arrangement, while "When I'm Not Near the Girl I Love" and "I've Never Been in Love Before" bring Sinatra into worthwhile new territory. All four volumes could be justified merely on the strength of one solitary track, the Sinatra–Billy May "Luck Be a Lady" (the only cut from any of the four LPs to make it onto the *Reprise Years* compendium), which, as we've seen, became an instant Sinatra classic.

The following year Sinatra also "conceived and produced" two deadly serious sets with Bing Crosby and Fred Waring's Pennsylvanians and Glee Club: *America, I Hear You Singing* and *The Twelve Songs of Christmas*, as well as *Frank Sinatra and His Friends Want You to Have Yourself a Merry Little Christmas*, a somewhat lighter seasonal sampling. *America* was a patriotic collection apparently inspired, like Judy Garland's "Battle Hymn of the Republic," by the murder of the President but which mysteriously did not include Sinatra's stunning Riddle-arranged readings of "California" (a Cahn–Van Heusen original) and "America the Beautiful" taped at one *Concert Sinatra* session in 1963.

And apart from all these albums, Sinatra continued to turn out singles, continuing his Columbia and Capitol policy of using this medium for newer songs. He also used the format to try out new arrangers; there was such a surfeit of talent even as late as the '60s that many of the better orchestrators he collaborated with never got the call to do an entire album. Torrie Zito, for instance, who would later go on to do great things with Tony Bennett, and Marty Paich, who had already written many masterful scores for Mel Tormé and Ella Fitzgerald (and, on Reprise, for Sammy Davis), were each assigned to score one ballad and one uptempo for Sinatra. "He had his favorite arrangers," Paich recalled recently, "but once in a while when he couldn't get them, then the rest of us would have a chance to slip in."

In 1965, Zito tackled "Everybody Has the Right to Be Wrong" and "I'll Only Miss Her When I Think of Her," both from *Skyscraper*, Cahn's and Van Heusen's most significant bid for a Broadway hit. (The show was shot down, according to showbiz lore, not just by the unwieldy length of the titles of its two key songs but by the unfortunate choice of the non-musical Julie Harris as its leading lady.) Two years before, Paich had worked on "Here's to the Losers" (coincidentally co-written by another Tormé collaborator, Bob Wells) and "Love Isn't Just for the Young."

"Apparently he heard something that he liked that I did, and called me to do these two things," Paich said. "So we went in with a large orchestra, and we just had this brief encounter. The whole thing was a little quick for me. I usually like to work a little slower. But the sides came out very nicely, very musical—and that was the last time I worked with him." The two swingers, Zito's "Right to Be Wrong" and Paich's "Here's to the Losers," came out especially well, showing both men to be keen students of the Sinatra-Riddle style: Zito dropped hints via Nelsonian trombones (the bass trombone in particular), and Paich had saxes and trumpets echo each other in round harmony on the central theme in the intro.

"Here's to the Losers," like "Ring-a-Ding Ding" and "Come Blow Your Horn" (a theme song for a Sinatra movie, put together around this time for the Chairman by Cahn, Van Heusen, and Riddle to a Neil Simon title), is almost a perfect piece of manufactured Sinatriana. If the payoff line had only gone "Here's to the losers—bless *us* all," instead of "bless *'em* all," it would have given the text the ironic edge it needs to become an impeccable Sinatra setpiece. The charming "Right to Be Wrong" has that edge, and so does "I'll Only Miss Her," which fares even better, setting Sinatra against a curtain of shimmering strings (sounding slightly Jenkinsian near the end) and flamenco-dancing Spanish guitar from Laurindo Almeida and Al Viola.

Unfortunately, other singles from the period—even on the same pickup albums these four were collected onto, *Softly, As I Leave You* and *My Kind of Broadway*—show Sinatra moving in far less appetizing directions as he began to betray his own superior musical taste in an attempt to capture the youth market that was more and more dictating the shots for the entire music industry in 1964 and 1965. He inaugurated a policy of polarization between the comparatively high-brow masterpieces he continued to sweat over with Riddle, May, and Jenkins, and the ephemera—often other people's hits—he knocked out to feed the jukeboxes. It seems strange to see Sinatra looking down these avenues at the same time that he was celebrating his maturity in such ventures as the *Man and His Music* double LP and a series of television specials. One hand acts as if it doesn't know what the other one is doing. One grabs for the same audience that is buying his daughter's discs and making her a platinum pop star; the other pats himself on the back for having both the panache and the forbearance to do it *his* way all these years. Even in the midst of sessions contemplating the *September of His Years*, he takes time out to tape the tacky "Forget Domani."

Sinatra had first made noises that sounded vaguely like rhythm and blues in the '50s, with the likes of "Bim Bam Baby" (1952), "Lean Baby" (1953),"Hey! Jealous Lover" (1956), and that egregious 45-rpm pairing of "Two Hearts, Two Kisses" and "From the Bottom to the Top" (1955). In the mid-1960s however, when pop music had evolved into an amalgam of spineless sounds that could no longer claim any connection to the blues—which had been the sole positive element of '50s rock—Sinatra started to go into the "youth music" business wholesale. Irv Cottler categorized the singer's efforts in this area as "ballad rock," saying, "I don't know why they call it rock because it's not rock at all. It just has that contemporary feel."

Sinatra selected producer and former pop star Jimmy Bowen as his first captain on this journey, and Bowen summarily recruited arranger-conductor Ernie Freeman as navigator. Born in New Mexico in 1937, Bowen had been, along with Buddy Holly, a progenitor of the short-lived genre known as Texas rock and roll. He served as bass guitarist, composer, and vocalist with the Rhythm Orchids, a threesome individually and collectively responsible for a number of top ten hits, circa 1957, such as "Party Doll" and "I'm Sticking with You" (both written by Bowen and Jimmy Knox). "My problem was that I sang a little flat. I could hear it, but I couldn't do anything about it," Bowen recalled recently. "So I knew that [my career as a singer] was a short-term thing. And then after about two years, the girls quit screaming and they started listening. Then I knew I was in trouble. So I said to myself, 'I'd better find something else to do.'"

Over the next few years, Bowen built up a reputation as a composer and producer, primarily for a Los Angeles label called Chancellor Records. An associate there named Murray Wolf, who happened to know Sinatra, was responsible for letting Bowen know that Sinatra was looking for a producer who was more in tune with the contem-pop culture. "When Frank first started Reprise, he said, 'No rock and roll on this label,' but obviously that changed," said Bowen. He told Wolf he was interested, and "about five or six weeks later I get a call one night from Murray, talking softly. He said, 'Listen, you got the job. Hang on, Frank wants to talk to you.' Sinatra came on and said, 'James? Glad to have you aboard.' Click! That was it."

Bowen began by producing strictly rock-style hits for the label, such as Jack Nitzsche's 1963 "Lonely Surfer," which was, he said, "a hit wherever there was water." He would attain some of the label's biggest sellers by virtue of his concept of repackaging the star power of the biggest classic pop names in terms that the current audience could accept. Not having the nerve to approach Sinatra with this idea first, Bowen initially asked if he could do a date with Reprise's crooner *numero dos,* Dean Martin. According to Bowen, a lot of the rockabilly types had been Dino diehards since childhood, not least among them the Pelvis himself.

Bowen was already working in tandem with orchestrator Ernie Freeman. "I had used other arrangers, but Ernie was my favorite," he said, "because we communicated so well. Ernie had the temperament to sit with me a couple of hours while we went over things: 'I want this and I want that.' It was a give-and-take, and a lot of arrangers won't do that. Plus, I like simplicity with a big orchestra, and Ernie would do it for me. He was just an incredibly talented man." A veteran of Los Angeles' Central Avenue jazz scene of the '40s, Freeman (born 1929) recorded with Dexter Gordon and singer Helen Humes. Throughout the '50s, he starred on a long series of blues sides for the "race records" label Imperial, one of which, an R&B "cover" of the country instrumental hit "Raunchy," made him a star under his own name.

In the '60s, Freeman specialized in helping white teen favorites like Bobby Vee and Paul Anka pass themselves off as rock and rollers, and then pulled off a comparable caper in making Sinatra and Dean Martin palatable to teenagers. "He'd been around a long time," said Bowen. "I first became aware of Ernie when he did Gene MacDaniels and Johnny Burnett arrangements for Snuff Garrett at Liberty Records, a big hit called 'Dreamin'' by Johnny Burnett. I remember when I heard that, and I said, 'Whoa, is that wild? Strings on rock and rockabilly records!' So when I got the opportunity, I went right to him." Bowen's and Freeman's first coast-to-coast mega-hit for Reprise was Dean Martin's Nashville-style update of his theme song, "Everybody Loves Somebody Sometime."

"So I did Dean, and since I was making hits for Frank's buddy," said Bowen, "I think Frank said, 'Well, I should give the kid a try.' He called me one day and asked if I'd come over for a meeting, and I grabbed a tune out of my good song file, called 'Softly As I Leave You,' that I knew Frank would just love. I took it over and we talked a bit, and he said, 'Listen, if you're going to produce some music for me, what would you do?' I said, 'Well, I wouldn't bastardize you. I'd change the music around you but keep you who you are.' He said, 'Well, that makes sense. What do you have?' Thank God I picked up that song. I played 'Softly As I Leave You,' and he said, 'Fine, let's do it.' So we went in a week or two later and recorded 'Softly As I Leave You.'"

Sinatra's first session with Freeman and Bowen took place in July 1964, when they did "Softly," an Italian song that had already charted in England thanks to Matt Monro,[14] as well as two newer items with *Billboard* potential, "Then Suddenly Love" by Roy Alfred (author of such classics in the genre as "The Hucklebuck" and "The Rock and Roll Waltz") and Sammy Cahn's "Available." If all three had been orchestrated in other eras, they might have proved acceptable Sinatra material. Rather than having to employ Sinatra's regular rhythm section, Bowen was given a free hand to bring in his own Nashville rock-style players, such as drummer Hal Blane and keyboardist Leon Russell, along with concertmaster Sid Sharp, who knew how to get fiddlers "who didn't mind busting a string."

While Sinatra is superlative on all three, the quality of the finished disc has less to do with the singing than the accessories: on "Softly" we hear monotonous rock drumming, a cloying choir, and the same kind of trite, nails-on-chalkboard string figures that plague, for instance, Belford Hendricks' charts for Dinah Washington and Nat Cole. The overdone chorus and strings do the same for the other two songs, both of which use a prominent Sy Oliver–like baritone. Ten years earlier, "Then Suddenly Love" would have been the basis for a brisk Sinatra frolic à la "Ya Better Stop," and while it retains some deft touches (such as an Edisonian bleating in the coda), it remains an unsuccessful attempt to marry ring-a-ding ding to yeah-yeah-yeah. Sinatra exclaims "Hot damn! I wish you love" when singing to his own generation, but when trying to contact the now generation, he feels obliged to tone down his juice to a piddling "Hot dog!"

"When we finished cutting 'Softly,'" said Bowen, "we were listening to the playbacks and Frank said, 'Well, James, what do you think?' And I said, 'I think it's [only] about a number thirty record, but it'll get us back on radio.' He looked at me like that didn't please him too much, and he left. And I think the record went to twenty-seven or twenty-eight. But with Sinatra that would be important because your word is very important to him, and that's what I felt. We had a challenge to get Sinatra on top-forty radio when the Beatles were happening."

---

14. It was the second hit by Monro, the talented crooner widely regarded as the "British Sinatra" (though because of the often sleepy quality of his records, he would have been better labeled the "Somnambulent Sinatra"), to be covered by the original FS, the first being "My Kind of Girl" on *Sinatra-Basie*, while a third was the 1968 "Born Free." Of course, that's nothing compared to the number of songs associated with Sinatra that Monro subsequently recorded.

The Bowen-Freeman sessions suggest how later generations will regard the '90s *Sinatra Duets* discs: after their novelty and hit value have faded, we'll be wondering why anyone ever made such a fuss about them. One's joy in the fact of Sinatra returning to the charts is severely hampered by the sacrifices in the quality of his work that made these achievements possible. In the mid-1960s, the public obviously wanted countrypolitan cadenzas, a doo-wah choir, ya-ta-ta ya-ta-ta tub pounding, and wimpy strings, and Freeman delivers these goods on such singles as "Somewhere in Your Heart," "Tell Her You Love Her," and "When Somebody Loves You."

"It's one of those things where you grasp the moment," said Bowen. "I had about a four- or five-year period where I had the feel of how to take these kinds of artists into the marketplace, to top-forty radio, at a time when top-forty radio didn't want to play them." "Forget Domani" and "Strangers in the Night" exemplify the worst of psychedelic '60s movie music. "Domani," from the 1965 Rex Harrison epic *The Yellow Rolls-Royce*, at least offers something in the way of camp value in the way it intermingles a Neapolitan mandolin sound with that of a discotheque. As Bowen himself clarifies, these sessions were never attempts to make classic Sinatra music for the ages (the Chairman would work with Sonny Burke on those projects) but were quick shots intended to move product in the moment. "We were just experimenting in all those sessions," he said. "If you listen to them, you can hear that. Basically, it was my idea of how I heard him in the marketplace at that time."

Bowen succeeded most spectacularly with "Strangers in the Night," the only one of the Old Man's singles from this period to have a long-lasting impact on his career. The song originated as the title music of a forthcoming James Garner spy comedy called *A Man Could Get Killed*, with a score by Burt Kaempfert. Considered the German giant of easy listening (sort of a Deutschlander Percy Faith, remembered by history as the first man to stick a microphone in front of the Beatles and the composer of Nat King Cole's last hit, "L-O-V-E"), Kaempfert already had several international instrumental hits. Bowen first heard the tune when the composer's manager and American publisher, Al Fine, sent a song plugger to Bowen's house to demonstrate it. "I said, 'Man, get me the lyric on that, and I'll do it with Sinatra.' I'd never said that to anybody because, obviously, nobody knows what Frank is going to do till he says what he's going to do. [But] I knew that melody [would be a hit]. So they sent me a couple of lyrics I didn't like, but then finally they got me one that I thought was right. And we went in and did that song."

The biggest battle to land the hit, however, occurred after the recording. Sinatra had made "Strangers in the Night" on a Monday, but Jack Jones recorded his version the previous Friday and immediately mailed out copies to the leading radio stations. Bowen quickly mixed the Sinatra performance, cut a few acetates, and thanks to obliging flight attendants and couriers racing to and from airports all over the country, actually had the Sinatra record in the hands of disc jockeys hours before the competitor's product arrived.

Sinatra, as he has said at numerous concerts, didn't care for the song and had recorded it only reluctantly.[15] But Freeman and he capitalize on the strength of the central hook, which the singer exalts with an effectively forlorn sound and the arranger supports with a chinking rhythm guitar and repetitious percussion pattern. Luckily, the string lines are several notches more bearable than those of the team's usual efforts, and Sinatra fades out with a surprisingly quixotic scat coda that quickly replaced "ring-a-ding ding" as the crowning Sinatraism of the '60s: "dooby-dooby-do." (Sinatra had uttered his first documented "oo-be-doo-be" a year earlier as a spontaneous interjection in a television performance of "Please Be Kind" done with Basie.)

While Freeman's chart was nowhere near as swingingly bluesy as the instrumental that Chico O'Farrell wrote around the same time for Count Basie, Sinatra's "Strangers" was an almost unprecedented, resoundingly massive hit—Sinatra's first number one single since an entire generation ago—and it went on to provide the title and opener to his final album with Nelson Riddle, a set so beautifully done it almost seemed as if Sinatra were apologizing for the original track. As Bowen recalled, the rest of the *Strangers* album had been originally earmarked for another project; Sinatra and Reprise annexed the material under the "Strangers" banner out of a quick need for an album to complement his megahit single.

After "Strangers," ballad-rock established itself as the dominant mode of Sinatra's singles and, eventually, his albums as well. When he turned "Strangers" into an album, Sinatra subtitled it *Sinatra Sings for Moderns*, and many of the songs for swinging moderns turned out to be the work of Johnny Mercer and Walter Donaldson. But when it came time to produce an album around the next Sinatra-Freeman-Bowen hit, "That's Life," instead of going again to one of his high-grade arrangers, the threesome contrived an entire set of material on the same low level as the title track.

15. The best live versions are the ones where he switches from "Love was just a glance away / a warm embracing dance away" to "a lonesome pair of pants away."

Sinatra himself had discovered "That's Life" in the summer or fall of 1966, around the time it was recorded by blues singer O. C. Smith, and premiered it on the 1966 edition of his *Man and His Music* series of TV specials. The original arrangement, presumably by Nelson Riddle (the musical director for the bulk of the program), used a bluesy sound underscored by an electric organ, in the tradition of the *Strangers* album charts. But when Sinatra decided to record it, he brought it to Bowen and Freeman, who modified the Riddle chart considerably for hit-single purposes, adding, among other elements, a fake gospel choir behind Sinatra's solo.

Bowen has recalled that when he walked into the recording session, which took place at a spanking new facility, he was informed that the only working mikes were for the vocal and rhythm section. Although a full contingent of horns, strings, and backup singers had been assembled, the producer concluded that it didn't matter: given the right performance by Sinatra, he could overdub the other elements of the performance at a later time (including an organ part by Mike Melvoin). Sinatra arrived, went to work, and soon came up with a performance of "That's Life" that almost all present were sure was "the one." "We played it back, and Frank said, 'Boy! That's a hit, isn't it!' And I said, 'Well, no. If you want a hit, you're going to have to do it one more time.' Everybody got real quiet, and he gave me the coldest look an artist ever gave me. But he went right out, and instead of singing it hip—he was pissed now—he *bit* it! *That's* when he sang 'That's Life!'"

The "That's Life" track features Sinatra's most concerted effort to approximate a blues sound. On songs like "My Kind of Girl" and "My Heart Stood Still," he's competing successfully with the likes of Nat King Cole and Peggy Lee; here he's not doing this particular tune anywhere near as soulfully as Aretha Franklin (on Atlantic). In the '40s, Sinatra and Nat Cole envied each other's roles, and now he's doing the same thing with Ray Charles. (And not merely by reprising one of Charles' hits, as he did earlier and later with "I Can't Stop Loving You" and "Hallelujah! I Love Her So.") Just as Charles added strings and started singing ballads, now Sinatra is shouting the blues over a background of pseudo Raelettes.

The Riddle arrangement of "That's Life" (which paid homage to Louis Armstrong with a descending paraphrase of the classic Satchmo coda "Oh, yeah!") had Sinatra getting merely sensually funky. The Freeman-Bowen treatment shows that he has come a long way from The Voice sound of the '40s (as in the 1945 "Try a Little Tenderness") and now gasps, growls, grunts, snarls, and all but spits at the audience: *The Antisocial Sinatra*.

After the *Strangers* album, Bowen was resolved not to again surround a contem-pop hit with traditional Sinatra material. As he told the singer, "We can't do just one thing that's modern and innovative for the times and then go back and do 'Wee Small Hours' for the other nine tunes." The rest of *That's Life* consists of orchestrations that are more brassy and less discothequey than other Freeman-Bowen-Sinatra items, although the songs themselves are the sort Sinatra would do had he deigned to portray a singing villain in *Batman*. It's a strange combination of material from American, British, and French sources, which testifies to the monotony of internationally homogenized mono-culture. However, where Eurotrash like the New Vaudeville Orchestra's "Winchester Cathedral" is insipid beyond the call of duty—even for this package—"You're Gonna Hear from Me" is surprisingly substantial. This André and Dory Previn movie theme works like "Hey! Look Me Over" (a hit Cy Coleman show tune from 1960), with its march tempo surgically removed in order to make it suitable for Sinatra.

"The Impossible Dream" reuses the steadily building pattern Sinatra had employed on the Riddle version of "Where or When," in a song that, like "Dancing in the Dark," keeps steadily modulating upward. The format helps him to turn this *Man of La Mancha* hit into a pre–"My Way" exhibition of pure ego—for the first time operating unfettered by such unnecessary appendages as a song. (Or at least a good song that might threaten to distract attention away from said ego.) According to collectors' lore, Sinatra couldn't stand this thing either but taped it at the insistence of his new third wife, Mia Farrow.

"We didn't cut it twenty-seven times or anything like that," said Bowen. "We broke it up into three or four sections. Then we just recorded the sections, and I edited it together. That was a crazy song to sing, plus he was not in great voice that particular week. I was afraid if we tried to get a whole take, it'd turn into agony, and he'd throw it out. He had promised somebody to do it, so he wasn't going to throw it out, but I didn't find that out until later." The impossible dream, indeed.

That's Life has its moments, which indicates that Sinatra had still not reached the nadir of his indulgence in the rock era. In fact, he would begin and end 1967 with two superb discs with similar titles, *Francis Albert Sinatra & Antonio Carlos Jobim* and *Francis A. and Edward K.* While the first concluded the singer's '60s cycle of one-shot collaborations, the two sets as a pair would unfortunately be regarded as the final two classic Sinatra concept albums for at least a decade.

The Brazilian musical style known as the bossa nova qualifies as one of the few musical trends of the '60s to impact beneficially on adult popular music. As with many other musical movements, jazz musicians were the first Americans to dabble in this form imported from Brazil, particularly the Brazilian-born Laurindo Almeida and Bud Shank, the first of a series of jazz guitar and "cool" saxophone combinations to explore the bossa idiom. In 1962, Stan Getz recorded *Jazz Samba,* launching a number of discs which reinvented the saxophonist into a gold-plated pop star. In the process, Getz also elevated Antonio Carlos Jobim and Astrud Gilberto, respectively the music's most accessible composer and flattest femme singer, as well as the bossa nova itself to international status.

The bossa nova eventually made its widest impact stateside as an additive, an element that interacted with better-established American genres, and was rarely presented in its pure form. By the mid-1960s, jazz and pop stars as diverse as Miles Davis and Eydie Gorme, Gil Evans and Ella Fitzgerald, Zoot Sims and Mel Tormé, Vic Damone, Perry Como, Kenny Dorham, and Peggy Lee were all blaming it on the bossa nova. Even the Pelvis found himself a "Bossa Nova Baby."

Only thirty in 1967, the Rio-born Jobim had written virtually all of the music's trademark hits, including "The Girl from Ipanema," "One-Note Samba" ("Samba de Una Nota Só"), "Quiet Nights of Quiet Stars" ("Corcovado"), "How Insensitive" ("Insensataz"), and "Meditation" ("Meditação"). As the German arranger Claus Ogerman recalled, "Frank really liked these strong and famous songs by Jobim and wanted to do an album with them." Sinatra worked out the details in his head and eventually decided to invite Jobim himself, who played guitar and, in a manner of sorts, sang, to participate in the sessions. "I came along with Antonio," added Ogerman, "because Frank had heard earlier albums I had done with Antonio and liked what I did."

Rather than tentatively dipping his toes into this particular lagoon, Sinatra elected to dive in headfirst. His rationale seemed to be that although other singers—particularly Tony Bennett (who could compile an entire CD of his fine Brazilian-style tracks)—had gotten there first, he would get there with the most. No other American pop star would so thoroughly immerse himself in the world of bossa; he not only recorded two whole albums' worth of the stuff but sacrificed his signature stylistics in order to more smoothly fit into the new vernacular. The two albums were *Francis Albert Sinatra & Antonio Carlos Jobim* (1967) and *Sinatra-Jobim* (1969), although the latter was not issued as Sinatra had originally intended.

While Sinatra used different arrangers on each set, namely Ogerman in 1967 and Eumir Deodato two years later, Jobim himself can be heard throughout both, supporting Sinatra with his guitar, which operates in both background and foreground capacities. What Jobim actually does vocally is difficult to describe. The track listing for the first album places an asterisk on four cuts on which the composer's voice is heard, explaining, "Vocal support by Antonio Carlos Jobim." The Brazilian either hums or sings softly in Portuguese, sometimes behind Sinatra, other times filling in between his lines, the way an obligatist like Sweets Edison would on a more assertive Sinatra set (or the way Sy Oliver does vocally on "The One I Love," from *I Remember Tommy*). Only one track, the originally unissued "Desafinado" (1969), qualifies as a true duet between the two men. Jobim plays a far more important role as the chief supplier of material, having written seven of the first album's ten tracks and all ten on the second.

Sinatra worked with Ogerman much as he had with Hefti and Mandel, supplying him with a list of songs and the keys he wanted them in, leaving everything else pretty much up to the arranger. Other decisions had already been predetermined, as Ogerman explained, in that "in a way, the tempos are locked in on the Jobim songs. You can't do them faster or slower." Sinatra also commissioned Ogerman to orchestrate three American standards—"Baubles, Bangles and Beads," "I Concentrate on You," and "Change Partners"—in the bossa idiom. "At that time," said Ogerman, "there were not enough Jobim songs with good English lyrics. Antonio has about four hundred songs that are great, but most of them had no English words because Antonio is very hard to please in that respect. It's very hard to translate Antonio's Portuguese into decent English. Unless you can get it into the hands of a master like Johnny Mercer, you're almost lost. So Frank decided to do some Cole Porter and Irving Berlin in addition to Antonio's songs."

Whereas Stan Getz had explored the harder-hitting angles of the bossa nova (particularly in the original *Jazz Samba* set), Sinatra uses the form as the vehicle for the softest singing he had ever done—with the possible exception of his original "chamber" sessions with Stordahl for *The Voice* album in 1945. As he says in the album's notes, "I haven't sung so soft since I had the laryngitis." All twenty bossa ballads feature Sinatra's sensual, supple, and super-subdued vocals atop sensitive strings, very understated brass (only the quietest of all brass instruments, a single trombone, played by Dick Noel, is audible), and gently undulating Brazilian rhythm, as expressed by Jobim on guitar and his "personal drummer," Dom Romano.

The miraculous "Dindi" is so supremely soft it could be heard on a tissue commercial; you almost have to listen twice to be sure that it's Sinatra. As on the *Edward K.* set recorded that December, Sinatra offers his most uncharacteristically reverential singing here, devoid of Frankish interjections and the familiar swagger. When he throws in an extra beat on the end of "Baubles, Bangles and Beads" on the phrase "I *have* heard," it derives both from the inherent playfulness of the Brazilian form and the Sinatra tradition of expanded contractions. Again, as with other arrangers, Sinatra gave Ogerman only a pitifully brief time in which to write the charts, but surprisingly the arranger feels that this actually contributed to the high quality of the work. "I had to write so fast that I didn't have time to put down millions of notes," said Ogerman, "so I left my arrangements extremely transparent, and that made it nice for the singer."

Throughout, Sinatra's lines display a startling flexibility and delicacy, as if they could be blown about by a soft Brazilian breeze. It's not even surprising when Jobim joins him on the climactic phrases of "Girl from Ipanema," transforming his solo vocal into a harmony line. Likewise, Sinatra presents himself as a wide-eyed innocent here, which is the only way he could make "Girl from Ipanema" work for him. He even utters an "ooh" that's entirely worshipful and not at all leering.

Sinatra is never at a loss for exactly what to do, even when the dynamic options only run the gamut from *piano* to *pianissimo*. While his phrasing is about as far removed from the Basie albums as Rio is from Kansas City, Sinatra is no less of a jazz singer here, particularly when he subtly emphasizes the syllables "tall" and "tan" (dropping the "and" between them) in "Ipanema" and similarly stressing the "you've" (in "you've been locked") and "in" (as in "in his arms") in "Change Partners." He so completely reconstructs this 1938 classic that despite Fred Astaire and *Carefree,* an entire generation has grown up unable to conceive of "Change Partners" as anything other than a bossa nova. (The talented contemporary jazz singer Jeanie Bryson, for one, performs it as such on her first album, *Love Being Here with You.*)

Ogerman's elegant orchestrations indicate that he could have been the next great Sinatra collaborator. On an '80s talk show appearance, Jobim observed that the most important element jazz shared with the bossa nova was a pliant, malleable rhythm, which he distinguished from European, and particularly Teutonic, music with its unrelenting oom-pah. Paradoxically, *FAS & ACJ*, the greatest of all bossa-pop records, was arranged by a Polish-born and Munich-based orchestrator. Born in 1930, Claus Ogerman had played piano with the big bands of the swing-oriented Kurt Edelhagen (a sort of German Ted Heath) and the funkier Max Greger before immigrating to the United States in 1959. Ogerman had grown up with American jazz and pop, listening to it even during the

Nazi regime (he could have been one of the "swing kids"). He had been a Sinatra fan since the Harry James days and cited Riddle as his favorite orchestrator, praising *In the Wee Small Hours* as "the pinnacle of everything in pop music."

Working primarily for Verve/MGM's Creed Taylor, Ogerman established himself as one of the few orchestrators of the '60s who seemed comfortable with contemporary developments in both rock and the new thing in jazz and yet remained relevant to what Sinatra called "the good pop music." In addition to arranging albums for Johnny Hodges, Donald Byrd, Jimmy Smith, Cal Tjader, and Bill Evans, Ogerman worked with Stan Getz on *Reflections* in 1963. In the same month as his Sinatra-Jobim set, Ogerman taped *Voices*, a program of orchestrations originally intended for Wes Montgomery but transferred to Getz when the guitarist switched label affiliations.

For Ogerman, working with Sinatra was a dream come true, and the reality of arranging and conducting for him was better than anything he had imagined. When Ogerman went to Sinatra's office at Warner Bros. to help pick the key for "Drinking Again," he sat down at the piano at one point and started noodling around with what he described as "very modern jazz harmonies." Sinatra then announced to the others in the room, "Listen, this guy isn't from Germany, he's from Brooklyn. He's just faking with that accent."

That song, "Drinking Again," makes it clear that Sinatra and Ogerman should have moved on to conventional ballads after completing the *Jobim* project. They taped this little-known gem of a Johnny Mercer song at the end of the first round of Jobim dates in 1967, but with studio guitarist Al Caiola replacing the Brazilian. Ogerman had known the song's composer, Doris Taubert, in New York. "She worked for many years as a staff pianist and song demonstrator for [music publisher] Harms Inc., which is the job Gershwin had earlier. She was practically Gershwin's successor." At that time, "Drinking Again" was primarily remembered for Dinah Washington's recording (done with Don Costa's orchestra) of five years earlier.

Ogerman created a light, stringy background every bit as colorful and supportive as the best of Costa, bringing together Mercer's on-target lyric and Bill Miller's always welcome saloon piano to inspire a Sinatra vocal that's stunning even by his own standards. The singer tempers his perfectly poised declamation with just the right amount of self-pity and self-consciousness, and with minuscule, never overtly noticeable tinges of the inebriate's slightly sloshed phrasing. By the fadeout, in which—replete with self-crucifying humor—he inwardly intones "Look at me,

I'm drinkin' again," Sinatra has concocted a perfect cocktail of tragedy and noir comedy, followed by a chaser of irony.[16]

Sinatra would have done well to give Ogerman the call two years later for his second set with Jobim, though it's foolish to suggest that there was any room for improvement on the ten orchestrations written by Eumir Deodato and conducted by movieland veteran Morris Stoloff. While Ogerman, whom Jobim might have classified as coming from the country of the "oom-pah," wrote the softer set, the Latin American Deodato and Sinatra turn up the voltage for a brassier and more high-powered one.

"One-Note Samba" and "This Happy Madness" swing almost like '40s swing tunes, while eloquent lines like "I fell gaily, gladly, madly into love"[17] in the second point to the great tradition of song lyrics in that era. Jobim told Jonathan Schwartz that Sinatra was having a tough time learning new tunes at this particular point (thanks to the temporary unavailability of Jimmy Van Heusen), which, Schwartz feels, explains why Sinatra plays it comparatively cautiously on "One-Note Samba."

"Drinking Water," which has Sinatra singing several lines in Portuguese; "Triste," where Sinatra emphasizes the rests and pronounces "airplane" as if it were spelled "aeroplane"; and "Don't Ever Go Away," which builds to a conventional Sinatra-type climax, are all typical of an even more danceable album with a stronger beat than the first Jobim collaboration. "Someone to Light Up My Life" doesn't shine quite as brilliantly as Tony Bennett's earlier reading, but then the piece became one of Bennett's signature tunes. However, "Wave" may well be the dramatic apex of the entire Sinatra-Jobim cycle, with Sinatra diving deep for a spectacular low note an entire octave beneath the tonic.

It's impossible to speculate why Reprise elected not to release this second album, to be titled *Sinatra-Jobim*, especially when the earlier set had charted quite respectably at number 19—and this in the face of formidable competition now that the pop album charts, no less than the singles, were dominated by uncopasetic sounds. (Sinatra, in the 1965 *Man and His Music* set, gives thanks to "DJs brave enough to give me equal time in Beatle land.") Although a cover was designed and, according to

---

16. "Drinking Again" came off as especially memorable as a gem buried in a trash bin when Reprise issued it on *The World We Knew*, otherwise an eminently forgettable album of soft-rock.

17. Lyricist and sometime singer Gene Lees has recalled that Jobim and Ogerman used him as a stand-in for Sinatra when working out the charts for the original *FAS–ACJ* sessions.

one discography, a handful of eight-track cartridges made it into stores, *Sinatra-Jobim* was never issued.

Perhaps Sinatra wasn't happy with the cover, which depicted him leaning against a Greyhound bus (what were they thinking?), or perhaps he wanted to remake "Desafinado," which remains the only one of the ten *S-J* tracks that has not been issued anywhere. In any case, Reprise put seven of the ten on the A side of a set called *Sinatra and Company,* the flip of which contained seven unmemorable kiddie-pop numbers with Don Costa that could have been called *Cycles II.* "Desafinado" has thus far only privately circulated among Sinatraphiles, and "Bonita" (issued on a domestic single) and "Song of the Sabia" have come out only on Italian Reprise LPs.

Which is our loss. Rumor has persisted that "Desafinado," the track that most prominently features the voice of Jobim, has lain unissued because to hear two male voices go to work on a love song (not a comedy number like "Well, Did You Evah" or "Guys and Dolls") sounds homoerotic to some ears. Compounding the problem, Sinatra and Jobim were singing a new American lyric (called "Off Key") by Gene Lees to a tune that had been published originally in this country in 1962. Jon Hendricks wrote the original libretto (with the publisher prompting, "You're the guy who writes the words to this kind of goofy shit") called "Slightly out of Tune."

The quality of Jobim's intonation, which suggests why he thought the totally tuneless Astrud Gilberto was a good singer, may also be the culprit, however. Jobim, who justifies Lees' title "Off Key," is so far away from any concept of pitch that he even throws Sinatra off.

Sinatra should have redone the piece as a solo; that would have suited the album better anyhow. "Bonita" and "Song of the Sabia" require no adjustments, the former being a straightforward love song while the latter is a soft, mystical piece on the order of the first album's "Dindi." "I'm not sure what was on his mind," said Milt Bernhart, who played on the dates. "He was unhappy because there were a couple of very difficult songs. These weren't just ballads, these were art songs that Jobim had written. He fought that one because it was very hard. It just was not reading right." The trombonist felt, however, that the results justified the effort, and he named "Sabia" (a Brazilian bird) one of the most gorgeous things he ever heard Sinatra sing. It's indeed beautifully gnomic, revealing Jobim as a Brazilian Billy Strayhorn who intrigues without ever quite explaining what's going on. "Sabia" underscores the need for the complete album *Sinatra-Jobim,* even with the suspect "Desafinado," to be restored and issued like a lost film classic.

*   *   *

With the *Jobim* albums (as well as Jobim's appearance on Sinatra's 1967 *A Man and His Music + Ella* TV special), Sinatra had proved he could address at least one contemporary trend. Likewise, parts of *Francis A. & Edward K., Strangers in the Night,* and all of *It Might As Well Be Swing* showed that he had no problem with making the better recently minted songs work for him. Yet these were to be practically the last times he was able to do that. After *Strangers* and *That's Life* came sets like *The World We Knew, My Way,* and others that continued to blur the distinction between singles and albums. Now Sinatra was recording like Tony Bennett and the late Nat King Cole: when a hit came his way, he built his latest album around it. Bennett and Cole, however, never seemed as if they were compromising when they adhered to this practice, mainly because they included so many good standard songs in their albums. And also because, as with any singer who isn't Sinatra, the stakes are considerably lower.

Sinatra, by now convinced he could break through to the under-thirty generation again and again, rarely recorded any decent standards after the excellent *Strangers* set. And when he did, it was to no avail: "Some Enchanted Evening" (included on *The World We Knew*), for instance, is encased in an H. B. Barnum arrangement so atrocious that one is tempted to believe the old wives' tale that Sinatra recorded it primarily to tick off the ever-deserving Richard Rodgers. It seems like a bad joke that the masterful "Enchanted Evening" he recorded in 1963 for the *Reprise Repertory Theatre: South Pacific* has been out of print for thirty years and that this mockery has always been available.

The World We Knew was the pop project that followed on the heels of the art project *Francis Albert Sinatra & Antonio Carlos Jobim.* Since the set contains both "This Is My Song" and "This Is My Love," one would have expected Sinatra to title the set *This Is My Album.* Instead, he named it after the latest potential hit by Burt Kaempfert. When the song came along, Bowen recalled, "Sinatra used to laugh at me. I think he was just challenging me to see if we could do it or not. And he used to laugh because Kaempfert's melodies were always testy. 'Strangers in the Night' is not easy to sing. And 'The World We Knew'—oh, God, what a hard song to sing!" Although that single reached the charts, it was by no means another "Strangers."

The album *The World We Knew* contained a mishmash of movie-title songs and other people's hits, somehow requiring the talents of five arrangers, including three familiar ones. Gordon Jenkins makes his first appearance as a *frankenrocker* (complete with snare drums), while Claus Ogerman scores heavily with "Drinking Again," a leftover from the *Jobim* sessions that is by far the best track on all of *The World We Knew.*

Ernie Freeman, in his now familiar role, arranged the title track as well as "Don't Sleep in the Subway" and "This Is My Song." Lyricist Carl Sigman fittingly subtitled "The World We Knew" as "Over and Over," and the song does repeat its hook, which Freeman accentuates with fuzz guitar and a blaring choir, a little too over and over even for kiddie pop. Once you get as far away from the hook as possible, as in the bridge sections, Sinatra almost makes it sound like a real song, receiving help from a Sweets Edison–style trumpet obligato. Similarly, a well-placed tuba helps Sinatra and Freeman turn Petula Clark's lightweight hit homage to the homeless, "Don't Sleep in the Subway," into a sort of more tender "That's Life," with the word "darling" in the original transmuted to "baby." But try as Sinatra may, the mood is sabotaged by the go-go chorus chanting "come on baby" and wordlessly harmonizing with the high brass.

Sinatra and Bowen chose to record one session for *The World We Knew* in New York, the singer's first date on the East Coast in almost fifteen years. While Big Apple studio greats like Clark Terry and Bucky Pizzarelli participated, *World We Knew* feels less like a jazz album than a Nancy Sinatra pop project. Several other producer-arrangers, including H. P. Barnum, Billy Strange, and the younger Sinatra's most frequent collaborator, Lee Hazelwood, all worked under Bowen. For that matter, so did Sinatra's firstborn herself, twisting a tonsil with dear old Dad on their number one hit duet, "Somethin' Stupid." Written by Carson Parks, it may be the most un-Frankish performance Sinatra ever recorded, with the two Sinatras chanting away in bland folkish harmony.

If "That's Life" finds Sinatra more sexually charged than ever, "Somethin' Stupid" presents him as completely neutered when the male and female voices merge. Still, the warmth that father and daughter feel for each other shines through, making the track almost charming in a savorless way—it could have been from an album called *Songs for Singing Nuns.*[18] Bowen, who coproduced the selection with Hazelwood, has reported that the taping was indeed a Kodak moment in the studio. As opposed to *Duets*, "we had two microphones set up in the studio, and they were singing side by side. It should have been filmed. It would have been a great TV spot."

In contrast, "This Town" rates as one of Sinatra's more successful

---

18. Frank Sr. and Nancy Jr. sang together on two other flower-child-style singles in 1970, "Feelin' Kinda Sunday" and "Life's a Trippy Thing," which have not yet been issued in album form. She also made an impressively visual appearance, "Bang Bang"-ing on his 1966 TV special *A Man and His Music Part 2*.

assimilations of blues feeling, with harmonica joining the electric organ (à la *Strangers*) and soaring Basie-style brass. "Lee Hazelwood wrote it," said Bowen, who commissioned Billy Strange to orchestrate it because "Billy did the best arrangements of Hazelwood songs—he did 'These Boots Were Made for Walking' with Nancy Sinatra. So I hired him to do 'This Town' with Sinatra. I didn't think it ever quite came off, but the idea was good on paper." It's far from classic Sinatra, but it has a beat and you can dance to it.

In 1968, Bowen left Reprise and stopped working with Sinatra; other than a cut on *Ol' Blue Eyes Is Back*, *The World We Knew* was their last project together. "Frank was pleased with the results of 'Softly,' 'Strangers,' 'That's Life,' and 'Somethin' Stupid.' I don't know about the other things," Bowen very astutely said of the sessions he produced for Sinatra, which totaled parts of four albums (not including two packages of *Greatest Hits*) and many singles over three years. "A lot of the other things we did together were not nearly as wonderful as what he did when Sinatra was in charge of Sinatra. My guess would be that it was just something he was doing at that time in his life." The producer added that the one thing he saw him really get into was not a Bowen project at all but a more traditional Sinatra taping he attended strictly as a guest, namely the *September of My Years* album.

It's left for longtime Sinatra listeners to postulate that the now-vanquished "world we knew" which the song refers to is the world of good music. The major innovation of this album was the placement of its handwritten liner notes on the front cover and an especially boyish-looking photo of Sinatra on the back. Apart from Jenkins, none of the set's mixmasters—Hazelwood, Strange, Barnum, and Freeman—would work with Sinatra beyond 1967.

From that year until his retirement, Sinatra concentrated on making kiddie-pop sides with Don Costa, which was both better and worse. While Costa's orchestrations of these rock and pseudorock songs are generally less irritating than Freeman's, they also have less in the way of balls. Again, it's rarely the fault of the arranger or the singer (in his capacity as singer, anyhow); in fact, the arrangements and the singing are beautiful. It's just that there's nothing to be arranged or sung. In the words of Gertrude Stein, there's no there there.

Apart from a slew of singles, Sinatra and Costa created two complete albums of timely tunes in these years, *Cycles* (1968) and *My Way* (1968–69), as well as the lesser half of *Sinatra and Company* (1969–70) and all of Sinatra's strangest-ever concept album, *A Man Alone* (1969). *Cycles* is the worst of the first three, not having even one standout track worthy of inclusion on the *Reprise Collection,* while *My Way* boasts the most good moments. The front cover of *Cycles* shows a serious-seeming Sinatra (looking as if he has just been handed a parking ticket) in a photo taken about two seconds after the one on the back cover of *The World We Knew,* and the disc also includes a clone of the previous set's title track, "My Way of Life," the third and least successful Sinatra-Kaempfert chart number.

Cycles should have been titled *The Soft Sinatra* or *Somethin' Even More Stupid,* illustrating that there's a difference between being soft and sensual, as on the Jobim albums, and indulging in wimp-rock, as he does on *Cycles* and the B side of *Sinatra and Company.* These discs suggest a complete turnabout from "That's Life." On that track a defiant Sinatra threatens to chomp your arm off; nothing on *Cycles* has any bite whatsoever. Here he's covering the likes of Pat Boone (the exceptionally awful "Moody River," where Sinatra twists the word "friend" as if to confide in those paying attention that he's not taking it seriously). There are also two tunes that provided hits for Glen Campbell (who, earlier in his career, had himself worked as a session guitar with Sinatra), "By the Time I Get to Phoenix" and "Gentle on My Mind"—and the whole shebang is just too gentle.

"(From) Both Sides Now," a hit associated with Joni Mitchell and Judy Collins, throws Sinatra a little bit of a philosophical bone to gnaw on, on top of a harpsichord underpinning apparently inspired by the Rolling Stones' "Lady Jane." Here Sinatra finds infinite variety even when limiting himself to the smallest part of his voice and the tiniest portion of his emotional spectrum. Still, it can't be true Sinatra material unless it builds to some sort of climax or at least a conclusion, which "Both Sides Now" refuses to do, preferring to just drone on and on.

Whereas "Both Sides Now" purports to challenge conventional mores, "Little Green Apples" could be a commercial for middle-class values. "I Will Drink the Wine" on *Sinatra and Company* takes yet another tack, being a put-down of flower-child mentality ("I'll give you back your flowers / and I will take the land") that Jerry Rubin could have claimed as he switched from yippie to yuppie—or that Sinatra might have intended as a kiss-off to Mia Farrow. But Sinatra will never convince us that he has ever eaten a little green apple. Likewise, in the title song "Cycles" (though nobly backed by pianist Ernest Hayes, mimicking Bill Miller, who is here conducting), it's hard to believe that he would ever actually use a phrase like "my gal just up and left."

While the Jobim side of *Sinatra and Company* contains some of Sinatra's most exquisite work of the late '60s, the B side unfortunately consists of yet more *Cycles* that continue to repeat themselves meaninglessly. The Carpenters' hit "Close to You" is so thin, it's actually an insult to the classic tune that bears that title, recorded by Sinatra in 1943 and 1956, while "Sunrise in the Morning" makes for the most redundant text Sinatra sang since Sammy Cahn let "each little small café" slip past him in "Only the Lonely." He also does two tunes by Henry John Deutschendorf, Jr., also known as John Denver, which made it for other people: "My Sweet Lady" hit four years later for Cliff DeYoung but does nothing for Sinatra, and the Peter, Paul and Mary charter "Leaving on a Jet Plane," which unfortunately is hardly "Come Fly with Me."

If Sinatra was intent on reverting to a second childhood, he achieves it with "Bein' Green"—written to be sung by Kermit the Frog—on which arranger Costa and songwriter Joe Raposo concoct what could have been the basis for a Reprise set called *The Sesame Street Sinatra.* On one level Sinatra distends its message from "It isn't easy bein' green" to "It isn't easy bein' *me.*" Still, he stays true to the juvenile aesthetic, singing the piece with a confined, naive quality. By abandoning his dynamic range, Sinatra sounds at once folkish and childlike. He doesn't even put the expected emotional accents on phrases like "big like an ocean or tall like a tree."

"Lady Day," originally written and recorded in a different arrangement for *Watertown,* stands out as the side's most disappointing track. Sinatra had already paid tribute to the late Billie Holiday in interviews as well as in practically everything he had ever sung, the 1945 "You Go to My Head" in particular. It seems more like an insult than an homage to summon up her memory with this simpering soft-rock ballad. Although Sinatra surges commandingly near the end, "Lady Day," with its Jenkinsian pseudo-classical strings and pretentious attitude, seems to epitomize everything that the real Lady Day wasn't.

Fortunately, there's better stuff on *My Way,* an album recorded in February 1969, when the single of that song, recorded the previous December, began selling. Costa's uptempos, even on worthwhile songs like "Watch What Happens" and "For Once in My Life" (a song that has truly left its Smokey Robinson roots behind), are problematic, as we'll explore in the postretirement period, but in light of *Cycles* and *Company,* Sinatra deserves credit for at least trying to do something with a little excitement to it.

The more directly rockish fast numbers are the less successful. "Hallelujah! I Love Her So" remains utterly unsuited to the Sinatra-Costa combo (Freeman would have been a better choice—not to mention Billy May[19]), while "Mrs. Robinson" qualifies as an infamous example of Sina-

19. May devised swinging orchestrations of many of these late '60s hits for singer Nancy Wilson that are light-years ahead of the Sinatra-Bowen versions.

tra's audacity. Sinatra turns Simon and Garfunkel's nonlinear assemblage of non sequiturs into a jivey nonsense number, extracting far more humor from it than the comparatively simple Mr. Simon ever did. Costa could do with a little more of that sense of outrageousness, for the chart seems lame in comparison to Sinatra's audacious vocal, in which he substitutes "Jilly" for "Jesus" (sounds reasonable) and fades out with Dean Martin's catchphrase, "Keep those cards and letters coming."

However, it's *My Way*'s ballads that constitute the truly worthwhile additions to the Blue Eyes canon. "All My Tomorrows" is a full minute longer and ten years darker and deeper than the classic 1958 original; when Sinatra gets to the phrase "arms that cling," he makes that last word into an incredibly potent, not to mention grabbing, verb in this heartfelt vocal. Likewise, "Yestarday," the only John Lennon–Paul McCartney song he would record (perhaps inspired by the visit of George Harrison to the taping of *Cycles*), rates a first-class Costa treatment, one excellent enough to make it worthy of the *Sinatra and Strings* set.

While there are two mediocre *Cycles*-level pieces—"Didn't We" and "If You Go Away"—Luiz Bonfa's "A Day in the Life of a Fool" compensates. With its beautiful piano work and gentle bossa nova background, the song (also known as "Manha de Carnival") suggests that rather than devoting themselves to this teeny-bopper jive, Sinatra and Costa, himself a recording star in Central America, should have invested their energies in a third album of Brazilian material, this time getting into some of the great bossa ballads by composers other than Jobim. All told, *My Way* has enough memorable moments, even without taking into account its formidable title track.

If "Somethin' Stupid" led to *Cycles*, then what track from *My Way* would Sinatra pick to lead into his next album, *A Man Alone*? Unfortunately, it turns out to be "If You Go Away," a dismal French melody with even drearier lyrics by pop poet Rod McKuen. At the time it was recorded in February 1969, McKuen was working on the words and music to *A Man Alone*. (In 1970, Sinatra also recorded "I'm Not Afraid" by Jacques Brel and McKuen; this single should have been added to the CD release of *A Man Alone*.) Sinatra and McKuen had met the previous April when Bennett Cert, publisher and member of the Sinatra inner circle (he was in attendance with his wife at *The World We Knew*'s New York session), introduced them at a birthday party for McKuen. "I had tried for years to reach Frank; wrote songs with him in mind, but could never get to him," McKuen told Leonard Feather at the time. "When we finally met, instead of just offering to do just one or two [of my songs], he promised

me an entire album, which he'd never done before for any other composer. It was incredible."

Incredible indeed—in the *Laugh-In* era, McKuen had established
himself as the most pecuniarily successful poet-songwriter of all time:
helped by Herculean promotional skills, three books of his poetry had sold
a million copies by 1968 plus two million LPs of those verses spoken and
sung in that year. McKuen made himself the McDonald's of poetry and got
rich marketing his McPoems. One doesn't imagine Sinatra took a lot of convincing to realize it would be worth his while to grab a piece of that action.

About the quality of McKuen's verses one can only echo the sentiments of Walter Burns in *The Front Page:* "Tell him his poetry stinks and
kick him down the stairs." To anyone who considers Whitman, Hart
(Lorenz), or Dylan (Thomas, not Bob) their idea of a poet, McKuen offers
slim pickings. His music likewise offers little that one would walk away
from humming. Yet no Sinatra album has absolutely nothing to recommend it, and even *A Man Alone* has much that is worth hearing. To paraphrase Shaw on Wagner, it's an album of brilliant minutes and
excruciating half-hours.

A Man Alone consists of eleven pieces revolving around the subject of
loneliness, the first of which, the title cut, Sinatra briefly reprises at the end,
making a total of twelve tracks. Of the eleven, McKuen wrote six in song
form to be sung by Sinatra and four in blank verse for Sinatra to recite over
an orchestral background. The remaining piece, "Empty Is," which, like
most of the album, is about as profound as "Happiness Is a Warm Puppy,"
contains both a sung and a spoken section, rendered without the band.
Going from words without music to music without words—definitely an
improvement—"Some Traveling Music" consists of a vocal and then a long
instrumental section. The latter piece could be a dedication to Jackie
Gleason, not only in its appropriation of catchphrases from the Great One's
variety show but in its Gleasonian *Martinis and Memories* Muzakiness.

To put it succinctly, most of the songs are absolutely nothing. "Lonesome Cities" is one of the more melodic items and virtually the only one
with any kind of beat. Boosted by solid barroom piano from Bill Miller,
it's a desouled version of "Any Place I Hang My Hat Is Home." "The
Beautiful Strangers" amounts to a philosophical discourse on the subject
of broads and hotel rooms. And the poems are even less: "From Promise
to Promise," better delivered in the whiny tones of an Andy Rooney,
contemplates the delivery of laundry, or rather the lack of it. Didn't Sinatra feel embarrassed reciting this poetry jazz in front of professional studio musicians—real artists and poets—who must have been fighting
back the giggles?

Yet two factors save *A Man Alone* from being a total epistemological clambake. The first is Sinatra's remarkable conviction; he's in beautiful voice throughout, and unlike the way he seems to distance himself from some of the quasi-rock numbers from this period, he makes us believe that, far from pulling our collective leg, he takes the stuff quite seriously. The second is Costa; where Riddle would have gagged on the naïveté of the material and Jenkins might have imposed his own pomposity on pieces already pontifical enough, Costa gets it just right.

As a result, although "I've Been to Town" suffers from an unengaging hook, Sinatra comes to life on the bridge, and pianist Miller and Lestorian tenor Ted Nash get in some good solos. "Love's Been Good to Me" is as good as any piece of Sinatra folk music, set in a convincingly simple ABABAB form and backing the star with another harpsichord (or similar-sounding electronic keyboard) and prominent guitar. In itself it's no more or less than any other pseudo-ancient air concocted for, say, Guy Mitchell, although Sinatra brings to it uncommon tenderness and sensitivity.

While "Love's Been Good to Me" rates as the Sinatra side most heard on easy-listening stations and in coffeeshops, the title song, "A Man Alone," makes the disc's one significant contribution to Sinatra's catalogue. For once the melody is strong, worth paying attention to, and the lyrics, as Sinatra told McKuen, "really get inside me." Both Sinatra and Costa attack with just the right dynamic of force and volume. Without disrupting McKuen's withdrawn, low-key mood, they still unearth all sorts of possibilities to display the differences between loud-soft and soft-soft. Even the wordless choir adds something for once. And while putting the strongest track at the beginning leaves one with a funny taste for the next forty minutes, it's a satisfying touch to fade away with a reprise of this opener—and more icing on the cake when Sinatra returns with a different set of lyrics. It's one of those perfect balances of man, music, and orchestration that were starting to get rarer and rarer for the Old Man.

For instance, there's nothing as good on *Watertown*, Sinatra's final full-dress production of the pre-retirement period. But if that 1969 album boasts nothing as strong as the title track of *A Man Alone*, its predecessor of several months, at least there's nothing as embarrassing as those poetry recitations, or "Pretty Colors" on *Cycles*. A soft-rock song suite, *Watertown* marks Sinatra's most ambitious foray into post–*Sergeant Pepper* "concept album" territory.

Watertown is essentially a Four Seasons album done for Sinatra. Nearly all the major creative talents on the project had been with that pop act, described by one encyclopedia as, "with the Beach Boys, the

most successful American male vocal group of the rock and roll era, selling some 80 million records in the course of their career." Writer and
producer Bob Gaudio, in addition to singing with the group, composed
nearly all of their big bubble-gum hits (such as "Big Girls Don't Cry,"
"Can't Take My Eyes off You," "Short Shorts," and "Walk Like a Man").
Co-writer Jake Holmes replaced Bob Crewe as Gaudio's collaborator
and had a major hit himself as a singer-songwriter in 1970's "So Close."
Producer-arranger Charles Calello had done the charts on most of the
Four Seasons' hits from the beginning. Lead singer Frankie Valli filled
the most important function of all: he "sold" Frank Sinatra on Gaudio's
work.

Although part of the rock era, the Four Seasons (named after a New
Jersey bowling alley) were all Jersey Italian-Americans who had grown
up on Sinatra's music and considered it a lifetime dream to work with
him. The genesis of *Watertown* begins with Valli, who, as Calello
described him, "had this uncanny ability . . . or the balls, really, to go up
to and talk to anybody. But anyway, Frankie had a lot of confidence in my
ability, and he also had a lot of confidence in Gaudio's ability. So he told
Sinatra they had all these hit records because Bob Gaudio wrote and
produced all their songs. And Sinatra said, 'Well, could he write some
songs for me?'"

Gaudio went to work writing songs for Sinatra with Holmes, who had
recently collaborated with him on the Four Seasons' *Genuine Imitation
Life Gazette*. Calello said, "I think they wrote about four songs, and Sinatra liked them. And then Gaudio laid on him the concept of doing it as
the *Watertown* album." Eventually Gaudio came up with the idea of
putting Sinatra "in a small town"—as Gaudio told Sinatraphile Ed
O'Brien, "having a small-town approach and taking it down as much as
we could to basic life in middle America." Gaudio also recalled that Sinatra initially thought the team was merely preparing an album's worth of
individual songs for him; he didn't realize until he heard all the demos
that he was getting a concept album.

Gaudio had gotten to know Sinatra personally some months earlier by
hanging out with him for a few weeks between shows in Las Vegas, but
Calello, who was conducting, did not meet him until the first session.
"Came the night of the date, he was supposed to be there at seven
o'clock. Three minutes after seven, the orchestra is playing, and Frank
walks in the back door. As he walked in, I felt the air in the studio
change—evidently the musicians caught him walking in because they
started to play with an entirely different intensity. My back was to him, so
he walked towards the orchestra as I was conducting on the podium. He

taps me on the leg because I was elevated and says, 'You Calello?', I turned around to go shake hands with him and say hello, but nothing came out of my mouth. Literally, nothing came out, I was so intimidated!"

The orchestra laid down tracks for eleven numbers over four dates in New York in July 1969; it's not known how many of them Sinatra recorded vocals for at this time. He felt he could do better in terms of his singing, and not wanting to hang around the East Coast (Calello remembers somebody was trying to serve him with some papers at the time), he decided to overdub new vocal tracks in Los Angeles. "He didn't know the songs well enough," said Calello. "One of the things I found out about working with him is that it took him a long time to learn a song. But I had spoken to Sammy Cahn about that. I asked him, 'How long does it take you to teach a song to Sinatra?' He said, 'Well, Frank doesn't like to speed-learn a song. He takes his time so he can really get it, to appreciate the value of the song. Sometimes it takes him a good week before he gets it under his belt.' So for him to learn all originals for a new album was a major task." Along the way Gaudio substantially remixed the orchestrations from the original tracks taken down by engineer Frank Laico; Sinatra also "produced" his own backings to several verses, employing Al Viola and his acoustic guitar.

Sergeant Pepper, long regarded as the definitive concept album of the rock epoch, had been a collection of whimsical psychedelia, while other famous thematic packages, such as The Who's *Tommy* and Pink Floyd's *The Wall,* addressed the issue of adolescent alienation. Sinatra's "rock-concept" set deals with more mature themes, and while the songs never spell out a crystal-clear story, the lyrics repeatedly suggest such issues as divorce in a small town, custody of the children, and a man and woman who grow up together only to grow apart. The cover artwork, depicting a train station where much of the action (such as it is) transpires, as well as a montage of marriage memorabilia (a photo album, anniversary cards, dolls) on the inside of the gatefold, delineates at least as much of the narrative as the texts. (For that matter, so does an inserted poster that shows a '60s casual Sinatra in a windbreaker, standing by those self-same railroad tracks.) Overall, the mood is halfway between the Beatles' "She's Leaving Home" and virtually every country-western song ever written. In both attitude and its Costa-like orchestrations ("I was always a fan of Don's," said Calello. "Don was my all-time favorite."), *Watertown* could be called *By the Time I Get to Phoenix—the Album.*

By its own standards, *Watertown* isn't bad. The songs on the whole are better than most of *Cycles, A Man Alone,* and the B side of *Sinatra and Company.* Sinatra shows his tender and paternal side in "Michael &

Peter," making for a marvelously effective vocal in spite of a rambling
and unfocused—not to mention pretentiously cryptic—piece of material. The title cut boasts an attractive solo by clarinetist Phil Bodner and
an evocative use of a train sound effect in the coda. "Goodbye (She Quietly Says)" and "I Would Be in Love (Anyway)" are both at least adequate
love songs.

The 1994 CD issue of the set includes "Lady Day," originally written
by Gaudio and Holmes for the *Watertown* suite. Sinatra eventually
decided the song would make an interesting tribute to Billie Holiday,
even though that was far from what the authors had intended. "Gaudio
didn't know they referred to Billie Holiday as Lady Day," said Calello.
"It was a coincidence, because Gaudio was not a jazz lover, and he didn't
really know who Billie Holiday was." Sinatra rerecorded "Lady Day" a
few months later with a more opulent orchestration by Don Costa, and it
eventually wound up on the *Sinatra and Company* package.

"She Says" may be the weirdest thing—though far from the worst—
Sinatra ever recorded. It's an aphoristic haiku-like text accompanied by
what sounds like a Japanese samisen (a string instrument that sounds
like a banjo; but this might be guitarist Vinny Bell playing what Gaudio
has identified as a "bellzuki") and a combination of flute and repercus-
sive percussion like something in an Ennio Morricone score for a
spaghetti Western. While a children's choir also participates, this is far
from "High Hopes"; you could call it "Low Hopes." This leads to "The
Train," a closing track that starts optimistically but leads only to a
reunion that ultimately isn't. *Watertown*'s strongest contender for a classic cut, apart from "Michael & Peter," is "Elizabeth," a lovely ballad
Sinatra intones convincingly. The singer could have revived this track
for his unfinished collection of song titles after girls' names (it's certainly
better than Van Heusen's "Barbara"), and it also would have been worthy
of inclusion on *The Reprise Collection*.

By the singer's own yardstick, *Watertown* hardly rates as essential
Sinatra, though it probably doesn't deserve its status as the most
neglected of his albums and the last to be issued on CD. As Gaudio and
Holmes recalled, *Watertown* was originally conceived as a TV special,
and Sinatra, on the verge of his retirement, ultimately decided not to go
through with the multimedia part of the project and released just the
album itself. They should have held it back until the special could be
produced, Gaudio feels, because without the proper launching pad
Watertown was a commercial disaster. In retrospect, the set amounts to
merely one more entry in a long era of unimportance. In the five years
between the last album with Riddle in 1966 and Sinatra's retirement in

1971, apart from the Jobim and Ellington sets Sinatra came out with only one song of any lasting significance. That was "My Way," which, although it first hit the charts (in a very minor way) in 1969, really belongs to the post-retirement period.

Thus Sinatra's recording career had been taking a disappointing turn as Reprise neared its tenth anniversary, not only in terms of artistic endeavor but also in sales. While *My Way* reached number 11 on *Billboard*'s album charts, the more ambitious *A Man Alone* charted only at number 30, selling 63,500 copies, while *Watertown* washed up at number 101 and 35,000 units. His film work, which had not been central to his career since *From Here to Eternity* (and had not resulted in a really good picture since 1962's *The Manchurian Candidate*), was coming up equally dry. He also burned several bridges in Las Vegas, getting into a tiff with a casino manager at Caesar's Palace that left him vowing never to return to Nevada.

In interviews, Sinatra railed against the "protestations" of young people marching in opposition to the "establishment." They never realized that by the end of the '60s the former counterculture now *was* the establishment, and Sinatra was the one reacting against the status quo. He seems to have known, by 1970, that "Sinatra music," as Jimmy Bowen calls it, had assumed the role of an alternative expression. Sinatra rebelled against rebellion and, disenchanted with the Camelot he had helped create, he began a gradual switch to the G.O.P., embracing Nixon, Agnew, and Reagan. One suspects (or at least hopes) that he neither agreed with nor personally liked any of these people, that he was just reaching out for shock value. He was just as determined to upset the apple carts of those who thought they could predict his next move as he had been when he made liberal waves twenty-five years earlier.

Thus the '60s, certainly Sinatra's most amazingly diverse epoch as a performer, would end as it began, with him calling a one-man strike— only this time, rather than just refusing to record, he announced his complete retirement from show business, effective March 1971.

In a masterful piece of public relations, Sinatra gave what was to be his final appearance as a benefit for the Motion Picture and Television Relief Fund at the Los Angeles Music Center on June 13. The circumstances surrounding the "farewell appearance" were the usual combination of events that could have happened to nobody but Sinatra. At the Oscar ceremony that spring, Sinatra was awarded the Jean Hersholt Humanitarian Award; a few months later he was subpoenaed to appear before the House Select Committee on Crime.

While "My Way" was his most recent, important hit, it was not the climax of his "farewell" concert; instead, that honor went to "Angel Eyes."
Thanks to stagecraft and the majesty of his singing, Sinatra stage-man-
aged a perfect coda. As the song wore on, Sinatra gradually faded out,
both aurally and visually. He sang the number accompanied only by a
pin spot and, if memory serves, just Bill Miller's piano (no band). As he
delicately entered a diminuendo, the smoke from his cigarette gradually
enveloped him as both the volume and the spotlight grew smaller and
smaller. Finally, when Sinatra uttered the last line, "'Scuse me while I
disappear," he was gone.

CHAPTER TEN

"OL' BLUE EYES IS BACK"
AND THE CONCERT YEARS, 1973–1994

> *On the day I decided to put my youth behind me, I immediately*
> *felt twenty years younger. You'll say the bark of the tree has to*
> *bear the ravages of time. I don't mind that—the core is sound and*
> *the sap goes on doing its work, as in the old apple trees in my*
> *garden: the more gnarled they grow, the more fruit they bear.*
>
> —GEORGE SAND TO GUSTAVE FLAUBERT

Sinatra made the headlines twice in one week in March 1994—which must be a record for any near-octogenerian entertainer, even the world's last living celebrity on the level of Elvis, JFK, and Marilyn. The first resulted from the 1993 Grammy Awards ceremony, held on March 1, when Frank Sinatra received the Grammy Legend Award. Both the show's producers and, supposedly, Sinatra's own "people," terrified of any moment smacking of genuineness, abruptly yanked the Old Man from the stage in midramble. The second happened five days later in Richmond, Virginia, when an overheated Sinatra blacked out for a few seconds in the middle of a performance.

Even the two New York tabloids that front-paged the occurrence surprisingly didn't make that much of the song Sinatra happened to be singing at the time of his brief collapse: "My Way." If there's any number that could provide an ironic spot for Mr. Very Old Blue Eyes to fall down during, it's "My Way." For the last twenty-five years the song has served as the major mantra, the idée fixe, the recurring motif of Sinatra's career; or, as Sinatra announced in his 1974 *Main Event* concert, "We're about to sing the national anthem, but you needn't rise."

One should be careful in ascribing autobiographical underpinnings to singers and their songs. Could it be mere coincidence, for instance, that Billie Holiday's line of lovermen exhibited a sadistic streak both in her lyrics and in her life? Yet Sinatra conspicuously treats "My Way" as a deliberately reflexive text, taking full advantage of how Paul Anka concocted the English lyrics to this French *chanson* with the Chairman of the Board in mind.

Fueled by the belief that Sinatra is singing about his own life, telling us his own story, his concert audience extracts a doubly cathartic response from "My Way." When he sings of the dejection and failure which led to his transforming tragedy into triumph, we not only feel it along with him but we give vent to our own inner longings to redirect rejection into redemption. Sinatra is a mythological figure who faces impossible odds and is very nearly beaten, yet undergoes a heroic transmutation and is born anew. Here he is, living proof that a nobody from nowhere can not only become a crucial figure in American culture but do it twice.

"My Way" originated as a French song by Gillis Thibault, Jacques Revaux, and Claude François, the last of the trio being a *chanteur* who introduced it in Europe under its first title, "Comme d'Habitude" ("As Usual"). Like most French songs, "My Way" has the kind of droning rhythm and minimal melodic content that made it acceptable to kiddie-pop ears (which also explains why they seem so appropriate with country-western settings; "c'est la guerre, pardners"). Two seasons later, "Puppy Love" poet Paul Anka, who unlike Lennon and McCartney (authors of "Yesterday" on the *My Way* album), was only a lightweight even in that shallow area, devised an English lyric and title. Don Costa, who had worked with Anka at the very start of his career, served as the connection between the teen idol and the Chairman of the Board.

A few days after Christmas 1968, Sinatra and Costa committed the piece to tape. Milt Bernhart, on seeing that there was a single piece of music on the stand—meaning they would likely get out quickly—remarked to the rest of the band that here was a Christmas present indeed. "Bud Brisbois played the lead trumpet on that," the trombonist recalled. "It was a Maynard Ferguson–type thing, and it wasn't easy." The band and Sinatra ran through two takes, and the whole process was completed in less than half an hour. Bernhart feels that the performance—issued and reissued on numerous singles, LPs, and CDs all over the world—is actually a composite of the two takes, noting a change in vocal quality. The only obvious splice in the piece occurs right before "I've loved, I've laughed, I've cried," where Sinatra cuts down instantly from a really big voice to a small voice in less time than he or anyone else could do naturally.

In its first release, "My Way" didn't chart as high as "Cycles" and was mainly notable as the first important Sinatra side in some time on which Bill Miller did not play. (The pianist was in the hospital at the time.) Lou Levy, an ace accompanist best known for his work with Peggy Lee and Ella Fitzgerald, deputized for Miller on the session.

When *Variety* attended one of the earliest concerts to include the anthem, the reviewer noted that Sinatra referred to both "My Way" and "Cycles" as intended "for the kids." The paper also noted that the two tunes received polite applause but nothing compared to the tumult that greeted "The Lady Is a Tramp" and "I've Got You Under My Skin."

But the combination of Sinatra and the song gradually snowballed. Musically, it's an underwhelming composition that contains five nearly identical stanzas, each consisting of a string of very monotonous four-note phrases. (Small wonder that as he gradually loses his memory and his ability to concentrate, the seventy-nine-year-old Sinatra can often be counted on to get lost in "My Way.") Yet the way he transforms this unpromising source material takes him beyond alchemy and into the realm of sheer magic. Musically, it has no more content than most rock and roll, yet Sinatra pumps it up with the grandeur of an operatic aria, a five-minute exercise in self-indulgence that starts quietly, even intimately, and ends enormously. It became the centerpiece of Sinatra's act when he took to playing rock venues, eighteen-thousand-seat amphitheaters and sports stadiums, rooms that were a mite too spacious for "Try a Little Tenderness."

It's as if you're standing in front of Macy's on Thanksgiving morning, watching the Frank Sinatra balloon float by. Nothing gets in the way of this choreographed exhibition of burgeoning ego, which is a risk he might run if the song had a strong melody or a witty text, or something akin to a sense of irony. It's conceivable that one could be critical when contemplating "My Way" from a distance, as when hearing it on the album or the radio. However, it's impossible not to be overwhelmed by it in person: how can you not stand up and cheer at the sight of a man who can, at will, grow to be ten stories tall?

Whatever deficiencies "My Way" may have as a piece of music, Sinatra soon inflated it into an irresistible piece of theater. Anka's self-congratulating lyrics had the desired effect of making the song both a summation of and a metaphor for Sinatra's entire career. And in the months following his 1971 retirement, Sinatra soon learned that millions of people would pay dearly for the privilege of experiencing him singing it in person.

*   *   *

It's difficult to know exactly how much concertizing meant to Sinatra's career before his aborted retirement. He first became a sensation thanks to live appearances, and all of his subsequent success in radio, recordings, and movies can be traced back to his triumph at the New York Paramount Theatre at the dawn of 1943. By the early '40s, "vernacular" entertainments had evolved into a modus operandi that would seem baffling to later generations. We can understand how the "legitimate" theater, meaning full-length musicals and straight plays, occupied the Broadway venues that still serve that purpose today. Big bands spent a chunk of their schedules in ballrooms, generally associated with the classier metropolitan hotels, and there still were a few all-live vaudeville houses here and there. But for the most part, vaudeville, swing bands, and movies had evolved into an entertainment amalgam unique to the '30s and '40s: a combination of a full program of films and a live show. While double features (usually a major release and a smaller "programmer" for the bottom half of the bill) were the norm at the less important theaters, the big houses typically presented roughly two and a half hours of film (including an important feature and several shorts and cartoons) and at least a full hour, or even ninety minutes, of live entertainment. Generally musically oriented, the live portion of the program would often include a dance team, singers, musically backed acrobats (the sort of act that later found a home on *The Ed Sullivan Show*), but the featured attraction was always the big band. It could have been swing (Benny Goodman) or sweet (Eddy Duchin) or both (Glenn Miller), but the most popular bands were those that comprised entire variety shows in themselves, like Tommy Dorsey or Swing and Sway with Sammy Kaye.

In a sense, Sinatra didn't emerge just from the Dorsey orchestra, he graduated from the Dorsey vaudeville entourage. He also made the transition from doing three or four songs per show to filling the entire star spot—forty minutes to an hour—all by himself. What drove both the bands and then Sinatra (the first solo singer to occupy the star spot, considering that Bing Crosby had long since stopped touring in this fashion) to distraction was the number of shows they had to do every day, from early in the morning to late in the evening. Indeed, it was a reprieve when Sinatra was able to leave early to do a broadcast or a mere couple of supper club sets at the Waldorf.

Alvin Stoller first worked with the singer at the New York Capitol (no relation) Theatre in 1945 and remembered those performances vividly: "The orchestra would play his theme song, 'Night and Day,' the stage would come up and the orchestra would rise, and he'd be standing on top of the piano, with everything lit from underneath. Frank was the act, he was *it*, he was the whole show. The Will Mastin Trio [the only other act on the bill] gained recognition [at that engagement]. Sammy [Davis, Jr.] was hoofing and doing imitations and all that stuff. But the Mastin Trio was only out for maybe ten minutes [as an opener], and the whole rest of the show was Frank."

While that was unusual for the period as a whole, according to Stoller, it was typical of Sinatra's theater appearances. "Every show was a Sinatra concert," as the drummer put it, "and the place used to be jam-packed with people." Incidentally, despite Sinatra's bringing in more bobby-soxer business than anyone could compute, he did not consistently break his own box-office records, because theaters found it impossible to eject fans between shows. "The theater tries to book as inferior a movie as possible to complement Sinatra," *The New Yorker* observed in 1946, "hoping (vainly) that the recurring flashes of mediocrity on the screen will discourage fans from waiting around for the next show."

In some instances, as on several occasions in Atlantic City (particularly on the Steel Pier), theater owners dispensed with the movie altogether. "[I used to do] eleven shows a day," Sinatra reminisced in the middle of a show in the same city around 1983.[1] "In those days they used to run people in and out so fast that you barely had time to turn around between shows. . . . I remember one day I had just gotten a bottle of soda and a sandwich, and I was still up on the stage; the curtain had come down. I was hungry. So I'm there, munching on this sandwich, and I turn around to say something to somebody and up goes the curtain. They were so fast that they had brought in a whole new audience, seated them and everything. The band starts up, and I'm expected to sing with a sandwich in my mouth. Well, I finished that sandwich. Believe me, I needed it. It was brutal then. But let me tell you something: I treasure those days. We did it—we got the job done."

These appearances constituted Sinatra's bread and butter throughout the Columbia period; indeed, he made considerably more money from accompanying pictures than he did from starring in them, even such blockbusters as *Anchors Aweigh* and *On the Town*. This tradition continued into the '50s; in 1951, Sinatra used his CBS TV show to hawk his May appearance at the Paramount (doing one show with the full cast of that revue, including the virtuosic Joe Bushkin, the vivacious Eileen Barton, and the indescribable Dagmar). However, television would soon put an end both to the big bands and to the movie business as it had been. In 1956, Sinatra reunited with the Dorsey band and the onetime "home of

1. As quoted in *Philadelphia* magazine, September 1983.

swoon" in an appearance motivated more by nostalgia and his desire to promote his current picture (the lamentable *Johnny Concho*) than by the bucks brought in by fans.

As live shows in movie theaters gradually faded away, it took Sinatra some time to find a permanent replacement as his central venue for in-person appearances. He had given his first actual "concert" in 1943, doing a tour in conjunction with a specially assembled Philharmonic orchestra. Being the first pop singer to engage in such a venture at that time and for many years after, he never would have imagined that con-certizing in this fashion would become the staff of his life. Indeed, the first nonclassical singing star to make a big splash at Carnegie Hall wouldn't get there until 1962, and he wouldn't be Sinatra but Tony Bennett.

"The problem was, we could never find places that were big enough," said Frank Military. "There was no Carnegie at that time; they weren't doing that then. So we worked at places like the Cal-Palace in Nevada. I remember one time in El Paso when we played some kind of bull arena, and occasionally large concert halls, like in St. Louis, before Frank started doing stadiums." He regularly worked the Copacabana in New York and the 500 Club in Atlantic City, even though these places were hardly enough to accommodate everyone who wanted to see Sinatra. "You couldn't get anyone in with a shoehorn," added Military, explaining why he had to do so many shows a night.

Thus, for most of the '50s and '60s Sinatra was a performer who made albums and pictures—at least two of each a year; was somewhat less suc-cessful on television; and made as many live appearances as he could, though these were generally for the high-rollers and rarely for the masses. Bill Miller remembers that Sinatra spent so much time on location and in the studios that "we hardly ever worked [on the road] in those days."

The equation only began to change after Sinatra's twenty-nine-month hiatus, from 1971 to 1973. Sinatra had spent much of the early '70s bud-dying up to Spiro Agnew and Richard Nixon, whom he had campaigned against vehemently in 1960. (Earl Wilson devoted a column to describing how Sinatra could barely bring himself to shake Nixon's hand when they bumped into each other in Toots Shor's in 1962.) It was at a White House gala (given in honor of Prime Minister Giulio Andreotti of Italy on April 17, 1973), at which Sinatra and Nelson Riddle performed, that the singer is said to have realized he wasn't ready to forsake the limelight. Riddle, having observed the president serve as cheerleader in a standing ovation, remarked to the singer, in his usual dry martini fashion, "You can't do much better than that." Ironically, just as Agnew and then Nixon were forced to resign Sinatra reemerged from his aborted retirement.

For the remainder of the '70s, Sinatra would be asked about the retirement and the subsequent "unretirement," and his official answer to interviewers invariably ran along the following lines: I started getting a lot of mail from people, and they would make suggestions like "We know you don't want to make live appearances anymore. But won't you consider doing us, your fans, a favor by making a new album?" So I began to think about recording, and then I gradually came around to the idea of touring again.

Given these statements, one would conclude that after Sinatra returned to performing he would make recording his primary activity and touring only a secondary consideration. And by May 1974, Sinatra had recorded two entirely new albums. But such assumptions proved short-lived; the situation worked out in exactly the opposite way. The Voice, now known as Ol' Blue Eyes (a monicker dreamed up by publicity man Lee Solters), continued to thrill millions—but now almost exclusively in concert. From 1974 to 1979, Sinatra would venture into the record studios only occasionally; when he did, the results impressed very few at the time, and even fewer since.

"What most of these [pre-rock] artists really didn't understand was that as the record business changed, the way of selling music also changed," observed arranger Charles Calello. "The record-buying audience is from an age of, let's say, ten years to about twenty-six. Then after you get out of college and get on your way, start your life, the chance of your running into a record store or really being interested in music is sort of limited, based on your romantic attachment. And after people start their adult lives and their families, then the new generation of people start to come in and buy their own generation. So if you go to see Sinatra, the audience will be a bunch of blue-haired people. If you go see the Four Seasons, you'll see a bunch of Italian-looking guys with mustaches and polyester clothes. And so Sinatra's record-buying audiences dried up. It wasn't so much that he needed to change his product, he needed to change his marketing."

Accordingly, the major breakthrough for this period was Sinatra's transformation from saloon singer to stadium singer—the realization that he could play the same venues the major rock acts played, the sports stadiums. According to most accounts, promoter Jerry Weintraub deserves most of the credit (after Sinatra, that is) for pulling this off. "When Frank came out of retirement and started doing stadiums, he didn't know if he would draw," recalled guitarist Al Viola. "He was going to have to pull in fifteen thousand or eighteen thousand people every place he went. But Jerry Weintraub handled the promotion and booking when he started to tour. Jerry was involved with rock groups. He knew all the stadiums from one part of the country to another, and he knew what he could sell. But in 1974, neither Frank nor anybody else had any idea what he could actually do in a room where they sold hotdogs."

Obviously, Sinatra went over spectacularly in this new forum, so well that he continued to be one of the world's strongest concert attractions more than twenty years later. It's difficult now to name many rival acts from 1974 who were still giving him competition, let alone performers from the late '30s, when Sinatra first began his career. The major selling point was that now you didn't have to go to Las Vegas and know somebody who knew somebody. Now if you could come up with the asking price—and had no objections to waiting on line all night for tickets—you could get in to see Sinatra.

In the '50s and '60s, after the rise of television and the decline of movie-vaudeville appearances, performing live was a mere supplement to Sinatra's income. The real dough came from his multimillion-dollar, multipicture deal with Reprise and Warner Bros. After 1974, when the concert circuit became the single biggest subsidizer of jewelry for Barbara Sinatra, he began to take these live shows more seriously. "He stayed more aloof from the musicians," percussionist Emil Richards explained. "He no longer called me 'Dag' [short for 'Dago'], he would just say 'hello' and never call me by name. Don't get me wrong, he was always friendly. It just was a whole different bag. He was rubbing noses with the Republicans and stuff. Now it was time to make some heavy bucks, and he started to do concerts. I think that the musical integrity suffered a little bit from then on."

Richards' observations should be placed in context. "Frank's entourage treated him like God and, in a sense, he was," said arranger and trombonist Billy Byers. "He'd been exalted so long he didn't act like he was just another guy in the band any more. But he still was terrific. He was way above the usual kind of guy you work for—who treats you like a waiter, like you ought to come in through the servants' entrance."

In the '40s, Sinatra had occasionally traveled with a regular big band, such as his 1945 East Coast tour of movie theaters with Jan Savitt's orchestra. Savitt, like Woody Herman in the 1974 *Main Event* tour, served as both secondary attraction and accompaniment via the employment of local "pickup" string sections. But more often Sinatra traveled with a regular rhythm section. From that rhythmic center, sometimes abetted by one or two horn section leaders, such as trumpeter Charlie Turner, the entourage would annex regional brass, reed, and string contingents. Sometimes Sinatra would change nearly the entire orchestra from city to city, although he preferred to keep one semipermanent band on the East Coast, one on the West Coast and Las Vegas, and a third, London-based orchestra to cover Europe.

Getting the right musicians was paramount; the problem was that most musicians of Sinatra's caliber preferred not to go on the road and were generally able to land enough studio work on either coast not to have to. As we've seen, having to fight with the Copacabana house orchestra in 1950 contributed greatly to the vocal breakdown Sinatra suffered during that engagement, and the locals hired to accompany him in Atlantic City that September weren't any better. "We [Sinatra's rhythm section] went up and rehearsed the band," drummer Johnny Blowers recalled. "The stage band was pretty bad. They were good guys, but they didn't give a damn. They sloughed off a lot of things, and you don't slough off with Frank! So when he got there, he called me and said, 'How's the band?' I was trying to think what kind of an answer to give him, and I didn't answer right away. Then he said it a little strongly: 'All right, did you hear? I said, "How is the band?" I said, 'Well, it's *comme ci, comme-ça.*' He said, 'What the hell does that mean?' I said, 'Well, I think you'd better hear it.' Well, we barely got through the first show and—whew—they were pretty bad." At this point, Sinatra did what situations like this frequently forced him to do. "After we finished that first show, he said, 'Fellows, we won't use the band anymore. Just have them come in on the closing chords.'"

When Sinatra began playing Las Vegas the following year, he similarly dreaded dealing with local players. "In the beginning, in Las Vegas, they didn't have enough musicians to go around," explained Milt Bernhart. "It was still a small town in the '50s, and believe me, Frank's standards were high. So after a rehearsal prior to opening night, there would be a call out in Hollywood for players that he wanted, to come to Las Vegas in a hurry. And money was paid; he paid very handsomely. It was almost a regular event. If he was going to open in Vegas, I almost expected it. And a couple of trumpet players, trombone players, and several fiddle players, and a fiddle section for sure, and maybe a saxophone—it depends on the band. But usually the local band just couldn't handle his music, not to his satisfaction. He'd even go so far as to rehearse with them [something he rarely had to do in the concert years]. But the orchestra there never satisfied him."

From 1974 onward, Sinatra's main accompaniment was the "New York" band assembled for him by contractor and concertmaster Joe Malin (until the violinist's death in 1994). Based in New York, this ensemble would travel with Sinatra to any gigs that happened to be closer to New York than Los Angeles, including many engagements in Europe, Africa, and South America. He would also use a permanent rhythm section for all gigs. In selecting this section in 1973, Sinatra naturally went with musicians he was already comfortable with, beginning with the six men who had accompanied him on his 1962 World Tour. As he had since 1951, Bill Miller would head the rhythm section on piano (with the exception of a few years in the late '70s and early '80s), Al Viola would grace the guitar chair until he tired of the road not long after Miller left (temporarily, it turned out), to be replaced by another tristate Italian, Tony Mottola. For a time, Emil Richards traveled with the unit on vibes, until Sinatra's accountants ascertained that a permanent mallet man was unnecessary. Charlie Turner also traveled with all editions of the Sinatra band for many years as the Chairman's preferred lead trumpeter (and frequent soloist). Ralph Pena, bassist with the '62 sextet, had been killed in a tragic accident in Mexico in the mid-1960s, so Gene Cherico played bass with the group for roughly a decade, and when he retired, Sinatra ceased employing a full-time bull-fiddler.

But the rock of the Sinatra rhythm section was always Irv Cottler. Sinatra depended so completely on the drummer's ultrareliable rhythm patterns that they became a veritable road map to the singer. He could practically pass out and then wake up in the middle of any number and know exactly where he was and what he had to do. Cottler's unswerving solidity gave Sinatra the support he needed to continually take chances, to improvise and crawl out on whatever limb happened to catch his musical fancy. "Irv was a great big-band drummer. I mean, the tempo really didn't move—it stayed where it was supposed to be," observed engineer Lee Hirschberg, himself a former drummer and a lifelong percussion connoisseur. "He really was a dictator of tempo. Once he set it down, that was where it stayed. And he knew what was going to be sung and where to put in the crashes of cymbals and stuff like that. He was really excellent at that."

Emil Richards told a similar story. The vibist and Cottler worked together frequently on variety shows, for television and elsewhere, in which they were required to play for all sorts of dancers. As the vibist recalled, "The dance acts would come up to Irv and say, 'Faster! Faster! I want it faster!' Irv would then stop playing. Then they'd say, 'What are you doing? Keep going, only faster!'" Cottler would then glare at the hapless terpsichoreans and inform them, in no uncertain terms, "'Don't tell me to play faster or slower. You show me where you want it, and I'll put it there and I'll keep it there!' Irv had a metronomic mind as far as knowing where the beat was, and Frank always depended on him. Frank would go into a song and just bring his hand down, and Irv would take up the tempo. Irv was right every time! He would lock into the tempo that he knew Frank wanted, and I think that's what Frank misses about Irv the most. I don't think there's another drummer anywhere who could do what Irv did as far as knowing the tempo that was gonna make it really cook for Frank."

Cottler's predecessor, Johnny Blowers, felt that of all the instruments the drums were the ones Sinatra empathized most with; he described the singer, like many show business icons (including Bing Crosby, Johnny Carson, and Bill Cosby), as "a frustrated drummer." "Drums are very important to Frank," said Blowers, "because he digs time and he likes rhythm. Yes, Frank was strong on drums. So was Berigan. So was Goodman. So was Dorsey. They all were. The heart of the band is the drum. If you've got a good drum, you've got a good band. If you've got a bad drum, you've got a bad band."

Between 1956, when Cottler first appeared on a Sinatra date, and 1971, the drummer and the singer worked together frequently if not religiously. On studio sessions Sinatra preferred the more flexible Alvin Stoller. Both were firmly rooted band-pushers in the Buddy Rich manner, yet while Stoller knew more different ways around the beat, on the road Cottler was Sinatra's man.

As for his personality, Cottler represented the opposite of Bill Miller, his partner of more than thirty-five years (off and on) in the Sinatra rhythm section. The Old Man himself, who has at times described himself as a manic-depressive, could have discerned his own reflection in each of the two men. At certain times Sinatra identified with a retiring loner like Miller; other times he saw something of himself in the always aggressive, occasionally hot-headed Cottler.

As Miller put it, "Oh, Irv hated to be told what to do." For instance, there's Billy May's favorite Irv Cottler story, about a date that the arranger conducted for the late Bobby Darin. Said May, "We called Irv 'Grump' because he was so congenial. Anyhow, the first date we did started out with some bright tune, and it had a big fat introduction, and Irv had a drum break in bars seven and eight of this introduction. So we played the introduction, and Irv played the drum break. Then Darin, who was a smart asshole kid, stopped the band and walked over to Irv and said, 'Now I'll tell you how I want this played.' Oops! And Irv stood up and stared him down and said, 'You sing the songs, I play the drums, see? Don't fuck with me.' That was the end of it. There was no trouble after that. Irv was wonderful! I think he'd even tell Frank where to go if Frank ever pulled that shit."

While neither Sinatra nor Cottler was known to pull his punches, they got along famously with each other. "He's beautiful," the drummer said in 1979. "I worked a lot of shows with a lot of singers, and I've never seen anything like him. You could never get bored with Frank. You could do the same songs day in and day out with him, but each time there's a different level. And I'm talking about twenty-five years here!"

In interviews, Cottler tended to exaggerate his curriculum; he wanted people to think that he had played on most of Sinatra's albums and had been the drummer who replaced Buddy Rich in Tommy Dorsey's band when actually Alvin Stoller deserved the credit for both those achievements.[2] Yet Cottler's accomplishments were formidable enough that they hardly required inflating. "In the music business," he said, "I got my four biggest thrills with Red Norvo, Claude Thornhill, Tommy Dorsey, and Frank Sinatra"—listing the thrills in chronological rather than quantitative order.

Cottler was first inspired to play the drums by the great black swing drummers. "The first drummer I ever saw play was Chick Webb," he said, "and then Jo Jones, the original drummer with the Basie band. I'll never forget the first time Basie came to town. He and Jo opened everybody's eyes with a new sound and a new approach." Talking some years ago about other percussionists he admired early on, Cottler mentioned that "Sid Catlett was a beautiful drummer. Shadow Wilson played with Basie a little later; he died at an early age, but he was a dynamite drummer." But Cottler reserved his greatest praise for Buddy Rich: "He *is* a genius. He's something else! When you talk about drummers, you put him on the side, then you start with the rest. He's a fine man and a beautiful human being. Buddy's like Frank, they're both perfectionists, they're great musicians. Hell, they're geniuses! I hope Buddy goes on forever because the young kids who are coming up should make it their business to see him, to know what the drums are. It's not the sixteen tom-toms that they've got going and all that bullshit. There are a couple of young drummers around, but for the most part it's amateur time!"

Stoller himself had recommended Cottler to Sinatra. "My dad was sick in New York," Stoller recalled not long before he died in 1992, "and I went back for a day. I sent Irv in to sub for me." Cottler first appeared with Sinatra in 1955 on half of the tracks used on the album *Songs for*

2. Cottler recalled playing for Dorsey in 1944. Since the personnel of Dorsey's band in this year hasn't been definitively documented, it's possible Cottler could have briefly substituted for Rich when the latter was in the service. When Rich left Dorsey for good, the Smiling Irishman hired Stoller as his permanent replacement.

Swingin' Lovers! From that point on, Cottler turned up occasionally on Sinatra Capitol albums, although Stoller continued doing the bulk of them. Cottler placed himself at Sinatra's disposal more often in terms of appearances outside the Los Angeles area. "When I didn't want to travel," said Stoller, "Irv jumped in because he wanted the job." Cottler made the famous 1962 World Tour with Sinatra, the first occasion that the two men had to get to know each other well, but as Cottler noted, "I never got to play the 500 Club [in Atlantic City] with Frank because we were all too busy in the studios."

The music industry itself was going through a severe shake-up around the time of Sinatra's retirement. The studio scene of the '40s and '50s was quickly being fazed out by developments like rock and roll (in which being a traditional musician became a liability) and electronics. Many musicians, even those whose skills had been as in great demand as Cottler's, panicked. "Irv had gotten very panicky," said Milt Bernhart. "Frank wasn't working, and the record dates were slowing down. Everybody was looking around for something else to do. So Irv bought a liquor store, and he lost everything he had on it." (Bernhart has had better luck with his own postmusic venture, a travel agency that he has operated for more than twenty years.)

When Sinatra began to plan for his reemergence in mid 1973, he and Cottler decided to commit to each other full-time. "In the early days," he said, "I couldn't get away from the studios often enough to go on the road. But then the studios became a real drag to go into, music-wise. So when Frank came out of retirement, I said, 'Forget it, I'm gonna have a ball!'"

For roughly fifteen years the routine was the same: Sinatra's regular men would rehearse with the locals, and the star himself would do only the actual show itself with the full contingent. Yet in the earlier part of the "Concert Years," Sinatra would run through at least part of the program with the full contingent. "The band would rehearse one day without Frank just to run down a chart," said Cottler. "He doesn't like to over-rehearse, which I agree with. When Frank walks in and he does rehearse, it becomes a different band. We have the same guys, but it sounds different. The minute he walks in, everybody just goes up a level, even two levels. The rehearsals are like a performance on stage."

For over a decade and a half Cottler was the force that propelled the Chairman and his board. It wasn't always "a ball": In the '70s, he hated playing the rock-oriented numbers that Don Costa arranged for Sinatra. Cottler, who occasionally rankled fellow sidemen as affable as Miller and Viola, was bound to butt heads with the more assertive Frank Sinatra, Jr., who began conducting the band in 1988. Cottler hardly kept it a secret that he didn't get along with the Old Man's son. "Junior took years off Irv's life," one old-time sideman (who prefers to remain anonymous) put it. Cottler was also considerably demoralized by the death of Buddy Rich in 1987. "Irv felt as if he and I were the only two drummers in the world," said Alvin Stoller. "He would always say, 'There are only two of us left.'"

"Irv worked with the Old Man so long that he just couldn't stop," said drummer Sol Gubin, who worked with Sinatra many times in the '60s and eventually succeeded Cottler. "Irv had arthritis very badly in his hands, and that's why that thing got to be that constant backbeat and pounding and shit. Irv really didn't have any chops left, and I knew he didn't like his own playing anymore, and I was really sorry. As a matter of fact, I ran into him a couple of times, and he said he wanted to quit and he wanted me to take the job. At the time I said I really didn't know if I wanted to go back on the road again."

The loss of Cottler can be partly blamed for the erratic quality of Sinatra's performances in the 1990s. His going through over a dozen drummers in the early '90s can be described as a continual search for another Irv Cottler. "He'll never find one," pianist Lou Levy said. "No way. Irv fit him like a glove. But there's only one glove, and he had it!" Not for nothing did Sinatra regularly introduce Cottler as "the best drummer I ever worked with in my entire career."

The papers saw fit to publish many Frank-should-retire editorials even as he unretired in 1974; many newspaper folk were gunning for him to step down even as he went into the concert arena. Columnists (most virulently the late Ralph J. Gleason, who had all but worshiped at the Sinatra shrine on the notes to *No One Cares* in 1959) complained that he was now a caricature of his former self, strutting around boxing rings—a judgment not born out by concert recordings of the period—and on top of that had the temerity to challenge the authority of the news media. He had begun daring reporters to knock the chip off his shoulder back in the '40s when the bulk of the media was controlled by ultra-right-wingers such as noted Sinatra hater William R. Hearst. That he had gone on attacking them now that he had switched sides only seemed to aggravate his precarious relationship with the liberal and youth cultures.

To a certain extent, Sinatra served as both the Howard Stern and the Rush Limbaugh of the '70s, using his inter-song spieling to vent against the unfortunate subjects of his personal wrath; the attacks took a misogynistic slant when he concentrated on female reporters. (Not to argue in his defense, but the most famous female journalists until recently were often gossip columnists.) And yet there's evidence that Sinatra was keeping the vituperation flowing not just because he couldn't control himself but as a deliberate means of keeping his name in the papers. Sinatraphile and writer Arnold J. Smith remembers seeing Sinatra at the miraculous Uris Theatre engagement (with Count Basie and Ella Fitzgerald) in September 1975: the first thing Blue Eyes did upon starting his opening number ("Where or When") was take note of the notetakers in the audience. He then made sure they caught his every movement—and not necessarily when talking but in the actual performance of each song. Then, despite having carefully played up to the reviewers in the house, he would launch into a diatribe concerning the mating habits of scribes in skirts.

Sinatra was getting more play in the press than ever before, and he didn't have to punch or marry anybody or even show up before an organized-crime commission. He was also exploiting the public's suspicions of the mass media. Sinatra's most disastrous blow-up ever—one of the few that actually hurt him more than it helped him—occurred in July of 1974. For this particular tour, Sinatra brought eight musicians, his usual four-piece rhythm section (Miller, Viola, Cherico, and Cottler) and three horn section leaders, Marvin Stamm on trumpet, Billy Byers on trombone, and Bud Shank on lead alto. "In Britain, there's a yellow press, and in Australia, the press is eight shades yellower," as Byers recalls the altercation. "Sinatra had a chauffeur who was supposed to let us off at rehearsal hall at top of a hill. But the press paid off the driver to let us off at the bottom of hill where the reporters were waiting. So here's Sinatra, who was no longer a young man, on a brick road running up a steep hill away from the reporters. Naturally, he got very angry and called one of them a whore. The Minister of Labor got wind of what happened and said Sinatra had insulted all Australian workers." Byers feels the whole thing was a scheme concocted by an ambitious politician to get his name in the headlines by attacking Sinatra.

When, at the concert of July 9, 1974, Sinatra exploded at some length, offering his inflammatory opinion of the local press, the entire collected force of Australian labor unions decided to boycott him. Without organized electricians and stagehands, Sinatra had to postpone his remaining appearances; the airport workers refused to sell him fuel or fill his tanks, so he couldn't even leave the continent. "Believe me when I say Frank was one hundred percent right," Cottler, who was unabashedly biased in favor of his boss and friend, insisted. "The people, the public, were marching in the street in Sydney with cards and signs printed that said, 'We want Sinatra! Down with the press!' Naturally, they didn't put pictures of that in the papers or on the air." While Sinatra never apologized—not in so many words—for his statements, he did make a peace offering to the Aussie media by doing a television appearance "on the house." Whatever the case, Sinatra's tirades were not only keeping him on the front pages, they ensured his continued status as an inciter of international incidents. "Or, as they say in Australia," Blue Eyes jokes in *The Main Event*, "Ol' Big Mouth is back."

As Andy Kostabi has often said, the important thing is to be talked about, even if the talk is something positive. Ultimately, the publicity—adverse or otherwise—amounted to icing on the cake. Sinatra's infamy and living-legend status brought in the cash customers in the first season or so of touring, but what kept them coming back was his continually riveting performances. He didn't change the repertory much—"New York, New York" could be heard in every show from 1979 on, while "My Way" turned up in nearly every single performance of the two decades of the concert years—but he went on instilling the feeling in his audiences that he was creating each song anew every time they heard it.

While each Sinatra concert cost as much to see as any Broadway show, apart from his opening acts (as weak as over-the-hill Vegas funnymen barking impotence jokes or as strong as Basie's orchestra), there was no filler, and there was more laughter, drama—even really scary moments (musical and otherwise)—in a one-hour set with Sinatra than in two acts of almost any musical spectacle. Although he sounds considerably better on the White House concert of 1973 (where he still had much of his fuller '60s voice) than he does in *The Main Event* in 1974, it's also amazing how long he kept being at his best. There are two beautifully recorded 1985 Tokyo concerts that may come close to ranking as Sinatra's all-time greatest live performances (although they have yet to be commercially issued by Reprise). Even in 1994, despite clamorings for a second retirement by those presumptuous enough to imagine that Sinatra might actually listen to them, Sinatra still has more than his share of "on" nights, even if at seventy-nine he can hardly be expected to hit the bull's-eye every time out.

Nearly six months before the official end of the retirement in 1973, Sinatra began taping his comeback album, *Ol' Blue Eyes Is Back*, which dovetailed with a TV special released in November with the same title. Despite the odd combination of the generally infantile songs of Joe Raposo with the often grandiose orchestrations of Gordon Jenkins, neither of those men dominated the proceedings. Rather, Don Costa, credited as producer on *Blue Eyes* (and arranger of three tracks), served as Sinatra's most-heard-from collaborator here and on nearly all of his '70s recordings.

As we've seen, Costa and Sinatra began their association with the 1961 *Sinatra and Strings,* one of Sinatra's most outstanding sets of the early Reprise years. At the end of the decade, he appointed Costa a one-man replacement for the producer-arranger team of Jimmy Bowen and Ernie Freeman, employing him as such on *Cycles, A Man Alone,* and *My Way.* By the end of the retirement, Costa's role as Sinatra's second-in-command was firmly established. Sinatra's retirement was partially an admission that he couldn't understand the youth culture that had come to dominate the music industry. Perhaps if he had decided, in coming out of retirement, to stay with his traditional venues, he might have simultaneously resolved to revert back to his earlier recording habits; that is, make classy albums and do the ephemeral songs of the day either only on singles or, better still by this time, not at all. Instead, the idea that he was charging into the home turf of the rock and rollers unfortunately reinforced the idea in his head that he had to tackle contemporary material both in the studios and in the stadiums. Yet while only a portion of his live performances consisted of forgettable material, nearly nothing that Sinatra put down on tape during these years had any lasting substance.

And, as Viola put it, "Don had helped Paul Anka get started, and he had an ear for that kind of music. Nelson didn't. Billy May didn't. Gordon Jenkins didn't. But Don Costa did. He had that extra talent. He was also younger. Unfortunately, that [soft-rock style] didn't fit with what Irv Cottler and I wanted to do, and though I liked Don personally, both Irv and I agreed that it didn't fit Sinatra." Charles Calello elaborated: "Don supplied Sinatra with contemporary arrangements that were musical enough for him to sing, which was good. The market had changed to such a degree that when it came to picking the new songs that would have any kind of longevity, he really needed someone who had some [modern] song sense."

Sinatra and Costa first met when the latter, born in 1925, was in his early twenties and working with a local theater band in his native Boston. "Axel Stordahl and I were doing a theater date in Boston, and we used a local orchestra and Costa was the guitarist. And that's when we first met," Sinatra told deejay Sid Mark not long after Costa's untimely death. "And Don later told me that he was terrified because he was such a big fan of Axel's. Don was thinking about writing and orchestrating in those days, and he finally met with Axel who was his idol. And Don was shaken when he met him and the great New York musicians we had brought up."

Like other arrangers, Costa worked with dozens of singers (including Paul Anka in his first stab at a career), but he first came to fame as the arranger-conductor for Eydie Gorme and Steve Lawrence at the time the two singers hit the national scene, both individually and as a couple. As Lawrence said, "The three of us—especially Eydie and Don—kind of grew up together musically." Sinatra and Frank Military had known Gorme and, subsequently, Costa and Lawrence since the late '40s when Sinatra's Barton Music office was down the hall from Gorme's first agent, Ken Greengrass, in the Brill Building. Said Billy May, "Don did a lot of wonderful things for Steve[3] and Eydie before he went to work for Sinatra." May added, only half-kidding, "For a guitar player, he turned out really good."

"Actually," said Eydie Gorme (who is also Mrs. Steve Lawrence), "I first heard of Don when I was singing with Tex Beneke's band in 1950 because he was sending in original arrangements, as were a lot of other arrangers, for the band to play. And I kept seeing his name on these charts. He kept calling them things like 'Costa's Last Stand,' 'Costa's Retreat,' Costa's this, Costa's that . . . and the stuff was wonderful, I mean, really wonderful. Unfortunately, Tex never used any of Don's charts because they really weren't Tex's style." (Slightly earlier, Costa and Bucky Pizzarelli had played tandem guitars on Vaughn Monroe's hit "Riders in the Sky.")

Gorme next encountered Costa when she was singing and he was doubling on bass and guitar for WPIX radio in New York. When she and Lawrence began recording for Coral Records, she recalled, "Don said, 'Hey, can I do some charts for you?' And I said, 'Sure.' And we started to do a record here and a record there for Coral." Within a few years, Costa had become not only their musical director but their producer and A&R man as well. In the mid 1950s, Costa, Gorme, and Lawrence started ABC-Paramount Records, and five years after that launched another disc operation under the aegis of a movie company, United Artists Records.

In both ventures Costa served as house arranger, conductor, and much more: "Don really was the chief cook and bottle washer," said Lawrence. "He ran artists and repertoire, he signed new artists and did the orchestrations, and he searched for songs written by other composers, hired other producers. Where the other guys [Riddle, Jenkins, and so forth] basically were orchestrators—and did that miraculously

---

3. Costa came up with one of the wittiest—and most Billy May–like—arrangements ever recorded by that Frank-enstyle funster Steve Lawrence on his United Artists album *Lawrence Goes Latin:* On the song "Small World," the key word of the lyric is "funny," and whenever Steverino hits it, Costa has a female choir in the background chant "ha! ha! ha!" as if it were "cha-cha-cha!"

well—Don had a greater thirst for knowledge and a greater, wider, broader gift than that of arranger. He orchestrated, composed, produced, and had a knowledge of electronics and studios and sound boards. Don really was very, very inventive, and ahead of his time." (Costa also recorded his own albums for these labels, such as *Don Costa and His Freeloaders Play Music to Break a Sub-Lease By.*)

As his career proceeded, Costa continued writing arrangements but increasingly preferred to let others conduct them. "Don just wasn't very good at conducting, and he didn't like to do it," said Lee Hirschberg. "He liked to be able to sit in the control room and listen to what was going on. Don was a big help with a lot of things, particularly on arrangements of his that were fairly intricate, that might be balanced in different ways. He wanted to hear all the specifics, things that a lot of the other writers didn't worry too much about. He felt that his contribution would be more in the booth than in conducting an orchestration he had already written." Costa would carefully rehearse his musicians, who hardly required a conductor to begin with, and then pass the baton to a specialist like Nick Perito (who later became Perry Como's musical director) or Joe Guercio, in the United Artists period, or Sonny Burke or Bill Miller on the Sinatra sessions.

As has been noted, Riddle and May weren't any Bruno Walters, either, in terms of their own conducting prowess, and Costa's decision to remain in the booth is no reflection on his ear or his skills as an orchestrator. The last arrangement that Costa wrote for the Lawrences was "Again," which Steve introduced at Carnegie Hall in the early '80s. While the band rehearsed the chart in the main auditorium, Costa sat in one of the subbasements, hundreds of feet below, poring over a pile of musical manuscripts. What was going on upstairs reached his ears only as a muffled morass of noise, and when he finally emerged, he informed the conductor exactly which string player hit precisely which note flat in which specific measure.

"You know, Don never used a piano," recalled fellow guitarist Tony Mottola. "If you were sitting next to him and had your radio on, you're listening to some rock and roll station, Don could still write an arrangement. He would be oblivious. No matter what was going on in the room, he could sit there and score an orchestration." Billy Byers calls Costa "The Puccini of pop," adding that Costa's orchestrations are "seething with melody" as opposed to those of Riddle, who, Byers feels, used comparatively little melody in the actual arrangements themselves, primarily supplying background harmonies while the soloist up front assumed most of the melodic responsibility.

Why and how did Sinatra decide to give Costa a shot? As with everyone else he worked with from Axel Stordahl onward, as Military explained, "he heard something by Don that he liked." As Lawrence semisarcastically answered the question, "Frank stole Don from us!" Costa seemed to be the perfect musical director for the post-retirement Sinatra: Jimmy Bowen and Ernie Freeman could help him make pop hits, but, as Bowen said, he never would have attempted making traditional "Sinatra music" with the Chairman. Riddle and May could make high-class music, but their textures weren't what was selling in the leisure-suit '70s. Costa, Sinatra hoped, could help him do both. "Don brought all these songs [that Sinatra tried in the '70s] to him, and there were others he turned away," said pianist Vincent Falcone. "But most of what Sinatra did were things that the two of them agreed upon. He trusted Don's taste far more than you would believe."

Also, in using Costa, Sinatra would not be wed to any one particular sound. Nelson Riddle sounds completely different on *Swing Easy* than he does on *Moonlight Sinatra,* but in both cases he was making an automatically identifiable Sinatra-Riddle kind of music. One can likewise spot Jenkins or May (though the latter is also an ace musical mimic). "Harmonically," longtime friend Falcone felt, "Costa was probably the most inventive and aggressive of them all." Yet, for all his technical prowess, Costa remained an invisible arranger: he wrote *Sinatra and Strings* with a style that remains unique to that album, but on the whole, as Lawrence said, "Costa had everything the other writers had, and he wrote in a way that was very identifiable to me. However, I think probably most listeners wouldn't recognize his work—not like you could Gordon or Billy. Don was a lot more flexible and versatile than some of the other guys. They seemed to have gotten locked into their own identities early on. Costa had much greater horizons that he was exploring. He didn't settle into a niche."

Costa not only followed Stordahl and Riddle as Sinatra's central arranger-conductor, he also replaced Sonny Burke as Sinatra's main producer. He joined Jimmy Van Heusen and Sarge Weiss (who looked after Sinatra's publishing interests) as a member of Sinatra's intimate business and music circle. "Don loved the Old Man to the point where he would sit like a dog at his master's knee," one member of the touring group recalled. "Great man that Don was, when he was around Sinatra, he was a puppy dog."

In both capacities, Costa was responsible for most of the production and arrangements of the two immediate postcomeback projects, *Ol' Blue Eyes Is Back* and *Some Nice Things I've Missed,* although Burke, Jimmy

Bowen, and Gordon Jenkins also had a hand in them. At the time of their release, the two sets (especially the first) were eagerly anticipated as the first new Sinatra albums since 1969; since then it is the rare Sinatraphile indeed who listens to the two sets with any regularity.

Both the truly great ("There Used to Be a Ballpark") and the truly abysmal ("Noah") moments on *Ol' Blue Eyes* go to Jenkins, who scored six of the set's nine tracks. Costa's three contributions include "Winners," the only one of the four Joe Raposo pieces on this set arranged by Costa. The derivative lyric, which opens with the line "Here's to the winners," suggests an antidote to "Nobody Wins," the track that follows it here, as well as the 1963 "Here's to the Losers." Both "Winners" and Costa's chart of "Dream Away" reflect '70s-style bell-bottom optimism and seem naively jingoistic today, like the score to a commercial or a TV movie opening title from that period ("Dream Away" was, in fact, introduced in the film *The Man Who Loved Cat Dancing*).

"Dream Away" is a hippy-dippy lullaby with lots of guitars and muted brass, a folk wannabe without the majesty (and the pomposity) that Jenkins would have brought to it. (In a radio interview at that time, Costa named it his favorite tune on the album.) "Let Me Try Again" is an attempt to make "My Way" magic happen twice, with a monotonous French-fried melody, a Paul Anka lyric (abetted by Sammy Cahn, no less), a Costa orchestration, and a dramatic performance from Mr. Blue Eyes. The protagonist of this text isn't quite as defiantly self-assured as that of the 1968 lyric, but the craftsmanship of the piece would hardly justify any confidence whatsoever: "To beg is not an easy task / But pride is such a foolish mask."

Some Nice Things I've Missed reverses the equation, with two charts by Jenkins and eight by Costa. The concept rates as the lamest that Sinatra would ever hang ten tunes on—glomming chart hits from the two years of his absence, as if all he did before he retired was cover other people's contem-pop charters. Worse, the package disingenuously suggests that Sinatra might have been the one who had the hits on the likes of "Sweet Caroline" and "Bad, Bad Leroy Brown" if he just hadn't been out of the picture.

To start with the worst, Costa arranged five uptempo pieces that are so trite one is embarrassed even to mention the titles: "Sweet Caroline (Good Times Never Seemed So Good)," Neil Diamond's 1969 hit; two especially forgettable items by Floyd Huddleston (like Raposo, best remembered for children's songs, in his case, from Disney cartoons), "Satisfy Me One More Time," which is heightened only by a brief Jackie Gleason impression, and "I'm Gonna Make It All the Way," published by

Sergeant Music, which Sinatra co-owned; "Tie a Yellow Ribbon Round the Ole Oak Tree," the ultimate hymn to the era of platform shoes (which uses a hardly John Cage–style example of *musique concrète* in applause that sounds dubbed from a baseball game); and the unspeakably shameful "Bad, Bad Leroy Brown."

While all except the Huddlestone opuses had been hits for younger pop stars, none come close to working for Sinatra in his idiom. "Sweet Caroline," for example, finds Costa using Billy May–style whimsical flutes and wah-wah brass, as the singer, who gets in some tasty low notes ("grand"), at once bites into the lyric with both his '60s-style aggression and an overcasual off-the-shoulder attitude. The pieces sound very assembly line, as if Sinatra had been handed the lyric sheet moments before tape started rolling and was trying to bang them out as fast as he could. All in all, the charts, the songs, and the singer aren't even remotely in the same ballpark; worse, Sinatra's swing-era rhythm section (particularly Cottler) offers little assistance in connecting the singer to this material.

Overall, these pieces justify Irv Cottler's contention that Costa was incapable of writing a swinging jazz chart. "He's a fine musician, and I wish I had his knowledge of music," the drummer said. "If I were a singer and I wanted a ballad, I would definitely have Costa write it. For instance, 'Lady Day' is a beautiful chart. But he's just not a jazz writer! He overwrites. His jazz writing is like trying to push a Mack truck with four flats uphill! Unlike Nelson, he doesn't know what to leave out." Al Viola elaborated: "We were essentially doing a copy of what Elton John or some other rock guy had done, which didn't make sense to me. That's what really upset Irv, because he had to play all the same drum breaks that the original rock drummer played."

Things pick up considerably when the tempo slows down. The love songs include "If," which Gordon Jenkins' chart substantially inflates, although not quite to the point of interest. Two Michel Legrand pieces also up the ante: "What Are You Doing the Rest of Your Life?" (soon to become *de rigueur* for all jazz singers, although only Sinatra seems to have recorded the verse); and "The Summer Knows" (a cover of a movie-derived hit by pianist Peter Nero). These are precisely the kind of kinky, Legrand-standing good-bad '60s melodies that Tony Bennett did best. "You Turned My World Around," the most respectable rock-beat item here, is a Sinatra–Jimmy Bowen–Burt Kaempfert item, the only one to be arranged by Costa (or anyone besides Ernie Freeman). Sinatra's biggest hits of the psychedelic era had been German ("Strangers in the Night") and French ("My Way"), and this piece attempts to blend the composer of the one with the arranger of the other. Sinatra escapes with a pleasant enough hook, if little else.

Cotter's comments aside, it must be said that Costa had few opportunities to orchestrate any worthwhile swinging pieces for Sinatra. After their sumptuous all-ballad debut, *Sinatra and Strings*, everything else, fast or slow, was all kiddie-pop. Only one in-tempo item rises above the pack here, namely, "You Are the Sunshine of My Life," which builds on a solid dance-band foundation—he could have arranged it for Tex Beneke or Les Brown in 1949. Wisely, Costa doesn't try to make it a real superswinger but rather instills the piece from the Stevie Wonder years with a gently rocking, Riddle-Dorsey-Lunceford two-beat. Here, Sinatra's hale and hearty Hobokenisms, such as his odd emphasis on the second syllable on "you came to my res-cue" and the *Love Supreme*–like incantation of "light my fire" at the coda, become "Sunshine"'s equivalent to the references in "Mrs. Robinson" to Jilly Rizzo. While they're not the most endearing asides he ever made, at least they help convince us that he gives a damn about the song. Anybody wanna dance?

The nineteen Costa cuts on *Ol' Blue Eyes* and *Some Nice Things* support the observations of Ted Nash. Having agreed that Costa wasn't as inventive as Riddle or May (with Sinatra), the saxophonist added, "Well, he was more commercial. He never did anything outstanding *musically* that the musicians could relate to, but he did a good job and came up with nice backgrounds, and Frank seemed to like the way he wrote. But it was sort of all the same. He just didn't have that much imagination." Or, to be more charitable, the circumstances didn't allow Costa to function at his best. Costa did little with Sinatra after 1961 that's as good as even the routine albums of standards he turned out for Steve and Eydie in the '50s. Judy Tannen, the Lawrences' manager for more than thirty years, may have been biased toward her clients when she said, "As good as Don's work was for Sinatra, he did his best charts for Steve and Eydie." However, she is, in fact, correct.

Whereas *Ol' Blue Eyes Is Back* made it to number 13 on the pop album charts, the overtly commercial *Some Nice Things* climbed only as high as 48—doing considerably worse than the more esoteric *A Man Alone* of only a half-decade earlier. In September 1974, Sinatra did one date with Jenkins (no tunes of which were issued until the '90s) and then spent the early part of October touring and gathering live material for what eventually became *The Main Event* album. Then, for the next five years, Sinatra did the most surprising and disappointing thing of all: he recorded next to nothing. The Voice was in great shape, and he obviously was in the mood to work, being on the road continuously. But the total scorecard of these years rings in at only sixteen generally unspectacular singles-directed songs and one aborted album, *Here's to the Ladies* with Nelson Riddle.

That count of sixteen includes only items that have been released; it omits tracks that may have been completed but still remain in the can. Virtually none of these was commonly available at the time or since; most came out only as singles, to be collected onto LPs only in Italy, on two albums that became instant collectors' pieces (both on WEA Italiana/Reprise, titled *I Sing the Songs* and *The Singles*); a few more saw the light of day only in 1990 on the four-CD *Frank Sinatra: The Reprise Collection*. To further confuse the issue, many "Sinatra sessions" from this period consist only of an arranger laying down orchestral tracks for which Sinatra never got around to doing his vocal part. (This was contrary to the way he liked to work, and while it may not have been the best way to tackle Cole Porter, it did fit the material he was recording.) Dick Nash remembers several sessions with Costa that "never came to fruition. I think they threw them out because Frank wasn't in great voice. That happened a lot, too. You know, he'd have a session all planned and set up, and he'd show up and go for about an hour, whatever, and the scratches would come in, and he'd say, 'Thanks a lot, guys, but this ain't it tonight.'"

Why the music from this period remains so obscure is a mystery. Most of it is no worse or better than what is available on the two 1973–74 albums. The exceptions to this are minor. The disco treatments of "Night and Day" and "All or Nothing at All" are generally viewed as the nadir of Sinatra's recording career, though in retrospect the disco genre isn't necessarily less suitable for him than soft-rock. The 1974–79 period encompasses a mere threesome of Sinatra classics, each the result of a renewed collaboration with old friends: with Bill Miller on the 1974 "Send in the Clowns" and "Empty Tables," and with Nelson Riddle on "I Love My Wife." These rank among the strongest performances that Sinatra recorded in any era. All three, it's pleasing to note, utilize contemporary songs; however, they're also songs written either for the Broadway stage or by old masters, and by that time musical comedy, even when it was written in rock style, was as far alienated from the record-buying mainstream as jazz.

But by and large, the 1974–79 tracks could easily have been put into albums with titles like *Ol' Blue Eyes Is Still Back* or *Some More Nice Things I Missed*. We have the same basic elevator-rock concept in which Sinatra is still resigned to the idea, unfortunately, that the only way to sell records is by making Muzak—soothing sounds for baby boomers. All these songs sound the same; they're all wishy-washy, sing-songy, not-quite-melody lines set in a just-plain-folk (ABAB) structure. That means each one consists of a "hook," which isn't nearly as catchy as its composer would like to think it is (and which isn't a tenth as good as the kind of melodic lines that Irving Berlin or Paul Gonsalves would throw away), and a lot of filler. They all have an especially pasty-sounding choir chiming in with the Chairman on the hook or B section.

Considering that Sinatra continues to rely primarily on Costa, with Jenkins occasionally pinch-hitting, we can truly say that never before have so many talented individuals attempted to do so much with so little. In addition to using the songs Costa steered him to, conductor-pianist Vincent Falcone noted, "Frank would listen and find out whoever was the hot writer at the time. Peter Allen, Carol Bayer-Sager, they were all hot at one point. Most of those songs were forgettable." So forgettable that most of them never even made it into the studio, surviving only on privately taped concert recordings. As far as commercial sessions went, Sinatra relied mainly on the same singer-songwriter standbys as he had for the 1973–74 dates, particularly Neil Diamond and Paul Anka.

Apart from giving us the French imports, Anka wrote words and music to two Sinatra tracks that Barney or Raffi or some other unsurnamed entity could use to entice Gerber dribblers to gurgle along with in a day-care center, "Everybody Ought to Be in Love," with its pseudo–Tijuana Brass figures, and "Anytime." Neil Diamond supplied the comparatively catchy "Stargazer," in which R&B tenor saxophonist Sam Butera helps Sinatra dispel the Beverly Hillbilly mood instilled by the tuba and banjo, marking the first Sinatra disc to include that instrument since 1952's "Tennessee Newsboy." (One is reminded of Mel Tormé's joke, "What do you call five thousand banjos at the bottom of the ocean?" Answer: "A good start.")

Snare drum and tambourine figure on Diamond's other song for Sinatra in this period, "Dry Your Eyes," which turns out to be pure pseudo-religious babble. While the piece would aspire to be saintly, lines such as "That distant falling angel / Who descended much too soon" seem to allude to Lucifer instead. Sinatra tries to instill some dynamics and drama into the thing, but Diamond's ditties aren't written to be intoned so much as interred as their composer would, in a droning, underpitch monotone.

On a similar note, Sinatra attempted a mock-sacred Christmas song by another "hot new writer" he favored in 1975 and 1976, namely, John Denver. In this overserious disaster, the Blue-eyed Patriarch croons sternly to his granddaughter (the newly born Angela, whom he mentions by name) that the Christ child was—and here's the title, folks—"A Baby Just Like You." To accompany this profound poetry, Costa supplies a synthesizer

line that mimics a child's toy piano. Costa came up with both the arrangement and the original melody for the flip side, "Christmas Mem'ries,"
to a lyric by Allan and Marilyn Bergman. It amounts to a dreary rip-off
of "The Christmas Song," being a fragmented mosaic of unconnected
yuletide imagery.

Some of the pieces work better than others, but there's nothing as
good as even the weakest Jimmy Van Heusen opus. As with the 1973
"You Will Be My Music," Sinatra gets his teeth deeper into pieces that
use a music-life metaphor, however transparent. The hillbilly lament
"The Only Couple" ("We were the only couple / On the floor that night,"
by John Durrill, who wrote hits for Cher) has one interesting musical
device in a fermata that occurs, appropriately, after the phrase "The
music stopped" (shades of 1943!). The other Denver piece, "Like a Sad
Song," engages Sinatra in a memorable monologue—and quite a rambling one at four minutes. The melodic content is negligible, however,
and the production begs for a Gordon Jenkins arrangement to bless it
with something in the way of personality; Sinatra can't do it without a
good song or at least a strong chart to help him.

But he seems determined to animate the Barry Manilow hit "I Sing
the Songs" via sheer force of personality, finding a reflection of himself
in lines like the opening, "I've been alive forever / And I sang the very
first song." He'd like the piece to become another autobiographical exhibition à la "My Way"—and he certainly plugged the hell out of it at
enough concerts (even using it as his opener). But here again Sinatra is
trying to drive a tank across a rope bridge, and the obvious lack of craftsmanship, indicated by the way he is forced to awkwardly bend a note on
the much-repeated phrase "and special" things, mark this as one of the
most amateurish pieces Sinatra ever tortured his tonsils on. After a few
tunes like this, even Michel Legrand, on his typically understated (read:
French) "The Saddest Thing of All," sounds like a master melodist.

As we've seen, the most embarrassing discs are the two best songs—
and the only standards—he recorded in this entire period, on Joe Beck's
1977 disco Sinatra session. Cottler recalled that "when disco became
popular, he decided to do two disco tunes. I think he was talked into it by
Don Costa. But when he mentioned the idea of doing two of the standards that were associated with him, I mentioned 'Night and Day' and
'All or Nothing at All.' It sounded like a great idea at the time. That was
the only time I ever suggested any tunes to him." This "Night and Day"
was issued briefly on an American single and on the Italian *Singles* collection, while "All or Nothing at All" came out unofficially on several
under-the-counter collectors' issues.

When the session actually happened, Cottler was the first to voice his adamant disapproval. Calling attention to the interviewer's tape recorder on the table, Cottler declared of the producer-arranger, "You want it on tape? I'll put it on tape! I think he's the worst writer I ever heard in my life! He's not a writer, he's a bricklayer. If it were up to me I'd ban all [that stuff] and ship it to an island!" Vincent Falcone's opinion was equally decisive, if less vehemently phrased: "They were just horrible. I don't understand how Sinatra ever got hold of Beck, but he did. Those charts were my nemesis! I kept beating on the Old Man to get rid of them. And finally, one day in a rehearsal at Caesar's Palace, we were doing the thing, and I made some kind of face, and he stopped the band. He said, 'Throw it on the floor!' And we never did those disco things again. We got the old 'Night and Day' back out!"

It was plain that Sinatra just didn't know what he should be recording. Actually, he had already found the answer to his problem, yet for whatever reason he refused to take advantage of it. At the beginning of this particular "comeback" in October 1974, Sinatra did a tour of the East Coast, as he would innumerable times over the next twenty years. This particular series of concerts climaxed in his debut at New York's major superstadium, Madison Square Garden. Employing Woody Herman and his Herd, augmented by his regular rhythm crew, three studio ringers (trombonist Urbie Green, taking the solo on "Skin," saxist Jerry Dodgion,[4] and percussionist Dave Cary), and a string section, Sinatra taped all six concerts. He then utilized the audio tapes of the six shows and the video of the last for his album and TV special combo *The Main Event*, in which he was introduced by that vulture of culture Howard Cosell.

It may seem a trifle deceitful to take the highlights of six shows and pass them off as a single concert (on "Let Me Try Again" and "I Get a Kick out of You," different sections of the same songs were patched together from different nights). But apart from Cosell's ludicrous intro (now I know why I'm not more of a fight fan), the results more than justify the means. Sinatra is electric from beginning to end, even to the point of demonstrating what he was trying to get out of "Bad, Bad Leroy Brown" and "Let Me Try Again." Dodgion concurred: "On a normal [nontelevised] concert, Frank establishes his own rhythm in how he builds from song to song. But at the Garden, every time he was ready to

---

4. Dodgion described an event that followed a long-established pattern of Sinatra's relationships with musicians: "I hadn't seen him in about fourteen years when I got the call to tour with him and Woody. Anyhow, at the rehearsal he came right up to me and said hello. That kind of shocked me. We had only worked together briefly much earlier."

go into a song, the director had to stop him and say, 'Oh, no, hold that.' He couldn't build up his usual momentum because of the TV crew. Anyway, that's why the special isn't as good as it should be. I know his performances were really a lot better on all the other concerts."

"I don't care how long you've been in this business, there's nothing like singing to live people," Sinatra said after "Angel Eyes." Pastiche that it may be, *The Main Event* disc builds beautifully in excitement and intensity, and, apart from *Trilogy*, is the only really worthwhile Sinatra album in all of the '70s. And this, my friends, is what Sinatra should have gone on doing, following this set with *The Main Event 1975*, *The Main Event 1976*, and so on. Each set would have concentrated on Sinatra's usual concert program, which was roughly sixty percent classic songs and the rest new material.

In this context, even the new stuff sounds good. This live "Sunshine of My Life" emits considerably more sunshine than the studio take, particularly when the Chairman interjects one of his Louis Prima impersonations. For that matter, the established Sinatra songs include many '50s Riddle classics that he had not yet rerecorded for Reprise. In addition, at least two of the old-timers are heard in newly minted charts, Billy Byers' hard swinging "Lady Is a Tramp" and a souped-up revamp of "My Kind of Town" by Riddle himself that even inspires twenty thousand hardened New Yorkers to cheer for Chicago. The new "Tramp" had been the sole benefit to come out of the July Australia-Japan tour. "Frank said he needed a 'hipper' arrangement," Byers recalled, "although he said, 'Make sure that the last two bars are the same because I have my choreography.' He used to like to give a little kick with his foot at the end." But though Sinatra had taped one earlier engagement, a Carnegie Hall benefit from the previous April, where he's much less sure-footed than in the fall tour despite a standout "Ballpark," yet he did not officially release another concert until 1995. According to Falcone, it wasn't just that things like "Autumn in New York" seemed irrelevant in the era of the Bay City Rollers but that Sinatra felt that he couldn't do anything that would appeal to '70s record buyers. By that time, even "nostalgia" meant Elvis Presley and the early rock era.

As late as the end of the '60s, Falcone said, "there were still two distinct audiences. There was the rock and roll audience, and there was also the traditional, Sinatra audience. So in those days you could have hits with songs that weren't straight rock." And Sinatra could at least land hits that were only semi-tacky: "That's Life," "My Way," and "Strangers in the Night" may have kowtowed to the kiddie crowd, but at least they weren't mere covers of other people's hits. As Cottler put it, "He's a leader, not a follower." Unfortunately, as Falcone reminded us, "by the late '70s the market for our kind of music was just completely gone. Nobody could make a record that didn't have 'Song Sung Blue' on it. You couldn't turn a radio on without hearing that thing forty-five times a day!" Sinatra had worked on a succession of classier album projects at this time, but none made it as far as a single session.[5] At one point he began planning an all-Latin set with Tito Puente. "We talked about it several times," *El Rey de Mambo* recalled, "but we never got around to making it. We both were always on the road, and we never could get together."

Sinatra got considerably further with *Here's to the Ladies*, which would have been his final complete album with Nelson Riddle. He devoted three dates in March 1977 to this collection of distaff appellations, although accounts differ as to how much of the set he actually completed. The most optimistic account is that Riddle arranged and laid down orchestral backings for ten songs of which Sinatra recorded vocals for approximately five (three were released on the 1990 *Reprise Collection,* the others not at all). It would have been the perfect album for him to make at this time, renewing his association with Riddle and with class material in general. Sinatra doesn't stoop to the trendy depths of any contemporary femi-names, although he did commission that Van Heusen and David Mack song named for his new bride, "Barbara." Luckily, the marriage made more of a hit than the song, which, though not one of the team's better efforts, at least ranks many notches higher than Barry Manilow's "Mandy."

It made for a depressing paradox: Sinatra not finishing (and not issuing) his projects involving class material, and just barely releasing the commercial dreck that he was able to get through. All the while, we have to remember, Sinatra still had a voice—one in fine shape, in fact—and he could still attract twenty thousand people to a single concert. If both supply and demand existed, why did this pattern consistently fail to result in any new product? Sinatra's brief return to a more sensible recording situation followed his switching to a new pianist and conductor in Vince Falcone, which occurred in October 1978.

---

5. Many of these allegedly planned albums may exist only in the imaginations of Sinatra fans. Albert I. Lonstein catalogued some of these rumored projects in his 1983 *Sinatra: An Exhaustive Treatise* (independently published), including "an album to be produced by Beatle George Harrison, a country-western LP to be produced by Snuff Garrett, an album to be titled 'Saloon Songs'" (which may have become *She Shot Me Down*), and an all-ballad set that was to have been arranged and conducted by Michel Legrand.

A native upstate New Yorker, Falcone was born in 1938 (the year Irv Cottler played his first major band gig) and was attracted early on to the piano. Although he studied for many years with the intent of becoming a "legitimate" (Falcone's word) concert soloist, he discovered contemporary jazz piano purely by accident in the mid-1950s, progressing from Stan Kenton to Erroll Garner, Horace Silver, Bobby Timmons, Art Tatum, and Hank Jones, as well as "every jazz piano record I could get my hands on." He went to college and then played in his native Syracuse, his career interupted by a stint in the army. He briefly played in Las Vegas but grew frustrated with the music scene and decided to support his family with a steady nine-to-five job selling pianos.

By the time he was thirty-two, Falcone had moved up the retail ladder to the point where he managed a multimillion-dollar chain of music stores. "But I was afraid that the next morning I would wake up and be fifty and never have done what I really wanted to do," Falcone said. "So I chucked it all. Nobody could believe that I would give up that kind of financial security, but there was just no choice as far as I was concerned. I packed up my stuff, packed up my family, and moved to Las Vegas, with no job, no place to live, nothing." He soon began playing in the lounge of the Thunderbird Hotel, which turned out to be, he said, "absolutely the worst musical experience I ever had in my life! After six months of that, I was really ready to blow my brains out." Things improved when he switched to the Dunes and then Caesar's Palace.

Shortly after starting at Caesar's in 1973, the first act he was called upon to accompany was Frank Sinatra, at a time when Bill Miller was conducting and only occasionally sitting at the keyboard. Falcone later learned that one of his mentors, Nat Brandwynne, who had conducted for Sinatra at the Waldorf-Astoria in the mid-1940s, was enthusiastically talking him up to the Old Man. Over the next five years, Falcone's playing at Caesar's justified his rabbi's recommendation. The Sinatra people began hiring him with increasing frequency, not just to work in Vegas but for traveling gigs as far as London.

Falcone took advantage of a unique opportunity to impress his new boss when Sinatra came up with a medley based on two classic charts by Nelson Riddle that he had recorded nearly twenty-five years earlier: "The Gal That Got Away" and "It Never Entered My Mind." Costa pieced the two together, taking the most liberties with the Riddle treatment of "Never Entered" in that he arranged it so that the full orchestra could either stay or drop out entirely, leaving only a solo piano behind Sinatra. To Falcone's surprise, Sinatra chose to use the piano version, especially after he heard Falcone play it, and it became a regular feature of the concerts.

In July 1978, Falcone was even more astounded to receive a call from Costa informing him that Sinatra wanted him to conduct, for the first time, on a recording session. He flew from Vegas to Burbank for the date and ran down three Costa charts with Sinatra and a typical fifty-piece orchestra of highly venerated Los Angeles studio musicians who had never heard of him. When, halfway through the date, the air-conditioning system broke down, Falcone was already perspiring so much from sheer nervousness that he never noticed the difference. "I was sweating so heavily on the podium that the drops of perspiration were blotting the music!" he said. "Of course, Sinatra told me later that the whole recording session was bogus; he just set it up to test me out. The Old Man decided that he wanted to see what I could do." (Of the three tunes, "That's What God Looks Like," Elton John's "Remember," and "You and Me," only the second was never remade.)

Falcone flew home to Vegas that night wondering what Sinatra had thought of his work and perplexed that Bill Miller wasn't there. The next time Sinatra played Lake Tahoe not long afterward, things were back to normal: Miller was conducting, and Falcone was at the keyboard. Then, a week after Tahoe, Sinatra's business manager, Mickey Rudin, notified Falcone that Sinatra wanted him as his permanent conductor, beginning in four days at Radio City Music Hall. Falcone accepted only after being assured that Miller had left of his own accord. "That was a hell of a place to open!" he said. "Talk about starting at the top. It's one thing to break in in Grand Rapids, Michigan, and quite another to open at Radio City. And I don't think I could ever have explained to anybody what a feeling it was when opening night came and Sinatra said to me, 'Are you ready, Vincenzo? Let's go!' And I realized, as I walked out on that stage, that there was no turning back, there was no stopping the orchestra if you didn't get something right. I mean, this was it, pal. This would either be a feather in my cap or the end of a very promising career. Fortunately, it went very well."

Falcone recalled that after he had been conducting for Sinatra for a few months, he and the Old Man happened to be doing another recording session. He doesn't remember what songs they were working on (and no information concerning this date has ever been documented anywhere), only that the whole date was scrapped after Sonny Burke went into the booth and suggested something called *Trilogy* to Sinatra. "Sonny explained it to Sinatra. He had it all laid out, he showed it to him," said Falcone. "And at that point, if my memory serves me correctly, Sinatra was so taken by Sonny's project that he ended that recording session right then. He said, 'We will not do another thing until we do this.'"

When finally released in 1980, *Trilogy* was a smash hit, going gold in a matter of weeks (meaning that it sold a minimum of 500,000 units or a million and a half individual LPs), which at $21 a pop added up to a lot of lettuce. That price becomes all the more exorbitant when one considers that people were really paying for just one record, Billy May's *The Past*. Most listeners could get through only a track or two of *The Future* and probably played *The Present* all the way through once or twice, but *The Past* was the disc that rated as essential Sinatra, worth reprising again and again.

Yet, Costa's *The Present*[6] had to be better than *Some Nice Things* and *Ol' Blue Eyes,* because the parameters of what it included were wider and the pickings not necessarily so slim. Covering the entire rock era, the material goes back as far as the 1956 Elvis Presley hit "Love Me Tender." Still, that fact also works against the concept, because in 1980 a song from twenty-four years earlier could hardly be described as part of *The Present.* (It's only two years younger than "All of You," the newest song on *The Past.*) While *The Present* may have earned Sinatra some commercial leverage at the time, it was obsolete long before *Trilogy* was even released. "Song Sung Blue" had won Neil Diamond the Record of the Year Award in 1972, so what the hell was the point of singing this drivel in 1980? *The Past* is an epic triumph and *The Future* a spectacular disaster, but at least with all its pretentiousness and ambition, it's a spectacular.

But there is no justification for *The Present.* Although it represents a much higher level of craftsmanship (particularly in the rhythm section) than *Ol' Blue Eyes* or *Some Nice Things,* it's merely a more professional presentation of the same old bubble gum. That description particularly fits the set's two fastest pieces, "Just the Way You Are" and "Song Sung Blue." Throughout the '70s, Sinatra fans of every stripe, including all his regular rhythm section, wondered why he couldn't simply concentrate on good songs. This thought was articulated at the time by David McClintick in *The Wall Street Journal.* As producer Clyde Otis once said of Aretha Franklin, artists who make it to the "living legend" level shouldn't have to worry about kowtowing to the marketplace when they, in fact, "*are* the market."

Yet in writing the notes for *Trilogy,* McClintick slightly altered this tune, explaining that "[Sonny] Burke understood Sinatra's reluctance to

---

6. The booklet claims that Costa conducted all but two tracks on *The Present,* but knowing the arranger's indifference to conducting, it seems more likely that Falcone led most of the sessions.

record only old songs. That would be as limiting as doing only new ones." Although it might have made sense at the time, fifteen years later that phrase can be read as "Sinatra's insistence on doing only good songs was as limiting as the idea that he should record only crap." Unfortunately, the good new songs of the period—and Sinatra could have filled an album with just Cy Coleman's best efforts of the '80s and '90s—are even less commercial than the good old ones. As Tony Bennett's valiant efforts to make a hit out of Charles DeForrest's "When Will the Bells Ring for Me" prove, well-written songs of the current era are doomed never to find a market or even a niche beyond the connoisseurs and theater crowd.

If *The Present* works better than the rest of Sinatra's forays into popsville, it's only because greater care was taken with it. Where *Some Nice Things* seems to have been ground out, many of *The Present* arrangements, like those for "Summer Me, Winter Me" and "New York, New York," had been in the book long before the sessions. It's also the only time that Sinatra seems to be working with the contemporary rhythmic feeling rather than fighting it. Normally, he used Cottler and bassist Gene Cherico, who were perfect on swing material but no more used to the '70s sound than the Old Man was; for *The Present*, Costa insisted on employing a more flexible bassist and drummer in George Duvivier and Jimmie Young. While the late, great bull-fiddler would have been aghast to learn he got the gig because of his capacity for rock rhythms, the flexible Duvivier (who also played—and hated—electric bass) could handle anything.

"Just the Way You Are" (forever associated with Dolores Hope) and "Song Sung Blue" rate as the set's least successful pieces.[7] Falcone has recalled that Costa originally intended to record the first piece in the same slow fashion that author Billy Joel had used until Falcone demonstrated to Sinatra how it might work in a swing tempo. Sinatra instructed Costa to revamp it into a Basie-like dance pattern. "Don was already fifty percent into the chart," said Falcone, "and he got a little angry with me because I caused him to have to redo the whole thing." They might as well have left it the way it was. Although they make the melody move lyrically, it was born a stupid song, and in lines such as "I don't want clever conversation," it remains a veritable ode to imbecility. Likewise, Costa and Sinatra take the hokey-pokey "Song Sung Blue" and give it

---

7. Sid Cooper disagrees. "I thought 'Just the Way You Are' was a wonderful arrangement, although nobody ever made much of it. I liked the way the saxophones were written there. It was one of the few times that we could swing a little bit."

something of a beat, and a touch of dramatic push. And then what have they got? A piece of junk with a beat and a little dramatic push.

"I couldn't stand 'Song Sung Blue' at the time, and I still hate it!" said Falcone. "The only thing that made it worthwhile was Don's chart. But you just couldn't do much with that song." In fact, "Isn't She Lovely?," a 1976 Stevie Wonder song that Sinatra recorded for *The Present* but never released, comes off as a substantially more convincing swing number, using electric keyboard and a Basie-like *whomp!* at the end. Wonder's lyrics (except for several trivializing and out-of-place references to the deity) fit into the tempo nicely, and the piece has the same feeling as any of those marvelously ephemeral rhythm singles that Sinatra cut for Capitol.

Of the ballads, "For the Good Times" ranks as a noble but unsuccessful effort. With its clever use of soprano Eileen Farrell as a counterpoint voice, what we have here is a legendary popular singer and a great opera singer wasting their time on hillbilly horror. When they invest the musicianship to sing a genuine harmony line on the phrase "lay your warm and tender body next to mine," it's as embarrassing as watching your parents making love—and for five full minutes at that. Live concert versions from this period (which do not feature Farrell) are inevitably much better.

The song's author, Kris Kristofferson, had already written a tune based on a line from Sinatra's 1962 *Playboy* magazine interview (allegedly a piece of expository writing by Reprise ad-copy writer Mike Shore), namely, his 1970 hit "Help Me Make It Through the Night." "That's What God Looks Like" seems similarly inspired by that "interview" in which a strangely atheistic Sinatra (meaning Shore) refers to intermediaries between man and God, such as priests, rabbis, and CPAs, as "witch doctors." Written by two unknowns who, according to legend, walked in off the street and anonymously submitted it to Sinatra's office, the text is so ludicrous one would swear, as far as halfway through it, that it's a joke—that any second, Spike Jones is going to burst in, shooting off popguns and emitting rude noises. (Much earlier, Reprise artist Tiny Tim had come up with a similar but more entertaining musical dialogue between father and son on the subject of God, entitled "[Daddy] What Is Heaven Like?") When someone once described the content of "That's What God Looks Like" to Billy May, his reaction was a simple "Oh, shit!"

But it gets better. The opener, "You and Me," isn't much of a song, but it does have a story and mood that Sinatra can sink his teeth into, while "Love Me Tender" finds Francis having fake folkie fun. To be sure, Costa's chart isn't up to the uptempo medley arrangement that Riddle wrote for a 1960 Sinatra TV show. Sung in a once-in-a-lifetime meeting with Elvis (on which Presley mangled one of Sinatra's hits, "Witchcraft," in unintentional self-parody), that treatment could have been titled "Love Me Tender Trap." But Costa keeps it simple, with a gently pulsating beat, backing Sinatra with guitar and choir, and then adding very subtle strings.

"MacArthur Park" merits attention as an offbeat experiment, one that doesn't work but was nonetheless worth trying. This ambitious art-rock aria, written by Jimmy Webb for nonsinging actor (and refugee from *Camelot*) Richard Harris, had been a most unlikely hit single back in 1968. Following the example set by Tony Bennett in his 1969 version, Sinatra elects to tackle only a brief excerpt from this seven-minute pop epic. Like a psychedelic answer to "Lush Life," the complete text depicts a reflection on a long-ended love affair. Where Strayhorn's lovers jet off to Paris for jazz and cocktails, Webb's boy and girl enjoy their romantic rendezvous in a rather seedy Los Angeles public park, where they dine on cake made soggy by liquid precipitation. Sinatra eliminates those very lengthy passages of the elegy that explain the narrative, instead finding autobiographical relevance in lines such as "I will win the worship in their eyes / And I will lose it." Like "There Used to Be a Ball Park" on *Ol' Blue Eyes*, "MacArthur Park" represents the only time on *The Present* where Sinatra actually takes the high road—which admittedly leads him nowhere. One perversely wishes that he had tried to bite off the entire work—goofy and pretentious as it is, he might have been able to make something out of it.

The two unqualified triumphs of *The Present* are obvious: "Summer Me, Winter Me" and Nelson Riddle's orchestration of "Something" (the sole non-Costa work on *The Present*). Both pieces use a very classical string orchestra (bereft of brass, reeds, or anything resembling a jazz big band), "Summer Me" being the only post-1961 Costa-Sinatra item to harken back to the glory days of *Sinatra and Strings*. He doesn't exactly make "Something" out of nothing, but he greatly embellishes two unspectacular melodies with his characteristic rising and surging through mountains and valleys of emotional crescendos and decrescendos, flowing in and out of tempo, sometimes only for a few bars at a time, before drifting to a whole new melodic current.

On "Something," Sinatra goes into an incredibly dramatic diminuendo, emerging from the bridge in a tiny, trembling voice. On "Summer Me" he expresses profound thoughts in a deliberately repetitious nursery rhyme of a lyric that becomes one of the most powerful love songs he has ever sung. "Something" would be the last great Sinatra-Riddle collaboration (considering that the "Gal That Got Away" medley was merely stitched together from older charts), and "Summer Me, Winter Me" indicates to posterity that Costa could compete with such stylistic masters as Riddle and Jenkins when provided with the appropriate opportunity.

"'Summer Me' was an exciting, marvelous arrangement," said lead saxist Sid Cooper. "Costa really entwined himself in that arrangement, and we had played it for a year before we recorded it. Oh, it's fantastic, just fantastic." Falcone explained why this well-received piece was so infrequently performed after the release of the album: "It was magnificent, but to this day nobody really knows how to perform that chart. The orchestral application is just missed. That chart takes two hours of rehearsal and a great deal of explanation before it gets performed the way it's supposed to be. But it is a masterpiece."

By far the most commercially successful number on *The Present*—on all of *Trilogy,* in fact—was not any kind of youth-directed pop-art at all but what amounts to a show tune from a flop film, "New York, New York." Frank Military, who had left Sinatra's employ at the end of the Capitol era, rightfully busts his buttons with pride at having been the first to pull Sinatra's coattails to this piece of material. "I sent him the song, and he said he would listen to it. I kept calling Dorothy [Uhlmann, Sinatra's secretary] to find out what was happening, and she said, 'It's on the turntable. He's getting to it.' It took him a while, but he finally got to it, and now it's probably the most popular thing he's ever done."

Written for Liza Minnelli (who had a minor hit with it) in Martin Scorsese's unfortunate 1977 musical of the same name, "New York, New York" marked the second show-type tune of that title to be associated with Sinatra (the first was from his 1949 film *On the Town*) and is more correctly titled "Theme from *New York, New York.*" In some early concert performances, Sinatra opened with the Bernstein-Comden-Green song to lead into the soon-to-be familiar John Kander–Fred Ebb introductory vamp.

Sinatra began doing the new "New York, New York" in concert in October 1978, around the time Falcone joined him, and initially used it as his opening number. "We were rehearsing up at NBC, and he brought the sheet music up to the piano and said, 'Here, play this for me,'" the pianist recalled. Around that time, Sinatra commissioned Costa to assemble an instrumental "overture" medley of New York songs for the Radio City engagement, which would include "Autumn in New York" and "Sidewalks of New York" and conclude with the now internationally known vamp to "New York, New York." The Chairman would enter the boardroom on top of the riff, the audience would begin applauding, and Sinatra would, to coin a phrase, start spreading the news.

"After that engagement," Falcone continued, "he said to me, 'Man, this thing is getting big. We have to take it out of the overture.' So I wrote a new ending for Don's overture. And then he said, 'We gotta put this further down in the show.' So it went down about halfway into the program because 'My Way' was still the closer. But 'New York' just kept getting bigger. Of course, all during this period, all during that year, he started to grow with the song, and he started to put it into the shape that it eventually took. It didn't start out being as dramatic at the end as it is now, with a much, much slower tempo. That's why he likes to do a song on stage for several months before he records it; he feels that he develops the song. And he doesn't want to record it too early because then he figures he'll change it." Once the record is released, Sinatra usually becomes locked into the rough form of the arrangement. (Of course he may decide a number of years later to start all over again with a completely new treatment.)

Sinatra had originally recorded "New York, New York" in New York, appropriately, in August 1979, along with most of the rest of *The Present*. Between August and September of that year, however, he felt his take on the tune had so improved that he should remake the number, doing it on the same date that he was also tackling part of the Billy May portion of the package. Said Falcone, "The Old Man didn't like the way it came off in New York. He wasn't satisfied with the way he did it. He had kept growing with that song, and by the time we were recording in Hollywood, it had grown that much more. So he said, 'The hell with it. I want to do it over again.' So I conducted it and [veteran West Coast jazzman] Pete Jolly played piano."

By 1980, when *Trilogy* finally came out, "New York, New York" was a bona fide hit—one that now concluded every Sinatra concert. Released as a single, "New York, New York" together with *Trilogy* marked Sinatra's biggest record triumphs in a decade, and a double whammy at that. He can be counted on to bring down the house with it at every show, particularly those in the New York City area. As sung by Minnelli, it's just your average da-da-da show tune. In the hands—or tonsils, rather—of Sinatra, it exemplifies the anger and the optimism, the ambition and the aggression, the hostility and the energy, the excitement and the excrement that is New York. And that also is Sinatra. By the time he reaches the outchorus, and the modulation that occurs with the second line he sings "those little town blues," the excitement of the crowd is impossible to contain. "New York," as Military suggests, has become more closely identified with Sinatra than any other song, even perhaps more than "My Way." (As late as 1990, in the horror comedy *Gremlins 2,* when the army of furry little killer *mesquites* are about to invade Fun City en masse, their head honcho cheers them on by donning a trench coat and fedora and breaking into "Start spreading the news . . .")

By 1980, Sinatra was on a recording roll again with the success of both the single and the multiple album set. Apart from stepping up TV and concert appearances, he soon began planning another album. For a while there was talk of going back to work on *Here's to the Ladies;* after the success of *Trilogy,* he had briefly considered expanding it into another three-LP box, this one containing thirty-six songs. Falcone recalled that Sinatra occasionally mentioned the *Ladies* project in the early '80s, thinking of a song that should go into it, but it never went any further than that. It certainly didn't help the project any that he and Nelson Riddle were no longer on speaking terms.

But while he should certainly have finished *Ladies* (at least in its single disc incarnation), the project he did concentrate on was precisely the right one for the time. Rather than an epic miniseries of a package covering all time periods and moods, *She Shot Me Down* would focus on what Sinatra did best: an intimate and sad set of what he correctly described as "saloon songs." As we've seen, the desire to make this final set with Gordon Jenkins also grew out of Sinatra's desire to vindicate the aging arranger after the trouncing that "The Future" had received.

While *Shot Me Down* was primarily Jenkins' show, Costa made the next most significant contribution. He received credit as producer, he arranged the opening track (Stephen Sondheim's "Good Thing Going"), composed the song "Monday Morning Quarterback," and assembled the closing medley of "The Gal That Got Away" and "It Never Entered My Mind" from vintage Nelson Riddle charts. Costa wrote the arrangement of the *Merrily We Roll Along* tune on an airplane as the Sinatra entourage returned from Rio (circa January 1980).

The lightest-weight entry on the set, "Good Thing Going," may deceive first-time listeners into thinking they're going to get another elevator-rock session. Compared to the increasingly moody Jenkins scores that follow, it's like opening a wine-tasting event with a bottle of Snapple. Costa's composition, "Monday Morning Quarterback," especially as magnified by a typically morbid string arrangement by Jenkins and a real in-your-gut interpretation by Sinatra, is one of the most gloriously emotional performances in the collection.

Like *The Present, She Shot Me Down* concentrated on new songs, although these would be completely unknown works by practiced hands in Sinatra's circle. As with *The Present*, Sinatra made the decision to tape the bulk of the album in New York, where he hadn't recorded an LP since 1950's *Sing and Dance with Frank Sinatra.* At the time, he let it be known that he was far from happy with the recording studios in Fun City. "There are maybe three decent studios in all of Manhattan that you can work in, and they're not the best," he told interviewer Arlene Francis. "The sound is not good, they're old, and they've been tinkered with and fooled with. The walls have been changed. They've been ruined, actually." Coincidentally, Sinatra happened to film his last movie in New York at around the same time, *The First Deadly Sin* (released in 1980), which costarred Francis' husband, Martin Gabel, and featured a score by Gordon Jenkins. (Sinatra also said that he was going into a partnership with real estate baron Harry Helmsley to build a state-of-the-art studio to his specifications on some "property behind Lincoln Center that's owned by *The New York Times.*")

But the glories of recording with "the New York band" made up for his dissatisfaction with the facilities. "We had been working a lot together at the time," said Sid Cooper. "We had just come back from Africa and also played Rio de Janeiro, Argentina, São Paulo, and then did some things in New York. So the band was very tight. And Frank loved that particular band, he was really very enamored of it. He spent a lot of time with us, did a lot of rehearsing, a lot of conducting, in his own fashion. He made very specific demands in terms of dynamics and things that he enjoyed hearing in back of him. And he was very much a part of the orchestra at that time."

Cooper may be understandably partial toward the New York band, whose sax section he led for seventeen years (1974–91), but his claims are more than supported by Falcone, who conducted for all of Sinatra's bands. "The New York group was by far the best band ever!" Falcone averred. "Los Angeles had great musicians, but those guys never learned how to 'band' together, and that was the problem. Too many egos, too many players who have reputations that certainly are deserved. They never learned that New York attitude of burying one's ego in favor of the finished product. And although you'll hear the bands in L.A. sound wonderful, when you're actually inside a band and hear the intricacies of an orchestra when it's playing together to make everything work, there's just no comparison between the New York guys and the L.A. guys."

The decision to do *The Present* and *She Shot Me Down* in New York was foremost an economic one. "As I always say," as Sid Cooper always says, "the bottom line, as far as management was concerned, is what it would cost. And that band was ready to go. We could go in and do anything in one take. If we went to California, they would sit down and make six takes, and take three hours to do one number, and we would do six numbers in three hours. It made more sense just to fly Gordon in."

Falcone said, "These guys are close friends of thirty and forty years, and they think nothing of saying to one another, 'Hey, this isn't right,' 'You better do that again,' and 'Watch this over here.' I mean, there's nothing personally connected, no egos. The section leader has the responsibility. And Sid Cooper is, in my view, probably the greatest lead alto player that ever lived. Sid would run the saxes, and all the guys in that section were stellar people, all stars in their own right. Yet when Sid said, 'Do it this way,' they did it that way. If you tried to do that in L.A., they'd just look at you out of the corner of their eye. The New York band was just the rompin' stompin' band of all time." Cooper concluded, "I remember, on a number of performances that were really unusually great, that Frank came up to me and kissed me!"

Though unfortunately Sinatra did not elect to do another live recording, which would have documented this formidable unit in performance, its contributions to the greatness of the two studio albums are inestimable. The concerts themselves had been strengthened by the presence of guitarist Tony Mottola, who joined the rhythm section around 1980. Sinatra and Viola went back to 1932 together when, as seventeen-year-old-hopefuls, they performed together on Jersey City radio station WAAT. They bumped into each other frequently in the studios in the '40s and early '50s, most famously on "S'posin," "We Just Couldn't Say Goodbye," and the immortal "My Cousin Louella." Released as by Frank Sinatra and the Tony Mottola Trio, these 1947 sides represent the best of Sinatra's early attempts to assimilate the style of the King Cole Trio.

In 1980, Mottola, who was then sixty-five, considered himself retired. Though he held on to his home in Denville, New Jersey, he stayed in Florida most of the time and hadn't actually touched a guitar in several years. Then to his surprise he received a call from Joe Malin. The contractor informed Mottola that an old friend of his wanted to work with him again. "Who's that?" asked Mottola. "Frank Sinatra!" said Malin. "You're kidding!" said Mottola. Malin assured him that he wasn't and told him that Al Viola had left the group and that Sinatra wanted him to fill in for a week at Resorts in Atlantic City and then a week at Carnegie Hall. Mottola recalled, "'Well,' he said, 'it's been a long time. Listen, now that I got you here, I want you to do a spot in the show.' I said, 'With you, like we used to do on *Vimms* [Sinatra's 1944 CBS radio series], just the guitar and voice?' 'Yeah,' he said, 'but I want you to do a solo spot, too.'"

When Rudin made Mottola an offer to go on the road with the Sinatra group, Mottola agreed, with the stipulation that he could bring his wife, Mitzi, with them. "It was great when Tony came along," said Falcone, "and, if you'll pardon the observation, in my humble view Tony was *the* quintessential guitar player for Sinatra. Not that Al wasn't, of course; they had two different styles." Viola is unbeatable as a jazz rhythm master, after the fashion of Freddy Green in Count Basie's band, whereas Mottola was celebrated as a virtuoso soloist. Before long, Mottola was enjoying two featured spots in each concert, one a feature for himself (such as "Concierto de Aranjuez," a traditional guitar solo, or "Manha de Carnaval") and the other a duo between himself and Sinatra, such as "September Song" and "As Time Goes By" (which Sinatra also performed as a duet with Teddy—not Dooley—Wilson in a TV tribute to *Casablanca* star Ingrid Bergman), in the tradition of the 1962 Sinatra-Viola "Night and Day."

While they had done several of these pieces on the road, the duo that they would perform on an official studio session was not a previously performed piece but originated as a complete impromptu. Longtime Sinatra buddy Jule Styne had started his career with the hit "Sunday" back in 1926, and now, nearly sixty years later, he returned to the same topic with "It's Sunday," using a lyric by future *Jelly's Last Jam* collaborator Susan Burkenhead. Impressed with the song, Sinatra first commissioned an arrangement from Peter Matz, a Hollywood orchestrator who, though he apparently hadn't worked with Sinatra before or since, had written beautifully for Bennett, Streisand, and many others. "So we ran the arrangement down," said Mottola, "but Frank didn't seem too pleased with it."

The troupe happened to be in Vegas at the time, and since Costa was handy, as always, Sinatra asked him to write a chart for "It's Sunday." "We ran it down again," Mottola said, "and again Frank wasn't happy with it. He said, 'You know, you're missing the whole point. I want this to be a very intimate thing. Let me do it with Tony for a little bit to show you what I mean.' So I played it, and he said, 'That's the kind of intimacy I want.' So Don wrote yet another chart! We were going to do it at the next record date, which was going to be in New York. However, we didn't have a chance to rehearse that one." Sid Cooper described Costa's chart as "a big orchestration. We recorded it with the orchestra, and Frank said, 'Tony, why don't we just dismiss the band and see what happens with the two of us?' And that's the way it came out—just wonderful."

Not quite—Sinatra liked the spontaneous duo treatment but felt he could improve on it still, and he redid it at the next session, this one in Hollywood a month later (February 1983). He and Mottola went to the Warner Bros. recording studio without the rest of the orchestra. "And it turned out beautifully," the guitarist commented. "It's what I call a love song for mature people, not teenagers. I mean, like older people in love, people talking about things: 'It's Sunday morning, I wake her up with a rose, bring her breakfast in bed.' It's a very difficult song to sing. In the first couple of bars there's something like eight words in every measure! It's the first time that he's ever recorded anything with a solo guitar, and it makes me very proud. And it's a beautiful song and a beautiful rendition." It's actually a "Sunday Kind of Love" kind of song, expressed so simply and directly in both the vocal and the accompaniment that it becomes almost monumental in its vivid exaltation of homely virtues.

It shows how much work Sinatra had to put into a song to get it exactly right—and why there are so many unfinished projects from this period. Apart from that gorgeous single, Sinatra released only two tracks between 1981 and 1984: "To Love a Child" and "Here's to the Band." In the same way that the lyrics to "New York, New York" *sell* that city as if in a chamber of commerce ad campaign (Sinatra's treatment of the text is quite another matter), these two pieces take an oddly jingoistic bent. "To Love a Child"—the last officially released Sinatra piece to be either written by Joe Raposo or arranged by Costa, whose daughter, Nikki,[8] sang in the children's choir here—served as a dedication to First Lady Nancy Reagan's Foster Grandparent Program. It could also have been the theme song of the many children's charities chaired by Barbara Sinatra.

One might hope that the title and text of "Here's to the Band" would contain some kind of metaphoric conceit in the same vein as Irving Berlin's "Let's Face the Music and Dance" or Abbey Lincoln's "You Gotta Pay the Band" (not a bad song for Sinatra, now that you mention it). But no. Three otherwise unknown Jerseyites, S. Howe, Alfred Nittoli, and Artie Shroeck, conceived "Band" as a vehicle for Sinatra to pay homage to the members of the American Federation of Musicians. Neither "Child" nor "Band" is a particularly marvelous piece of songwriting, and neither gives Sinatra the opportunity to take it beyond the commercial announcement and tap into something deeper, the way he does on "New York, New York." Neither made any impression at the cash register, either.

But even though Sinatra was, once again, under-recorded, he and his musical entourage had hit yet another peak in the early '80s. The only thing missing in those years was the familiar sound of Bill Miller's soft chords emanating from the keyboard; Sinatra and Rudin would have

8. Apart from Sinatra, Don and Nikki Costa enjoyed a substantial hit when the ten-year-old girl's debut album as a vocalist sold a reported three million copies, primarily in Latin America, where Costa's wife, Terry, and Nikki happened to be touring at the time of his death.

done well to keep both Falcone and Miller on the payroll, with them alternating in the roles of pianist and conductor where appropriate. Miller would play on the saloon songs and classic '50s and '60s arrangements; Falcone was just right for the more contemporary material and items that required more of a modern jazz sensibility.

Surprisingly, such things were beginning to turn up in his repertoire. "When I left Tommy, we went with the full [string] orchestra at all times," Sinatra said in 1980, "and now I'm thinking of going the other way, going with a good jazz band, a Basie-type band and stay with that for a while. And if something soft has to be done, we would use a rhythm section, just a piano, drums, guitar, and bass, and do all the ballads quietly." For a time Sinatra put the emphasis on hard swing by dropping his string section and whittling his accompaniment into what he called "the hot band." As he told Sid Mark, "The people [in the audience] are excited by the sound. I can see their faces from the stage. And I am excited by it. It really pushes you along when you are up there on a stage and the band is blowing away behind you. So I feel that we made the right move."

In the very early '80s, Sinatra showed more interest in out-and-out jazz than he had in twenty years, doing a number of quartet-only uptempos such as "Lover, Come Back to Me," yet another new variation on "Night and Day," and "I Get a Kick Out of You." (This latter piece was done with just the rhythm section, as on the 1981 *Man and His Music* TV special, and with the addition of Al Klink's golden-toned tenor on at least one concert recording.) Where we expect to hear Sinatra with the familiar sound of Miller's playing, which comes out of the era of Teddy Wilson and Earl Hines, here the singer utilized pianistic underpinnings closer to Wynton Kelly or Sonny Clarke. Falcone and Miller would have complemented each other well.

But what really made the *Trilogy/She Shot Me Down* era so special was that, all these years after the comeback, Sinatra himself had reached a new peak. The idea that he was getting older may actually have been a blessing because it made him work all the harder to remain in top condition. "I first met him when he was fifty-nine years old, and by that time he was already starting to suffer some vocal deterioration," said Falcone. "But it didn't matter because he worked so hard at keeping his voice in shape in those days. He got excited about what we were doing and began to do vocal exercises again. We used to spend several hours every day in vocal exercises. I'd meet him every afternoon, and we would spend a couple of hours going over scales and arpeggios, et cetera. And then later, for at least an hour immediately prior to every performance, he would do still more exercises.

"These were the kind of exercises that had been taught to him by classical singers over the years. I even went with him one time when he went to visit Pavarotti. We were doing a concert with him in New York, and we went to his apartment because the Old Man was having a particular problem with something and wanted to discuss it with him. Robert Merrill was another one whom he'd always go to for advice about the use of the voice and so forth. He knew that they didn't know how to do what he did, but he knew that they knew about the voice and how to maintain the equipment." Sinatra went as far as to temporarily quit smoking (except to use a cigarette as a prop in "The Gal That Got Away") during this period. He also refused to drink when he had a show coming, knowing that whiskey was bad for the throat, and even kept tea in his glass on stage. Falcone emphasized, "I mean, he really toed the line."

Falcone's conducting also served to bring up the quality level of the concerts. Sid Cooper, who traveled with Sinatra through four orchestra leaders, described Falcone as the most "serious" of the bunch. "Vincent was probably the one who cared the most about the position he had. He was always trying to make Frank happy. He made himself available all the time. He would leave messages about where he was in case the Old Man wanted him. He really cared for his position." Falcone explained that his philosophy on conducting had been imparted to him by Gordon Jenkins, who taught the young musician to watch Sinatra like a hawk. "Sinatra never got away from me," he said. "He's done this with other conductors over the years. He absolutely demands that you stay with him on every phrase that he makes, every breath, every movement. He wants that orchestra deadlocked to him. It used to get to be a game between him and me, where he would actually try to get away from me, and he couldn't because I had learned how to keep up.

"I think that was one of the things that kept me in his good graces all those years. He knew that he didn't have to worry about changing a phrase here or there, or if his voice wasn't quite up to par on this particular night and he didn't want to hold a note as long as he might have held it the night before. He didn't have to worry about having to let me know about anything like that because he never told you anything. He just went out and did it. Gordon taught me to watch his mouth, to watch his chest when he breathed so I would know when he was going to do what he was going to do. As a tip, it was priceless. Gordon told me many other things, but that's probably the most important thing that he ever laid on me."

The rapport between Sinatra, at the top of his form vocally, and his team was perfect, and the performances were extraordinary. They took chances together: in 1982, Sinatra and Falcone experimented with a ten-minute *Porgy and Bess* medley, using only voice and piano. But it was all too good to last. There was bad feeling between certain members of the group who were jealous when any of the others received any attention, one in particular. Eventually it became unbearable for Falcone, who left at the very end of 1983 after playing for Sinatra as occasional pianist and then conductor for a total of ten years. Falcone was only the first to go as the team gradually broke up; next was Cherico, then lead trumpeter Charlie Turner, then Mottola. "And unfortunately," said Falcone, "when that group disbanded, the replacement musicians were a considerable step down." Finally, in 1989, Irv Cottler died.

That was the other problem: in 1980, all of the people Sinatra counted on to make music with were still active. By 1989, virtually all of them had gone: Sonny Burke, Don Costa, Gordon Jenkins, Nelson Riddle, Irv Cottler, and, within a few years after that, Jimmy Van Heusen, Sammy Cahn, and Jule Styne. It has long been averred that *Trilogy* in effect killed Sonny Burke—it was such an enormous project, biting off three albums at a time when one would have been difficult. (Of course, in 1961, Sinatra and Burke could have done the whole thing in three weeks, tops.) It left the near-seventy veteran completely drained. It was also ironic that Riddle succumbed to cancer just as he was starting work on a new album for Sinatra.

The death of Costa, only fifty-seven, hit Sinatra particularly hard. Those close to the late arranger are too protective of him, even in death, to tell any outsider what killed him, though one gets the impression that had he been blessed with another kind of personality, he might have saved himself. But then, he might not have been what he was. "Don's heart was bad," said Sid Cooper, "and he was a very stressed guy, a very tense guy, and I don't think he took care of himself. He had marital problems [he had children with two different wives], and this and that. He was not a drunk by any means, and he wasn't on drugs, outside of his medicines. He just didn't lead the kind of life you lead if you want to hang around for a while."

By 1981, said Cooper, Costa's health was bad and getting worse. "Don was conducting a number for Frank in Rio, and he really didn't want to do it. At that time he already wasn't feeling that well. And he came to the end of the bandstand and looked over to me and said, 'Would you finish up?' So I stood up, and he walked offstage, and I conducted till the end of the show. In other words, he just wanted to get off there as soon as he could. And he liked [being able to leave] so much that we did it that way on every show."

The last project he and Sinatra worked on was an album the singer produced and conducted for his old friend, cabaret legend Sylvia Sims, taped in April 1982. Costa did the charts but was already too sick to attend the sessions; during the recording, Sinatra would occasionally phone him and hold the receiver up to the proceedings so he could hear how everything was going down. Costa held on for another eight months, and after undergoing multiple bypass surgery, died in January 1983.

Yet the decline of the Sinatra road company was hardly immediate, and they would have many spectacular nights yet. Warner Bros.' Japanese affiliate issued a commercial video (which American Reprise should rightfully issue on CD and laser disc) of Sinatra in Tokyo in 1985 that's even more powerful than *The Main Event* or *Sinatra at the Sands.* (Befitting a visiting dignitary, Sinatra doesn't share his feelings regarding the mating habits of lady gossip columnists in Japanese, but he does sing "Ruck Be a Rady"—I kid you not.)

Sinatra also participated in an inspired series of concerts with his old nemesis-turned-pal, Buddy Rich, climaxing in the deservedly frequently-aired video *Concert for the Americas.* According to Sid Cooper, who, like Sinatra, had worked with the superdrummer in the Tommy Dorsey days, Rich's band was exciting as an opening act, but the reed section couldn't cut Sinatra's charts. "Steve Marcus was a good [saxophone] soloist, but he couldn't play the clarinet to save his ass," said the saxist. "They couldn't play the flutes, and they couldn't play the woodwinds. So they called me out, and I stayed a week with them and taught the guys how to do it." Cooper was miffed, however, that after providing the Rich sax section with such brilliant tutelage, he was not invited to join them on that South American tour.

Joe Parnello, conductor, pianist, and arranger, took over from Falcone around December 1982 or January 1983. His roughly three years with Sinatra are best summed up by Cooper: "Joe Parnello was somebody who was used to other singers, and his writing was good, although it wasn't in the same class [as Sinatra's regular writers, Riddle, Jenkins, Costa, and so forth]. Joe seemed a little frightened most of the time. He didn't seem to have the confidence that was necessary, and you had to have that around Frank. If he sensed that you were insecure, he could lay a number on you! But Joe was good. He worked very hard, and he did a very good job." Parnello, who contributed a red-hot treatment of "Change Partners," left in 1985, dying not long after.

In the meantime, Sinatra had determined that for his next recording project he would go beyond his usual pool of orchestrators—the waters of which were rapidly draining anyhow. In many ways, Quincy Jones must have appeared a logical successor to Costa. He'd had considerable experience in both classic pop (or, in Jones' case, pure jazz) and baby-boomer pop; in addition to writing arrangements, he had a vast track record of hits as a producer and A&R man (earning his initial reputation at Mercury Records). In 1982, Jones had become the most successful music man in the industry with the release of *Thriller*, the LP that made Michael Jackson a superstar.

Dwelling as he has in two worlds, Jones has the unique distinction of being extremely well compensated in the pop world and underappreciated among jazz fans. In jazz, they pay you off with critical kudos that won't buy you a Xerox of a cup of coffee; in pop, what's best is what sells the most, and they pay you off with something called money—lots of it. From Jones' '60s hits with Leslie Gore (such as "It's My Party") to his 1985 superproduction "We Are the World" (which, with the exception of Frank Sinatra, utilized nearly all of the then-current biggest names in pop, almost all of whom had become Trivial Pursuit questions by decade's end), Jones has been incredibly well remunerated for his parade of pop successes. More powerful than even a mogul, Jones is a multimedia baron whose controlling interests extend to film and television projects as well as music.

In the day-for-night world of jazz, however, such achievements tend to be held against you. In Jones' case, his accusers can't make up their minds whether he was a major talent who sold out or a no-talent who sold out (in both scenarios he is often compared to Mitch Miller). Jones himself deprecates his work as an arranger, and as Rosemary Clooney has observed, with no disrespect intended, "It's impossible to pick out a Quincy Jones arrangement," because he never had a signature sound as identifiable as Riddle or May (another trait Jones shares with the late Don Costa).

"He doesn't [give himself a lot of credit as a writer], but he was really great," Frank Foster said. "When people compare me to him, they say, 'Hey, man, you got a whole lot more on the ball than Quincy,' and I say, 'Well, I don't really think so.' Quincy was really a wonderful arranger. He just put it all aside to do something else, to come into the contemporary era. He took it somewhere else. When he wrote for the Basie orchestra, you couldn't exactly tell [which charts] were Quincy's; all you could tell was that they were very good. With his own band he seemed to have more of an individual trademark. When people hear things like 'The Midnight Sun Will Never Set,' 'Nasty Magus,' 'Rat Race,' and 'I Needs to Be Be'd With,' they say, 'Man, those are dynamite charts. Who did them?'"

"Quincy was an excellent arranger, but he doesn't write anymore," adds Billy Byers. "He found a better and easier way to go. Quincy is highly motivated and finds it tough to sit down long enough to write a whole chart. You've got to be a recluse like Nelson was, to do orchestrations. Quincy would much rather be up front with the clients, doing what I call his 'floor show.'"

Jones seems to have reattracted Sinatra's attention through his work with another showbiz legend whom Sinatra had long admired, Lena Horne. Jones had produced the hit album of her 1981 one-woman Broadway show, with its Sinatra-inspired title, *The Lady and Her Music,* and the success of the disc cemented the success of that Horne "comeback." The earliest project that Sinatra discussed with Jones (since the 1964 *It Might As Well Be Swing*) was to team up with Horne. Long a supporter of the lady in both her music and her liberal politics, Sinatra had employed both Horne and Eleanor Roosevelt in his 1960 television special *Here's to the Ladies,* a bold gesture even at the dawn of Camelot.

Like the aborted album that shared the same title of *Here's to the Ladies,* the Lena Horne project at one point expanded into a three-disc set in the wake of *Trilogy.* In a 1983 interview with Washington, D.C., deejay Ed Walker, Sinatra reported, "We were ready to do the album about two months ago, and she had a vocal problem, a nodule that grew on a vocal chord or something, and she had to get off the road with her show. Consequently, we didn't do the album with Quincy Jones. That's quite an undertaking, by the way, with thirty-eight songs involved in it. He thinks he's gonna do it in two weeks. I say if we do it in four months we're lucky!"

If Jones and Sinatra had been able to stick to a small-scale scenario—a one-disc set of duos—they might have been able to pull it off. As it was, they kept expanding the project until it was set to become another Quincy Jones superspectacular. "We were planning on a really big extravaganza there," said the producer. "It was going to be an incredible mixture of jazz musicians and duets. We had Lionel Ritchie involved and Michael Jackson, Cynthia Weil and Barry Manilow, and lots of people." In addition to the duets, the set was supposed to include a number of solo selections, on which Sinatra would sing numbers associated with Horne (of which, truth to tell, there aren't many after "Stormy Weather") and vice versa, climaxing in a gala medley. While most Sinatra and Horne fans could live without Jackson and Ritchie, one still feels Jones is entirely justified when he said, "If we had been able to pull it all together, it would have been a great album."

Unfortunately, the Sinatra-Horne package never made it to the studio (even to lay down tracks), becoming another Sinatra project to have been kiboshed by overplanning. The next album that Sinatra and Jones worked on, *L.A. Is My Lady,* reached fruition for the same reason in reverse—they came up with an idea, struck while the iron was hot, and crafted a perfectly respectable release without a lot of bother or superfluous production. This album began with a song, "L.A. Is My Lady," credited to Jones and his wife, the former Peggy Lipton (who, as an actress, had costarred on TV's *Mod Squad*). Jones had written the piece for a civic celebration in Los Angeles, which involved the city's mayor, Tom Bradley. Although the Bergmans received credit for the text, Jones said that the song wasn't written specifically for Sinatra or indeed anybody to sing on a specific record. "They might have written a different song if they had known that at the time," he said.

Jones doesn't recall passing the song on to Sinatra himself, only that the singer had heard it and called him suggesting that they use it as the title track for an album. "His mind was focused on the project, and he wanted to do it right then, you know?" said Jones. The two then set out to select the repertoire, Sinatra picking "How Do You Keep the Music Playing," among others, and Jones' suggestions, including "Mack the Knife." As producer and conductor, Jones assumed responsibility for "casting" four arrangers on various tracks, including two fellow Basieites, Frank Foster and Sam Nestico, plus Torrie Zito (who had scored a single for Sinatra some twenty years earlier and then worked more extensively with Tony Bennett), and Sinatra's current musical director, Joe Parnello. (Jones also arranged for the set to be released on his Warner Bros. subsidiary, Q-West Records, rather than Reprise, which was Sinatra's.)

In its roughest form, *L.A. Is My Lady* suggests the same outline as *Strangers in the Night:* Sinatra and Jones start with a new potential hit, rendered in the contemporary style. They use this to lead off an album of standards that Sinatra had not previously recorded, rendering the whole package in swinging dance tempos. Even the ballads have a beat. Whereas Tony Bennett treats "How Do You Keep the Music Playing" as a dramatic show-stopper (in crawl tempo with a roof-rattling closer), Sinatra keeps his danceable. The only thing wrong with this plan is that the title track failed to materialize as the hit that Sinatra and Jones hoped for. They were clearly looking for a lotusland follow-up to "New York, New York," but the obvious geographic "hook" tended to work against the song rather than for it. Then, too, the disco-y nature of the melody and the arrangement, while considerably better than the Beck treatment of "Night and Day," is the kind of thing that might have hit for Sinatra and Jones in the '70s but seemed a beat behind the times in the mid-1980s.

As a piece of music that was neither especially good (nor, it must be admitted, particularly bad) nor a pop hit, the title track unfortunately served to drag down the entire set in the minds of most listeners. A decade after it was recorded in 1984—particularly in the wake of *Duets*—the rest of *L.A.* seems like an undiscovered minor classic. (Although available in Japan, *L.A.* is the only Sinatra concept album not to be issued on domestic CD.) It doesn't have the depth of any of the uptempo sets written by Riddle or May, particularly *Strangers in the Night*, but it's bright and brassy and a ball to listen to.

Although Jones corralled a quartet of ace arrangers, the biggest star recruited to operate behind the scenes, after Jones himself, was Phil Ramone. He had long since established himself as a hit-making producer on the same level as Jones or Jimmy Bowen, but he had begun his career as a recording engineer and had, in fact, served in that capacity on the New York session for Sinatra's 1967 *The World We Knew*. To work with Sinatra again, Ramone volunteered to be temporarily demoted from calling the shots to twisting the dials. "Quincy and I have been close friends for a long time," said Ramone, "and he called me and said, 'Would you like to be involved in [this album]? You know how to make a band holler on tape.' I said, 'If you want me to fix microphones, that's where I'll be. I don't care, I just want to be there.'"

Jones assembled an all-star aggregate of the hottest New York players. Selecting the cream of the city's studio giants, he leaned toward veterans of the bands of Basie, Hampton, Herman, and Goodman. He also enticed a number of players who had formidable careers as recording stars in their own right, such as Randy and Michael Brecker and George Benson (Benson solos on "It's All Right with Me," a Sam Nestico chart on a classic Cole Porter piece that can be viewed as a sequel to "All of You" on *Trilogy: The Past*)—not to mention Lionel Hampton himself. While this provided Sinatra with yet another of his greatest recording bands, at the time Jones failed to note the paradox that "New York, New York" had been recorded in Los Angeles while "L.A. Is My Lady" was taken down in New York.

As we have seen, the idea was to do for Los Angeles what Sinatra had previously done for New York (and in 1964 for Chicago in "My Kind of Town"). The set also includes a further New York follow-up in the bouncy "The Best of Everything," written by Kander and Ebb, and other than the two Bergman pieces ("How Do You Keep the Music Playing?" and the title track), those constitute the only material from what Mel Tormé calls the "RRP" (relatively recent past). Without a new Cahn and Van Heusen track, Sinatra gets around to two vintage Cahn jobs.

On "Teach Me Tonight" (Cahn's sole collaboration with Gene

DePaul), arranger Zito employs Riddlesque flutes, while the second, "Until the Real Thing Comes Along" (by Cahn and his original partner, Saul Chaplin), has the Chairman really zinging it to us via his emphasis on the rhyme on "sigh" and "cry" in the second chorus. Sammy adds extra sauce to both with additional new sets of lyrics that expand the texts in a racy, Sinatra-at-Vegas fashion—the first extending the original's classroom metaphor with a triple rhyme ("graduate," "articulate," and "matriculate") that's a typically ingenious Cahn job. Frank Foster, who had written some additional lyrics as part of his chart to "Mack the Knife," recalled, "I had thought the words that I added to 'Mack' were pretty out there, but Sammy's (on 'Teach Me Tonight') were really 'hellified!' Yeah, they were pretty risqué."

New lyrics also figure on Foster's arrangement of "After You've Gone," on which Benson and Hampton solo. Foster explained that he approached the song "as sort of a departure. It was. There were no other charts in the whole production that were quite like that. I was just trying to put a heavy personal Frank Foster touch on it. I try not to borrow from anybody else. I just went down into my own arsenal of licks and said, 'I'm just going to make this a bad motherfucker!' I liked the challenge of writing the uptempo arrangement. I didn't know how it would be accepted, but I thought, if it goes out strong, they can't turn it down."

Sam Nestico's "If I Should Lose You," with Sinatra giving out with the opening phrase (and the first first line of each A section) in a well-timed orchestral rest, also goes out strong. (This 1935 Leo Robin and Ralph Rainger classic is a song that has certainly made the rounds, having been introduced by mega-stiffs Gladys Swarthout and John Boles in the 1935 horse operetta *Rose of the Rancho,* and finally put on the map nearly fifteen years later by Charlie Parker.)

Nestico also provided two slightly slower pieces, the blues ballad "Stormy Weather" and the shuffle-rhythmed "One Hundred Years from Today" (with a trombone part by Benny Powell), which utilizes an effective ritard in the coda. Sinatra's third commercial cutting of Harold Arlen's "Stormy Weather" can be seen as an obvious holdover from the aborted Lena Horne project. It finds Sinatra in a searingly slow tempo, the scratchiness of his sixty-eight-year-old chops not only very much in evidence but contributing to the intensity of the piece. Still, there's more than a hint of a swing feeling to it, with Sinatra not trying to get anywhere near as dark as he does on Arlen's "Blues in the Night" or as deep as he does on his "Come Rain or Come Shine."

"Stormy Weather" was the only track on the disc to be cut in Los Angeles. Initially, it was one of two performances recorded on the first date that had to be rejected. The other was "Body and Soul," the only piece ever arranged for Sinatra by jazz-pop pianist Bob James (best known for his theme from the TV series "Taxi"). "Body and Soul" (which Sinatra hadn't recorded since 1947) was successfully taped; Ramone described Sinatra's vocal as "beautiful. He sang his ass off." Upon listening to a playback, however, the producer and engineer realized that the orchestration was a half-step or so higher than it ought to be.

Jones convinced Sinatra to rerecord "Stormy Weather" after he had returned to Los Angeles, but "when he recut it, it was not as great," Ramone said. Sinatra elected not to try again with "Body and Soul," perhaps because the piece, which opens with eight bars of Sinatra accompanied only by arranger James' electric Rhodes keyboard and a tenor solo, probably by George Young, is the slowest and the most overtly ballady in the set.

"Mack the Knife" had long been indirectly associated with Sinatra by way of Bobby Darin. The younger singer had used an overtly Sinatra-styled type of arrangement of "Mack" as the vehicle for his transition from kiddie pop to classic pop. This left Sinatra in a strange relationship with the Weill-Brecht theater piece. He had never gone near it, and yet in a certain sense a lot of people seemed to think they had already heard him sing it. When Jones suggested "Mack the Knife" to Sinatra, he didn't immediately consent. "He said," Jones recalled, "'Louis [Armstrong] and all of them did it so well, what the hell can we do with it?'" Further, unlike "It Had to Be You" or "After You've Gone," "Mack" is a very specific theater piece, being Kurt Weill's dramatic/musical introduction to *Die Dreigroschenoper,* which details the bloodthirsty deeds of the gangster Macheath. Originally written in a medium-slow drone, the piece assumed a new life when Louis Armstrong made it into a Dixieland hit. Dick Hyman refashioned it as an instrumental pop hit, and then Bobby Darin did a hugely successful *Swingin' Lovers*–style treatment. However, Jones contends that he said, "'I still think you can do a version that would be distinctively yours.' So Frank Foster wrote [that] into the lyrics, to acknowledge that all these other great singers had done such a great job with it and now he was trying 'Mack.'"

Upon assigning Foster to do "Mack the Knife," the producer gave the arranger only three words of instruction: "Make it funky." Foster complied. Whereas the 1959 Darin version, arranged by Richard Wess, incorporated a Louis Jordan–style shuffle underpinning, the Sinatra-Foster version is pure swing à la Basie. "I made it as funky as possible," stresses Foster. "I stole some licks from Lionel Hampton's 'Flying Home,' and I just put a whole potpourri of stuff in there [as countermelodies]. When the band played it, it was swinging so hard and so was Frank, and when he got to the end of it, he was so delighted with it, he threw the whole arrangement up in the air!"

Director Billy Wilder once said that Frank Sinatra, "is beyond talent. It's some sort of magnetism that goes in higher revolutions than that of anybody else in the whole of show business. There's a certain electricity permeating the air. It's like Mack the Knife was in town and the action is starting." (When this statement was repeated to Sinatra, the singer's characteristic response was, "I think that Wilder's a drunk for saying such things.") Louis Armstrong once said that he related to the song because it reminded him of some of the more sharkish types he observed from as far away as possible in the wide-open New Orleans of his childhood. Sinatra, who had known his share of wise guys with no necks and broken noses, could also relate.

Foster's supplementary libretto (heard at the end) reflects on Armstrong, Darin, and Ella Fitzgerald, who had a concert version from 1959 that was nearly as famous as theirs; it was recorded live in Berlin, the very city where Mr. Mack first knifed. Forgetting the lyrics halfway through, Fitzgerald spontaneously improvised a set of words that reflected on the nature of the song itself, including her own commentary on its previous interpreters. Sinatra's version not only discusses all three earlier singers but goes on to drop the names of the "bad cats" in the band backing him up. (Foster justifiably included his own name in the list, although he preceded it with trumpeter Joe Newman, so less-informed listeners might think Sinatra is referring to a single "cat" named "Newman Foster.") Since Sinatra has always been careful to give credit to his accompanists, the song provided a perfect vehicle for him in concert to introduce Bill Miller, Irv Cottler, Frank Sinatra, Jr., and the other members of his regular company.

"Mack" went over so well in concert that Sinatra kept singing it until, after two and a half years, he felt he was doing it much better than in the original 1984 session and decided to remake it. He laid down a new vocal part on top of the original orchestral track (complete with Major Holley's bass-bowing and harmonic-humming, à la Slam Stewart, in the introduction) in 1986. Since the album had already come and gone, it's hard to speculate exactly why. Perhaps he knew that the compact disc was going to be a big deal, and maybe he thought he could use this "upgrade" to make the CD a superior release. (This one track made it to *The Reprise Collection* four years later.) Whatever the case, it's a stunning improvement. By now Sinatra has come up with that especially winning patter ending in which he informs his audience, "You better lock your door/And call the law" in anticipation of the dreaded yet revered Captain Macheath.

While neither the single nor the album *L.A. Is My Lady* qualifies as a hit, "Mack the Knife" became an instant classic in Sinatra's terms. It has outlived the rest of the set by far, particularly the title track, and it never fails to, in Sinatrian terms, knock the crowd on its collective ass. It is the last in the series of rock-era show-stoppers that he has paraded since "Strangers in the Night" and "That's Life" in the late '60s. Not counting *Duets,* the '86 retrack is the final Sinatra performance to be widely released commercially. More important, it is also the last new piece of material added by Sinatra to his regular repertoire (as of 1995, at least).

Had *L.A.* been a big hit, one can readily imagine Sinatra and Jones returning to the studio for a succession of albums. As it was, the set was their last project together. As Jones said, "He has my number, and I'll be there anytime he wants me." With Costa gone and Jones involved with other artists, Sinatra seems to have felt he had no one to work with. Charles Calello, who had last worked with Sinatra in 1978, recalled running into the singer around the time of the Jones album. "I tried many times to get Frank interested in making more records, but he said to me, 'You know, I really don't sing so good anymore. I don't feel my voice can handle being with the strings. [This was perhaps one reason they weren't used on *L.A.*] I really don't want to make records.'"

From 1984 to 1993, Sinatra participated in only three known sessions, two items of which have been heard: the 1986 redo of the vocal track on "Mack the Knife" and a semiprivately released version of "Silent Night" from 1991. He had arrangements and orchestral tracks made on several new tunes, including Lieber and Stoller's "The Girls I Never Kissed," Jule Styne's "One to a Customer" (in a swinging Billy May chart), and four standards, primarily arranged by May. One run-through take of "Cry Me a River," which somehow leaked out, reveals that Sinatra was doing exactly what he should have been: jazzy and bluesy treatments of standards. May's chart of this 1953 Julie London hit swings considerably harder than the bulk of *L.A. Is My Lady.* Like "Mack," it would have been a perfect song for Sinatra to add to his book at this point in his career. In 1988, Sinatra taped "Leave It All to Me," a Paul Anka piece (and Torrie Zito arrangement) with the feeling of a Jerry Herman pseudo-French show tune. A surreal, almost hallucinatory experience, with both melody and lyrics spinning off a carnival barker's shpiel, it amounted to a great single that should have been released.

In 1985, Joe Parnello left the entourage and Falcone returned, staying for only a year. "It didn't work out too well with Joe," said Falcone (who added that there were no hard feelings; he and Parnello remained friendly up to the latter's death). "And they asked me to come back. But when I did, there were so many things that needed to be fixed. Also, I knew when I went back that I could never put my future completely in the hands of one client."

It seemed as if Sinatra was reinstating his accompanists in reverse order: from Miller to Falcone to Parnello to Falcone back to Miller. At the age of seventy-one, Bill Miller went into his own unretirement and back on the road with Sinatra. From 1986 to 1988, he conducted, while a number of capable hands sat in the keyboard chair. Among them were Bernie Leighton, one of the most recorded pianists of all time (a New York studio man, he seems to have done at least ten sessions a week in the '50s and '60s), and Mike Renzi, an exceptionally gifted virtuoso whose prodigious technique sometimes leads him to a deliberately over-busy approach.

On several occasions, such as an April 1987 engagement in Las Vegas, Sinatra's people even enticed the legendary Lou Levy to take to the road. Perhaps the most revered accompanist of all time—a claim challengeable only by Hank Jones and Tommy Flanagan—Levy had worked with Lee and Ella Fitzgerald on many of their most important albums (as well as Sinatra's "My Way").

In 1988, Frank Sinatra, Jr., then forty-four, began conducting for his father. Some twenty-six years previously, the younger Sinatra had decided he wanted to follow in his father's footsteps as a jazz-pop singer. He was certainly as talented as many singers who made it, and less derivative of Sinatra Senior than many (although, unlike Gary Crosby, he never went out of his way to avoid sounding like his famous father). Unfortunately, Sinatra Jr.'s career was almost totally sabotaged by the youth revolution of the '60s as well as by the adverse attention unfortunately generated by his 1963 kidnapping.[9]

(Sadly, the defense's totally fictitious countercharge that the Sinatra family had staged the crime to stir up publicity for the fledgling singer's career had a devastating effect on his professional life. In 1964, Sinatra Jr. told the *Los Angeles Times* that he feared the kidnapping had nurtured "a seed of doubt about my integrity that will stay with me for the rest of my life.")

"I've never been much of a success," Sinatra Jr. once told the *National*

---

9. Unlike his sister, in her late '60s success as a rock-country hit maker, Sinatra Jr. elected to remain in the classic pop idiom; he was actually younger than most of the rock stars of the era.

Enquirer, "but I'm still in the running." At the time he began conducting for his father, one of his managers, Andrea Kauffman, told one paper, "I see him as an opening act. He'll never say, 'I wanna be a superstar.' He opened for George Burns at Caesar's. I see him opening for Buddy Hackett, Alan King."

Unlike Senior, however, Junior was a formally trained musician who, apart from his singing career, can play the piano and read printed music on a professional level. "He is a fine pianist and has a sense of composition," Sinatra Sr. said in 1977. "I would like to see him achieve status as a composer, for movies or TV more than anything else, rather than [singing]." Sinatra Jr. eventually assembled his own jazz orchestra, which worked primarily in the lounge showrooms of Las Vegas. He established his new identity as his father's conductor over the course of two tours that received a lot of attention even by Sinatra standards: the "Ultimate Event" tour, which costarred Sammy Davis, Jr., and Dean Martin (quickly replaced by Liza Minnelli) of 1988–89 (Cottler's final tour), and the "Golden Jubilee" tour of 1990–91, celebrating the Old Man's seventy-fifth birthday.

Gradually, Sinatra Jr. began replacing the men who left the classic New York band of the early '80s with musicians who had served in his Vegas band. "I hesitate to bad-mouth anybody, so the only thing I can say is when [Junior] first came with the band," said Sid Cooper, "he didn't know his ass from his elbow. We carried him for a couple of years until he learned. And then, once he learned how to do what he had to, he started bringing in the Vegas guys that played with his band out there." In defense of Sinatra Jr., one feels obliged to add that the New York band, apart from Cooper, had already deteriorated since the *Trilogy-Shot Me Down* years and that, as conductor, he certainly had the right to work with the musicians he wanted, as long as his dad didn't mind.

The most radical personnel change resulted from a higher authority than either Sinatra. While at the home of his daughter in 1989, drummer Irv Cottler, then seventy-one, died of cardiac arrest. The choice to replace him was obvious. "I think Sol Gubin is the best drummer that Sinatra could possibly have had," opined Falcone. "In my view Sol should have been with him all those years. To me, there's just no comparison. He was the best drummer that ever played for Sinatra, the quintessential Sinatra drummer." Although younger than Cottler, Gubin was also a veteran of the swing era, having played with such bandleaders as Charlie Barnet, Sonny Dunham, Elliott Lawrence, Hal McIntyre, Stan Kenton, and Count Basie. He worked for Sinatra on East Coast dates throughout the late '50s and the '60s. Gubin recalled that the Sinatras were so anxious to have him get started that Junior presented the drum parts to him at Cottler's funeral.

That rosy glow of enthusiasm quickly faded, however. Sinatra Jr. and Gubin seem to have hated each other from the first day. They tolerated each other for sixteen months, which might be described as Sinatra's last stand—regarded by some as the final opportunity the Old Man had to work with a drummer who gave him exactly what he needed. "I loved Sol," said Cooper, speaking for the band. "He played the book the first time in Atlantic City as if he had been playing it all his life."

By all accounts, some of the concerts from the period were truly sainted. For instance, although Sinatra had been relying on tele-prompters for the lyrics for many years, Gubin recalled a show they gave in Sweden that was performed "entirely without the monitors. We worked in an outdoor arena, and he jumped off the stage and went down on the track and mingled with the people. And then he got an ovation [that even for him] was incredible. In fact, he cried after the show. He cried on the plane coming back to the States. He just couldn't get over the ovation and how these people loved him. To me, every time I worked with him, I just enjoyed the hell out of it."

After nearly a year and a half, according to Gubin, Sinatra Jr. waited for him to ask for a raise and when he did, used that opportunity to fire him. Gubin sued for breach of contract, and though he eventually won a financial settlement, he didn't get the prize he wanted, which was to keep playing for Ol' Blue Eyes. "The power had to be in Junior's hand, not the new drummer," said one member of the band. "If he beat it off the wrong tempo, Sol would play the right tempo." Both Bill Miller and Falcone took exception to the breakup. Miller, while admitting that Junior acted like a "cement head," felt that Gubin's "big mouth did him out of the job. And he's a good player, you know, but a constant complainer." (Anyone would seem like a *kvetch* compared to Miller's zenlike tranquility.)

Falcone felt that Gubin was no more or less difficult than most creative people and that the drummer was worth special handling. "Sol has a temperament like every musician has a temperament. The challenge for the leader is to learn how to take these temperaments and meld them together into a team that works out. You don't have to eat dinner with him, you don't have to sleep with him, you've got to play with the guy. When he gets on the stand, if he kicks the hell out of the band, that's all you've got to care about as the leader. You don't care whether the guy parts his hair on the left side, you don't care whether the guy's a pain in the ass. You care how he plays the show! That's what the primary consideration is. You get your problems solved off the bandstand, and you take care of business. The guy who plays the show the best, that's the guy who sits in my drum chair. And to me, to not have Sol Gubin playing for the Old Man these days is a travesty!"[10]

After Gubin left, the Sinatras went through drummer after drummer; their current percussionist, Gregg Field, who plays on the *Duets* albums, has lasted the longest. At one point, Alvin Stoller replaced Cottler, who, ironically, had been the one who took his place to begin with. Stoller, who hadn't played with Sinatra since the '60s, also had his difficulties with the younger Sinatra ("He talks like a colonel in the Marine Corps!" said Stoller). The real problem, though, was that the veteran percussionist was simply too old and too sick to play. "I told Junior, 'Let's try Alvin,'" Bill Miller recalled. "[In his prime] Alvin could have done it, but he wasn't well. Alvin was just *old* up there. It might have worked out, but the timing was bad. So he was out." Not long after, "I had to stop," Stoller reported in July 1992. "Doctor's orders are that I can't play. I have to sit back and get well, so that's what I'm doing. I don't even listen to anything." Stoller died early in 1993.

If finding a suitable drummer has been Sinatra Jr.'s greatest problem, by many accounts his greatest ambition as musical director was to make a new record with his father. "All the years that I've known [Junior]," said Sol Gubin, "he's been talking about trying to get the Old Man into the studios again." In August 1991, Senior and Junior recorded "Silent Night" together in a rather bare-bones arrangement for voice and piano (on the same date Sinatra recorded other takes using Bill Miller, but Junior plays on the final version). This painful although certainly moving performance suggests that the deterioration of Sinatra's voice was even worse than his concerts of the period revealed. So far the track has been released only on a special charity fund-raising disc, one that has gotten into few hands even among Sinatra fans. Around 1991 or 1992, Sinatra expressed interest in doing a new album of rhythmic treatments of ballads, including some numbers he had never sung in that style before, as well as some songs new to his repertoire. The project got only as far as Bill Miller putting together a list of suggested tunes.

By the spring of 1993 it seemed as if Sinatra's career was trapped in reissue land; he hadn't even made a new album since the introduction of the compact disc. While fans waited for new product, nearly everything he had ever sung in a studio saw the light of day on a digital disc. (And a great deal more besides, including acres of unauthorized concert and

10. It should be pointed out that in the course of an interview that lasted over three hours, this was the only time Falcone was even remotely critical of Sinatra Jr.

broadcast material, much of which is just as essential to any understanding of the Sinatra universe as the officially sanctioned product.) It was at this point, after a few particularly weak shows at the Westbury Music Fair in Long Island, New York, that the latest and probably last Sinatra controversy appeared. A writer for the local paper, *Newsday*, started what might be called a "press-roots" movement promoting the idea that Sinatra should stop performing.

Thus, for a few months, the only time Sinatra made it to the media was as part of a mandatory-retirement—or, in this case, re-retirement—debate. The tone of the papers changed in the summer and fall of 1993 with the announcement and then the release of *Duets*. Star-to-star duos had long been a staple of the pop-singing industry, from Johnny Mercer and Margaret Whiting to Mickey and Sylvia. Recent years have seen such megahits as "You Don't Bring Me Flowers" (1978) by Barbra Streisand and Neil Diamond and "To All the Girls I've Loved Before" (1985) by Willie Nelson and Julio Iglasias—and note that all four of these stars were recruited for the Sinatra project. Sinatra himself had recorded duets occasionally (both Columbia and Reprise could easily assemble their own *Sinatra Duets* CDs from their vaults), although not as frequently as Bing Crosby. The electronically crafted combining of two voices not present in the same room at the same time also has a considerable history; Doris Day and Buddy Clark's 1948 hit "My Darling, My Darling" was assembled at three different sessions, one for each singer and a third for the band.

The '90s kind of electro-duet has a slant that's not so much technological as economical. The idea is to capture two audiences at once by electronically suturing the biggest stars of the past with the biggest names of the present, thereby doubling potential sales. The trend was launched in a spectacular fashion with 1991's sensation, *Unforgettable*, in which Natalie Cole dueted electronically with her long-deceased father, Nat King Cole. Sinatra himself had indirectly participated in such a project in 1992 when Cyndi Lauper dubbed her voice over Sinatra's 1947 Columbia record of "Santa Claus Is Coming to Town."

Duets apparently originated as an idea for the Sinatra organization to pick up a piece of the *Unforgettable* action. Phil Ramone, who produced the album, doesn't take credit for the concept; he says it was one of the ideas raised when he first started talking with the "Sinatra people," including general manager Eliot Weisman, Charles Koppelman, and Don Rubin in 1991.[11] Although Ramone had worked on two earlier Sina-

11. The Sinatra "team" also includes business manager Sonny Golden and public relations person Susan Reynolds.

tra albums (*The World We Knew* and *L.A. Is My Lady*), he was better known as a top-flight producer, often referred to as "The Prince of Pop." (Ramone shares one compliment, of sorts, with Sinatra: both have had new-wave rock bands named after them.)

Originally, Ramone had an entirely different idea in mind. "I went to Frank and said to him, 'I know it's impossible, but conceptually what I'd love to do is a *Wee Small Hours* kind of album with just a rhythm section and maybe a string quartet and a couple of great soloists.' I had all these grandiose ideas of doing Sinatra easily. [Frank] said, 'I don't know, I don't think so.' And then about three months later we talked again, and the concept of other artists singing with him came to the table, and I said, 'Jesus, I want to be there. I want to make sure we make this album because I feel that if I can convince him that he will be in and out of that studio, we'll do it.' It took another six months of dialogue back and forth."

After several months of discussions, primarily with Weisman, Ramone had another opportunity to talk it over with the Old Man himself. "I went down to Palm Beach, Florida, where he was playing," Ramone said. "And I really faced him head-on and talked it through. And although he was quite enthusiastic at that point, he kept checking it over as to why anybody would want to sing these songs, why they would want to sing with him, and how he would match these modern-day artists." While many assumed the project would go to Warner Bros.–Reprise, the Sinatra office surprised the industry by deciding to go with Capitol Records, thereby rebuilding a bridge Sinatra had incinerated thirty years earlier. Capitol actively "pursued" the project, Ramone reported, promising not only loot for production but considerable promotion— which they more than delivered.

The "concept" for *Duets,* as it developed, might more accurately be described as a set of ground rules. First, as the title implies, Sinatra would sing with other artists. Second, they would be stars of comparable drawing power—which automatically eliminated virtually every other performer in Sinatra's field. Third, the material would basically consist of very familiar Sinatra standards and hits. Fourth, because of the logistics of getting the Old Man into the studio, Sinatra would lay down his vocal tracks (in some cases on top of orchestral parts that had already been put down), and the other singers would overdub their parts of these electronically created "duets" at convenient intervals. Pat Williams, a veteran TV incidental-music writer whose credits include *The Mary Tyler Moore Show* (and who had also arranged such terrific pop LPs as *Steve and Eydie Together on Broadway*), served as musical director, conducting and occasionally revising familiar Sinatra charts.

After one aborted attempt in early 1993 (Ramone described the first date as a "total disaster"), the producer and the singer tried again in July. Recording at night, when Sinatra was used to working, the first two summer sessions were also unsuccessful in that Sinatra was uncomfortable and complained of a sore throat. According to some stories, on at least one occasion he forgot the purpose of the tracks he was creating and wondered aloud why he was rerecording pieces he had so often done before. Why, indeed. Finally, on the third night (July 1), co-producer Hank Cattaneo got the idea to set the studio up like a concert stage, complete with a wireless, handheld microphone.

That was the night the Ol' Frank magic started to happen. When Sinatra arrived, said Ramone, "he put me through hell for about ten minutes while the orchestra waited, asking why we were doing this again, why we would subject ourselves to this kind of possible ridicule, what would happen if it didn't work. And I said to him, 'You know, you have the final say on everything we're doing here. The most important thing is that if it's musically not there, we're not putting it out. If the duets don't work, nothing's going to happen.' And he said, 'All right, we'll try one, but you'd better be right.' I went into the control room. We did a take of 'Come Fly with Me,' played it back, and you could see the eyes start to light up. That's because the band was smokin'. They were right next to him. He said, 'All right, we'll do one more.' Well, we did nine more tunes. And, you know, that's the historic night. We had the best time with each other."

Some of the vocals he laid down justified the criticism of the *Newsday* reviewer; others (particularly "One for My Baby") were among the most remarkable things Sinatra recorded in his entire career. Yet all were defaced by overdubbed vocal tracks rendered by some of the least appropriate pop acts imaginable. When rumors of *Duets'* imminent production began to spread among the Sinatra constituency, many of Blue Eyes' staunchest supporters assumed it could only be a joke.

Many critics also pointed out that *Duets* didn't consist of true duets at all but what *The New York Times* techno-critic Hans Fantel has labeled "sonic collage." "I think it's a little scary that this technology exists," as even Nancy Sinatra has admitted (to Michael Musto). "They can pair Dad with Newt Gingrich. He wouldn't have to know about it until it's too late." However, Tony Bennett has pointed out that the producers weren't just taking two random pieces of tape and sticking them together; he worked to make his vocal fit in very specifically with the one Sinatra had given him to work with. The two voices on one selection, "They Can't Take That Away," with the original electro-duetist, Natalie Cole, match so closely you might think the two singers actually were in the studio together. But that can't be said for the tracks on which the shortcomings of the process are immediately evident and the interartist rapport is lost, a failing particularly evident on *Duets II*. Many of the duetists insisted on acknowledging their ghostly partner (referring to him as Francis or Frank, as if they had ever met him or had ever been within a hundred feet of him), and these asides seem especially disingenuous.

In the summer of 1993, Capitol's PR crew seems to have realized that they couldn't suppress the truth. They turned an obvious liability into an asset by ballyhooing the idea that the *Duets* weren't real duets and promoting the set as a technological achievement. (What they were loath to discuss is the degree to which Sinatra's own vocal tracks were tampered with—not only spliced and diced but pitch-altered to improve his fading intonation.) A year later, their tune had changed: they were no longer playing up the techno angle, the fiber-optic phone lines, and the digital multitracking. Both the liner notes to *Duets II* and *Frank Sinatra Duets*, the CBS TV Thanksgiving weekend (1994) special, completely skirt the issue and rather dishonestly lead the audience to believe that the contempo artists were actually singing in tandem with Sinatra, thereby giving one reason to invoke the old discussion regarding the distinction between telling a lie and not telling the truth.[12]

There is nothing wrong with using available technology. Perhaps you've heard of an art form known as the movies, where performances are made up of zillions of tiny fragments edited together, and no one claims that Laurence Olivier can't act. As Johnny Mandel has pointed out, technology is used in kiddie-pop as a substitute for talent and technique, but who is to say that major artists like Bennett and Sinatra should not be allowed an occasional techno-dabble to enhance what they do?

When Sinatra finally warmed up to the *Duets* concept, said Ramone, the Chairman's first question was "How is Ella [Fitzgerald] doing?" The First Lady of Song had apparently hung up her microphone for the last time, but other great artists in Sinatra's area were more than available— Peggy Lee, for instance. The fact that Luther Vandross, of all inappropriate people, was the first artist to actually finish his "duet," perfectly illustrates what went wrong with the project.

In the end, *Duets* fails not in concept but in execution. On some levels

12. The *Duets* TV special took great pains to avoid the truth: during shots of Sinatra doing "The Best Is Yet to Come" in his isolation booth, the image of Jon Secada was superimposed onto such a booth on the other side of the studio.

the idea wasn't bad: Sinatra encountering the leading figures in other music genres, much the way Bing Crosby teamed with such greats as Louis Jordan, Louis Armstrong, and Woody Herman fifty years earlier. *Duets* was conceived as a cross-genre project as well as an intergenerational one. But that wasn't the way it worked out. Instead of encountering the leading lights of, for instance, soul and Latin music, Sinatra is teamed with the likes of Vandross (who makes an exceedingly sorry contribution to "Lady Is a Tramp," based on the 1974 Billy Byers arrangement) and Julio Iglesias, who amount to rather sorry representatives of their respective fields. Regarding the Sinatra-Iglesias "Summer Wind," one Capitol Records executive commented sardonically, "To think I've been listening to Frank's old record of that all these years and I never realized it was a buddy song!"

Sinatra does toss tonsils with several of his peers in other areas, such as Aretha Franklin (who should have been given "That's Life" to sing with the Chairman instead of "What Now My Love," which is hardly a Sinatra classic) and Charles Aznavour (whose vocal deterioration is considerably worse than the Old Man's). Unfortunately, the canned "duet" process prevents Sinatra from meeting them halfway, and they sound uncomfortable and unconvincing in his milieu.

He also confronts the closest thing to '90s celebrities in his own idiom in Barbra Streisand, a technically gifted, emotionally barren superstar with ties to both kiddie and grown-up pop, and the great Tony Bennett. While the Streisand-Sinatra "I've Got a Crush on You" includes more back-and-forth than the other tracks (thanks to Sinatra's re-overdubbing lines on top of the vocal that Streisand had already dubbed on top of his original vocal, if you can follow all this), it ends up as nothing but a battle of egos: Streisand, with her acres of chops, sounds as if she's trying to overwhelm Sinatra. She just doesn't get it, and simply by being his plain old ultracool self, the Chairman makes her look sick.

Throughout, there are surprises: who knew that Latin-disco queen Gloria Estefan, who does shockingly well on "Come Rain or Come Shine," could even sing at all without the electronic ephemera she usually employs? But these exceptions are far outweighed by the disappointments: while Tony Bennett is by far the most sympatico of all possible Sinatra partners, their "New York, New York" produces no magic. In nearly four decades of being in the spotlight, Liza Minnelli has completely failed to establish any sort of aural identity for herself, and her intrusion on the classic Sinatra-Riddle 1953 "I've Got the World on a String" shows why: mindlessly belting for three minutes, Minnelli is all energy (which sometimes has its charm, to be sure) and no style.

This is a set that aspires to the mediocre, with far more lows than highs. While the Sinatra solo "One for My Baby (and One More for the Road)," when separated from the unspeakably awful Kenny G. instrumental it's attached to, constitutes a classic Sinatra performance, there are more epic disasters here than in a *National Geographic* special. As far as choosing the single worst item on the set, it's a toss-up between "I Guess I'll Hang My Tears out to Dry" with Carly Simon and "I've Got You Under My Skin" with Paul Hewson, better known as Bono from the rock group U2.

In listening to the Carly Simon track, one can't help but be prejudiced by the story (reiterated in Stephen Holden's *New York Times* review) that Ms. Simon was originally asked to sing "One for My Baby" with Sinatra. While we should be grateful that she had the decency to leave this track unpolluted, the explanation for her switching to another song is dumbfounding. According to Simon, the Mercer-Arlen classic is politically incorrect because it advocates drinking and driving. The '70s pop star understated her case; apparently she didn't realize that "One for My Baby" clearly encourages alcoholic *infants* to operate heavy machinery while intoxicated.

Even if she hadn't provided us with this philosophical gem, Simon would be bad enough. She has a nasal voice that can be effective with the kind of folky material that put her on top, but watch out when she attempts Sinatra's kind of music. More important, for much of the track Simon sings a melody line directly on top of Sinatra's original melody line. You read that right—not a harmony line that might work with what Sinatra is singing, but two melody lines at once, in obvious musical conflict. It's earsplitting to say the least.

Yet the bottom of the barrel, the all-time worst thing Sinatra has ever been involved with—worse than the horrors of the '50s, '60s, and '70s combined—is this "I've Got You Under My Skin." Forget that Bono can't sing, forget that he doesn't even have a name. There's no way his rape of the *Songs for Swingin' Lovers!* masterpiece can be construed as anything but a sledgehammer attack on Sinatra and everything he stands for. It begins with the rocker moaning along with the Sinatra track as if he were some stoned punker with a karaoke machine, and from there it escalates not into "sonic collage" but aural graffiti of the most offensive kind. Worse than attempting to sing with Sinatra, which he is completely incapable of doing, the Irish rocker tries to scat alongside him, resulting in nightmarish screams that suggest live animal vivisection.

Duets II was released in the fall of 1994, based on Sinatra vocals taped at that highly productive July 1993 date and other, subsequent sessions over the next twelve months. (In July 1994, Ramone reported he had fifteen unused Sinatra vocals in the can, most from 1993—including one from "just before Christmas.") All around, *II* was a considerable improvement over *I* in that it had no embarrassingly unlistenable moments, no Bono equivalents. The set didn't do as well in sales as its predecessor, even though Capitol promoted it equally heavily. It also didn't rack up as many rave reviews, perhaps because, as one editor at *Entertainment Weekly* privately postulated, critics who felt that they had gone overboard on *Duets I* somehow felt obliged to blame the faults of the first on the second, superior as that sequel happened to be.

First the bad news: for the most part, *Duets II* is just as pointless as the original. Unlike Bono, most of the singers here—such as Patti Labelle, and even Jon Secada and Luis Miguel, who are described as "Latin boy-wonders" in the notes—are competent enough to get through their numbers (respectively: "Come Fly with Me," "The Best Is Yet to Come," on which Sinatra sounds raw and powerful, and "Bewitched"). There's just no musical reason for them to be there. Even if they don't take anything away from Sinatra, they don't add anything, either. It's as if the Yankees were to hire Cindy Crawford to pitch naked; she would certainly bring in crowds, but she can't play the game.

The problem is exacerbated on the medley of "How Do You Keep the Music Playing?" and "My Funny Valentine." The former is sung by talented country chanteuse Lorrie Morgan, and it's a perfectly acceptable Nashville-Paris conjunction in an AM radio sort of way. The latter is a newly revised arrangement by Pat Williams for Sinatra (whose voice is captured at its weakest) with a Mel Tormé–style coda that detours through "Bess, You Is My Woman Now." There just is no earthly reason for these two tracks to be spliced together.

Those tracks amount to the average, being neither the best nor the worst nor the weirdest on *Duets II*. The worst would have to be "The House I Live In" with Neil Diamond, an unbearable drone who cuts the thin cord of suspended disbelief that the song hangs from, letting it drop into the domain of pedantic pretentiousness. "Fly Me to the Moon" with Carlos Jobim scores as the set's biggest letdown; the guitarist-composer (who died shortly after the album was released) leads a contigent of fellow Brazilians in a very out-of-place prelude to the Quincy Jones/Basie arrangement. Two meetings with Nashville giants are equally frustrating: Willie Nelson can certainly sing standards after a countrypolitan fashion, but he swings like an outhouse door, and Jimmy Buffet has no business being on "Mack the Knife." It's easy to imagine Sinatra singing their music—Nelson's "On the Road Again" (recorded by Rosemary Clooney) and Buffet's "Margaritaville" hinge upon Sinatra-sympatico themes—but Nelson and Buffet themselves are just not universal enough in their approaches to work in his world.

Linda Ronstadt, vapid as ever on "Moonlight in Vermont," is the one who initiated the concept of rock stars covering Sinatra-era music, which might be deemed the first step on the road to *Unforgettable* and *Duets*. Chrissie Hynde was perhaps anticipating that trend when she named her rock band The Pretenders; fifteen years after that group's first album, here she is, like Ronstadt and Simon, pretending to be able to sing Sinatra's music. Her annoying vocal on "Luck Be a Lady" sounds every bit as perfectly ghastly as Patrick Dennis' preppy girlfriend in *Auntie Mame* or William F. Buckley in drag. The strangest cut is "My Kind of Town," a duet between Frank Jr. and Frank Sr. It somehow summons up an image that could be the cover of a '60s DC comic, depicting a *bizarro* Superman locked in mortal combat with a superannuated Superman.

Ah, but there's good news tonight, folks. As a completely unexpected bonus, three of these tracks are actually worth the time it takes to listen to them. It's no surprise that the long-awaited Sinatra–Lena Horne duet, "Embraceable You," would turn out to be as warm and winning as we'd hoped, even if it's not as tender and passionate as it might have been had these two fellow travelers of the long, long road actually met face to face. It's quite a surprise that "For Once in My Life," the least likely of these items, sung with Gladys Knight and prefaced by a harmonica prelude by Stevie Wonder, works out so well. While Knight isn't the same kind of supreme talent that Aretha Franklin is, this more directly soulful song happens to suit her perfectly. As with many of the darker tunes in his repertoire, old age has been kind to Sinatra's readings of this song, giving him the power to instill it with far more punch and passion than he could muster in 1969. His vocal here exposes all the nerve endings and is full of the time-tempered vehemence of an old blues singer.

Hynde and Bono may purport to be ground-breaking new-wavers, but the only real innovating going on around here occurs in "Where or When," Sinatra's encounter with Steve Lawrence and Eydie Gorme (who shared the Diamond Jubilee Tour with him in 1990). Designated representatives of the demographic group heaved out the window by the mass media when Johnny Carson went off the air, they're generally considered members of Sinatra's generation, although Lawrence is actually younger than Willie Nelson. Lawrence and Gorme begin with a rubato verse accompanied by an electric keyboard, which, for once, fits. When the piece moves into tempo with the refrain, Sinatra, Lawrence, and Gorme make like Lambert, Hendricks, and Ross. The same way that this innovative singing group of the '50s attached words to the instrumental portions of Count Basie–Joe Williams classics, Lawrence and Gorme use Billy Byers' 1966 treatment of "Where or When" (recorded by Sinatra and Basie *At the Sands*) as a template. They also convincingly incorporate Sinatra's mannerism of throwing in the extra syllable "once" in front of "before" and make it a formal part of the chart. Unlike most of the *Duets* participants, they know how not to intrude on Sinatra or the band but instead complement their colleagues with ingenious harmony lines.

Best of all, they don't insist on addressing Sinatra by his first name, even though in their case the familiarity would be far from false. In effect, it's a total 180-degree turn away from Bono, who, in trying to compete with Sinatra-style lyric-altering intimacy, has the effrontery to address Sinatra as "you old fool." Yet considering that Sinatra allowed himself to be suckered into this clambake, one wonders how far off the mark Bono's accusation really is.

Foolish, that is, like a fox. In a single swipe the albums (the first in particular) did miraculous things for Sinatra's credibility as a force in the 1993 record industry. At one point reaching as high as number two on the pop album charts, *Duets* was by and large considered the album of the year. Yet within a few months, most Sinatra-style radio stations, such as New York's WQEW, stopped playing the *Duets* versions of these songs in favor of the original classics, which underscores the point: the only level on which *Duets* succeeded was purely economic.

"On 'Tramp,' the tempo is wrong, the band ain't swinging and on most of the album, you don't even hear the drums. They're just not rhythmically convincing," says Billy Byers, whose arrangements of "Tramp" and "Where or When" are included in *Duets I* and *II*, respectively. While he agrees that *II* is a considerable improvement over *I* (adding that he was flattered by Steve and Eydie's adaption of his 1966 "Where or When" arrangement), Byers has reservations regarding the whole concept. "Phil is a smart guy and Pat is excellent, but I'd rather hear Sinatra do some new stuff. I think everybody's getting a free ride: everybody's doing the same concept, somebody with somebody else. It's just a way to get all the names on one CD cover." (Other arrangers whose work was used on the album feel the same way—although they asked not to be quoted.)

In making money and not making art, *Duets* violates the essential tenet of Sinatra's career. Duke Ellington was a major artist of comparatively limited commercial success, especially during the last twenty years of his life when he failed to compose a single hit song. Elvis Presley was and is a major commercial entity, although his artistic abilities remain questionable if not negligible. Sinatra is both a major artist and a commercial giant. If he has to make money by stooping to the shallowest means, in a very real way he has failed his public—no matter how much money *Duets* happens to make. Jimmy Bowen made the point that he doesn't consider the hit singles he produced with Sinatra in the '60s to be "real Sinatra music"; *Duets* ultimately doesn't amount to Sinatra product at all, but rather greedy rap-era "samplings" in which his voice and oeuvre have been appropriated. It's the kind of cheap-shot route to mass-market, multimedia success in the '90s that detracts from, rather than contributes to, his legacy.

Yet Sinatra is far from an otherworldly presence on these albums the way he is on his daughter Tina's movies *Sinatra* and *Young at Heart*. His voice may be stronger on some tracks than others, but the feeling and overall *there*ness of the Old Man can't be debated. Rumors have it that his current contract with Capitol calls for three albums: two sets of duets and one lacking other vocalists, which might be called, in a stroke of marketing brilliance, *Frank Sinatra Solos*. Ramone might even get to produce that *Wee Small Hours*–type album he dreamed of making. Bill Miller, who has never been one to whitewash the Sinatra situation, feels that the Old Man is more than up to it, that he can still sing; the only problem is firing him up to want to put in the time and effort it would take to cut a new album. If he were to work hard to learn new material or arrangements and be satisfied to bite off only a tune or two per session, Sinatra could probably finish an entire set over the course of a few months.

Says Byers, "*Duets* would be valid artistically if only the kids were learning to appreciate Frank Sinatra. But they're just buying it for their favorites, they're not investigating other Sinatra albums." Ironically, the *Duets* albums come at a time when Tony Bennett is having great success with Generation X strictly on his own terms; if the kids are buying Bennett on his own merits, it doesn't seem unreasonable to assume that they'd react equally enthusiastically to new *real* Sinatra product.

If he does record again, we can hope it won't be another set of redos, with or without artificial additives. He may finally get around to standards he has never done before, of which—as he consistently refuses to acknowledge—there are hundreds. There are also songs from recent shows by the same writers he has long favored, such as Jule Styne ("To a Small Degree"), Cy Coleman ("Without You, I'm Nothing" and others from *City of Angels*), Betty Comden and Adolph Green, or non–show songs by Alan and Marilyn Bergman and/or Michel Legrand. Even Stephen Sondheim has one or two tunes up his sleeve (like "Losing My Mind") that could be potential Sinatra masterpieces.

There may be one or two songs from the more melodic members of the pop-rock crowd, such as John Denver ("Perhaps Love"), Paul Simon ("Still Crazy After All These Years," which Rosemary Clooney has sung to good effect), or Elvis Costello ("Almost Blue"), while Willie Nelson and other cowboy poets have also written a few verses that would lie easily on Sinatra's tongue. "There are some singers who don't believe that any great songs are being written anymore," Frank Sinatra, Jr., said coyly in his own act (adding, in his counterpart to his father's lifelong obsession with "Amos 'n' Andy," "If I keep on like that, I'm gonna be an orphan in the morning").

It seems an odd comment to make about a singer who spent the '70s recording nothing but new songs, but we know what he means. Sinatra may even find some new songwriters who don't yet have a reputation in any field. While no kid, Charles DeForrest some years ago wrote a perfect Sinatra song called "(Don't Fight It) It's Chemistry," a "Tender Trap"–like ringer-dinger that has Blue Eyes written all over it.

Still, learning new material may pose a problem, because Sinatra has trouble remembering songs he has been doing for decades. He has difficulty following the Teleprompter monitor much of the time these days, and when he does, nearly everyone in the room becomes aware that he needs this crutch. Bill Miller insists the problem rests solely with the Old Man's declining optical powers. His intonation has been declining steadily during his late seventies, but even without Irv Cottler, he can still find his way around the beat. There are nights when he coasts; sometimes he just seems to be going through the motions. Ironically, it's on the shows when he isn't trying to dig too deeply that he gets through without losing his place too often. When he takes chances and invests more of himself emotionally in the material, that's when he risks blowing his concentration. In the moments he connects the most deeply, both with his material and his audience, that's when he gets thrown.

And yet there are still nights when he's incredible—when he is, in fact, Frank Sinatra. Although he gave a good accounting of himself in April 1994 at New York's Radio City Music Hall, the best performances he has given in the '90s have been at Atlantic City and Las Vegas. Obviously, the comparative intimacy of these auditoriums and the familiarity of the casino-saloon setting give him warmer vibes than an enormous, antiseptic stadium. He does so well at these venues that at the time one wished he would just confine himself to the gambling houses and perhaps one or two big cities and cut down on the constant touring that is clearly wearing him out. One member of the current company told Sol Gubin about a recent performance in Salt Lake City. The crowd reaction was even more overwhelming than usual. "The people were screaming and yelling and throwing flowers at him and everything," said the drummer, "but when they got on the jet, the Old Man was very sad about it. He turned around to this guy and said, 'Jesus, these people make me feel as if they're coming to see me for the last time.'" They had learned the wisdom of George S. Kaufman's pronouncement that "one should always listen closely when people say good-bye."

Frank Foster, who shared the stage with Sinatra as leader of the Basie orchestra on many occasions (most recently at Radio City in April 1994), put it this way. "After all these years, his voice is going, and at seventy-eight what do you expect? But he still has the same charisma, the same ability to stir a crowd that he had years ago. It may seem like a shame that they have to have four monitors on stage to flash the lyrics in front of him and that he makes heavy use of them. Hey, man, if you're still going professionally at seventy-eight, it's no disgrace to use whatever props are necessary, especially when you can still fill Radio City Music Hall for an entire week."

Three Sands shows from 1992, 1993, and 1994 are among the most sensational Sinatra sets I've ever experienced (to be sure, there were also disappointing performances at Madison Square Garden in 1991 and the Garden State Arts Center in 1993). On the opening night of one run, November 11, 1993, he had only one embarrassing moment—when he got lost in the out-of-tempo verse to "I've Got a Crush on You," a notoriously sing-songy, amelodic intro that has thrown many a younger rider. In a misguided attempt to offer aid, one fan in the house yelled "Get Barbra, Frank!" Sinatra thought the guy meant his wife, Barbara, and responded pretty much to himself, "I wish she were here. We'd be havin' a drink right now," making it obvious that he was oblivious to the fact of having made a record of "Crush on You" with Barbra Streisand.

Yet for the rest of the evening, Sinatra was totally on target. His "For Once in My Life," which usually suits Tony Bennett much better than it does Sinatra (Old Blue, in fact, originally encouraged Bennett to do this 1965 song), was practically the best performance he has ever given of it, displaying a more potent combination of tenderness and bite than any other documented Sinatra reading. In place of "One for My Baby" in this particular show, his big saloon song was "Guess I'll Hang My Tears out to Dry," and it was every bit as moving as Sinatra has ever sung it.

Not all of his recent performances have been as successful. According to several accounts, the August 1994 concert at New Jersey's Garden State Arts Center found Sinatra momentarily singing into the wrong end of his handheld mike. Yet October and November appearances in

Chicago and the Sands were spectacular. At the Sands, Sinatra was so sure of himself he even had the chutzpah to poke fun at his own memory and/or vision problems by daring the audience to remember the words to "All or Nothing at All." (Around this time he was also singing Pat Williams' lovely new revision of "My Funny Valentine," happily shorn of "How Do You Keep the Music Playing.")

Yet two nights in Japan, shortly after his seventy-ninth birthday, in December 1994, were the all-time nadir. Sinatra was tired and, perhaps for the first time in his life, jet-lagged, and could hardly get through any songs without badly and obviously losing his way. He then stayed off the road for two months, not singing again until his wife's annual charity combination golf event and concert at the end of February 1995. Although this Palm Springs miniconcert was a rousing success (as Bill Miller testifies), as of May, Sinatra has not booked any further engagements. According to his office, "it's about fifty-fifty" as to whether he'll work again.

Even in 1994, Sinatra refused to do the same ending twice to "Mack the Knife"; there was always some sort of extra twist in the windup that has to be created spontaneously. As always, even in the very big rooms, "Come Rain or Come Shine" remained defiant and triumphant. "My Way," with its so-hard-to-remember and so-easy-to-forget melodic line, represents a major problem for the senior Sinatra. The song made him lose his bearings several times during an otherwise excellent set in March 1992, yet in May 1994 he delivered one of the best renditions of his career. Haughty, arrogant, aggressive, and irresistible, it was everything that Frank Sinatra singing "My Way" ought to be.

Throughout the recent Sands shows, the audience was far from just pulling for Sinatra to make it through the set without too many screwups. They were too busy being entertained, thrilled, and moved by him. And they were reminding us that we have to stop thinking of him as some kind of trimmed-down, incapacitated version of the old Sinatra; the Sinatra of today is completely different from the artist he was thirty years ago. He has an all-new set of considerations, and he's reacting to what the current crowd is feeding back to him, not limiting himself to what he did decades ago. His place is here. His time is now.

In his perfection of the art of singing barroom ballads, Sinatra has tapped into the same truths that Elwood P. Dowd espoused in *Harvey*. Speaking not just of six-foot rabbits and arriving icemen, Dowd explained how those who frequent public establishments usually talk about "the big terrible things they have done, and then they talk about the big wonderful things they will do, because nobody ever brings anything small into a bar."

Even if he never works again or, worse, continues to desecrate his legacy with a *Duets III* and *IV,* Frank Sinatra has already proven himself a thousand times over. In addition, he has often captured our imagination with his extramusical activities, which involve close associations with the movers and shakers of Hollywood, Washington, and the underworld. Well, perhaps "the big, terrible things" he has done will be canceled out by "the big, wonderful things" he has also done.

Sinatra's accomplishments apart from his singing—his highly erratic film career, for instance—can be said to leave his account with us as even. It's as a musical artist that he'll ultimately be remembered. Like Ellington and Armstrong, he is indisputedly a great artist. The Chairman of the Board triumphs eternally as the definitive voice of the American experience. In the words of movie director Peter Bogdanovich, "His songs are not only his biography but ours as well."

As Sinatra approaches his ninth decade, his once awesome pipes have frazzled. Yet even now, no other performer can get his listeners to *feel* as much as he does. When he loses that—and not before—then he'll know it's time to pack it in. To conclude with what is currently Sinatra's favorite toast, raise your glasses, please, ladies and gentlemen: may we all live to be four hundred years old, and may the last voice we hear be his.

A NOTE ON SOURCES

All unattributed quotes come from interviews conducted (with the kind folks listed in the acknowledgments) by myself and Mr. Granata. Only two individuals I wanted to talk with directly turned me down: Mo Ostin, of Warner Bros.-Reprise Records, and Frank Sinatra himself. In the case of Mr. Sinatra, it wasn't such a loss as I might have imagined: on the one hand I doubt that he'd remember the answers to my questions, and, on the other, I have been enormously fortunate to excavate a series of interviews (never published in print form) with the singer going back fifty years. Because it's been a kind of Sinatra tradition for those around him to put words in his mouth, I have tried my best to stick with radio interviews in which he's clearly speaking for himself.

Herewith is a list of the interviewers and approximate dates, and, in some cases, the subject matter:

Dave Garroway, from late 1945, on Glenn Miller.
Jack Ellsworth, New York, July 11, 1949.
Ben Heller, Atlantic City, Labor Day Weekend, 1950.
Larry King, 1965.
Paul Compton, KGIL, San Francisco, June 5, 1970, and December 30, 1973.
William B. Williams, U.S. Army Reserve recruiting program, syndicated, July 1976.
Suzy Visits the Sinatras (TV show), May 25, 1977.
Arlene Francis, WOR NY radio, January 10, 1977, September 24, 1980 (with Martin Gabel), and September 15, 1981.
Sid Mark, September 1981.
William B. Williams, WNEW AM, New York, November 13, 1981.
Ed Walker, WMAL, April 19, 1983, Washington, D.C.
Sid Mark, taped November 1983 (mostly on Don Costa).
Sid Mark, April 28, 1984, backstage in Philadelphia (mostly on Gordon Jenkins).
Sidney Zion, one-on-one "seminar" done before an audience of students at Yale University, April 15, 1986.
Jonathan Schwartz, WNEW AM, New York, on Irving Berlin's 100th Birthday, May 11, 1988.

Other interviews consulted (other than my own) include Nelson Riddle (with Robert Windeler and Jonathan Schwartz), Gordon Jenkins (with Wink Martindale), Irv Cottler (with Richard Apt), and Alan Freeman (with Stan Britt).

CONSUMER GUIDE
AND COMPACT DISCOGRAPHY

A complete Sinatra discography would, naturally, take up this entire book—in fact, many book-length, independently manufactured Sinatra discographies have already been published. The most comprehensive volume currently on the market is the *Sinatrafile Part 2* (Second Edition, Commercial) (John Ridgway, John Ridgway Books, Birmingham, U. K., 1991). Be warned: it's frightfully expensive, hard to find, unwieldy, and already out of date (so much product has been released or re-released between then and now). The work was originally part of a series that included two earlier companion volumes, *The Sinatrafile 1* and *3* (which document non-commercial material and films, respectively) which are now even harder to come by.

Sinatra: The Man and his Music, The Recording Artistry of Francis Albert Sinatra (Ed O'Brien and Scott P. Sayers, TSD Press, Austin, Texas, 1992) is also recommended. While considerably smaller, cheaper, and easier to find, it unfortunately omits many necessary details—such as session personnel. (Although it does have plusses such as a complete accounting of Sinatra's soundtrack sessions.)

As far as this current volume is concerned, there's only room here for a quick read-through of CDs currently available. As I did in *Jazz Singing*, I have indicated all releases that have my name on them with a + sign. (However, I leave it to the reader to ascertain whether this in fact amounts to a plus or a minus.)

THE UTMOST ESSENTIAL SINATRA

If, for some reason, you've decided to limit your Sinatra purchases to three sample packages, fortunately there are multiple sets that present a good cross section of the best of what Sinatra recorded during the three most important label affiliations of his career. It should also be noted that in conjunction with the very silly 1992 TV miniseries *Sinatra*—don't get me started—Reprise has also issued an unusual double-disc sampler which contains tracks from all of Sinatra's myriad periods, from Tommy Dorsey on up to "My Way." The full title is *Sinatra: Music from the CBS TV Miniseries* (2 CDs, Reprise 45091-2 +. Another double, the recommended *Sinatra Saga* (39 tracks on 2 CDs, Bravura CD2-104) offers concert highlights from the '50s to the '80s, covering many stages of Sinatra's career evolution.

The Voice, 1943–52 (72 tracks on 4 CDs, C4K-344240) Although superseded by the superior *Complete Columbia Sessions* box (below), this collection provides an enjoyable basic sampling of the early years. However, you're probably better off if you realize now rather than later that you *will* eventually have to have the complete works. (In the late '80s, Sony also released three additional single volumes of Sinatra music: *Hello, Young Lovers* [CGK-40897]; *Christmas Dreaming* [CK-40707], which has been replaced by the superior *Christmas Songs by Sinatra,* listed below; and *Sinatra Rarities* [FC 44236]. Again, however, rather than investing in seven individual discs, you're better off going straight for the big *Complete* box.)

For 1995, Columbia has announced a four CD (100 track) compilation of Sinatra's most memorable tracks from the '40s, using the masters from the 1993 *Complete* box, and listeners are advised to wait for this package.

The Capitol Years (75 tracks on 3 CDs, C2-94777 +) A bargain, with the most tracks crammed onto the fewest discs, this 1990 set is offered for the Sinatraphile who has everything—containing one brand new Sinatra-Billy May discovery and lots of singles not otherwise available on CD—and nothing, with many classic cuts selected for benefit of the neophyte who wants to sample the classic Capitol "concept" albums before buying all of them. Again, trust me, you will eventually want them all. Maybe not today, maybe not tomorrow, but soon—and for the rest of your life. However, even then this sampler will still contain some goodies unavailable anywhere else.

The Reprise Collection (81 tracks on 4 CDs, 926340-2) As with *The Capitol Years,* it's a very listenable mixture of the rare and the familiar. Another 75th birthday compilation, the most interesting and unusual material, surprisingly, comes from the '70s, making the point that this was a much more rewarding era in Sinatra history than the regularly released tracks from these years would lead us to believe.

THE NEARLY COMPLETE WORKS

Corresponding with the outline of this book as a whole, this section is organized by either collaborator or period, whichever seems the most sensible. Reprise albums with more than one arranger, such as *Trilogy,* will usually be found in the "general" sections for the '60s ("Looking for the Hook") and '70s-'80s-'90s ("The Concert Years").

HOBOKEN AND HARRY

While we wait for Columbia's complete accounting of the Sinatra-James sessions, two European producers have taken advantage of the fact of these items slipping out of copyright overseas. (However, all of the James-FS material is due to be included in the 1995 Columbia compilation.) *The Beginning and Harry James* (English JRR Records FS-1939-2) and *Frank Sinatra Volume 1, 1935–1940* (French Media 7 MJCD 35) collate nearly all then-known pre-Dorsey material, the JRR including more of the pre-James stuff as well as two James-FS aircheck items. *Harry James and His Orchestra* (Hindsight HBCD503) contains three CDs of excellent live James from 1938 to 1948, among them seven Sinatra vocals, all on tunes not commercially recorded by the band.

WITH TOMMY DORSEY

In the mid- to late 1980s, RCA/BMG issued a rather ghastly series of discs of Sinatra-Dorsey items, called, for no apparent reason, *All Time Greatest Hits Vol. 1* (8324-2), *Vol. 2* (8554-2), *Vol. 3* (9679-2), and *Vol. 4* (2269-2). Since these are randomly programmed, with poor sound, incomplete and with poor packaging, the listener is advised to flee from these as he or she would a social disease. At least two more coherent sets of the same material were issued internationally, one in England (in two double disc packages: *The Sinatra Archive, Vol. 2—1940* [JRR FAS-1940-2] and *Vol. 3—1941* [JRR FAS-1941-2], which do contain a few unique alternate takes), and the Japanese *Tommy Dorsey and His Orchestra with Frank Sinatra* (5 CDs, BMG BVCJ 7042-46). But don't buy any of these.

All these sets pale beside *Tommy Dorsey-Frank Sinatra: The Song Is You* (5 CDs, RCA 07863 66353-2 +), which offers all the master takes complete, in excellent sound, with a 90-page booklet and a bonus disc of previously unheard live radio performances. Unfortunately, RCA has yet to release a good one-volume set of highlights from the Sinatra-Dorsey sessions.

Other live performances by the Dorsey orchestra, with occasional vocals by Frank Sinatra, can be heard on the following unofficially released discs: *The Tommy Dorsey Orchestra Vol. 2 (Featuring Frank Sinatra)* (Echo Jazz EJCD 09); *Tommy Dorsey 1940* (Danish Tax CD 3705-2); *Tommy Dorsey and His Orchestra—1942 War Band Broadcast*, featuring "Blues in the Night" (Jazz Hour JH-1013), and *Nov. 26, 1940—Jan. 6, 1943* (Jazz Hour JH-1035); *The All-Time Hit Parade Rehearsals*, including a 1944 Sinatra-Dorsey reunion (Scottish Hep CD 39). *This One's for Tommy* (Voice V-CD-1103) features the 1955 reunion, a 1958 FS-TD tribute, and other rarities.

Not to forget: *I Remember Tommy* with Sy Oliver (Reprise 45267).

WITH AXEL STORDAHL AND
ALL THE IN-BETWEEN YEARS (1943–1952)

I'm understandably prejudiced by having worked on it, but I don't think many Frankophiles would disagree with the assertion that *Frank Sinatra: The Columbia Years 1943–1952, The Complete Recordings* (approximately 285 songs on 12 CDs, Columbia Legacy CXK 46873 +) ranks as one of the great achievements of the modern recording industry. Including the master take of every song Sinatra recorded for Columbia in the best possible sound, the set includes scores of rarities, among them dozens of selections that were either previously only issued on 78 or not at all; with a 140-page booklet. I can't recommend this set too highly.

Sony has also issued four one-disc samplers of highlights culled from the big blue box, including the *Frank Sinatra: The Columbia Years 1943–1952, The Complete Recordings* sampler (which was supposedly noncommercial, but should be findable) (CSK 5224 +); *The Essence of Frank Sinatra* (CK 57152), *I've Got a Crush on You* (CK 66964), and *16 Most Requested*. As mentioned above, Sony is also planning a 4-CD set of highlights from the Columbia years for 1995.

The corporation has announced further plans to supplement the box with a follow-up series of material from outside its scope, of which *Christmas Songs by Sinatra* (CK 66413), including some alternate takes and radio items not on the box, and *Frank Sinatra: The V Discs* (2 CDs, C2K 66135 +) have already been released. A godsend for collectors, this second set contains radio performances and an original session as mastered for an all-serviceman audience during World War II. Be aware that while the performances are often fascinating and even revelatory, the sound isn't always up to the commercial masters. Also available: *Frank Sinatra Conducts the Music of Alec Wilder* (Sony Music Special Products A 4271).

As far as noncommercial material goes, the 1940s is the most prolific period of Sinatra's career, considering that Sinatra had a weekly radio slot and then TV show going straight for nearly a decade. For two seasons, in fact, Sinatra even did two shows at once, as well as dozens of unsalaried appearances on the Armed Forces Radio Network. The cream of that often-wonderful material is sampled on the following unauthorized releases:

JRR Records of England, which specializes in highly recommended compilations of unrecorded songs gathered chronologically, currently has the following discs available: *Your Hit Parade, 1944* (JRR-144-2), *Songs by Sinatra, 1945* (JRR-145-2), *Your Hit Parade, 1947* (JRR-147-2), *Your Hit Parade, 1948* (JRR-148-2), *Your Hit Parade, 1949* (JRR 249-2), and *Light Up Time, 1949* (JRR-145-2).

VJC: *The Unheard Frank Sinatra Vol. 1: As Time Goes By* (VJC-1004), *Vol. 2: The House I Live In* (VJC-1007), *Vol. 3: Long Ago and Far Away* (VJC-1030), *Vol. 4: I'll Be Seeing You (Songs of WW2)* (VJC-1051), and *The Songs of Sammy Cahn and Jule Styne* (VJC-1045).

Also worth finding: *Portraits from The Past* (Bravura BCD-101); *Frank Sinatra "The Voice" 1943–1947* (Decade DCD-102); *The Rarest Sinatra* (Decade DCD-103, which is true to its title); *Live Duets, 1943–1957* with Bing Crosby, Nat Cole, Louis Armstrong, etc. (Voice V-CD-1101); *There'll Be Some Changes Made* TV tracks 1950–51 (Voice V-CD-1102); *Frank Sinatra Live 1942–46* (JRR-149-2); *Frank Sinatra Hit Parade Shows* (Jazz Hour JH-1036); *Frank Sinatra 1946 Old Gold Shows* (Jazz Hour JH-1040); *1949 Lite Up Time Shows* (Jazz Band EBCD 2116-2, English), featuring several tracks with Bobby Hackett; *In the Blue of Evening: The War Transcriptions* (Natasha Imports NI-4007); and *Sinatra: The Radio Years 1939–1955* (6 CDs, Meteor CDMTBS 001, English), which is as hard to locate as the sound is bad, but it contains lots of interesting stuff.

GENERAL CAPITOL

In 1992, EMI gathered all sixteen of the classic Sinatra "theme" albums made for Capitol, into an imposing wooden box they called *Sinatra Concepts* (+). While the box does include the otherwise unreissued instrumental set *Tone Poems of Color*, the set unfortunately omitted the singles compilations (such as the *This Is Sinatra!* albums), and the three soundtrack LPs Sinatra released on that label. Still, the set is recommended for those who don't happen to already own the CD issues of the individual albums. Between the enormous boxes offered by both Sony and Capitol (and Reprise has also announced a megabox for the eightieth birthday in 1995), when you buy Sinatra product you're not merely acquiring software, you're investing in furniture (although they're not for sale at your local Ikea).

However, almost all of the original Capitol theme albums are available individually, if you prefer to go that route. Be advised, however, that in the '80s Capitol frequently added what they called "bonus tracks" to many of these sets. In some cases, these make perfect sense—such as restoring the originally deleted tracks to *Close to You* and other tracks from the same sessions as *Sinatra's Swingin' Session.* Yet in other cases, these after-the-fact additions are completely inappropriate, and in a few instances they even serve to bring down what was already a perfectly programmed original album. However, it's good to have these masterpieces, as well as the "supplementary material," on CD, and generally speaking, they sound better than ever. (Reprise, it should be noted, has also added "bonus" cuts on some of their original-cover reissues, but generally theirs tend to be more of a piece with the original LPs.)

WITH NELSON RIDDLE

The classic, original Capitol albums:

Songs for Young Lovers and *Swing Easy* (on one CD, CDP-748470-2)
In the Wee Small Hours (CDP-746571-2)
Close to You (CDP-746572-2, although this may have been withdrawn)
Songs for Swingin' Lovers! (CDP-746570-2)
A Swingin' Affair (CDP-794518-2)
Only the Lonely (CDP-7484471-2)
Nice 'N' Easy (CDP 7 96827 2, now including "The Nearness of You")
Sinatra's Swingin' Session (CDP-746573-2)

Capitol Singles and soundtracks:

All the Way (CDP-791150-2, now withdrawn), a classic singles anthology
Capitol Collector's Series (CDP-792160-2), a recent singles anthology
Frank Sinatra at the Movies (CDP-99374-2), another new compilation
Can-Can (CDP 7 91248 2), original soundtrack, now withdrawn
Pal Joey (CDP 7 91249 2), original soundtrack, now withdrawn

The Reprise albums:

The Concert Sinatra (FS 1009-2)
Sinatra's Sinatra (FS 1010-2)
The Days of Wine and Roses (FS 1011-2)
Moonlight Sinatra (FS 1018-2)
Strangers in the Night (FS 1017-2)

WITH BILLY MAY

On Capitol:

Come Fly with Me (CDP-748469-2)
Come Dance with Me (CDP-748468-2)
Come Swing with Me (CDP-794520-2)

On Reprise:

Sinatra Swings/Swing Along with Me (FS 1002-2)
Francis A. & Edward K with Duke Ellington's Orchestra (FS 1024-2)

WITH GORDON JENKINS

On Capitol:

The Sinatra Christmas Album (originally released as *A Jolly Christmas with Frank Sinatra*) (CDP-748329-2)
Where Are You? (CDP-791209-2)
No One Cares (CDP-794519-2)

On Reprise:

All Alone (27022)
September of My Years (FS 1014-2)
She Shot Me Down (FS 2305)

MISCELLANEOUS '50S NONCOMMERCIAL MATERIAL   Concerts on JRR: *Monte Carlo, 14 June, 1958,* a classic concert with Quincy Jones (158-2), and *Melbourne, 19 January, 1955,* a surprisingly disappointing concert (155-2). On Bravura: *A Tour De Force—The Legendary Concert with Red Norvo, Australia, 1959,* the greatest concert of the Capitol years (BCD-102); *Perfectly Frank,* unique small group tracks done for radio, 1953–55 (BCD-103); *The Television Years,* late '50s, that is (BCD-105); *The Soundtrack Sessions* (BRCD-7106); *Frank Sinatra Live Vol. 4* (Fremus CDFR 0485, Italian) contains a great concert from Seattle, 1957, although the disc has a few engineering problems. Expensive and impossible to find, but worth it: *From the Vaults,* pressed only in a limited edition of 750 copies.

LOOKING FOR THE HOOK

Other '60s albums (all Reprise except the second):

Ring-a-Ding Ding! with Johnny Mandel (27017-2)
Point of No Return with Axel Stordahl (Capitol CDP-748334-2)
Sinatra and Strings with Don Costa (27020-2)
Sinatra-Basie arranged by Neil Hefti (FS 1008-2)
Sinatra and Sextet Live In Paris (45487-2)
Sinatra Sings Great Songs from Great Britain with Robert Farnon (9 45219 2)
Sinatra and Swingin' Brass with Neil Hefti (27021-2)
Sinatra-Basie: It Might As Well Be Swing arranged by Quincy Jones (FS 1012-2)
Softly As I Leave You with Riddle, May, Emie Freeman, Marty Paich, etc. (1013-2)
My Kind of Broadway with Torrie Zito and others (FS 1015-2)
A Man and His Music with various arrangers (two CDs, FS 1016-2)
Sinatra-Basie at the Sands conducted by Quincy Jones (two LPs on one CD, FS 1019-2)
That's Life with Ernie Freeman (FS 1020-2)
Francis Albert Sinatra & Antonio Carlos Jobim with Claus Ogerman (FS 1021-2)
The World We Knew with Ernie Freeman, Gordon Jenkins and others (FS 1022-2)
Cycles with Don Costa (FS 1027-2)
A Man Alone with Don Costa (FS 1030-2)
Sinatra & Company with Don Costa, Eumir Deodato, Antonio Carlos Jobim (FS 1033)
Greatest Hits Vol. 1 (FS 2274-2)

Greatest Hits Vol. 2 (FS 2275-2)
My Way (FS 1029-2)
Watertown (45689-2)
The Sinatra Christmas Album (45743-2). A 1994 compilation, primarily from *12 Songs
of Christmas* (1964) and *The Sinatra Family Wish You Happy Christmas* (1068).
Inside Great Songs (Artisan 605-2)
Inside Tommy (Artisan 606-2)

OTHER '60S CONCERTS *London Royal Festival Hall, 1 June, 1962,* far superior to the
officially released Paris concert of a few days later (2 CDs, JRR 162-2); *Saloon Singer,*
from the Sands, 1961 and Chicago, 1962 (Encore ENCD-1001); *Frank Sinatra, Dean
Martin and Sammy Davis, Jr. at Villa Venice Chicago, 1962, Volume One* (Jazz Hour JH-
1033) and *Volume Two* (Jazz Hour JH-1034); though the sound is superb on both, be
warned that volume two consists primarily of ethnic jokes.

'60S TV TRACKS *Christmas in California* (Fremus SAS CDFR 0500, Italian) containing
the 1967 Dean Martin X-mas special with Sinatra and family and *Sinatra: The Classic
Collection: A Man and His Music* (Fremus CDFR 0503, Italian), the 1965 special.

OTHER '60S SESSION MATERIAL: The following are all very underground: *Sinatra Sessions*
(Decade DCD 100); *On the Inside Volume 1* (Artisan 601-2); *On the Inside Volume 2*
(Artisan 602-2); *Inside Brass* (Artisan 603-2); and *Inside Basie* (Artisan 604-2).

THE CONCERT YEARS

Ol' Blue Eyes Is Back with Gordon Jenkins & Don Costa (FS 2155-2)
Some Nice Things I've Missed with Don Costa & Gordon Jenkins (FS 2195-2)
The Main Event Live with Woody Herman's Young Thundering Herd (FS 2207-2)
Trilogy: Past, Present & Future with Billy May, Don Costa, and Gordon Jenkins
(two CDs, FS 2300-2)
L. A. Is My Lady Produced & conducted by Quincy Jones (Japanese QWest/Warner
Bros WPCP-3604)
Frank Sinatra Duets (Capitol CDP 89611-2)
Frank Sinatra Duets II (Capitol CDP 7243 8 28103 2 2)

OTHER '70S AND '80S CONCERTS AND RARITIES *The White House, 17 April 1973* (JRR
173-2), a concert so great even Tricky Dick can't screw it up; *The Sinatra Saga Volume 2*
(Bravura BRCD 7107); *For The Good Times, Resorts International 1979* (Boardwalk
501); *A Swingin' Night At The Sabre Room* (MAC 200). *The Unissued Sinatra* (Ty D100)
contains an interesting plethora of studio rarities in fairly mushy sound.

Sources The International Sinatra Society, PO Box 7176, Lakeland, FL 33807-7176;
Select Circles, PO Box 302, Riverside, CT 06878; Jazz M/O, 140 W 22nd St, 12th Floor,
New York, NY 10012. Sinatra fans with internet access are invited to subscribe to the
Sinatra Electronic Mailing List. Send e-mail to *listserv@vm.temple.edu,* with the only
content of the note being: *subscribe sinatra.* Once you are subscribed you may send mes-
sages to *sinatra@vm.temple.edu.* Also of interest is Rick Apt's Sinatra Collectibles,
P.O. Box 620, Pomona, NJ 08240.

A YEAR IN THE LIFE OF A FRANKIE FAN

The twelve months between July 1995, when the first edition of this book was "put to bed," and July 1996, when this current paperback edition was prepared, have been particularly rewarding ones for Sinatra collectors. Following is a list of recommended recent releases (assembled with the aid of the tireless Ken Hutchins).

THE UTMOST ESSENTIAL SINATRA

The Best of the Columbia Years (C4K 84681+) is a highly recommended sampling of 93 of The Voice's key classics from 1943–'52 on four CDs with a 68-page booklet.

HOBOKEN AND HARRY

Sony's *Harry James and his Orchestra featuring Frank Sinatra* (CK66377 +) features 21 songs, including seven radio performances from 1939 as well as all the master recordings and alternate takes. Hindsight's *Harry James and his Orchestra featuring Frank Sinatra: All Or Nothing At All* (HCD–263) features seventeen airchecks by the '39 band, nine with Sinatra vocals.

WITH TOMMY DORSEY

Frank Sinatra and Tommy Dorsey GREATEST HITS (BMG/RCA 09206-68487-2) doesn't have all the songs you or I would have picked, but it is a worthwhile sampler to the big *Song Is You* box. 15 tracks, including two remotes.

WITH AXEL STORDAHL AND
ALL THE IN-BETWEEN YEARS (1943–1952)

In addition to *The Best of the Columbia Years* described above, Columbia has also issued *Frank Sinatra Sings Rodgers and Hammerstein* (CK 64661+) and *Swing And Dance With Frank Sinatra* (CK 64852+). Both contain numerous previously unissued alternate takes, while the latter show-driven collection works in five airchecks of R&H arrangements otherwise unsung by The Voice. *Swing And Dance* is particularly valuable as a summary of Sinatra's early jazz work as well as of the artistry of the great "missing link" of Sinatra arrangers, George Siravo.

1940s Radio Material: *A Treasury Of Sinatra "Vomume 1"* (sic) (JRR 001-2) commemorates the 40th anniversary of the Sinatra Music Society with many rare radio and tv broadcast items, including the 1943 FDR 61st-birthday tribute version of "Night And Day." *In Celebration* (Exclusive EXC101) includes the complete October 17, 1945 Songs By Sinatra show, with twelve other songs from various radio shows. *Frank Sinatra And Friends* (Hallmark 300022) includes 21, mostly radio, duets taken from Voice 1101. *There'll Be Some Changes Made (The Rarities 1950–51)* (Voice 1102) comes from early TV tracks.

1940s Soundtracks: The Turner/Rhino alliance has produced *That's Entertainment* (Rhino R2 72182), a six-disc set containing all the numbers from the three so-titled features, among them six Sinatra vocals, most in genuine stereo. Less officially you can get: *Ship Ahoy and Las Vegas Nights* (Hollywood Soundstage 4006), *Reveille with Beverly* (Hollywood Soundstage 4007), and *On the Town/Anchors Away* (Bluemoon BMDC 7007).

GENERAL CAPITOL

Sinatra 80th All The Best (Capitol CDP 7243 8 35952 2 8) is a fairly useless two-CD compilation, including a disingenuous pseudo-duet of "The Christmas Song," produced by mangling together separate tracks by Sinatra and Nat King Cole (with the Sinatra track pitched higher than actually recorded). As compensation, however, Bing Crosby's spoken line, "You must be one of the newer fellows" has now been restored to "Well Did You Evah?"

A mess of Sinatra singles were issued on the double UK set *This Is Sinatra 1953–1957* (Capitol/EMI CD DL1275), which contains all of the LPs *This Is Sinatra!*, *This Is Sinatra Volume Two*, and *Look To Your Heart*. However, Capitol's own *Sinatra Singles* (four CDs 38089 +) rather literal-mindedly gathers all of Ol' Blue Eyes's 45s from 1953–1961. The only drawback is that it omits many miscellaneous "orphan" tracks that were neither originally on singles nor concept albums, but the plus is that there's a generous seventy-page booklet.

Miscellaneous '50s: the *High Society* soundtrack is now on Japanese Capitol (TOCP-6587); hopefully there will be an expanded U.S. release before the millenium. There's also a private issue of the *Guys and Dolls* soundtrack (M.P.T.1). *From The Vaults Two and More* (Audio Archive 202) combines eight recording session outtakes with ten broadcast items. For more radio tracks, *Frank and Bing* (Boardwalk 503) collects both Bing Crosby shows with our boy from 1954 along with a 1953 transmission of Sinatra in Italy. *FS After Hours* (Artistry 3001) offers 33 more cuts from the *To Be Perfectly . . . Frank* show, fifteen ballads, and the rest with rhythm section. Also live is *Frank & Dean's Hollywood Party / Sinatra & Dorsey Historic Reunion* (MAG 500). Most importantly, there has been an excellent, if unofficial, release of what is easily the most amazing Sinatra concert of the era, *Frank Sinatra Live! Seattle, Washington Concert, June 9, 1957* with Nelson Riddle (Jazz Hour JH-3001), which replaces an earlier and inferior version on the Italian Fremus label.

LOOKING FOR THE HOOK

In honor of the big 80th, Reprise entered the luggage business with *Frank Sinatra: The Complete Reprise Studio Master Recordings* (Reprise 46013-2), a limited-edition, twenty-disc package. The CDs, carrying 452 songs (among them eighteen never-before-released titles), came in an overdone suitcase package (putting new meaning to the term "traveling music") but with a rather minimal booklet and, unfortunately, without the magnifying glass necessary to follow the track listing. It's not the way I recommend hearing these albums, but it's the only way to acquire 99.9% of FS's issuable Reprise master takes in one fell swoop. Reprise also issued a single CD collection, *Everything Happens to Me* (Reprise 9 46116-2), purportedly programmed by The Man himself. The very dark 1981 reading of the title cut is the highlight here.

Other '60s Concerts: *Cole Porter—You're the Top: A Testimonial* (Viper's Nest VN-180) includes five Sinatra vocals, among them a rare ballad/solo piano version of "I've Got You Under My Skin." An abridged version of the Villa Venice concert is now available, *The Clan In Chicago* (Timeline TL 1339), which thankfully eliminates much of the non-music. *Sinatra In The Sixties* (Virtuoso-5001) collects live songs from Vegas; several TV shows; the 1961 Inaugural Gala; and concerts from Sydney, Australia; St. Louis; Oakland; and The United Nations in New York.

Other '60s session material: *Inside Great Songs from Great Britain* (Artisan 605) and *Inside Tommy* (Artisan 606), both pressed in Italy.

THE CONCERT YEARS

On November 16, 1970 Old Blue gave two concerts in London—the second is available on video from Warner Bros./Reprise and unofficially on a CD, *My Way Frank Sinatra* (The Entertainers CD 322); the first show has recently been released as *The Lost London Concert* (Esquire 2200). The limited edition *See The Show Again* (Boardwalk 502) features 24 generally unusual songs in generally poor quality, some from audience-made recordings, concentrating on unrecorded charts of ephemeral '70s songs. *A Jumpin' July 4th* (MAC2100) features a complete concert (July 4, 1986) from the Golden Nugget in Atlantic City. *Sinatra and Sammy: North Country Concert* (Matdant 586) features the March 22, 1988 concert, taped just after Dean Martin dropped out of the "Together Again" tour.

Capitol's *Sinatra 80th Live In Concert* (Capitol CDP 7243 8 31723 2 0), comes from two sources: the Dallas Reunion Theatre concert of October 1987, which also featured Sammy Davis, Jr. and Liza Minelli (not heard on the Capitol disc), and a show from the Fox Theatre, Detroit in November-December 1988. On the whole, the disc is fine, but hardly what it could have been. The inclusion of the horrendous faux-duet of "My Way" with Pavarotti hardly helps. (For extreme completists an alternate mix of "Fly Me To The Moon" with country star George Strait is on the latter's *Strait Out Of the Box* set [MCA MCAD4-11263, 4 CDs].) The limited-edition *Sinatra Unreleased* (GETZEL #1) offers studio rarities in varying quality, including the intriguing "Leave It All To Me" and other cuts that didn't make the Reprise suitcase. There's also an "undercover" CD rather pessimistically titled *The Last Performance* (no label and no number), containing the Old Man's most recent public appearance, given at the Frank Sinatra Golf Tournament on February 25, 1995.

GREAT SONGS FROM GREAT BATONS

The following CDs feature Sinatra in his secret identity as conductor: *Frank Sinatra Conducts The Music Of Alec Wilder* (Columbia Special Products A4271), *Sleep Warm* with Dean Martin (Capitol CDP 7243 8 37500 2 3), and *The Man I Love* with Peggy Lee (available on a Capitol/EMI Japanese import TOCJ-5356). Some of these songs can be heard on *Great Ladies of Song: Peggy Lee* (Capitol CDP 28533).

Addendum: The following have all been released very recently indeed: *The Sinatra Songbook Live* (Artistry), *Francis Albert Hall* (Melcone 401), *FS Spectacular*, containing the 1965 Dismas House benefit with the Rat Pack and Count Basie (Shine Box 61170).

INDEX

The week Will Friedwald was born, Frank Sinatra commemorated the occasion by recording *Point of No Return.* The author of *Jazz Singing: America's Great Voices from Bessie Smith to Bebop and Beyond*, and a regular contributor to *The Village Voice* and *The New York Times*, Friedwald has also written for *New York* magazine, *Entertainment Weekly*, *New York Newsday*, *L.A. Weekly*, *The New York Observer*, and for numerous music and film journals. He has been a consultant on many television documentaries, and has produced and annotated hundreds of compact disc reissues, including several Grammy-winning packages. In 1990, Nancy Sinatra Lambert invited him to write an essay for *Frank Sinatra: The Capitol Years*. Since then he has contributed to compilations of the music of Frank Sinatra on the four labels on which Sinatra has recorded. He has a recurring dream in which he visits Mr. Sinatra's home and discovers that the walls are covered with photos of Italian restaurants.